Sustainable Design for Interior Environments

Sustainable Design for Interior Environments

SUSAN M. WINCHIP

Professor, Department of Family and
Consumer Sciences, Interior and Environmental
Design Sequence, Illinois State University

Fairchild Publications, Inc.
New York

Director of Sales and Acquisitions: Dana Meltzer-Berkowitz
Executive Editor: Olga T. Kontzias
Acquisitions Editor: Joseph Miranda
Senior Development Editor: Jennifer Crane
Development Editor: Barbara A. Chernow
Art Director: Adam B. Bohannon
Production Manager: Ginger Hillman
Senior Production Editor: Elizabeth Marotta
Copyeditor: Shelley Flannery
Cover Design: Adam B. Bohannon
Cover Art: Corbis
Text Design: Andrew Katz
Additional Text Illustrations: Tim Bayley, Ron Carboni, and
  Alan Reingold

The paper used in this publication is acid free.

Illustrations from *The Little Prince,* by Antoine de Saint-
Exupéry, are used by permission of Harcourt, Inc.

Library of Congress Catalog Card Number: 2006932414
ISBN: 978-1-56367-460-0
GST R 133004424

Printed in Canada
10 9 8 7 6 5 4 3 2 1
CH01, TP14

CONTENTS

EXTENDED CONTENTS

PREFACE

The vast majority of educators and practitioners concur that the interior design profession has a social and moral responsibility to help protect our planet and the health, safety, and welfare of people. Recently this ethos has become even more critical because of the concerns related to global warming, the increases in natural disasters, and soaring energy costs. In response to the serious global environmental problems, many professional organizations associated with the built environment have prioritized sustainable design and development, including the Council for Interior Design Accreditation, the former Foundation for Interior Design Education and Research (FIDER). A thorough knowledge of sustainable development is imperative for the welfare of current and future generations. To engage in meaningful practice requires a comprehensive knowledge of the principles of sustainability and an understanding of how to integrate the principles with design solutions. Acquiring this level of expertise is a challenge because most practitioners and educators were not formally prepared to design sustainable interiors. Individuals may have an awareness of "green" design, but sustainable development is a concept that is far more comprehensive than the traditional environmental perspectives. Sustainable development and designs require a cultural transformation that involves society, the environment, and economics.

For the purpose of this textbook, the concept of sustainable design is derived from the principles established at the 2002 World Summit on Sustainable Development in Johannesburg, South Africa, which was sponsored by the United Nations:

Changing unsustainable patterns of consumption and production. Fundamental changes in the way societies produce and consume are indispensable for achieving global sustainable development. All countries should promote sustainable consumption and production patterns, with the developed countries taking the lead and with all countries benefiting from the process (2002, p. 13).

Protecting and managing the natural resource base of economic and social development. Human activities are having an increasing impact on the integrity of ecosystems that provide essential resources and services for human well-being and economic activities. Managing the natural resources base in a sustainable and integrated manner is essential for sustainable development. In this regard, to reverse the current trend in natural resource degradation as soon as possible, it is necessary to implement strategies that should include targets adopted at the national and, where appropriate, regional levels to protect ecosystems and to achieve integrated management of land, water, and living resources, while strengthening regional, national, and local capacities (2002, p. 20).

Health and sustainable development. The Rio Declaration on Environment and Development states that human beings are at the center of concerns for sustainable development, and that they are entitled to a healthy and productive life, in harmony with nature (2002, p. 39).

For more than 25 years I have had an affinity for environmental initiatives, concerns, and designs. My commitment to the planet evolved as a result of experiencing the energy crisis in the 1970s. As a consequence of the crisis and the increasing degradation of natural resources, I became engaged in environmental research and practice. This knowledge was transferred to the courses I was teaching at the collegiate level. Since the early 1980s I have been teaching environmental principles in interior design courses without an appropriate textbook. Comprehensive environmental textbooks written for the interior design profession did not exist. The lack of a textbook focused on understanding sustainable design within the context of interior design presented challenges in the classroom. The many books and resources available on ecology, environmental science, and sustainable architecture/construction are meaningful to students in their respective disciplines, but they fail to provide the background, essential components, terminology, and applications that are needed by interior designers. Furthermore, current "green" books are generally written for the general public and primarily focus on residential interiors. The lack of relevance to the profession of interior design is further exacerbated by the assortment of resources that are available in libraries, professional organizations, retail stores, and electronic formats. Identifying and analyzing the enormous quantity of diverse resources can discourage professors and students from incorporating the principles of sustainability in design solutions.

Sustainable development and design are complex topics, which are not easily understood by students of interior design. Consequently, a project might include terminology associated with sustainable design, but the design solutions may not accurately reflect the principles of sustainability and may have a negative impact on the built environment. Teaching the principles of sustainable design can be difficult for professors who did not receive formal training on the topic. This is fairly common because an emphasis on understanding sustainable design is a relatively new addition to the interior design curriculum. Teaching and learning sustainable design is further complicated by the variety of terms associated with the concept, such as green design, sustainable development, sustainable architecture, eco-effectiveness, LEED (Leadership in Energy and Environmental Design) rating system, cradle-to-cradle, biomimicry, green development, green architecture, responsible design, socially responsible design, environmental design, ecological thinking, technological sustainability, ecological sustainability, and ecological design. The diversity in terminology creates confusion and presents the impression that environmental issues are fads rather than problems that must be continuously addressed.

To incorporate sustainable principles in courses, I developed materials from a variety of sources. This methodology lacks the focus and integration that is required to understand the principles of sustainability. Moreover, the lack of accompanying pedagogical features limits the intrinsic teaching and learning process. Students, professors, and practicing professionals need a comprehensive textbook that is written with an emphasis on the principles of sus-

tainability within the context of the design process. *Sustainable Design for Interior Environments* delineates the information that an interior designer needs to design environmentally responsible interiors. I have found that the principles of sustainable design can be taught effectively using the following approaches: a) establish the importance of the concepts, b) demonstrate how the principles relate to the work of an interior designer and the design process, and c) incorporate hands-on activities that require an integration of sustainability, design fundamentals, ethics, professional values, social responsibility, regulations, and business principles. *Sustainable Design for Interior Environments* explains the principles of sustainability, provides case studies demonstrating best practices, and explains how to apply this knowledge to the design process.

CONCEPTUAL DESCRIPTION

Sustainable Design for Interior Environments equips professors, students, and practitioners to design sustainable interiors. This requires an understanding of environmental concerns, ecosystems, ethics, values, worldviews, and examples of how science and technology can be used to address environmental problems. Environmental science serves as the foundation for understanding how interior products and designs impact the environment. Knowledge of the fundamentals of environmental science enable practitioners to intelligently design interiors that are environmentally responsible within the context of new technologies and the term du jour. Demonstrating how the practice of interior designers affects the environment is critical to the successful application of the principles of sustainability. The content, organization, and pedagogical features of the textbook integrate the complex topics of sustainability with the design process. This enables students to apply the concepts of sustainability with the same ease as they apply the elements and principles of design.

Sustainable design should be viewed as an interdependent component of the built environment. *Sustainable Design for Interior Environments* focuses on the importance of designing interiors within the context of the surroundings, conditions, and influences. The emphasis is on the environment rather than the space, room, or interior. Studying the interior environment prompts a holistic examination of the factors that can impact people, spaces, materials, and the quality of life.

Sustainable Design for Interior Environments is written for the college students who will soon shape the built environment as interior designers, architects, environmental designers, contractors, and facility managers. The textbook is written for individuals who are familiar with the design process and have fundamental drafting skills. The text is intended for a comprehensive course on sustainability and can serve as a reference in any architectural/interior design course that requires students to complete interior design projects. The interdisciplinary nature of the content makes the book an excellent choice for reinforcing content throughout the curriculum. In addition, professional interior designers, architects, builders, contractors, and facility planners can use this text as a reference manual.

ORGANIZATION OF THE TEXTBOOK

The interdisciplinary nature of the content makes the textbook an excellent choice for reinforcing concepts throughout the interior design curriculum. The text is organized to enable an instructor to incorporate the content in a variety of courses and formats. Furthermore, the content addresses several indicators that are required for programs accredited by the Council for Interior Design Accreditation. For example, accreditation requirements focus on increasing the level of understanding of sustainable design through the following indicators that are associated with six of the eight educational program standards:

Standard 2. Professional Values

The program **must** provide learning experiences that address *environmental ethics* and the role of *sustainability* in the practice of interior design.

The program **must** provide learning experiences that address a *global perspective* and approach to thinking and problem solving (viewing design with awareness and respect for cultural and social differences of people; understanding issues that affect the *sustainability* of the planet; understanding the implications of conducting the practice of design within a world market).

Standard 3. Design Fundamentals

Student work **must** demonstrate understanding of the principles and theories of *sustainability*.

Standard 4. Interior Design

Student work **must** demonstrate programming *skills*, including information gathering research and analysis (functional requirements, code research, *sustainability* issues, etc.).

Standard 6. Building Systems and Interior Materials

Students **must** demonstrate understanding of the concept of *sustainable* building methods and materials.

Standard 7. Regulations

Student work **must** demonstrate the appropriate application of codes and regulations (for example, International Building Code [IBC]) and standards (for example, American National Standards Institute [ANSI]).

Students **must** demonstrate understanding of the impact on health and welfare of indoor air quality, noise, and lighting.

Standard 8. Business and Professional Practice

Students **must** demonstrate understanding of project management practices: assessment processes (for example, post-occupancy evaluation, productivity, square-footage ratios, life cycle assessment) (Professional Standards, 2006, pp. II-8–17).

The textbook is sequentially written and organized to develop the expertise and skills needed to design interior environments that embody the principles of sustainability. Unit I introduces sustainable design by reviewing the global perspectives associated with sustainable development, environmental concerns, regulations, programs, and transformational principles and strategies. Unit I provides the scientific, philosophical, political, and ethical background that is necessary for a fundamental understanding of global environmental problems, issues, and solutions. Knowledge gained in Unit I serves as the foundation for understanding how the practice of interior design impacts the environment and what an interior designer should consider when designing sustainable interior environments.

Unit II examines elements that are involved in the design process from a sustainability perspective. Unit

II introduces sustainability considerations of the built environment, including assessment standards, various strategies for the conservation of natural resources, and indoor environmental quality. Unit II also focuses on sustainable strategies for specifying building components, finishes, and furnishings. The author acknowledges and commends the work of the Building Green company for their pioneering efforts in developing specification criteria for green interior and architectural projects (Wilson, Malin & Piepkorn, 2005). Unit III serves as the integrative section of the textbook. The reader will learn how to apply the principles of sustainability to the design process. Unit III reviews strategies for integrating the principles of sustainability into residential and commercial interiors and the major phases of the design process. Sustainable strategies are identified for each phase of the design process, including comprehensive planning, programming, schematics, design development, contract documents, contract administration, and post-occupancy.

Chapters in the textbook have pedagogical features that are designed to assist teaching and enhance learning. To help explain concepts and techniques, the textbook includes tables, figures, and illustrations. Each chapter begins with a list of objectives, which can be used as an assessment tool at the beginning and end of a lesson. Chapters have a list of key terms, a summary, and exercises that are designed to reinforce the content and develop important professional skills. The appendices are important for learning the content of the book and can be an excellent reference for practicing professionals. The appendices include a substantial list of Internet addresses for professional organizations, government agencies, and trade associations that are associated with the environment and sustainability. The extensive bibliography provides an excellent reference for literature related to sustainability. The glossary includes important terms related to sustainability that an interior designer should know when designing sustainable interior environments.

The Instructor's Guide that accompanies the textbook provides suggestions that can facilitate the student's ability to learn the knowledge and skills required to design sustainable interior environments. The activities and assignments in the Instructor's Guide were developed to assist teaching and enhance learning. Suggestions provided in the Instructor's Guide were formulated to develop and measure cognitive skills of diverse learners by identifying a wide range of activities and assignments for teaching and learning the principles of sustainable design. A variety of pedagogical techniques are required to address diverse learners, teaching styles, course objectives, class schedules, technologies, and classroom environments, including online activities. By emulating the philosophy demonstrated in the textbook, suggestions in the Instructor's Guide are derived from theory, research, and practice. I used Benjamin Bloom's *Taxonomy of Educational Objectives: The Classification of Educational Goals, Book I: Cognitive Domain* (1956) as a theoretical framework to develop intellectual abilities and skills.

Based upon Bloom's taxonomy, the objectives of each chapter serve as the foundation for the learning experiences described in the Instructor's Guide. Learning experiences can be adapted for use both in and out of the classroom. Suggested activities and assignments are designed to help a student progress through Bloom's six major classifications. This is accomplished by providing a variety of test items, exercises, approaches to active learning, and assessment techniques. Test items include multiple-choice and essay questions. Generally, the multiple-choice items are testing for knowledge and comprehension, and the essay questions test for application, analysis, synthesis, and evaluation. In addition, exercises presented at the end of each chapter are a means to measure students' cognitive domain. Activities outlined in the exercises are especially important in developing Bloom's highest levels of the taxonomy. Approaches to active learning include ways to enhance lectures, problem-based learning, team-based learning, multimedia suggestions, and online activities. The bibliography in the Instructor's Guide includes articles and books that focus on research related to learning and educational strategies.

ACKNOWLEDGMENTS

I'm thrilled to have the opportunity to write a textbook on a topic that is very important to my personal and professional philosophies. I extend a heartfelt thank you to Olga Kontzias, executive editor, and Joseph Miranda, acquisition editor. I am very grateful for their vision in understanding the importance of sustainability and for asking me to write this textbook. I also extend my gratitude to the external reviewers and the many staff members at Fairchild who worked professionally and expediently to complete the project in a timely manner.

I would not have been able to write this textbook without the support of my husband, Galen. I genuinely thank him for being understanding and supportive of my many, many hours of research and writing. I am grateful that he shares my concerns for the environment and that he recognizes the importance of disseminating sustainable practices. I dedicate the book to him with all my love.

UNIT I Exploring Sustainable Development: Transformational Perspectives

CHAPTER 1

Introduction to Sustainable Development

In order to make his escape, I believe he took advantage of a migration of wild birds. On the morning of his departure, he put his planet in order. He carefully raked out his active volcanoes. The little prince possessed two active volcanoes, which were very convenient for warming his breakfast. He also possessed one extinct volcano. But, as he said, "You never know!" So he raked out the extinct volcano, too . . .

Of course on our Earth we are much too small to rake out our volcanoes. That is why they cause us so much trouble.

—ANTOINE DE SAINT-EXUPÉRY

In order to make his escape, I believe he took advantage of a migration of wild birds.

Fig. 1.1. Frontispiece from *The Little Prince*.

Objectives

- Comprehend the scientific theories associated with sustainability, including ecology and environmental science.
- Apply an understanding of environmental science to sustainability concepts and terminology.
- Describe the history of environmental movements and legislation in the United States.
- Synthesize the most significant global initiatives for sustaining the planet.
- Analyze the relationship between sustainability and economics.
- Understand the principles associated with environmental responsibility, including stewardship, ethics, and social justice.

TO BEGIN the *journey* of understanding sustainable development, start by thoughtfully reading *The Little Prince* by Antoine de Saint-Exupéry. This story embodies the principles of sustainable development and has been cherished by generations of people throughout the world. The parallel connections are reinforced in this textbook by including illustrations and quotes from *The Little Prince*.

The primary goal of Unit I in this textbook is to provide the background of **sustainable development** in order to apply **sustainability principles** to **sustainable design**. The overall philosophy of this textbook is that the values and principles embedded in the concept of *sustainable development* serve as the foundation for *sustainable designs*. Hence, Unit I reviews sustainable theories, policies, global concerns, strategies, and business practices. The knowledge gained in Unit I serves as the basis for applying sustainability principles to the *practice* of interior design in Unit II and the *design process* as presented in Unit III.

Chapter 1 introduces and provides the background for beginning to understand the principles of sustainable development. This is accomplished by focusing on the three interdependent components of sustainable development: society, the environment, and economics. Understanding the integration of these three areas is critical to being able to apply the principles to the practice of sustainable design. Frequently, sustainable design is inaccurately perceived as a substitute for *green design* or *environmental design*. Thus, to gain a comprehensive understanding of sustainable development, this chapter explains the concept within the context of its three integrative areas.

SUSTAINABLE DEVELOPMENT: SOCIETY, ENVIRONMENT, AND ECONOMICS

To understand the interrelated and interdependent elements of sustainable development, Chapter 1 begins by exploring global societal concerns. This area is the heart of sustainable development. Environmental and economical solutions must be determined within the global context of the current and future needs of people.

Defining Sustainable Development

The *Merriam-Webster's Collegiate Dictionary, 11th Edition* (2005), defines *sustainable* as "a: relating to, or being a method of harvesting or using a resource so that the resource is not depleted or permanently damaged" and "b: of or relating to a lifestyle involving the use of sustainable methods (*sustainable* society)." The same dictionary lists some of the definitions for *develop* as:

- "To make active or promote the growth of"
- "To make available or usable (*develop* natural resources)"
- "To make suitable for commercial or residential purposes"
- "To cause to unfold gradually"
- "To expand by a process of growth (*developed* a strong organization)"

These two basic definitions of *sustainable* and *develop* serve as a good foundation for understanding the concept of sustainable development. The combination of the two words together describes a concept that is focused on sustaining any of the resources that are growing or expanding. *Resources* can include people, the environment, financial capital, and technology. In practice, people refer to sustainable development's triad as: society/environment/economics; or the three P's, people/planet/profit; or the three H's, humanity/humility (referring to respect for the environment)/honesty (being ethical, truthful, and *transparent* in economical activities).

The origin of sustainable development is credited to the 1987 report of the **World Commission on Environment and Development (WCED)**, entitled "Our Common Future." Today this document is often called the **Brundtland Report** in honor of the chairperson of the commission, Gro Harlem Brundtland, from Norway. The report reviews some of the most critical issues related to sustainability: identification of common concerns that threaten our future; the role of the international economy; equality; managing the shared oceans, space, and Antarctica; security; and institutional and legal proposals. Major themes in the report were connections between poverty, inequality, and environmental degradation.

In describing sustainable development, the Brundtland Report states: "Humanity has the ability to make development sustainable to ensure that it meets the needs of the present without compromising the ability of future generations to meet their own needs. The concept of sustainable development does imply limits—not absolute limits but limitations imposed by the present state of technology and social organization on environmental resources and by the ability of the biosphere to absorb the effects of human activities. But technology and social organization can be both managed and improved to make way for a new era of economic growth" (WCED, 1987, p. 24).

The commission further notes that sustainable development is not a permanent state but "a process of change in which the exploitation of resources, the direction of investments, the orientation of technological development and institutional change are made consistent with future as well as present needs" (WCED, 1987, p. 25). The commission defined the *environment* as the place "where we all live" and indicated that *development* is "what we all do in attempting to improve our lot within that abode." Thus, the report explains that many of the "development plans" of countries are not sustainable, yet for economical and political reasons these development decisions are enacted and have a profound effect on people.

There are many aspects of the Brundtland Report that are important for understanding sustainable development and how to integrate sustainability into policies, procedures, and practice. First and foremost, the report is the collaborative endeavor of people representing countries throughout the world. To successfully develop a consensual document, which reflects a compromise of diverse self-interests, is a remarkable feat. This accomplishment speaks to the commitment of the participants, the importance of the issues, and a shared purposefulness of having a prosperous world for future generations. Love for children may be the single unifying commonality of people worldwide.

Developing a universally accepted concept, with volunteer participants, is a transformational methodology. To implement the philosophy requires unique approaches and global involvement. Consequently, this textbook attempts to include international perspectives whenever it is feasible, while addressing many of the sustainable issues within the United States. In reflecting the perspectives of the environmental international summits, issues related to people focus on the importance of developing policies by collaborating with all of the **stakeholders**. The inclusive list of stakeholders, or all the people affected by decisions, is global and intergenerational.

Sustainable Development and Business Practices

Integrating sustainable development into a lifestyle and business practices policies requires a focus on continuous improvement, while developing long-term strategies. Continuously focusing on improving products, processes, and practices is vital to sustainability. While this statement appears obvious, there are many examples of environmental issues that are gradually forgotten or ignored after a *crisis*. For example, Chapter 2 describes a historical case study of how Southern California has been trying to resolve a serious water shortage. Once community efforts helped to resolve excessive pollutants in Mono Lake, which is a primary source of water for the region, some officials perceived the problem as solved. Improving the condition of Mono Lake helps to ensure a healthy water supply, but the water shortage problem still exists in Southern California. Water shortages, or any other issues, require strategies that include plans for continuous improvement.

The world cannot be sustainable without planning for the future. Strategic thinking is planning for the future. Solutions for environmental, societal, and economic issues must be approached holistically. This requires an analysis of a system's strengths, weaknesses, opportunities, and threats (SWOT). The SWOT findings are used to establish goals and a strategic plan for the future. Simplistically, a strategic plan examines the "what-ifs" and then identifies approaches to help resolve an issue or opportunity. For example, what-ifs could be: "What if a hurricane strikes a community?" "What if new forms of energy are developed?" or "What if all waterways are polluted?" Strategic plans are the means for identifying the *how*, *what*, *who*, and *when* of what-ifs. Hence, a strategic plan for dealing with a hurricane should include: *how* to safely evacuate people, *what* means of transportation will be needed, *who* is responsible for executing the evacuation plan, and *when* the evacuation will occur.

Strategic thinking is an approach to identifying predictions to avoid problems in the future. To instill this philosophy into practice, many professionals discuss environmental issues from a management perspective. Hence, frequently recommendations for dealing with an environmental concern are reframed by concentrating on *managing* the problem. For example, water management is the sustainable approach to resolving too much water (flooding) or too little water (shortages). A focus on managing a problem reflects an acknowledgment of an issue and implies continuous and conscious efforts toward resolutions.

Systems Analysis

To include all stakeholders requires a holistic approach to problem solving. Fundamental to holistic thinking is an understanding of the structure and behavior of systems. **Systems analysis** is the study of elements and the interactions among them. The elements can be abstract concepts, such as analyzing the components of a design, or concrete, such as studying ecosystems. The underlying principle of systems analysis is examining all of the factors that affect an issue, policy, or decision. To think systemically requires identifying the relevant variables, and then understanding how they interact.

Elements in a system are interrelated and interdependent. Thus, systemic thinking requires analyses that examine what an element needs to exist independently, and then how elements relate and affect the other elements in the system. For example, successful designs of interior spaces reflect thoughtful systemic analyses. An interior designer identifies all of the elements in a space, such as the color of walls, carpeting, and upholstery. To decide which colors to specify requires an analysis of how each color independently exists in the room, and how each color interacts with all of the other colors in the space. Since the room has been designed holistically, an interior designer would also have to analyze what would happen to the entire design if one aspect were changed, such as a different paint color. An analysis of how this color alteration affects the room is examining the interdependent components of the design composition.

Understanding how to apply systems analysis to the concepts of sustainable development is essential. In order to develop solutions that can affect the global population, environment, and economic conditions, a holistic approach is required. An es-

sential component of balancing diverse self-interests is systemic thinking. Trying to identify solutions that appease competing interests requires an understanding of how compromises can be made by careful balances. Issues related to balancing self-interests will be apparent by examples provided in this textbook, which involve financial interests of a business versus the needs of people and/or the natural environment.

To help the visually oriented interior designer to better understand systems analysis and the fragility associated with balancing elements in a system, an excellent analogy is a mobile sculpture invented by Alexander Calder. Figure 1.2 is a representation of Calder's creation. Designing an art object that is suspended in air is extremely complex. An artist has to consider the beauty of the sculpture and the functional aspects related to maintaining perfect balance while floating in air. The entire mobile could be perceived as an entire system. Each sculptural piece on the mobile is independent, but it is still connected to the other elements by the thin wires. This connectedness or interrelationship is required to have the entire sculpture balanced. The sculptural pieces are dependent upon one another for a balanced arrangement. Hence, the perfect balance is lost if one of the sculptural pieces is removed or changed.

Imagining that the mobile is an ecosystem that can perform a parallel comparison. Each of the colored sculptural pieces on the mobile could represent the components of an ecosystem, such as land, animals, and sunlight. As with the mobile, an eco-system in perfect balance has the ideal quantity and quality of natural resources. Each member of an ecosystem, such as water, is unique, but it is connected to the other elements in the system. Thus, water has an interaction with land and sunlight. The perfect balance of the system is gone if one of nature's elements is removed or altered too rapidly. For example, removing too many trees at one time creates an imbalance to ecosystems. Eventually, this alteration affects many entities, such as waterways, insects, soil, and animals.

Collaborative Partnerships: International Summits

The first global environment summit was the **UN Conference on the Human Environment** (1972)

Fig. 1.2. A reproduction of a mobile created by Alexander Calder. The entire mobile could be perceived as a system.

in Stockholm, Sweden. The primary outcome of this summit was the urgent need to respond to problems associated with degrading the environment. In 1987 the WCED sponsored *Our Common Future* and produced the Brundtland Report. In addition to developing this document, the WCED was charged with identifying recommendations for the following: (1) long-term environmental strategies for achieving sustainable development by the year 2000 and beyond; (2) identification of ways that concerns for the environment can be translated into enhanced cooperation among developing countries and between countries at different stages of economical and social development; (3) policies that lead to the achievement of common and mutually supportive objectives by reflecting the interrelationships between people, resources, the environment, and development; (4) effective means for the international community to use when dealing with environmental concerns; (5) definitions of shared perceptions of long-term environmental issues and the appropriate efforts required to deal with the problems of protecting and enhancing the environment; and (6) a long-term agenda for action and inspirational goals for the world community (1987, p. 11).

To examine the progress of the commission's recommendations, global participants reconvened in Rio de Janeiro, Brazil. The **UN Conference on Environment and Development** (1992), informally referred to as **Earth Summit**, was extremely well attended and focused on numerous environmental concerns. A variety of documents were developed at the summit, including **Agenda 21** and the **Rio Declaration on Environment and Development**. Agenda 21 (1992) delineates four major areas: (1) *social and economic dimensions*, including poverty, consumption patterns, demographics, human health, and international cooperation to accelerate sustainable development; (2) *conservation and management of resources for development*; (3) *strengthening the role of major groups* in sustainable development including women, children, youth, business, and nongovernmental organizations; (4) *means of implementation* with a concentration on financial resources, environmentally sound technology, science, and promoting education, public awareness, and training. Five years later the UN reported that the summit's concerns have produced results that include a systematic review of the production of toxic components; alternative sources of energy; a new emphasis on public transportation to reduce air pollution and smog; and a greater awareness of and concern over the growing scarcity of water (United Nations, 1997).

Ten years after the Rio summit, the United Nations sponsored the 2002 World Summit on Sustainable Development in Johannesburg, South Africa. Global participants reaffirmed the commitment to sustainable development and further explored: (1) poverty eradication; (2) changing patterns of consumption and production; (3) protecting and managing the natural resource base of economic and (4) social development; and (5) health and sustainable development (UN, 2002). The report suggests that to achieve global sustainable development, all countries need to be involved, but developed countries should take the lead in promoting sustainable consumption and production patterns. Human activities have an impact on the integrity of ecosystems. Sustainable development requires careful management of natural resources. To reverse the current trend in natural resource degradation, strategies should be implemented that protect ecosystems, strengthen capacities, and achieve integrated management of components of the environment. Finally, in concurrence with the Rio declaration, human beings are at the center of concerns for sustainable development. All generations are entitled to a healthy and productive life in harmony with nature.

Most recently, the UN disseminated a report that describes the progress of another suggestion from the Rio Conference: Partnerships for Sustainable Development (2005). The entity is a voluntary, multistakeholder partnership that works toward the goals of sustainable development, specifically the globally agreed commitments in the Johannesburg Plan of Implementation and Agenda 21 (UN, 2005). Three hundred partnerships have been registered from five continents (see Figure 1.3). The partnerships examine "global economic, social, and environmental concerns by strengthening cooperation in areas of institutional and human capacity-building, research and information-sharing and technology transfer" (UN, 2005, p. 9). The update summary describes progress of the partnerships that involves organizational development by outreach to new partners and establishing principles to promote collaboration. Coordination and implementation activities include conducting meetings, pilot projects, workshops, and

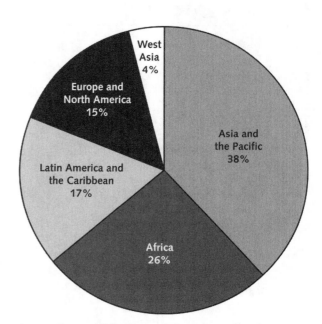

Fig. 1.3. The regional distribution of the UN Partnerships for Sustainable Development.

information dissemination via websites, directories, and educational materials (UN, 2005).

SUSTAINABLE DEVELOPMENT: ENVIRONMENT, ECONOMICS, AND SOCIETY

The Brundtland Report, "From One Earth to One World," focused on the need for global collaboration and solutions. In addition to the commonalities related to people and society, international concerns focus on how impacts to the environment affect the planet. This is especially important when analyzing aspects of the environment that are universally shared, such as air, weather, sunlight, and water; however, scientists have been very definitive about the fact that the world knows very little about ecosystems. Thus, it is uncertain how a seemingly small change in one location in the world affects global systems.

Science of Sustainability: Ecology and Environmental Science

Ecology is the science that studies the interrelationships between organisms and their interaction with an environment. Ecology is a biological discipline with origins in the late nineteenth century; however, the term did not become popular until the 1960s.

Ecologists study the population of species and explore the factors that affect their growth, demise, and extinction. The origin of the word *ecology* provides further insight regarding the purpose of the science. *Eco* and *logy* are derived from the Greek meaning for *house* and *study*, respectively. For the purpose of ecology, a *house* is the environment that shelters all living organisms. The environment consists of **biotic** and **abiotic** elements. Biotic is the living organisms, and abiotic is the nonliving attributes of the planet, such as sunlight, the atmosphere, soil, minerals, and water.

Organisms, Populations, and Communities

The science of ecology is organized by the following natural systems: **organisms**, **populations**, **communities**, **ecosystems**, and the **biosphere** (see Figure 1.4). The study of organisms involves exploring the behavioral traits of living things, including animals, insects, birds, plants, or microbes. Ecologists study how an organism functions and examine requirements for shelter, sustenance, reproduction, and creating populations. Effective environmental conditions result in the development of populations.

A population is one species that is capable of interbreeding and living in a specific region. Generally, geographic factors affect the formation of populations. In analyzing the interactions of populations with the environment, some of the key variables are growth patterns, size, and density of the population. To sustain a healthy ecosystem, it requires the appropriate balance between the number of organisms within an area and the environmental resources that are needed for sustenance. A population growth that proceeds too quickly for the environmental conditions eventually results in extinction.

Ecologists study conditions that are required for a population to survive. This research is critical to populations that are identified on the endangered species list. For example, in analyzing annual counts of the Alaskan Steller sea lions (see Figure 1.5), the National Marine Fisheries Service (NMFS) determined that the sea lions were an endangered species. To help recover and preserve the population of Steller sea lions, NMFS created a *Steller Sea Lion Recovery Team*. The goals of the recovery team centered on identifying the actions and conditions that would help save the sea lions that were living in Alaska.

The focus of community ecology is studying the **biodiversity** of an environment. This involves understanding how different populations coexist within a prescribed area. The setting could be a forest, lake, coral reef, or tundra. In studying the community, ecologists examine how different species interact with each other, including the identification of prey and predators. Since the 1980s, scientists have been

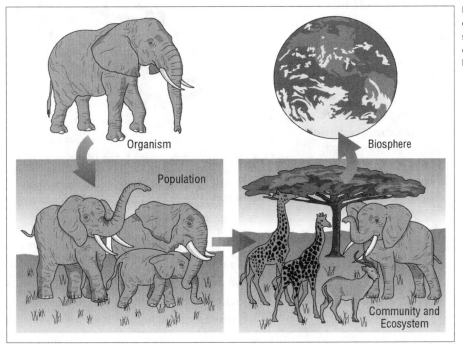

Fig. 1.4. The science of ecology is organized by the following natural systems: organisms, populations, communities, ecosystems, and the biosphere.

Organism

Population

Biosphere

Community and Ecosystem

Fig. 1.5. Alaskan Steller sea lions. To help recover and preserve the population of Steller sea lions, the National Marine Fisheries Service (NMFS) created a Steller Sea Lion Recovery Team.

concerned about the negative consequences associated with a reduction in biodiversity. In understanding the interrelationships of species, ecologists have determined that natural systems require diverse organisms for optimum performance. Therefore, any environmental condition that can eliminate a species has a dire effect on a community. Eventually, these occurrences can be harmful to other ecosystems and to the planet.

From a humanistic perspective, an important reason for biodiversity is the exploration for future medicinal chemicals. Scientists have only begun to research the chemicals that are contained in natural systems. Thus, retention of various species provides researchers with the opportunity to determine the pharmaceutical value of an organism. Furthermore, scientists do not know enough about natural systems to understand how the extinction of even the smallest species or microbes could affect life on the planet.

Ecosystems and the Biosphere

The next organizational level, ecosystems, includes a community and its abiotic elements. Ecosystem ecologists research behavioral characteristics of species in a community and their interactions with the land, air, and water (see Figure 1.6). Specifically, scientists study the effects of energy and nutrients within the natural system. Ecosystems are specific to

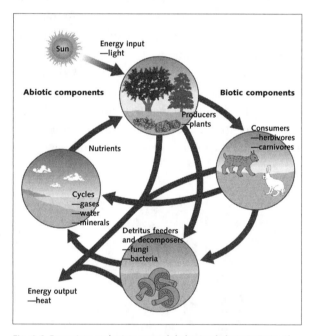

Fig. 1.6. Ecosystem ecologists research behavioral characteristics of species in a community and their interactions with the land, air, and water. This includes examining the effects of energy and nutrients within the natural system.

a geographic area and place in time. For example, vastly different ecosystems exist in the South Pacific and Iceland. In addition, the existing conditions are very different from what they were 100 years ago. An ecosystem can exist in an extremely large area encompassing thousands of miles, with millions of species. In contrast scientists might study the specific ecosystem of a small pond or a decaying log. Regardless of the size of an ecosystem, or the number of species, the interactions between organisms are extremely complex. **Autotrophic** organisms, such as plants, produce their own food as a source of nutrition. In contrast, **heterotrophic** organisms obtain their nutrients from feeding on other organisms. The source of nutrition could be plants, meat, or a combination of plants and meat. Furthermore, some organisms consume only waste material or dead organisms. The **nutrient cycle** is used to describe this energy, or nutritional flow between organisms.

Transitional ecosystems are formed when different types of ecosystems blend together. For example, this can occur in the coastal areas surrounding a lake (see Figure 1.7). For the unique characteristics of water and land to coexist requires the development of a different ecosystem. This ecosystem, the marshlands, thrives by creating a system that blends water with land. To survive, organisms must live in their natural ecosystem. Optimum environmental conditions must be present for the community to thrive, including proper nutrients, healthy air, suitable sunlight levels, and the appropriate quality and quantity of water. Alterations to prescribed conditions, including the introduction of exotic species or toxins, impact the ecosystems of communities.

The biosphere is all of the earth's ecosystems, including the interactions between organisms, land, air, and water. The biosphere extends from the bottom of the ocean to the top of the highest mountain. Any shared global commodity, such as air and water, can impact the quality of environmental conditions throughout the world. The biosphere has several regional ecosystems, such as forests, tundras, deserts, grasslands, and tropical rain forests. Marine and freshwater aquatic ecosystems include coastlines, marshes, coral reefs, oceans, and freshwater lakes. Within ecosystems, organisms compete for nutritional needs and reproduction. Thus, to determine growth and death rates of populations, ecologists study the **carrying capacity** of ecosystems. This involves identifying the environmental conditions that are needed for an optimal balance.

Many environmental conditions are studied at the biosphere level, including global warming and ozone depletion. As a means to monitor consumption rates of natural resources, researchers examine the **ecological footprints** of a country. This calculation is determined by the average amount of land and ocean needed for each person to live. Thus, the ecological footprint reflects the amount of natural resources required for shelter, food, transportation, energy, and waste. The ecological footprint difference between developing and highly developed countries is significant. For example, the ecological footprint for people living in the United States is significantly greater than for people living in the country of India.

Environmental Science

Environmental science is a specialization of ecology that focuses on the interaction of people and ecosystems. The **environment** is all of the factors or conditions that surround an organism. This can include air, temperature, light, sound, plants, animals, and people. In addition, cultural, psychological, and social conditions are factors affecting the environment. Collectively the components of an environment affect an organism's behavior, reproduction, and survival. Current and future conditions of the global environment determine the sustainability of the planet.

A distinction is made between ecology and environmental science. Ecologists provide the scientific theories that can be applied to environmental science. Environmental science is an interdisciplinary study integrating the theories, research, and practices associated with various disciplines, including law, economics, ecology, chemistry, sociology, politics, and ethics. Environmental scientists study environmental problems, determine the factors that

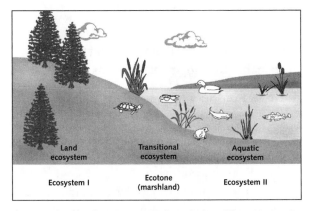

Fig. 1.7. Transitional ecosystems are formed when different types of ecosystems blend together.

contribute to the problems, and then identify solutions that reflect the realities of germane conditions. For example, in analyzing the problem of air pollution, an environmental scientist could suggest a solution that addresses the airborne toxins within the context of the society's economic position, political circumstances, and current or proposed legislation.

The field of environmental science focuses on ecosystems, populations, resources, energy, and pollution. To study ecosystems, environmental scientists rely heavily upon the science of ecology. The emphasis is on understanding how ecosystems function, and determining the factors or conditions that can affect any element of the system. This involves studying the flow of energy through the system, characteristics of living organisms, and the interactions with the physical environment.

In operating as a system, organisms react and adapt to environmental conditions. For example, Figure 1.8 illustrates a water cycle, which includes the interactive processes of precipitation, wind, runoff, evaporation, and percolation. Precipitation in the form of rain, sleet, or snow falls from the sky to the ground and waterways. Wind can blow water from waterways onto the land. Water on higher elevations can flow, or run off, to lower ground and any waterways. Evaporation occurs when water from soil, vegetation, and the waterways is transferred to the air. Percolation can happen by runoff seeping into the ground and by flowing to bodies of water. A conceptual understanding of the water cycle is very useful in studying how pollutants interact with the environment.

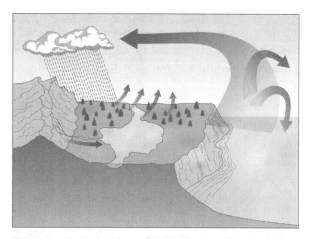

Fig. 1.8. A water cycle includes the interactive processes of precipitation, wind, runoff, evaporation, and percolation.

Human populations have a significant positive and negative impact on ecosystems. To understand the consequences of human behavior, environmental scientists analyze growth patterns of people and their effect on the environment. This analysis is conducted for a specific area of land and period of time. The number of births and deaths determines the population of the earth. For a given period of time an environment has a maximum capacity for living organisms. As a finite entity, the earth has a maximum amount of land, water, and air for a given number of people. Since 1800 human population has increased significantly. The United Nations predicts that the world population will be seven billion by the year 2013. Overpopulation and unnecessary consumption patterns affect food supplies, resource utilization, the environment, and economics.

Environmental scientists study the problems associated with many resources, including food, water, soil, minerals, species, and land use. The primary goal is to establish policies and practices that preserve, restore, and conserve vital resources. To accomplish this goal, scientists analyze problems associated with limited resources, including population growth, consumption patterns, conservation laws, cultural attitudes, and economic conditions. Environmental scientists study the effects of population on **nonrenewable** and **renewable resources**. Nonrenewable resources include **fossil fuels** (oil, natural gas, coal) and various minerals. The earth has a limited supply of resources, such as oil or aluminum. Once these resources are depleted, they are gone forever. Renewable resources, such as water, trees, or soil, have the potential to be replenished. However, careless stewardship of renewable resources could endanger their existence.

Historical Overview of Environmental and Sustainable Development Concerns

The historical roots of sustainable development can be traced to several environmental initiatives, movements, catastrophes, and legislation. Initially, the emphasis was on how development was degrading natural resources and what should be done to prevent the problems. As this understanding advanced, the focus expanded to include environmental concerns related to the interrelationships between in-

Fig. 1.9. A painting done by John James Audubon, who introduced the beauty of birds thriving in their natural habitat by painting, describing, and cataloguing numerous species of North America.

U.S. Environmental History

When colonists arrived in the New World, the abundant soil, forests, and water supplies appeared to be infinite. Thus, a lack of respect for natural resources resulted in polluted waterways and depleted forests from rampant logging operations. To acquire more resources, pioneers moved west rather than practicing conservation. By the nineteenth century, naturalists understood the disastrous environmental implications of these actions. To rally support for the natural resources, and their inhabitants, many individuals started to communicate with the public via books, paintings, and speeches. For example, John James Audubon, an artist and ornithologist, introduced the beauty of birds thriving in their natural habit by painting, describing, and cataloguing numerous species of North America (see Figure 1.9). Henry David Thoreau wrote about the beauty of Walden Pond and eloquently described the beauty of living simplistically with nature. George Perkins

Marsh is responsible for initiating ecological discussions by writing the book *Man and Nature* in 1864, and subsequently the revised edition in 1874, entitled *The Earth as Modified by Human Action: Man and Nature*.

Also in 1874, explorer and conservationist John Muir started an extraordinarily successful career as a writer by describing the beauty of the Sierra in a series of articles, entitled *Studies of the Sierra*. The uplifting quality of Muir's writings inspired many people to appreciate nature and conserve the natural beauty of mountains, meadows, and forests. Muir's influence was responsible for the concept of developing national parks and was involved with starting Grand Canyon, Sequoia, Mount Rainier, and the Petrified Forest. Muir's focus on national parks prompted Theodore Roosevelt to become involved with preservation by creating federal conservation programs (see Figure 1.10).

To use and preserve "wild nature," Muir and other naturalists founded the Sierra Club in 1892. John Burroughs, a friend of Muir and Roosevelt, was another naturalist and writer who was very influential in preserving nature. Forests and wildlife were also the focus of the important writings of Aldo Leopold. Leopold is best known for his writings in

Fig. 1.10. John Muir's focus on national parks prompted Theodore Roosevelt to become involved with preservation by creating federal conservation programs.

dividuals, societies, natural resources, and the built environment.

A Sand County Almanac (1949), but during his lifetime he wrote for *Journal of Forestry, Journal of Wildlife Management,* and *American Forests.*

In the 1950s, Barry Commoner became very well known for his protest of nuclear testing. Subsequently, Commoner wrote several books on "surviving science" and problems associated with energy. Biologist, writer, and ecologist Rachel Carson is celebrated for writing *Silent Spring* in 1962. Carson exposed the very serious health and environmental hazards of the pesticide DDT. Chemical manufacturers refuted Carson's writings, but her perseverance eventually led to the acknowledgment of the dangers of pesticides. In 1972 the United States banned the use of DDT. In response to the strength of the environmental movement in the 1970s, Denis Hayes coordinated the first *Earth Day* in 1970 and is currently the chair of the *International Earth Day Network.*

R. Buckminster Fuller, an inventor, architect, and engineer, was a true visionary whose lifelong goal was developing his concept of a *Comprehensive Anticipatory Design Science* (Buckminster Fuller Institute, 2005). The goal of Fuller's science was an "attempt to anticipate and solve humanity's major problems through the highest technology by providing more and more life support for everybody, with less and less resources" (Buckminster Fuller Institute, 2005, p. 2). To fulfill this goal, Fuller invented many products and building systems, including the geodesic dome (see Figure 1.11). The dome is the strongest, lightest,

and most cost-effective structure ever designed. The dome does not require internal supports, and it becomes stronger as its size increases. Currently, there are more than 300,000 geodesic domes, including *radome* weather stations in the Arctic, which can deflect winds up to 180 miles per hour. The adaptability of the dome is also evident by the $350 corrugated metal domes that people in Africa use for shelter.

Fuller's sustainability philosophy is also demonstrated by his focus on renewable energy sources, including solar, wind, and wave energy. Fuller's research indicated that these sources could meet the world's demands for energy, while eliminating a dependency on fossil fuels and atomic energy. Fuller commented, "There is no energy crisis, only a crisis of ignorance" (Buckminster Fuller Institute, 2005, p. 2). Fuller's sustainable development philosophy is emphasized by how he described his work: "An experiment to discover what the little, penniless, unknown individual might be able to do effectively on behalf of all humanity." Most of Fuller's work was done from the 1930s to the 1970s; however, his work to "advance humanity's option for success" is still being carried out by the Buckminster Fuller Institute.

Victor Papanek is world renowned for his perspectives regarding sustainable design. Papanek focused on "designs for the real world" by designing products through the *lenses* of human ecology, nature, and social change. Papanek wrote numerous books, which

Fig. 1.11. Buckminster Fuller invented many products and building systems, including the geodesic dome. The dome is the strongest, lightest, and most cost-effective structure ever designed.

have been published in several languages throughout the world. As a reflection of his sustainable philosophy, Papanek notes, "In this age of mass production when everything must be planned and designed, design has become the most powerful tool with which man shapes his tools and environments (and, by extension, society, and himself). This demands high social and moral responsibility from the designer. It also demands greater understanding of the people by those who practice design and more insight into the design process by the public" (1985, pp. ix–x). Papanek's books have numerous illustrations that demonstrate his "designs for the real world" by focusing on designing for a safe future, spirituality in design, unnecessary products, and problems with excessive consumption patterns (see Figure 1.12).

The general public became very concerned with energy and the environment when OPEC (Organization of Petroleum Exporting Countries) imposed an oil embargo in 1973. This action significantly impacted the quantity and availability of petroleum for transportation and heating buildings. The lack of gasoline for cars resulted in high prices, hours of waiting in long lines, theft by siphoning gas from cars, and on occasion gasoline pumps that were totally empty. This crisis prompted consumers to conserve all forms of energy, including gasoline, fuel for heating, and electricity. People demanded fuel-efficient cars, and research initiatives focused on energy conservation. Engineers focused on developing technologies for passive solar energy, improved building insulation, and energy-efficient windows. After oil prices were lowered, people lost interest in conserving energy, and they have been buying cars without worrying about the miles per gallon. Spikes in gasoline prices may prompt people to refocus their attention on conservation initiatives.

The Brundtland Report inspired many governments, scientists, architects, and engineers to research the benefits of sustainable development. Recently, the writings of Janine Benyus, Sarah Susanka, and William McDonough with Michael Braungart have been very influential. Benyus describes how the new science **biomimicry** can be applied to the problems of sustainability (1997). Biomimicry scientists examine how nature functions, and then identify ways the processes can be adapted to human needs. Since nature is the foundation in developing biomimical

Fig. 1.12. A reproduction of a design created by Victor Papanek, whose focus on "designs for the real world" involved designing for a safe future, incorporating spirituality in design, avoiding unnecessary products, and addressing excessive consumption patterns.

products and processes, the results should be sustainable and environmentally friendly. In writing several popular contemporary books, the architect Susanka has brought attention to reducing consumption patterns by designing residential spaces that are smaller, yet "personalized and well-crafted" (Susanka and Vassallo, 2005). Susanka's approach is to counteract homes that have "superfluous square footages," or what is commonly referred to as McMansions.

In the book *Cradle to Cradle*, McDonough and Braungart postulate that industrial practices, which produce cradle-to-grave products, should be eliminated and substituted for eco-effective processes. These processes involve converting waste into nutrients for the purpose of providing beneficial resources to the environment. McDonough and Braungart propose five steps to eco-effectiveness: (1) "get 'free' of known culprits" by removing harmful substances, (2) "follow informed personal preferences" in determining eco-effective design solutions, (3) "create a 'passive positive' list" that includes substances that are healthy and safe for use, (4) "activate the positive list," and (5) "reinvent" products and processes to generate nutritious effects on the environment (2002, pp. 166–180).

As a result of the naturalists' actions, environmental organizations, and presidential initiatives, the federal government established environmental legislation. Conserving land through the **General Revision Act** of 1891 was the first environmental legislation, followed by a focus on water quality with the **Refuse Act** of 1899. Subsequent legislation categories and the year of the first act are pesticide control (1938), wildlife conservation (1956), air quality and noise control (1965), solid and hazardous waste management (1965), and energy conservation (1975). Environmental legislation related to green building initiatives are the **National Environmental Policy Act (NEPA)** of 1969; energy conservation laws of the **Energy Policy Act** of 1992; air quality laws associated with the **Clean Air Act (CAA)** of 1970 and its amendment of 1990; and solid and hazardous waste laws delineated in the **Resource Conservation and Recovery Act (RCRA)** of 1976 and its amendment of 1994.

Environmental Ethics

A major goal of the UN global summits is to develop ethical policies and practices. A subdiscipline of philosophy, environmental ethics is the study of conduct that is right or wrong with respect to natural resources. Ethics are the principles or standards of conduct that preside over individuals or groups of people in a society. Concerns regarding a "land ethic" can be traced back to the work of John Muir and Aldo Leopold. The discipline of environmental ethics started in the 1970s. Theorists in environmental ethics study the moral relationship between human beings and the environment. These arguments center on the ethical obligations to the environment. Some theorists contend that the earth exists for people to use, and others postulate that people have a moral responsibility to be good stewards of natural resources. Leopold's perspectives regarding a "land ethic" succinctly summarize environmental ethics:

> Conservation is getting nowhere because it is incompatible with our Abrahamic concept of land. We abuse land because we regard it as a commodity belonging to us. When we see land as a community to

which we belong, we may begin to use it with love and respect. There is no other way for land to survive the impact of mechanized man, nor for us to reap from it the ethical harvest it is capable, under science, of contributing to culture.

> That land is a community is the basic concept of ecology, but that land is to be loved and respected is an extension of ethics. That land yields a cultural harvest is a fact long known, but latterly often forgotten (1949, p. xiii–ix).

The moral obligations and responsibilities formulated in environmental ethics translate to justice, equity, and stewardship. The **Environmental Protection Agency (EPA)** defines **environmental justice** as "the fair treatment and meaningful involvement of all people regardless of race, color, national origin, or income with respect to the development, implementation, and enforcement of environmental laws, regulations, and policies" (EPA, 2005). The federal government initiated laws that uphold environmental justice. Concerns focus on an increasingly disproportionate amount of pollution and waste that exists in communities serving minority and/or low-income populations. For example, many municipal and hazardous waste landfills are located near these populations because the cost of land is relatively low. Many disadvantaged homes are located close to polluted waterways and the air from the emissions of manufacturing plants. The problem becomes even more complex because these populations do not have the economic means to clean their environment.

The principles embedded in environmental justice were created to ensure all people are treated fairly, regardless of race, ethnicity, age, or socioeconomic status. All people should have healthy living conditions and experience aesthetically pleasing environments. Leopold noted, "The chance to find a pasqueflower is a right as inalienable as free speech" (1949, p. vii). Environmental justice is important for current and future generations. This intergenerational equity is reflected in the principles of sustainable development. To implement environmental justice, the EPA has established the **National Environmental Justice Advisory Council**. This organization and various UN committees are committed to the fair treatment of all people on concerns related to environmental justice.

Environmental Stewardship

One approach to ethical environmental behavior is stewardship. **Environmental stewardship** is the management and care of our natural resources. Effective stewardship results in a healthy planet for future generations. To restore, maintain, and preserve natural resources requires everyone to be a steward. Some countries or organizations refer to this responsibility as global environmental citizenship. As members of the global community, everyone must take responsibility for engaging in decisions and behaviors that are healthy for people, land, air, and water.

To foster wise management of our resources, many governmental agencies have developed environmental stewardship programs. For example, the United Kingdom has a stewardship program that is an "agri-environment scheme." This program provides incentives to land owners, such as farmers, who enact sustainable practices. The program's objectives include conserving biodiversity, protecting natural resources, and promoting public access and understanding of the countryside [Department for Environment, Food, and Rural Affairs (DEFRA), 2005]. The University of Michigan has established an aggressive environmental stewardship program that emphasizes, "Everyone is a steward of the environment," and suggests, "We need to manage our resources in a manner that is fiscally responsible" (University of Michigan, 2005).

SUSTAINABLE DEVELOPMENT: ECONOMICS, SOCIETY, AND ENVIRONMENT

The Brundtland Report was very cognizant of the importance of the interrelationships between sustainable development and the international economy. Life-enhancing development can occur only within the realities of how goods and services are produced and distributed among people.

Environmental and Economic Global Interdependence

The traditional economic theory postulates that the basic elements of production include natural resources, labor, and capital. To produce products and services requires people and natural resources. In exchange for goods and services, consumers pay the business sector. To reflect the true value of the environment, ecological economists developed an economic theory. The theory demonstrates how natural resources are essential to the production and disposal of goods and services. The finite nature of many materials affects productivity and the international economy. A focus on the interdependency of the economy and limitations of natural resources reinforces the importance of sustainable development.

A robust global economy depends upon sustainable ecosystems and equitable economic exchanges. A healthy and productive ecosystem is necessary for the production of goods and services. For example, products made from wood require trees from various ecosystems. To enhance economic conditions, the speed of logging operations may exceed the time that is required to replenish the stock of trees. Consequently, this inequitable economic exchange can result in a serious depletion of this natural resource. In the long term, a reduction in supply will increase the price of lumber and eventually will raise the cost of products made from wood. Steep increases in costs can cause consumers to reduce or eliminate purchases. In a global economy these fluctuations can impact the quality of life for people throughout the world.

Sustainable ecosystems help to maintain a healthy economy, and they have an important role in equitable economic exchanges between countries. This is especially problematic for developing countries. For example, many people living in highly developed countries desire exotic woods for furniture inlays. Many exotic woods are grown in developing nations with people living in poverty. To acquire the money to buy the essentials of life, people in developing countries have been willing to sell high quantities of exotic woods at low prices. This can result in exploitation of forests and degrading of nutrients in the soil. The problem is exacerbated by the fact that many of these developing countries do not have the proper agricultural conditions or technologies to produce food in abundant quantities. As a result, people in poverty are paying very high prices for food that is imported from other countries. Thus, an inequitable economic exchange of commodities occurs due to the high price of food and the low cost of the exotic wood. In focusing their expenditures on the essentials of life, people in developing countries cannot afford to spend resources on sustaining their environment. Therefore, the people living in developing countries can experience even greater problems if the valuable exotic woods become extinct or they must wait many years for the forests to be replenished. The global circle of economic interdependency not only impacts the nonessential supply of exotic wood. The lack of money due to not being able to sell exotic woods affects the farmers in the developing countries who were selling their crops to developed countries.

Direct and Indirect Costs

There are direct and indirect costs associated with maintaining and conserving natural resources. In 2003 *Building Design and Construction* (BDC) surveyed its readers to determine their perceptions of sustainability and their firms' extent of involvement in green building (BDC, 2003). Ninety-seven percent of the respondents viewed green building as a growing phenomenon; however, 42 percent indicated that "the market was not interested in sustainability or not willing to pay a premium to achieve it" (2003, p. 15).

All sustainability costs affect the international economy. Some of the most significant costs are associated with pollution and waste. Economic activities such as manufacturing, farming, and services deplete and degrade natural resources. This can occur at the point of production, with the use of a product/service, or when depositing the waste. To conserve natural resources at any point in the life of a product or service has a price. Reducing or eliminating pollutants can be employed at various points in the life cycle of a product or service. For example, a carpet manufacturing plant could invest in equipment that would reduce or eliminate pollutants. The equipment initially could be expensive, but could save costs in the long term and be environmentally responsible. A company unwilling to invest in pollution-reduction equipment might have to pay fines, penalties, and for cleanup activities. When a community is unable to identify the source of the pollution, taxpayers pay the cost of pollution and waste.

As a result of irresponsible polluting and waste,

governments have enacted policies and legislation to help protect the health of people and the environment. Environmental regulations concentrate on reducing or eliminating the sources of pollution. Governmental policies also regulate the use of natural resources. These laws affect the international economy by increasing the cost of products and services. However, the laws and regulations are essential to safeguard the lives of people and the sustainability of the planet. To enforce environmental laws and regulations, governments have *command-and-control* policies and *market-based* strategies. Command-and-control regulations stipulate the maximum levels of pollution or toxic waste. Generally, corporations conform to these regulations. However, the lack of incentives often discourages businesses from enacting sustainable practices that exceed the requirements. Market-based policies allow a corporation to select its best means for profitability. As a result, corporations have financial incentives to engage in sustainable practices, which conserve natural resources and help to reduce or eliminate pollutants.

Eventually, costs associated with protecting the environment are borne by the consumer. For interior design professionals, this affects the budget of their firm, their clients' budgets, and the budget of any users of their commercial interiors. Therefore, it is imperative for an interior designer to be knowledgeable regarding the enhanced costs associated with sustainable design. This is important because clients expect an interior designer to justify the cost of a project. An effective approach to rationalizing cost increases for sustainable design is to relate the enhanced prices to the priorities of the client. For example, a client who is concerned about their company's public image might be willing to pay the extra costs for sustainable design if the practice is promoted in the media. Many consumers are impressed with a corporation that is willing to be environmentally responsible. A positive image can be very profitable and have a positive effect on regional, national, or international economics.

Case Study: Integrating Society, Environment, and Economics

Fundamentally, the concept of sustainability has always been central to the motives and behavioral

Fig. 1.13. On Easter Island numerous moai statues were built by a civilization centuries ago. The moai were carved from extremely heavy volcanic rock.

patterns of civilizations. People and the planet would not exist today without sustainability. This supposition can be studied by examining the hypothesized history of the inhabitants of Easter Island in the South Pacific Ocean. The island is approximately 2,300 miles (3,700 kilometers) from Chile, and is the most remote location in the world. In the 1700s a Dutch explorer, Jacob Roggeveen, discovered the island and found very few people. However, Roggeveen postulated that a very advanced society must have existed on the island because he found hundreds of statues, or *moai*, scattered throughout the island (see Figure 1.13). The *moai* were carved from extremely heavy volcanic rock.

Many scientists have researched Easter Island in order to explain what happened to all of the people who were responsible for building the *moai*. Scientists hypothesize that at some point in time there were too many people living on the island for the available natural resources. To provide adequate resources for the vast numbers of people, it appears the ecosystems of the island were essentially destroyed. For example, scientists have learned that almost all of the trees were cut down to provide shelter and heat energy. Land without trees caused soil erosion. Wind blew the soil away and rainfalls caused the soil to flow to the ocean. Soil degradation prohibited the growth of crops and the available water was tainted. The lack of a fertile soil reduced the quantity of food and created great hunger in an overpopulated island. In addition, the inhabitants could not travel to another island because they were unable to construct boats without the lumber from trees. Consequently, these events triggered wars and the death of hundreds of people. In a short period of time, a population that had grown to approximately 1,400 was diminished to 350.

The dire situation that occurred on Easter Island is an excellent example to explain the integration of society, the natural environment, and economics. A lack of sustainable practices led to the elimination of nearly an entire population. Most of the people died on the island because natural resources were depleted. Natural resources were depleted to support the economic activities required for food and shelter.

Figure 1.14 graphically illustrates changes that can occur without sustainable practices. *Circle A* represents a harmonic relationship between the needs of people, economic activities, and the environment. Economic activities can be any task or service that is performed by people. For Easter Island the economic activities focused on farming and logging operations. As the arrows suggest in *Circle A*, there is a balance between competing interests. *Circles B* and *C* illustrate

Fig. 1.14. A series of changes that can occur without sustainable practices. Circle A represents a harmonic relationship between the needs of people, economic activities, and the environment. Significant increases in the growth of people and economic activities result in the imbalance that is shown in Circle E.

a shift in the balance when people while engaged in economic activities start to impose too many demands on the environment. Note that the environment is nearly depleted in *Circle C. Circles D* and *E* demonstrate how the balance changes when the environment is depleted. As shown in *Circle E*, the depletion of natural resources eventually triggers the elimination of people and all economic activities.

Summary

- The origin of sustainable development is credited to the 1987 report of the World Commission on Environment and Development (WCED), entitled "Our Common Future."
- Integrating sustainable development into a lifestyle and business practices policies requires a focus on continuous improvement, while developing long-term strategies.
- To include all stakeholders requires a holistic approach to problem solving. Fundamental to holistic thinking is an understanding of the structure and behavior of systems. Systems analysis is the study of elements and the interactions among them.
- The first global environment summit was the UN Conference on the Human Environment (1972) in Stockholm, Sweden. The primary outcome of this summit was the urgent need to respond to problems associated with degrading the environment.
- Ecology is the science that studies the interrelationships between organisms and their interaction with an environment.
- The science of ecology is organized by the following natural systems: organisms, populations, communities, ecosystems, and the biosphere.
- Environmental science is a specialization of ecology that focuses on the interaction of people and ecosystems. The environment is all of the factors or conditions that surround an organism. This can include air, temperature, light, sound, plants, animals, and people.
- The historical roots of sustainable development can be traced to several environmental initiatives, movements, catastrophes, and legislation. Initially, the emphasis was on how development was degrading natural resources and what should be done to prevent the problems.
- As a result of the naturalists' actions, environmental organizations, and presidential initiatives, the federal government established environmental legislation. Conserving land through the General Revision Act of 1891 was the first environmental legislation, followed by a focus on water quality with the Refuse Act of 1899.
- A major goal of the UN global summits is to develop ethical policies and practices. A subdiscipline of philosophy, environmental ethics is the study of conduct that is right or wrong with respect to natural resources.
- One approach to ethical environmental behavior is stewardship. Environmental stewardship is the management and care of our natural resources. Effective stewardship results in a healthy planet for future generations.
- Sustainable ecosystems help to maintain a healthy economy, and they have an important role in equitable economic exchanges between countries.
- All sustainability costs affect the international economy. Some of the most significant costs are associated with pollution and waste.

Key Terms

Abiotic

Agenda 21

Autotrophic organisms

Biodiversity

Biomimicry

Biosphere

Biotic

Brundtland Report

Carrying capacity

Clean Air Act (CAA)

Communities

Department for Environment, Food, and Rural Affairs
    (DEFRA)

Earth Summit

Ecological footprints

Ecology

Ecosystems

Energy Policy Act

Environment

Environmental justice

Environmental Protection Agency (EPA)

Environmental science

Environmental stewardship

Fossil fuels

General Revision Act

Heterotrophic organisms

National Environmental Justice Advisory Council

National Environmental Policy Act (NEPA)

Nonrenewable resources

Nutrient cycle

Organisms

Populations

Refuse Act

Renewable resources

Resource Conservation and Recovery Act (RCRA)

Rio Declaration on Environment and Development

Stakeholders

Systems analysis

Sustainable design

Sustainable development

Sustainable principles

UN Conference on the Human Environment

UN Conference on Environment and Development

World Commission on Environment and Development
    (WCED)

Exercises

1. To better understand how elements of a system are interrelated and interdependent, the assignment is to design and construct a functional mobile sculpture. The mobile should consist of pieces that are various shapes, sizes, and colors. The sculpture should be balanced when suspended from a ceiling. Provide the mobile sculpture and a written summary that describes how the sculptural design relates to elements of a system.

2. Review the international environmental conferences that have occurred since the UN Conference on the Human Environment (1972) in Stockholm, Sweden. In a written report, summarize the results of the conferences and identify how to apply the findings to sustainable interiors.

3. Draw a conceptual illustration that demonstrates the relationships between organisms, populations, communities, ecosystems, and the biosphere. Write a report that summarizes how the natural systems affect one another.

4. Research an individual who has made a significant impact on conserving natural resources. Develop an oral presentation that describes the person's contributions and how his or her efforts have impacted sustainability.

CHAPTER 2

Environmental Issues

"GOOD MORNING," said the little prince.

"Good morning," said the salesclerk. This was a salesclerk who sold pills invented to quench thirst. Swallow one a week and you no longer feel any need to drink.

"Why do you sell these pills?"

"They save so much time," the salesclerk said. "Experts have calculated that you can save fifty-three minutes a week."

"And what do you do with those fifty-three minutes?"

"Whatever you like."

"If I had fifty-three minutes to spend as I liked," the little prince said to himself, "I'd walk very slowly toward a water fountain . . ."

—ANTOINE DE SAINT EXUPÉRY

Objectives

- Analyze sources of energy and describe energy consumption patterns.
- Understand population growth rates of highly developed and developing countries, and their relationship to sustainability.
- Describe the factors that affect annual world population change.
- Analyze the characteristics and problems associated with natural resources, including air, water, soil, minerals, biodiversity, and land.
- Describe environmental concerns and challenges related to natural resources, including atmospheric changes, waste, and air, water, and soil pollution.
- Define indoor air quality (IAQ) and its related health concerns.

INTERIOR DESIGNERS have a responsibility to safeguard the health, safety, and welfare of the user's interior environment. To design sustainable interiors requires knowledge of problems associated with natural resources, and an understanding of the most effective conservation and preservation methods. Energy conservation is one of the most pressing challenges facing the world today.

Products and mechanical systems associated with the built environment consume high quantities of energy and have a significant impact on the environment. To specify sustainable products and processes requires knowledge of the interactions between people, energy, natural resources, and pollutants. Chapter 2 explains the interactions between people and the natural environment. This includes an examination of how pollutants affect human health, especially the consequences of indoor air pollution.

ENERGY AND PEOPLE

Chapter 1 explained the importance of solving global problems by considering the interrelated aspects of society, the environment, and economics. Many of the world's sustainability problems are connected to its demands for energy. For thousands of years people basically had adequate resources for energy. The current energy crisis started about 200 years ago when the Industrial Revolution advanced production and technological processes. To meet the current and future needs of people, sustainable energy policies must be enacted today.

Sources of Energy and Consumption Patterns

Basically energy is the capacity to do work. Forms of energy are used to heat and cool buildings, provide electricity, produce light, and transport people, products, and services. Energy is acquired by direct or indirect means. For example, heat energy can be directly obtained from fire. Gasoline for transportation is indirectly derived via the refinement of crude oil.

Sources of Energy

The world's primary sources of energy are fossil fuels, which include oil, natural gas, and coal. Other sources of energy include waterpower, nuclear en-

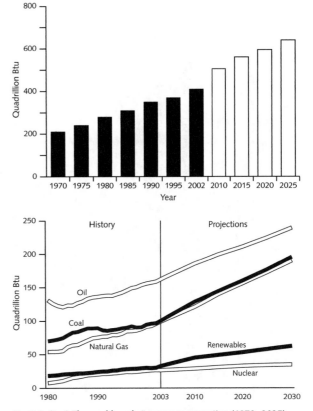

Fig. 2.1. (top) The world market energy consumption (1970–2025).
Fig. 2.2. (bottom) The world market energy use by fuel type (1980–2030).

ergy, wood, solar, wind, tidal, chemical, and geothermal (see Table 2.1). In projecting the future, potential energy sources include fuel cells, wastes, and hydrogen generation. Table 2.1 provides a summary of these sources of energy by focusing on consumption patterns, usages, pollutants, and challenges.

The **Energy Information Administration (EIA)** has been monitoring international energy demands. The findings of their work are published in a report titled *International Energy Outlook (IEO)*. The 2005 report summarizes the use of all energy sources and projects strong growth for worldwide energy demands from 1970 to 2025 (see Figure 2.1). Specifically, energy demands in China and Asia are expected to more than double during the forecast period.

As illustrated in Figure 2.2, oil, natural gas, and coal continue to supply most of the world's energy needs. Oil has the highest consumption due to the needs associated with transportation and industrial production. Compared to oil and coal, natural gas is "projected to be the fastest growing component of world primary energy consumption" (EIA, 2005, p. 3).

Table 2.1

Sources of Energy and Their Characteristics, Percentages of Use in the World, and Primary Uses

Sources of Energy	Characteristics / Advantages and Disadvantages	Percentage of Energy Used in the World	Primary Uses
Nonrenewable			
FOSSIL FUELS			
Petroleum (Oil)	Removed from deep in the earth, termed crude oil. Refineries process into gasoline and other products.	40% of commercial energy 40% of this used in U.S.	Transportation fuels, such as gasoline, diesel fuel, and heating fuel.
Coal	Mining for coal is a dangerous occupation. Releases sulfur and other pollutants.	26% of commercial energy 23% of this used in U.S.	Used to produce steam in boilers. Steam generates electric power. Heat homes in Asia and Europe. Generate steam for electric power.
Natural Gas	Comes from deposits in the earth. Refined naturally during its formation in the earth.	21% of commercial energy 25% of this used in U.S.	Heat buildings, cooking, and other household needs.
NUCLEAR ENERGY	**Nuclear fission**—splitting of atomic nuclei, such as uranium. Great amount of energy from small quantities of fuel. Problems: Thermal pollution and radioactive waste generation. Accidents can cause harmful radioactivity into the air. **Nuclear fusion**—combines atomic nuclei. Produces the heat and light of the sun and stars. Working to control reactions.	6% of commercial energy 8% of this used in U.S.	Nuclear fission: Power ships and generate electricity. Nuclear fusion: still developing.
Renewable			
DIRECT SOLAR			
Infrared Radiation	Capture energy and convert the sun's energy into heat or electrical energy.	Used throughout the world for various applications.	
Passive Solar Heating	Passive: Heat buildings without pumps or fans.		Flat or sloped plate collectors: convert solar energy to heat water and air in buildings.
Solar Thermal Generation (STG)	STG: Solar energy captured with lenses onto a fluid-filled pipe (generates electricity).		
Photovoltaic (PV) Solar Cells	PV: Solar energy captured with wafers or thin-film devices (generates electricity). **PV: Fastest growing of all renewable technologies.**		Solar cells (photovoltaic cells) convert daylight into electric energy.
Solar-Generated Hydrogen	Hydrogen: Uses PV-generated or wind-generated electricity to produce hydrogen fuel from water. Darkness and weather conditions affect success.		
INDIRECT SOLAR			
Biomass Energy/Bioenergy Wood, Plants, Crops, Sawdust, Wood Chips, Animal Wastes	Solid, liquid, or gas forms. Wood: Was the chief fuel of the world. Still main source for many developing countries. Residues from sawmills, paper mills, and agricultural industries used in power plants to generate electricity. Burning trash can produce heat and electrical energy. Liquid organic wastes (sewage) produce methane gas for fuel. Bioconversion: plant and animal wastes into fuel: methanol, natural gas, and oil. Reduces dependence on fossil fuels and reduces waste. Production requires land and water. Burning faster than replenishing is a problem.	At least half of the human population relies on biomass as main source of energy. 3% of total U.S. energy	Wood: Heating homes and cooking in developing countries. Highly developed countries limited to mainly fireplaces. Converted to liquid fuels—methanol and ethanol. Methane-rich biogas burned in a heat and power engine to power generators for electricity.

Energy Source	Description	Details	Notes
Wind Energy	Harness wind energy to generate electricity. Must have strong and steady winds to be functional. Great potential.	Most profitable in rural areas that receive continual winds. Working on technology for tall urban buildings.	Wind farms. Vertical axis wind turbines used to generate electric power. Heavy-duty turbines.
Waterpower (Hydropower)	Energy from water flowing from a higher place to a lower location. Gravity of the falling water is captured and used to produce energy. Needs dams or other structures to harness power. Dams have a negative impact on the environment.	7% of commercial energy 4% of this used in U.S.	Generate electric power.
Tidal Energy	Energy from high tide to low tide. Few geographical locations have large enough differences in water levels. High costs with building power stations and can cause environmental problems.	France, Russia, China, and Canada	Tidal: Generate power for electricity during falling tides.
Geothermal	Generated when water in contact with hot rocks in the ground. Only in locations with hot rocks near the surface. Seasonal underground heat and cold storage (summer heat stored for winter use and winter cold stored for summer use). Groundwater systems for heat pumps. Enormous quantities. Environmentally benign.	U.S. world's largest producer of geothermal electricity.	Steam created can generate electricity. Heat and cool buildings.

Future Energy Sources

Energy Source	Description	Details	Notes
INDIRECT SOLAR			
Ocean Waves	Waves can turn a turbine to generate electricity.	Norway, Great Britain, Japan, Scotland, and other countries are pursuing the technologies.	More testing is needed to be cost-effective.
Ocean Thermal Energy	Uses ocean temperature gradients to generate power (ocean thermal energy conversion—OTEC).	Hawaii is exploring ocean thermal energy.	
Bituminous Sands and Oil Shale	Sands: deposits of sand covered with an oil-producing substance. Oil shale: type of rock processed for crude oil and natural gas.		
Fuel Cell Technology	Batterylike devices: gas or liquid combine to generate electricity.		Limited. Very expensive.
Hydrogen	Hydrogen removed from water (hydrolysis) by passing an electric current through water. Burns easily, emits huge amounts of heat, water is by-product.		Requires enormous amounts of electricity—very costly. Could someday replace gas and oil.
Magnetohydrodynamic (MHD) Generators	Converts fuel directly to electric energy.		Technical problems must be solved before use.

SOURCES: Catania, P. (2002), Energy Supply; Raven & Berg (2004), Environment.

Coal consumption will continue to increase at a rate of 2.5 percent per year. As noted in Figure 2.2, consumption of renewable and nuclear energy is expected to be very low.

Fossil fuels were formed about 360 million years ago from the decay of organisms, such as skeletons and plants. Every process that uses fossil fuels as an energy source impacts the environment. For example, extracting the fuels from the earth can destroy the vegetation and topsoil. Extraction processes can also introduce toxins to nearby streams, rivers, or lakes. In transporting oil or natural gas, a potential collision can pollute the air, waterways, and land. Burning fossil fuels creates pollution and increases the levels of carbon dioxide in the atmosphere. The aftereffects from using fossil fuels also pose environmental problems. Abandoned underground gas tanks or offshore oil platforms can cause unrecoverable toxic seepage.

The EIA (2005) estimates the generation of electricity will nearly double between 2002 and 2025. Economic growth in developing countries is expected to increase demands for electricity to operate equipment and appliances. To generate electricity, natural gas is expected to be the preferred energy source. The EIA notes the important link between economic growth and the world's energy consumption. To analyze these energy consumption patterns, the EIA provides projections of energy consumption by "end-use," which includes the residential, commercial, and industrial sectors.

The EIA (2005) notes that the energy use in these three sectors "can vary widely from country to country, depending on a combination of regional factors." The EIA groups regions of the world by relative levels of economic development (see Figure 2.3). The new nomenclatures for the regions, as of 2005, are "mature market economies," "transitional economies," and "emerging economies." The EIA indicates that mature market economies "include nations whose energy markets are generally well-established and whose industrial sectors have trended away from more energy-intensive manufacturing industries toward less energy-intensive service industries" (2005, p. 2). Transitional economies include nations that are moving away from centrally planned economies and converting to free market economies. Nations in the emerging economies region have less

developed economies, but energy consumption patterns are expected to shift to practices that are exhibited by mature market economies.

An analysis of the residential sector includes all energy consumed by households, including heating, air conditioning, lighting, and high-energy-using appliances. The type and amount of energy consumed is dependent on the region, income levels, size of residential structure, and available energy infrastructure (EIA, 2005). As shown in Figure 2.4, residential energy use is generally higher in the mature market economies. However, the EIA projects that worldwide residential energy consumption will continuously increase due to the proliferation of electricity-using appliances. The EIA also notes, "In the United States, which is by far the largest residential energy consumer in the region (and the world), total residential electricity use is projected to grow on average by 1.6 percent per year" (2005, p. 17).

The commercial or service sector includes businesses, institutions, and organizations. Commercial sector examples include schools, retail stores, hotels, restaurants, hospitals, and office buildings. In commercial buildings, energy is used for heating, cooling, water heating, lighting, and cooking. The EIA (2005) explains that economic and population growth trends stimulate activities of the commercial sector and affect energy consumption patterns. For example, increases in the population require more services, such as health care, education, and retail stores. Communities with fairly affluent households generally have businesses that are supported by disposable income, such as restaurants, hotels, theaters, and fitness/training facilities. The mature market economies consume the greatest amount of commercial

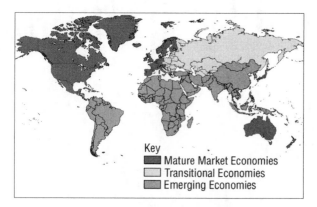

Fig. 2.3. The EIA 2005 world regions by mature market economies, transitional economies, and emerging economies.

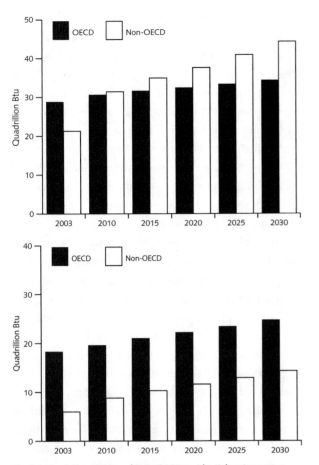

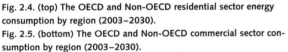

Fig. 2.4. (top) The OECD and Non-OECD residential sector energy consumption by region (2003–2030).
Fig. 2.5. (bottom) The OECD and Non-OECD commercial sector consumption by region (2003–2030).

energy (see Figure 2.5). The industrial sector includes manufacturing, agriculture, mining, and construction. Worldwide energy consumption in the industrial sector is projected to increase. However, the EIA projects that emerging economies, including China and the Middle East, will have the most growth. Furthermore, in the transportation sector "China is the key market that will lead regional consumption."

Energy Consumption and Challenges

The amount of energy consumed for electricity is a serious concern. According to EIA projections, "world net electricity consumption will nearly double over the next two decades." In analyzing electrical consumption patterns by region, the EIA estimates that more than half of projected growth of demand for electricity will occur in the emerging economies. The mature market economies will account for approximately 28 percent of the demand for electricity, followed by the transitional econo-

mies at 14 percent. The EIA also notes that "to meet the world's projected electricity demand over the 2002 to 2025 forecast period, an extensive expansion of installed generating capacity will be required" (2005, p. 67).

Worldwide, coal is the fuel that is used the most to generate electricity, and the EIA projects that this dominance will continue to at least 2025. Electricity generated from nuclear power rapidly increased during the 1970s and 1980s, and use of natural gas expanded during the 1980s and 1990s (EIA, 2005). The EIA also reported that due to high prices and international conflicts, oil for electrical generation has been slowly declining. In considering nonrenewable sources, the EIA projects "moderate growth in the world's consumption of hydroelectricity and other renewable energy resources." Most of the projected growth is attributable to countries with emerging economies, particularly in China, India, Laos, Brazil, Peru, and Venezuela.

Energy consumption depletes natural resources and has a negative impact on the environment. These problems affect the quality of life for people, and eventually can have a substantial impact on economics. One of the most significant problems is emissions from energy-related carbon dioxide. As one of the most dominant **greenhouse gases** in the atmosphere, carbon dioxide in large amounts is significantly contributing to global climate changes (see the next section for more information). According to the EIA, "world carbon dioxide emissions from the consumption of fossil fuels are expected to grow at an average rate of 2.0 percent per year from 2002 to 2025" (2005, p. 78). Recently, several nations signed an international agreement, the **Kyoto Protocol**, for the purpose of reducing or eliminating emissions of carbon dioxide and other greenhouse gases. Originally, the United States supported and signed the protocol in 1998. Subsequently, President Bush withdrew the United States from its commitment to the Kyoto Protocol.

Sustainable strategies for the energy crisis focus on energy conservation, improving efficiency, and developing new energy sources. These strategies should be accomplished with the least impact on the environment. Unit II provides suggestions for conserving energy and purchasing energy-efficient products and equipment. Energy conservation is especially important in this era of terrorist attacks. The U.S. economy is dependent on imported fossil fuels for energy. As a result, the United States is very vulnerable to disruptions in oil supplies, which may occur in troubled areas of the world. In addition, destruction of power plants in the United States would also place the nation in a perilous situation.

Human Populations

Many of the problems associated with energy consumption are due to the dramatic increases in the world's population. More energy is needed to meet the demands of additional people and the subsequent need for increases in products and services. Human beings are in the unique position to maintain, improve, or destroy the environment. Significant increases in the human population could degrade global ecosystems, create widespread famine, and promote disease. To avoid catastrophic conditions, people must understand world population growth rates and manage the planet within the constraints of its natural resources.

Demographics

Demography, a subdiscipline of sociology, is the study of population statistics. Demographers analyze a variety of statistics related to the populations of communities, regions, countries, and the world. In this text, the statistical tables for 227 countries and areas are derived from the **U.S. Census Bureau's International Data Base (IDB) (2005)**. In regard to sustainability, a very important statistic is the world population growth rate. The most basic formula for determining population growth (not including migration) is population growth = birth rate − death rate.

Demographers and sociologists research a variety of factors that affect population size, including capacity of the earth, standards of living, resource consumption, technological innovations, waste generation, natural disasters, and manmade disasters such as terrorist attacks. Population growth rates are critical to determining the point of **environmental resistance**, or the limits imposed by the environment. When organisms are not able to reproduce, the problem can be attributed to diseases and/or inadequate food, water, or shelter.

Global Demographics

Human beings have inhabited the earth for thousands of years. Prior to the last 200 years, birth and death rates were fairly equal. The world's population did not reach one billion until 1800. Since 1800 the world's population growth rate has been rising rapidly. Improvements in the medical field and technology have significantly affected population rates. From 1900 to 2000 the world's population rapidly increased to 6.1 billion. Once the world population reached one billion, significantly less time was required to add another billion people. At this rate of growth, demographers estimate that the world's population will be over 9.2 billion in 2050. From the sustainability perspective, the current requirements of an ecological footprint are impossible for 9 billion people.

Table 2.2 provides statistical data for the most relevant factors that affect sustainability. As a global concern, sustainability must be analyzed by examining the conditions of developed and less developed countries. Everyone is directly or indirectly impacted by the environmental and socioeconomic conditions of all nations. Thus, to have sustainable development, people living in highly developed countries should provide assistance to the less advantaged. To compare and contrast the two groups, Table 2.2 includes data from the world, less developed countries, and more developed countries. To create the regions, the U.S. Census Bureau utilizes the criteria established by the United Nations. The more developed countries or continents are Australia, Europe, Japan, New Zealand, North America, Georgia, Uzbekistan, and the other Soviet republics of the former Soviet Union. The less developed areas are Africa, Latin America, and the Caribbean, Mexico, and most of Asia and Oceania.

Table 2.2 includes total midyear populations, area, and density for every 10 years from 1950 to 2050. The density data in Table 2.2 reveal that people living in less developed countries have always had more crowded conditions than people in highly developed countries. Moreover, the projections illustrate this condition will continue until at least 2050. For example, in 2050 people in less developed countries will have 98.4 persons per square kilometer. In contrast, people in more developed countries will have 24.8 persons per square kilometer. The same population groups and time frames or periods are provided for vital rates and events from 1950 to 2050 (see Table 2.3).

Table 2.2
Midyear Populations for the World, Less Developed Countries, and More Developed Countries

Year	Population	Area (sq. km.)	Density (persons per sq. km.)
	World		
1950	2,556,517,137	131,003,018	19.5
1960	3,040,966,466	131,003,018	23.2
1970	3,708,751,360	131,003,018	28.3
1980	4,452,645,562	131,003,018	34.0
1990	5,282,765,827	131,003,018	40.3
2000	6,081,527,896	131,003,018	46.4
2010	6,825,750,456	131,003,018	52.1
2020	7,563,094,182	131,003,018	57.7
2030	8,206,457,382	131,003,018	62.6
2040	8,759,140,657	131,003,018	66.9
2050	9,224,375,956	131,003,018	70.4
	Less Developed Countries		
1950	1,749,772,512	81,166,205	21.6
1960	2,130,595,054	81,166,205	26.2
1970	2,705,547,634	81,166,205	33.3
1980	3,371,854,801	81,166,205	41.5
1990	4,139,736,415	81,166,205	51.0
2000	4,888,071,832	81,166,205	60.2
2010	5,601,672,047	81,166,205	69.0
2020	6,320,210,048	81,166,205	77.9
2030	6,957,380,835	81,166,205	85.7
2040	7,512,797,412	81,166,205	92.6
2050	7,988,909,895	81,166,205	98.4
	More Developed Countries		
1950	806,744,625	49,836,813	16.2
1960	910,371,412	49,836,813	18.3
1970	1,003,203,726	49,836,813	20.1
1980	1,080,790,761	49,836,813	21.7
1990	1,143,029,412	49,836,813	22.9
2000	1,193,456,064	49,836,813	23.9
2010	1,224,078,409	49,836,813	24.6
2020	1,242,884,134	49,836,813	24.9
2030	1,249,076,547	49,836,813	25.1
2040	1,246,343,245	49,836,813	25.0
2050	1,235,466,061	49,836,813	24.8

SOURCE: U.S. Census Bureau, International Data Base.

Table 2.3
Vital Rates and Events for the World, Less Developed Countries, and More Developed Countries

Year	Births (per 1,000 population)	Deaths (per 1,000 population)	Net Number of Migrants (per 1,000 population)	Rate of Natural Increase (percent)	Growth rate (percent)
		World			
1950	29.9	12.7	0.3	1.72	1.75 (183)*
1960	31.5	12.6	−0.0	1.90	1.89 (169)*
1970	31.1	11.0	−0.3	2.01	1.97 (139)*
1980	31.0	11.9	−0.1	1.91	1.90 (80)*
1990	26.1	9.3	0.2	1.68	1.70 (15)*
2000	21.2	8.9	0.0	1.23	1.23
2010	19.6	8.6	−0.0	1.11	1.11 (3)*
2020	17.6	8.4	0.0	0.92	0.92 (3)*
2030	15.9	8.8	0.1	0.71	0.72 (3)*
2040	15.1	9.4	0.1	0.57	0.58 (3)*
2050	14.4	10.0	0.1	0.44	0.45 (3)*
		Less Developed Countries			
1950	42.5	16.9	1.2	2.56	2.68 (157)*
1960	44.6	16.8	−0.3	2.78	2.76 (143)*
1970	41.2	12.9	−0.4	2.82	2.78 (114)*
1980	36.9	13.1	−0.9	2.37	2.29 (58)*
1990	28.8	9.2	−0.4	1.96	1.92 (1)*
2000	23.6	8.6	−0.4	1.50	1.46
2010	21.5	8.1	−0.4	1.34	1.30 (3)*
2020	19.1	7.9	−0.3	1.11	1.08 (3)*
2030	17.0	8.3	−0.2	0.87	0.85 (3)*
2040	16.0	8.9	−0.1	0.70	0.69 (3)*
2050	15.0	9.5	−0.1	0.55	0.54 (3)*
		More Developed Countries			
1950	25.1	11.1	0.0	1.40	1.40 (26)*
1960	19.5	8.7	0.2	1.08	1.10 (26)*
1970	18.1	8.5	−0.2	0.95	0.93 (25)*
1980	15.1	8.6	2.0	0.65	0.85 (22)*
1990	13.8	9.5	2.8	0.43	0.71 (14)*
2000	11.1	10.2	2.1	0.09	0.30
2010	11.0	10.4	1.6	0.05	0.21
2020	10.3	10.9	1.6	−0.06	0.09
2030	10.0	11.7	1.8	−0.16	0.02
2040	10.3	12.6	1.8	−0.23	−0.06
2050	10.4	13.2	1.7	−0.28	−0.11

*Data missing for one or more variables for the number of countries shown.

SOURCE: U.S. Census Bureau, International Data Base.

As shown in Table 2.3, the world growth *rates* are projected to decrease. This table is a means to study the birth and death rates of less and more developed nations.

Table 2.4 provides a list of the top 10 countries, ranked by population, for the years 1950, 2000, and 2050. The purpose of Table 2.4 is to summarize the countries that will require the greatest resources in the future and examine expected changes in the rankings. The countries requiring the greatest resources and their stage of development significantly affect the success of sustainable development. In

Table 2.4

Countries Ranked by Population, 1950, 2000, 2050

Rank	Country	Population
Countries Ranked by Population: 1950		
1	China	562,579,779
2	India	369,880,000
3	United States	152,271,000
4	Russia	101,936,816
5	Japan	83,805,000
6	Indonesia	82,978,392
7	Germany	68,374,572
8	Brazil	53,443,075
9	United Kingdom	50,127,000
10	Italy	47,105,000
Countries Ranked by Population: 2000		
1	China	1,268,853,362
2	India	1,002,708,291
3	United States	282,338,631
4	Indonesia	224,138,438
5	Brazil	175,552,771
6	Russia	146,731,774
7	Pakistan	146,342,958
8	Bangladesh	130,406,594
9	Japan	126,699,784
10	Nigeria	114,306,700
Countries Ranked by Population: 2050		
1	India	1,601,004,572
2	China	1,424,161,948
3	United States	420,080,587
4	Nigeria	356,523,597
5	Indonesia	336,247,428
6	Pakistan	294,995,104
7	Bangladesh	279,955,405
8	Brazil	228,426,737
9	Congo (Kinshasa)	183,177,415
10	Mexico	147,907,650

NOTE: Data updated 4-26-2005 (Release notes).
SOURCE: U.S. Census Bureau, International Data Base.

studying patterns for the years 1950 to 2050, China, India, and the United States are consistently ranked as the countries with the world's greatest populations. After the 1950 census, the United Kingdom, Germany, and Italy no longer appear in the list, and are replaced by Pakistan, Bangladesh, and Nigeria. The population projection indicates that by the year 2050, Russia and Japan will be replaced by Congo (Kinshasa) and Mexico.

U.S. Demographics

Data specifically related to the United States are critical to sustainable development and for understanding consumption rates of a highly developed country. Table 2.5 is IDB summary demographic data (2005 and 2025) for the United States. In comparing actual data for 2005 and estimated statistics for 2025, the number of births is the same (14), but the total fertility rate per woman is expected to increase to 2.2. The increase in the number of deaths in 2025 from 2005 helps to explain the decrease in the annual rate of growth. As shown in Table 2.5, the growth rate percentages have been decreasing since 1950. Many sociologists believe the reduced growth rate is a reflection of an increase in the use of contraceptives and various other factors. The demographics also indicate an increase in life expectancy from 77.7 to 80.5 years for someone born in 2005 and 2025, respectively. Figures 2.6 a, b, and c provide illustrations of life expectancies and demonstrate differences between genders. Increases in years of life can dramatically affect resource requirements and subsequently sustainable development.

Population increases result in higher levels of the consumption rates of natural resources, such as fossil fuels and nonrenewable minerals. However, population alone does not address consumption rates. Developed countries with high income levels consume more resources than developing countries. For example, according to the Population Reference Bureau, "more than half of the world's population lives on less than $2 per day" (2005) (see Table 2.6). Developed countries have consumed a disproportionate quantity of resources compared to less developed countries. For example, in 2002 the energy use per capita in more developed and less developed countries was 4,878 and 893, respectively (see Table 2.6). As shown in Table 2.6, energy consumption differences

Table 2.5
United States Demographic Indicators: 2005 and 2025

	2005	2025
Births per 1,000 population	14	14
Deaths per 1,000 population	8	9
Rate of natural increase (percent)	0.6	0.5
Annual rate of growth (percent)	0.9	0.8
Life expectancy at birth (years)	77.7	80.5
Infant deaths per 1,000 live births	6	5
Total fertility rate (per woman)	2.1	2.2

Midyear Population Estimates and Average Annual
Period Growth Rates: 1950 to 2050
(Population in thousands, rate in percent)

Year	Population	Year	Population	Period	Growth Rate
1950	152,271	2005	295,734	1950–1960	1.7
1960	180,671	2006	298,444	1960–1970	1.3
1970	205,052	2007	301,140	1970–1980	1.0
1980	227,726	2008	303,825	1980–1990	0.9
1990	250,132	2009	306,499	1990–2000	1.2
2000	282,339	2010	309,163	2000–2010	0.9
2001	285,024	2020	336,032	2010–2020	0.8
2002	287,676	2030	363,811	2020–2030	0.8
2003	290,343	2040	392,173	2030–2040	0.8
2004	293,028	2050	420,081	2040–2050	0.7

SOURCE: U.S. Census Bureau, International Data Base (IDB).

Table 2.6
Regional Comparisons of Economy, Area, Density, and Environment

Estimates	World	More Developed	Less Developed	Less Developed (excluding China)	United States
ECONOMY					
2004 gross national income PPP per Capita (US$)	$8,540	$26,320	$4,450	$4,100	$39,710
% population living below US$2 per day	53%	—	56%	59%	—
AREA AND DENSITY					
Area of countries (square miles)	51,789,601	19,814,584	31,975,017	28,278,917	3,717,796
Population density per square mile	125	61	165	140	80
ENVIRONMENT					
Urban					
Pop. with access to improved drinking water source (%) 2002	94%	100%	92%	92%	100%
Rural					
Pop. with access to improved drinking water source (%) 2002	71%	—	69%	70%	100%
Energy use per capita 2002 (kg oil equivalent)	1,669	4,878	893	869	7,943

SOURCE: 2005 World Population Data Sheet of the Population Reference Bureau.

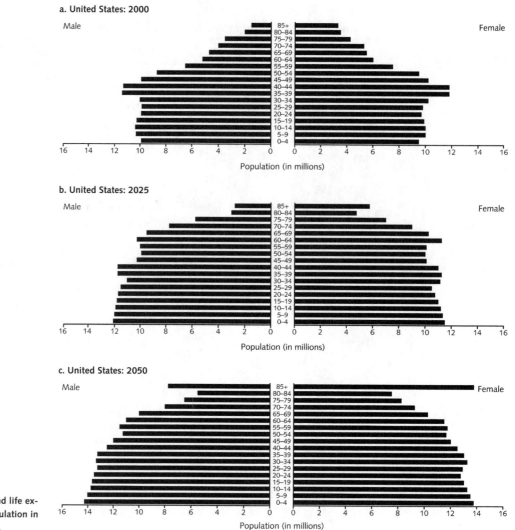

a. United States: 2000

b. United States: 2025

c. United States: 2050

Fig. 2.6a–c. Gender and life expectancies of U.S. population in 2000, 2025, and 2050.

are even greater when comparing the United States and developing countries. Interior designers are in a position to help reduce consumption rates, because a high percentage of their clientele have the financial resources to purchase substantial quantities of products and services.

High consumption of fossil fuels translates to higher levels of toxic emissions. The United States represents approximately 5 percent of the world's population but is responsible for emitting about 25 percent of the global emissions of carbon dioxide. This situation is a good example of environmental injustice. People in developed countries, including interior design professionals and their clients, should address the inequities by seriously engaging in environmental stewardship.

NATURAL RESOURCES: AIR

Demographic data must be applied to environmental concerns. High population growth and consumption rates contribute to pollution, deforestation, a reduction of biodiversity, and increases in solid and toxic waste. Pollutants significantly affect human health and the environment by creating acid rain, holes in the ozone layer, and changes in the global climate. In urban areas, numerous abandoned sites and buildings, or **brownfields**, pose significant problems for people and the entire ecosystem. In addition, pollutants in buildings have become a very serious problem. Interior designers must be involved in helping to reduce pollutants, including the problems related to the quality of indoor air.

Air Pollutants

It is a statement of the obvious that people need clean air. However, as evidenced by air pollution and changes to the climate, many people, communities, and countries tend to ignore the importance of air. The apparent apathy may be a reflection of an individual's lack of knowledge of the problem, or not understanding how to help eliminate pollution. The availability of air can give people the impression that cleanup activities are the responsibilities of governments or the polluting industry. Governmental agencies and many manufacturing companies have worked to improve air quality, but to adequately address the problem requires global collaborative initiatives.

To help contribute to improving air quality necessitates a basic understanding of air pollutants, consequences of the toxins, and approaches to controlling air pollution. Pure air is composed of water vapor, nitrogen, oxygen, argon, and a very small amount of carbon dioxide (0.4 percent). An essential interdependent relationship exists between air and the other elements of the natural environment (see Figure 2.7). As an element of the ecosystem, air quality affects and is affected by the other components in the environment. Thus, pollutants in the air affect all of the parts of the system, including water, soil, and people.

Pollutants can come from either a **point** or **nonpoint source pollutant**. Point source pollution is derived from one main source, such as a factory chimney or sewage pipe. Nonpoint source pollution is the result of the combined effect from various sources. For example, water pollution in a pond could be the result of toxins from a nearby landfill, pesticides used on farmland, and/or poisons from the residue of rainwater. Point and nonpoint sources of pollutants contribute to air pollution. Outdoor and indoor air pollution is the presence of contaminations that come from a variety of natural and human sources, such as volcanic eruptions, forest fires, gasoline fumes, **radon**, and **asbestos**.

The major categories of air pollution produced by people are **air toxics**, **carbon oxides**, **hydrocarbons**, **nitrogen oxides**, **ozone**, **particulate matter**, and **sulfur oxides**. Table 2.7 summarizes the major categories of outdoor air pollution by including compositional characteristics and their effects on people and the environment (EPA, 2005; Raven & Berg, 2004). Air pollution exists in the form of gases, or

Fig. 2.7. A model of the interdependent relationships between air and the other elements of the natural environment.

Table 2.7

Major Categories of Outdoor Air Pollutants and Their Effects on People, the Environment, and the Built Environment

Factors	Air Toxics	Carbon Oxides (CO: CO2, CO)	Hydrocarbons	Nitrous Oxides (NOX: NO, NO2)	Troposphere Ozone	Particulate Matter	Sulfur Oxides (SOX: SO2)
Description	Various chemicals: Chlorine Lead Formaldehyde	Chemical interaction between carbon and oxygen	Solid, liquid, or gas	Chemical interaction between nitrogen and oxygen Nitrogen dioxide NO2: dissolves in water vapor in air to form acids. Contributes to (O3)	Ground-level ozone (O3): Interaction between sunlight, air, nitrogen oxides, and VOCs	Solid particles Liquid droplets floating in air	Chemical interaction between sulfur and oxygen Sulfur dioxide (SO2): Formed from sulfur in coal, oil, and ores during combustion
Primary Sources	Industrial processes Burning of solid wastes	Transportation vehicles Burning of waste paper and plastic Carbon Dioxide (CO2): Heating/Cooling Electric power plants	Transportation vehicles Methane: Microbes from cattle and rice fields	Transportation vehicles Heating/Cooling Electric power plants	Smokestacks Cars Paints and solvents	Heating/Cooling Electric power plants Industrial processes	Heating/Cooling Electric power plants Industrial processes Volcanoes
Effects on People	Potential for long-term health problems Lead poisoning: mental retardation and learning disabilities	Carbon monoxide (CO): poisonous Reduces transfer of oxygen in blood Heart disease	Some dangerous to human health	Constrict airways Impair exchange of gases in lungs Affect immune system	Contributes to health problems: Colds Pneumonia Emphysema Inflammation of lungs Fibrosis of lungs	Constrict airways Impairs exchange of gases in lungs Cardiovascular pathology Microscopic especially harmful	Constrict airways Impair exchange of gases in lungs Bronchitis
Effects on Natural Environment		Smog CO2: Most important contributor to greenhouse gas due to high quantities. Contributes to global warming CO: Indirect global warming	Smog Methane (CH4): greenhouse gas and contributes to global warming	Smog Acid Deposition Nitrous oxide (N2O): greenhouse gas Damage plants	Smog Reduces air visibility Stresses plants	Industrial smog	Industrial smog Acid deposition Damaged vegetation Contributes to global warming
Effects on Built Environment	Dissolve concrete and stone Corrode metals Damage fabric, rubber, and plastics	Dissolve concrete and stone Corrode metals Damage fabric, rubber, and plastics	Dissolve concrete and stone Corrode metals Damage fabric, rubber, and plastics	Corrode metals Fade fabrics and dyes Weaken textile fibers Damage buildings and materials	Dissolves concrete and stone Corrodes metals Damages rubber, plastics, textiles, including cotton, acetate, nylon, polyester	Dissolves concrete and stone Corrodes metals Damages fabric, rubber, and plastics	Corrode metals Dissolve stone and concrete Fade fabrics

SOURCES: EPA (2005), Raven & Berg (2004).

particulates of solid or liquid matter. In general, air pollution can cause eye irritation, emphysema, chronic bronchitis, heart disease, and asthma, and can impair the functions of the respiratory and immune systems. Some chemicals can cause cancer, birth defects, and death. Air pollution contributes to smog, greenhouse gases, **atmospheric changes**, **acid deposition**, and the degradation of plants and reduces visibility. In addition, air pollution deteriorates materials used in the built environment, such as metals, stone, concrete, paints, and textiles.

Sources of Outdoor Air Pollution

As illustrated in Table 2.7, there are several primary sources of outdoor air pollution. Sources include modes of transportation, such as automobiles, trucks, airplanes, boats, and trains. Burning coal or oil for the production of electricity causes air pollution. Industrial processes can also produce pollutants in the air by burning solid wastes. Smog dramatically affects visibility, and at high levels smog can cause respiratory diseases (see Figure 2.8 a and b). The two major types of smog are **industrial smog** and **pho-**

Fig. 2.9. Photochemical smog is created by the interaction between sunlight and various chemicals in the air.

tochemical smog. The primary source of industrial smog is the combustion of household fuel. Serious dangers associated with industrial smog were made very apparent by London's "killer smog" in the winter of 1952. During this very short period of time, approximately 4,000 people died from respiratory diseases. Photochemical smog is created by the interaction between sunlight and various chemicals in the air (see Figure 2.9). Photochemical smog is more prevalent in the summer, and is visible as a brownish-orange-colored haze. The primary sources of photochemical smog are car emissions, yeast by-products from bakeries, and toxic fumes from dry cleaners.

Another serious environmental problem associated with air pollution is acid deposition, or acid rain. The primary sources of acid rain are sulfur and nitrogen oxides, which are produced by burning fossil fuels and other industrial processes. Acid rain exists in wet and dry forms. Wet acid deposition occurs when rain, snow, sleet, mist, or fog has acidic chemicals. Dry acid deposition occurs when particles float in the air or when they land on earth. Rain can wash off the dry, acidic particles from trees and buildings. A very toxic situation can occur when precipitation combines wet deposition of acids with dry acidic particles. Toxicity levels are significantly increased when the acidic runoff water is combined with acidic rain. In the United States, acid deposition is primarily created by motor vehicles and by burning fossil fuels such as coal for electric power.

Acid deposition is a major global problem for urban and rural areas because the oxides in the air can travel great distances. For example, acid emissions of the United States have traveled to Canada.

a

b

Fig. 2.8a. Visibility without high levels of smog.
Fig. 2.8b. Smog dramatically affects visibility, and at high levels smog can cause respiratory diseases.

Fig. 2.10. As illustrated by damage to the Parthenon in Athens, Greece, acidic particles contribute to the corrosion of metals, stone, and building materials.

Acid deposition affects ecosystems, especially aquatic organisms, birds, and forests. Acidic particles contribute to the corrosion of metals, stone, and building materials. Consequently, acid deposition is responsible for severely damaging buildings, monuments, and historic sites throughout the world. Significant examples include the Parthenon in Greece, the Statue of Liberty in New York City, and the ancient Mayan ruins in Mexico (see Figure 2.10).

Atmospheric Changes

Scientists believe that air pollution is contributing to global atmospheric changes. This is primarily evident by increases in greenhouse gases and the deterioration of the **stratosphere** ozone. The **greenhouse effect** (see Figure 2.11) occurs when solar radiation is absorbed and reflected by the earth. Greenhouse gases help to warm the earth by retaining some of the infrared radiation. The naturally occurring greenhouse effect requires some greenhouse gases; however, the additional amounts of gas from pollution alter the balance of the system. As evidenced by global changes, including the size of the polar cap, scientists contend that the greenhouse gases are retaining too much of the infrared radiation (see Figure 2.12). In September 2005, an article in the *Chicago Tribune* noted, "Scientists suggest Arctic cap is smallest in century." Mark Serreze, a scientist, reported, "This summer was the fourth in a row with

ice cap areas sharply below the long-term average" (Revkin, 2005, p. 10). The negative consequences of warmer temperatures are (1) increases in infectious diseases such as malaria, (2) more frequent tropical storms, (3) floods from higher water levels, (4) the retention of destructive insects, and (5) a loss of biodiversity. According to the **National Energy Information Center (NEIC)**, in the United States 82 percent of the greenhouse gases are related to energy, including fuel for generating electricity and the carbon dioxide emissions from oil and natural gas.

Air pollution is also creating holes in the earth's ozone. Ozone exists in the earth's **troposphere** and stratosphere. However, ozone in the troposphere is not good and ozone in the stratosphere is essential. As shown in Table 2.7, troposphere ozone is one of the primary categories of air pollution and, consequently, negatively affects human health and the

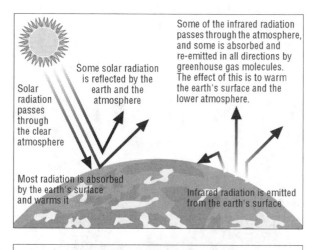

Fig. 2.11. (top) The greenhouse effect occurs when solar radiation is absorbed and reflected by the earth.

Fig. 2.12. (bottom) As evidenced by global changes, including the size of the polar cap, scientists contend that the greenhouse gases are retaining too much of the infrared radiation.

environment. Detrimental ozone is created by the combination of sunlight and chemical reactions between oxides of nitrogen and **volatile organic compounds (VOCs)**. The major sources of troposphere ozone are industrial plants, electrical utilities, transportation vehicles, and chemical solvents.

The ozone in the stratosphere is a protective layer that helps to filter harmful rays of the sun. Destroying the ozone could result in more skin cancer, cataracts, and the elimination of some plants. Scientists in the 1970s found that chlorofluorocarbons (CFCs), aerosol propellants used in products such as hairspray, were destructive to the ozone. In 1978 the U.S. government prohibited the use of CFCs as propellants in aerosol cans, but the substance remains in the atmosphere for a long period of time. Other substances that deplete the ozone are used in pesticides, fire extinguishers, and appliances with refrigerants, such as refrigerators, humidifiers, and window air conditioners.

Indoor Air Pollution

Naturally, indoor air quality is affected by outdoor pollution. However, in recent years scientists have been concerned about indoor air pollution that is attributable to interior materials and substances. Research indicates that some interiors have a much higher level of pollution than outdoors. This situation is compounded by the fact that currently people spend about 90 percent of their time indoors. This percentage reflects people who have chosen this lifestyle and individuals who are essentially confined to the indoors, such as young children, the elderly, and people afflicted with an illness. For the latter group, spending a majority of time indoors is especially problematic, because these are the people who are very susceptible to the health problems associated with pollutants. Children can have long-term health problems due to indoor air pollution, because pollutants can impair the growth and development of their respiratory system.

Building-Related Illnesses (BRI) and Sick Building Syndrome (SBS)

Indoor air quality (IAQ) environmental problems can be divided into two categories: **building-related illnesses (BRI)** and **sick building syndrome (SBS)**. Symptoms associated with BRI require a physician's diagnosis and are considered more serious than SBS. Some of the illnesses associated with BRI are asthma, carbon monoxide poisoning, Legionnaire's disease (type of pneumonia), hay fever, and other infectious or allergic diseases. Most illnesses appear soon after exposure, but some, such as cancer, may not appear until after a prolonged period of time. The causes of BRI can be identified, such as the detrimental effects from radon. Sick building syndrome occurs when people who are working or living in the same building experience similar health problems, such as headaches, dizziness, nausea, depression, or eye irritations. When people who experience SBS leave the building, they no longer have the shared symptoms. Sick building syndrome cannot be traced to any specific cause.

Indoor air pollution can occur from a variety of sources and conditions. The most common indoor contaminants are **formaldehyde**, radon, **biological agents**, carbon monoxide, cigarette smoke, household pesticides, nitrogen dioxide, cleaning solvents, ozone, asbestos, lead, and VOCs. Table 2.8 provides a summary of indoor contaminants, including descriptions, sources, and health effects (Aerias, 2005; EPA, 2005; Health Canada, 2005). Contaminants that are often associated with the field of interior design are explained in greater detail in the next section of this chapter. Health problems associated with contaminants vary according to the overall health and age of an individual, and the characteristics of the chemicals. Variations in health effects can also include the quantity of the chemical and the length of exposure.

In addition to pollutants, humidity and moisture affect the quality of indoor air. This is especially problematic in spaces where water is involved with performing tasks, such as kitchens and bathrooms. Basements and crawlspaces are also areas where water can be a problem, in particular in spaces without moisture barriers. Some of the indicators of problems with moisture and humidity are condensation on windows and wall surfaces, wet stains, moisture blisters, rust, rotted wood, cracked masonry, mold on objects, and musty-smelling odors. High levels of moisture are detrimental to people with allergies or asthma and can degrade interior materials such as fabrics, plaster, and wood.

Table 2.8

Major Categories of Indoor Air Pollutants, Sources, and Their Effects on People and the Built Environment

Indoor Contaminants	Description	Primary Sources	Health Effects
Formaldehyde	One of the VOCs Colorless gas chemical used to produce building materials and household products	Some carpets Carpet backings Vinyl wall covering Some textile fabric finishes (i.e. permanent-press) Vinyl flooring Fabrics Furniture Plastics Hardwood plywood Softwood plywood Particle board Medium-density fiberboard Insulation Varnishes Furniture stains Floor finishes Water-based paints (especially gloss finish) Glues/adhesives/binders Cigarette smoke Household products Fire retardants Cardboard and paper Unvented fuel-burning equipment (i.e., gas stoves; kerosene space heaters)	Irritant Headaches Sore throat/coughing/wheezing Eye irritation
Radon	Colorless, odorless, and tasteless radioactive gas that occurs naturally from the breakdown of uranium in soil, rock, and water	Radioactive gas that is emitted from the ground into the air and soil Within a building, the primary sources are exposed soil/rock in crawlspaces; cracks in foundation walls and floors; holes in wall joints, support posts; and floor drains.	Lung cancer
Biological Agents	Fungi (yeasts, molds, and mildew); dust mites, pet dander, rodent/pests/insect droppings	Areas that possess moisture or water Cooling coils Humidifiers Condensation collectors Unvented rooms with high moisture content such as bathrooms, kitchens Window treatments Bedding Carpets Windows	Asthma from mold, dust mites, pet dander Tuberculosis Measles Staphylococcus infections Legionnaire's disease Influenza

Carbon Monoxide	An inorganic compound that is a by-product of the burning of fossil fuels.
	Colorless gas or liquid
	Close to odorless
	Tasteless
		Fuel-burning equipment (natural gas, propane, oil)
		Unvented gas space heaters
		Unvented kerosene heaters
		Cigarette smoke
		Leaking chimneys
		Leaking furnaces
		Gas water heaters
		Wood fireplaces and stoves
		Burning coal and charcoal
		Generators
		Gasoline-powered equipment
			Can inhibit oxygen intake
			Fatigue
			Chest pains—people with heart disease
			Higher concentrations:
			  Impaired vision
			  Impaired coordination
			  Headaches
			  Dizziness
			  Confusion
			  Nausea/Vomiting
			Extreme exposure:
			  Brain damage
			  Coma
			  Death

Table 2.8 (continued)

Indoor Contaminants	Description	Primary Sources	Health Effects
Household Pesticides	Products used for insecticides and disinfectants Available in sprays, liquids, sticks, powders, crystals, balls, and foggers Origin can be from use in a building or brought into a space from products used outdoors.	Pesticide sprays (insects, termites, rodents, fungi) Lawn and garden chemicals Household cleaners	Skin, throat, and eye irritation Respiratory problems Digestive tract problems Damage to nervous system and kidney Increase risk of cancer Headaches
Nitrogen Dioxide	A red-brown-colored gas or a yellow colored liquid A highly reactive oxidant and corrosive	Unvented gas stoves and heaters Kerosene heaters Carbon monoxide gas appliances Cigarette smoke Vented appliances with faulty installations	Respiratory problems Skin, throat, and eye irritation Fatigue Dizziness
Asbestos	A mineral fiber used for construction materials and fire-retardant applications Disturbing materials containing asbestos creates airborne asbestos.	Insulation Floor and ceiling tiles Acoustical materials Fireproofing Textured paints Millboard Pipe and furnace insulation materials Roof shingles Coating materials Thermal and electrical insulation	Long-term effects include chest and abdominal cancer Lung diseases Mesothelioma (cancer of the chest and abdominal linings) Asbestosis (irreversible lung scarring)

Lead	Metallic element of the periodic table that is highly toxic, particularly in young children. Removing lead-based materials, such as paint, releases toxic lead dust in the air.	Air, water, and soil
		Food
		Lead-based paint
		Dust
		Gasoline
		Soldering
		Stained-glass production
			All systems of the body
			Low levels:
			  Impair mental and physical development
			Mid-levels:
			  Affects central nervous system, kidney, and blood cells
			High levels:
			  Convulsions
			  Coma
			  Death

Mercury	Odorless gas or liquid metal	Vapor lamps Some fluorescent lamps Batteries Thermometers Some glassware Latex paint prior to 1991	Eye, skin, and lung irritation Damage to the nervous system Increase in blood pressure Kidney damage

Volatile organic compounds (VOCs)	INDOORS
	Organic chemicals used in interior products
	Can include methane, propane, pentane, ethylene, acetylene, benzene, ethanol, formaldehyde, ether, and ketones
	Products can release VOCs during use and at times when in storage.
	OUTDOORS
	Gasoline fumes
	Smog former
		Color pigment in paint is dissolved in a mixture of VOCs.
		Varnishes
		Wax
		Paint strippers/thinners and solvents
		Wood preservatives
		Aerosol sprays
		Plastics
		Lacquer production
		Degreasing
		Moth repellents
		Air fresheners
		Stored fuels
		Automotive products
		Dry-cleaned clothing
		Contained in some products:
		  Cleaning
		  Cosmetics
		  Hobby Supplies
			Eye, nose, and throat irritation
			Headaches
			Irritability; difficult to concentrate
			Loss of coordination
			Nausea
			Damage to liver, kidney, and central nervous system
			Some can cause cancer in humans and animals
			Limits the growth of plants

SOURCES: Aerias (2005); EPA (2005); Health Canada (2005).

Formaldehyde, Radon, and Noise

Formaldehyde is a chemical that is frequently used in materials for construction and products specified by interior designers, such as furniture and textiles. The two primary sources of formaldehyde resins are urea-formaldehyde (UF) and phenol-formaldehyde (PF). Urea-formaldehyde is present in the adhesives used to produce interior pressed wood products, such as particleboard and hardwood plywood paneling. According to the EPA, medium density fiberboard, which is used for furniture drawer fronts, cabinets, and tops of furniture, "contains a higher resin-to-wood ratio than any other UF pressed wood product" (2005). In addition, this fiberboard is generally recognized as being the "highest formaldehyde-emitting pressed wood product." Phenol-formaldehyde resin is used in pressed wood products for exterior construction. The PF resins in pressed woods release formaldehyde at a lower rate than products with UF resins. However, the EPA reports that the rate of emissions can change depending on the age of a product and room temperatures. Generally, formaldehyde emissions will decrease with time, but high room temperatures or high humidity levels can accelerate the discharge of the chemical.

Radon is considered one of the most serious contaminants that can be present in an interior. The **World Health Organization (WHO)** reported that radon is attributable to approximately 15 percent of lung cancers in the world. The potential of having lung cancer is exacerbated by the combination of radon and cigarette smoke. Radon is a radioactive gas that is derived from the natural breakdown of uranium in soil, rock, and water. The breakdown of uranium emits radon gas into the air and in soil. This is a safe emission because radon combines with other atmospheric conditions. However, radon that is emitted to an enclosed space, such as a school, becomes dangerous to the inhabitants. The primary source of radon in a building is from the breakdown of uranium in the soil. Through this process, radon primarily enters a building through any opening close to the ground. According to the EPA, the most common sources for the emission of radon into a building are construction joints; cavities inside walls; cracks in floors or walls; exposed soil or rock in crawlspaces; gaps in suspended floors, posts, or serv-

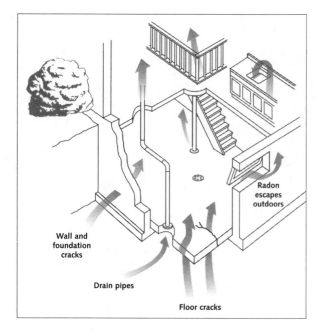

Fig. 2.13. Some of the most common sources for the emission of radon into a building.

ice pipes; the water supply; and floor drain pipes and sumps (see Figure 2.13).

Various types of buildings can have high levels of radon. Buildings that shelter people for the greatest amount of time are the most critical. Generally this group includes residences, office buildings, and schools. Within these structures, radon can be present in buildings that are new, old, well insulated, drafty, and with or without basements. The radon levels can vary from house to house within a neighborhood. The levels of radon in a building from soil gas are dependent on the amount of uranium contained in the soil and the number of points of entry. Other factors include the exchange rates of indoor and outdoor air, the condition of the foundation, and weather conditions. Unfortunately, the goal of creating energy-efficient buildings has contributed to escalation in the levels of radon gas. Buildings that allow for a high exchange rate between indoor and outdoor are less susceptible to problems with radon gas. Radon gas emitted through soil is the most serious form of the contaminant; however, radon can enter a building through the water supply. This is most likely to occur when a building is connected to a groundwater source, such as a well.

Noise pollution is also an environmental problem that can affect the mental and physical well-being of people, including inducing stress-related illnesses. Noise can be any disturbing sound that is loud, annoying, interferes with tasks, or damages hearing. In addition to permanent hearing loss, noise can increase blood pressure, dilate the pupils of the eyes, and cause migraine headaches. Noise is most problematic when exposure to the sound is for a long duration. Some of the factors that affect perceptions of noise are physical attributes of someone's hearing and subjective impressions. Activities taking place and equipment used outdoors contribute to most noise pollution, but an interior designer should survey an interior to determine sources of indoor noise. Sources of indoor noise can be echoes from the configuration of voluminous space; sound reflecting from hard materials; and humming from HVAC (heating, ventilating, and air conditioning) systems, lighting systems, appliances, and equipment.

NATURAL RESOURCES: WATER AND SOIL

Interior designers must be cognizant of how the products and processes associated with interiors contribute to polluting air, water, and soil. Water and soil are essential to the lives of people and are critical components of ecosystems. Sustainability cannot be achieved without healthy water and fertile soil. To foster sustainable designs, interior designers must understand the value of natural resources, sources of

pollution, and methods that can be used to prevent pollution.

Water Pollution and Management

All organisms on earth require water for existence. Approximately three-quarters of the earth is water, but most of this is salt water, which is not suitable for drinking or irrigation. The amount of freshwater (~2.5 percent) on Earth is very limited, and could become very scarce with a simultaneous occurrence of increases in global population and pollution. The horrors of polluted water were very evident when hurricane Katrina ravished the Gulf Coast in 2005 (see Figure 2.14). In the City of New Orleans, the EPA tested the floodwaters to determine the presence of more than 100 priority pollutants, such as VOCs, metals, pesticides, herbicides, and **polychlorinated biphen-yls (PCBs)**. The EPA reported that the quantities of lead, hexavalent chromium, and arsenic in the water exceeded EPA "drinking water action levels" (2005).

In analyzing chemicals and bacteria, the EPA also found the levels of *E.coli* in sampled areas greatly exceeded the EPA's recommended levels for contact. Therefore, the EPA suggested that "every effort should be made to limit contact with floodwater due to potentially elevated levels of contamination associated with raw sewage and other hazardous

Fig. 2.14. The horrors of polluted water were very evident when Hurricane Katrina ravished the Gulf Coast and the city of New Orleans in 2005.

substances" (2005). In addition, excessive moisture from the rains and floods prompted health and environmental problems associated with biological agents, such as mold and mildew.

Surface water, groundwater, and precipitation are the major sources of water. Surface water includes bodies of water that are above the earth's surface, such as lakes, rivers, and streams. Groundwater is the water supply that is underground, and provides a great amount of drinking water. Precipitation soaks into the ground, falls into surface water, or becomes runoff from hard surfaces. To conserve water and reduce pollution requires careful analysis of what transpires at every source.

Water pollution occurs when chemical or physical changes in the water's environment adversely affect aquatic ecosystems. As described in the previous section of this chapter, acid deposition is a serious problem that affects air and water quality. The primary sources of water pollutants are airborne particles and contaminants derived from agricultural production, industry, and sewerage outlets. The pollutants include toxic chemicals, heavy metals, and various other contaminants. For example, chemical fertilizers and pesticides from farming operations can pollute groundwater and numerous other sources of water. Groundwater can be polluted when excessive concentrations of animal waste and agricultural chemicals are repeatedly applied to the soil. Other waterways can be contaminated when these pollutants combine with water, and then flow into a pond, river, lake, or ocean.

Water Management

In addition to problems associated with water pollution, the world has serious issues with managing water. Too much or too little water is equally devastating. The Gulf Coast floods in 2005 reflect what can happen when too much water must be managed. Flooding destroyed many communities, and the excessive contaminations resulted in very unhealthy conditions. Another concern is not having enough water to meet the needs of people, farming, industry, and the environment. In the United States, the largest use for water is agricultural irrigation, followed by electric power production, industrial use, and then residential usage.

Water shortages that exist throughout the world

are attributed to population growth, inadequate purification processes, or arid conditions. Water resources may not be able to accommodate the significant population growth rates of countries such as Brazil, India, and China. The World Health Organization (WHO) reports that in 2002, 1.1 billion people, or 17 percent of the world's population, lacked access to improved water sources. Two-thirds of this group lived in Asia. In sub-Saharan Africa, the region south of the Sahara desert, 42 percent of the population was without improved water. A lack of safe drinking water and sanitation facilities is responsible for millions of people becoming ill or dying each year. Water-related diseases can include diarrhea, malaria, and hepatitis A.

Approximately 40 percent of the world's population lives in arid or semiarid countries. To compound this situation, many of these countries are still developing, which generally means their primary focus is trying to feed people. Farming in arid conditions requires irrigation methods that consume high quantities of water. In addition to reducing water supplies for drinking and bathing, developing countries do not have the resources to build and operate water treatment facilities. In the United States, many of the arid and semiarid areas in the West and Southwest also have high population densities, such as Arizona and California.

Case Study: Complexities of Water and Sustainable Development

Developing and implementing water management strategies are critical, yet very difficult to accomplish. To better understand the challenges of water management, an effective approach is to study the situation that has been occurring in Southern California. This case study is especially useful in understanding sustainable development, because California's water management issue incorporates societal and environmental issues. Historical data for the following analysis are derived from a speech titled *Stepping Outside the Box: Water in Southern California*, presented by Martha Davis at a UCLA Environment Symposium on March 3, 1998. The complete Davis transcription is available at www.monolake.org/waterpolicy/outsidebox.htm.

According to Davis, the land area of the Los Angeles basin is 6 percent of California's total land area. In

Fig. 2.15. Los Angeles attempted to acquire adequate water by extracting water from numerous sources.

1998, the basin had .06 percent of the state's stream flow to serve the needs of 16 million people, which represents more than 45 percent of the people living in California. Davis indicated that the basin's population was expected to increase to more than 24 million people. In considering the ecological footprint of either population size, and the amount of stream water in California, it is apparent that the basin has serious water shortages. As Davis quoted Carey McWilliams, "God never intended Southern California to be anything but desert. . . . Man has made it what it is" (1946).

Efforts to have adequate water in a desert started during the settlement years of Los Angeles and continue today. In the earliest years, solutions focused on satisfying the supply of water by building artesian wells and aqueducts. Extensive pumping was used to mine for the underground water supply. In the late 1800s and early 1900s, Los Angeles attempted to acquire adequate water by extracting water from numerous sources, including the San Fernando Valley (originally separate from Los Angeles), the Owens Valley, Owens River, Owens Lake, and, via Boulder Dam, the Colorado River. This required hundreds of miles of aqueduct to transport the water (see Figure 2.15). Just the aqueduct from the Owens River to the edge of the San Fernando Valley was 238 miles long. Originally the aqueduct was used only for agricul-

tural purposes in the valley, not to supply water to the people of Los Angeles.

The lack of sufficient water for people stimulated the process of seeking more water from external sources. To help accomplish this goal, in 1928 Los Angeles helped to create the Metropolitan Water District (MWD) of Southern California. The MWD was instrumental in helping to finance the Colorado River project. The MWD also extended the Owens aqueduct to the Mono basin and Mono Lake, which is 350 miles from Los Angeles. The Owens aqueduct was expanded again in the 1950s, when water was diverted from Northern to Southern California. By the 1970s, Southern California "was connected by a vast network of federal, state, and local dams and aqueducts to water supplies from Northern California and the Colorado River watersheds."

Unfortunately, these "rearview mirror" strategies never resolved Southern California's water shortage problems and created environmental disasters. Davis explained that the first 50 years in the state's history focused on the construction of dams and aqueducts. The second 50 years focused on "coping with the environmental problems created by those projects" (1998). The water diversions to Los Angeles resulted in converting the agricultural land of Owens Valley into brush. Furthermore, Owens Lake became a hole filled with dirt. Other aquatic ecosystems affected by the diverted waters were San Francisco's Bay Delta and Mono Lake. As illustrated in Figure 2.16, the aqueduct diversion resulted in severe drops in the water level of Mono Lake. Local economies were devastated by the lack of water for crops and fisheries. Multiple problems stimulated litigation and water battles, and yet officials continued to request the construction of more dams and aqueducts. Officials thought this was necessary because Southern California still did not have an adequate supply of water for people.

In the 1990s, the people of California responded to their problems by developing comprehensive strategic plans that involved all the stakeholders. Legislation was enacted that required existing water projects to return water to the environment. The MWD imposed water rationing and established a water conservation program. In addition MWD developed a groundwater management program and created water-recycling programs. These strategic plans, which emphasized decreasing demand, were very successful. Davis indicated that in 1998, the MWD service area was using approximately the same

Fig. 2.16. The city of Los Angeles aqueduct diversion resulted in severe drops in the water level of Mono Lake.

amount of water that was used in 1983 "despite an almost 30 percent growth in its population." Davis added that in 1998 the city of Los Angeles also had success with water conservation. Moreover, investments in the 1990s resulted in new locally based water supplies that were reliable. Davis concluded her speech by suggesting that California should always have "aggressive water conservation and recycling programs that will reshape demand in California."

Industrial Waste

Industrial waste that enters the waterways can come directly from sewage pipes or from acid rain, which originated from smokestacks. Some industries dump waste or heated water directly into bodies of water. Waste materials can include radioactive substances, heavy metals, and various toxic chemicals. Drinking water with chemicals that contain carbon can cause cancer and could attack the body's nervous system. Furthermore, chemicals can be toxic to fishes, plants, and animals living in bodies of water. Industrial processes that emit heated water into the waterways, called **thermal pollution**, are also detrimental to aquatic ecosystems. An unnatural water temperature alters the ecosystem's balance in a variety of ways, including accelerating the rate of decomposition and decreasing the supply of oxygen. In addition, unsuitable water temperatures can kill or shorten the life span of some species. Thermal pollution is especially problematic with the addition of other nutrients, such as fertilizers, that stimulate plant and algae growth. An overabundance of fish, plants, animals, or algae creates an unbalanced ecosystem, which eventually can result in a body of water with no oxygen or life.

Sewage dumped into waterways is a major source of water pollution. The contents of sewage primarily are derived from storm drains and sanitary sewers. Storm drains collect precipitation and any runoff from hard surfaces. Thus, acid rain and any contaminants collected from runoff, such as gasoline or oil on a driveway, can flow into storm drains and then become part of polluted sewage. Wastewater from sinks, toilets, showers, dishwashers, and washing machines from buildings flows into sanitary sewers. Wastewater contains soap, detergent, human waste, and any other substances deposited into drains. A wastewater treatment process extracts approximately 95 percent of the waste in sewage. The treated water is then dumped into waterways, such as rivers or lakes. To protect water quality, the two most important federal laws are the **Safe Drinking Water Act (SDWA)** and the **Clean Water Act (CWA)**. To continuously improve the quality of water, the acts have been amended several times. For example, in 1988 the law banned the use of lead solder in water pipes used for water in new construction projects.

Soil

Soil is a terrestrial system of layers that is composed of minerals, organic matter (i.e., worms, insects, fungi, algae), water, and air. Soil composition can vary greatly depending on multiple factors, including the age of the soil, type of minerals, weather conditions, organisms, decomposition rates, topography, and the quality and quantities of water and air. To grow crops, which feed people and animals, requires fertile soil. Sustainable soil practices are essential to meet the needs of people today and future generations. Sustainability is especially important because to make soil requires hundreds or thousands of years.

Most soil degradation is caused by irresponsible agricultural practices, deforestation, and overgrazing of animals. Some of the agricultural methods that degrade soil are tillage methods that cause soil loss, and depleting the nutrients in the soil by continuously planting the same crops. Trees and vegetation help to prevent soil from being blown or washed away during a rainstorm. Some of the serious environmental problems that have occurred in California have resulted from deforestation of hillsides and mountains. A great number of trees and brush were removed to build houses and roads along the sides of mountains. Consequently, during the rainy seasons disastrous mudslides may occur because there isn't enough soil and vegetation to absorb the rain. Eventually, soil erosion can create gullies that are barren and dry. The problems continue during the hot and dry times of the year, because the lack of vegetation can create the ideal conditions for starting and spreading fires.

Sustainable soil practices must include preventing pollution. As an interdependent element of ecosys-

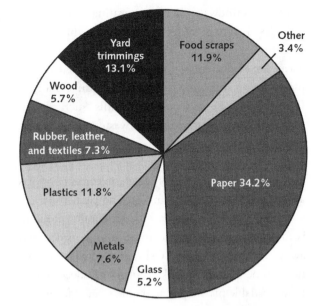

Fig. 2.17. 2005 Total MSW Generation, 246 Million Tons (Before Recycling). Most municipal solid waste is composed of paper (34.2 percent), yard trimmings (13.1 percent), metals (7.6 percent), plastics (11.8 percent), food scraps (11.9 percent), glass (5.2 percent), and other (3.4 percent).

tems, soil quality affects air, water, plants, animals, and people. As discussed in previous sections of this chapter, contaminants in air and water can pollute soil. Other sources of soil pollution are solid and hazardous wastes. These sources pollute the soil, and then further environmental damage can occur when the poisoned soil emits pollutants to the air, groundwater, and bodies of surface water. **Municipal solid waste** is debris from residential and commercial buildings. As illustrated in Figure 2.17, most municipal solid waste is composed of paper (34.2 percent), yard trimmings (13.1 percent), metals (7.6 percent), plastics (11.8 percent), food scraps (11.9 percent), glass (5.2 percent), and other (3.4 percent) (EPA, 2005). The greatest amount of solid waste is from industry, which includes mining, agriculture, and manufacturing. Solid waste from the industrial sector includes fossil fuel combustion waste, medical waste, and construction/demolition debris. Solid waste can be hazardous or nonhazardous.

Solid and Hazardous Waste Management

The United States leads the world in the amount of solid waste. The primary means to dispose of municipal solid wastes are sanitary landfills (55.4 percent), recycling (30.1 percent), and combustion (14.5 percent). Sanitary landfills are designed to protect soil and groundwater by incorporating several technologies. Drainage pipes are buried in the ground to collect the liquid wastes and then transport the waste for treatment. The ground is covered with a plastic lining and compacted clay. To reduce many of the problems associated with landfills, such as rats, odors, and fires, applications of waste are alternated with soil.

Some of the major problems associated with landfills are the production of flammable methane gas and toxins that can seep into groundwater from defects in the liners. Plastics are a considerable problem because of the escalating amount that is thrown away, and their extremely slow rate of decomposition. Some plastics can take centuries to decompose. Biodegradable plastic polymers have been developed to try to solve the problem; however, scientists have found biodegradable products in landfills that should have decomposed years ago. Some materials are reduced through incineration, but this process produces air pollution, and the ashes create solid waste. Some facilities have **waste-to-energy** equipment, designed to convert the heat that is generated from the burning waste into energy. This process still emits air pollutants, but the amount of contaminants is less than from coal-burning plants.

Solid waste can be nonhazardous and hazardous. According to the EPA, a waste is hazardous if the material has any of the characteristics of hazardous waste: ignitability, corrosivity, reactivity, or toxicity. Hazardous waste can be a liquid, solid, or gas. There are thousands of hazardous substances, including nerve gas, acids, mercury, lead, and PCBs. The characteristics and health effects associated with mercury and lead are illustrated in Table 2.8. PCBs were made for a variety of uses, including in inks, ballasts in lamps, adhesives, and fire retardants. The EPA banned the use of PCBs in the 1970s; however, enormous amounts of products containing PCBs still exist in current buildings and landfills.

Solid Waste Regulations

In the United States, the laws that regulate the management of hazardous waste are the Resource Conservation and Recovery Act (RCRA) and the **Comprehensive Environmental Response, Compensation, and Liability Act (CER-CLA)**, or what is referred to as the **Superfund Program**. The primary purpose of the RCRA is to regulate the standards for disposing of hazardous waste. The RCRA enables the EPA to identify hazardous wastes and develop procedures for proper protective treatment, disposal, and long-term management of hazardous waste. The Superfund Program was enacted to regulate cleanup procedures for sites that already have hazardous waste. The EPA estimates that the United States has approximately 400,000 hazardous waste sites, which could be leaking toxic chemicals or radioactive substances. Many of these sites are close to housing developments, and thus are potentially dangerous to health, especially in the developing bodies of young children.

The cost of cleanup is very expensive and time consuming, and the danger always exists that traces of the toxins may remain in the environment. The cleanup process is impeded by the availability of federal dollars, and every day of delay allows pollutants to emit toxins in the air and infiltrate the waterways. Therefore, individuals, businesses, industries, communities, and countries must adhere to the policies and practices related to the safe management of hazardous wastes. Reducing the use of hazardous waste is critical, but when a product is necessary, disposal of the material must be handled using the safe procedures outlined by the EPA. The EPA's goals of safe management include the safe recycling, storage, and disposal of hazardous waste. Chapter 4 reviews integrated management strategies for sustaining the environment, including the safe disposal of solid and hazardous waste.

Summary

- The world's primary sources of energy are fossil fuels, which include oil, natural gas, and coal. Other sources of energy include waterpower, nuclear energy, wood, solar, wind, tidal, chemical, and geothermal.

- The amount of energy consumed for electricity is a serious concern. According to EIA projections, "world net electricity consumption will nearly double over the next two decades." In analyzing electrical consumption patterns by region, EIA estimates that more than half of projected growth of demand for electricity will occur in the emerging economies.

- Demography, a subdiscipline of sociology, is the study of population statistics. Demographers analyze a variety of statistics related to the populations of communities, regions, countries, and the world.

- The world's population did not reach one billion until 1800. Since 1800 the world's population growth rate has been rising rapidly. From 1900 to 2000 the world's population rapidly increased to 6.1 billion.

- High consumption of fossil fuels translates to higher levels of toxic emissions. The United States represents approximately 5 percent of the world's population, but is responsible for about 25 percent of the global emissions of carbon dioxide.

- Pollutants can come from either a point or nonpoint source pollutant. Point source pollution is derived from one main source, such as a factory chimney or sewage pipe. Nonpoint source pollution is the result of the combined effects from various sources.

- The major categories of air pollution produced by people are air toxics, carbon oxides, hydrocarbons, nitrogen oxides, ozone, particulate matter, and sulfur oxides.

- A serious environmental problem associated with air pollution is acid deposition, or acid rain. The primary sources of acid rain are sulfur and nitrogen oxides, which are produced by burning fossil fuels and other industrial processes.

- Scientists believe that air pollution is contributing to global atmospheric changes. This is primarily evident by increases in greenhouse gases and the deterioration of the stratosphere ozone.

- Air pollution is creating holes in the earth's ozone. Ozone exists in the earth's troposphere and stratosphere.

- Indoor air pollution can occur from a variety of sources and conditions. The most common indoor contaminants are formaldehyde, radon, biological agents, carbon monoxide, cigarette smoke, household pesticides, nitrogen dioxide, cleaning solvents, ozone, asbestos, lead, and VOCs. In addition to pollutants, humidity and moisture affect the quality of indoor air.

- Noise pollution is an environmental problem that can affect the mental and physical well-being of people, including inducing stress-related illnesses.

- In addition to problems associated with water pollution, the world has serious issues with managing water. Too much or too little water is equally devastating.

- Industrial waste that enters the waterways can come directly from sewage pipes or from acid rain, which originated from smoke stacks. Some industries dump waste or heated water directly into bodies of water. Waste materials can include radioactive substances, heavy metals, and various toxic chemicals.

- The United States leads the world in the amount of solid waste. The primary means to dispose of municipal solid wastes are sanitary landfills (55.4 percent), recycling (30.1 percent), and combustion (14.5 percent).

- In the United States, the laws that regulate the management of hazardous waste are the Resource Conservation and Recovery Act (RCRA) and the Comprehensive Environmental Response, Compensation, and Liability Act (CER-CLA).

Key Terms

Acid deposition

Air toxics

Asbestos

Atmospheric changes

Biological agents

Brownfields

Building-related illnesses (BRI)

Carbon oxides

Clean Water Act (CWA)

Comprehensive Environmental Response, Compensation, and Liability Act (CER-CLA)

Demography

Energy Information Administration (EIA)

Environmental resistance

Formaldehyde

Greenhouse effect

Greenhouse gases

Hydrocarbons

Indoor air quality (IAQ)

Industrial smog

Kyoto Protocol

Municipal solid waste

National Energy Information Center (NEIC)

Nitrogen oxides

Noise pollution

Nonpoint source pollutant

Ozone

Particulate matter

Photochemical smog

Point source pollutant

Polychlorinated biphenyls (PCBs)

Radon

Safe Drinking Water Act (SDWA)

Sick building syndrome (SBS)

Stratosphere

Sulfur oxides

Superfund Program

Thermal pollution

Troposphere

U.S. Census Bureau's International
   Data Base (IDB)

Volatile organic compounds (VOCs)

Waste-to-energy

World Health Organization (WHO)

Exercises

1. Create an illustration or a model that demonstrates how greenhouse gases affect global warming. The depiction should include alterations to the polar ice caps. Provide a written summary of how greenhouse gases are affecting the planet.

2. The world's population did not reach one billion until 1800. Since 1800, the world's population growth rate has been rising rapidly. Create a graphic that depicts the rapid escalation in the rate of the world's population growth. Include projections to 2050.

3. Develop a written report that describes for a client the predominant sources of indoor air pollution. Include how the pollutants affect people and provide recommendations for creating a healthy indoor environment.

4. Water pollution occurs when chemical or physical changes in the water's environment adversely affect aquatic ecosystems. Create an illustration that demonstrates how surface water and groundwater become polluted. Include in the illustration the sources of pollution and how pollutants can affect natural ecosystems.

CHAPTER 3

Regulations, Programs, and Organizations

But if it's the seed of a bad plant, you must pull the plant up right away, as soon as you can recognize it. As it happens, there were terrible seeds on the little prince's planet . . . baobab seeds. The planet's soil was infested with them. Now if you attend to a baobab too late, you can never get rid of it again. And if the planet is too small, and if there are too many baobabs, they make it burst into pieces.

—ANTOINE DE SAINT-EXUPÉRY

Objectives

- Describe policies, legislation, and labeling related to sustainable design.
- Summarize the purposes of agencies and organizations that are related to sustainable design.
- Understand sustainability perspectives of organizations and professionals associated with the field of interior design.
- Compare and contrast sustainable resources and assessment tools.
- Understand the goals, policies, and procedures of selected sustainability assessment tools.

CHAPTERS 1 AND 2 provide an introduction to the global problems and concerns of sustainable development. In response to the seriousness of working toward a sustainable future, governments, organizations, and agencies have been developing policies, laws, regulations, and building codes. The goals of these initiatives are to improve the well-being of people and protect the natural environment. To achieve these goals requires the efforts of everyone, including interior designers.

For interior designers to successfully apply the principles of sustainable design to interiors requires an understanding of environmentally related laws and regulations. The chapter begins by reviewing important legislative actions, including global policies. To comprehend how laws are implemented, the next section of the chapter describes sustainable initiatives of organizations and corporations. This section also includes examples of sustainable policies of major interior design firms and sustainability perspectives of leading interior designers.

Policies, legislation, and research related to sustainability are constantly evolving; thus, it is imperative to keep abreast of the field. The resources identified in this chapter can be referenced when studying the content of future chapters. The chapter concludes by reviewing sustainable practices of communities, organizations, corporations, and professionals.

SUSTAINABLE POLICIES, LEGISLATION, AND ORGANIZATIONS

Specifications for sustainable interiors have to be in compliance with laws, regulations, and state and local building codes. These doctrines can provide valuable support for sustainable initiatives, but some regulations and codes can hinder innovative solutions. An interior designer must be knowledgeable about both situations and understand how to practice within the given parameters.

Laws and Regulations

Mandated laws, regulations, and codes can be very helpful to interior designers when they are working with a client who is reluctant to approve sustainable design solutions. Opposition to sustainable products is frequently based on real or perceived higher costs.

In addition, building codes can be a hindrance to sustainable initiatives when builders do not have the option to pursue nonconventional construction. For example, many communities prohibit a **gray water** system, which is a method to direct water from sink or tub drains to secondary usages, such as flushing toilets or watering the landscape. In these situations an interior designer can play an advocate role by encouraging state and local representatives to create building codes that support sustainable design.

U.S. Environmental Laws

Many factors can influence U.S. environmental laws, including natural disasters, environmental accidents, an energy crisis, war, societal attitudes, politics, and international summits and treaties. In the United States, environmental laws are created when both houses of Congress and the president approve a bill. New laws become acts, such as the Clean Water Act. Congress delegates the development of the act's regulations to a governmental agency, such as the EPA. After establishing the regulations, the agency is responsible for enforcing the law and working with people to help them comply with the laws. States, cities, and towns are responsible for developing codes that comply with the laws. All laws and codes must require the standards prescribed in the federal laws, but a community can create codes that are stricter than federal mandates.

Chapter 1 identified some of the important acts related to the environment, such as the **Refuse Act of 1899** and the **National Environmental Policy Act (NEPA)** of 1969. The EPA is responsible for approximately 12 statutes or laws. The NEPA is the charter act for protecting the environment. A purpose of NEPA is to encourage productive and enjoyable harmony between people and the environment. The 1969 act serves to promote efforts to (a) prevent or eliminate damage to the environment and biosphere, (b) stimulate the health and welfare of people, (c) enrich the understanding of ecological systems and the importance of natural resources, and (d) establish the **Council on Environmental Quality (CEQ)**. The NEPA policies affect all branches of government prior to engaging in any major federal action that can affect the environment, such as constructing a federal building. All federal agencies must conduct environmental assessments and develop environmental impact statements (EISs) when proposing a federal activity.

Recently, the CEQ created a document that is very important to sustainable design. The CEQ developed a framework for improving the process of an environmental impact assessment by addressing cumulative effects. The CEQ defines cumulative effects as "the impact on the environment which results from the incremental impact of the action when added to other past, present, and reasonably foreseeable future actions regardless of what agency (Federal or non-Federal) or person undertakes such actions" (1997, p. v). This perspective is important to sustainable design, because the focus includes futuristic actions and an examination of all of the factors that can affect the environment.

The Clean Air Act (CAA) of 1970, which was amended in 1990, identifies the standards for air quality and emissions. Aspects of the CAA include clean-up programs that address smog, particulates, carbon monoxide, and hazardous air pollutants. The CAA identifies sources of air pollution and delineates guidelines for reducing pollution. Sources include transportation vehicles, pollutants from smokestacks, acid rain, consumer products, and residential woodstoves. The CAA regulates consumer products that release VOCs and ozone-destroying chemicals, such as paints and foam plastic products. The 1990 amendment addresses global climate protection by stipulating a phase-out of the production of substances that deplete the ozone layer. The CAA is responsible for the dramatic reduction in the amount of lead in the atmosphere, especially in cities such as Los Angeles, California, which had some of the worse conditions in the country.

Currently federal regulations do not include standards for indoor air quality (IAQ); however, various councils, agencies, and nonprofit associations have suggested standards, procedures, and protocols for air quality. For example, the **Occupational Safety and Health Administration (OSHA)** is a division of the U.S. Department of Labor. The OSHA has proposed standards addressing indoor air quality in indoor work environments. The OSHA's regulations would ban smoking indoors, control measures for special contaminants, and include operational plans. This would include IAQ compliance plans, periodic testing, and maintenance of written records. The

OSHA and the **American National Standards Institute/American Society of Heating, Refrigerating, and Air-Conditioning Engineers (ANSI/ASHRAE)** have ventilation standards for the general and construction industries. Standard 62-2001 of ANSI/ASHRAE sets minimum ventilation rates and other requirements for commercial and institutional buildings (OSHA, 2005).

Water Management

The **Clean Water Act (CWA)** of 1977 and the **Safe Drinking Water Act (SDWA)** of 1974 are the two most important legislations created to protect the quality of water. The objective of the CWA, formerly known as the Federal Water Pollution Control Act of 1972, is to "restore and maintain the chemical, physical, and biological integrity of the Nation's waters" (U.S.C. 1251, Sec. 101, 2002). To accomplish this objective, the act delineates several national goals, which fundamentally aim to (1) eliminate the discharge of pollutants into navigable waters; (2) provide "for the protection and propagation of fish, shellfish, and wildlife"; (3) provide "for recreation in and on the water"; and (4) prohibit "the discharge of toxic pollutants in toxic amounts" (U.S.C. 1251, Sec. 101, 2002). Some of the elements of the CWA are minimum national waste standards for industries and discharge permits with enforceable limits. In addition, the CWA has provisions for problems such as toxic chemicals (DOE, 1996).

An interdependent relationship exists between the CWA and SDWA, because the success of the CWA affects drinking water quality. The SDWA was established to protect the quality of water in the United States by setting minimum standards for healthy water. The 1974 act enabled the EPA to establish safe standards of purity, including maximum contaminant levels. Owners or operators of public water systems must adhere to the regulations of the SDWA (EPA, 2005). A shared concern, which affects clean water and safe drinking water, is nonpoint source pollution. Generally, the EPA can identify point source water polluters; however, nonpoint source pollution is very difficult to trace because the pollutants can come from multiple sites that are miles apart. Point and nonpoint sources pollute surface water and groundwater. Groundwater pollution, especially from hazardous waste, is especially problematic because toxins in the ground can contaminate drinking water. This can occur when there are holes or cracks in water pipes that are buried in soil that contains polluted groundwater. Thus, after a community water supplier has treated water, this pure water can be contaminated before it reaches a home or business by flowing through damaged pipes.

Knowledge that these laws exist is useful to interior designers when they are working with a client whose business discharges pollutants into water. Legal requirements are needed to specify sustainable products and services. Furthermore, an understanding of lawful water disposal practices, and any other environmentally related concern, can be applied when assessing sustainability processes of a company or manufacturer.

Conserving Energy and Natural Resources

The federal government's focus on conserving energy started during the energy crisis in the mid-1970s. The **Energy Policy and Conservation Act (EPCA)** of 1975 initiated a series of important federal environmental legislation related to energy conservation, including the **National Appliance Energy Conservation Act (NAECA)** of 1987 and the **Energy Policy Act** of 1992. In 2005, President Bush signed into law a national energy plan that (1) encourages energy conservation and efficiency, (2) promotes alternative and renewable energy sources, (3) reduces dependence on foreign sources of energy, (4) increases domestic production, (5) modernizes the electricity grid, and (6) encourages the expansion of nuclear energy (White House, 2005).

The national energy plan was based on the findings and key recommendations of the **National Energy Policy Development Group (NEDP)** in 2001 (**National Energy Policy (NEP)**, 2001). NEDP identified many important issues related to sustainable design and development. For example, the report outlines some of the most serious energy shortage problems that people throughout the country faced in 2001, such as rolling blackouts or brownouts, employee layoffs or reductions in production, and high gasoline prices. In 2005, energy shortage problems were exacerbated by the war in Iraq and hurricanes Katrina and Rita. Cities experienced significant in-

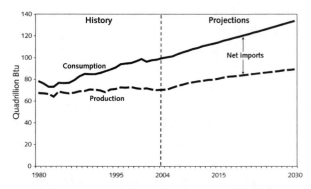

Fig. 3.1. Total energy production and consumption, 1980–2030 (quadrillion Btu). The Department of Energy (DOE) projects that U.S. energy consumption will increase to approximately 130 quadrillion Btu annually by 2020.

creases in gas prices, with hours of waiting in a line to fill up a car's gas tank, and some stations ran out of gasoline. Concerns focused on the potentially excessive prices for home heating oil and natural gas for the future winter months. To deal with problems associated with Hurricane Rita, such as high gasoline prices and shortages, the governor of Georgia declared that schools should be closed September 24–27, 2005. The governor thought eliminating bus transportation would save gasoline and taxpayers' money. Unexpected price increases are a challenge to school districts, because typically, administrators plan their budgets a year in advance.

The fact that schools were closed because of energy shortages demonstrates the need for strategic planning and supports NEDP's finding that the "growth in U.S. energy consumption is outpacing production." As illustrated in Figure 3.1, the **Department of Energy (DOE)** projects that U.S. energy consumption will increase to approximately 130 quadrillion Btu annually by 2020. However, by using 1990–2000 energy production growth rates, the projected energy shortage in 2020 is approximately 55 quadrillion Btu annually. These projections illustrate very serious problems facing the United States and the world. If the projections are accurate, significant energy shortages will affect not only the United States but also all of the nations in the world. As described in the study, if this imbalance continues, significant energy shortages will "undermine our economy, our standard of living, and our national security" (NEP, 2001).

As noted earlier, the energy shortage projections were based on 1990–2000 energy production growth rates. If the projections are not accurate and energy shortages are even more severe, the world could experience a graver situation. Concerns related to the accuracy of the projections focus on many of the assumptions associated with using 1990–2000 data, and applying a level application of the 1990–2000 growth rates. Global conditions during 1990–2000 were fairly stable and the United States experienced great prosperity. Using the 1990–2000 growth rates assumes that the same global conditions will exist in 2000 and until 2020. This is an improbable assumption. Global conditions that can affect the supply of energy include demographics, environmental sustainability, weather conditions, war, technological capabilities, sociopolitical issues, the economy, standards of living, and global energy consumption.

The United States has already experienced several significant disasters in the twenty-first century that impact energy production, such as the 9/11 terrorist attack, the war in Iraq, and the dramatic increase in the number of and devastation caused by hurricanes. Hurricanes striking the Gulf of Mexico can cause significant damage to oil operations (see Figure 3.2). For example, the United States anticipated that more than 500 oil rigs, located in the waters of the Gulf of Mexico, could have been destroyed by Hurricane Rita. Obviously many unexpected situations can occur that impact energy supplies. However, there

are expected conditions that should be considered when projecting energy shortfalls. For example, as discussed in Chapter 2, the world's population is growing and the most significant increases are expected to occur in the developing countries.

This is a very significant situation because developing countries with large populations, such as China and India, are also becoming more industrialized. A shift to industrialization translates to demanding more energy. In 1990–2000, most developing countries demanded relatively little energy, because they were not engaged in economic activities that required high-energy consumption. In contrast, during the same decade and continuing through 2005, the United States consumed more energy than any other country. Thus, transforming countries with enormous populations will affect global energy consumption patterns.

Supply and Demand Policies

The previous discussion illustrates how supply and demand policies affect energy consumption. To better understand these policies and their effect on sustainable design, a good source is the NEP. Some of the 2001 recommendations of the NEP were developed to meet energy needs by investing in initiatives that focus on increasing the *supply* of energy, such as increasing domestic production, modernizing the

Fig. 3.2. Hurricanes striking the Gulf of Mexico can cause significant damage to oil operations.

electricity grid, or encouraging the expansion of nuclear energy. When people can get cheap energy, in the desired quantities, they do not have incentives to reduce consumption. In the United States this is a very serious concern because we must import more than half of the oil produced in the world in order to have enough fuel to meet the needs of transportation. Policies such as "increasing domestic production," which focus on meeting insatiable demands, fail to provide the impetus required to change consumption behaviors. Based on the expected shortfalls between energy consumption and production growth rates, the first priority should be to reduce and conserve energy.

To meet future energy needs, other 2001 recommendations of the NEP include strategies intended to decrease the *demand* for energy, such as encouraging energy conservation and efficiency. From the sustainability perspective, to have adequate resources requires policies and practices that encourage people to consume less energy and natural resources. Thus, sustainable strategies focus on reducing the demand for energy by encouraging conservation and energy efficiency. Reducing the dependency on fossil fuels is critical for pollution prevention, atmospheric conditions, and the global environment. Thus, sustainable solutions emphasize the advancement of alternative and nonrenewable energy sources. The NEP advocates research, investment, and tax credits for using renewable energy sources, including wind, solar, and **biomass** energy. Biomass is "any organic matter that is available on a renewable or recurring basis (excluding old-growth timber, or timber of a forest from the late successional stage of forest development)" (Executive Order 13134, 1999). The NEP suggests more money for research that includes energy efficiency and expanding knowledge of hydrogen technologies.

In promoting the principles of sustainable design, interior designers must reflect on global energy problems, and then determine solutions for their clients that conserve natural resources and are energy efficient. The objectives of energy conservation are to engage in practices that reduce or eliminate energy consumption. Examples include weatherproofing a building, adding insulation, lowering a thermostat in the winter, and turning off lights or an air conditioner. Energy efficiency focuses on using technologies that use less energy. For example, a client can be

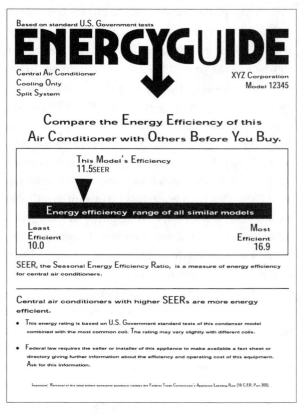

Fig. 3.3. The National Appliance Energy Conservation Act of 1987 (NAECA) establishes efficiency standards for appliances. To comply with NAECA, appliance manufacturers must delineate annual operating costs and efficiency levels on Energy Guide labels.

energy efficient by using appliances, HVAC (heating, ventilating, and air conditioning) units, and lighting systems that are specifically designed to be energy efficient.

The National Appliance Energy Conservation Act of 1987 (NAECA) establishes efficiency standards for appliances, such as refrigerators, freezers, dishwashers, washing machines, dryers, and air conditioners. To comply with NAECA, appliance manufacturers must delineate annual operating costs and efficiency levels on Energy Guide labels (see Figure 3.3). These labels allow a consumer to easily compare and contrast the energy efficiency of various appliances while shopping online or in a retail store. Additional information regarding energy conservation and energy efficiency is discussed in Unit II of this text.

Managing Waste

The U.S. government's efforts to manage solid and hazardous waste are legislated by the laws of the Resource Conservation and Recovery Act (RCRA) of 1976, which was amended in 1994. The RCRA was created to (1) protect human health and the environment, (2) reduce/eliminate the generation of hazardous wastes, and (3) conserve energy and natural resources (Department of Energy, 2003, p. 1). The RCRA enables the EPA to control hazardous waste from "cradle-to-grave," which includes procedures related to generation, transportation, treatment, storage, and disposal (EPA, 2005).

To help facilitate the management of hazardous waste, the EPA designates some widely used products as **federal universal wastes**. The regulations of universal wastes govern the environmentally sound collection and management of batteries, pesticides, thermostats, and lamps. Management regulations focus on proper recycling or treatment of universal wastes. The regulations provide information for businesses, communities, and residences. According to the EPA, the regulations are intended to ease the regulatory burden on businesses, such as retail stores, that collect or generate the universal wastes (2005). Wastes are to be transferred to an appropriate treatment or recycling facility. As a result, the regulations help to reduce the quantity of wastes going to municipal solid waste landfills or combustors.

In working with clients, interior designers may have to provide recommendations for the collection and management of batteries and lamps. As prescribed by 40 CFR 273, the EPA describes the waste requirements for these products. The requirements include (1) when the regulations apply to the product, (2) labeling/marking specifications for lamps, and (3) waste management of products for small and large quantity handlers. The EPA indicates that universal waste batteries include nickel-cadmium (Ni-Cd) and small sealed lead-acid batteries. Many of these are in commercial and residential interiors, including electronic equipment, mobile telephones, portable computers, and emergency backup lighting (EPA, 2005).

Universal waste lamps include bulb or tube electric lighting devices that have a hazardous component, such as mercury or lead. These lamps include fluorescent, high-intensity discharge, neon, mercury vapor, high-pressure sodium, and metal halide. Interior designers might also be working with a lighting system that has ballasts that were manufactured prior to 1978. These ballasts were made with the toxic material polychlorinated biphenyls (PCBs). Ballasts without PCBs are labeled "No PCBs." Due to the hazardous components, federal and state laws regulate the disposal of ballasts with PCBs. At the federal level, the **Toxic Substances Control Act (TSCA)** and the Superfund Law regulate proper disposal of PCBs.

SUSTAINABLE POLICIES AND PROGRAMS

Numerous public and private organizations have been created to address the importance of sustainable development. These entities are at the global, national, regional, and local levels. These organizations provide the opportunity for communities, businesses, and individuals to be involved with various aspects related to sustainable policies and practices. Activities could include being involved with developing sustainable policies, advocating for environmental laws, or encouraging sustainable practices in the local government.

Pollution Prevention

In developing sustainable policies, a critical achievement was enacting laws that demonstrated the importance of preventing pollution. In 1990, the **Pollution Prevention Act (PPA)** was created to focus attention on "reducing the amount of pollution through cost-effective changes in production, operation, and raw materials use." This act represents an important transformation in the way that industry, communities, government, and individuals perceive pollution. EPA regulations include pollution prevention, waste minimization, and recycling practices.

Since the 1970s, most legislation and regulations have focused on approaches to manage existing pollution. Many improvements have occurred, such as the reduction of lead pollutants from gasoline emissions of automobiles; however, **rearview mirror thinking** causes people to constantly reflect on past bad practices. Rearview mirror thinking is an analogy conceived by W. Edwards Deming, a management expert, to illustrate the risk of not focusing on the future (1986). To emphasize the importance of planning for the future, Deming suggests that one should think about how dangerous driving would be if people only watched the road through the car's rearview mirror. In applying the analogy to the environment, individuals, businesses, communities, and countries must focus on a quality existence for future generations. The PPA encourages a philosophy that is focused on identifying strategies, policies, and procedures that attempt to avoid pollution. The emphasis is on source reduction, which is preferred to managing waste or controlling pollution. The EPA identifies other means of preventing pollution, including efficient energy consumption and conserving water and other natural resources.

To help prevent pollution, President Clinton enacted several executive orders that focus on "greening the government" by (1) waste prevention, recycling, and federal acquisition (Executive Order 13101 in 1998); (2) efficient energy management (Executive Order 13123 in 1999); and (3) leadership in environmental management (Executive Order 13148 in 2000). On the surface, it might not appear that greening the government would have a significant effect on preventing pollution. In contrast, an examination of the size of the government makes it apparent how federal greening initiatives can positively impact the global environment. The federal government is the "nation's largest energy consumer" as reflected by owning, operating, and managing more than 500,000 buildings and spending $200 billion per year on products and services (Presidential Documents, 1999). Thus, the federal government acknowledges that "greening" initiatives can save taxpayer dollars; reduce emissions that contribute to air pollution and global climate change; help foster markets for emerging technologies; and promote energy efficiency, water conservation, and the use of renewable energy products (Presidential Documents, 1999).

"Greening" Executive Orders

Interior designers can apply many aspects of the executive orders to the practice of sustainable design. The orders are good resources for identifying goals for pollution prevention, technical definitions, specifications, product descriptions, and standards. This information can serve an educational purpose and can provide guidance for writing sustainability guidelines, specifications, and contracts. These documents are especially important to refer to when an interior designer is working with the federal government on a project. The orders focus on preventing pollution by "greening the government" and promoting technologies that reduce pollutants from fossil fuels.

To conserve energy and water at federal facilities, President Clinton established Executive Order 12902 (1994). The order delineates (1) energy consumption reduction goals, (2) descriptions of energy and water surveys, and (3) guidelines for implementing energy-efficient and water conservation projects. An emphasis on energy conservation continued with Executive Order 13134, "Developing and Promoting **Bio-based Products** and **Bioenergy**" (1999). This order was created to encourage the development and adoption of technologies needed to manufacture biobased products and economical bioenergy. For example, the 1999 order identifies that a biobased product "utilizes biological products or renewable domestic agricultural or forestry materials." Bioenergy utilizes biomass for the production of energy, including electricity, fuels (liquid, solid, and gaseous), and heat (Executive Order 13134, 1999). Biomass matter can include "dedicated energy crops and trees, agricultural food and feed crop residues, aquatic plants, wood and wood residues, and animal wastes" (Executive Order 13134, 1999).

Sustainable Policies, Politics, and Economics

The development of sustainable policies and laws is very complex and time consuming. It requires the collaborative efforts of global participants. Desirable goals are easy to identify: Everyone wants clean water, pure air, access to beautiful recreational areas, and healthy homes and businesses. Conflicts arise when decisions must be made regarding how, when, and who will perform the goals. Conflicts become even more intense when the costs are high, when boundaries are involved, and when regulations affect the special interests of business and industries. For these reasons and many other factors, the development of sustainable and environmental policies is frequently contentious. Thus, to be successful in developing sustainable policies and regulations requires collaboration, perseverance, and reasonable compromises.

How federal, state, or local governments respond to issues determines the number of environmental laws, the effectiveness of the proposed initiatives, and the extent of implementation and enforcement. Fundamentally, the stages of policy development can be divided into four areas: (1) conceptualization, (2) legislation, (3) implementation, and (4) enforcement.

For example, in the United States, the conceptualization and implementation of environmental policies started in the nineteenth century. This legislation reflects the initiatives and perseverance of many of the individuals discussed in Chapter 1, including the political involvement of Theodore Roosevelt. Implementation and enforcement of environmental legislation developed in the 1970s has been successful in various areas, including reducing pollution and protecting natural resources. To achieve success with enforcement, the EPA needs the willingness of people, resources, and political support.

Many factors affect the outcomes of every stage of policy development: economic conditions, natural disasters, societal attitudes, availability of funding, and politics. For example, it appears the disaster in the city of New Orleans from Hurricane Katrina could be an example of how multiple factors can affect policies. A great deal of the devastating flooding that filled New Orleans occurred because of several breaches in the levees, which separate the city from Lake Pontchartrain. To control flooding, the federal government is working with the city of New Orleans to reconstruct the levee. In 2005, a U.S. Senate proposal was drafted that would grant the EPA the right to "waive or modify requirements for any emergency response related to Hurricane Katrina" (Green Party, 2005). In response to a waiver that would create dire consequences to the environment, the cochair of the Louisiana Green Party commented, "The first disaster to hit our state was a natural one. The one following suspension of EPA rules will be a human-generated environmental disaster" (Green Party, 2005, p. 1).

The people of New Orleans and all communities affected by catastrophes deserve a healthy and safe place to live. Cleanup activities and new construction must reflect the best interests and the well-being of people living in the community, and its surrounding natural resources. The next several years will determine the EPA's success with being able to help Gulf Coast communities to implement environmental regulations and whether the EPA will be able to apply environmental enforcement laws. In contrast to eliminating EPA regulations, the federal government could take this opportunity to proclaim that the Gulf Coast communities would be rebuilt by applying the principles of sustainable design and development. Given the global publicity and the wide-reaching interest in rebuilding these devastated areas, these showcase communities could be highly influential in encouraging sustainable practice throughout the world.

Sustainable Organizations and Professional Perspectives

Interior designers are in a formidable position to influence sustainability practices by collaborating with their professional organizations and educating stakeholders. This can be especially important when an organization is working with legislators who can create sustainability regulations. Designers can educate stakeholders by using their firm as a showcase for exemplary sustainability business practices. In addition, an interior designer can encourage suppliers to engage in sustainable processes.

Educating the profession, clients, and users regarding sustainable design/development appears to be very necessary. In the 2003 *Building Design and Construction* (BDC) survey, the results indicate that 33 percent of the 498 respondents were "somewhat experienced" with sustainable design and 39 percent had "not much experience, but interested." In reporting their firms' involvement with sustainable design, approximately half of the respondents indicated working on at least one green project, and 57 percent of the firms encouraged staff to learn more about the topic.

To support sustainability activities requires keeping abreast in multiple disciplines. There are hundreds of agencies, organizations, and programs dedicated to sustainability and the environment. These entities are in every highly developed country and many of the developing countries. To provide an overview of available resources, the proceeding sections highlight the major categories, purposes of selected organizations, and descriptions of activities. Extensive lists of resources and contact information are provided in Appendix C.

Global Perspectives

Interior designers should analyze the sustainable information developed by other countries. Multiple sources provide new perspectives, which can be applied to practice. Knowledge of international sustainable policies can be very useful when an interior designer is working with a client from another country and when a client's facilities serve users from throughout the world.

The United Nations (UN) is an excellent resource for international environmental programs. Specifically, the UN has a **Division of Environmental Information, Assessment, and Early Warning**, which supports the **UN Environment Programme (UNEP)**. In 1995, the UNEP initiated the **Global Environment Outlook (GEO)** Project. A major function of the project is to coordinate a global environmental assessment process (the GEO process). In addition, the project is responsible for developing reporting mechanisms, including the GEO report series, technical reports, a website, and a publication for youth (see Figure 3.4). A very important component of the GEO process is the comprehensive input from representatives of regions throughout the world. Numerous experts in disciplines that affect environmental policy, such as environmental scientists, ecologists, economists, sociologists, engineers, and policy makers, work together to analyze global data. For example, more than 850 people and approximately 35 centers were involved with the production of *GEO-2000*.

A full participatory process results in consensus on prioritized issues and recommended actions. Therefore, the information disseminated by GEO is thoroughly researched, comprehensive, and reflects the best sustainability practices of the world. The *GEO-2000* report includes a summary of global perspectives from these regions: Africa; Asia and the Pacific; Europe and Central Asia; Latin America and the Caribbean; North America; West Asia; and the Polar Regions (UNEP, 1999).

Another excellent international source for sustainable design/development information is the **World Green Building Council (WorldGBC)**. Established in 1999, the mission of the nonprofit organization is to provide "a federation union" of national green building councils whose common goal is the sustainable transformation of the global property industry (WorldGBC, 2005). The national members of WorldGBC are Australia, Canada, India, Mexico, Taiwan, and the United States. Some of the objectives of WorldGBC are to (1) "create a global market for green building through the creation of successful national Green Building Councils"; (2) "be the peak global voice for global green building issues"; (3) have a dynamic Web presence; and (4) develop "collaborative relationships with all other complementary global organizations." Interior designers can acquire information from the WorldGBC website, which includes green building information, case studies, government initiatives, construction projects, rating systems, and technologies.

The **International Initiative for a Sustainable Built Environment (iiSBE)** is a nonprofit organization whose overall aim is to "actively facilitate and promote the adoption of policies, methods, and tools to accelerate the movement toward a global sustainable built environment." The iiSBE's board of directors has a member from almost every continent. The objectives of iiSBE are to (1) "map current activities and establish a forum for information exchange on

Fig. 3.4. An outline of the Global Environment Outlook (GEO) process for environmental assessment.

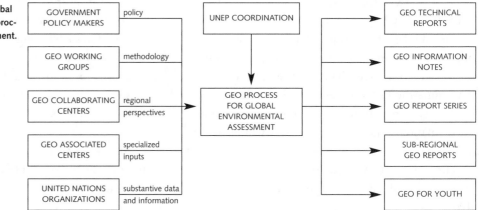

Fig. 3.5. The European Union (EU) is an international organization composed of European countries, or "Member States." Members of the EU collaborate for "peace and prosperity." As of 2004, there are 25 countries that have joined the EU.

SBE initiatives," (2) "increase awareness of existing SBE initiatives and issues," and (3) "take action on fields not covered by existing organizations and networks." Some of the iiSBE activities that are valuable to interior designers include research and development databases, the international *Green Building Challenge* program, and an international program for identifying policy initiatives in the area of sustainable built environments.

The **European Union (EU)** is an international organization composed of European countries, or "Member States." Members of the EU collaborate for "peace and prosperity." As of 2004, 25 countries have joined the EU (see Figure 3.5). The Member States have identified issues that affect Europe, such as air pollution, and have granted the EU the authority to make a decision that serves the best interest of all of the Member States (EU, 2005). The EU refers to this delegation of authority to one entity as "European integration." One of nine major activities of the EU is "caring about our environment" (EU, 2005). The EU approach to environmental issues is that "pollution has no respect for national frontiers" (EU, 2005). Thus, the EU serves as the objective entity that coordinates all of the environmental strategies of the Member States. Most of the EU environmental "di-

rectives," or laws, focus on reducing waste, water management, and reducing air pollution.

In working with European clients, an interior designer must be aware of laws that are enacted by the EU and enforced by its *Member States*. For example, the EU has more than 200 "environmental protection directives" that can affect The Netherlands. Thus, when The Netherlands creates environmental laws, the minimum standards must comply with the laws of the EU. Adhering to the standards of the EU can be costly and time intensive and can consume the expertise of a country's best scientists. Thus, it is commendable that 25 countries are willing to support the EU for the good of the continent, world, and future generations. The philosophy and values of the EU reflect the essence of sustainable development: "Europe is a continent with many different traditions and languages, but also with shared values. The EU defends these values. It fosters cooperation among the peoples of Europe, promoting unity while preserving diversity and ensuring that decisions are taken as close as possible to the citizens. In the increasingly interdependent world of the twenty-first century, it will be even more necessary for every European citizen to cooperate with people from other countries in a spirit of curiosity, tolerance, and solidarity" (EU, 2005).

Global collaborative initiatives require standards that can be applied and understood in every country. An organization that affects the work of interior designers is the **International Organization for Standardization (ISO)**. The ISO's commitment to establishing equitable standards is reflected in its choice of a headquarters. The organization is located in Geneva, Switzerland, which has an international reputation for neutrality. The ISO is a nongovernmental organization for developing standards for a variety of industries and governments. As an international organization, the ISO is a "network of the national standards institutes of 156 countries, on the basis of one member per country" (ISO, 2005). The ISO develops standards for the private and public sectors. Most of the standards are specific to "a particular product, material, or process." Generally sustainability-related standards are subsumed in **ISO 14000**, "environmental management." The standard focuses on "what the organization does to minimize harmful effects on the environment caused by its activities, and continually to improve its environmental performance." Unit II of this text provides examples of ISO standards that are applicable to products and processes in the field of interior design.

National Organizations

Most countries in the world have environmental/sustainable agencies, organizations, and programs. For example, founded in 1971, **Environment Canada (EC)** is a "science-based department" to preserve and enhance the environment, enforce the rules of Canada, and coordinate federal policies and programs. In 1997, EC published a document titled *Sustainable Development Strategy*. This document outlines Canada's vision of sustainable development: (1) protect Canadians and ecosystems, (2) contribute to the protection of the global environment, (3) promote fairness in sharing the costs and benefits of development, (4) enhance Canada's productivity, (5) promote renewable resources, and (6) encourage the efficient use of nonrenewable resources. In addition, the document indicates that the three major challenges to sustainable development are (1) developing approaches to integrating environmental, economic, and social issues; (2) facing environmental problems that are very complex and have expanded to become global issues; and (3) transferring more environmental responsibility to communities and individuals. An understanding of these challenges is very helpful when an interior designer is trying to encourage a client to implement sustainable design and development. Based on the needs of the client, an interior designer can develop strategies that address the challenges. Suggestions for encouraging clients to invest in sustainable design are covered in Unit III of this text.

As identified in previous chapters, there are many U.S. federal agencies dedicated to develop, implement, and enforce environmental regulations. In addition to federal agencies, such as the EPA and the DOE, interior designers can obtain excellent sustainability information from the **United States Green Building Council (USGBC)**, **Building for Environmental and Economic Sustainability (BEES)**, **Government Services Administration (GSA)**, and ANSI/ASHRAE/IESNA 90.1-2004. Table 3.1 includes some of the federal agencies and programs related to sustainable design, and a brief summary of their missions and goals.

Sources of sustainability information and best practices include agencies that are chartered to emphasize sustainability, such as BEES, and many programs in the military. The Department of Defense (DOD) and the U.S. Air Force, Army, and Navy all have sustainability programs. Frequently, sustainability initiatives are attributed to the "greening the government" programs in the 1990s. Various federal agencies focus on attaining **LEED (Leadership in Energy and Environmental Design)** certification, such as the National Aeronautics and Space Administration (NASA) and the **National Park Service, U.S. Department of the Interior (DOI)**. The federal government estimates that since 1985 the government's building-related energy costs have dropped 23 percent per square foot because of the "greening" movements and other initiatives focused on sustainable design.

An example of a recent federal government initiative related to **high-performance green buildings** was the 2002 **Green Building Roundtable**. The purpose of the roundtable was for members of the USGBC to educate the U.S. Senate Committee on Environment and Public Works. A trend identified during the roundtable was that in the United States "the built environment accounts for approximately one-third of all energy, water, and materials consumption and generates similar proportions of pollution" (USGBC, 2003). In addition, the EPA determined indoor air quality "as one of the top five environmental health risks today, affecting the health and performance of occupants" (USGBC, 2003).

Indoor air quality has serious consequences for children in U.S. schools and productivity in the workplace. The roundtable also identified barriers to implementing green buildings, including costs associated with integrating high-performance features and insufficient research. Unfortunately, the National Institutes of Health (NIH) and National Science Foundations (NSF) have not prioritized research dollars to the built environment. In contrast, the EU spends six times more than the United States (USGBC, 2003). The roundtable emphasized the importance of documented research related to the relationships between IAQ and improved productivity, health, and learning.

Table 3.1
Federal and Private Agencies and Programs Related to Sustainable Development/Design

U.S. Departments and Agencies	Sustainable Program	Missions/Goals	Website
American Society of Heating, Refrigerating and Air-Conditioning Engineers/ Illuminating Engineering Society of North America (ASHRAE/IESNA) 90.1-2001	N/A	ASHRAE: To advance the arts and sciences of heating, ventilation, air conditioning, refrigeration, and related human factors to serve the evolving needs of the public and ASHRAE members and to provide a permanent financial resource to support the Society and its mission to benefit the public To be the global leader in the arts and sciences of heating, ventilation, air conditioning, and refrigeration To be the foremost, authoritative, timely, and responsive source of technical and educational information, standards, and guidelines To be the primary provider of opportunity for professional growth, recognizing and adapting to changing demographics, and embracing diversity IESNA: To communicate information on all aspects of good lighting practice to its members, to the lighting community, and to consumers through a variety of programs, publications, and services To advance knowledge and disseminate information for the improvement of the lighted environment to the benefit of society	www.iesna.org www.ashrae.org
ENERGY STAR	N/A	A government-backed program that helps businesses and individuals protect the environment through superior energy efficiency	www.energystar.gov
Federal Trade Commission (FTC)	N/A	Seeks to ensure that the nation's markets function competitively, and are vigorous, efficient, and free of undue restrictions Works to enhance the smooth operation of the marketplace by eliminating acts or practices that are unfair or deceptive Stops actions that threaten consumers' opportunities to exercise informed choice Undertakes economic analysis to support its law enforcement efforts and to contribute to the policy deliberations of the Congress, the Executive Branch, other independent agencies, and state and local governments when requested Carries out its statutory enforcement responsibilities Advances the policies underlying Congressional mandates through cost-effective nonenforcement activities, such as consumer education	www.ftc.gov
National Fire Protection Act (NFPA) 5000	N/A	To reduce the worldwide burden of fire and other hazards on the quality of life by providing and advocating consensus codes and standards, research, training, and education	www.nfpa.org
National Institute of Standards and Technology (NIST)	N/A	To develop and promote measurement, standards, and technology to enhance productivity, facilitate trade, and improve the quality of life To be the global leader in measurement and enabling technology, delivering outstanding value to the nation	www.nist.gov

(continued)

Table 3.1 (continued)

U.S. Departments and Agencies	Sustainable Program	Missions/Goals	Website
National Park Service, Department of the Interior (DOI)	N/A	To protect and provide access to our Nation's natural and cultural heritage and honor our trust responsibilities to Indian tribes and our commitments to island communities Protect the nation's natural, cultural, and heritage resources Manage resources to promote responsible use and sustain a dynamic economy Provide recreation opportunities for America Safeguard lives, property, and assets, advance scientific knowledge, and improve the quality of life for communities we serve Manage the department to be highly skilled, accountable, modern, functionally integrated, citizen-centered, and result-oriented	www.doi.gov
Partnership for Advancing Technology in Housing (PATH)	N/A	Dedicated to accelerating the development and use of technologies that radically improve the quality, durability, energy efficiency, environmental performance, and affordability of America's housing Improves new and existing homes and strengthens the technology infrastructure of the United States Identifies and reduces barriers that impede innovation, including regulatory barriers Disseminates information to speed the development and adoption of advanced building technologies Focuses on the innovation process and aims to institutionalize sustained investments in housing with public and private funding	www.pathnet.org
President's Council on Sustainable Development (PCSD) 1993–1999	N/A	Develops bold new approaches to achieve economic, environmental, and equity goals Committed to the achievement of a dignified, peaceful, and equitable existence	http://clinton4.nara.gov/PCSD
U.S. Air Force	Cleanup: Installation Restoration Program (IRP) Compliance: Air Force Environmental Compliance Assessment and Management Program (ECAMP) Conservation: Environmental Impact Analysis Process (EIAP) Pollution Prevention: Qualified Recycling Program (QRP)	IRP: sites are restored through an intensive, and often lengthy, program of identification, investigation, and cleanup ECAMP: places a high priority on self-inspection and total workforce adherence to regulatory and permit requirements EIAP: involves the community in a comprehensive analysis of proposed projects to ensure minimal disruption to fragile ecosystems, archaeological artifacts, and historical structures QRP: takes new recycling initiatives—which include collection of brown glass, media such as floppy disks and video and audio tapes—far beyond initial paper and aluminum can recycling efforts	www.af.mil
U.S. Army	The Army Strategy for the Environment: Sustain the Mission—Secure the Future	A policy enforced so that the Army will move beyond traditional environmental compliance to balance mission requirements, community needs, and natural resource protection	www.army.mil
U.S. Department of Defense (DOD)	Green Procurement Policy—September 2004	Affirms a goal of 100 percent compliance with federal laws and executive orders requiring purchase of environmentally friendly, or "green," products and services	www.dod.gov www.defenselink.mil/releases/2004/nr20040901-1208.html

Table 3.1 (continued)

U.S. Departments and Agencies	Sustainable Program	Missions/Goals	Website
U.S. DOD (continued)		Outlines a strategy for meeting those requirements along with metrics for measuring progress	
U.S. Department of Energy (DOE)—Office of Energy Efficiency and Renewable Energy (EERE)	N/A	To strengthen America's energy security, environmental quality, and economic vitality in public-private partnership that enhances energy efficiency and productivity, brings clean, reliable, and affordable energy technologies to the marketplace, and makes a difference in the everyday lives of Americans by enhancing their energy choices and their quality of life Dramatically reduce or even end dependence on foreign oil, also reduce burden of energy prices on the disadvantaged Increase the viability and deployment of renewable energy technologies and increase the reliability and efficiency of electricity generation, delivery, and use Increase the efficiency of buildings and appliances and increase the efficiency/reduce the energy intensity of industry Create the new domestic bioindustry, lead by example through government's own actions, and change the way EERE does business	www.eere.energy.gov
U.S. Department of Health and Human Services (DHHS) Sustainability Program	The National Institute of Environmental Health Sciences (NIEHS)	NIEHS: uses environmental sciences to help people live longer and healthier lives	www.os.dhhs.gov
	The U.S. Environmental Protection Agency (EPA)	EPA: to protect human health and the environment, works for a cleaner, healthier environment for the American people	www.epa.gov
	The Division of Extramural Research and Training (DERT)	DERT: plans, directs, and evaluates the Institute's grant program, which supports research and research training in environmental health	
U.S. Department of State	Bureau of Oceans and International Environmental and Scientific (OES)	Responsible for international ocean law and policy, marine pollution, marine mammals, polar affairs, maritime boundaries, and marine science	www.state.gov
U.S. Environmental Protection Agency (EPA)	N/A	To protect human health and the environment Works for a cleaner, healthier environment for the American people	www.epa.gov
U.S. Federal Facilities Council (FFC)	N/A	To identify and advance technologies, processes, and facilities management practices that improve the performance of facilities over their entire life cycle, from planning to disposal	http://www7.national academies.org/ffc/ index.html
U.S. General Services Administration (GSA)	N/A	Secures the buildings, products, services, technology, and other workplace essentials federal agencies need Provides superior workplaces for federal workers Facilitates procurement of state-of-the-art commercial products and a wide range of services Offers best value and innovative solutions on IT products and services Develops and implements government-wide policies	www.gsa.gov
U.S. Green Building Council (USGBC)	N/A	The nation's foremost coalition of leaders from across the building industry working to promote buildings that are environmentally responsible, profitable, and healthy places to live and work	www.usgbc.org

(continued)

Table 3.1 (continued)

U.S. Departments and Agencies	Sustainable Program	Missions/Goals	Website
U.S. National Aeronautics and Space Administration (NASA)	NASA Environmental Tracking System (NETS)	NETS: automated application and database supporting: ■ Mandatory agency environmental reporting ■ Agency-wide performance metrics ■ Environmental Functional Management	www.nasa.gov
	Kennedy Space Center (KSC) Environmental Program Branch	Environmental Program Branch: provides center-wide policy development, interfacing with regulatory agencies, program management of remediation activities, development assistance and review of environmental permits, over-seeing the conservation of natural and historical resources at KSC, and development of programs to reduce future environmental burden	

Private Agencies	Sustainable Program	Missions/Goals	Website
ASTM (originally known as the American Society for Testing and Materials)	N/A	To be the foremost developer and provider of voluntary consensus standards, related technical information, and services having internationally recognized quality and applicability that: ■ Promote public health and safety, and the overall quality of life ■ Contribute to the reliability of materials, products, systems, and services ■ Facilitate national, regional, and international commerce To provide the optimum environment and support for technical committees to develop needed standards and related information and to ensure ASTM products and services are provided in a timely manner and meet current needs	www.astm.org
Federal Energy Management Program (FEMP)	N/A	To reduce the cost and environmental impact of the federal government by advancing energy efficiency and water conservation, promoting the use of distributed and renewable energy, and improving utility management decisions at federal sites	www.eere.energy.gov/femp
National Association of Home Builders (NAHB)	N/A	To represent the building industry by serving its members and affiliated state and local builders associations To achieve an overall mission of member satisfaction, NAHB concentrates on: ■ Balanced national legislative, regulatory, and judicial public policy ■ Public appreciation for the importance of housing and those who provide it ■ The premier resource for industry information, education, research, and technical expertise ■ Improved business performance of its members and affiliates ■ Effective management of staff, financial, and physical resources to satisfy the association's needs NAHB strives to create an environment in which: ■ All Americans have access to the housing of their choice and the opportunity to realize the American dream of homeownership ■ Builders have the freedom to operate as entrepreneurs in an open and competitive environment	www.nahb.org

Table 3.1 (continued)

Private Agencies	Sustainable Program	Missions/Goals	Website
NAHB (continued)		▪ Housing and those who provide it are recognized as the strength of the nation	
Natural Resources Defense Council (NRDC)	N/A	To safeguard the earth: its people, its plants and animals, and the natural systems on which all life depends To restore the integrity of the elements that sustain life—air, land, and water—and to defend endangered natural places To establish sustainability and good stewardship of the earth as central ethical imperatives of human society; NRDC affirms the integral place of human beings in the environment To protect nature in ways that advance the long-term welfare of present and future generations To foster the fundamental right of all people to have a voice in decisions that affect their environment To break down the pattern of disproportionate environmental burdens borne by people of color and others who face social or economic inequities To help create a new way of life for humankind, one that can be sustained indefinitely without fouling or depleting the resources that support all life on Earth	www.nrdc.org
The Sustainable Buildings Industry Council (SBIC)	N/A	To advance the design, affordability, energy performance, and environmental soundness of America's buildings	www.sbicouncil.org

Approaches to conserving energy have been a significant priority for federal governments. The **International Energy Agency (IEA)** serves as an energy policy advisor for 26 countries. The purpose of the organization is to "ensure reliable, affordable, and clean energy for their citizens" (IEA, 2005). IEA staff members are from the 26 countries and have expertise in energy and statistics. An interior designer could reference this organization when seeking sustainable information, including "climate change policies, market reform, energy technology collaboration," and global outreach activities.

The **U.S. ENERGY STAR** is a program supported by the U.S. federal government that assists businesses and individuals to reduce energy costs. Results have been positive. ENERGY STAR reports that "in 2004 alone, Americans, with the help of ENERGY STAR, saved enough energy to power 24 million homes and avoid greenhouse gas emissions equivalent to those from 20 million cars—all while saving $10 billion" (2005). Interior designers can reference ENERGY STAR to obtain information regarding the energy efficiency of household products, residences, HVAC systems, and energy management. In partnership with the EPA's LEED rating system, the *Buildings Upgrade Manual ENERGY STAR* is used as a guide for energy-efficient strategies in top-performing buildings.

Interior designers can contact state and local authorities to learn about the sustainable policies specific to their client's community, including zoning regulations, tax incentives, grant programs, and local environmental experts. The 2002 roundtable identified states and counties focused on green initiatives: California, Colorado, Maryland, New York, Pennsylvania, and Wisconsin; and the counties included Alameda, California; King, Washington; and Cook, Illinois. Numerous major cities in the United States are involved with sustainable development, including Austin and Frisco, Texas; Boulder, Colorado; Portland, Oregon; Los Angeles, Santa Monica, and San Francisco, California; Scottsdale, Arizona; Chicago, Illinois; Seattle, Washington; and Minneapolis/St. Paul, Minnesota.

Major cities with large populations present incredible opportunities and challenges. To initiate, implement, evaluate, and constantly improve a green program requires committed leadership. For example, Chicago is a very good model of how green initiatives can occur in a major urban environment (see Figure 3.6). The mission of Chicago's Department of the Environment (DOE) is "protecting human health and the environment, improving the urban quality of life, and promoting economic development in Chicago" (Chicago, 2005). The DOE has several divisions that are responsible for establishing policy, developing strategic direction, providing information, delineating operational procedures, and enforcing regulations. The DOE divisions include Energy Management and Air Quality; Natural Resources and Water Quality; Urban Management and Brownfields Redevelopment; External Government Relations and Policy; and Community Programming and Education Outreach. One of the most recent initiatives is the **green roof** program (see Figure 3.7). For example, owners of commercial, industrial, and residential buildings can contact the city of Chicago to acquire information regarding financial assistance, designing roof gardens, maintenance, and zoning requirements.

Colleges and Universities

An example of the vast extent of interest in sustainability is evident by the 1990 international conference in Talloires, France. The **Talloires Declaration (TD)** is the first official statement regarding higher education's commitment to environmental sustainability. University administrators declared that they are "deeply concerned about the unprecedented scale and speed of environmental pollution and degradation and the depletion of natural resources" (Talloires, 2005). Creators and original signatories included representatives from Africa, Brazil, China, Costa Rica, India, France, Ghana, Lebanon, Mexico, Nigeria, South Africa, Thailand, the United States, and the former USSR.

The TD is a 10-point action plan for colleges and universities: (1) increase awareness of environmentally sustainable development; (2) create an institutional culture of sustainability; (3) educate for environmentally responsible citizenship; (4) foster

Fig. 3.6. (top) Chicago is an excellent model of how green initiatives can occur in a major urban environment. The mission of Chicago's Department of the Environment (DOE) is "protecting human health and the environment, improving the urban quality of life, and promoting economic development in Chicago" (Chicago, 2005).
Fig. 3.7. (bottom) One of the most recent initiatives in Chicago is the green roof program. This green roof is on top of city hall in Chicago.

environmental literacy for all; (5) practice institutional ecology; (6) involve all stakeholders; (7) collaborate for interdisciplinary approaches; (8) enhance capacity of primary and secondary schools; (9) broaden service and outreach nationally and internationally; and (10) maintain the movement (Talloires, 2005). The TD continues to be supported by more than 300 university presidents and chancellors in more than 40 countries (TD, 2005).

An important aspect of the TD is the focus on acquiring an understanding of sustainable practices for all citizens, including children in primary and secondary schools. Learning about sustainability at the earliest ages sets the stage for expecting sustainable design throughout their lives. Informed citizens help interior designers when they are specifying sustainable design. In addition, knowledge of the actions of the TD document can help interior designers when they are working with educational facilities.

PROFESSIONAL ORGANIZATIONS, CORPORATIONS, AND RESEARCH

The importance of sustainability design is very evident when examining the philosophies and initiatives of professional organizations associated with interior design. The principles of sustainable development are evident in the most prominent interior design firms and leading manufacturers of products for interiors. The examples that follow demonstrate the extent of commitment to sustainable design and provide excellent examples of how organizations and industry are embracing sustainability.

Professional Organizations

The vast majority of educators and practitioners concur that the interior design profession has a social and moral responsibility to help protect our planet and the health, safety, and welfare of people. Hence, sustainable design is required in the curriculum of programs accredited by the **Council for Interior Design Accreditation** [formerly **Foundation for Interior Design Education and Research (FIDER)**] and is a content area of professional examinations. The importance of incorporating the principles of sustainable design in the interior design curriculum is evident by the recently enacted requirements of the Council for Interior Design Accreditation standards. Revisions to the accreditation standards emphasize increasing the level of understanding of sustainable design (see Table 3.2).

Table 3.2

Sustainability Content Areas of the Council for Interior Design Accreditation (Formerly Foundation for Interior Design Education and Research [FIDER]) Accreditation Requirements

Council for Interior Design Accreditation Standard	Description
Standard 2. Professional Values	The program **must** provide learning experiences that address (c) *environmental ethics* and the role of *sustainability* in the practice of interior design.
	The program **must** provide learning experiences that address (d) a *global perspective* and approach to thinking and problem solving (viewing design with awareness and respect for cultural and social difference of people; understanding issues that affect the *sustainability* of the planet; understanding the implications of conducting the practice of design within a world market).
Standard 3. Design Fundamentals	Student work **must** demonstrate understanding of principles and theories of *sustainability*.
Standard 4. Interior Design	Student work **must** demonstrate programming skills, including (f) information gathering research and analysis (functional requirements, code research, *sustainability* issues, and so forth).
Standard 6. Building Systems and Interior Materials	Students **must** demonstrate *understanding* of the concept of *sustainable* building methods and materials.
Standard 7. Regulations	Students **must** demonstrate the appropriate application of codes, regulations, and standards.
Standard 8. Business and Professional Practice	Students **must** demonstrate understanding of project management practices: (f) assessment processes (for example, post-occupancy evaluation, productivity, square-footage ratios, *life cycle assessment*).

SOURCE: Council for Interior Design Accreditations 2006, www.accredit-id.org.

The **Interior Design Educators Council (IDEC)** is a professional organization "dedicated to the advancement of interior design education" (IDEC, 2005). The importance of applying the principles of sustainable design to interiors came to the forefront at IDEC's 2005 annual conference. The two keynote speakers, William McDonough and Janine Benyus, focused on the importance of preserving our planet for future generations. The IDEC members demonstrated their support for educating interior design students regarding the concepts of sustainable design by voting to endorse the **Cradle to Cradle (C2C)** Design Paradigm developed by William McDonough and Michael Braungart. To provide easy access to interior sustainability information, the IDEC developed the "Green Design Education Initiative" website, www.idec.org/greendesign/, which includes green/sustainable interiors, resource links, and educational materials.

The **American Society of Interior Designers (ASID)** is the first and largest professional organization for interior designers. In connecting sustainable design to the practicing profession, the ASID has demonstrated extensive support for the principles of sustainable design. For example, the *Sustainable Design Information Center* on its website, www.asid.org, provides information on sustainable design and several links to Internet resources, including solar energy, IAQ, sustainable business, and news. At the 2004 *ASID Conference on Design*, Ray C. Anderson presented a speech on the topic of sustainability. Anderson is the founder of Interface, which is the largest commercial carpet manufacturer in the world. In his speech, *Towards Ethical Design*, Anderson described a brief summary of the environmental movement and environmental consequences of industrialism. Anderson noted that he is in the process of transforming Interface into a "wholly sustainable company by 2020, taking nothing, doing no harm" (ASID, 2005, p. 8). Anderson read an ancient quote from the Native American Cree prophecy that succinctly integrates sustainability, economics, and business practices:

> *Only after the last tree has been cut down,*
> *Only after the last river has been poisoned,*
> *Only after the last fish has been caught,*
> *Only then will you find money cannot be eaten.*
>
> (ASID, 2005, p. 8)

The **International Interior Design Association (IIDA)** is a professional interior design organization that "advocates for interior design excellence; provides superior industry information; nurtures a global interior design community; maintains educational standards; and responds to trends in business and design" (IIDA, 2005). The IIDA is another professional interior design organization that is committed to sustainable design as indicated by the adoption of a sustainability policy statement: "IIDA seeks to promote awareness and knowledge of interior design strategies that reduce negative impacts on our natural environment and improve the health and well-being of all people" (IIDA, 2005, p. 1). In addition, to enhance the education of sustainability, the IIDA established the *Sustainable Design Education Fund*. Maharam, a textile manufacturer, and *Interior Design* magazine provided financial support for the IIDA's educational program.

In response to the 1992 *Earth Summit* in Rio de Janeiro, Brazil, the **International Union of Architects (UIA)** and the American Institute of Architects (AIA) cosponsored a meeting in Chicago to focus on sustainable development for the twenty-first century (UIA-Architects, 2005). The 1993 conference theme was *Architecture at the Crossroads: Designing a Sustainable Future*. The conference resulted in an agreement titled *Declaration of Interdependence for a Sustainable Future*, which recognizes, "A sustainable society restores, preserves, and enhances nature and culture for the benefits of all life, present and future; a diverse and healthy environment is intrinsically valuable and essential to a healthy society; today's society is seriously degrading the environment and is not sustainable" (UIA-Architects, 2005). This UIA/AIA sustainability document is an excellent resource for understanding global perspectives of the principles of sustainability. The declaration emphasized the importance of understanding the interdependent elements of humanity and the natural environment. In addition, the UIA/AIA stated that "sustainable design integrates consideration of resource and energy efficiency, healthy buildings and materials, ecologically and socially sensitive land-use, and an aesthetic sensitivity that inspires, affirms, and ennobles" (1993).

The AIA demonstrates a continuous commitment to sustainable design by sponsoring a division titled the **Committee on the Environment (COTE)**. The committee "works to sustain and improve the environment by advancing and disseminating environmental knowledge and values and advocating best design practices to integrate built and natural systems to the profession, industry, and public" (2005). Annually, outstanding examples of sustainable design are presented with the AIA/COTE Green Project Award. The 2005 Green Project Awards were presented to eight projects, including the Austin Resource Center for the Homeless in the City of Austin, Texas (see Figure 3.8).

Interior Design Firms

Globally, numerous interior and architectural firms have embraced the principles of sustainability. However, there are firms that identify "sustainability" in their promotional materials but may not have extensive experience with executing a sustainable project. Thus, when seeking employment opportunities, it is important to thoroughly study a firm's promotional materials and the multiple divisions of its website. Generally, interior design firms that have a commitment to sustainability have a sustainable philosophy and provide a range of services related to sustainable design. In addition, these firms can demonstrate experience in integrating sustainable design practices with solutions for the built environment. A review of several websites reveals that many of the leading firms identify sustainable design as one of their primary services. Examples of primary service areas are architecture, interior architecture, and

historic preservation. To be exclusively listed as a primary service area demonstrates the importance of sustainable design. Intensely studying green materials is also important when reading product and service literature.

The critical importance of designing sustainable interiors is apparent by the commitment of the world's largest firms. For example, Gensler Architects has a portfolio that includes architecture, corporate office, retail, and entertainment (www.gensler .com). The 2003 annual sales of Gensler exceeded $250 million and the firm employs approximately 900 employees. Globally, offices are located in Hong Kong, London, Tokyo, and the United States. In 2001, Gensler won the *AIA Firm of the Year 2000* Award. An example of Gensler's sustainability philosophy is reflected in their statement, "Environmental responsibility is in OUR NATURE" (Gensler, 2005). This philosophy is expanded by explaining, "We're devoted to taking a sustainable approach to the design of places for people, helping us meet our needs today without preventing future generations from meeting their needs" (Gensler, 2005). Gensler clarifies that a "sustainable approach" enables its clients to reduce energy and operating costs, improve corporate image, create a market advantage, and improve workplace performance and the quality of life (Gensler, 2005). Figure 3.9 illustrates an example of a project planned by Gensler that embodies the principles of sustainable design.

Leo A Daly is a major firm with offices in Berlin,

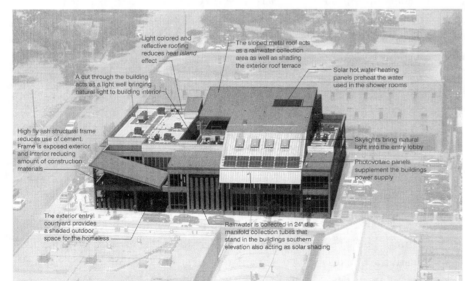

Fig. 3.8. Outstanding examples of sustainable design are presented annually with the AIA/COTE Green Project Award. The 2005 awards were presented to the Austin Resource Center for the Homeless in the City of Austin, Texas. The multipurpose facility has a 100-bed shelter for men, a day resource center, and a health clinic.

Fig. 3.9. An example of a Gensler project that embodies the principles of sustainable design. The PNC Financial Services Group is the first U.S. bank to design and construct environmentally friendly branches.

Dubai, Hong Kong, Madrid, Spain, Tokyo, United Arab Emirates, and the United States. Leo A Daly is engaged in architecture, engineering, interiors, and planning. As "stewards of the environment," Leo A Daly indicates that "responsible and appropriate use of materials has been an integral part of Leo A Daly's practice since our earliest days. The notion that a building should respect and enhance its natural environment has always been a part of our design philosophy" (Leo A Daly, 2005, p. 2). Leo A Daly's commitment to sustainability is reflected in the firm's extensive history of "incorporating respect and concern for energy efficiency into our designs." For example, in 1976 Leo A Daly received an award from the AIA for the firm's "vision and leadership to lead the AIA to take its first steps in the field of energy conservation in the built environment" (Leo A Daly, 2005, p. 2). Leo A Daly has received many other awards for incorporating energy efficiency and sustainability into its projects, including the *Excel Energy Assets Award* from Northern States Power.

Corporations and Industry

Sustainability is an important business practice for many corporations throughout the world, including companies that manufacture products for interiors. As with any business or industry, an interior designer must study a corporation's views toward the practice and integration of sustainability. Specifying sustainable products requires a thorough assessment of a corporation's manufacturing processes and attributes of a product.

Sustainable Manufacturers

The importance of sustainable design is evident by reviewing some of the world's leading manufacturers of interior products. For example, Herman Miller is a major company with $1.34 billion in net sales during fiscal year 2004. The corporation designs and manufactures furnishings, interior products, and related services. Products include office furniture systems, freestanding furniture, filing products, and office seating. An excerpt from *Herman Miller's Corporate Values Statement* explains, "We contribute to a better world by pursuing sustainability and environmental wisdom. Environmental advocacy is part of our heritage and a responsibility we gladly bear for future generations" (Herman Miller, 2005).

Herman Miller's corporate values are reflected in its business practices and the company's *Environmental Policy Statement*: "At Herman Miller respecting the environment is more than good business practice—it is the right thing to do. We believe that continued economic growth and environmental protection are inextricably linked—that the quality of life depends on meeting human needs without destroying the environment on which all life depends" (Herman Miller, 2005). To demonstrate its commitment to sustainability, Herman Miller has been engaged in several endeavors, such as providing financial support to the establishment of USGBC and owning LEED-certified buildings. Herman Miller was awarded Gold LEED certifications for renovating the MarketPlace and Building C1, which are located in Zeeland, Michigan. In addition, in 1995 Herman Miller's manufacturing facility, Greenhouse, was selected as a pilot for the development of the LEED certification process (see Figure 3.10).

In fall 2005, the EPA's *WasteWise Program* presented Herman Miller with its *Product Stewardship Gold Achievement Award* in the *Design* category. A factor in receiving the award was the work of Herman Miller's **Design for the Environment (DfE)** protocol, which focuses on developing "sensitive design standards for new and existing Herman Miller products." Futuristically, Herman Miller is "committed to building or renovating its facilities to achieve at least a 'Silver' LEED rating" and the company has identified "the year 2020 as the deadline to achieve a range of sustainability targets, including zero landfill and zero hazardous waste generation."

Interface also demonstrates a commitment to sustainable development and design. In business for more than 30 years, Interface designs and produces modular carpet, broadloom carpet, panel fabrics, and upholstery fabrics. The company's vision is to become the "world's first environmentally restorative company by 2020." The vision of Interface is "to be the first company that, by its deeds, shows the entire industrial world what sustainability is in all its dimensions: people, process, product, place, and profits—by 2020—and in doing so we will become restorative through the power of influence" (Interface, 2005).

Interface has published an essay that provides an overview of sustainability, including a comparison of current conditions in the world and the Industrial Revolution. Compared to the world today, the industrial era had "fewer people, less material well-being, and plentiful resources." As a result, manufacturing processes became a "highly productive, take-make-waste system that assumed infinite resources and infinite sinks for industrial waste" (Interface, 2005). Interface acknowledges being part of the problem; thus, it is committed to helping to create solutions. Suggestions focus on creating a company that "addresses the needs of society and the environment by developing a system of industrial production that decreases our costs and dramatically reduces the burdens placed on the systems" (Interface, 2005). Interface contends that this approach will make "precious resources available for the billions of people who need more."

Fig. 3.10. To demonstrate their commitment to sustainability, Herman Miller has been engaged in several endeavors. In 1995 Herman Miller's manufacturing facility, Greenhouse, was selected as a pilot for the development of the LEED certification process.

Sustainability Research Resources

As evidenced by the TD, universities throughout the world have a major role in the education, research, and service aspects of sustainability. The continuous flow of new knowledge regarding sustainability requires an interior designer to stay abreast of the field. Excellent sources are the reports, articles, books, and workshops disseminated by colleges and universities. For an interior designer, many of the resources are easily accessible online. For example, an excellent resource is the website for the **Lawrence Berkeley Laboratory (Berkeley Lab)**, which conducts research in science and engineering (www.lbl.gov). The Berkeley Lab is a national laboratory of the U.S. Department of Energy and is managed by the University of California (see Figure 3.11). Currently there are 10 Nobel laureates engaged in scientific research at the Berkeley Lab. Based on the beliefs of its founder, Nobel laureate Ernest Orlando Lawrence, research is conducted through teams of individuals with diverse backgrounds in basic and applied technologies.

Many research activities related to the sustainability practice are conducted in the divisions of earth science, environmental health and safety, environmental energy technologies, and advanced light source. The mission of the Earth Science Division is to develop "earth technologies for production of energy in an environmentally responsible manner and to deploy these technologies through partnership of industry, government, and academia" [Lawrence Berkeley Laboratory (Berkeley Lab), 2005]. A unit in this division is the Environmental Science Program (ESP), which conducts research with an emphasis on contaminants and water resources. As described in ESP's website, much of its research is "applicable to problems faced by the private sector" (Berkeley Lab, 2005). For example, the ESP website has an excellent drawing that illustrates a complex process with graphics that are appealing to the general public (see Figure 3.12).

Rocky Mountain Institute (RMI), a nonprofit organization, has its headquarters in a building with advanced energy- and water-conserving features. RMI's headquarters is a research center and serves as an educational facility for people who seek to learn about sustainability design (see Figure 3.13). The purpose of the research center is to "foster the efficient

Fig. 3.11. An excellent resource for research results is the Lawrence Berkeley Laboratory (Berkeley Lab). The Berkeley Lab, a national laboratory of the U.S. Department of Energy, is managed by the University of California.

and restorative use of resources to make the world secure, just, prosperous, and life-sustaining" (RMI, 2005). Research information is available on the RMI website, www.rmi.org. Some of the topics of interest to interior designers include energy, climate, water, buildings, and green development services. The sustainability design features of the institute's headquarters can be applied to various buildings. In reporting the energy-efficient features, RMI reported that "almost all the space and water-heating energy uses solar, it uses about a tenth the usual amount of household electricity (mostly solar-generated), and it uses less than half the normal amount of water" (2005).

Another valuable sustainability resource for interior designers is the **International Design Center for the Environment (IDCE)**, located in Research Triangle Park, North Carolina. The IDCE was created to advance sustainable designed buildings and products (IDCE, 2005). The IDCE's mission is "to integrate life cycle environmental stewardship, economic performance, and social equity into the design, construction, and furnishing of buildings in corporations, on campuses, and in communities" (IDCE, 2005). Research activities focus on structures built for a variety of purposes because IDCE contends that buildings are responsible for approximately "50 percent of all environmental degradation caused by human activity." The IDCE's first building was an exhibit for the EPA on "Sustainability Building Design, Construction, Furnishing and Operations." Designed as a traveling exhibit, "the KnowRoom" has been displayed in various locations throughout the country. Recently IDCE developed the eLCie Web-tool for product evaluation and selection. For more information on eLCie, see Unit II of this text.

An excellent online resource for assistance in identifying sustainability research related to the field of interior design, as well as numerous other topics, is **InformeDesign**, www.informedesign.org (see Figure 3.14). The goals of InformeDesign are to (1) "Collect, interpret, and disseminate information that will improve the design of the built environment and its support of human behavior, protect the health, safety, and welfare of the public and protect the earth, and expand the body of knowledge of the profession of interior design"; (2) "Improve communication and enhance knowledge sharing among practitioners, researchers, educators, students, code officials, allied practitioners, industry partners, legislators, and the public"; and (3) "Utilize input from interior design practitioners, design firms, and industry partners to identify research issues and increase the perceived value of research" (2005).

The University of Minnesota, with the support

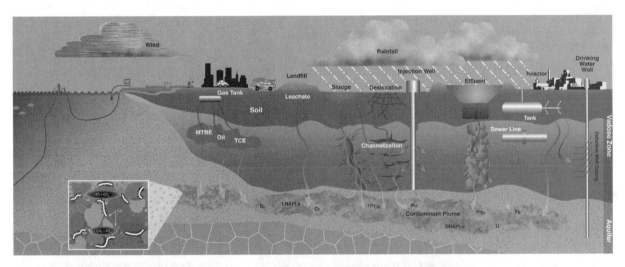

Fig. 3.12. (above) The Berkeley Lab's Environmental Science Program (ESP) conducts research with an emphasis on contaminants and water resources. This ESP illustration depicts a complex process associated with environmental remediation.

Fig. 3.13. (left) Rocky Mountain Institute (RMI), a nonprofit organization, has its headquarters in a building with advanced energy- and water-conserving features.

Fig. 3.14. An excellent online resource for assistance in identifying sustainability research related to the field of interior design, as well as numerous other topics, is InformeDesign.

of its founding sponsor, American Society of Interior Designers (ASID), and founding contributors created InformeDesign. The industry support from founding contributors included Armstrong World Industries, Inc.; Carpet and Rug Institute (CRI); Sherwin-Williams Company; and Vista Window Films. Financial support from ASID and ASID's "Industry Partners" for InformeDesign demonstrates the importance of interior designers' applying research to practice. As explained on InformeDesign's website, "There is a broad range of benefits to be gained by the design community, clients, occupants, participants, and other users through the interior designer's use of research" (InformeDesign, 2005).

As illustrated in Figure 3.14, InformeDesign's research database is organized into three major categories: "Space," "Issues," and "Occupants." Articles categorized in the Space section relate to building type/design specialization, such as sustainable design, corporate facilities, and residences. The Issues category focuses on specific design topics such as codes, safety, and design business. Articles that focus on Occupants present research findings related to how interiors affect people of different ages, disabilities, and socioeconomic standing.

Each category has numerous articles that have been analyzed and summarized by professors at the

University of Minnesota. For example, in fall 2005 there were 16 research summaries listed under the topic of sustainability. Each summary of an article includes citation information and brief descriptions of the "design issue," "design criteria," "key concepts," "research method," "limitations," and "commentary." The two-page summaries provide an excellent resource for interior designers who seek to keep current in the field but lack the time or interest to read the original academic research article. The complete citation for every article allows an interior designer to read the entire article for in-depth content. To receive updates of information posted on the website, individuals can register for automatic e-mail notices.

Indoor air quality (IAQ) is a very important concern of the interior design profession. To obtain information regarding low-emitting products, an excellent source is the **GREENGUARD Environmental Institute (GEI)**. GEI is an industry-independent, nonprofit organization created to manage the *GREENGUARD Certification Program*. GREENGUARD certification is a voluntary program for manufacturers and suppliers of interior products. Corporations can submit their product to GREENGUARD for testing of chemical and particle emissions. The results of testing are published in the *GREENGUARD Product Guide*, which is an IAQ resource for indoor environments. According to the GEI (2005), disseminating the research results related to low-emitting products and materials will help architects, interior designers, and purchasing units to improve the quality of life by having safer products. This can be very useful to consumers who are uncertain regarding the manufacturers' claim of producing products with low emissions. Uncertainties related to information disseminated by product manufacturers and their representatives are further discussed in Unit II.

Summary

- The National Environmental Policy Act (NEPA) is the charter act for protecting the environment. The act serves to promote efforts to (1) prevent or eliminate damage to the environment and biosphere, (2) stimulate the health and welfare of people, (3) enrich the understanding of ecological systems and the importance of natural resources, and (4) establish the Council on Environmental Quality (CEQ).

- The Clean Water Act (CWA) of 1977 and the Safe Drinking Water Act (SDWA) of 1974 are the two most important legislations created to protect the quality of water. The objective of the CWA is to "restore and maintain the chemical, physical, and biological integrity of the Nation's waters" (U.S.C. 1251, Sec. 101, 2002).

- The Energy Policy and Conservation Act (EPCA) of 1975 initiated a series of important federal environmental legislation related to energy conservation, including the National Appliance Energy Conservation Act (NAECAA) of 1987 and the Energy Policy Act of 1992.

- To meet future energy needs, other recommendations of the NEP (2001) include strategies intended to decrease the demand for energy, such as encouraging energy conservation and efficiency.

- The National Appliance Energy Conservation Act of 1987 (NAECA) establishes efficiency standards for appliances, such as refrigerators, freezers, dishwashers, washing machines, dryers, and air conditioners.

- The U.S. government's efforts to manage solid and hazardous waste are legislated by the laws of the Resource Conservation and Recovery Act (RCRA). The RCRA was created to (1) protect human health and the environment, (2) reduce/eliminate the generation of hazardous wastes, and (3) conserve energy and natural resources (Department of Energy, 2003, p. 1).

- Numerous public and private organizations have been created to address the importance of sustainable development. These entities are at the global, national, regional, and local levels.

- In 1990, the Pollution Prevention Act (PPA) was created to focus attention on "reducing the amount of pollution through cost-effective changes in production, operation, and raw materials use."

- To support sustainability activities requires keeping abreast in multiple disciplines. There are hundreds of agencies, organizations, and programs dedicated to sustainability and the environment.

- The United Nations (UN) is an excellent resource for international environmental programs. Specifically, the UN has a Division of Environmental Information, Assessment, and Early Warning that supports the UN Environment Programme (UNEP).

- Generally sustainability-related standards are subsumed in ISO 14000, "environmental management." ISO 14000 focuses on "what the organization does to minimize harmful effects on the environment caused by its activities, and continually to improve its environmental performance."

- The U.S. ENERGY STAR is a program supported by the U.S. federal government that assists businesses and individuals to reduce energy costs.

- The importance of sustainability design is very evident by examining the philosophies and initiatives of professional organizations associated with interior design.

- The principles of sustainable development are evident in the most prominent interior design firms and leading manufacturers of products for interiors.

- Sustainability is an important business practice for many corporations throughout the world, including companies that manufacture products for interiors.

- The continuous flow of new knowledge regarding sustainability requires an interior designer to stay abreast of the field. Excellent sources are the reports, articles, books, and workshops disseminated by colleges and universities.

Key Terms

American National Standards Institute/American Society of Heating, Refrigerating and Air-Conditioning Engineers (ANSI/ASHRAE)

American Society of Interior Designers (ASID)

Biobased products

Bioenergy

Biomass

Building for Environmental and Economic Sustainability (BEES)

Clean Water Act (CWA)

Committee on the Environment (COTE)

Council for Interior Design Accreditation [formerly Foundation for Interior Design Education and Research (FIDER)]

Council on Environmental Quality (CEQ)

Cradle to Cradle (C2C)

Department of Energy (DOE)

Design for the Environment (DfE)

Division of Environmental Information, Assessment and Early Warning

Energy Policy Act

Energy Policy and Conservation Act (EPCA)

Environmental Canada (EC)

European Union (EU)

Federal universal wastes

Global Environment Outlook (GEO)

Government Services Administration (GSA)

Gray water

GREENGUARD Environmental Institute (GEI)

Green Building Roundtable

Green roof

High-performance green building

InformeDesign

Interior Design Educators Council (IDEC)

International Design Center for the Environment (IDCE)

International Energy Agency (IEA)

International Interior Design Association (IIDA)

International Initiative for a Sustainable Built Environment (iiSBE)

International Organization for Standardization (ISO)

International Union of Architects (UIA)

ISO 14000

Lawrence Berkeley Laboratory (Berkeley Lab)

LEED (Leadership in Energy and Environmental Design)

National Appliance Energy Conservation Act (NAECA)

National Energy Policy (NEP)

National Energy Policy Development Group (NEDP)

National Environmental Policy Act (NEPA)

National Park Service, U.S. Department of the Interior (DOI)

Occupational Safety & Health Administration (OSHA)

Pollution Prevention Act (PPA)

Rearview mirror thinking

Refuse Act

Rocky Mountain Institute (RMI)

Safe Drinking Water Act (SDWA)

Talloires Declaration (TD)

Toxic Substances Control Act (TSCA)

UN Environmental Programme (UNEP)

United States Green Building Council (USGBC)

U.S. ENERGY STAR

World Green Building Council (WorldGBC)

Exercises

1. Research local state laws and regulations affecting sustainability and interior environments. In a written report, summarize the findings and discuss how the laws and regulations affect practice in commercial and residential interiors.

2. Research the most prevalent global energy problems. Identify energy-efficient recommendations that could be provided to a residential client living in a cold and warm climate. In a written report, provide the energy-efficient recommendations and include any relevant product specifications.

3. In the 2003 Building Design and Construction (BDC) survey, the results indicate that 33 percent of the 498 respondents were "somewhat experienced" with sustainable design and 39 percent had "not much experience, but interested." Approximately half of the respondents indicated working on at least one green project and 57 percent of the firms encouraged staff to learn more about the topic. Conduct interviews or distribute a questionnaire to local businesses to determine the extent of their experience with sustainable design. In a written report, summarize the results and provide recommendations for encouraging sustainable practices.

4. Research several major interior design firms and determine their level of commitment to sustainability. In a written report, compare and contrast the firms' approaches to sustainability. Provide recommendations for future practice.

CHAPTER 4

Transformational Sustainable Principles and Strategies

Your planet is so small that you can walk around it in three strides. All you have to do is walk more slowly, and you'll always be in the sun.

When you want to take a rest just walk . . . and the day will last as long as you want it to.

—ANTOINE DE SAINT-EXUPÉRY

Objectives

- Comprehend the importance of applying a set of sustainable principles to the practice of interior design.
- Describe the process associated with a sustainability life cycle assessment (LCA).
- Understand the strategic relationships between sustainable design, economics, and benefits.
- Apply an understanding of environmental management systems to the practice of interior designers.
- Understand how to apply LCA to sustainable design.
- Determine a strategy for integrating the principles of sustainability, economics, and systems.

FOR INDIVIDUALS, professionals, industry, and governments to reframe their way of thinking about environmental responsibility requires novel approaches to leadership, management, and practice. Chapter 3 provides examples of how international governments, organizations, and industry have embraced sustainability. These examples offer the framework for exploring strategies for integrating the principles of sustainability with the practice of interior designers.

This chapter explores principles of sustainability, and then examines various strategies that should be used when applying the principles to practice. Important principles of sustainability include a committed leadership, a consistent focus on the future, global collaboration, and strategic planning for continuous improvement. An effective strategy for implementing sustainability principles is to use various tools, including the **PDCA (Plan, Do, Check, Act) Cycle,** the **life cycle assessment (LCA),** and the **cost-effectiveness analysis (CEA).** These tools are very useful to an interior designer because they provide a framework for understanding essential elements of a system and sustainable processes. In addition, the graphics associated with these tools help to illustrate the holistic nature of sustainability and the fluidity between the interdependent elements of the system.

TRANSFORMATIONAL ELEMENTS

For many interior designers and their clients, sustainable design is a new concept that requires fresh ways of thinking about decision-making processes, business protocols, and lifestyles. Systemic and meaningful transformation, as opposed to mere revisions, requires principles and a path focused on the future. Fortunately, the substantial literature related to sustainability provides an interior designer with inspiration from a variety of global perspectives.

Principles of Sustainability: Interior Applications

To successfully integrate sustainability with practice requires interior designers to develop a set of principles that are based on the unique aspects of their firm and their clients. This is not difficult to conceptualize because interior designers already have a working knowledge of applying the *principles of design* to practice. For example, an interior designer applies the principles of emphasis and unity when planning space, selecting colors, and specifying furnishings.

To successfully apply a new concept to practice necessitates a process that involves extensive learning, followed by allocating enough time to analyzing how the concept can be integrated into one's practice (Fullan, 1991). For example, if interior designers want to apply sustainable development to the practice of their firm, the process should involve (1) studying the various global aspects related to sustainability, (2) analyzing the philosophy of sustainability to the extent that the concept becomes intuitive, and (3) a strategic plan that prescribes sustainability policies and practice.

Sustainable design principles can serve as a guide for making decisions related to business practices and designs for commercial and residential interiors. The principles can be used to make decisions on a daily basis, or they can become the criteria for long-term decisions. To establish consistency in decision-making, the principles should be (1) enduring, (2) well understood by the stakeholders, and (3) reflective of the needs of the firm and its clients. An essential component of sustainable design is an emphasis on continuously enhancing the environment for the needs of the current and future generations. To carry out this goal requires constant monitoring and assessment of policies, processes, and practice. For sustainability purposes, the assessment criteria should reflect the values of people, a respect for the environment, and economic development. Box 4.1 has a suggested list of sustainable design principles. To reflect the practice of the profession, the 10 sustainable principles are divided into three primary areas: *operational, philosophical,* and *practice.*

Transformational Tools

For the purpose of studying sustainability models, the word *tools* is not used within the usual operational definition. Rather than an "instrument, such as a saw that is used by hands to do work," *tools,* within the sustainability context, refers to an assortment of resources that can help the mind "to do work." For example, ISO provides this description of a product developed for one of the series in ISO

Box 4.1

To embrace sustainability, an interior design firm should have the overarching operating principles:

- Apply systemic philosophies and long-term perspectives to all decision-making processes.
- Collaborate with various stakeholders involved with decisions related to sustainable design.
- Constantly scan the world to incorporate the most appropriate solutions for improving the health of people and minimizing the direct and indirect impacts on the environment.

To embrace sustainability, an interior design firm should have the following philosophical principles:

- Respect the needs of current and future generations of people throughout the world by taking responsibility for being an exemplary steward of the environment.
- Embrace environmental practices that encourage conscious consumption, manage natural resources, and promote energy-efficiency.
- Encourage sustainable solutions that are cost-effective, facilitate adaptability, and serve the functional needs of the end users.

To embrace sustainability, an interior design firm should have the following practice principles:

- Design healthy interiors that promote quality of life for the current and future generations.
- Promote design solutions that eliminate or reduce pollutants in all stages of the life of products, materials, finishes, and building systems.
- Promote the long-term benefits of investing in durable products, materials, and processes while respecting the budgetary limitations of the client.
- Provide preference for sustainable products from manufacturers that engage in sustainable practices.

To provide tools that will help organizations to implement standards is an excellent approach for reframing perspectives toward standards. *Standards* are frequently associated with requirements that are costly, time consuming, unduly complicated, and difficult to implement. Generally, compliance is not voluntary; thus, implementation occurs only when governments mandate compliance via laws and their respective financial penalties. Punitive strategies are typically not an effective means to motivate people. Consequently, organizations find loopholes in the standards, or avoid implementation for years while fighting the laws in court. For some organizations, the fines are cheaper than compliance. Therefore, the corporation never complies with the standards and simply pays the fines and penalties.

If environmentally related laws are ever suspended, corporations typically suspend the mandated operations and then return to their previously detrimental practices. Unfortunately, due to the examples described above, and various other factors, legislation is either weakly implemented or ignored. Thus, laws that are intended to improve the health of people and the environment fall short of meeting their objectives. Within this context, it is extremely difficult to successfully implement the principles of sustainable design. Systemic and meaningful implementation begins with individuals who *choose* to engage in sustainability practices, because they respect and value a quality life for people and the environment for thousands of years.

Depending on the client, to advocate for meaningful sustainable design an interior designer could use approaches that may help an individual or corporation to reframe their attitudes toward "mandated" sustainability practices. People must be motivated to work with standards because they "want to do the right thing," not because the laws mandate compliance. The ISO provides excellent examples of taking proactive approaches to standards, because the *toolkits* are designed to explain how the standards can help them to do the right thing. The ISO's website for resources that are available for the ISO 14000 series has a tone that is helpful and polite and frames descriptions in an extremely positive manner. For example, in trying to empathize with someone's frustration with understanding the complexities associated with standards, ISO indicates, "ISO 14000,

standards: "Every organization determined to embrace ISO 14000 should have a supporting policy manual, procedures, data collection forms, etc. The *ISO 14000 Toolkit* provides all of these, along with training presentations, checklists, and a comprehensive implementation guide."

ISO 14001, ISO 14004 . . . the myriad of ISO 14000 standards and information related to environmental management can sometimes hinder progress and cause confusion. This website is designed to untangle and simplify these—to make environmental management using the above standards a much easier task" (2005).

To ease an introduction to standards, ISO indicates that standards and items are explained with a series of simple-to-use resources. In taking a very positive approach to implementing standards, ISO suggests that an organization is "determined to embrace" the standards and that ISO has "supporting" policy manuals. To be respectful of readers and their occupational responsibilities, ISO concludes, "Hopefully, these pages will help you ensure that you meet your obligations diligently and professionally, but with the minimum of fuss" (2005). These examples demonstrate the subtle nuances that can make the difference between an individual being intimidated by complex standards and being encouraged to adopt the standards. Interior designers should apply ISO's *gentle* approach to standards when they are working with clients, industry representatives, and policy makers. Working with people in a helpful and positive manner encourages a transformation in behavior that is meaningful, systemic, and long lasting.

Environmental Management System (EMS)

To manage the interactions between an organization and the natural environment, many businesses utilize the **environmental management system (EMS)**. The EMS is utilized to help a business strategically manage all aspects associated with production processes, including planning, implementation, controlling costs, evaluating outcomes, and identifying future opportunities. The **International Finance Corporation (IFC)** is an example of an organization that supports utilizing EMSs and provides helpful information regarding EMS on its website, www.ifc.org. For an interior designer who seeks to apply the principles of sustainable design to practice, IFC is an excellent resource because the organization has a "core commitment to sustainable development" and is extensively involved with financing projects throughout the world. The IFC's mission is to "promote

sustainable private sector investment in developing countries, helping to reduce poverty and improve people's lives" (IFC, 2005).

The IFC defines EMS as "a comprehensive approach to managing environmental issues, integrating environment-oriented thinking into every aspect of business management" (IFC, 2005). The IFC indicates that the EMS approach prioritizes the environment while integrating other aspects that are important to a business, such as costs, productivity, and investments. The EMS approach can increase efficiency and focus on "customer needs and marketplace conditions, improving both the company's financial and environmental performance" (IFC, 2005). The EMS utilizes the PDCA cycle within the context of environmental matters. As with any initiative where meaningful adoption is important, EMS requires a commitment from top management and the involvement of its stakeholders.

SUSTAINABLE PROCESSES: PDCA CYCLES

An essential tool associated with sustainable design principles is the PDCA cycle. To understand the extent of success associated with the PDCA methodology, it is useful to briefly trace the tool back to its origins of practice.

PDCA: Plan, Do, Check, Act

Walter A. Shewhart developed the concepts associated with PDCA in 1930 (see Figure 4.1). In the early 1950s, **Shewhart's cycle** became very popular when the renowned statistician, W. Edwards Deming, used the model to help the Japanese improve the quality

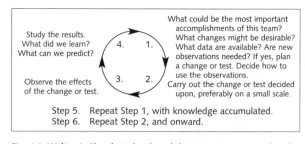

Fig. 4.1. Walter A. Shewhart developed the concepts associated with PDCA in 1930. In the early 1950s Shewhart's cycle became very popular when W. Edwards Deming used the model for quality improvement processes.

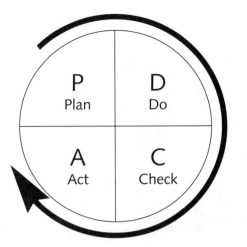

Fig. 4.2. The Deming cycle, or Deming's "plan for action," was simplified to PDCA (plan, do, check, act). Each stage receives input from the previous stage, performs a transaction, and then submits the outcome, or output, to the next stage.

of their products. At this time the Japanese had an international reputation for manufacturing inferior products. For example, there was a strong association between "cheap" and the frequently seen product label: "Made in Japan." Deming used Shewhart's cycle to explain that work at any stage should have "continual improvement of methods and procedures, aimed at better satisfaction of the customer (user) at the next stage" (Deming, 1986, p. 87). Since Deming was using Shewhart's cycle, the Japanese renamed the concept the **Deming cycle**.

By the 1980s, the dramatic transformation in the quality of Japanese products prompted attention to Deming's management philosophy and the Deming cycle. Subsequently, the Deming cycle, or Deming's "plan for action," was simplified to PDCA and also became the **ISO 14001 PDCA** (see Figure 4.2). Deming explained that within a process, activities occur in various stages (1986). As illustrated in Figure 4.2, each stage receives **input** from the previous stage, performs a *transaction*, and then submits the outcome, or **output**, to the next stage. Deming suggests that to have optimum outcomes, methods and processes should be continuously improved at each stage throughout the cycle. The goal should always be to improve an outcome for the *customer* who receives the product or service in the next stage. Thus, all stages collaborate to continuously improve quality and optimize the satisfaction of a customer. The Deming or

PDCA cycle is a procedure designed to continuously help improve activities at each stage of a process and assist in identifying problems.

The basic PDCA cycle is divided into four stages: plan, do, check, and act. The activities in the "plan" stage include identifying objectives, processes, resources, and associated costs. The outcomes of the plan stage are transferred to the "do" stage, which involves the processes related to the production of products or services. The purpose of the "check" stage is to evaluate the outcomes from the do stage, by comparing the results with the objectives that were identified in the plan stage. At the last stage, "act," the outcomes from the evaluation process are used to take any corrective actions. The continuous improvement cycle advances by providing the new knowledge gained in stage four to the first stage: "plan." The circular format of the PDCA model suggests that the process is never ending. Management must continuously review and contemplate the inputs and outcomes of each stage of the process. Unfortunately, corporations or institutions do not always follow this methodology. For example, it is very common for an organization to develop a planning document that sits on a shelf and is rarely revised to improve practice. The simplistic format of the PDCA helps organizations to understand what should be done to have continuous improvement, and that all stages require constant scrutiny.

ISO 14000 Model and the 14001 PDCA Cycle

To manage business procedures and operations, multiple corporations, firms, organizations, and institutions throughout the world have adopted the fundamental elements of the PDCA (see Figure 4.3). As shown in Figure 4.3, ISO developed a model to graphically depict the *14000 Family of International Standards* (see Table 4.1). The overall format of the ISO 14000 model illustrates which ISO series connects with the PDCA cycle. For example, people working in the "do stage" need information related to environmental performance communication. This content is available in the ISO 14020 and ISO 14063 series.

The ISO utilizes the basic components of the PDCA for the foundation of the ISO 14001 International Standard. An explanation of ISO's version of the PDCA is provided because ISO developed the

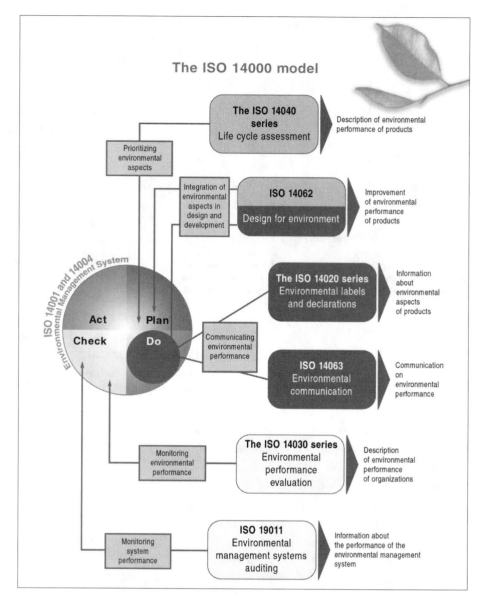

Fig. 4.3. The ISO 14000 model. The overall format of the ISO 14000 model illustrates which ISO series connects with the PDCA cycle.

Fig. 4.4. The ISO partnered with ArTech to develop the Kids' ISO 14000 Programme. The ISO has lent its name and provides support for the Kids' ISO 14000 Programme, which was created and is operated by ArTech.

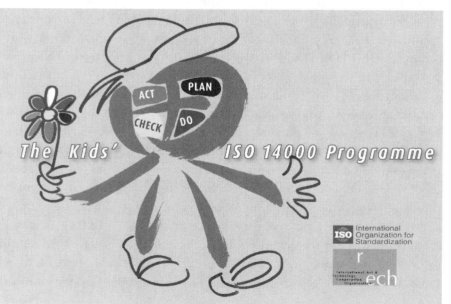

standard within the context of the EMS. The ISO's standards represent the work of a global alliance of national standards bodies. Thus, knowledge of the PDCA cycle, within the ISO context, is an excellent foundation for understanding the elements of the process from an international perspective while gaining knowledge of important standards. In addition, the ISO program is designed for a variety of public and private organizations, including households. For example, recently ISO partnered with ArTech (2005), an international art and technology organization, to develop the **Kids' ISO 14000 Programme** (see Figure 4.4). The purposes of the program are to (1) develop an environmental awareness among children;

Table 4.1

The ISO 14000 Family of Standards, Guides, and Technical Reports (Including Drafts)

ISO 14001:1996	1996 Environmental management systems—Specification with guidance for use
ISO 14004:1996	1996 Environmental management systems—General guidelines on principles, systems, and supporting techniques
ISO 14010:1996	1996 Guidelines for environmental auditing—General principles
ISO 14011:1996	1996 Guidelines for environmental auditing—Audit procedures—Auditing of environmental management systems
ISO 14012:1996	1996 Guidelines for environmental auditing—Qualification criteria for environmental auditors
ISO 14015:2001	2001 Environmental management—Environmental assessment of sites and organizations (EASO)
ISO 14020:2000	2000 Environmental labels and declarations—General principles
ISO 14021:1999	1999 Environmental labels and declarations—Self-declared environmental claims (Type II environmental labeling)
ISO 14024:1999	1999 Environmental labels and declarations—Type I environmental labeling—Principles and procedures
ISO/TR 14025:2000	2000 Environmental labels and declarations—Type III environmental declarations
ISO 14031:1999	1999 Environmental management—Environmental performance evaluation—Guidelines
ISO/TR 14032:1999	1999 Environmental management—Examples of environmental performance evaluation (EPE)
ISO 14040:1997	1997 Environmental management—Life cycle assessment—Principles and framework
ISO 14041:1998	1998 Environmental management—Life cycle assessment—Goal and scope definition and inventory analysis
ISO 14042:2000	2000 Environmental management—Life cycle assessment—Life cycle impact assessment
ISO 14043:2000	2000 Environmental management—Life cycle assessment—Life cycle interpretation
ISO/TR 14047	Environmental management—Life cycle assessment—Examples of application of ISO 14042
ISO/TS 14048:2002	2002 Environmental management—Life cycle assessment—Data documentation format
ISO/TR 14049:2000	2000 Environmental management—Life cycle assessment—Examples of application of ISO 14041 to goal and scope definition and inventory analysis
ISO 14050:2002	2002 Environmental management—Vocabulary
ISO/TR 14061:1998	1998 Information to assist forestry organizations in the use of the Environmental Management System standards ISO 14001 and ISO 14004
ISO/TR 14062:2002	2002 Environmental management—Integrating environmental aspects into product design and development
ISO/WD 14063	To be Environmental management—Environmental determined communications—Guidelines and examples
ISO/AWI 14064	Guidelines for measuring, reporting, and verifying entity and project-level greenhouse gas emissions
ISO 19011:2002	2002 Guidelines for quality and/or environmental management systems auditing (This standard replaces ISO 14010, 14011, and 14012.)
ISO Guide 64:1997	1997 Guide for the inclusion of environmental aspects in product standards
ISO/IEC Guide 66*	1999 General requirements for bodies operating assessment and certification/registration of environmental management systems (EMS)

NOTES: AWI = Approved Work Item; WD = Working Draft; CD = Committee Draft; DIS = Draft International Standard; FDIS = Final Draft International Standard; DTR = Draft Technical Report; TR = Technical Report

* ISO/IEC Guide 66 was developed by the ISO Policy Development Committee on conformity assessment (ISO/CASCO).

SOURCE: ISO (2002), Environmental Management, Geneva, Switzerland: ISO.

(2) educate children how to implement ISO 14000 in their homes and communities; and (3) "open them to the value of networking with young people in other schools, communities, and countries in order to bring the force of collective action to global environmental issues" (ArTech, 2003).

The starting point for developing the EMS model for the ISO 14001 standard is establishing an environmental policy. This policy serves as the framework for "implementing and improving an organization's environmental management system" (ISO, 2004, p. 11). According to the ISO, the environmental policy should address several areas, including a commitment to preventing pollution, the provision of a framework for environmental objectives, compliance with legal requirements, and dissemination to internal and external constituents in an easily understood manner (2004). Furthermore, the ISO recommends that any contractors assigned to work at a facility should be informed about the environmental policy, but the format of communication could be via contracts or project requirements.

The environmental policy should be developed in a collaborative effort with the stakeholders. For example, in 1991 Herman Miller, Inc., established the **Environmental Quality Action Team (EQAT)** to create the corporation's first environmental policy. The EQAT is a steering committee of Herman Miller employees that establishes the corporation's environmental goals and priorities and reviews environmental impacts. Important components of the committee's governance structure include the "team-based approach" and participation from each of the corporation's primary functional areas, such as "indoor air," "packaging/transportation," and "design for environment" (see Figure 4.5). To conduct its work, EQAT has several teams, such as the "design for the environment (DfE) team," "green buildings team," and an "environmental low impact processing group."

Frequently, the ISO standards prescribe that an organization should "establish, implement, and maintain" procedures or documents. These three verbs concisely describe the type of work that is often required in each stage of the process. For example, the planning section states, "the organization shall establish, implement, and maintain a procedure to determine those aspects that have or can have signif-

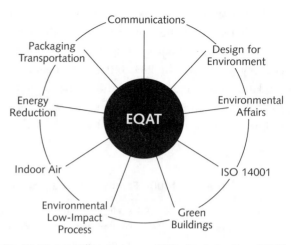

Fig. 4.5. Herman Miller's Environmental Quality Action Team (EQAT).

icant impact(s) on the environment" (ISO, 2004, p. 4). *Maintain* is an excellent word for describing actions that should occur when an organization is involved with sustainable design. To maintain a procedure or document suggests that care will be taken to continuously review and monitor the activities. Thus, ISO requires an organization to *maintain* procedures or documents related to environmental systems.

PDCA Stages

As illustrated in Figure 4.3, ISO's *plan* stage consists of environmental aspects; legal and other requirements; and objectives, targets, and programs. Environmental aspects in design/development, and data derived from a life cycle assessment (LCA), provide the inputs for the planning stage.

The "Plan" Stage

ISO defines environmental aspects as any element of an organization's "activities or services that can interact with the environment" (2004). Environmental aspects have the potential to significantly impact the environment. In the plan stage an organization identifies "the environmental aspects of its activities, products, and services" within the EMS (ISO, 2004). The organization also identifies any legal requirements and how they apply to its environmental aspects. The organization's environmental policy, environmental aspects, and legal requirements are the basis for the organization's objectives and targets. The ISO stipulates that these elements should be measurable and specific to functions and to organizational levels. To ensure that objectives and targets are met, organizations must identify programs that delineate methods, a timeline, and the roles and responsibilities of people (ISO, 2004).

To gather all the information that is required for the plan stage, a recommended practice in the area of sustainable design is a **charrette**, which is the French word for *cart*. The word *charrette* is derived from design processes in Parisian art and architectural studios during the nineteenth century [National Charrette Institute (NCI), 2005]. Students were required to work quickly on their projects in the studio. Once the deadline for completion approached, a proctor walked through the studio with a cart to collect the projects (see Figure 4.6). Thus, *charrette* is the term used to describe an interdisciplinary, collaborative activity that results in a plan. According to the NCI, various professional units engage in a charrette, including interior designers, planners, and architects (2005). Generally, as with the art students in Paris, a charrette is used to quickly create or develop a product in a few days. Charrettes have become popular with sustainable design projects because of the focus on the holistic process involving multistakeholders.

The "Do" Stage

The *do* stage, or the implementation and operation phase, consists of the following categories: (1) resources, roles, responsibility, and authority; (2) competence, training, awareness, and communica-

Fig. 4.6. In nineteenth-century art and architectural studios in Paris, students were required to work quickly on their designs and then place the completed projects in a charrette. The charrette concept is now applied to the design of sustainable interior environments.

tion; (3) documentation and control of documents; and (4) operational control and emergency preparedness and response (ISO, 2004). The ISO standards that affect the do stage are *design for environment* (ISO 14062), and the series related to communicating environmental performance. The first category, *resources, roles, responsibility, and authority*, deals with governance and allocating the resources needed to accomplish the tasks of the **stakeholders**. This involves identifying people who have the appropriate skills, allocating adequate time, and providing sufficient financial resources. To organize the multiple processes requires a well-conceived governance structure, or meaningful work will never be accomplished. As demonstrated by the international summits, sustainable development was established using communication processes, which involved stakeholders and consensus. As explained by Hemmati, "sustainable development requires a process of dialogue and ultimately consensus-building of all stakeholders as partners who together define the problems, design possible solutions, collaborate to implement them, and monitor and evaluate the outcome. Through such activities, stakeholders can build relationships and knowledge which will enable them to develop sustainable solutions to new challenges" (2002, p. 40).

To engage in all of the important processes that Hemmati identified necessitates an organizational structure, or governance, that facilitates the processes. This is accomplished by establishing *how* processes will be conducted, including the identification of roles, responsibilities, and authority. Meaningful work can never be accomplished without an understanding of *who* is responsible for *which* activities. In addition, the organizational structure must identify who has the *authority* to ensure that decisions are implemented and maintained. For example, in the *contract and implementation phases* of the design process, roles and responsibilities must be clearly understood to complete a project. All of the stakeholders involved with the project, such as the client, contractors, and electricians, must know *who* has authority and responsibility for operations. This involves knowing who is responsible for tasks such as signing contracts, ordering furniture, delivering merchandise to the site, and installing the building systems.

A very important component of ISO's *competence,*

training, and awareness category is ensuring that the participants have significant knowledge of environmental impacts. Furthermore, this category stipulates that an organization has an extensive program for continuous education. *Awareness* involves enacting policies and procedures that ensure an understanding of the EMS and various aspects related to the organization's environmental policy. For example, the ISO indicates that people should be aware of the importance of conforming to the organization's environmental policy, impacts associated with environmental aspects, and environmental benefits (2004). The *communication* category focuses on ensuring effective communication between internal and external constituents in every division of the organization. In a governance document, communication channels and methods can be integrated with the roles and responsibilities of the stakeholders.

Areas connected to communication are found in the *documentation and control of documents* category. The ISO indicates that EMS documentation should include all items related to environmental policies, including objectives, the main elements of the EMS, and records related to the "planning, operation, and control of processes that relate to its significant environmental aspects" (ISO, 2005). The document control category provides the requirements associated with developing and maintaining records. An organization should have procedures to approve, revise, publicize, and distribute all documents related to the EMS.

A primary purpose of the *operational control* category is to establish operations that will ensure the organization's significant environmental aspects will be maintained in the prescribed manner. An organization should develop documents and procedures that address operational criteria and disseminating information to external suppliers. The last category of the do stage is *emergency preparedness and response*. This category focuses on procedures related to any emergencies or accidents that have a negative impact on the environment. The ISO indicates that an organization should have emergency policies and procedures that focus on (1) identifying potential problems, (2) describing appropriate responses if an emergency occurs, and (3) continuously reviewing policies, procedures, and responses.

The "Check" Stage

The primary purpose of the *check* stage is to conduct an assessment of how well an organization is supporting its environmental policy and the EMS. This assessment process involves (1) monitoring and measurement; (2) evaluation of compliance, nonconformity, corrective action, and preventative action; and (3) control of records, internal audit, and management review (ISO, 2004). Monitoring environmental performance and system performance are covered in the ISO 14030 and 19011 series, respectively. The *monitoring and measurement* category refers to the environmental impact requirements associated with compliance of objectives and the proper monitoring of performance and operations. In addition, procedures must be enacted that ensure that monitoring equipment is maintained and operational.

The *compliance* category reviews the requirements related to ensuring that an organization is in compliance with legal statutes and procedures for taking corrective action in the occurrence of nonconformity (ISO, 2005). In the event of noncompliance, procedures should identify (1) steps for correcting the actions; (2) investigative policies and evaluation methodologies; (3) documentation requirements; and (4) guidelines for reviewing corrective strategies. The *control of records* category indicates that an organization must document its conformity to the EMS. To properly maintain EMS activities, an organization must have procedures for the "identification, storage, protection, retrieval, retention, and disposal of records" (ISO, 2004). Further documentation of the EMS is delineated in the *internal audit* category. At planned intervals, an internal audit examines whether the EMS is complying with several requirements. Areas can include International Standards, appropriate implementation procedures, and adequate maintenance.

The results of an internal audit, and data from various other sources, are submitted to management for review and evaluation. The *management review* category includes procedures and items that should be included for the evaluation process. Generally, a manager should review all of the processes, procedures, and actions that affect the organization's EMS. Thus, a thorough review should include a close examination of all activities associated with the *plan, do,* and *check* stages. For example, the ISO suggests that a manager should review (1) how well an organization achieved its objectives, (2) the adequacy of planned resources, (3) environmental performance and compliance status, and (4) communications from people external to the organization (2004). Upon completing an EMS review, management provides suggestions for improving operations, and these initiatives are forwarded to the *act* stage. The PDCA cycle continues when the corrective actions performed in the act stage serve to inform the next EMS plan for the organization.

Life Cycles and Sustainable Design

Interior designers are placed in a very complex situation when a client wants the designer to specify products that are "green," or "environmentally friendly." Requests for sustainable design will become even more frequent because of the ever-increasing energy costs and the extensive environmental damage from some of the most recent disasters: the World Trade Center in New York City (September 2001); the tsunami in and around the Indian Ocean (December 2004); Hurricane Katrina in the Gulf Coast (August 2005); and the earthquake in Kashmir, an area between India and Pakistan (October 2005) (see Figure 4.7a and b). To provide answers to a client's sustainability questions is very difficult, because there are so many variables that affect the environment. To present more complexity to the situation, many manufacturers market their product as green but may in fact harm the environment at some stage of the product's life. To evaluate the degree of impact on the environment, an interior designer must have a good understanding of the processes involved with producing, using, and disposing of a product.

The life cycle assessment (LCA) tool is used to help determine the environmental impact of products, services, or processes. The results of an LCA study can help to identify ways to reduce burdens on the environment. To explain the LCA in this text, the term *entity* will be used to collectively represent products, services, and processes. The analysis involves identifying each phase that occurs in the life of a product, and then determining the natural and

a

b

Fig. 4.7a. Examples of devastation in 2005. Muslim children after an earthquake in Kashmir, an area between India and Pakistan. Pakistani rescue workers gather at the site of the quake.
Fig. 4.7b. A child evacuates during Hurricane Katrina, which hit the Gulf Coast.

human-made resources that are required for each phase. For this purpose, a product's *life* starts at the "cradle" or extraction of the raw material. A product's life ends when the product is in a "grave," which could be a landfill or the bottom of an incinerator. Thus, a popular term for LCA is **cradle-to-grave**. The objectives of an LCA are to (1) identify and examine the interactions between natural resources and the life of a human-made product, service, or process; and (2) determine how these interactions affect the environment.

The ISO indicates that an LCA study involves four sequential phases: (1) the goal and scope definition phase, (2) the inventory analysis phase, (3) the impact

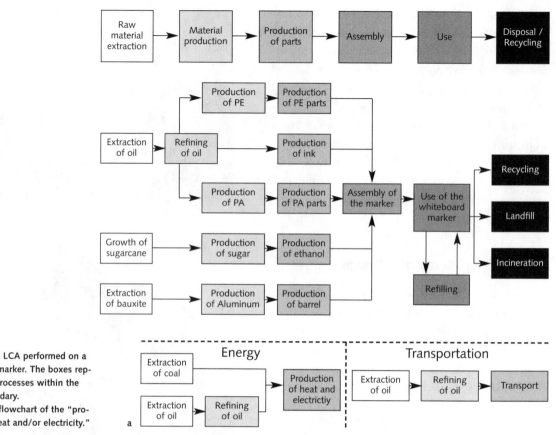

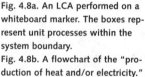

Fig. 4.8a. An LCA performed on a whiteboard marker. The boxes represent unit processes within the system boundary.
Fig. 4.8b. A flowchart of the "production of heat and/or electricity."

assessment phase, and (4) the interpretation phase (2005). The goals developed in the first phase of the LCA establish the basis of the methodology for the succeeding four phases. This is an important undertaking because the processes of the entire study are dependent on the purpose of performing the LCA. An LCA study can be very simplistic or complex depending on how an organization intends to utilize the results. For example, a very detailed LCA would be conducted when a carpet manufacturer intends to use the results of the study to attain an *environmental performance declaration* from an independent party. In contrast, a less intensive LCA study can be conducted when a manufacturer needs the results for brainstorming new products via internal processes.

Phase I of the LCA

To determine the magnitude of the study, the variables to consider are the (1) **scope** of the life of an entity, (2) **system boundaries**, and (3) extent of details (ISO, 2005). The scope includes items that address the goals of the study, including quantities involved with product systems, boundaries of the systems, and functions of the production system. For

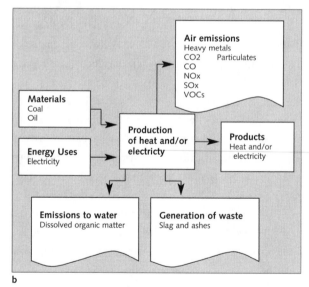

example, a technological scope of a project would include information related to the type of machinery and mode of transportation. The location of a manufacturing plant is an example of a geographical scope.

System boundaries identify the unit processes that are involved with the study. Units process the inputs and outputs of an activity. For example, the two illustrations for Figure 4.8 demonstrate an LCA performed on a whiteboard marker. Figure 4.8a is a linear flowchart of the life of a whiteboard marker, which is adapted from the website http://www.howproductsimpact.net. The boxes represent unit processes within the system boundary. Thus, the system boundary includes "the growth of sugar," "the use of the whiteboard marker," and "production of heat and electricity." Note that the boundary of the system includes processes associated with "recycling," "refilling," "energy," and "transportation."

This interactive website, http://www.howproductsimpact.net, allows a user to click through numerous levels of the analysis. An examination of processes begins by clicking on one of the boxes in the flowchart. Thus, clicking on "production of heat and/or electricity" prompts the image in Figure 4.8b. This flowchart allows the user to click to categories, such as "particulates" or "coal." Clicking on "particulates" brings the user to a description of suspended particulates—". . . reactions in the environment . . . impacts to humans . . . impacts on materials. . . ." This comprehensive website is an excellent resource for understanding the complexities associated with LCAs and environmental interactions.

Phase II of the LCA: Life Cycle Inventory (LCI)

After the LCA goals have been established, the study can proceed to Phase II, or the **Life Cycle Inventory (LCI)** phase. The purpose of the LCI phase is to gather data regarding each stage of an entity. Generally, most examples of life cycles depict five stages: (1) extraction of raw materials, (2) refining the raw materials, (3) manufacturing the product, (4) consumer use of the product, and (5) disposal and/or recycling (see Figure 4.9). As illustrated in Figure 4.9, the basic LCA model has been expanded to include two additional stages. The primary reason for adding these stages is to focus attention on activities that are associated with packaging and marketing. Activities associated with packaging and marketing can cause considerable burdens to the environment. Packaging in particular is a concern to the interior design profession, because many of the products are shipped in large quantities of packaging, such as sofas or office workstations. Impacts on the environment due to marketing activities can vary depending on the manufacturer and the product. Thus, marketing is included in the model to help ensure that the resultant impacts to the environment are considered when a product has an extensive marketing program.

To help understand the stages of a product's life cycle, the explanation that follows uses as the model product a solid wood conference table (see Figure 4.10). A *solid* wood table is used to concentrate on studying the LCI. In reality most furniture today is constructed using particleboard with either a wood

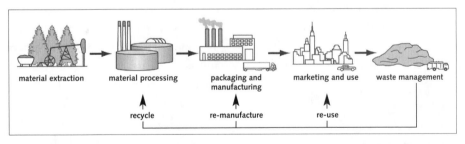

material extraction   material processing   packaging and manufacturing   marketing and use   waste management

recycle   re-manufacture   re-use

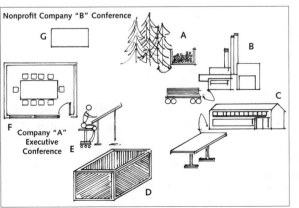

Fig. 4.9. (above) Most examples of life cycles depict five stages: extraction of raw materials; refining the raw materials; manufacturing the product; consumer use of the product; and disposal and/or recycling. This model also includes activities associated with packaging and marketing.

Fig. 4.10. (left) A–G represent the life cycle stages of a wood conference table.

veneer or plastic laminate. An LCI that includes these additional materials would be very complex. The life of a table begins by cutting down trees and transporting the logs to a lumber mill (stage 1). The wood is processed at the mill, sawed into planks, kiln-dried for several weeks (consuming large quantities of electricity), and then transported to a furniture manufacturer (stage 2). The furniture manufacturer builds the table using glued joints and then may apply a stain, lacquer, or varnish to its surfaces. Other materials used for the table could be metal hardware (stage 3). Prior to shipping the furniture, the manufacturer crates the table for shipment to a client, a furniture store, or a warehouse (stage 4). Simultaneously, product information is prepared that could include product labels, brochures, websites, maintenance instructions, and sometimes advertisements for publication in various media (stage 5).

When a table is shipped to a furniture store for display purposes, the shipping materials may be discarded. In this situation, new packaging material is needed to deliver the table to the client. After the table is purchased, delivery is made to the commercial building. The client utilizes the table and may apply various cleaning materials to the surfaces (stage 6). When a client elects to no longer use the table, a decision is made to find a reuse application or the table becomes solid waste (stage 7). Thus, the table's *life* could end by being dumped in a landfill or burned in an industrial waste incinerator.

Within each of the stages identified above, the LCI

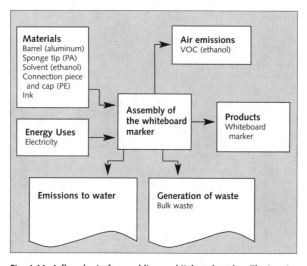

Fig. 4.11. A flowchart of assembling a whiteboard marker. The inputs include aluminum, ethanol, and electricity. The outputs are the whiteboard marker, bulk waste, VOC emissions, and discharges to water.

phase includes a close examination of the inputs and outputs of the system. The inputs of a system are the resources that processes utilize to produce an outcome. This could include fossil fuels, materials, water, land use, and electrical energy. Outputs of a system include the product, solid waste generation, and emissions to water and air. For example, to assemble the whiteboard marker, inputs include aluminum, ethanol, and electricity (see Figure 4.11). The outputs are the whiteboard marker, bulk waste, VOC emissions, and discharges to water. The LCI process conducts an inventory of all the inputs and outputs of a system, which includes quantities of a material or substance.

Phase III of the LCA: Life Cycle Impact Assessment (LCIA)

The third phase of the LCA is the **Life Cycle Impact Assessment (LCIA)**. At this phase, data collected in the LCI phase are analyzed to determine the environmental exchanges, or the impacts that are associated with the life cycle of an entity. The analysis requires a thorough examination of the production, transportation, energy consumption, and disposal processes. This entails all of the materials, natural resources, energy, emissions, and waste that are required for each process. For example, in analyzing the extraction stage of the conference table, considerations would include environmental exchanges between ecosystems and the processes used to remove the trees. Thus, the analysis would include an examination of the effects on the ecosystem of the forest, and perhaps nearby freshwater ecosystems, due to the logging activities. The LCIA process would examine the environmental exchanges between ecosystems and pollutants from the equipment used to fell the trees. An LCIA would also analyze what may occur to the environment of the forest and its inhabitants after the removal of trees. For example, a change from a shaded setting to full sunlight would have a significant impact on plant life, animals, and insects.

All human-made processes affect ecosystems; however, to reduce detrimental impacts to the environment requires an understanding of interdependent systems and the importance of balancing inputs and outputs. For example, all of the plants, trees, insects, and soil in a forest exist in an interdependent

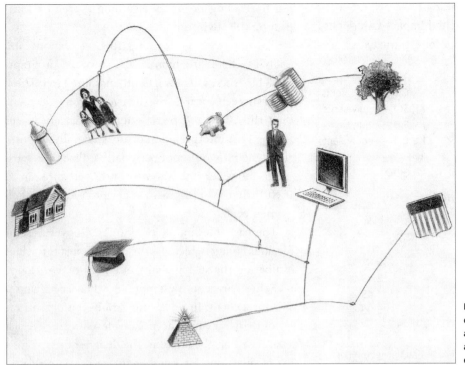

Fig. 4.12. The natural occurrences of interdependent systems require an appropriate balance of inputs and outputs with environmental exchanges.

ecosystem, with a unique climate and atmospheric conditions. Within an interdependent system, all living organisms require one another to exist. In addition, an impact on one organism affects all of the other organisms. For example, a tree needs soil to exist. Without the tree, soil would not have the required nutrients for its plants and insects. If a tree is impacted by pollution, eventually chemical changes to the tree will affect the soil and subsequently its insects. Therefore, the natural occurrences of interdependent systems require an appropriate balance of inputs and outputs within environmental exchanges.

To better understand the complexities associated with balancing environmental exchanges, see the elements on the mobile in Figure 4.12. As shown in the conceptual drawing, imaginary lines between the pieces of the drawing represent several inputs and outputs that can affect a life cycle (for example, the life cycle of the conference table in Figure 4.10). The pieces represent processes and the natural environment. The sculptural pieces show external factors that can affect the life cycle at every stage, such as economic conditions, energy costs, availability of resources, or sociological factors. In *normal* conditions life-cycle stages are balanced and in harmony with

external factors. An external phenomenon, such as a depression, affects every stage of a life cycle.

As with the perfect balance of the mobile, when appropriate environmental interchanges occur between inputs and outputs of a system, the elements are harmoniously balanced. A disturbing imbalance can occur when too many natural resources are extracted from the environment, or production processes emit too many pollutants to the environment. As with the mobile's design, any alteration to the individual pieces creates an imbalance to the stability of the mobile. Use the beauty of this sculpture as a means to reinforce the importance of giving thoughtful consideration to balancing natural and human-made systems.

Phase IV of the LCA: Interpretation

The last phase of the LCA is to summarize the results of the LCI and LCIA studies and to provide recommendations for reducing burdens on the environment. Typically, summaries focus on an assessment of environmental impacts and an inventory of inputs and outputs (see Table 4.2). Conclusions should be confined to the goals and scope of the study. The LCA interpretation is similar to what occurs in the *check* phase of the PDCA. Thus, recommendations

Table 4.2

LCA Summaries: Environmental Impact Categories, Inputs, and Outputs for Electricity

Environmental Impact Categories	Unit
Global Warming	Kg CO_2—equivalents
Acidification	Kg SO_2—equivalents
Eutrophication	Kg PO_4—equivalents
Smog Formation	Kg C_2H_4—equivalents
Solid Waste Generation	kg
Oxygen Depletion	kg COD

Exchanges per kWh (year 1999)

Inputs	Unit
Resources:	
Fuel Oil	39.81 g
Diesel	2.69 g
Natural Gas	111.43 g
Lignite	182.05 g

Outputs	Unit
Product: Electricity	1.00 kWh
Emissions to Air:	
CO	0.16 g
CO_2	0.71 kg
N_2O	22.15 mg
NO_x	2.27 mg
NMVOC	33.80 mg
CH_4	14.82 mg
Dust	0.12 g
SO_2	1.21 g
As	6.87 µg
Cd	0.41 µg
Cr	3.89 µg
Hg	0.02 µg
Ni	3.89 µg
Pb	22.00 µg
V	7.77 µg
Zn	34.40 µg

SOURCE: http://www.howproductsimpact.net.

can inform future policies and practices. The complexity of an entity's life cycle prohibits conclusions that specify definitive answers. For example, the type and quantity of emissions to air is a variable, which is affected by the measurement instrument, atmospheric conditions, and numerous other uncontrollable factors. Hence, the conclusions must be written within the context that many known and unknown factors affect the life cycle of an entity. In addition, it is important to not **greenwash** the results by making misleading promises regarding a product's impact on the environment.

To help with performing the calculations and analysis, there are many LCA software programs available, such as GaBi, LCAit, and SimaPro6. These programs can compile the life-cycle inventories, conduct the LCIA, and provide reports that are useful for the LCA interpretation phase. Generally, an interior designer would not personally utilize these programs; however, an awareness of the software can be useful when working with other professionals, such as engineers.

The basic methodology of an LCA is very useful for identifying which factors are important when evaluating the sustainability of an entity. For example, there are countless options when specifying a sofa for a client. In reviewing various options, an interior designer can conceptually develop an LCA of a sofa. Based on the analysis, the designer can create a list of questions for manufacturers that are related to the interactions between the sofa's life and the natural environment. The list of questions can become the basis for comparing production processes of several manufacturers. Examples of questions are: What materials were used for the sofa's frame? What is the transportation distance between the warehouse and the client's building? During the construction of the sofa, how did the manufacturer deal with emissions or solid waste? What is the composition of the crating materials? Were recycled materials used for production or transportation purposes? On the basis of the answers, or no response, an interior designer can specify the sofa that appears to have the least impact on the environment. A no-response to questions related to environmental exchanges is cause for concern.

SUSTAINABLE STRATEGIES: INTEGRATED WASTE MANAGEMENT AND ECONOMICS

To practice the principles of sustainable design requires an understanding of economics. Economics is the reason why natural resources have been depleted and polluted. Clean water, pure air, and healthy interiors come with a price. The world would be in pristine condition if there weren't costs associated with having a sustainable environment.

Economics drives decisions and investments. To convince a client to invest in sustainable design requires strategies that integrate environmental protection, societal needs, and economic development.

Integrated Waste Management

The results of an LCA can help to demonstrate the sources of pollution and how waste reduction processes affect environmental exchanges. To handle municipal solid waste, the EPA suggests an **integrated waste management plan**, which is prioritized in this order of importance: (1) **source reduction**, (2) **recycling**, and (3) waste combustion and landfilling (2005).

Fig. 4.13. The semi-trucks are filled with extremely compacted waste. The trucks are traveling to a landfill 100 miles away, at an approximate rate of one truck per minute during operational hours. The landfill is only one of many in the country.

Integrated Waste Management:
Source Reduction

First and foremost in reducing waste is to buy fewer products and services. The EPA defines source reduction as "the design, manufacture, purchase, or use of materials (such as products and packaging) to reduce the amount of toxicity of trash generated" (2005). *Source reduction is so vitally important to sustainable design and development* that the strategy is woven into numerous topics in the next two units of this text. Source reduction helps to reduce pollution and conserve natural resources. Source reduction helps to reduce the quantity of land that is needed for landfills. Source reduction helps to reduce the amount of toxins from hazardous waste that can leach into the ground of landfills.

Source reduction is better than recycling, because the life cycle of a recycled product requires resources and burdens the environment. Source reduction is a means to avoid more waste in landfills and the subsequent environmental consequences associated with the landfills. In addition, semi-trucks generally are used to transport waste to landfills and the quantity is staggering. For example, in Figure 4.13 the semi-trucks are filled with extremely compacted waste. The trucks are traveling to a landfill 100 miles away, at an approximate rate of *one truck per minute* during operational hours. The landfill is only one of many in the state and country. Moreover, trucks require great quantities of fuel and can emit some of the worst pollutants.

There are many solutions for reducing solid waste. For example, designing and manufacturing products that are durable, adapt to various purposes, and possess timeless qualities are strategies of source reduction. Source reduction also includes diminishing or eliminating unnecessary packaging. Frequently, a product is packaged in a means that does not support sustainability. For example, in a recent purchase of an energy-efficient compact fluorescent lamp (CFL), the packaging consisted of cardboard made from nonrecyclable products, and a nondegradable plastic. An effort to produce an energy-efficient product should be complemented by sustainable packaging properties.

Frequently, a product would not need any packaging. Consumers and manufacturers should start to question some of the assumptions associated with the need for packaging. For example, my first exposure to understanding excessive consumption patterns occurred in Paris in the 1970s. Upon buying a loaf of bread in a Parisian bakery, the salesclerk gave me the bread without any packaging. Being accustomed to purchasing practices in the United States, I expected wrappings. However, in contemplating the *naked* loaf of bread, I realized that wrappings were not necessary. For centuries the French have bought bread, without any packaging, and have lived extremely well. Consequently, the experience stimulated a process of questioning long-term assumptions regarding what materials and products are *truly* necessary. This very simplistic example demonstrates a paradigm shift that can occur when identifying approaches to source reduction. A focus on sustainable design prompts questions regarding assumptions that people have indoctrinated into practice. Identifying what can be eliminated is fundamental to source reduction and sustainability.

Some other very important approaches to source reduction are reuse and recovery. There are numerous ways an interior designer can create a design that includes reusable products and interiors. Adaptive reuse buildings are excellent examples of this strategy and are reviewed in more detail in Unit II. **Recovery** is a strategy related to renovation work. An interior designer can support recovery strategies by identifying ways to renovate interiors and furnishings, such as tables, wood floors, and broken stained glass windows. Architectural salvage stores are becoming extremely popular as a resource for products that can be reused and recovered.

Integrated Waste Management: Recycling

When source reduction is not an option, the next best sustainable solution is to recycle. Of all the sustainable strategies, recycling appears to be the most popular with the general public. Communities throughout the world have recycling programs that encourage people to sort and save waste. Paper, plastic, glass, and aluminum cans are the most frequently recycled materials. Globally, depending on the socioeconomic conditions of a country, recycling can have different purposes. For example, in poverty-stricken areas, out of necessity, people frequently rely on recycling for their income. In contrast, the affluence in highly developed countries provides the financial means for some people to routinely throw away products and then replace the items with new products. Thus, due to economic conditions, developing countries are frequently more motivated to recycle than highly developed countries.

The basic recycling process consists of four stages: (1) collecting recyclable materials from consumers, (2) sorting by the material composition, (3) cleaning and reprocessing the materials into a new form, and (4) using the product made from recycled materials. Many products from residences, commercial buildings, and industrial sites can be reprocessed into new products. For example, cellulous insulation for buildings is made from recycled newspapers, with a fire retardant additive. Recycled tires make an excellent base for playgrounds. **Glassphalt** contains recycled glass, and the various colors produce an interesting roadway material. Important considerations for determining the practicality of recycling a material are the environmental exchanges associated with recycling processes. The LCA of the whiteboard marker described earlier in this chapter included a recycling processing unit. To recycle the marker eliminates some of the unit processes associated with extraction and refinement. To convert the marker into another use requires some form of energy to facilitate the process, and the transaction will produce emissions and waste.

To address a sustainable approach for the life of a product after use, William McDonough and Michael Braungart converted *cradle to grave* into *cradle to cradle (C2C)*. The C2C concept focuses attention on product developments that are designed to return to the earth without harmful effects. The book titled *Cradle to Cradle* is a stimulating approach to questioning assumptions related to product design and environmental exchanges. The C2C concept is an excellent sustainable approach for new products. For example, in 2005 Herman Miller received the Gold Achievement Award from the EPA for the company's "environmentally sensitive product design standards" (Herman Miller, 2005). The company developed the standards based on the C2C protocol. The standards evaluate new and existing products based on their "material chemistry, ease of disassembly, recyclability, and recycled content." For example, Herman Miller's *Cella* chair, introduced in 2005, is "composed of 33 percent recycled content, is 99 percent recyclable, can be disassembled in less than five minutes, is PVC free, and is also produced using alternative energy" (see Figure 4.14; Herman Miller, 2005).

Integrated Waste Management: Landfilling

Waste management requires a means to dispose of any waste that is not reused or recycled. Disposal in landfills is the most common method for waste management. Waste deposited in a landfill creates pollution and consumes large quantities of land. As discussed in Chapter 2, hazardous waste is an extremely serious problem and proper disposal practices are mandatory. Many factors affect the

Fig. 4.14. Herman Miller's Celle chair, introduced in 2005, is "composed of 33 percent recycled content, is 99 percent recyclable, can be disassembled in less than five minutes, is PVC free, and is also produced using alternative energy" (Herman Miller, 2005).

chemical and biological reactions that occur in a landfill, such as atmospheric conditions, climate, composition of the materials, and time. Depending on the interactions of the combined factors, which are always unknown, a product can remain in the landfill for one day or thousands of years.

Scientists have a good understanding of how pure materials react to certain conditions, but a landfill's setting is so unpredictable that it is impossible to predict chemical interactions or environmental exchanges. For example, some communities have tried to reuse the land consumed by a landfill by converting the area into recreational facilities, such as golf courses. Long after the construction was completed, management noticed settling of grassy surfaces and some sinkholes, which developed from decomposition of the materials that existed in the landfill.

Depositing waste in landfills prompts questions regarding degradable products. Scientists are knowledgeable of the degradation of many materials in their pure state. For example, many foods and plant materials are biodegradable, thus are excellent materials for **composting**. Nature is able to compost organic materials and convert them into the humus substance, which enriches the soil. However, the EPA reports that scientists have found "biodegradable" materials in landfills after 30 years (2002). Researchers understand that the amount and duration of exposure to sunlight dramatically affects degradation. This is especially problematic with plastics. Some plastics are not able to degrade without the ultraviolet rays of sunlight. Therefore, without contact with sunlight, plastic products buried deep in the landfill

will remain in the ground indefinitely. These situations reinforce the unknowns related to how products in a landfill interact with other materials and environmental conditions.

Sustainable Economic Strategies

The environmental economist Alan Gilpin explains, "the factors of production are defined as natural resources (traditionally land), labor including managerial and entrepreneurial skills, and capital" (2000, p. 3). The four types of capital are human-made capital, natural capital, human capital, and social capital. According to Gilpin, *human-made capital* is a commodity such as machines, factories, and materials, which are used to produce goods and services. *Natural capital* is environmentally provided assets, such as ecosystems, air, oceans, minerals, and forests. The skills and energy of people are embodied in *human capital*. *Social capital* is the group of factors that collectively define a society (2000).

Many of the factors of production, such as natural resources and capital, described earlier, were discussed in the explanation of an LCA. To analyze the factors of production within the context of sustainability, a useful profile is provided by Gilpin's description of the functions of an economic system (see Table 4.3). As identified in Table 4.3, to encourage individuals and businesses to "use natural resources and environmental assets of society within a framework of sustainable development" is a challenge for interior designers. In trying to specify sustainable products and designs, a client frequently asks an

Table 4.3
Functions of an Economic System

- Match supply to effective demand for goods and services, at home and overseas, in an efficient manner and to an acceptable quality.
- Allocate scarce resources among industries and activities producing and distributing goods and services.
- Provide channels for fruitful capital investment and transactions in financial instruments.
- Fully utilize the human resources of society, endeavoring to provide adequate employment opportunities, both full-time and part-time, for men, women, and school-leavers, with adequate training facilities.
- Utilize the natural resources and environmental assets of society within a framework of sustainable development; convey to consumers information on which goods and services are available for best value, within a socially responsible framework.
- Promote research and development aiming at improved, safer, environmentally friendly products and services, better designed to meet society's objectives.
- Increase productivity in all sectors, easing distress resulting from downsizing, restructuring, devolution, off-shoring, and competitive failure.
- Conserve raw materials, achieve cleaner production, reduce waste, encourage reuse and recycling, minimize waste disposal problems, and generally protect the environment in all stages of activities.
- Control all emissions from activities to meet statutory requirements and social aspirations.
- Relate to the affected community through regular meetings and open-days.
- Promote fair trading in all markets.
- Cooperate with government in improving the performance of the economic and financial system and promoting the interests of the nation.

SOURCE: Gilpin, A. (2000), *Environmental Economics: A Critical Overview*. New York: John Wiley & Sons.

interior designer: "How much will it cost us?" and "How will this expense affect our profits?" For the sustainability proposal to be successful, an interior designer must be prepared to answer with a response that demonstrates sound business management. Unfortunately, responding to the client that "It is the right thing to do" rarely works, and generally this rationale is even more unacceptable to the stockholders.

Sound business responses require an understanding of profits and the methods that can be used to analyze costs, benefits, and effectiveness. Profit maximization (or satisfactory levels of profit) is the driv-

ing force of corporations. Fundamentally, a business cannot exist or grow without maximizing returns of profits and investments. Stockholders and a company's lending bank expect profits. Thus, an interior designer must work with clients to help them understand how sustainable design can produce profits for the company. To demonstrate the business benefits of implementing EMS, the ISO reported that "there is mounting evidence that companies which manage not only the standard economic factors but also the environmental and social factors affecting their business show financial performance superior to those which fail to manage all three" (2005, p. 7).

Financial Analysis Frameworks

To identify the most effective strategy for maximizing profits, economists have developed various methodologies, such as **cost-benefit analysis (CBA)** and cost-effectiveness analysis (CEA). The CBA is a tool that can be used to evaluate the data that are related to sustainability development processes and then translate the information into monetary terms. An important element of the CBA is to quantify the valuation of environmental assets. Quantifiable answers can help clients to determine the feasibility of a project. In performing the calculations, costs are considered a negative, and benefits are positive. Typical costs can include inputs, labor, insurance, taxes, and pollution prevention equipment. Benefits can include products, services, improved productivity of employees, employment opportunities, and clean waterways. The nonmonetary values are difficult to determine; thus, generally a subjective value is calculated that reflects what is believed society is willing to pay for the outcome.

A CBA cost-benefit ratio is calculated by dividing the benefits by the costs. A positive answer generally indicates support for an action, and a negative answer may suggest that an activity should not occur. However, before stopping an activity, an analysis should be conducted to determine whether costs could be reduced, such as reducing the number of people engaged in the activity. A CEA is a means to determine the lowest cost for a given objective. Thus, the methodology compares the cost of purchasing a product, such as an air conditioner, by examining various options. The CEA calculations are frequently used to evaluate new building technologies. Unit II discusses some of the energy simulation software tools that are available for this purpose.

Economic Principles and Responsibility

Sustainable economic principles that can be applied to encourage more responsible consumption and practices are the **user-pays principle** and the **polluter-pays principle** (Gilpin, 2000). The user-pays principle proposes that consumers should pay the social costs that are associated with resources. For example, there could be a basic charge for the *use* of resources, such as land and water. In a public location, such as a hotel room, an individual would pay the exact cost associated with the amount of water or electricity he or she consumed. The premise of the strategy is for a consumer to become aware of costs associated with natural resources, and to encourage conservation practices. The user-pays principle is economically efficient, and the approach has been very helpful in changing consumption behaviors.

Another approach to "internalizing environmental costs" is the polluter-pays principle (Gilpin, 2000). According to Gilpin, this principle has two versions. The first version "equates the price charged for the use of environmental resources with the cost of damage inflicted on society by using them" (2000, p. 101). Gilpin indicates that there are several problems with this principle, including difficulties with identifying appropriate costs and determining the original source of the pollution. In addition, Gilpin suggests that this perspective indirectly supports pollution, because people assume that it is acceptable to pollute as long as the polluter pays for the damage.

The second perspective "asserts that the full cost of controlling pollution by whatever means to an adequate degree shall be undertaken by the polluter, preferably without public subsidy or tax concession" (2000, p. 102). This principle eventually distributes the cost of controlling pollution to the consumer. Thus, a company lacks a financial incentive to reduce pollution. Gilpin concludes the description of the polluter-pays principle by indicating that the concept has international endorsement, but current attitudes support regulatory pollution control regulations.

Responsible business practices have also focused on strategically planning for risk. The global problems associated with terrorists, health risks of HIV/AIDS, and environmental issues have prompted companies to develop new approaches for handling risks. **Risk management** is the approach business is using to help avoid risk or minimize any adverse impacts from a disaster. From a sustainability perspective, the **World Business Council for Sustainable Development (WBCSD)** explains, "There is a new recognition among companies that the achievement of their objectives depends on being able to deal with risks of a more 'systemic' nature. These are the risks that cannot by tackled in isolation from each other, and which need to be addressed through an alliance of business and society working in unison. Achieving sustainable development falls squarely into this category" (WBCSD, 2004, p. 3).

To be "risk enabled," the WBCSD suggests the following approaches: (1) develop a wider appreciation of risk, (2) focus on the long term, (3) create an appropriate culture, (4) develop a performance-focused approach to megarisks, (5) recognize that risks also present opportunities, and (6) recognize the need to engage with multistakeholders (2004). The emerging importance of risk management is also evident by the ISO's establishment of a working group on *Risk Management Terminology* and the publication of *ISO/IEC Guide 73, Risk Management Vocabulary Guidelines for Use in Standards*. According to Knight, the chairman of the ISO Technical Management Board, risk management is an "integral component of corporate governance and good management" (2003, p. 21).

Time = Finances = Sustainability

The **payback principle** is a strategy for comparing short- and long-term costs of a product or service. In applying the payback principle, costs to be considered include energy consumption, capital investments, operational costs, and maintenance. Payback analyses examine the **first costs** and **operating costs**. Typically, first costs refer to expenses related to purchasing, transporting, and installing a product. Operating costs include energy consumption, maintenance, and repair. Unfortunately, many businesses in the United States base procurement decisions solely on first costs. Many new construction projects are based on first costs, rather than examining how reduced operating costs will reduce the overall expenses of a project over a designated period of time.

The amount of time that a business or individual is willing to wait for a return on their investment varies tremendously. Some people do not want to wait for a return on their investment; thus, they will purchase the least expensive product even though the operating costs will be very high. This frequently occurs when lamps are purchased. Many incandescent lamps have inexpensive first costs, but the operating costs are extremely high. In contrast, the first costs of a compact fluorescent lamp are comparatively high, but the operating costs for electricity are much lower and the lamps have an extremely long life.

Frequently, a focus on short-term *first* costs, rather than long-term *operational* costs prompts the consumer to select the most inexpensive choice. Discrepancies between first and operating costs are a major concern to successfully practicing the principles of sustainability. An interior designer must very diligently demonstrate to a client the benefits of purchasing products and services that optimize the total costs.

As reviewed in Unit II of this text, time perspectives vary among cultures, political beliefs, and generations. For example, at the 2005 *Sustainable Water-fronts: Learning from the Dutch Experience* conference in Chicago, an engineer from The Netherlands explained that his firm was designing technology that is expected to last hundreds of years and possibly 1,000 years (see Figure 4.15). In explaining the validity of this assertion, he noted that his engineering firm has performed maintenance on technology in England that is more than 800 years old. Generally, for people living in the relatively new United States, the concept of designing something to last 1,000 years is inconceivable. Implementing meaningful sustainable design requires a paradigm shift that can project a future that is generations away from the present. Examples of how interior designers can inspire clients to purchase products and services based on the inclusion of operating costs appear in Unit II of this text.

When an industry is interacting with the environment, there must be an appropriate balance to sustain the ecological systems. When it is possible to recover from human-made interventions, natural processes require time to *heal* the ecosystems. Too much pollution or excessive removals of species, such as with extensive logging operations, can destroy ecosystems. Time is a key element for maintaining a proper balance. Ecosystems cannot adequately react to human-made interventions that occur in excessive amounts, or within a short period

Fig. 4.15. The Netherlands is world renowned for engineering technological systems that last for hundreds of years.

of time. For example, applying a pesticide to a garden must be done in small doses over a period of time. If the same amount of pesticide were applied at one time, typically all of the plants would die. In another example, when trees are gradually removed from a forest, nature is able to grow new trees before environmental changes destroy the biodiversity of its ecosystem.

The interrelationships between time and an ecosystem also affect costs. This concept was understandably illustrated by a presentation at the 2005 *Sustainable Waterfronts: Learning from the Dutch Experience* conference in Chicago. Harry Vermeulen, a Dutch engineer, explained a soil remediation program that involved a comparison of the cost of cleanup and time. Through various charts, Vermeulen demonstrated that to immediately clean the soil was very expensive because the process involved human-made interventions. However, by allowing the environment time to *naturally clean* the soil significantly reduced remediation costs. In addition, a natural process eliminates solid waste and possible pollutants from the substances that would have to be used to quickly clean the soil. Vermeulen emphasized that the cost of remediation can be very little when people are willing to wait for nature to heal itself. Thus, identifying long-term solutions can result in source reduction, fewer pollutants, and cost savings.

The aforementioned economic frameworks and principles are tools that can be used to provide quantifiable rationales to clients. However, as noted by Thomas, "economics can demonstrate the benefits of using alternative environmental technologies, but the application of such measures requires more— the commitment of consumers to a culture of resource conservation" (2002, p. 211). Transforming behavior to a "culture of resource conservation" is difficult to achieve in financial systems that are driven by quantities of consumption. Brown explains, "two concepts that emerged during the mid-twentieth century have shaped the evolution of the global economy—**planned obsolescence** and **throwaway products**" (note: bolding done by author; 2001, p. 123). As noted by Brown, to recover from the disastrous effects of World War II, both practices were purposefully developed to stimulate economic growth and provide employment opportunities for thousands of people who were un-

employed. Unfortunately, this strategy encourages repeatable consumption patterns, which results in wasting natural resources, increasing pollution, and overloading landfills.

Planned obsolescence refers to products that are intentionally designed for short-term use. This could include throwaway products, but planned obsolescence generally is associated with objects that can be repeatedly used for a short duration. Immediate or short-term throwaway products ensure future sales for a manufacturer; however, the societal and environmental costs can be disastrous. The reason for the obsolescence can be functional or psychological. For example, most personal computers are designed to be obsolete in a very short period of time. Typically, for a consumer to have the most updated software requires purchasing a new computer and all of the peripheral equipment. This planned functional obsolescence has contributed to large quantities of solid waste in landfills. The problem is compounded by the fact that the material composition of computers is not biodegradable and has considerable quantities of toxic materials.

In the field of interior design, examples of psychological planned obsolescence include any trendy-colored product or style. For example, to encourage new sales prior to the end of an appliance's life, manufacturers change the colors of new products. In the 1970s, popular appliance colors were *avocado green* and *harvest gold*. When people became tired of these colors, products in new colors replaced the appliances. Subsequently, appliances in the avocado green and harvest gold colors were considered "outdated." The psychological impact of these colors is so strong that when manufacturers seek to *recycle* the same colors they are given new names, such as *moss green* or *golden yellow*. To reduce waste, interior designers must work with their clients to encourage purchasing classic furnishings and maintainable equipment and appliances.

In addition, interior designers must adopt sustainable practices for their own firm by establishing policies and procedures that encourage a culture of resource conservation. For example, the costs of products and services could be formulated to encourage clients to buy furnishings that are sustainable. Quantity discounts should be transformed to sustainable discounts. An interior designer could also encourage manufacturers to shift paradigms by suggesting a restructuring pricing plan that provides discounts for sustainable products rather than quantity purchases.

Case Studies: Transformational Business Strategies

Convincing a client that sustainable design is good business requires an interior designer to suggest long-term economic strategies that can transform traditional management practices. One approach to demonstrating to clients that sustainability can be profitable is to share with them examples of corporations that have embraced the philosophy and are successful. For example, at the ASID conference the president of Interface, Ray Anderson, indicated that he has "made the business case for sustainability over and over, in terms of survival (macro), risk management, markets, people, processes, products, profits, and purpose" [American Society of Interior Designers (ASID), 2005, p. 9].

Another corporation that is incredibly successful and embraces sustainability is ABN AMRO, an international bank with more than 3,000 branches in 60 countries. ABN AMRO is the eleventh largest bank in Europe and twentieth in the world (ABN AMRO, 2004). ABN AMRO demonstrates its commitment to sustainable development in numerous ways. ABN AMRO's definition of sustainable development is "to live our Corporate Values and Business Principles and to meet the needs of the organisation and our stakeholders, thus seeking to protect, sustain, and enhance human, natural, and financial capital needed in the future" (2004, p. 9).

In addition to the typical *Annual Report*, which all corporations distribute, ABN AMRO publishes a *Sustainability Report*. The purpose of the document is to demonstrate how ABN AMRO embraces sustainable development through various avenues: (1) reporting financial, social, and environmental facts and figures; (2) outlining corporate values and business principles; (3) describing sustainability educational programs for employees; and (4) providing examples of how they "live" their values. The *facts and figures* summary includes the number of employee volunteers and the bank's *Dow Jones sustainability indexes (DJSI)* rating. This rating provides an assessment of a com-

pany's sustainability strategies. The DJSI weighting scheme examines the social, environmental, and economic dimensions of an industry.

ABN AMRO's report also includes a summary of the company's electricity consumption, energy consumption through other sources, and miles of business air travel. Accompanying these figures is each activity's carbon dioxide emissions. In 2004, ABN AMRO also started to record total water consumed. To provide greater detail regarding the corporation's interaction with the environment, the report also includes a summary of sustainable criteria for their suppliers.

Also in 2004, ABN AMRO introduced its new global tagline: "Making more possible." ABN AMRO explains that the tagline "stands for customers and the bank together achieving goals and taking up challenges. 'Making more possible' also articulates the importance we attach to sustainable development: financing the future." ABN AMRO also acknowledges a responsibility for "protecting the environment for future generations and in reducing the number of people living below the poverty line." This philosophy is supported by the corporation's philanthropic efforts and by the approach ABN AMRO uses when evaluating a customer who needs a loan. For example, the report includes examples of the criteria the corporation used for financing projects. ABN AMRO was considering financing a mining project in a developing nation. ABN AMRO denied financial support because its analysis revealed that the project "compromised a degree of environmental and social sensitivity."

ABN AMRO's commitment to sustainability demonstrates that a large corporation can be *eco-successful*. Many of the corporation's activities related to sustainable development can serve as a guide to companies that would like to embrace the principles. This is especially important for a relatively new concept. Many businesses need examples of how to integrate sustainable development with business practices. The fact that the corporation is in the financial industry is even more important to the integration of sustainable development. ABN AMRO is in a formidable position to significantly impact the enculturation of sustainable development, because it is able to deny financial assistance to any business project that does not fulfill the principles of sustainability. Given the grand scale of ABN AMRO worldwide, the results can be extraordinary.

Summary

- Sustainable design principles can serve as a guide for making decisions related to business practices and designs for commercial and residential interiors.
- The basic PDCA cycle is divided into four stages: plan, do, check, and act. The activities in the "plan" stage include identifying objectives, processes, resources, and associated costs. The outcomes of the plan stage are transferred to the "do" stage, which involves the processes related to the production of products or services. The purpose of the "check" stage is to evaluate the outcomes from the "do" stage, by comparing the results with the objectives that were identified in the "plan" stage. At the last stage, "act," the outcomes from the evaluation process are used to take any corrective actions.
- To gather all the information that is required for the plan stage, a recommended practice in the area of sustainable design is a charrette.
- The life cycle assessment (LCA) tool is used to help determine the environmental impact of products, services, or processes. The results of an LCA study can help to identify ways to reduce burdens to the environment.
- The ISO (2005) indicates that an LCA study involves the following four sequential phases: (1) the goal and scope definition phase, (2) the inventory analysis phase, (3) the impact assessment phase, and (4) the interpretation phase.
- The purpose of the LCI phase is to gather data regarding each stage of an entity. Generally, most examples of life cycles depict five stages: (1) extraction of raw materials, (2) refining the raw materials, (3) manufacturing the product, (4) consumer use of the product, and (5) disposal and/or recycling.
- The third phase of the LCA is the Life Cycle Impact Assessment (LCIA). At this phase, data collected in the LCI phase are analyzed to determine the environmental exchanges, or the impacts that are associated with the life cycle of an entity. The analysis

requires a thorough examination of the production, transportation, energy consumption, and disposal processes.

- To handle municipal solid waste, the EPA (2005) suggests an integrated waste management plan, which is prioritized in this order of importance: (1) source reduction, (2) recycling, and (3) waste combustion and landfilling.
- To identify the most effective strategy for maximizing profits, economists have developed various methodologies, such as cost-benefit analysis (CBA) and cost-effectiveness analysis (CEA).
- Sustainable economical principles that can be applied to encourage more responsible consumption and practices are the user-pays principle and the polluter-pays principle (Gilpin, 2000).
- Interior designers must adopt sustainable practices for their own firm by establishing policies and procedures that encourage a culture of resource conservation.

Key Terms

Charrette
Composting
Cost-benefit analysis (CBA)
Cost-effectiveness analysis (CEA)
Cradle-to-grave
Deming cycle
Environmental management system (EMS)
Environmental Quality Action Team (EQAT)
First costs
Glassphalt
Greenwash
Input
Integrated waste management plan
International Finance Corporation (IFC)
ISO 14001 PDCA
Kids' ISO 14000 Programme
Life cycle assessment (LCA)
Life Cycle Impact Assessment (LCIA)
Life Cycle Inventory (LCI)
Operating costs
Output
Payback principle
PDCA (Plan, Do, Check, Act) Cycle

Planned obsolescence

Polluter-pays principle

Recovery

Recycling

Risk management

Scope

Shewart's cycle

Source reduction

Stakeholders

System boundary

Throwaway products

User-pays principle

World Business Council for Sustainable Development
(WBCSD)

Exercises

1. An effective strategy for implementing sustainability principles is to use various tools, including the PDCA (Plan, Do, Check, Act) Cycle, and the life cycle assessment (LCA). Create illustrations or models that demonstrate the PDCA cycle and the LCA. Provide a written summary of how an interior designer can implement the PDCA cycle and the LCA in practice.

2. Sustainable design principles can serve as a guide for making decisions related to business practices and designs for commercial and residential interiors. Develop sustainable design principles that could be used in your future practice of interior design.

3. To gather all the information that is required for the plan stage, a recommended practice in the area of sustainable design is a charrette. Develop a format for a charrette that could be used for a commercial client. The format should include the purpose of the charrette, participants, agendas, and intended results. Develop a plan that would be presented to the client.

4. The purpose of the life cycle inventory (LCI) phase is to gather data regarding each stage of an item. Identify a common product that is specified for interiors and create a graphic depiction of the LCI phase. The illustration should minimally include these five stages: (1) extraction of raw materials, (2) refining the raw materials, (3) manufacturing the product, (4) consumer use of the product, and (5) disposal and/or recycling.

UNIT II Sustainability and the Interior Environment

CHAPTER 5

Building and Product Assessment Standards

The LITTLE PRINCE crossed the desert and encountered only one flower.

A flower with three petals—a flower of no consequence . . .

"Good morning," said the little prince.

"Good morning," said the flower.

"Where are the people?" the little prince inquired politely.

The flower had one day seen a caravan passing.

"People? There are six or seven of them, I believe, in existence. I caught sight of them years ago. But you never know where to find them. The wind blows them away. They have not roots, which hampers them a good deal."

—ANTOINE DE SAINT-EXUPÉRY

Fig. 5.1. "He carefully raked out his active volcanoes."

Objectives

- Understand how the built environment affects people and the natural environment.
- Compare and contrast environmental assessment methods.
- Describe global building assessment tools and standards.
- Understand the categories associated with Leadership in Energy and Environmental Design (LEED). Synthesize the requirements for acquiring LEED certification.
- Understand how the Global Ecolabeling Network (GEN) functions and requirements of its members.
- Compare and contrast organizations that certify equipment and finishes.

UNIT I PROVIDED an overview of sustainable development and design by examining the global origins of the perspective. This background serves as the basis for understanding the impact that buildings have on society, the environment, and the economy. The multidisciplinary and interrelated components of sustainable design present numerous challenges to successful implementations. Unit II serves as a guide for understanding how to design interiors that promote the health and well-being of people, respect the natural environment, and provide economic benefits.

In expanding on content presented in Unit I, Chapter 5 begins by providing an in-depth analysis of the effects of the built environment on society, the environment, and the economy. This background serves as the basis for understanding how interior designers can play a critical role in sustaining the planet for the current and future generations. The chapter continues by reviewing global resources that interior designers can use to help guide best sustainable practices. Based on research, numerous governments, agencies, and nonprofit organizations provide suggestions for sustainable design and construction practices. These recommendations are outlined in various sources, including environmental assessment tools, standards, and green product certification programs. The growing use of building certification programs such as LEED reflects the interest in sustainable designs and the subsequent future of the interior design profession.

IMPACT OF THE BUILT ENVIRONMENT AND ASSESSMENT METHODS

To design sustainable interiors requires an understanding of how buildings and development affect people and the environment. Generally, statistics related to the built environment are derived from various governmental agencies, such as the Census Bureau, Department of Energy (DOE), and Environmental Protection Agency (EPA). These data help to provide an excellent rationale for designing sustainable buildings and serve as the basis for the development of formal environmental assessment methods.

Summary of the Impact of the Built Environment

In a 2004 report the EPA succinctly identifies some of the most salient effects of the built environment on the natural environment, human health, and the economy. In addition to identifying important environmental considerations, the report provides statistical data that quantify the various impacts. Table 5.1 provides a summary of statistics provided in the report and demonstrates the relationships between the built environment and the effects on people, the economy, and the natural environment. As illustrated in Table 5.1, statistics reveal that the United States has millions of existing buildings and millions are constructed annually. The number of buildings reflects land use, water usage, the rate of economic activity in the country, and increases in the population.

The location of buildings impacts lifestyles and the environment. For example, for people to get to commercial buildings that are located far from residential areas requires transportation other than walking or biking. This location affects their lifestyle by eliminating the possibility that they will engage in exercise on their way and by requiring that they spend money for an automobile or public transportation. Any transportation that requires the use of fossil fuels contributes to polluting the environment and depleting nonrenewable resources. Buildings located in areas that require people to drive to the site are particularly detrimental to the environment because of the energy consumption and emissions. In addition, resources are consumed to manufacture the automobile and to construct the infrastructure required to operate a car, including roads, parking lots, gas stations, and repair shops. Roads, driveways, and parking lots are especially problematic because their impermeable surfaces contribute to polluting waterways. A serious environmental concern is shopping malls and their large parking lots (see Figure 5.2). To build these structures and surfaces requires enormous amounts of resources and large quantities of land, which often was once farmland. A very unfortunate aspect of these large parking lots is that the enormous size was designed to accommodate only a few weeks during the year—the Christmas season. For most shopping malls, the majority

Fig. 5.2. Serious environmental concerns are the impermeable surfaces of shopping malls and their large parking lots. These elements require enormous amounts of resources and land, which often was once farmland.

of the lot is empty during the other 11 months of the year.

As shown in Table 5.1, the vast number and size of buildings have a significant impact on the environment by consuming energy and electricity. Consequently, energy consumption negatively impacts air and atmospheric conditions. In addition, the combination of outdoor and indoor air pollution negatively impacts the quality of interior environments. Pollutants in the interior environment have a more profound effect on people today because of the high percentage of time that is spent indoors. The potential health effects of **indoor environmental quality** include cancer, asthma, and other ailments delineated in Unit I of this text. In addition to the health effects on people, more time spent indoors also increases the consumption of energy and electricity.

The statistical report provided by the EPA identifies some of the factors that affect the indoor environmental quality (IEQ). However, as identified in the next sections of this chapter, there are many considerations that must be employed for the health and well-being of people. These include the availability of daylight, views to the outdoors, humidity levels, adequacy of ventilation, user control of human comfort, noise levels, and indoor air pollution. Due to the

considerable amount of time that people are indoors and the economic value associated with productivity, research has focused on identifying the elements of the built environment that affect behavior. Most of the studies have focused on offices, schools, healthcare facilities, and retail stores. Research indicates that various attributes associated with sustainable interiors can enhance productivity, improve learning, reduce illnesses, and decrease absenteeism.

A holistic approach is apparent when examining the benefits of sustainable or green buildings. For example, the EPA indicates that the potential benefits of green buildings focus on society, the environment, and the economy. Social benefits of green buildings include (1) enhance occupant comfort and health, (2) heighten aesthetic qualities, (3) minimize strain on local infrastructure, and (4) improve overall quality of life (EPA, 2005). Environmental benefits of green buildings are to (1) enhance and protect biodiversity and ecosystems, (2) improve air and water quality, (3) reduce waste streams, and (4) conserve and restore natural resources. The EPA postulates that the economic benefits of green buildings are to (1) reduce operating costs; (2) create, expand, and shape markets for green products and services; (3) improve occupant productivity; and (4) optimize life-cycle economic performance (EPA, 2005).

Table 5.1
Summary of Buildings and the Effects on People, the Economy, and the Natural Environment

Built Environment	Effects on People	Effects on Economy	Effects on Natural Environment
TOTAL NUMBER OF BUILDINGS			
~ 223,114 establishments/ businesses in the building industry	~$62 billion in annual payroll >1.7 million employees (2002)	>$531 billion in annual revenues ~$62 billion in annual payroll >1.7 million employees (2002)	Total land area in U.S. (excluding AK and HI) 1.983 billion acres ■ 107.3 million of these acres are developed ■ Increase of 24% in developed land over past 10 years (2002) **Energy** 39.4% total U.S. energy consumption (2002) 67.9% total U.S. electricity consumption (2002) **Air and Atmosphere** 38.1% of nation's total CO_2 emissions
Water 12.2% of total water consumed per day			**Water** Buildings and transportation infrastructure replace natural surfaces and create runoff that washes pollutants into waterways; urban runoff 4th leading source of impairment in rivers, 3rd in lakes, and 2nd in estuaries (2000)
Indoor Levels of Pollutants Most of an individual's exposure to air pollutants is derived from indoor air (World Health Organization, 1999).	~90% or more of time spent indoors; indoor levels of pollutant may be 2–5 times higher and occasionally more than 100 times higher than outdoor levels.		
Sources of Indoor Air Pollution	Combustion sources; building materials and furnishings; household cleaning, maintenance, personal care, or hobby products; central heating/cooling systems and humidification devices; and outdoor sources such as radon, pesticides, and outdoor air pollution		
Health Effects of Indoor Environmental Quality (IEQ) Radon	**Cancer** Radon 2nd leading cause of lung cancer and estimated to be responsible for ~21,000 deaths per year	Loss of life, cost of health care, loss of productivity from cancer and asthma	
Secondhand tobacco smoke Dust mites, molds, cockroaches pet dander	Environmental tobacco smoke **Asthma Attacks** >20 million people (>6 million children) accounts for >10 million outpatient clinic visits, ~2 million emergency visits, and ~4,500 deaths annually (2000)		
Waste Building-related construction and demolition (C&D) debris ~136 million tons per year This is ~60% of total non-industrial waste generation in the U.S. (1996)		**Waste** ~20–30% of C&D debris recovered for processing and recycling (1996) Materials most frequently recovered and recycled were concrete, asphalt, metals, and wood	**Waste** Sources of building-related C&D debris waste stream per year (1996): ~48% demolition ~44% renovation ~8% new construction ~20–30% of C&D debris recovered for processing and recycling (1996)

Table 5.1 (continued)

Built Environment	Effects on People	Effects on Economy	Effects on Natural Environment
EXISTING RESIDENTIAL BUILDINGS 116 million buildings (2000) Location of schools and housing development patterns	In 2001, <15% of students (ages 5–15) walked or biked to or from school, down from 48% in 1969 Vehicle use in U.S. has nearly tripled, from 1 to 2.85 trillion miles per year, between 1970 and 2002 (FBT)		**Energy** 54.6% of total U.S. energy consumption (2002) 51.2% of total U.S. electricity consumption (2002) **Air and Atmosphere** 20.6% of nation's total CO_2 emissions Vehicles are responsible for ~20% of U.S. greenhouse gas emissions annually (NRDC)
Water 74.4% of the 12.2% of the total water consumed per day **Indoor Levels of Pollutants** 64 million homes, 83% of privately owned units built before 1980, have some lead-based paint	In 1992, 1 of ~15 homes had radon concentrations > EPA recommended action levels 12 million occupied by families under the age of 7 years old		
Waste ~43% of C&D debris			
NEW RESIDENTIAL CONSTRUCTION >1.8 million built annually (2003) Site selection	Vehicle use in U.S. has nearly tripled, from 1 to 2.85 trillion miles per year, between 1970 and 2002 (FBT)	Production and labor rates	Impact natural resources Vehicles are responsible for ~20% of U.S. greenhouse gas emissions annually (NRDC)
EXISTING COMMERCIAL BUILDINGS 4.7 million office buildings (1999) Site Selection	Vehicle use in U.S. has nearly tripled, from 1 to 2.85 trillion miles per year, between 1970 and 2002 (FBT)		**Energy** 45.4% of total U.S. energy consumption (2002) 48.8% of total U.S. electricity consumption (2002) **Air and Atmosphere** 17.5% of nation's total CO_2 emissions Vehicles are responsible for ~20% of U.S. greenhouse gas emissions annually (NRDC)
Water 25.6% of the 12.2% of the total water consumed per day **Waste** 57% of C&D debris			
COMMERCIAL NEW CONSTRUCTION ~170,000 built annually Site selection	Vehicle use in U.S. has nearly tripled, from 1 to 2.85 trillion miles per year, between 1970 and 2002 (FBT).	Production and labor rates	Impact natural resources Vehicles are responsible for ~20% of U.S. greenhouse gas emissions annually (NRDC)
NUMBER OF COMMERCIAL DEMOLITIONS ~44,000 demolished annually		~44,000 demolished annually	
SCHOOLS ~117,007 public and private primary and secondary schools (2000) Location of schools and housing development patterns	~73 million Americans (68.5 million children) spend their days annually In 2001, <15% of students (ages 5–15) walked or biked to or from school, down from 48% in 1969		Impact consumption of natural resources Impact air emissions

(continued)

Table 5.1 (continued)

Built Environment	Effects on People	Effects on Economy	Effects on Natural Environment
SCHOOLS (continued)			
Indoor Levels of Pollutants	Mid-1990s, 1 in 5 schools reported unsatisfactory IAQ and 1 in 4 reported unsatisfactory ventilation.		
Health Effects of IEQ	Asthma is most serious chronic disease of childhood and 3rd ranking cause of hospitalization of children <15 years; ~14 million school days are missed each year due to asthma.		

SOURCES: U.S. Environmental Protection Agency (December 20, 1994), *Buildings and the Environment: A Statistical Summary.* Washington, DC: U.S. Environmental Protection Agency; Federal Bureau of Transportation; NRDC; World Health Organization (1999).

Overview of Environmental Assessment Methods

This chapter provides an overview of four major assessment methods, representing four continents of the world: BREEAM from the United Kingdom, Green Star from Australia, CASBEE from Japan, and LEED in North America (see Figure 5.3). Any client throughout the world can use these assessment methods. For example, as of 2005 LEED has been used to certify buildings in 13 countries. However, each system may have criteria that are unique to its country's lifestyle or environment.

There are many reasons for reviewing these four assessment methods. First, a global perspective demonstrates the world's commitment to sustainability. Second, a multicultural perspective helps to provide an awareness of varying perspectives and priorities regarding sustainability. This can be helpful to interior designers when working with global clients and when planning interiors for international end-users. Third, a comprehensive examination of environmental assessment methods enables interior designers to identify an extensive list of best sustainable practices. A comprehensive list provides interior designers with the opportunity to develop solutions that extend beyond the requirements of one specific assessment method. This can be very useful when an assessment method allows credit for innovative sustainable practices.

Generally, environmental assessment methods have similar goals, organizational structures, and operating procedures. The programs are voluntary rating systems that were created to promote sustainable design and performance of buildings. Goals of the assessment programs include promoting sustainable practices and identifying common sustainability language and standards of measurement. The programs are reviewed continuously for improvement. Criteria of the credit categories focus on (1) reducing pollution and building life-cycle impacts; (2) enhancing indoor environmental quality and the health and well-being of people; and (3) conserving energy, water, land, biodiversity, and raw materials. The credit categories are developed in a collaborative process with the assistance of professionals from many organizations. The credit categories reflect best principles, practices, and standards. Each credit category has a maximum number of available points. For example, up to three points could be awarded for a design that has good levels of daylight for users of the space. The total number of points awarded to a building determines the level of certification. Most systems have three to four levels of certification.

Crediting agencies rate buildings by type of structure, such as new construction, existing building, commercial interior, office, home, retail, industrial, school, and health. All of the methods employ a holistic approach to buildings and encourage collaborative processes with all of the stakeholders. Generally, certification processes proceed in three stages. The first stage involves registering a building with the certifying organization and payment of any registration fees. The second stage is to prepare the application by gathering information, completing the required forms, and preparing documentation. The third stage is the building certification process, which involves a review of the application and payment of any fees. To help assist with the assessment process, organizations provide materials and training workshops.

In addition to the benefits described by the EPA, there are many benefits associated with specifically attaining green certification of a building. The voluntary nature of the process reflects a genuine interest in sustainable practice and environmental stewardship. This concern for the planet and the well-being of people translates to economic benefits associated with people who want to do business with individuals who possess this ethos. Thus, businesses and corporations frequently market their building's environmental certification in promotional literature. The market value of property is also enhanced with environmental credentials.

Global Building Assessment Tools and Standards

An interior designer's work with commercial and residential buildings presents an opportunity to positively impact the environment, society, and the economy. Fortunately, to help guide good practice an interior designer can reference several sources on sustainable design. These sources include various environmental assessment methods that have been adopted throughout the world.

As described in the forthcoming sections of this chapter, credit categories vary depending on the certifying organization. All of the organizations focus on aspects of buildings that normally are not included in the work of an interior designer, such as site selection and HVAC systems. These categories are

briefly reviewed in this text, because as a member of a project's team an interior designer should be aware of all the elements that are involved with the certification process. This information helps to inform best practice for interior solutions and can be very helpful when educating a client regarding a holistic approach to sustainable design. An interior designer doesn't have direct responsibility for many aspects related to the construction of a building, but as a consultant on a project a designer can ask the appropriate questions related to sustainability, and subsequently influence attitudes and decisions. Holistic approaches to interior environments are needed to have buildings that are sustainable and healthy for the well-being of their users.

The British BREEAM system is the world's oldest method for assessing the environmental performance of buildings. As the originator of environmental assessment systems, BREEAM has been very influential in the development of methods used in other countries throughout the world. The BREEAM method contends its success is attributable to "its unique ability to cover a range of environmental issues within one assessment, and to present the results in a way that is widely understood by those involved in property procurement and management" (BREEAM, 2005, p. 1).

The BREEAM method assesses the performance of a building by examining the following categories: (1) *management*: overall management policy, commissioning site management and procedural issues; (2) *energy use*: operational energy and carbon dioxide (CO_2) issues; (3) *health and well-being*: indoor air affecting health and well-being; (4) *pollution*: air and water

Fig. 5.3. Four major assessment methods represent four continents of the world: BREEAM from the United Kingdom, Green Star from Australia, CASBEE from Japan, and LEED in North America.

pollution issues; (5) *transport*: transport-related CO_2 and location-related factors; (6) *land use*: greenfield and brownfield sites; (7) *ecology*: ecological value conservation and enhancement of the site; (8) *materials*: environmental implication of building materials, including life-cycle impacts; and (9) *water*: consumption and water efficiency. The BREEAM system has an environmental assessment method for offices, *Ecohomes*, industrial units, retail units, and schools. To provide examples of BREEAM's criteria, Table 5.2 is a summary of the assessment issues for homes. A summary of BREEAM's assessment issues for retail stores and schools is in Appendix A. Credits are awarded upon performance in each of the assessment issues. The following scale rates buildings: *pass*, *good*, *very good*, and *excellent*.

Green Star—Australia is one of the newest environmental assessment systems, hence the organization credits the development of its program to the British BREEAM system and the North American LEED system. The rating system was developed to establish a common language; set a standard of measurement for green buildings; promote integrated, whole-building design; recognize environmental leadership; identify building life-cycle impacts; raise awareness of green building benefits; and reduce the environmental impact of development [Green Building Council Australia (GBCAUS), 2005]. As of 2005 Green Star rating tools were developed for commercial office buildings in various stages in the building life cycle, including new construction, existing buildings, and office interiors. In the future, Green Star tools will be available for different stages of a building's life cycle and for different types of buildings, such as retail, industrial, and residential.

The framework for the Green Star rating tool includes the following categories: management; indoor environment quality; energy; transport; water; materials; land use, site selection, and ecology; and emissions. Table 5.3 provides an overview of Green Star's criteria within each category for office designs. Green Star uses six stars as a means to measure performance (see Figure 5.4). Projects that receive one, two, or three stars do not receive formal certification. Four stars recognizes *Best Practice*, five stars indicates *Australian Excellence*, and a six-star rating awards *World Leadership*.

The Japanese CASBEE system is also a new tool for

Fig. 5.4. Green Star uses six stars to measure performance. Australia's first six-star project is the Council House (CH2) office building in the city of Melbourne. The building's six-star rating, which denotes World Leadership, was announced in April 2005.

examining the environmental performance of buildings. In reporting the development of CASBEE, the chair of **Japan Sustainable Building Consortium (JSBC)** indicated, "Promoting sustainability is a major social challenge. As the building industry consumes large amounts of material resources and energy, specific technological and political means should be developed in order to promote sustainable buildings" (CASBEE, 2005, p.1). Thus, representatives from education, industry, and the government collaboratively developed CASBEE.

To promote sustainability, CASBEE reflects the following policies: (1) "the system should be structured to award high assessments to superior buildings, thereby enhancing incentives to designers and others"; (2) "the assessment system should be as simple as possible"; (3) "the system should be applicable to buildings in a wide range of applications"; and (4) "the system should take into consideration issues and problems peculiar to Japan and Asia" (CASBEE, 2005, p. 1). These policies serve to guide the framework of CASBEE, which includes the building life cycle and four assessment tools (see Figure 5.5).

Table 5.2

BREEAM EcoHomes 2005—Issue 1.1 Credit Categories and Aims

Credit Categories	Aim of Categories
ENERGY	
Energy 1 Carbon Dioxide	To minimize emissions of CO_2 to the atmosphere arising from the operation of a home and its services.
Energy 2 Building Fabric	To improve the efficiency of dwellings over their whole life and to encourage refurbished dwellings to improve their insulation standards.
Energy 3 Drying Space	To minimize the amount of energy used to dry clothes.
Energy 4 Ecolabeled Goods	To encourage the provision or purchase of energy-efficient white goods, thus reducing the CO_2 emissions from the dwelling.
Energy 5 External Lighting	The purpose of this credit is to encourage the provision of energy-efficient external lighting.
TRANSPORT	
Transport 1 Public Transport	To encourage developers to provide a choice of transport modes for residents, with the aim of reducing the level of car use.
Transport 2 Cycle Storage	To encourage the wider use of bicycles as transport, and thus reduce the need for short car journeys, by providing adequate and secure cycle storage facilities.
Transport 3 Local Amenities	To encourage developers to plan new housing developments that are close to, or include, local shops and amenities. This will help to reduce the reliance of local residents on their cars.
Transport 4 Home Office	To reduce the need to commute to work by providing residents with the necessary space and services to be able to work from home.
POLLUTION	
Pollution 1 Insulant ODP and GWP	To reduce the potential for long-term damage to the earth's stratospheric ozone layer and the potential for increased global warming from substances used in the manufacture or composition of insulating materials.
Pollution 2 NO_x Emissions	To reduce the nitrous oxides (NO_x) emitted into the atmosphere.
Pollution 3 Reduction of Surface runoff	To reduce and delay water runoff from the hard surfaces of a housing development to public sewers and watercourses, thus reducing the risk of localized flooding, pollution, and other environmental damage.
Pollution 4 Zero Emission Energy Source	To reduce atmospheric pollution by encouraging locally generated renewable energy to supply a significant proportion of the development's energy demand.
MATERIAL	
Materials 1 Timber: Basic Building Elements	To recognize and encourage the specification of timber from responsible forest sources and harvested forests/plantations for primary building elements.
Materials 2 Timber: Finishing Elements	To recognize and encourage the specification of timber from responsible forest sources for secondary building and finishing elements.
Materials 3 Recycling Facilities	To encourage developers to provide homeowners with the opportunity and facilities to recycle household waste.
Materials 4 Environmental Impact of Materials	To encourage the use of materials that have less impact on the environment, taking account of the full life cycle.
WATER	
Water 1 Internal Water Use	To reduce consumption of water in the home.
Water 2 External Water Use	To encourage the recycling of rainwater and reduce the amount of water taken from the mains, for use in landscape and gardening.
LAND USE AND ECOLOGY	
Land Use and Ecology 1 Ecological Value of Site	To encourage, wherever possible, development on land that already has a limited value to wildlife and discourage the development of ecologically valuable sites.
Land Use and Ecology 2 Ecological Enhancement	To enhance the ecological value of a site.
Land Use and Ecology 3 Protection of Ecological Features	To protect existing ecological features from substantial damage during the clearing of the site and the completion of construction work.

(continued)

Table 5.2 (continued)

Credit Categories	Aim of Categories
Land Use and Ecology 4 Change of Ecological Value of Site	The aim of this credit is to reward steps taken to minimize reductions in ecological value and to encourage an improvement.
Land Use and Ecology 5 Building Footprint	To promote the most efficient use of a building's footprint by ensuring that land and material use is optimized across the development.
HEALTH AND WELL-BEING	
Health and Well-being 1 Daylighting	To improve the quality of life in homes through good daylighting and to reduce the need for energy to light a home.
Health and Well-being 2 Sound Insulation	To ensure the provision of sound insulation and reduce the likelihood of noise complaints.
Health and Well-being 3 Private Space	To improve the occupiers' quality of life by providing a private outdoor space.

SOURCE: Building Research Establishment, Ltd. (March 2005), *EcoHomes 2005: The Environmental Rating for Homes*. United Kingdom: Building Research Establishment, Ltd.

Table 5.3
Green Star—Australia Office Design v2: Reference Title and Aim of Credit

Reference Title	Aim of Credit
MANAGEMENT	
Green Star Accredited Professional	To encourage and recognize the adoption of environmentally sustainable principles from the earliest project stages throughout design and construction.
Commissioning Clauses	To encourage and recognize improved building services performance and energy efficiency due to adequate commissioning and handover to the building owner.
Commissioning—Building Tuning	To encourage and recognize improved energy efficiency and comfort within the building in all seasons due to adequate commissioning.
Commissioning— Commissioning Agent	To encourage and recognize the appointment of an independent commissioning agent from design through to handover.
Building Users' Guide	To encourage and recognize the provision of guidance material to enable building users to achieve the environmental performance envisaged by the design team, and to manage future changes that promote efficiency and environmental quality.
Environmental Management	To encourage and recognize the adoption of a formal environmental management system in line with established guidelines during construction.
Waste Management	To encourage and recognize management systems that facilitate the reduction of construction waste going to landfill.
INDOOR ENVIRONMENT QUALITY	
Ventilation Rates	To encourage and recognize the provision of increased outside air rates, in order to promote a healthy indoor environment.
Air Change Effectiveness	To encourage and recognize systems that provide for the effective delivery of clean air through reduced mixing with indoor pollutants in order to promote a healthy indoor environment.
CO_2 Monitoring and Control	To encourage and recognize the provision of response monitoring of CO_2 levels to ensure delivery of minimum outside air requirements.
Daylight	To encourage and recognize designs that provide good levels of daylight for building users.
Daylight Glare Control	To encourage and recognize buildings that are designed to reduce the discomfort of glare from natural light.
High-Frequency Ballasts	To encourage and recognize the increase in workplace amenity by avoiding low-frequency flicker that may be associated with fluorescent lighting.
Electric Light Levels	To encourage and recognize base building provided office lighting that is not overdesigned.

Table 5.3 (continued)

Reference Title	Aim of Credit
External Views	To encourage and recognize reduced eyestrain for building occupants by allowing long-distance views and the provision of visual connection to the outdoors.
Thermal Comfort	To encourage and recognize the use of thermal control assessments to guide design options.
Individual Comfort Control	To recognize the benefits of individual control to provide good thermal comfort.
Asbestos	To encourage and recognize actions taken to reduce health risks to occupants from the presence of hazardous materials.
Internal Noise Levels	To encourage and recognize buildings that are designed to maintain internal noise levels at an appropriate level.
VOCs	To encourage and recognize projects that reduce the detrimental impact on occupant health from finishes emitting internal air pollutants.
Formaldehyde Minimization	To encourage and recognize projects that reduce the use of formaldehyde composite wood products in order to promote a healthy indoor environment.
Mold Prevention	To encourage and recognize the design of systems that reduce the risk of mold growth and its associated detrimental impact on occupant health.
Tenant Exhaust Riser	To encourage and recognize the provision of buildings designed with a general exhaust riser that can be used by tenants to remove indoor pollutants from printing and photocopy areas.
ENERGY	
Energy 1	To reduce base building operational energy and greenhouse gas emissions.
Energy Improvement	To encourage and recognize projects that contain design features that help to minimize operational energy consumption and greenhouse gas emissions of the base building over and above the Conditional Requirement in Energy 1.
Electrical Submetering	To encourage and recognize the provision of energy submetering to facilitate energy monitoring of base building services.
Tenancy Submetering	To encourage and recognize the provision of energy submetering to facilitate energy monitoring by tenants or end users.
Office Lighting Power Density	To encourage and recognize lighting design practices that lessen lighting energy consumption while maintaining appropriate lighting levels.
Office Lighting Zoning	To encourage and recognize lighting design practices that offer greater flexibility for light switching, making it easier to light only occupied areas.
Peak Energy Demand Reduction	To encourage and recognize projects that implement systems to reduce peak demand on energy supply infrastructure.
TRANSPORT	
Provision of Car Parking	To encourage and recognize building design that promotes the utilization of alternative modes of transport by limiting available car parking spaces.
Small Parking Spaces	To encourage and recognize building design that supports the use of smaller, more fuel-efficient vehicles for work commuting.
Cyclist Facilities	To encourage and recognize building design that promotes the use of bicycles by occupants and visitors by ensuring adequate cyclist facilities are provided.
Commuting Public Transport	To encourage and recognize developments with proximity and good access to public transport networks that have frequent services.
WATER	
Occupant Amenity Potable Water Efficiency	To encourage and recognize systems that have the potential to reduce the potable water consumption of building occupants.
Water Meters	To encourage and recognize the design of systems that monitor and manage water consumption.
Landscape Irrigation Water Efficiency	To encourage and recognize the design of systems that aim to reduce the consumption of potable water for landscape irrigation.
Cooling Tower Water Consumption	To encourage and recognize building design that reduces the potential demand on potable water supplies and infrastructure due to water-based building cooling systems.

(continued)

Table 5.3 (continued)

Reference Title	Aim of Credit
Fire System Water Consumption	To encourage and recognize building design that reduces potable water consumption of the building's fire protection and essential water storage systems.

MATERIALS

Recycling Waste Storage	To encourage and recognize the inclusion of storage space that facilitates the recycling of resources used within offices to reduce waste going to the landfill.
Reuse of Facade	To encourage and recognize the reuse of existing facades to reduce new material consumption.
Reuse of Structure	To encourage and recognize the reuse of existing structures to reduce new material consumption.
Shell and Core of Integrated Fitout	To encourage and recognize the reduction of material wastage during tenancy fitouts.
Recycled Content of Concrete	To encourage and recognize the reduction of embodied energy and resource depletion due to the use of concrete.
Recycled Content of Steel	To encourage and recognize the reduction in embodied energy and resource depletion due to the use of recycled steel.
PVC Minimization	To encourage and recognize the reduction of polyvinyl chloride (PVC) products in Australian buildings.
Sustainable Timber	To encourage and recognize the specification of reused timber products or timber that has certified environmentally responsible forest management practices.

LAND USE AND ECOLOGY

Ecological Value of Site	To encourage wherever possible development on land that already has a limited ecological value and discourage the development of ecologically valuable sites.
Reuse of Land	To encourage and recognize the reuse of land that has previously been developed.
Reclaimed Contaminated Land	To encourage and recognize positive actions to use contaminated land that otherwise would not have been developed.
Change of Ecological Value	To encourage and recognize the minimization of ecological impact from a development and maximize the enhancement of a site for both new and existing buildings.
Topsoil and Fill Removal from Site	To encourage and recognize practices that reduce the amount of topsoil and fill removed from development sites.

EMISSIONS

Refrigerant ODP	To encourage and recognize the reduction of potential long-term damage to the earth's stratospheric ozone layer through the accidental release of ozone-depleting substances to the atmosphere.
Refrigerant GWP	To encourage and recognize the selection of refrigerants that reduce the potential for increased global warming arising from the emission of refrigerants to the earth's atmosphere in the event of accidental release of intensive greenhouse gases to the atmosphere.
Refrigerant Leak Detection	To encourage and recognize systems that reduce the release of refrigerants to the atmosphere arising from leakages in a building's cooling plant.
Refrigerant Recovery	To encourage and recognize systems that reduce and prevent unnecessary loss of refrigerants in the event of a leak.
Watercourse Pollution	To encourage and recognize project design that reduces the potential of pollution in water running off from buildings and hard surfaces to natural watercourses.
Reduced Flow to Sewer	To encourage and recognize building design that reduces water flow to the municipal sewerage systems for treatment.
Light Pollution	To encourage and recognize lighting design that reduces pollution from unnecessary dispersion of light into the night sky and onto neighboring property.
Cooling Towers	To encourage and recognize building systems design that eliminates the risk of Legionnaires' disease from cooling towers.
Insulant ODP	To encourage and recognize designs that reduce the potential for long-term damage to the earth's stratospheric ozone layer from ozone-depleting substances used in the manufacture or composition of thermal insulation.

Table 5.3 (continued)

Reference Title	Aim of Credit
INNOVATION	
Innovative Strategies and Technologies	To encourage and recognize the spread of innovative initiatives for commercial building applications that improve a development's environmental impact.
Exceeding Green Star Benchmarks	To encourage and recognize design initiatives that demonstrate additional environmental benefit by exceeding the current benchmarks in Green Star—Office Design.
Environmental Design Initiatives	To encourage and recognize design initiatives that have a significant measurable environmental benefit and are not awarded points by Green Star—Office Design.

SOURCE: Green Building Council of Australia (2005), *Green Star: Office Interiors v1*. Australia: Green Building Council of Australia.

The CASBEE method defines the stages of the cyclical process of building design as pre-design, design, and post-design. The pre-design stage examines the background elements of the plan, including the "natural, social, cultural, and business environment." Design themes, shared conceptualization, and policies are developed at the pre-design stage. The design stage utilizes the outcomes of the pre-design stage to define "ecological, technical, social, cultural, aesthetic, and economic aspects." To integrate the design as "best practice" the design stage also includes a self-evaluation process. The post-design stage occurs after a design has been practiced. To evaluate sustainability, the design "is subjected to an overall verification followed by ongoing retrospective verification through its life cycle." A continuous improvement cycle occurs by utilizing the results of the verification to enhance the implemented design and concept.

As shown in Figure 5.5, CASBEE has four assessment tools, which correspond to the building life cycle. *Tool-0 CASBEE (CASBEE-PD)* is for pre-design applications, *Tool-1 CASBEE (CASBEE-NC)* is

used for new construction projects, *Tool-2 CASBEE (CASBEE-EB)* is for existing buildings, and *Tool-3 CASBEE (CASBEE-RN)* is intended for renovation. The CASBEE tool also has applications for special purposes: (1) "application to buildings for short-term use," (2) "simple assessment," (3) "consideration for regional character," (4) "detailed assessment of heat island impact," and (5) "extended tool for regional scale assessment." For example, the traditional CASBEE-NC can be revised for temporary construction activities, such as short-term exhibition facilities. Guidelines for this type of application focus on material use and recycling activities associated with construction and demolition. The *simple assessment*, or a brief version of CASBEE-NC, process can be used for situations when a quick (~2 hours) assessment is all that is necessary, such as a preliminary consensus between a client, designers, and builders.

To be applicable to the unique characteristics of local conditions, local authorities can also use a brief version of CASBEE-NC. Local conditions could include climate, the availability of materials, or policies. *CASBEE-HI* (heat island) is another example of

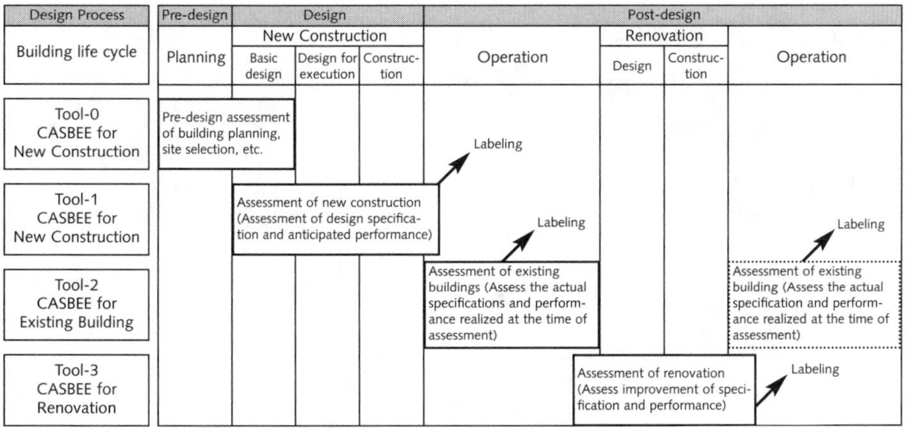

Fig. 5.5. CASBEE has four assessment tools, which correspond to the building life cycle. *Tool-0* is for pre-design applications, *Tool-1* is used for new construction projects, *Tool-2* is for existing buildings, and *Tool-3* is for renovation.

revising CASBEE for special applications. This unique application is very important to major urban areas such as Tokyo, due to the heat island–related concerns. The last specific purpose application represents an effort to assess building groups. The CASBEE system is in the process of developing a tool called *CASBEE for District/Regions*, which will expand assess-

ment to include "city-center renewal of urban districts, or development of large areas including multiple buildings" (CASBEE, 2005, p. 4).

In building on the work of BREEAM and LEED, the CASBEE tool reconstructs current environmental performance assessment frameworks by developing a new system that is based on the principles of sustainability. Fundamentally, this is accomplished by advancing the framework from "eco-efficiency" to building environmental efficiency (BEE). To accommodate this new perspective, CASBEE has two categories of assessment: *Q (Quality)*—building environmental quality and performance; and *L (Loadings)*—building environmental loadings (see Figure 5.6). *Q* evaluates "improvement in living amenity for the building users, within the hypothetical enclosed space (the private property)." *L* evaluates "negative aspects of environmental impact which go beyond the hypothetical enclosed space to the outside (the public property)."

The four assessment fields are (1) energy efficiency, (2) resource efficiency, (3) local environment, and (4) indoor environment. As shown in Figure 5.7, CASBEE recategorizes the four fields into *Q* and *L*. Note that for the BEE equation, *Q* is in the numerator and *L* is in the denominator. This equation represents a significant and important distinction from other assessment methods. Dividing the building's

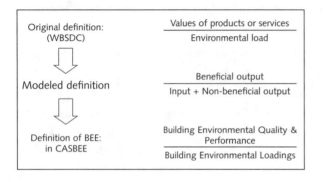

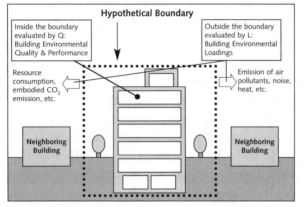

Fig. 5.6. (above) CASBEE has two categories of assessment: *Q (Quality)* – building environmental quality and performance; and *L (Loadings)* – building environmental loadings. *Q* evaluates improvement in living amenity for the building users. *L* evaluates negative aspects of environmental impact external to the hypothetical enclosed space.

Fig. 5.7. (right, top) CASBEE recategorizes the four fields into *Q* and *L*. Dividing the building's environmental quality and performance (*Q*) by the building's environmental loads (*L*) presents a clearer representation of the building's environmental performance assessment.

Fig. 5.8. (right, bottom) The outcomes of *Q*, *L*, and BEE result in the rating for a CASBEE building: Class C (poor) to class S (excellent).

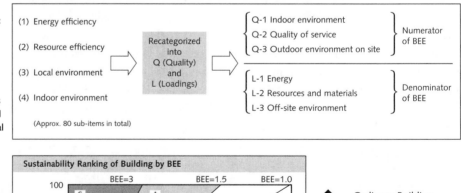

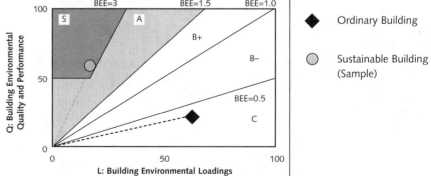

a

b

Fig. 5.9a. LEED Building Type: K–12 education. The Third Creek Clearview Elementary School in Hanover, PA, is a 43,600-square-foot (4,050 square meters) new construction project. The school replaces an existing facility at the same location. Rating: U.S. Green Building Council LEED-NC, v2—Level: Gold (42 points).

Fig. 5.9b. LEED Owner and Occupancy: City of Seattle, Local Government. The Seattle Justice Center in Seattle, WA, is a 288,000-square-foot (26,800 square meters) new construction project. Rating: U.S. Green Building Council LEED-NC, v2—Level: Silver (33 points).

environmental quality and performance (Q) by the building's environmental loads (L) presents a clearer representation of the building's environmental performance assessment. Thus, a building with a high Q value *and* a low L value will demonstrate the most sustainability for the environment. Figure 5.8 illustrates how the outcomes of Q, L, and BEE result in the rating for a CASBEE building: class C (poor) to class S (excellent).

LEADERSHIP IN ENERGY AND ENVIRONMENTAL DESIGN (LEED)

The LEED system of North America has been gaining significant interest in the past several years. As of 2005 there are approximately 260 certified projects and more than 2,000 registered projects. Every state in the United States has a registered project, and there are LEED certified projects in 13 countries. California has the most certified projects, and the other leading states are Pennsylvania, Washington, New York, Oregon, Texas, Massachusetts, Illinois, Michigan, and Virginia. Certified projects encompass more than 225 million gsf (gross square feet) of space. Figures 5.9a and b illustrate the registered projects by building and owner types, respectively.

The LEED system was created to (1) "define 'green building' by establishing a common standard of measurement"; (2) "promote integrated, whole-building design practices"; (3) "recognize environmental leadership in the building industry"; (4) "stimulate green competition"; (5) "raise consumer awareness of green building benefits"; and (6) "transform the building market" (USGBC, 2005, p. 1). The mission of LEED "encourages and accelerates global adoption of sustainable green building and development practices through the creation and implementation of universally understood and accepted standards, tools, and performance criteria" (USGBC, 2004, p. 3).

As a means to "define and measure green buildings," in 1998 the U.S. Green Building Council (USGBC) developed the first LEED Pilot Project Program (LEED Version 1.0) and subsequently in 2000 the LEED Green Building Rating System Version 2.0. Currently this rating system is called **LEED for New Construction and Major Renovations (LEED-NC)**. In 2005, USGBC published **LEED for**

Commercial Interiors (LEED-CI) and launched developments of **LEED for Core and Shell (LEED-CS)**, **LEED for Homes (LEED-H)**, and **LEED for Neighborhood Development (LEED-ND)**.

The USGBC explains that the LEED Green Building Rating System is a voluntary program that was developed by professionals in the building industry. The rating system is for new and existing commercial, institutional, and high-rise residential buildings. The LEED-H will cover single-family residences and multifamily structures up to three stories high. Environmental performance is based on a "whole building perspective over a building's life cycle" (USGBC, 2005, p. 12). The LEED rating system is organized by five core credit categories: (1) *Sustainable Sites*, (2) *Water Efficiency*, (3) *Energy and Atmosphere*, (4) *Materials and Resources*, and (5) *Indoor Environmental Quality* (see Table 5.4). *Innovation and Design Process* is an additional category developed to address "sustainable building expertise as well as design measures not covered under the five environmental categories."

The system is based on existing technology that has been proven to be successful. In addition, the ratings reflect "accepted energy and environmental principles" and allow for the inclusion of emerging concepts. To keep abreast of the ever-changing developments in sustainable performance, USGBC provides updates on its website, www.usgbc.org. The LEED rating structure is a performance-oriented system, which provides credits for satisfying criteria. For example, upon satisfying the criterion, "three points can be earned for locating the tenant space in a LEED Certified Building" (USGBC, 2005, p. 19). The LEED-CI ratings are awarded at the following levels: *Certified* (21–26 points), *Silver* (27–31 points), *Gold* (32–41 points), and *Platinum* (42–57 points).

As shown in Figure 5.10, addressing some of the core credit categories that are required to have a LEED certified project. The sections that follow provide an overview of each category and include a summary of how the *LEED Version 2* certified projects have approached fulfilling the credits within each category (see Table 5.5). The analysis provides an awareness of the credits that are the most frequently

Fig. 5.10. An abbreviated checklist that shows some of the core credit categories that are required to have a LEED certified project.

Project Checklist
LEED for HOMES (Version 1.73 - October 19, 2005)

Builder Name:		Maximum Points[2]	
Address (Street/City/State):		Dry Normal Wet	

Detailed information on the measures in the checklist below are provided in the companion document "LEED for Homes Rating System"

Yes ? No		Location and Linkages (LL)		OR	10
HOLD		LEED-ND Neighborhood		LL2-5	10
	2	Site Selection	Avoid Environmentally Sensitive Sites and Farmland	LL1	2
	3.1	Infrastructure	Site within 1/2 Mile of Existing Water, Sewer, and Roads	LL1	1
	3.2		Select an Infill Site	LL1	1
	4.1	Community Resources	Within 1/4 Mile of Basic Community Resources / Public Transportation	LL1	1
	4.2	OR	Within 1/4 Mile of Extensive Community Resources / Public Transportation	LL1	2
	4.3	AND/OR	Within 1/2 Mile of Green Spaces	LL1	1
	5.1	Compact Development	Average Housing Density >/= 7 Units / Acre	LL1	1
	5.2	OR	Average Housing Density >/= 10 Units / Acre	LL1	2
	5.3	OR	Average Housing Density >/= 20 Units / Acre	LL1	3
		Sub-Total			

Yes ? No		Sustainable Sites (SS)			14
Y	1.1	Site Stewardship	Minimize Disturbed Area of Site (If Site > 1/3 Acre)		Mandatory
Y	1.2		Erosion Controls (During Construction)		Mandatory
Y	2.1	Landscaping	Basic Landscaping Design		Mandatory
	2.2		Apply 3 to 4 Inches of Mulch Around Plants		1
	2.3		Limit Turf		3
	2.4		Minimize Landscape Water Demand		2
	3	Shading of Hardscapes	Locate and Plant Trees to Shade Hardscapes		1
Y	4.1	Surface Water Management	Install Permeable Material for at Least 65% of Lot (If Lot >/= 1/4 acre)		Mandatory
	4.2		Use Permeable Paving Materials		3
	4.3		Design and Install Permanent Erosion Controls		2
	5	Non-Toxic Pest Control	Select Insect and Pest Control Alternatives from Lis		2
		Sub-Total			

Notes: 1. **Certified** 30–49 points   **Silver** 50–60 points   **Gold** 70–89 points   **Platinum** 90–108 points
2. "Points" are shown for 3 precipitation zones: Dry (< 20 inches / year); Normal (20–40 inches / year); and Wet (>40 inches / year

I hereby attest that I have verified all of the indicated credits above as installed in the home identified above.		
Rater's Name	Company	
Signature	Date	

I hereby attest that I have verified all of the indicated credits above as installed in the home identified above.		
Provider's Name	Company	
Signature	Date	

Table 5.4
LEED—CI for Commercial Interiors: Categories and Intent Statements

Environmental Categories	Intent
SUSTAINABLE SITES	
Credit 1 Site Selection	Encourage tenants to select buildings with best practices systems and employed green strategies.
Credit 2 Development Density and Community Connectivity	Channel development to urban areas with existing infrastructure, protect greenfields, and preserve habitat and natural resources.
Credit 3.1 Alternative Transportation, Public Transportation Access	Reduce pollution and land development impacts from automobile use.
Credit 3.2 Alternative Transportation, Bicycle Storage, and Changing Rooms	Reduce pollution and land development impacts from automobile use.
Credit 3.3 Alternative Transportation, Parking Availability	Reduce pollution and land development impacts from single occupancy vehicle use.
WATER EFFICIENCY	
Credit 1.1 Water Use Reduction, 20% Reduction	Maximize water efficiency within tenant spaces to reduce the burden on municipal water supply and wastewater spaces.
Credit 1.2 Water Use Reduction, 30% Reduction	Maximize water efficiency within tenant spaces to reduce the burden on municipal water supply and wastewater systems.
ENERGY AND ATMOSPHERE	
Prerequisite 1 Fundamental Commissioning	Verify that the project's energy-related systems are installed, calibrated, and perform as intended.
Prerequisite 2 Minimum Energy Performance	Establish the minimum level of energy efficiency for the tenant space systems.
Prerequisite 3 CFC Reduction in HVAC&R Equipment	Reduce ozone depletion.
Credit 1.1 Optimize Energy Performance, Lighting Power	Achieve increasing levels of energy consumption below the prerequisite standard to reduce environmental impacts associated with excessive energy use.
Credit 1.2 Optimize Energy Performance, Lighting Controls	Achieve increasing levels of energy conservation beyond the prerequisite standard to reduce environmental impacts associated with excessive energy use.
Credit 1.3 Optimize Energy Performance, HVAC	Achieve increasing levels of energy conservation beyond the prerequisite standard to reduce environmental impacts associated with excessive energy use.
Credit 1.4 Optimize Energy Performance, Equipment and Appliances	Achieve increasing levels of energy conservation beyond the prerequisite standard to reduce environmental impacts associated with excessive energy use.
Credit 2 Enhanced Commissioning	Verify and ensure that the tenant space is designed, constructed, and calibrated to operate as intended.
Credit 3 Energy Use, Measurement, and Payment Accountability	Provide for the ongoing accountability and optimization of tenant energy and water consumption performance over time.
Credit 4 Green Power	Encourage the development and use of grid-source, renewable energy technologies on a net zero pollution basis.
MATERIALS AND RESOURCES	
Prerequisite 1 Storage and Collection of Recyclables	Facilitate the reduction of waste generated by building occupants that is hauled to and disposed of in landfills.

(continued)

Table 5.4 (continued)

Environmental Categories	Intent
Credit 1.1 Tenant Space, Long-Term Commitment	Encourage choices that will conserve resources, reduce waste, and reduce the environmental impacts of tenancy as they relate to materials, manufacturing, and transport.
Credit 1.2 Building Reuse, Maintain 40% of Interior Nonstructural Components	Extend the life cycle of existing building stock, conserve resources, retain cultural resources, reduce waste, and reduce environmental impacts of new buildings as they relate to materials manufacturing and transport.
Credit 1.3 Building Reuse, Maintain 60% of Interior Nonstructural Components	Extend the life cycle of existing building stock, conserve resources, retain cultural resources, reduce waste, and reduce environmental impacts of new buildings as they relate to materials manufacturing and transport.
Credit 2.1 Construction Waste Management, Divert 50% from Landfill	Divert construction, demolition, and land clearing debris from landfill disposal. Redirect recyclable recovered resources back to the manufacturing process. Redirect reusable materials to appropriate sites.
Credit 2.2 Construction Waste Management, Divert 75% from Landfill	Divert construction, demolition, and land clearing debris from landfill disposal. Redirect recyclable recovered resources back to the manufacturing process. Redirect reusable materials to appropriate sites.
Credit 3.1 Resource Reuse 5%	Reuse building materials and products in order to reduce demand for virgin materials and to reduce waste, thereby reducing impacts associated with the extraction and processing of virgin resources.
Credit 3.2 Resource Reuse 10%	Reuse building materials and products in order to reduce demand for virgin materials and to reduce waste, thereby reducing impacts associated with the extraction and processing of virgin resources.
Credit 3.3 Resource Reuse 30% Furniture and Furnishings	Reuse building materials and products in order to reduce demand for virgin materials and to reduce waste, thereby reducing impacts associated with the extraction and processing of virgin resources.
Credit 4.1 Recycled Content, 10% (post-consumer + ½ pre-consumer)	Increase demand for building products that incorporate recycled content materials, therefore reducing impacts resulting from extraction and processing of virgin materials.
Credit 4.2 Recycled Content, 20% (post-consumer + ½ pre-consumer)	Increase demand for building products that incorporate recycled content materials, therefore reducing impacts resulting from extraction and processing of virgin materials.
Credit 5.1 Regional Materials, 20% Manufactured Regionally	Increase demand for building materials and products that are extracted and manufactured within the region, thereby supporting the regional economy and reducing the environmental impacts resulting from transportation.
Credit 5.2 Regional Materials, 10% Extracted and Manufactured Regionally	Increase demand for building materials and products that are extracted and manufactured within the region, thereby supporting the regional economy and reducing the environmental impacts resulting from transportation.
Credit 6 Rapidly Renewable Materials	Reduce the use and depletion of finite raw materials and long-cycle renewable materials by replacing them with rapidly renewable materials.
Credit 7 Certified Wood	Encourage environmentally responsible forest management.

INDOOR ENVIRONMENTAL QUALITY

Prerequisite 1 Minimum IAQ Performance	Establish minimum indoor air quality (IAQ) performance to enhance indoor air quality in the occupant space, thus contributing to the comfort and well-being of the occupants.
Prerequisite 2 Environmental Tobacco Smoke (ETS) Control	Prevent or minimize exposure of tenant space occupants, indoor surfaces, and systems to Environmental Tobacco Smoke (ETS).
Credit 1 Outdoor Air Delivery Monitoring	Provide capacity for ventilation system monitoring to help sustain long-term occupant comfort and well-being.
Credit 2 Increased Ventilation	Provide additional air ventilation to improve indoor air quality for improved occupant comfort, well-being, and productivity.
Credit 3.1 Construction IAQ Management Plan, During Construction	Prevent indoor air quality problems resulting from the construction/renovation process in order to help sustain the comfort and well-being of construction workers and building occupants.

Table 5.4 (continued)

Environmental Categories	Intent
Credit 3.2 Construction IAQ Management Plan, Before Occupancy	Prevent indoor air quality problems resulting from the construction/renovation process in order to help sustain the comfort and well-being of construction workers and building occupants.
Credit 4.1 Low-Emitting Materials, Adhesives and Sealants	Reduce the quantity of indoor air contaminants that are odorous, potentially irritating, and/or harmful to the comfort and well-being of installers and occupants.
Credit 4.2 Low-Emitting Materials, Paints and Coatings	Reduce the quantity of indoor air contaminants that are odorous, potentially irritating, and/or harmful to the comfort and well-being of installers and occupants.
Credit 4.3 Low-Emitting Materials, Carpet Materials	Reduce the quantity of indoor air contaminants that are odorous, potentially irritating, and/or harmful to the comfort and well-being of installers and occupants.
Credit 4.4 Low-Emitting Materials, Composite Wood and Laminate	Reduce the quantity of indoor air contaminants that are odorous, potentially irritating, and/or harmful to the comfort and well-being of installers and occupants.
Credit 4.5 Low-Emitting Materials, Systems Furniture and Seating	Reduce the quantity of indoor air contaminants that are odorous, potentially irritating, and/or harmful to the comfort and well-being of installers and occupants.
Credit 5 Indoor Chemical and Pollutant Source Control	Maximize exposure of building occupants to potentially hazardous particulates, biological contaminants, and chemical pollutants that adversely impact air and water quality.
Credit 6.1 Controllability of Systems, Lighting	Provide a high level of lighting system control for individual occupants and specific groups in multioccupant spaces (e.g., classrooms and conference areas) to promote the productivity, comfort, and well-being of building occupants.
Credit 6.2 Controllability of Systems, Temperature and Ventilation	Provide a high level of thermal and ventilation control for individual occupants or specific groups in multioccupant spaces (e.g., classrooms and conference areas) to promote the productivity, comfort, and well-being of building occupants.
Credit 7.1 Thermal Comfort, Compliance	Provide a thermally comfortable environment that supports the productivity and well-being of tenant space occupants.
Credit 7.2 Thermal Comfort, Monitoring	Provide a thermally comfortable environment that supports the productivity and well-being of tenant space occupants.
Credit 8.1 Daylighting and Views, Daylight 75% of Spaces	Provide the occupants with a connection between indoor spaces and the outdoors through the introduction of daylight and views into the regularly occupied areas of the tenant space.
Credit 8.2 Daylighting and Views, Daylight 90% of Spaces	Provide the occupants with a connection between indoor spaces and the outdoors through the introduction of daylight and views into the regularly occupied areas of the tenant space.
Credit 8.3 Daylighting and Views, Views for 90% of Seated Spaces	Provide the occupants with a connection between indoor spaces and the outdoors through the introduction of daylight and views into the regularly occupied areas of the tenant space.

INNOVATION AND DESIGN PROCESS

Credit 1 Innovation in Design	Provide design teams and projects the opportunity to be awarded points for exceptional performance above the requirements set by the LEED Green Building Rating System and/or innovative performance in Green Building categories not specifically addressed by the LEED Green Building Rating System
Credit 2 LEED Accredited Professional	Support and encourage the design integration required by a LEED Green Building project and streamline the application and certification process.

SOURCE: U.S. Green Building Council (2005), *LEED-CI for Commercial Interiors: Reference Guide Version 2.0*. Washington, D.C.: U.S. Green Building Council.

Table 5.5

Summary of LEED Version 2 Certified Projects

Environmental Categories LEED Category (NC: New Construction) (Approximate number of projects and results as recorded November 2005)	Platinum: LEED 3	Gold: LEED 37	Silver: LEED 49	Certified: LEED 72	Platinum: LEED NC 4	Gold: LEED NC 17	Silver: LEED NC 18	Certified: LEED NC 29
SUSTAINABLE SITES								
Credit 1 Site Selection	3	33	45	59	4	15	13	23
Credit 2 Urban Redevelopment	1	7	10	9	2	3	4	4
Credit 3 Brownfield Redevelopment	0	5	5	10	2	2	3	3
Credit 4.1 Alternative Transportation, Public Transportation Access	2	19	33	49	4	11	10	24
Credit 4.2 Alternative Transportation, Bicycle Storage and Changing Rooms	3	32	43	58	4	16	17	23
Credit 4.3 Alternative Transportation, Alternative Fuel Refueling Stations	2	15	15	15	3	5	7	8
Credit 4.4 Alternate Transportation, Parking Capacity	3	29	35	37	4	16	9	18
Credit 5.1 Reduced Site Disturbance, Protect or Restore Open Space	2	19	11	14	1	9	4	7
Credit 5.2 Reduced Site Disturbance, Development Footprint	2	26	31	39	3	11	8	17
Credit 6.1 Stormwater Management, Rate and Quantity	3	21	16	17	4	7	7	10
Credit 6.2 Stormwater Management, Treatment	3	19	18	22	4	10	7	9
Credit 7.1 Landscape and Exterior Design to Reduce Heat Islands, Non-roof	3	27	30	30	4	10	14	19
Credit 7.2 Landscape and Exterior Design to Reduce Heat Islands, Roof	3	20	28	25	4	10	10	9
Credit 8 Light Pollution Reduction	2	23	23	34	4	6	7	8
WATER EFFICIENCY								
Credit 1.1 Water Efficient Landscaping, Reduce by 50%	3	34	43	58	4	16	14	20
Credit 1.2 Water Efficient Landscaping, No Potable Use or No Irrigation	3	29	28	39	4	15	10	15
Credit 2 Innovative Wastewater Technologies	3	16	8	7	3	8	3	2
Credit 3.1 Water Use Reduction, 20% Reduction	3	35	33	44	4	15	17	19
Credit 3.2 Water Use Reduction, 30% Reduction	3	29	27	29	4	15	11	9
ENERGY AND ATMOSPHERE								
Credit 1.1 Optimize Energy Performance, 20% New/ 10% Existing	3	37	47	56	4	17	17	21
Credit 1.2 Optimize Energy Performance, 30% New/ 20% Existing	3	33	41	42	4	16	16	16
Credit 1.3 Optimize Energy Performance, 40% New/ 30% Existing	3	26	25	12	4	13	7	6
Credit 1.4 Optimize Energy Performance, 50% New/ 40% Existing	3	16	12	7	3	7	3	0
Credit 1.5 Optimize Energy Performance, 60% New/ 50% Existing	3	9	1	2	1	3	2	0
Credit 2.1 Renewable Energy, 5%	3	12	7	2	1	4	0	0
Credit 2.2 Renewable Energy, 10%	3	9	2	1	1	3	0	0
Credit 2.3 Renewable Energy, 20%	2	9	2	1	1	2	0	0
Credit 3 Additional Commissioning	3	18	29	32	4	9	11	10
Credit 4 Ozone Depletion	3	19	28	36	4	6	6	15
Credit 5 Measurement and Verification	1	14	13	20	4	6	6	5
Credit 6 Green Power	1	15	21	23	1	12	11	14

MATERIALS AND RESOURCES

Credit								
Credit 1.1 Building Reuse, Maintain 75% of Existing Shell	0	4	8	9	0	3	2	0
Credit 1.2 Building Reuse, Maintain 100% of Existing Shell	0	4	2	4	0	2	0	2
Credit 1.3 Building Reuse, Maintain 100% of Shell and 50% Non-shell	0	0	2	1	0	1	0	0
Credit 2.1 Construction Waste Management, Divert 50% from Landfill	3	33	43	50	4	13	13	23
Credit 2.2 Construction Waste Management, Divert 75% from Landfill	3	27	37	29	4	9	11	16
Credit 3.1 Resource Reuse, Specify 5%	1	10	4	2	3	3	0	1
Credit 3.2 Resource Reuse, Specify 10%	0	6	1	1	2	1	0	0
Credit 4.1 Recycled Content 10% (post-consumer + 1/2 pre-consumer)	3	34	45	53	4	15	18	17
Credit 4.2 Recycled Content, 20% (post-consumer + 1/2 pre-consumer)	3	27	35	39	4	14	16	13
Credit 5.1 Local/Regional Materials, 20% Manufactured Locally	3	35	48	65	4	16	18	24
Credit 5.2 Local/Regional Materials, of 20% Above, 50% Harvested Locally	2	22	36	40	4	16	14	18
Credit 6 Rapidly Renewable Materials	1	3	3	3	3	2	0	0
Credit 7 Certified Wood	2	13	10	20	4	4	4	9

INDOOR ENVIRONMENTAL QUALITY

Credit								
Credit 1 Carbon Dioxide (CO_2) Monitoring	3	26	27	34	4	15	8	12
Credit 2 Increased Ventilation Effectiveness	1	15	19	10	2	6	4	3
Credit 3.1 Construction IAQ Management Plan, During Construction	3	24	24	37	4	12	10	15
Credit 3.2 Construction IAQ Management Plan, Before Occupancy	3	19	30	38	4	9	9	14
Credit 4.1 Low-Emitting Materials, Adhesives and Sealants	3	30	41	57	4	14	15	22
Credit 4.2 Low-Emitting Materials, Paints and Coatings	3	35	37	58	4	15	17	19
Credit 4.3 Low-Emitting Materials, Carpet Materials	3	35	45	67	4	17	17	24
Credit 4.4 Low-Emitting Materials, Composite Wood	3	19	21	23	3	8	8	11
Credit 5 Indoor Chemical and Pollutant Source Control	3	26	33	42	4	12	14	13
Credit 6.1 Controllability of Systems, Perimeter	2	19	11	18	4	4	6	5
Credit 6.2 Controllability of Systems, Non-perimeter	0	13	8	12	2	4	2	3
Credit 7.1 Thermal Comfort, Comply with ASHRAE 55-1992	3	30	33	30	4	15	14	16
Credit 7.2 Thermal Comfort, Permanent Monitoring System	2	26	24	26	3	13	6	10
Credit 8.1 Daylighting and Views, Daylight 75% of Spaces	3	19	17	25	2	10	9	13
Credit 8.2 Daylighting and Views, Daylight 90% of Spaces	2	31	34	49	4	12	11	18

INNOVATION AND DESIGN PROCESS 17

Credit								
Credit 1.1 Innovation in Design: Sustainability Education	3	37	47	58	4	17	18	25
Credit 1.1 Innovation in Design: Exemplary Performance WEc3	3	37	41	46	4	17	18	23
Credit 1.1 Innovation in Design: Exemplary Performance MRc5.1	3	27	28	27	4	16	15	16
Credit 1.1 Innovation in Design: Exemplary Performance MRc4	2	16	19	9	3	8	13	7
Credit 2 LEED Accredited Professional	3	26	49	72	4	17	18	29

SOURCE: www.USGBC.org.

implemented and the credits that are the least likely to be employed. This information can be very useful when an interior designer seeks to design sustainable interiors. For example, the analysis of the credits indicates that most projects do not get credit for "increase ventilation effectiveness." Thus, when an interior designer is working on a project that is seeking LEED certification, a careful analysis should be performed to determine any obstacles associated with increasing the effectiveness of ventilation. To provide an overview of the credit categories the explanations that follow are derived from *LEED-CI for Commercial Interiors, Reference Guide Version 2.0 June 2005.*

Sustainable Sites and Water Efficiency

As shown in Table 5.4, the *Sustainable Sites* category for commercial interiors provides credits for site selection, development density, community connectivity, and alternative transportation. The Sustainable Sites category is very important for examining how buildings affect ecosystems. The LEED-CI summarizes that selecting a site that has not been developed, or **greenfield,** reduces the amount of land that is available for agricultural purposes, wildlife habitats, or recreation (USGBC, 2005). Buildings and any transportation infrastructure required for the structure can cause stormwater runoff, erosion from sedimentation, and increases in temperatures from absorbing the heat from sunlight. In addition, buildings can increase light pollution in the evening hours.

The location of a building also affects the means of transportation. Car transportation results in more consumption of land and nonrenewable resources. Thus, to reduce the impacts on ecosystems, natural resources, and energy consumption, LEED-CI indicates that project teams should identify buildings with "high performance attributes in locations that enhance existing neighborhoods, transportation networks, and urban infrastructures" (2005, p. 17). Sustainable Sites credits can be attained by selecting a LEED certified building or meeting the requirements of various options, such as brownfield redevelopment, stormwater management, heat island reduction, or water-efficient irrigation.

Credit 2 of LEED-CI's Sustainable Sites category focuses on development density and community connectivity. The requirements for this credit focus on selecting a site that is in an urban environment, with walkable access to the building and community amenities. The LEED system's overview of alternative transportation includes a description of how the mode of transportation affects the environment, economy, and community. The LEED-CI reports, "As of the late 1990s, an estimated 200 million of the 520 million cars worldwide were located in the United States" (2005, p. 87). Decreasing the number of people driving cars reduces fuel consumption, air pollutants, stormwater runoff, and the effects from urban heat islands. Thus, LEED-CI provides credit for site selections that have access to public transportation and provide facilities for bicycle storage and changing rooms.

The LEED-CI reports that "in the United States, approximately 340 billion gallons of freshwater are withdrawn per day from rivers, streams, and reservoirs to support residential, commercial, industrial, agricultural, and recreational activities" (2005, p. 103). In addition, "Almost 65 percent of this water is discharged to rivers, streams, and other water bodies after use and, in some cases, treatment." In examining the sustainability of the situation, LEED-CI notes, "On an annual basis, the water deficit in the United States is currently estimated at about 3,700 billion gallons. In other words, Americans extract 3,700 billion gallons per year more than they return to the natural water system to recharge aquifers and other water sources."

To encourage water efficiency, LEED-CI provides credit for water use reduction. For commercial buildings, LEED-CI suggests that water usage can be reduced by at least 30 percent (2005). In providing suggestions for reducing water consumption, LEED-CI indicates that "in a typical 100,000-square-foot office building, low-flow fixtures coupled with sensors and automatic controls can save a minimum of 1 million gallons of water per year, based on 650 building occupants each using an average of 20 gallons per day." The LEED-CI also suggests that nonpotable water can be used for landscape irrigation, toilet flushing, and building maintenance.

Energy and Atmosphere

In citing the substantial amount of energy and electricity annually consumed by buildings, LEED-CI reviews many of the adverse environmental impacts associated with the production of energy (2005). Conventional methods used to produce electricity significantly impact the environment. The detrimental effects start at the extraction stage of fossil fuels and continue through the generation processes, which emit high levels of pollutants. In working with clients, interior designers can promote products, systems, and practices that reduce electrical consumption. In developing approaches to commercial interiors, which are generally part of a large building, LEED-CI suggests a focus on energy efficiency, lighting, HVAC, appliances, and equipment (2005).

To reduce the amount of energy and electricity consumed by buildings, LEED-CI promotes practices that optimize energy performance, enhance commissioning, reduce energy consumption, and increase the use of "green power." To optimize energy performance of lighting power and HVAC, LEED-CI utilizes **ANSI/ASHRAE/IESNA 90.1-2004** as the reference standard. The energy end uses include heating, cooling, fans/pumps, lighting, water heating, all equipment plugged into electrical systems (**plug loads**), and miscellaneous loads. For appliances and equipment, LEED-CI recommends products that are qualified by the EPA's ENERGY STAR program.

The LEED-CI system defines commissioning as the "process of ensuring that systems are designed, installed, functionally tested, and capable of being operated and maintained to perform in conformity with the design intent" (USGBC, 2005, p. 128). Commissioning processes focus on any energy-related systems, such as **HVAC&R (heating, ventilating, air-conditioning, and refrigeration)** systems, lighting controls, daylighting, domestic hot water systems, and renewable energy systems (PVC, wind, solar, and so on). According to LEED-CI, enhanced commissioning involves additional activities that result in verifying and ensuring that an interior space is "designed, constructed, and calibrated to operate as intended." Green power initiatives involve contracts with local utility companies that are generating electricity from renewable sources. The LEED-CI indicates, "Green power may be procured from a Green-e certified power marketer, a Green-e accredited utility program, through Green-e Tradable Renewable Certificates, or from a supply that meets the Green-e Renewable Power definition" (USGBC, 2005, p. 185).

Materials and Resources and Indoor Environmental Quality

There are many areas in LEED-CI's *Materials and Resources* category that pertain to the work of interior designers. Sustainable materials and products can significantly improve the environment by minimizing consumption of natural resources and reducing pollutants and waste. The LEED-CI system emphasizes that a very effective approach to minimizing impacts to the environment is the reuse of buildings, structural components, equipment, furniture, and furnishings. The LEED-CI defines furniture and furnishings as the materials included in **CSI Master-Format™ Division 12**. The list provided by LEED-CI is fabrics, key cabinets, hospital casework, display casework, window treatments, panels/dividers, furniture, furniture systems, furniture accessories, floor mats/frames, multiple seating, and chairs (2005). Interior designers have considerable experience with reuse applications, such as restoration/renovation projects, historic preservation, adaptive reuse buildings, architectural salvage operations, and antique furniture/furnishings auctions. All of these reuse applications are a means to reduce the consumption of virgin materials and reduce the quantity of products diverted to landfills. In addition, preserving interiors, furniture, and furnishings helps to retain society's cultural heritage (see Figure 5.11).

When reuse is not possible, sustainable designs should have materials and resources that are made from recycled content. Recycled content can be composed of **post-consumer** and **pre-consumer** materials. The LEED-CI system defines post-consumer recycled content as "consumer waste that has become a raw material (feedstock) for another product. It originates from products that have served a useful purpose in the consumer market" (USGBC, 2005, p. 236). Pre-consumer or **post-industrial content** is "output from a process that has not been used as part of a consumer product, that is sold, traded, or exchanged under commercial terms (including auditable transactions between profit centers within an organization) as feedstock for another industrial process, and that would otherwise be landfilled,

Fig. 5.11. The Sydney Opera House in Australia officially opened in 1973. This extraordinary building serves as an example of a preserved building.

incinerated, or somehow disposed of as a waste, as defined by the Federal Trade Commission" (USGBC, 2005, p. 236).

The source of materials and resources is also important for sustainable designs. This includes examining where materials are extracted and the location of the manufacturer. The LEED-CI system encourages locally sourced materials and suppliers. This helps to support the local economy and reduces the negative impact on the environment associated with transportation. In addition to the location of materials, the preferred source of materials is rapidly renewable vegetation. The LEED-CI defines rapidly renewable materials as fiber and animal products that take "10 years or less to grow or raise, and to harvest in an ongoing and sustainable fashion" (USGBC, 2005, p. 248). Some of the examples provided by LEED-CI include bamboo flooring, wool carpets, strawboard, cotton batt insulation, linoleum flooring, composite panels made from wheat rather than wood, and the emergence of bio-based plastics made from corn starch instead of petroleum (2005). When wood products are specified, LEED-CI recommends that the products are certified in accordance with the principles and criteria established by the **Forest Stewardship Council (FSC)**.

The LEED-CI system requires a certified building to have facilities and products for the collection and storage of recyclables. To determine appropriate solutions for managing recyclables, LEED-CI refers to the research conducted in 1999 by the **California Integrated Waste Management Board (CIWMB)**. This study determined the amount of waste generated by the type of business and number of employees. The research findings reveal that some businesses such as general offices and financial institutions generate the least amount of waste. Hotels, health services facilities, and educational institutions generate a moderate amount of waste. Retail stores, food stores, and restaurants were determined to be "heavy waste" generators. Therefore, occupancy and type of business affects the management of recyclables, and must be considered in order to successfully address prerequisite 1 of LEED-CI's Materials and Resources category.

Indoor Environmental Quality (IEQ)

Interior designers have a responsibility to the health, safety, and well-being of their clients. Therefore, IEQ is a major area of concern for the interior design profession. Researching the effects of materials and products on the health of people is a relatively new area of study. However, a great deal of information is available regarding the source of indoor contaminants and effective preventative measures. The LEED-CI system suggests that IEQ is affected by manufacturing processes, construction practices, and material composition of products. The LEED-CI also emphasizes the importance of preventing IEQ problems rather than trying to improve contaminated interiors. Preventative measures are viewed as the most cost-effective approach to IEQ. The LEED-CI identifies some preventative actions that can occur during the construction stage of a project (2005). For example, construction schedules can be planned to reduce materials exposure to moisture and **off-gassed contaminants**. Air handling systems should be protected during construction activities, and prior to occupation the system should be flushed out.

A very effective approach to preventing IEQ problems is to specify materials that release the least amount of harmful chemical compounds. Some of the products that require detailed evaluation are adhesives, paint, sealants, coatings, fiberglass, plastic foams, flooring, composite wood products, welded applications, furniture, and cleaning solvents. The LEED-CI (2005) requirements related to VOC content limits are prescribed in *Green Seal Standard GS-36* (2000) and *Adhesives, Sealants, and Sealant Primers: South Coast Air Quality Management District (SCAQMD) Rule #1168* (2003). The South Coast Rule #1168 VOC limits include architectural adhesives application; welding and installation; sealants; and substrates. References to interior paint and coatings include *Green Seal Standard GS-11* (1993), *GS-03* (1997), and *South Coast Air Quality Management District (SCAQMD) Rule #1113* (2004). Carpet systems, including carpet, carpet pad, and adhesives, must adhere to the requirements prescribed by *Carpet and Rug Institute's Green Label*.

Mechanical systems can be designed to improve IEQ. The LEED-CI recommends: (1) higher ratios of filtered outside air; (2) increasing ventilation rates; (3) monitoring and managing moisture; (4) automatic HVAC controls for temperature, humidity, rates of outdoor air, and lighting; and (5) sensors that signal problems with the IEQ (2005). The LEED-CI system also recognizes that IEQ is affected by the ability of users to see views to the outdoors, enjoy the benefits of daylight, and control the thermal comfort and illumination levels within their environment.

GREEN/ENVIRONMENT PRODUCT CERTIFICATION AND STANDARDS PROGRAMS

Many organizations have developed voluntary green or environmental performance certification programs. The information provided by these organ-

izations is very useful to the work of an interior designer. Prior to certification processes, a manufacturer could **greenwash**, or state unfounded ecological claims, regarding many attributes of a product, such as the percentage of recyclable content or its energy efficiency rating. By contacting an environmental certification program, an interior designer can learn which products have been certified, how the product satisfied the environmental criteria, and manufacturers' information. These data can help save an interior designer a great deal of time and help to ensure the specification of products that have the least impact on the environment.

Environmental certification programs are structured as third-party systems. The neutral nature of third-party testing procedures helps to ensure that the product is true to its claims. For example, **Green Seal**, a U.S. environmental testing organization, states in its informational profile, "Green Seal has no financial interest in the products that it certifies or recommends nor in any manufacturer or company" (2005, p.1). Generally, there are two basic types of testing organizations. Some organizations test and certify a consumer product by examining the stages of its life cycle. Other organizations specialize by testing a specific product, such as carpeting, or an attribute of a product, such as energy efficiency. Generally, to acquire certification a manufacturer completes an application and sends a product to a third-party testing organization. Upon completion of the testing procedures, a product may or may not be granted the right to use the label of certification. When a product meets the required criteria, the manufacturer has the right to affix the seal to the product for a designated period of time. Subsequently, to ensure that the standards are sustained, the certifying organization routinely monitors the product.

Global Ecolabeling Network (GEN)

Founded in 1994, the Global Ecolabeling Network (GEN) is a nonprofit association comprised of 26 national and multinational third-party environmental performance-labeling organizations (see Figure 5.12). The purpose of GEN is to "improve, promote, and develop ecolabeling of products and services" (GEN, 2005, p. 1). In supporting the mission, the 26 members of GEN (1) "set criteria for and certify products and services with lower environmental burdens and impacts than comparable products/services with the same function"; (2) "provide information, advice, and technical assistance to organizations contemplating or developing programs"; (3) "disseminate information to the public"; and (4) "represent the interests of ecolabeling in various international meetings and events" (GEN, 2005, p. 1).

All members of GEN subscribe to "protecting the environment"; "encouraging environmentally sound innovation and leadership"; and "building consumer awareness of environmental issues" (2004). To protect the environment, members aim to encourage the efficient management of natural resources, protect ecosystems, and promote the proper management of chemicals. Policies also focus on the reducing, reusing, and recycling of consumer wastes. To encourage innovation and leadership, GEN members establish criteria that reward the "top environmental performers in a product category" and continuously raise standards. Ecolabeling on products helps to build consumer awareness of environmental issues and can encourage people to routinely select certified products.

To have a credible ecolabeling program, organizations must adhere to several principles (GEN, 2004). The first principle is the voluntary participation of manufacturers, service providers, and any organizations involved with the ecolabeling program. The criteria of ecolabel programs must be in compliance with national, regional, and local legislation, while addressing the quality and performance of a product. Product testing methods must reflect sound scientific and engineering principles that are based on life-cycle considerations. Criteria must distinguish leadership in the field of products and the requirements must be "credible, relevant, attainable, and measurable/verifiable" (GEN, 2004, p. 7). A credible program and its board members must be independent of vested interests. Processes must be operated in an open and accountable manner with the flexibility to be cost-effective and responsive to the changes in technology. To keep abreast of new developments, GEN recommends that its members review standards every three years (2004). Finally, ecolabeling criteria should be guided by appropriate standards, such as ISO 14020 and ISO 14024.

The GEN website, www.gen.gr.jp, has a listing of product categories and criteria documents of ecolabeling programs worldwide (see Figure 5.13). Some of the product categories are building materials, carpet, residential appliances, lights, paint, and office furniture. The product category listing provides the programs that certify these items. For example, some of the countries that certify products in the construction/building category are Australia, Canada, China, Germany, and Thailand. Products related to the built environment that are certified by Green Seal include paint, commercial adhesives, compact fluorescent lamps, the operation/maintenance of green facilities, cleaners, floor-care products, lodging properties, occupancy sensors, windows, and HVAC systems.

Each program affiliated with GEN has a website that provides detailed information regarding the objectives of their ecolabel, product listings, standards,

Fig. 5.12. Founded in 1994, the Global Ecolabeling Network (GEN) is a nonprofit association comprised of 26 national and multinational third-party environmental performance-labeling organizations.

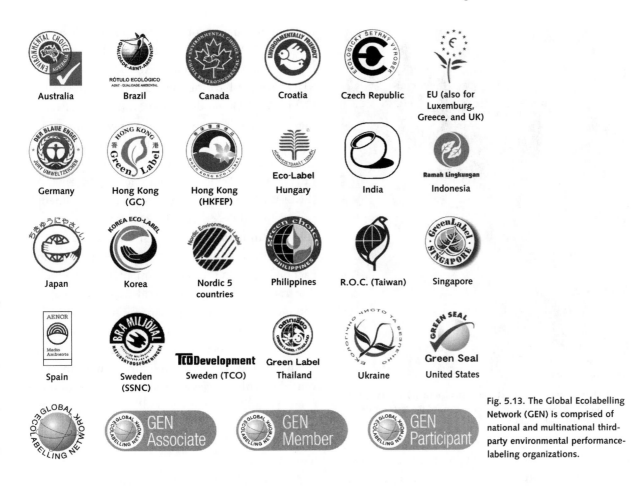

Fig. 5.13. The Global Ecolabelling Network (GEN) is comprised of national and multinational third-party environmental performance-labeling organizations.

news, and updates. For example, the *Australian Environmental Labelling Association (AELA)* has information regarding commercial adhesives and three categories of paint products or architectural coatings. Green Seal's specific programs include (1) *greening your government* to provide technical assistance to governmental agencies, (2) *product standards and certification* to identify leadership products in specific categories and certifications, (3) *product recommendations*, (4) *greening the lodging industry*; and (5) *policy development* (2005, p.1).

As illustrated in Table 5.6, the Australian Environmental Labelling Association provides detailed information of a product's test results. The AELA reports the product marketing name, use, application, date of certification, and manufacturer's contact information. Specifics about the product focus on comparing the tested material to conventional applications. For example, in certifying a product produced by Forbo Floorcoverings Pty Ltd (see Figure 5.14), AELA concludes, "In comparison to PVC and other petroleum based flooring surfaces Forbo produces a linseed oil base hard wearing surface suitable for walkway, commercial, and manufacturing flooring applications"

Table 5.6
Flooring Product Test Results Performed by the Australian Environmental Labelling Association

Material Contents of Linoleum 2,5 mm (Dutch System) 2.0 mm (Swedish System) in g/m 2

Contents	Linoleum 2.5 mm	Linoleum 2.0 mm
Tall oil	398	316
Gum resin	76	55
Linseed oil	588	452
Wood flour	901	688
Limestone	592	441
Pigment	101	76
Jute	233	260
Lacquer	12	12
TOTAL	2900	2300

Wood flour is supplied mainly by English and German suppliers, cork by Portuguese suppliers (all cork is produced in Portugal), jute is supplied by Indian, Dutch, and French suppliers (all jute is grown in India and Bangladesh), linseed oil is supplied by Dutch and German suppliers (all linseed is grown in Canada), gum resin is supplied by Dutch and German suppliers (all raw resin is produced in Indonesia).

SOURCE: Australian Environmental Labelling Association (2005), www.aela.org.

Fig. 5.14. In certifying a product, the Australian Environmental Labelling Association (AELA) provides a comparison of the tested material to conventional applications.

(2003, p.1). A product's impact on the environment is presented by analyzing its life cycle. For example, material extraction information includes the content and origin of materials. The Forbo flooring has cork content produced in Portugal, and the raw resins are produced in Indonesia. Packaging details are provided and reference is made to waste properties. The AELA's overall product assessment states, "Marmoleum and Artoleum display important environmental preferable attributes related to renewable and non-renewable raw material use, human toxicity, ecotoxicity, environmental loads associated from waste, toxicity of surface treatments, and longevity from a flooring product life cycle perspective" (AELA, 2003, p. 2).

ENERGY STAR

ENERGY STAR is an example of a certificate program that focuses on a specific environmental issue. This program is sponsored by the U.S. government for the purpose of "helping businesses and individuals protect the environment through superior energy efficiency" (ENERGY STAR, 2005, p. 1). In 1992, the U.S. EPA established ENERGY STAR in order to

have more energy-efficient computers. Currently, ENERGY STAR has more than 40 product categories for the home and workplace. According to ENERGY STAR, people have purchased more than 1 billion ENERGY STAR products and "thousands of buildings have undergone effective energy improvement projects" (ENERGY STAR, 2003, p. 1). Furthermore, "More than 1,100 buildings have earned the ENERGY STAR label for superior energy performance" (ENERGY STAR, 2003, p. 1). From an environmental perspective, these energy efficiencies translate to less emission from power plants, fewer power plants, and lower energy bills. This can have a significant impact on improving the environment. For example, as illustrated in Figure 5.15, residential, commercial, and industrial energy represent more than one-half the greenhouse emissions in the United States. ENERGY STAR has determined, "In 2002, with the help of the ENERGY STAR program, Americans prevented greenhouse gas emissions equivalent to those from 14 million vehicles and avoided using the power that 50 300-megawatt (MW) power plants would have produced, while saving more than $7 billion" (2003, p. 1).

To accomplish these energy efficiencies, ENERGY STAR has several initiatives. The most extensive program focuses on identifying which products are reliably energy efficient. The EPA and U.S. Department of Energy (DOE) work with product manufacturers

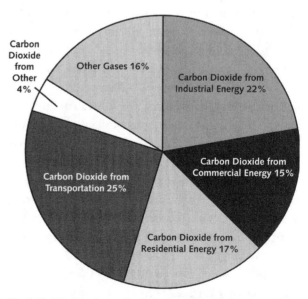

Fig. 5.15. U.S. Greenhouse Gas Emissions 2003. The EPA reports that residential, commercial, and industrial energy represent more than one-half of the greenhouse emissions in the United States.

Fig. 5.16. The ENERGY STAR label is awarded when a product attains efficiency standards, satisfies consumer-driven performance criteria, and provides a reasonable payback within a given period of time.

to "determine the energy performance levels that must be met for a product to earn the ENERGY STAR" (ENERGY STAR, 2003, p. 3). The ENERGY STAR label is awarded when a product attains efficiency standards, satisfies consumer-driven performance criteria, and provides a reasonable payback within a given period of time (see Figure 5.16). For easy access by consumers, products that qualify for the ENERGY STAR label are listed on the ENERGY STAR website. Product information includes the expected savings, retail stores that sell the item, and environmental benefits associated with the purchase. Educating the public focuses on savings that can be attained over the long term and the relationships between energy use and air emissions.

Once a product has the ENERGY STAR label, the EPA routinely monitors the use of products and selectively tests products to ensure that products continue to qualify for the label. To keep abreast of technological improvements and market changes, the EPA routinely updates performance specifications. In recent years, the EPA has been very focused on improving the energy efficiency of commercial and industrial buildings. This has been a formidable task because many companies have assumed that electrical usage is "the least controllable category of business costs," and prior to 1999 corporations did not have an appropriate tool for measuring energy performance or efficiency (ENERGY STAR, 2003). Currently, ENERGY STAR has home and buildings assessment tools, which can help to plan for energy efficiency and cost savings.

In recognizing the importance of business profits, ENERGY STAR has focused on initiatives that demonstrate to management how energy costs affect profitability. For example, the EPA has collaborated with a financial analysis firm to reveal that "leaders in corporate energy management outperform their competitors by 20 to 30 percent on Wall Street" (ENERGY STAR, 2003, p. 10). The EPA also has case studies of successful projects, such as the Starwood

Hotels & Resorts Worldwide, Inc., in White Plains, New York (see the description in Box 5.1). The EPA indicates that the key elements of superior energy

---

Box 5.1
Starwood Hotels & Resorts Worldwide, Inc., White Plains, New York

Starwood Hotels & Resorts Worldwide, Inc., is a leading U.S. hotel company owning, operating, and franchising more than 700 hotels in 80 countries. Its brands include Four Points, Sheraton, Westin, and W Hotels. Starwood received the ENERGY STAR Award for Excellence in Energy Management in 2002 and 2003. At the Energy Efficiency Forum at the National Press Club in June 2002, the EPA recognized Starwood's Sheraton Boston Hotel as one of the first hotels in the nation to earn the ENERGY STAR.

Starwood's "Energy Management Is Good Business" strategy is centered around its commitment to making energy management everyone's responsibility. The company has benchmarked all of its owned and managed hotels using EPA's energy performance rating system and will apply for the ENERGY STAR label for top-performing hotels (those scoring 75 or better) to demonstrate its environmental commitment to guests and the public. Starwood based a portion of its 2001 bonuses for its energy team on energy consumption reductions, and its "Watts for Wheels" contest created competition among the company's properties for energy efficiency accomplishments. Starwood also helped the EPA test the benchmarking system for hotels by providing energy data for all of its buildings.

Starwood's energy management initiatives are paying off. The company invested $8.5 million in energy projects completed in 2001 and saved $3.4 million—equivalent to renting 9,370 additional rooms. In 2002, Starwood invested approximately $4.6 million in energy projects and saved $1.3 million, the equivalent to renting 9,800 additional rooms.

SOURCE: U.S. EPA (2003), *ENERGY STAR—The Power to Protect the Environment Through Energy Efficiency.* Washington, DC: U.S. Environmental Protection Agency.

management are "top-level commitment to reduce energy waste"; "routine assessment of organization-wide performance, against competitors and across own portfolio"; and "use of a systems-integrated approach to upgrade buildings" (ENERGY STAR, 2003, p. 10). This information provides an excellent rationale for specifying energy-efficient products. Thus, interior designers can utilize EPA data when they are promoting energy-efficient environments to their clients.

Finishes and BEES Software

To determine the effects on IAQ, the **Carpet and Rug Institute (CRI)** has a *Green Label* testing program (see Figure 5.17). This program is an independent laboratory that tests carpet, adhesives, and cushion products for chemical emissions. The most common application for adhesives is in commercial interiors, but adhesives can be used in residential interiors when carpet is installed over concrete. Carpet is tested for VOCs, formaldehyde, styrene, and 4-PC (4-phenylcyclohexene), the compound that is associated with the odor of new carpet. A product type number on the label identifies the manufacturer and indicates that the product meets

Fig. 5.17. The Carpet and Rug Institute (CRI) Green Label testing program tests carpet, adhesives, and cushion products for chemical emissions.

the criteria for low emissions. A carpet that has the *CRI Air Quality Label* indicates that the product is a "responsible, low-emitting carpet." The Green Label program also tests vacuum cleaners and carpet cleaning products. To ensure continuous compliance with the standards, CRI retests products on a quarterly basis.

The CRI developed *Green Label Plus*, which is the highest standard for IAQ within the industry. Green Label Plus exceeds California's standards for low-emitting products used in commercial interiors, such as schools and office buildings. The Green Label Plus certification indicates that carpet and adhesives have passed a rigorous testing procedure. In comparison to the Green Label program, products certified as Green Label Plus are tested by examining additional chemicals, using more stringent criteria, and employing a Scientific Review Board. The CRI is also affiliated with **Carpet America Recovery Efforts (CARE)**, a voluntary program created to reduce the quantity of carpet in landfills. The program focuses on carpet reclamation and recycling methods.

The Forest Stewardship Council (FSC) is a nonprofit organization created to encourage the "responsible management of the world's forests." The mission of FSC is to "promote and enhance well-managed forests through credible certification that is environmentally responsible, socially acceptable, and economically viable" (FSC, 2003). By focusing on the triadic components of sustainable development, the FSC strives to (1) protect the natural environment, (2) encourage people who are affected by what happens to the forests to be involved with the decision-making process, and (3) sustain a means for people to continue to make a living from the forest. As of 2005, there are more than 39 million hectares of forest that are FSC certified. These forests are in 66 countries on 5 continents. The FSC is the world's first forest product labeling scheme and is supported by the World Wildlife Fund, Greenpeace, and Friends of the Earth.

The FSC defines good forest management by complying with principles that focus on (1) compliance with laws and FSC principles; (2) respecting rights to the land, indigenous people, community, and employees; (3) encouraging efficient use of the forest's resources while conserving biological diversity, water resources, soil, and ecosystems; and (4)

Fig. 5.18. Products that have wood from an FSC-certified forest *and* have the chain-of-custody (COC) certificate are labeled with the FSC logo. The FSC logo identifies products that contain wood from well-managed forests certified in accordance with the rules of the Forest Stewardship Council.

management, monitoring, and assessment plans that focus on long-term objectives and social and environmental impacts (FSC, 2003). National organizations utilize the principles of the FSC as the basis for defining forest management that is appropriate for their locality. Forests that meet the standards become FSC certified.

Products that have wood from an FSC-certified forest *and* have the **chain-of-custody (COC) certificate** are labeled with the FSC logo (see Figure 5.18). The FSC defines COC as the "path taken by raw materials harvested from an FSC-certified source through processing, manufacturing, distribution, and printing until it is a final product ready for sale to the end consumer" (2005, p. 1). Thus, a product that has the FSC logo represents sustainable practices through several stages of its life cycle. The FSC-certified forest component addresses good management of the growing process. The COC certificate covers the product's life cycle from extraction to consumer use. To ensure high standards, certified FSC-accredited certification bodies monitor forests and processing operations.

The sections above describe some of the organizations and agencies that can provide valuable information regarding a product's impact on the environment. In addition to this important information, a client is interested in knowing the cost-effectiveness of a product. To help provide this information, in 1994 the **Building for Environmental and Economic Sustainability (BEES)** software program was developed by the **U.S. National Institute of Standards and Technology (NIST)**. The purpose of BEES is to "develop and implement a systematic methodology for selecting building products that achieve the most appropriate balance between environmental and economic performance based on the

decision maker's values" (Lippiatt, 2002, p. 1). This publicly available software helps an interior designer to select for clients products that are environmentally friendly and cost effective.

The BEES software is developed on consensus standards and is formatted to be practical, flexible, and transparent. The Windows-based software has actual environmental and economic data for approximately 200 building products. Building products are defined and classified using the ASTM standard classification (UNIFORMAT II E-1557). Some of the products include partitions, floor coverings, paint, and office chairs. The environmental performance of building products is analyzed by applying ISO 14040 standards. The analyses of the product's life cycle include raw material extraction, manufacture, transportation, installation, use, and waste management (Lippiatt, 2002). Economic analysis is based on the ASTM International standard life-cycle cost method (E 917). These costs are the initial investment, replacement, operation, maintenance, repair, and disposal.

The BEES model examines multiple environmental and economic impacts over the life of a building product. As noted by Lippiatt (2002), examining the multiple impacts and life-cycle stages is important because selecting a product based on a single impact or life stage may not be the most sustainable solution. For example, a manufacturer might indicate that a product is green because recycled content has been used, or it has low VOC emissions. These attributes might be accurate; however, the product's manufacturing process, or the means of transportation, might have been very detrimental to the environment. Hence, any advantages to using a product with recycled content or low VOC emissions could be negatively offset by the environmentally unfriendly processes that were used during the product's life-cycle stages.

The BEES overall performance score for a product includes an environmental and economic performance score (see Figure 5.19). Box 5.2 presents an example of BEES product data for 3.9.2 generic virgin latex interior paint (C3012A). As shown in the box, the BEES software provides a user with the raw materials of the paint, the paint flowchart, and the market shares for the resins used for interior latex paint and

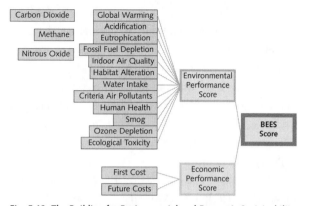

Fig. 5.19. The Building for Environmental and Economic Sustainability (BEES) overall performance score for a product includes an environmental and economic performance score.

primers. The BEES program also provides emissions, transportation, and cost projections. For the latex paint example, first costs include purchase price and installation. Future costs for the paint include replacement, estimates regarding the number of replacements, operations, maintenance, and repair.

Summary

- In a 2004 report, the EPA succinctly identifies some of the most salient effects of the built environment on the natural environment, human health, and the economy.
- The four major assessment methods, representing four continents of the world, are BREEAM from the United Kingdom, Green Star from Australia, CASBEE from Japan, and LEED in North America.
- The LEED system of North America has been gaining significant interest in the past several years. As of 2005, there are approximately 260 certified projects and more than 2,000 registered projects.
- LEED was created to (1) "define 'green building' by establishing a common standard of measurement"; (2) "promote integrated, whole-building design practices"; (3) "recognize environmental leadership in the building industry"; (4) "stimulate green competition"; (5) "raise consumer awareness of green building benefits"; and (6) "transform the building market" (USGBC, 2005, p. 1).
- The Sustainable Sites category is very important for examining how buildings affect ecosystems. The LEED-CI (2005) summarizes that selecting a site that has not been developed, or greenfield, reduces the amount of land that is available for agricultural purposes, wildlife habitats, or recreation.
- In examining the sustainability of water consumption rates, LEED-CI notes, "On an annual basis, the water deficit in the United States is currently estimated at about 3,700 billion gallons. In other words, Americans extract 3,700 billion gallons per year more than they return to the natural water system to recharge aquifers and other water sources."
- To reduce the amount of energy and electricity consumed by buildings, LEED-CI promotes practices that optimize energy performance, enhance commissioning, reduce energy consumption, and increase the use of "green power."
- The LEED-CI defines commissioning as the "process of ensuring that systems are designed, installed, functionally tested, and capable of being operated and maintained to perform in conformity with the design intent" (USGBC, 2005, p. 128).
- Commissioning processes focus on any energy-related systems, such as HVAC&R (heating, ventilating, air-conditioning, and refrigeration) systems, lighting controls, daylighting, domestic hot water systems, and renewable energy systems (PVC, wind, solar, and so on).
- There are many areas in LEED-CI's Materials and Resources category that pertain to the work of interior designers. Sustainable materials and products can significantly improve the environment by minimizing consumption of natural resources and reducing pollutants and waste.
- When reuse is not possible, sustainable designs should have materials and resources that are made from recycled content. Recycled content can be composed of post-consumer and pre-consumer materials.
- A very effective approach to preventing IEQ problems is to specify materials that release the least amount of harmful chemical compounds. Some of the products that require detailed evaluation are adhesives, paint, sealants, coatings, fiberglass, plastic foams, flooring, composite wood products, welded applications, furniture, and cleaning solvents.
- Founded in 1994, the Global Ecolabeling Network (GEN) is a nonprofit association comprised of 26

Box 5.2
3.9.2 Generic Virgin Latex Interior Paint (C3012A)

Major virgin latex paint constituents are resins (binder), titanium dioxide (pigment), limestone (extender), and water (thinner), which are mixed together until they form an emulsion. The figure below displays the system under study for virgin latex paint.

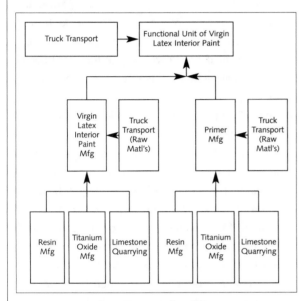

Fig. 3.23. Virgin Latex Interior Paint Flow Chart

RAW MATERIALS. The average composition of the virgin latex paint/primer system modeled in BEES is listed in the table that follows.

Virgin Latex Paint and Primer Constituents

Constituent	Paint (Mass Fraction %)	Primer (Mass Fraction %)
Resin	25	25
Titanium Dioxide	12.5	7.5
Limestone	12.5	7.5
Water	50	60

The table below displays the market shares for the resins used for interior latex paint and primer.

Market Shares of Resin

Resin Type	Market Share (%)
Vinyl Acrylic	40
Polyvinyl	40
Styrene Acrylic	20

The table below shows the components of the three types of resins as modeled in BEES. The production of the monomers used in the resins are based on the DEAM database.

Components of Paint Resins

Resin Type	Components (Mass Fraction)
Vinyl Acrylic	Vinyl Acetate (50%)
	Butyl Acrylate (50%)
Polyvinyl Acetate	Vinyl Acetate (100%)
Styrene Acrylic	Styrene (50%)
	Butyl Acrylate (50%)

EMISSIONS. Emissions associated with paint manufacturing, such as particulates to the air, are based on AP-42 emission factors.

TRANSPORTATION. Truck transportation of raw materials to the paint manufacturing site is assumed to average 402 km (250 mi) for titanium dioxide and limestone and 80 km (50 mi) for the resins.

COST. The detailed life-cycle cost data for this product may be viewed by opening the file LCCOSTS.DBF under the File/Open menu item in the BEES software. Its costs are listed under BEES code C3012, product code A0. First cost data are collected from the R.S. Means publication, *2000 Building Construction Cost Data*, and future cost data are based on data published by Whitestone Research in *The Whitestone Building Maintenance and Repair Cost Reference 1999*, supplemented by industry reviews. Cost data have been adjusted to year-2002 dollars.

SOURCE: Lippiatt, B. C. (2002). *BEES 3.0 Technical Manual and User Guide.* Washington, DC: National Institute of Standards and Technology.

national and multinational third-party environmental performance-labeling organizations.

- ENERGY STAR is an example of a certificate program that focuses on a specific environmental issue.

This program is sponsored by the U.S. government for the purpose of "helping businesses and individuals protect the environment through superior energy efficiency" (ENERGY STAR, 2005, p. 1).

- To determine the effects on IAQ, the Carpet and Rug Institute (CRI) has a Green Label testing program. This program is an independent laboratory that tests carpet, adhesives, and cushion products for chemical emissions.
- The Forest Stewardship Council (FSC) is a nonprofit organization created to encourage the "responsible management of the world's forests."

Key Terms

ANSI/ASHRAE/IESNA 90.1-2004

Building for Environmental and Economic Sustainability (BEES)

California Integrated Waste Management Board (CIWMB)

Carpet America Recovery Efforts (CARE)

Carpet and Rug Institute (CRI)

Chain-of-custody (COC) certificate

CSI MasterFormat™ Division 12

Forest Stewardship Council (FSC)

Green Seal

Greenfield

Greenwash

HVAC&R (heating, ventilating, air-conditioning, and refrigeration)

Indoor environmental quality (IEQ)

Japan Sustainable Building Consortium (JSBC)

LEED for Commercial Interiors (LEED-CI)

LEED for Core and Shell (LEED-CS)

LEED for Homes (LEED-H)

LEED for New Construction and Major Renovations (LEED-NC)

LEED for Neighborhood Development (LEED-ND)

Off-gassed contaminants

Plug loads

Post-consumer

Pre-consumer

Post-industrial content

U.S. National Institute of Standards and Technology (NIST)

Exercises

1. Research the requirements of the four major assessment methods: BREEAM, Green Star, CASBEE, and LEED. In a written report, compare and contrast the organizations' approaches to determining a building's sustainability. Provide suggestions for how the assessment methods affect the work of an interior designer.

2. The LEED rating system is organized by five core credit categories: (1) Sustainable Sites, (2) Water Efficiency, (3) Energy and Atmosphere, (4) Materials and Resources, and (5) Indoor Environmental Quality. In addition, LEED has a category titled Innovation and Design Process. Identify three suggestions for a commercial interior that could qualify for the Innovation and Design Process category.

3. Recycled content can be composed of post-consumer and pre-consumer materials. Research finishes and furnishings specified by interior designers that have post-consumer and pre-consumer materials. Develop a resource file that includes the specifications of post-consumer and pre-consumer products.

4. Many organizations have developed voluntary green or environmental performance certification programs. Research certification programs related to the field of interior design. Develop a portfolio of various certification programs that includes a summary of the organization and how the information can help to enhance the sustainability of a project.

CHAPTER 6

Sustainable Strategies for the Consumption of Natural Resources

Men occupy very little space on Earth. If the two billion inhabitants of the globe were to stand close together, as they might for some big public event, they would easily fit into a city block that was twenty miles long and twenty miles wide. You could crowd all humanity onto the smallest Pacific islet.

Grown-ups, of course, won't believe you.

They consider themselves as important as the baobabs.

—ANTOINE DE SAINT-EXUPÉRY

Objectives

- Understand sustainable strategies for land consumption and apply the criteria to the built environment.
- Identify the elements that contribute to thriving communities.
- Describe sustainable strategies for HVAC systems.
- Understand how to conserve energy and water when working with the built environment.
- Identify and describe the components of lighting systems.
- Apply the principles of sustainability to the components of the building envelope.
- Understand the energy-efficient strategies for windows and water technologies.

CHAPTER 5 INTRODUCED several environmental assessment methods (EAMs) and green labeling programs that are being used worldwide to promote sustainable practice. These initiatives serve as an excellent guide for an interior designer to use when working with commercial and residential clients. From a cautionary perspective, it is very important to view the criteria associated with EAMs as interconnected and interdependent. Each assessment methodology organizes the criteria into five to eight categories. This helps to simplify the assessment process and ensures that the most salient sustainable approaches are reviewed. However, this compartmentalization tends to promote an attitude that each category exists in isolation from the other factors. Thus, it is critical when determining solutions to one of the categories, such as having a sustainable site, that decisions reflect the other attributes of a sustainable project, including meeting the needs for a quality interior environment and conserving energy.

Chapter 6 begins an exploration of the assessment criteria by examining how the requirements impact the design of sustainable interiors. Ideally, by working in a collaborative manner with all of the stakeholders involved with a project, interior designers will have the opportunity to influence decisions that are not normally under their direction but affect the overall sustainability of a project. Thus, an interior designer should be involved with the decisions related to site selection, land use, ecological impacts, and mechanical building systems. Eventually, all of these considerations impact the design of the interior.

In taking a collaborative and holistic approach to sustainable design, Chapter 6 begins by exploring the important factors that should be considered when selecting the site for a project. The overarching theme for this consideration, as well as all the other elements of a sustainable interior, is *reducing consumption*. Thus, reducing consumption is also the point of emphasis for strategies related to energy and water expenditures. Reducing the consumption of natural and human-made resources plays a critical role in managing emissions, which is reviewed in the last section of this chapter.

SUSTAINABLE STRATEGIES FOR CONSUMPTION OF LAND

Frequently, an interior design project begins with site selection. A client needs to find a new location for either a business or a home. In consulting with the client, options should include identifying the site for the building that will optimize societal, environmental, and economic considerations. In focusing on consumption reduction practices, the first priority is selecting a site that has already been used or disturbed by construction activities. Currently, world land use is approximately divided between (1) agricultural/pastoral purposes; (2) natural ecosystems, including forests; and (3) nonproduction uses such as roads, buildings, deserts, and tundra. Using an existing structure, or constructing a new building on previously disturbed land, is becoming even more critical given the estimated population projections.

To accommodate the needs of people and economic activities, building sites in urban settings will have to be conserved, restored, and well planned. Moreover, the suburban sprawl that has been occurring in major metropolitan areas will cease to be a solution for population increases because the farmland will be needed to feed people. The abundant resources that are associated with new construction, such as new roads and utilities, will become scarce or extremely expensive. Depleting natural resources and increasing contaminated emissions have serious implications for the world's ecosystems. Some of the best examples for understanding effective conservation practices are small countries with no area to expand. For example, Japan is a small country that is highly populated. Yet, the surrounding waters prohibit any land expansion or access to other natural resources. Thus, for decades the Japanese have had to strategically manage their land use, conserve natural resources, minimize consumption practices, and maximize vertical space.

Sustainable Site Criteria

The substantial increases in the world's population will have an impact on society, the environment, and the economy. To lessen the impact requires sustainable solutions, which start with a close examination of how people can utilize the resources that have already been expended for the built environment. Thus, in working with a client, an interior designer should suggest a survey of existing structures and building sites. Some of the most important issues are the location of the site, environmental considerations, and the size of the building and interior spaces.

There are many factors that should be considered when selecting a site that promotes sustainability and sustainable practices. In approaching the project as an interconnected and interdependent system, all of the elements that create a sustainable project should be considered at these initial stages. Thus, prior to selecting a site a great deal of planning should be done to identify sustainable solutions, which are intended to be incorporated in the building but are not directly associated with purchasing the site. For example, a building site selected for its low ecological value must also be able to support daylighting and healthy indoor air quality. Thus, an interior designer should strategize with a client to determine how well the site itself fulfills sustainability qualities, as well as the future built environment.

In analyzing the sustainable criteria, which are specific to a site, an important consideration is the condition of the land and building. Environmental assessment methods discourage building on undeveloped land, or greenfields, especially sites that have a high ecological value. In contrast, EAMs allow credit for urban and brownfield redevelopments. This involves reusing land that has been occupied by a building, parking lot, or any condition that has polluted a site. Building on an empty lot, or **infilling**, is also a means of urban redevelopment. Brownfield redevelopment involves remediation procedures that remove contaminants and result in a safe site for a building.

Ecological factors must be considered during the construction phase and after the building exists. Frequently, a great deal of the ecological environment is disturbed during construction of a building. The environment can be negatively affected by the removal of habitats, erosion, changing the topography, reducing biodiversity, and depleting the valuable topsoil. Frequently, new construction requires the removal of trees and hedges, which can cause irrevocable damage to the other living organisms of the ecosys-

tem and destroys some of the natural beauty of the site. This can be especially problematic in areas of high ecological value, such as habitats with species on an endangered list, waterways, or meadows. To reduce the impact to the ecosystems, some EAMs indicate that trees larger than a specific diameter should not be removed. The USGBC is exploring LEED-ND credits for avoiding "environmentally sensitive sites," such as areas that are in floodplains or prime farmland.

Removing natural landscaping contributes to soil erosion and affects the natural flow of water on a site. Altering the flow of water can be very detrimental to the ecosystem and other structures surrounding the building site. Thus, stormwater management becomes a critical element of creating a sustainable site. Removing the topsoil affects the nutrient levels for future plantings and can affect the flow of water during a storm. Some contractors purposely remove the topsoil during construction and sell the valuable resource to people working in other industries. Subsequently, the consumer is left with an impermeable clay soil, in which it is very difficult to dig holes for vegetation, and clay lacks the nutrients required for proper growth. Furthermore, watering plants and trees is a problem because clay does not absorb water very well. Instead of penetrating the soil, water runs off the surface.

In addition to the problems associated with direct disturbance of the land for the **building's footprint**, the construction staging area can also impact the environment. This can occur with new construction or when renovating an existing building. Construction specifications should delineate how and where the staging should be conducted. Care should be taken to avoid the destruction of landscaping and the compaction of soil. Heavy trucks and equipment compact soil and create a surface that prevents the absorption of water. Consequently, water flows over the surface of the ground, and the runoff can create excessive sediment in adjacent ecosystems and/or storm sewers.

In urban settings a major concern is **heat islands**. This occurs from the significant amount of heat-absorbing materials, such as streets, roofs, and parking lots. These surfaces absorb the radiant heat of the sun during the day and then release the warmth

Fig. 6.1. Green roofs help to mediate the effects of heat islands by absorbing the radiant heat from the sun. The vegetation can help to insulate the building, attract wildlife, and absorb rainwater.

during the evening hours. As a result of this phenomenon, the temperature during the day and evening is warmer than what normally should occur in the environment. Consequently, this negatively impacts the ecosystems, people, and the cost of air conditioning. To counteract the effects of heat islands, some people are constructing green roofs, which are gardens constructed on the roof of a building (see Figure 6.1). Green roofs help to mediate the effects of heat islands by absorbing the radiant heat from the sun. The mass helps to insulate the building, and the plant materials attract wildlife. In addition, the garden absorbs rainwater, which helps to reduce negative effects from stormwater.

Sustainable Practices: Thriving Communities and Transportation

The location of the building should also help to sustain ecosystems by reducing the impact to the environment caused by cars traveling to and from the site. Cars emit various pollutants, and the infrastructure required for cars consumes valuable land and resources. Moreover, urban sprawl is promoted when cars are the primary or only mode of transportation to a building. In the United States, people are more willing to live far from a central business district when they can drive to and from work. This is apparent in the growing number of sprawling metropolitan regions in the country (see Figure 6.2). According to Ewing et al., some of the most sprawling areas in the United States include Riverside, California;

Greensboro, North Carolina; and Atlanta, Georgia (2002). Most suburban areas are specifically designed to accommodate cars and have very limited public transportation. Communities that are designed around automobile transportation consume huge amounts of land and resources for roads, driveways, garages, and parking lots. A focus on the importance of automobiles is evident by new homes that have multiple garages. Many homes in developments have a garage that is wider than the front of the house and have more driveway space than green areas (see Figure 6.3). All of the EAMs discourage this type of development and promote lifestyles that are healthy for the environment and people.

Some of the best examples of livable communities are cities developed prior to the mass production of automobiles. Every major city in the world was developed before the automobile. Without cars, cities were planned in a manner that enabled people to

Fig. 6.2. Sprawling metropolitan regions in the United States affect ecosystems, reduce farmland, and increase automobile transportation, and the impermeable surfaces create problems with stormwater runoff.

Fig. 6.3. Many contemporary homes reflect the unsustainable lifestyle associated with excessive consumption of resources. A focus on the automobile is evident by homes with garages wider than the front of the house and more area dedicated to the driveway than to green space.

walk from their homes to amenities, such as schools, stores, and churches. For people to get to work, municipalities had to develop public transportation systems. Thus, in order for people to be mobile it was essential that they lived and worked in the city. Since the city was their home, rather than a place to commute to for employment, people developed an affinity for their neighborhoods. Walking in their neighborhoods helped to foster these feelings. Cities that are designed for walking become livable communities. As people walk along the streets they develop a sense of ownership and pride in their neighborhood. In addition, the presence of many people walking along the neighborhood sidewalks also helps to reduce crime. Statistics reveal that crime is always lower in communities where people are constantly present. A connection to a city and its neighborhoods creates a strong sense of place. Consequently people develop a desire to maintain clean and attractive environments.

Livable communities promote sustainability by enhancing the lives of people, improving the local economy, and reducing the impact to the environment. For these reasons and many more, EAMs promote sites that encourage people to walk or use public transportation. Sustainable communities are diverse in their offerings. A neighborhood should have buildings for businesses, education, religious services, recreation, and housing that can accommodate various income levels. Diversity is also reflected

in modes of transportation, such as walking, mass transit, and bicycles. The availability of public transportation is especially important for people who are unable to drive a car due to a disability or age restrictions. Communities that encourage use of public transportation and cycling must have the infrastructure to support the activities. Mass transit must be at reasonable cost, reliable, safe, and convenient and maintain a schedule of frequent arrivals and departures. Facilities designed for waiting must be safe and protected from adverse weather.

To encourage cycling, a community must build and maintain paths and provide bike storage units and ideally accessible facilities for showering and changing clothes (see Figure 6.4). Lyon, France, has been very successful with a program that allows people to rent bicycles from publicly owned racks (see Figure 6.5). Patrons can rent the bikes for one euro ($1.20) per hour, but the first 30 minutes is free (Ó hAnluain, 2005). As of 2005, during a three-month period 15,000 individuals used the bikes for 4,000 trips per day. The trips totaled more than 24,800 miles per week using 2,000 bikes, located at 150 bike stations. Interior spaces should be designed to encourage this type of sustainable behavior. An employer or community that is interested in promoting cycling should have locked facilities for bike storage, locker rooms, and showers. Residential dwellings should have facilities that are designed to provide easy access to use and storage.

a

b

c

Fig. 6.4a–c. (left) To encourage cycling, a community must provide bike storage services and, ideally, accessible facilities for showering and changing clothes.
Fig. 6.5. (above) One of the 150 Vélo'v bike stations in Lyon, France. The city has been very successful with a new program that allows people to rent bicycles from publicly owned racks.

Sustainable Footprints and Interior Spaces

In focusing on reducing consumption of resources, site selection should also focus on smaller lots and reducing the square footage of a building. To reduce land consumption and the subsequent impacts on the environment, individuals and communities must address density issues. As noted in Chapter 2, the U.S.

population density per square mile is low compared to the world average. The less developed countries have the highest population density per square mile. Generally, cities and countries with high population densities per square mile, such as Tokyo, provide good examples of how to conserve space and resources (see Figure 6.6).

It is important for existing buildings and new construction to minimize the size of the buildings while maximizing the effectiveness of the interiors. In the United States, during the last half of the twentieth century, there has been a significant increase in the size of buildings, especially residential dwellings. A recent study conducted by the National Association of Realtors (2005) indicates that in 1950 the average house size was 1,905 sq. ft.; 18 percent had garages; and the average size of the lot was 17,600 sq. ft. In 2005, the average house size was 2,349 sq. ft.; 83 percent were built with garages; and the average lot size was 15,788 sq. ft. Thus, in 55 years the size of the average American home increased approximately 20 percent, and the number of garages increased about 80 percent.

These figures reflect very unsustainable practices. Residences have been increasing in size during the past 50 years, but the average number of people in a family has been decreasing. Furthermore, the 80 percent increase in garages reflects a focus on dedicating resources for the automobile. The minimal decrease in the size of the lot could indicate that many homes are built on a lot size that is too small for the building's footprint. This pattern is good for trying to reduce land use; however, larger residential structures require more finishes, furnishings, maintenance, and energy consumption. Larger structures require more energy for heating and air conditioning, which results in more emissions. Moreover, larger residences create more areas that are impermeable, which contributes to problems associated with stormwater. From an aesthetic perspective, a large structure built on a small lot is not in scale. The focus must be to encourage clients to reduce the size of buildings.

Reducing the size of buildings requires more attention to efficient space utilization, or **spatial strategies** (see Box 6.1). Spatial strategies are required for sustainable designs. The concept of spatial strategies is practiced in the European Union, where the land-locked countries are trying to maximize their limited resources. Spatial strategies are a dynamic participatory decision-making process that involves all the stakeholders. The essence of the concept is to make spatial decisions that are based on immediate needs of a client and forecasted long-term changes. Decisions are based on the goals of a client and the external environment, such as economic conditions, population changes, and technological advancements. The ongoing process monitors the success of spatial decisions and continuously implements adjustments to shifting conditions.

Implementing spatial strategies expands on the traditional practice of *space planning*. The principles of space planning started in the mid-twentieth century when interior designers created flexible layouts, which accommodated expansions and changes in workplace operations. To facilitate communication, small working units, and paper flow, the Quickborner Team developed the open office layout. These interiors, which supported the way that people work, became very popular, especially in the United States. Sustainable interiors should incorporate the principles of space planning and strategize space. Sustainable interiors require strategies for space planning that reduce the size of buildings and accommodate the diverse needs of people.

The conceptual perspective embedded in the term *spatial strategy* is an effective means to design sustainable interiors. To strategize the design of an interior necessitates a great deal of planning in the early stages of the project. Spatial strategies for sustainable designs begin with reducing square footage. Purchasing or building smaller buildings has a ripple effect on all of the other elements associated with structures. Smaller buildings lead to less construction materials, less materials for the building envelope, less flooring, less furnishings, less furniture, less accessories, less energy, less construction waste, and in the future less waste from renovation and/or restoration. To be successful, smaller-sized interiors must have spatial strategies. This involves designing spaces that are the appropriate size and shape for the purpose

Fig. 6.6. Cities that have high densities must learn to conserve resources.

Box 6.1
Principles of Spatial Strategies

Maximize Space by Strategizing a Space

- Plan the appropriate square footage for the required activities.
- Determine the size and shape of a room *after* developing the ideal furniture arrangement for the activities in a room.
- Determine the ideal proportions for the activities and furnishings.
- Identify effective use of vertical space.
- Reduce the number of objects in a room.
- Position doors, windows, and openings in locations that support furniture arrangements, activities, and circulation.
- Locate HVAC elements, electrical outlets, and lighting in locations that support furniture arrangements, activities, and circulation.
- Create an appropriate balance between positive and negative space.
- Base the size and shape of a room on needs of the users, rather than conforming to typical room dimensions.
- Plan nonrestrictive ceiling and flooring systems.
- Plan for anticipated changes in program requirements.
- Locate walls and partitions that support furniture arrangements, activities, circulation, daylight, views to the outdoors, natural ventilation, and safe egress.

- Plan appropriate locations for short- and long-term storage.
- Specify furniture that is the appropriate scale.
- Specify furniture that appears to have small mass.
- Lessen the perception of a small room by strategizing the elements and principles of design.
- Plan for the perceived weight that can be associated with the vertical dimension of objects.
- Plan for anticipated changes in equipment and technology.

Maximize Space by Strategizing the Integration of Multiple Spaces

- Reduce or eliminate transitional spaces.
- Reduce or eliminate hallways.
- Plan the most direct paths for circulation.
- Plan for versatile shared spaces.
- Plan vista openings to adjacent rooms.
- Use alternative methods to walls and partitions, such as steps with low risers; altering ceiling heights; or changing surface materials, colors, or textures.
- Determine the ideal number of rooms for the needs of the users.
- Design multipurpose rooms.
- Conform to the requirements of the ADA.
- Plan for safety, security, thermal comfort, noise reduction, daylighting, views to the outdoors, and natural ventilation.

---

of the room and its contents. In strategizing a floor plan, an interior designer should integrate the client's needs with the appropriate furniture and space needs. Spatial strategies involve integrating furniture placement with the location of openings, such as windows and doors. Circulation paths should be direct and no wider than what is necessary for safe passage. The size of furniture should be on an appropriate scale for smaller rooms.

Addressing the needs of end-users is critical for sustainable designs. People who are pleased with the built environment are more likely to stay in the building. This helps to save natural resources, because people who enjoy their interior space are less

inclined to construct a new building or remodel the existing space. Thus, a sustainable interior must address the multiple needs of its users, including functional requirements, accessibility, economics, thermal comfort, and maintenance demands. Encouraging a long-term commitment to a building also involves spatial strategies that enable users to modify rooms as changes occur in future years. For example, a residence could have spatial strategies that enable a family to alter the interior later in life. A business might need the flexibility to rearrange office space when the company either expands or reduces operations. A building might have multipurpose spaces that accommodate various activities and have the flexibility to meet the needs of ever-changing equipment and/or technology.

Increases in the size of buildings are reflected in the additional rooms in residences. Sustainable interiors should have spatial strategies that optimize the rooms that are needed while eliminating rooms that are not necessary. For example, in reflecting the lifestyles of people in the United States, most households do not need a living room and a family room. Commercial interiors should examine spaces that are no longer needed or operations that could be replaced by technological means. For example, an office that utilizes space to store files could transfer the material to electronic formats. In addition to reducing the number of rooms, spatial strategies should be applied to the amount of square footage allotted for activities. A thorough review should be performed to assess the rationale for the size of a room. This is especially important for rooms that have had significant increases in the last 50 years, such as kitchens, master bedrooms, and bathrooms. In addition to examining the rationale for large rooms the analysis should review how small spaces affect the functional and psychological needs of people. For example, businesses have reduced the work area for employees by substituting private offices for systems furniture. A spatial review would examine how these configurations affect job satisfaction and productivity. An analysis of space requirements is critical for rooms that are used infrequently. For example, frequently conference rooms may not be used on a regular basis. Most educational buildings are vacant for months during the summer. Starting at preschool through higher education, the educational sector represents extensive quantities of the built environment.

SUSTAINABLE STRATEGIES FOR MECHANICAL SYSTEMS AND LIGHTING

Smaller buildings reduce the amount of energy needed for buildings. This results in fewer pollutants and economic savings. In addition to reducing the size of buildings, there are many technical areas that are important for sustainable interiors. The areas include the mechanical systems, building envelope, lighting, and water technologies. Architects and engineers design most of these technical areas, but an interior designer should have an understanding of the critical elements that impact the design of interiors. This knowledge is important when communicating with a client and when serving as a member of the project's team.

Sustainable designs require a **whole building design approach**. This entails considering and planning all of the elements of a building, such as the site, orientation, building envelope, mechanical systems, equipment, products, needs of its users, and economic issues. The whole building design approach is necessary to ensure the appropriate integration of the equipment, products, and systems that are components of the built environment. For example, the size and orientation of a building affect the design of a passive or active solar system. The type and placement of windows can affect the design of a lighting system.

An important element of the whole building design approach is proper **commissioning**. Building commissioning is a process that helps to ensure that all of the systems in a building, including HVAC, lighting, and hot water equipment, are functioning and performing as intended. Commissioning is a prerequisite for LEED-CI and a credit is available for enhanced commissioning. Enhanced commissioning involves processes that extend beyond fundamental commissioning, such as designating a commissioning authority and developing a commissioning manual. The stakeholders involved with the project, including the interior designer, should be members of the commissioning team. The most effective commissioning process occurs in four phases: pre-design, design, construction, and warranty. The pre-design phase includes identifying a commissioning provider and determining key strategies that will conserve energy and facilitate operations. During the design phase it is imperative that the strategies identified in the pre-design phase are implemented throughout the design of the building. The construction phase involves testing the equipment and correcting any element of a system that does not perform as intended. The warranty phase occurs after a building is occupied and generally continues up to one year. The purpose of the warranty phase is to verify the intended functions of the systems and provide any training that might be necessary for operations and maintenance.

To maximize effectiveness, the whole building

approach must involve all of the professionals involved with designing the project as well as its stakeholders. A collaborative approach can employ a charrette to explore the most important issues that affect the client, architects, engineers, interior designers, and community representatives. The holistic approach involving all the constituents should be initiated during the earliest stages of the design process, and continue through post-occupancy evaluations. (See Unit III for more information regarding stages in the design process.)

Sustainable Strategies for Mechanical Systems

Buildings consume a large percentage of the energy consumed in the United States and are responsible for generating large quantities of carbon dioxide, sulfur dioxide, and nitrogen oxide. Given the depleting supplies of nonrenewable natural resources, increases in pollution levels, and the high cost of energy, buildings must be designed to optimize energy. To establish levels of energy efficiency, LEED-CI requires a minimum compliance with ANSI/ASHRAE/IESNA Standard 90.1-2004 or any local energy code that might be more stringent, such as California Title 24. Standard 90.1-2004 is the U.S. energy standard for buildings, except low-rise residential buildings. The standard provides the minimum requirements for the energy efficiency of buildings in the following categories: section 5: building envelope; section 6: heating, ventilating, and air-conditioning; section 7: service water heating; section 8: power; section 9: lighting; and section 10: other equipment.

To exceed Standard 90.1-2004 requires strategies that optimize energy performance. The LEED-certified buildings have been able to enhance energy performance by focusing on the following components: integrated HVAC systems, natural ventilation, raised flooring distribution methods, daylighting, electrical lighting sources, insulation, windows, and renewable energy sources. The accumulated savings from all the components in a building optimizes energy performance. Energy savings are based on regional climate zones. Energy costs for buildings in northern Minnesota are dramatically different from those in San Diego, California.

To optimize energy performance, LEED-CI provides credit for energy-efficient equipment and appliances. The credit includes ENERGY STAR eligible equipment and appliances, including refrigerators, freezers, dishwashers, clothes washers, office equipment, electronics, and commercial food service equipment. The credit does not include HVAC, lighting, and building envelope products. Credit is based on the rated power in watts, which is the nameplate power on appliances or equipment. In addition, LEED-CI examines the *plug load*, which represents all equipment and appliances that are plugged into the building's electrical system.

To reduce the depletion of the ozone layer, a holistic approach to buildings includes reducing chlorofluorocarbons (CFCs) in HVAC and refrigeration systems. The LEED-CI (2005) requires zero use of CFC-based refrigerants in new HVAC&R and fire-suppression systems; LEED-CI indicates that refrigerants should have a short environmental lifetime, low **ozone-depleting potentials (ODPs)**, and low **global-warming potentials (GWPs)**. However, based on a LEED Steering Committee study in 2004, an environmentally friendly refrigerant does not exist. The Montreal Protocol has banned CFCs, and another refrigerant, hydrochlorofluorocarbons (HCFCs), will be phased out by 2020 for new equipment. Refrigerants will still be able to use an alternative compound, hydrofluorocarbons (HFCs), but HFCs are greenhouse gases, and hence contribute to global warming. In addition, HFCs require more power than the other refrigerants; thus, HFCs cause more carbon dioxide emissions. Refrigerants are an environmental problem with no short-term solution. Substances either cause ozone depletion or global warming, and all refrigerants contribute to carbon dioxide pollution. The LEED Steering Committee encourages LEED users to evaluate both atmospheric effects when selecting a refrigerant. The committee also recommends that the current LEED *Energy and Atmosphere* credit be "renamed from its current 'ozone protection credit' to 'refrigerant selection credit' to reflect its broadened purview" (2004, p. v).

An integrated and holistic approach to energy efficiency requires strategies that focus on reducing the demands on HVAC systems. This requires buildings that are designed to be sensitive and responsive to climatic conditions. During the years of relatively inexpensive energy, buildings were designed to accommodate volumetric space without serious consideration to conserving energy. The evolving focus on sustainable design has initiated buildings that are designed to maximize energy performance. Thus, energy considerations are starting to stimulate the design of the architecture. For example, the Beddington Zero Energy Development (Bed ZED), an urban village in the United Kingdom, has numerous sustainable features that define the architectural design of the structure (see Figure 6.7). Passive solar benefits are derived from the wall of windows and the sun-space conservatories, which are located on the south side of the buildings. Photovoltaic modules installed on the facades of the units generate electricity. Extended cowls on the roof help to provide natural ventilation and expel stale air. New strategies for designing the shell of a building affect the work of an interior designer by impacting floor plans, furniture arrangements, and product selections.

The efficiency of the design of a building affects the loads on HVAC systems. Sustainable strategies for HVAC systems focus on optimizing energy use and maintaining healthy air quality. The four major ways to transfer heat are through convection, conduction, radiation, and evaporation. In convection a space becomes heated by warm air passing through a room. Conduction occurs by heat being transferred from one source to another solid mass. Heat is transferred by infrared radiation by passing through space, such as the generation of heat from a fire or the sun. Heat can be generated by evaporation, as when a body sweats. Heating systems produce warmth by heating air, water, or steam, or directly by radiation. A furnace creates heat by blowing air over warming units that is then circulated through the building. In hot-water heating systems, water is heated and then pumped through pipes. Radiators or heat exchangers transfer the heat into the space. Radiant heat can be derived from heated air or water. The pipes distributing the heat can be located in floors, ceilings, or walls. Heat pumps heat and cool buildings. To warm a building, heat is derived from outside air, or from water when a geothermal well is embedded deep in the earth. To cool a building, heat pumps reverse the operation.

Sustainable designs have prompted considerable attention to ventilation systems. This is due to the growing concern regarding indoor air quality and the high energy consumption rates associated with air-conditioning. Ventilation systems regulate the flow of air by controlling odors and contaminants. A special concern is maintaining healthy levels of carbon dioxide. Effective ventilation systems should remove stale air and balance thermal comfort, while

Fig. 6.7. The Beddington Zero Energy Development (Bed ZED) in the United Kingdom has numerous sustainable features, including passive solar benefits from the windows and sun-space conservatories; photovoltaic modules that generate electricity; and extended cowls on the roof to provide natural ventilation and expel stale air.

being unnoticed by the occupants. Systems are designed for natural and mechanically assisted ventilation. Natural ventilation is air movement that flows through a building without the assistance of mechanical means. Mechanically assisted ventilation includes a fan that forces air movement. Sustainable designs strategically position windows and skylights to maximize natural ventilation, without having to supplement with mechanically assisted systems. However, in analyzing energy consumption, mechanically assisted ventilation systems are preferable to air-conditioning.

A great deal of attention has focused on improving natural ventilation. An effective means to create the natural flow of air is through cross-ventilation. To create cross-ventilation, an effective approach is to locate windows across from each other in a room (see Figure 6.8). Tall towers can also be used to draw the air vertically through a building. These techniques are incorporated in many homes built in warm climates (see Figure 6.9). An excellent example of utilizing natural air to ventilate a building is the Coventry University Library in the United Kingdom. The building has natural cross-ventilation from windows surrounding the building. Several large light wells serve as shafts to deliver ventilation and provide daylight (see Figure 6.10).

Air-conditioning systems operate by removing heat and humidity from the air. In working like a refrigerator, heat is removed from the air and is exhausted to the outdoors, or to the ground via a geothermal system. Humidity is removed from the air by mechanical cooling or desiccant cooling/dehumidification. Mechanical cooling removes moisture by condensation, and the desiccant process works by absorbing moisture. Some sustainable strategies in large buildings have included desiccant dehumidification, because the system utilizes less electricity and the process reduces the growth of molds.

There are a variety of approaches that can be used to optimize the energy performance of HVAC systems. A high priority is specifying high-efficiency units. The LEED-CI (2005) indicates that efficiency requirements must comply with or exceed the New Buildings Institute's publication *Advanced Buildings: Energy Benchmark for High Performance Buildings (E-Benchmark)*, and ANSI/ASHRAE/IESNA Standard 90.1-2004. To conserve energy, HVAC systems should be properly sized for normal operating scenarios, rather than planning the system for the most severe conditions. In addition, when a client is anticipating an expansion, the system should be designed for the existing facilities, rather than oversizing the equipment to accommodate potential increases in square footage. History has demonstrated that frequently expansions do not occur. In situations when an addition has been built, typically technological improvements make the original system obsolete. Thus, a new and appropriately sized system should be installed. Operating some equipment during off-peak

Fig. 6.8. A great deal of attention has focused on improving natural ventilation. An effective means to create the natural flow of air is through cross-ventilation.

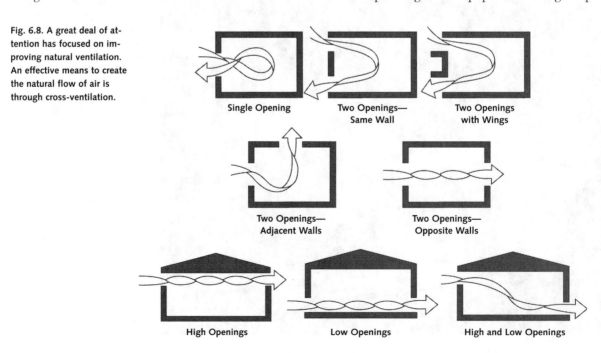

Single Opening Two Openings—Same Wall Two Openings with Wings

Two Openings—Adjacent Walls Two Openings—Opposite Walls

High Openings Low Openings High and Low Openings

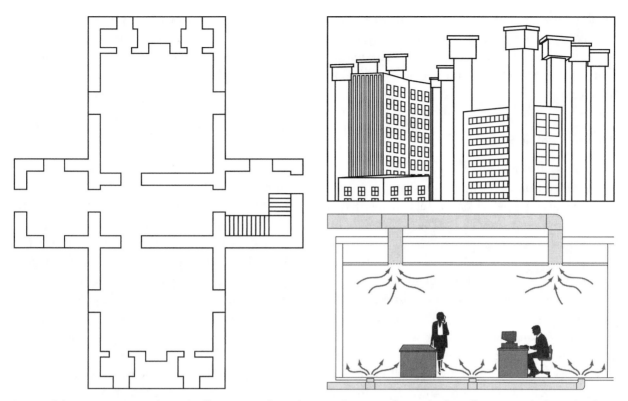

Fig. 6.9. (left) To create cross-ventilation, an effective approach is to locate windows across from each other. Tall towers can also be used to draw the air vertically through a building.

Fig. 6.10. (right, top) An excellent example of utilizing natural air to ventilate a building is the Coventry University Library in the United Kingdom. The building has natural cross-ventilation from windows surrounding the building. Several large light wells serve as shafts to deliver ventilation and provide daylight.

Fig. 6.11. (right, bottom) Underfloor systems deliver air through diffusers located in the floor. Air is returned through exhaust outlets in the ceiling. An underfloor air distribution system distributes the newly conditioned air in the areas where people are working.

periods and selecting equipment that can operate with partial loads can improve energy performance of HVAC systems.

Components of HVAC Systems

To accommodate the needs of HVAC systems, interior designers must plan for a variety of units, including registers, grilles, baseboard heaters, radiators, and returns. A common HVAC approach for commercial buildings has been to use overhead air distribution systems. These systems have diffusers and returns in the ceiling. In designing the lighting for a space, an interior designer must locate fixtures around these mechanical units.

To improve IAQ and the thermal comfort of people, sustainable design strategies have focused on *underfloor air distribution* and *access floor systems*. Underfloor systems deliver air through diffusers located in the floor, and air is returned through exhaust outlets in the ceiling. Distributing the newly conditioned air in

the area where people are working provides the optimum comfort level for users of the space (see Figure 6.11). One method for underfloor air distribution is the **displacement ventilation system**. This system provides two zones of air. The lower zone is where the fresh air exists and the upper zone contains the stale air. The displacement ventilation system is found to provide the healthiest air quality, because the pollutant levels are the lowest where people are standing or working in the space. Access floor systems are floor panels that are located above the structural floor. The space between the structural floor and the floor panels is used to house HVAC equipment and wiring for electrical power, voice, and data systems. Underfloor air distribution and access floor systems significantly affect the work of an interior designer. The floor area around diffusers must be clear for the appropriate flow of air. The easy availability of wiring through floor panels provides more flexibility when spaces are reconfigured. The elimination of diffusers in the ceiling provides more options for the placement of light fixtures. However, depending on the construction of the ceiling, it may not be possible to install recessed fixtures, and installing electrical wiring in the ceiling could also be problematic.

Interior Lighting Systems

Specifying efficient lighting systems can optimize energy performance. Lighting is responsible for approximately 40 percent of the electricity that is used in commercial buildings. Thus, efficient lighting systems have an important role in conserving nonrenewable resources that are used to generate electricity and reducing the pollutants emitted from power plants. A lighting system consists of electricity, lamps, luminaires or fixtures, ballasts, controls, maintenance, and service. Each component of the system should be energy efficient, and to maximize efficiencies it is very important that all of the elements of the system are compatible. Differences in product requirements can occur within a manufacturer's line and can vary between manufacturers. Daylighting should be used to illuminate interiors and, whenever possible, renewable energy sources should be used to power lighting systems.

The type of lamp used in the system can have a dramatic impact on the consumption of energy. In specifying a lamp, an interior designer should review the output, efficacy, lamp life, color, maintenance considerations, and cost. Most of these lamp data are available from manufacturers. The **light output** of a lamp is measured in **lumens**. The energy efficiency of a lamp is determined by its **efficacy**, or **lumens per watt (lpW)**. Thus, the most efficient lamps emit a high amount of lumens, while using a small amount of electricity. Efficient lamps should also have a long life. The life of a lamp is determined by how long it takes for approximately 50 percent of 100 lamps to burn out. Lamps with a long life help to save resources by reducing the number of lamps that are manufactured and decrease the amount of waste going to a landfill.

Color characteristics of a lamp are reflected in the **chromaticity** and **color-rendering index (CRI)**. Chromaticity of a light source indicates the degree of warmth or coolness, measured in kelvins (K). For example, cool daylight is 5,000 K and light emitted from candlelight is 2,000 K. The CRI is a means to indicate how well objects appear under a light source. The scale is 0–100, whereby 100 represents the best rendering ability. Generally, lamps that have higher CRI ratings consume more electricity than lamps with lower ratings.

Maintenance considerations include cleaning and relamping. For sustainable designs, lamps should be cleaned on a regular basis. Dust, dirt, and grease that accumulate on the bulb reduce the lumen output, yet the amount of energy used to illuminate the lamp remains the same. This results in a waste of electricity. The same situation can occur when a lamp is close to the end of its life. These lamps consume the same quantity of electricity, but operate at a reduced lumen output. Thus, to conserve electricity and promote safe interiors, lamp maintenance procedures should monitor the light output and relamping should occur at the optimum time. Controls and **building management systems (BMS)** provide a convenient and efficient means to monitor lighting systems. (Controls and energy management systems are reviewed later in this chapter.)

Cost of a lamp includes the initial purchase, installation, energy consumption, and replacement considerations. The cost of lamps is another important factor in sustainable designs. The initial cost of some efficient sources, such as **compact fluorescent lamps (CFLs)**, can be more than for lamps that use higher quantities of electricity. Thus, frequently people purchase the cheapest lamp, even though the overall lifetime cost of the lamp is higher. This results in higher energy consumption and the generation of more pollutants. In addition, generally lamps that have low lpW ratings do not have a long life. Consequently, more resources are used to replace the lamps and unnecessary waste is deposited in the landfills. Waste can be especially problematic when lamps contain hazardous materials such as mercury.

The **incandescent lamp** is the oldest electrical light source, and the operational components have not changed significantly since its invention by Thomas Edison and Joseph Swan. Light is created in an incandescent lamp by having an electric current heat a tungsten filament until incandescence. The lamps have excellent color rendering properties and a color temperature between 2,600 and 3,000 K. Incandescent lamps have several characteristics that do not support sustainable designs. Only about 10–15 percent of the energy that is consumed by the lamp results in illumination. The other 85–90 percent results in heat. Thus, the lpW is not efficient and the heat slowly destroys the tungsten filament. Once the filament is destroyed, the lamp burns out. Heat generated by an incandescent lamp results in a short lamp life and imposes additional loads on air-conditioning systems. **Halogen lamps** are in the incandescent family, but the lamp's regenerative cycle helps to improve its function by redepositing tungsten on the filament. Thus, halogen lamps are slightly more efficient than standard incandescent lamps. To improve the efficiency of the halogen lamp, the halogen infrared reflecting (HIR) lamp was developed. Halogen lamps become very hot; thus, dissipating the heat is a significant problem and a potential fire hazard.

Fluorescent lamps are a discharge source, thus they do not have a filament, and operate on low or high pressure. Originally, fluorescent lamps had poor color-rendering properties and relatively cool color temperatures. The development of triphosphors, which coat the lamp's glass tube, has improved color properties and efficacy ratings. Fluorescent lamps are very efficient compared to incandescent lamps. Fluorescents consume approximately 80 percent less energy and have a life that is 18 times longer than incandescent lamps. Some fluorescent lamps are rated to last over 20,000 hours. Moreover, fluorescent lamps generate very little heat, which has a positive impact on thermal conditions. The T12 (tubular shape with a 12"/8" (1½") diameter) lamp was a very common lamp used in commercial application. However, for energy conservation purposes, the T12 lamp is being replaced by the T8. The T8's lpW is approximately 25 percent better than the T12's. The T5 lamp is gaining popularity, but the lamp is only slightly more efficient than the T8 and poses retrofit problems.

To incorporate the efficiency of fluorescent lamps into incandescent applications, manufacturers created compact fluorescent lamps (CFLs), which are available in a variety of sizes and shapes (see Figure 6.12 a and b). Basically, bending the tube shape of the traditional fluorescent lamp creates CFLs. These lamps have a series of tubes or a circular shape. The Department of Energy (DOE) has provided efficiency

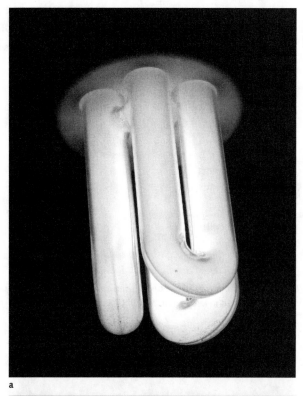

a

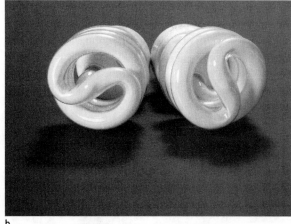

b

Fig. 6.12a–b. Compact fluorescent lamps (CFLs) are available in a variety of sizes and shapes. Bending the tube shape of the traditional fluorescent lamp creates CFLs.

recommendations for replacing incandescent lamps with CFLs (see Table 6.1). For emitting the same amount of lumens, CFLs consume considerably less electricity than incandescent lamps. The DOE has determined that CFLs are three to four times more efficient than standard incandescent lamps; CFLs last about 10 times longer than incandescent lamps and generate very little heat.

High-intensity discharge (HID) lamps are extremely efficient electrical light sources. The three basic HID types are mercury vapor, metal halide, and

Table 6.1

The Department of Energy (DOE) Efficiency Recommendations for Replacing Incandescent Lamps with CFLs

To Replace Incandescent Bulb Rated At:	Necessary Light Output (Lumens)	Typical CFL Replacement Wattage[a]	Recommended CFL Lumens per Watt (lpW)
Bare Bulbs[b]			
40 watts	495 or more	11–14 watts	45 lpW or more
60 watts	900 or more	15–19 watts	60 lpW or more
75 watts	1200 or more	20–25 watts	60 lpW or more
100 watts	1750 or more	≥ 29 watts	60 lpW or more
Reflector Type Bulbs			
50 watts	550 or more	17–19 watts	33 lpW or more
60 watts	675 or more	20–21 watts	40 lpW or more
75 watts	875 or more	≥ 22 watts	40 lpW or more

[a] Some more efficient lower wattage CFLs can produce equivalent light output to the corresponding incandescent (listed in left-hand column); to assure sufficient lighting, make sure the CFL replacement provides at least enough lumens.

[b] Covered bulbs have lower lumens per watt. Recommended lpW for covered lamps are as follows: ≤ 14 watts: 40 lpW; 15–19 watts: 48 lpW; 20–24 watts: 50 lpW; ≥ 25 watts: 55 lpW.

SOURCE: The Department of Energy (DOE) (2000), *How to Buy Energy-Efficient Compact Fluorescent Light Bulbs.*

high-pressure sodium. The least efficient, mercury vapor lamps, are being replaced by the other two HID lamps. The HID lamps are excellent choices for applications that require high efficacy, long life, operation in a range of temperatures, and economic savings. Color rendering has been a problem with HID lamps. Metal halide lamps produce a color close to white, but high-pressure sodium lamps emit an orange-gold color. The ceramic metal halide (CMH) lamp is an improved version of the standard metal halide. The CMH lamps have improved efficacy, lumen maintenance, color rendition, and lamp life. Due to the enhanced color-rendering properties, metal halide lamps are the preferred choice for interior applications.

Light-emitting diodes (LEDs) and **organic light-emitting diodes (OLEDs)** are electrical light sources that have the greatest potential to be an extremely efficient source for many interior applications. The LEDs and OLEDs are solid-state electronic light sources. The OLEDs are used in very thin applications, such as automobile dashboards. As a semiconductor device, LEDs have a chemical chip embedded in a plastic capsule (see Figure 6.13). An electrical charge energizes the chip and produces light. Light is focused, or scattered, by lenses or diffusers. The LEDs can last up to 100,000 hours and do not emit heat. The chemicals contained in the chip determine the color of light. Producing LEDs in an attractive white color has been one of the challenges for engineers. Another major problem with LEDs is the low lumen output. However, every year the industry introduces new and improved LEDs. Currently LEDs are an excellent sustainable choice for building exit signs and traffic lights.

Electric discharge lamps, such as fluorescent and HID sources, require ballasts for operation. A ballast is a device that starts a lamp and controls the electrical current during operation. Ballasts are available in magnetic and electronic versions. Electronic ballasts are preferred for sustainable designs because of the increases in energy efficiencies and the enhancement of lamp output and life. The high-frequency electronic ballast was designed to work with the efficient T8 lamp. The combination of the two components results in a system that is very energy efficient, easier to maintain, and demonstrates long lamp life. Fluorescent ballasts are available in several different types: rapid start, instant start, program rapid start, and dimming electronic. Rapid start ballasts are the most frequently used because they help to prolong the life of lamps and are economical. Instant start ballasts are inexpensive, but are most effective in applications where lights remain on for long periods of time. The system is not as effective when lights are frequently turned on and off.

Program rapid start ballasts are considered the best choice for sustainable designs because they are the most energy efficient and they help to prolong lamp life. Dimming electronic ballasts provide the flexibility to change the illumination levels on fluorescent lamps. The range of dimming is dependent on the type of ballast. Dimming can provide some energy savings. Multiple-lamp ballasts are available to accommodate several lamps. Electronic HID ballasts provide energy efficiency for metal halide lamps. However, there are dimming and wattage limitations. All ballasts require electricity for operation. Thus, in determining power loads, the energy needs of ballasts should always be included in calculations. In working as a system, the ballast must operate with the appropriate lamp, wattage, and controls.

The luminaire or light fixture is the device that coordinates the various components of a lighting system. Thus, for sustainable designs, careful consideration should be afforded to selecting the luminaire. Luminaires that are rated for high-efficiency should be specified for commercial and residential interiors. After an energy-efficient lamp has been selected, a luminaire should be selected that will maximize the lumen output for the intended lighting purpose. The primary methods for distributing light from a luminaire are direct, indirect, semi-direct, semi-indirect, and diffused. A direct distribution emits approximately 90 percent of the light down on a task or plane. In contrast, an indirect distribution results in most of the light upward. Semi-direct occurs when most of the light is direct, but some of the illumination is indirect. Semi-indirect is the opposite, whereby most of the illumination is indirect and some of the light is direct. Diffused sources emit light in all directions. For sustainable designs, selecting the type of distribution provided by a luminaire should be a priority, because an efficient distribution of light conserves energy. Light that exists in areas that do not require illumination wastes energy. The distribution of light from a luminaire should fall in the area where light is needed to perform a task or fulfill another purpose.

The distribution of light and the quantity of illumination are determined by the light source, the shape of the luminaire, the material used to house the lamp, and the type of device that might be shielding the light. Light sources with optical control, such as reflector lamps, have internal designs that distribute light in a specific beam spread. These lamps can emit light in a spot, which is a small concentrated area, or in a wide area, such as what occurs with a flood lamp. Some lamps, such as fluorescents, have a diffused spread of light with no optical control. The interior shape of the luminaire can affect the quantity and distribution of light. Luminaire manufacturers provide this photometric data by illustrating the candlepower distribution at the horizontal and vertical angles. This information can be especially useful when nondirectional light sources are used in the luminaire.

Light distribution and quantity are affected by the type of material and the color of the luminaire's interior housing. A smooth and light-colored surface will reflect the greatest amount of light. A rough surface and dark colors tend to absorb light. A smooth finish reflects light at a more direct angle. A rough finish tends to scatter the distribution of light. Luminaires have a variety of units to reflect, diffuse, or shield a light source. Each device has a unique way of directing the light, which affects the quantity of illumination. The placement of the luminaire affects the quantity of illumination within a specific area and contributes to the overall user satisfaction of the interior. For optimum performance, luminaires should be installed according to the manufacturer's specifications. This will help to ensure the proper amount of illumination required for an area and, hence, avoid wasting energy. Luminaire installation should also take into consideration air infiltration that can occur

Fig. 6.13. As a semiconductor device, LEDs have a chemical chip embedded in a plastic capsule.

in and out of the building's envelope. Energy can be wasted by leaks surrounding a luminaire or openings within the fixture itself. Energy-efficient luminaires are designed to control for air infiltration. Some applications require rated, **insulated ceiling–air-tight (IC–AC)** type housings.

To avoid excessive illumination levels, luminaires should be planned to accommodate a specific purpose. Frequently, a commercial interior has a symmetrical grid pattern of illumination, with a uniform distribution of light throughout the space regardless of varying needs and activities (see Figure 6.14). For example, in an office plan the hallways do not need the same amount of illumination as workstations. Sustainable designs require lighting plans that specify luminaires in the proper location, with the appropriate amount of lumens. Conventional layouts, which have a uniform distribution of luminaires with the same amount of illumination, are no longer a feasible approach to lighting interiors.

Controls are a very effective means to provide the flexibility in illumination levels that is needed for energy-efficient interiors. Research indicates that controls can save up to 45 percent of the electricity used for lighting (Agogino, 2005). Significant technological improvements in controls have led to the development of systems that are easy to use, conserve energy, and provide the flexibility to serve the unique needs of each user. Controls are available in conventional modes, automated, or a combination of both. In rooms with a variety of activities and/or spaces that are usually occupied, manual rather than automatic controls may be the best choice. Building networks or the Ethernet/Internet enable users to access controls from remote locations.

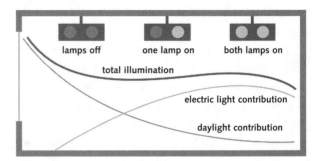

Fig. 6.15. A lighting plan can be designed to conserve energy when switching is circuited to turn some fixtures off while allowing other lamps to remain on.

The most basic control is the toggle on/off switch, which is limited in its ability to conserve electricity. However, a lighting plan can be designed to conserve energy when switching is circuited to turn some fixtures off while allowing other lamps to remain on. For example, energy can be conserved when fixtures located next to windows can be turned off while luminaires on the opposite side of the room remain illuminated (see Figure 6.15). Other controls include dimmers, occupancy sensors, timers, and centralized controls. Dimmers can conserve energy when power is reduced and can extend the life of some lamps. Timers turn lights on and off at designated times. The most effective location for timers is in spaces with predictable schedules, or for lamps that should not be switched frequently.

Occupancy sensors operate by keeping lights on when movement is detected, and fixtures are automatically turned off when no activity occurs in the space. Sensors can be programmed for the amount of time the lights remain on. There are various types of occupancy sensors that should be researched for the appropriate application. To detect motion, passive infrared sensors (PIRs) rely on detecting heat that is emitted from a person. The device can be mounted on various surfaces in a room; thus, the location should be carefully selected to ensure that the sensor is able to detect motion throughout the room. This can be a problem in offices with partitions. People might be working within a workstation and an improperly located sensor might not detect motion. Ultrasonic sensors emit a sound that is interrupted with movement. These sensors are able to detect more movement than PIRs. Some sensors combine

Fig. 6.14. Uniform distribution of light, regardless of the varying needs and activities within the room, wastes energy and might not be satisfactory for the users of the space.

Table 6.2

Equations for LEED-CI (2005) Energy and Atmosphere Credit 1.1: Optimize Energy Performance

---

Equation 1: Installed Interior Lighting Power

Installed Interior Lighting Power = Σ (Quantity by Type of Luminaires × Rated Wattage by Type of Luminaire)
    [Watts]   [Watts]

Equation 2: Interior Lighting Power Allowance Using the Building Area Method

Interior Lighting Power Allowance = Gross Lighted Floor Area × Building Area Type Lighting Power Density
    [Watts]   [sq. ft.]   [Watts/sq. ft.]

Equation 3: Interior Lighting Power Allowance Using the Space-by-Space Method

Interior Lighting Power Allowance = Σ (Space Floor Area × Space Type Lighting Power Density)
    [Watts]   [sq. ft.]   [Watts/sq. ft.]

Equation 4: Lighting Power Reduction Achieved [watts]

Lighting Power Reduction Achieved = Interior Lighting Power Allowance − Installed Interior Lighting Power
    [Watts]   [Watts]   [Watts]

Equation 5: Lighting Power Reduction Achieved [%]

Lighting Power Reduction Achieved = Lighting Power Reduction Achieved ÷ Interior Lighting Power Allowance
    [%]   [Watts]   [Watts]

SOURCE: U.S. Green Building Council (2005, p.145), *LEED-CI Reference Guide: Version 2.0.* Washington, D.C.: U.S. Green Building Council.

both technologies, which provides the most optimum situation.

Photosensors operate by switching or dimming lights according to the amount of daylight that is present in a room. Reducing electrical sources by using daylight conserves energy. This practice is a form of **daylight harvesting**, whereby electrical sources are dimmed or turned off depending on the level of daylight entering a space. To control glare from sunlight, frequently light sources are coordinated with automatic window shades. For the most precise readings, photosensors should not be located in direct view of electrical sources or sunlight.

A centralized control system can monitor and regulate lighting in various areas in a building. Some systems are integrated with mechanical, energy, and security programs. Digital addressable lighting interface (DALI) can help to conserve energy by individually addressing each ballast, and by having bi-communication between a control system and each ballast. An address for each ballast enables the lighting system to have a different illumination requirement for the lamps that are connected to each ballast. Bi-communication provides feedback from the ballast to the control system. For example, the DALI system can communicate with a building's

automation program when a light source is faulty. This is especially useful when the maintenance and service operations are at a remote location. The DALI system also allows *scenes* to be programmed for different activities. For example, in a restaurant, lighting scenes could be programmed for lunch service, evening dining, and after-hours cleaning. Scenes provide an easy format for instantly establishing a prescribed appearance to a space and can help to conserve energy by pre-controlling illumination levels.

To reduce excessive energy consumption, LEED-CI requires that the lighting power density be *below* what is allowed by ANSI/ASHRAE/IESNA Standard 90.1-2004. This can be determined by the whole building lighting power allowance to the entire space, or by applying the space-by-space method (2005). A computer simulation model can be used to determine the lighting power densities. The equations used by LEED-CI to calculate lighting powers are illustrated in Table 6.2. Equation 1 is the formula for determining installed interior lighting power, including the general, task, furniture lighting systems, and luminaires. As shown in Equation 2, the building area method is based on the type of building and lighting power density (W/sq.ft.).

The space-by-space method allows each space

type to be included in the calculations. Thus, as illustrated in Equation 3, the interior lighting power allowance is determined by the sum of each space, multiplied by the lighting power density for the space. Equation 4 is used to determine the achieved lighting power reduction, which is the difference between the installed and the code interior lighting power allowance. The last calculation, Equation 5, is used to calculate the percentage of the achieved lighting power reduction. For LEED-CI, the "credit thresholds for one, two, or three points are 15 percent, 25 percent, or 35 percent" (2005, p. 144).

In addition to considering the effects of electrical sources on the built environment, interior designers should consider how lighting affects the outdoors by producing **light pollution**. Generally the source is exterior lighting, but often an interior designer is involved with lighting solutions for landscape and/or illuminating the exterior facade of a building. As illustrated in Figure 6.16, there is a significant amount of illumination that is wasted by fixtures that are aimed toward the sky and lamps that are excessively bright.

From a different perspective, light trespass has become an issue for people who experience annoyance from a light source that is located adjacent to their property. For example, someone living in a residence might encounter light trespass from lights in a retail parking lot located close to their home. Light pollution and light trespass affect the quality of the interior and exterior environment and illustrate examples of wasted energy. In selecting exterior lighting, care should be taken to select lamps and luminaires that direct light in the required area with appropriate levels of illumination. The **Dark Sky Association (DSA)** is a good resource for information regarding light pollution and light trespass.

SUSTAINABLE STRATEGIES FOR BUILDING ENVELOPE AND WATER MANAGEMENT

A primary goal of sustainable interiors is to achieve zero emissions. This is difficult to accomplish, but efforts should focus on trying to have zero or minimum emissions. Zero emissions are most likely to occur with renewable resources, such as passive solar heating, or using a method that does not consume energy. For example, stairways could be designed to encourage use rather than elevators. This could be done by planning easy access, constructing comfortable steps, and creating an interesting design that attracts attention. Locating stairways close to entrances rather than in remote locations in the building could encourage use on a regular basis. The dimensions of treads and risers should be calculated to ease stair

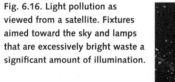

Fig. 6.16. Light pollution as viewed from a satellite. Fixtures aimed toward the sky and lamps that are excessively bright waste a significant amount of illumination.

climbing. Generally, low rises are the easiest steps to climb. A beautifully designed staircase, especially one that incorporates natural daylight, could entice people to climb steps for the pleasure of the experience.

Building Envelope

To minimize pollutants such as carbon dioxide, nitrogen oxides, and sulfur dioxide requires a reduction in energy consumption. An integrated whole building approach requires optimal energy performance from the building's envelope. The components of the building's envelope include the walls, floors, roof, doors, windows, skylights, and slabs. The design of the building's envelope is determined by the structure's climatic zone. A well-designed building envelope can significantly reduce the loads on the HVAC system. The primary goal is to select components that will eliminate leaks and reduce the transfer of heat or cooling to the outdoors. Leaks can occur at the interface between surfaces, joints, and fenestration openings. Weather stripping, caulk, and foam can help to reduce heat loss in the winter and heat gains in warm weather.

Analyzing energy-efficient approaches to the building envelope is an excellent way to examine passive solar heating. Passive solar heating is a strategy for providing heat to a building by using the energy generated by sunlight. The most successful passive solar heating applications are designed by considering all of the factors that impact the penetration and control of sunlight. The elements outside a building that affect passive solar designs include the topography of the site, location of trees, latitude of the site, local climate, and location of adjacent buildings. Factors related to the building that affect passive solar designs include the shape of the building, fenestration, orientation of the building, heat absorption characteristics of materials, insulation, and room configurations.

The fundamental design of passive solar heating in the Northern Hemisphere is to maximize the penetration of sunlight in the winter and control the heat in the summer. This is achieved by situating the building in the optimum position. The structure should be built on the east-west axis, with a large area of glazing on the south-facing wall. The structure should be positioned to ensure that adjacent build-

ings, geographical features, or evergreen trees do not block the sun from striking the south-facing wall during the winter. In colder climates, the shape of the building should minimize exposure to harsh winter winds. In warmer climates, the shape of the building should maximize cross-ventilation.

Rooms on the south-facing wall should have heat-absorbing materials that are exposed to the sunlight. Glazing properties should facilitate heat absorption, and floors and walls should be a material that absorbs heat. (Appropriate glazing materials are discussed later in this chapter.) Heat-absorbing materials for floors and walls include brick, concrete, stone, tile, and earthen. The distance from the south-facing windows and the opposite wall must be calculated to ensure that the wall is close enough to absorb solar energy. Window treatments should be specified that help to control heat gain or loss.

To help keep rooms cool during the summer months, sunlight control strategies must be incorporated within the design of the exterior and interior. These strategies can also be used in buildings located in warm climates. (Approaches to controlling sunlight are reviewed in Chapter 7 of this text.) Controlling sunlight during warm days includes shading solutions, such as deciduous trees, overhangs, and awnings. Light-colored roofs can help to reflect the heat from sunlight. Appropriate insulation and effective ventilation strategies also help to naturally cool a building.

Effective insulation in the walls and roof is an excellent approach to reducing thermal exchanges. An R-value, or thermal resistance, is a means to rate insulation materials. The highest R-values are assigned to the materials that provide the greatest amount of insulation and the greatest resistance to heat flow. Since heat rises, roofs require insulation with a higher R-value than walls. The R-values are determined by state codes and by ANSI/AHRAE/IESNA Standard 90.1-2004. R-values are based on the number of cooling and heating degree-days for a particular zone in the country. In addition to an energy-efficient R-value, sustainable designs should have insulation materials that are not harmful to the environment.

The manufacture or composition of some insulation promotes damage to the stratospheric ozone layer and potential global warming. Insulation materials that used chlorofluorocarbons (CFCs) in the manufacturing process should be avoided. Materials that have ozone-depleting substances, such as CFCs and HCFCs, should also be avoided. Sustainable insulation choices include recycled materials and organic insulants that are synthetic or natural. Examples of recycled materials are recycled cotton insulation, primarily made from used denim, and cellulose made from recycled newspapers. To apply insulation directly into walls or in roof cavities, a preferred material is sprayed polyisocyanurate/polyurethane foam (SPF). Straw bale insulation, which is biodegradable, is being used in many residences. Sustainable insulation should be used in roofs, interior walls, exterior walls, doors, floors, and hot water pipes. In addition, any openings to the exterior from electrical, plumbing, and heating systems should have caulk or foam surrounding the equipment. Insulation, caulk, or foam should also exist between jambs and the framing units of windows and doors.

Windows and Skylights

There are many important sustainable considerations related to windows and skylights. An adequate number of windows and skylights are required to have sufficient ventilation, improve indoor air quality, provide views, and maximize natural daylight. All of these attributes are critical to sustainable designs. Unfortunately, many residential and commercial buildings that have been constructed since the development of air-conditioning have either an inadequate number of windows or windows that are inoperable. Many developers construct homes with windows that simply meet the minimum local codes. Thus, it is very common to see large and expensive homes without any windows or with one small window on an entire side of a house (see Figure 6.17). The lack of windows inhibits the cross-ventilation of natural air flows and eliminates natural light from an entire side of a house. Moreover, from an aesthetic perspective the arrangement lacks balance and presents an unattractive elevation of a building. It is anticipated that the growing focus on sustainability will create a greater awareness of the importance of strategically located operable windows and skylights.

Sustainable designs require that windows and skylights are energy efficient. Improvements in the technologies of windows allow for the specification of many windows that are operable and energy efficient. The basic types of windows are casement, awning, hopper, double-hung, single-hung, and horizontal sliding. Sustainable designs require ventilation from windows and the avoidance of infiltration, or unwanted airflow, from leaks and cracks around windows. Generally, casement windows have the best design for ventilation, followed by awning windows. The operating principles of a casement window allow for ventilation in most of the open area of the sash. The design of hoppers, double-hung, and sliding windows allow ventilation to pass through less than half the size of the window. Energy loss through windows and skylights occurs by convection, conduction, thermal radiation, solar radiation, and infiltration.

The elements of a window that determine energy efficiency are glass coatings, **gas fills**, **warm edge spacers**, and framing materials. **Low-emittance (low-E)** is a microscopically thin glass coating that is applied to glazing to help retain heat in a building during the winter and reflect heat from sunlight in the summer. As shown in Table 6.3, the type of low-E coating is based on the climate of a region. To enhance insulation, air between panes of glass is replaced with a gas, such as argon or krypton. For optimum performance, ENERGY STAR recommends spacing between panes at least one-half inch for air or argon gas, and three-quarters of an inch for kryp-

Fig. 6.17. The lack of windows inhibits cross-ventilation of natural airflow and eliminates natural light from an entire side of a house. This has become a common practice of contemporary residences.

Table 6.3
U-factors and SHGC Ratings for Windows, Doors, and Skylights

Windows & Doors			
Climate Zone	U-factor[a]	SHGC[b]	
Northern	≤ 0.35	Any	
North/Central	≤ 0.40	≤ 0.55	
South/Central	≤ 0.40	≤ 0.40	Prescriptive
	≤ 0.41	≤ 0.36	Equivalent
	≤ 0.42	≤ 0.31	Performance
	≤ 0.43	≤ 0.24	(Excluding CA)
			Products meeting these criteria also qualify in the Southern zone.
Southern	≤ 0.65	≤ 0.40	Prescriptive
	≤ 0.66	≤ 0.39	Equivalent Performance
	≤ 0.67		
	≤ 0.68	≤ 0.39	
	≤ 0.69	≤ 0.37	
	≤ 0.70		
	≤ 0.71	≤ 0.36	
	≤ 0.72	≤ 0.35	
	≤ 0.73		
	≤ 0.74	≤ 0.34	
	≤ 0.75	≤ 0.33	

Skylights			
	U-factor[a]		
	2001 NFRC	RES97	
Climate Zone	rated at 20°[c]	rated at 90°[d]	SHGC[b]
Northern	≤ 0.60	≤ 0.45	Any
North/Central	≤ 0.60	≤ 0.45	≤ 0.40
South/Central	≤ 0.60	≤ 0.45	≤ 0.40
Southern	≤ 0.75	≤ 0.75	≤ 0.40

[a] Btu/h.ft^2.°F

[b] Fraction of incident solar radiation.

[c] U-factor qualification criteria based on 2001 NFRC simulation and certification procedures that rate skylights at a 20-degree angle. Although reported U-factor is higher than RES97 rated products, energy performance at the ENERGY STAR minimum qualifying level is equivalent.

[d] NFRC certification using the 1997 NFRC procedures for residential windows (RES 97) that rated skylights at a 90-degree angle. Skylights rated under this procedure may be present in the marketplace until March 31, 2008. NFRC labels for products using this procedure state: "RES97 rated at 90 degrees."

SOURCE: http://www.energystar.gov.

ton. Gas fills work best when the window has low-E coatings. Warm edge spacers are used to separate the panes of glass in a window. To prevent condensation, and to maximize insulation, spacers should be made of steel, foam, fiberglass, or vinyl. Framing materials affect the insulating ability of a window. In cold climates window frames should be made from wood, wood composites, fiberglass, or vinyl. Aluminum frames with thermal breaks can be used in regions with mild climates. Multiple panes improve the energy efficiency of windows. ENERGY STAR (2005) indicates that two rather than three panes is all that is needed when the window has low-E coatings, gas fills, warm edge spacers, and suitable framing materials.

Fenestration characteristics that affect energy performance are the **U-factor, solar heat gain coefficient (SHGC), visible transmittance (VT or T$_{vis}$),** and **air leakage rating**. From a whole building approach, the window's U-factor or **U-value** is very important. The U-factor is a measurement of the rate of heat loss. U-factor ratings range from .25 to 1.25, whereby the lower the rating, the better the

insulating value. Thus, to conserve energy, windows should be selected with a U-value that prevents heat from escaping in the winter and avoids heat gain in the summer. The U-value rating of a window should reflect all the components of the window, including the glazing, frame, and warm edge spacer. The **National Fenestration Rating Council (NFRC)** is an excellent resource for determining a window's insulation capabilities. The NFRC's U-factor ratings reflect all of the components of a window. Table 6.3 illustrates the U-factors for windows, doors, and skylights in various climate zones. Thermal window treatments and draperies fabricated with insulating lining can help to provide additional thermal comfort.

The SHGC is a rating that indicates how well a window or skylight blocks the heat from sunlight. The SHGC scale is 0 to 1, whereby the lower the rating, the less heat will enter a room. The appropriate SHGC is also dependent on the climate in a region (see Figure 6.18). Solar control can be obtained from a variety of materials applied to glazings, including tints, modified low-E films, and reflective coatings.

In warm climates, or during the summer in cold regions, in addition to glazing treatments there are many other ways to reduce solar heat gain. (See Chapter 7 for techniques to control sunlight.) Different SHGC ratings can be applied to various orientations. For example, the east and west facade of a building could have low-SHGC windows. For larger buildings the south side might need low-SHGC windows. When solar heat gain is desirable, windows with a higher SHGC and low U-factor might be specified.

Special glazings are available to reduce ultraviolet rays; however, the coatings do not prevent fading or fiber deterioration that occurs from sunlight. The VT indicates how much light penetrates the glazing. The rating scale is 0 to 1, whereby the higher the VT, the greater the amount of light that will enter a room. Tinted glass reduces the amount of light that passes through glazing. Spectrally selective coatings help to reduce solar gains while emitting a great amount of visible light. From a sustainability perspective, a higher VT rating is often preferred because this provides higher amounts of daylight.

The Northwest Energy Efficiency Alliance (NEEA) indicates that heating and cooling losses through windows in commercial buildings result in approximately 2 percent of the nation's energy use. In addition, the amount of glazing used in commercial buildings continues to increase. The NEEA's commercial windows initiative (CWI) was established to produce energy savings by encouraging new commercial fenestration technologies. For commercial windows, the guidelines suggest a SHGC of .40 or lower and a VT of .50 or higher. The recommended maximum U-factor is .35 for windows made with nonmetal, fiberglass, wood, or vinyl. For metal windows the recommended U-factor is .42.

Leaks and cracks around windows, frames, and sashes affect energy loss in a building. The AL rating indicates the equivalent cubic feet of air passing through a square foot of the product's area (cfm/sq. ft.). A low AL indicates little air infiltration. The type of window, quality of the unit, and installation techniques affect infiltration. Windows with compressing seals, such as casement or awning, provide the greatest protection from infiltration. To prevent infiltration with skylights, the unit should have continuous edge seals. Manufacturers provide air leakage ratings for windows and skylights. Windows with low ratings have the best protection against infiltration. To reduce infiltration, windows must be properly installed and cracks must be caulked. In addition to windows and skylights, doors must be planned to reduce air infiltration. For commercial buildings, entries should have revolving doors or air locks with two doors to reduce air infiltration.

Water Conservation and Technologies

Sustainable designs must conserve water. The LEED-CI indicates, "On an annual basis, the water deficit in the United States is currently estimated at about

Fig. 6.18. (right and opposite page) The National Fenestration Rating Council (NFRC) is an excellent resource for determining the insulation capacities of doors, windows, and skylights. Ratings are based upon climate zones, which have been coordinated with ENERGY STAR.

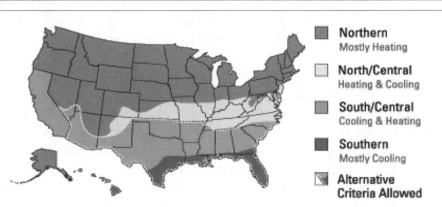

ENERGY STAR®
For Windows, Doors, and Skylights

Climate Zone Lookup for Major U.S. Cities

City	State	Zone
Albuquerque	New Mexico	North/Central
Anchorage	Alaska	Northern
Atlanta	Georgia	South/Central
Birmingham	Alabama	South/Central
Bismarck	North Dakota	Northern
Boise	Idaho	Northern
Boston	Massachusetts	Northern
Brownsville	Texas	Southern
Buffalo	New York	Northern
Burlington	Vermont	Northern
Charleston	South Carolina	South/Central
Cheyenne	Wyoming	Northern
Chicago	Illinois	Northern
Dayton	Ohio	Northern
Denver	Colorado	Northern
El Paso	Texas	South/Central
Fort Worth	Texas	South/Central
Fresno	California	South/Central
Great Falls	Montana	Northern
Honolulu	Hawaii	Southern
Jacksonville	Florida	Southern
Kansas City	Missouri	North/Central
Lake Charles	Louisiana	Southern
Las Vegas	Nevada	South/Central
Los Angeles	California	South/Central
Madison	Wisconsin	Northern
Medford	Oregon	Northern
Memphis	Tennessee	South/Central
Miami	Florida	Southern
Minneapolis	Minnesota	Northern
Nashville	Tennessee	North/Central
New York	New York	Northern
Oklahoma City	Oklahoma	South/Central
Omaha	Nebraska	Northern
Philadelphia	Pennsylvania	Northern
Phoenix	Arizona	South/Central
Pittsburgh	Pennsylvania	Northern
Portland	Maine	Northern
Portland	Oregon	Northern
Raleigh	North Carolina	North/Central
Red Bluff	California	South/Central
Reno	Nevada	Northern
Salt Lake City	Utah	Northern
San Antonio	Texas	Southern
San Diego	California	South/Central
San Francisco	California	South/Central
Seattle	Washington	Northern
Washington	District of Columbia	North/Central

3,700 billion gallons" (2005, p. 103). Thus, every year consumers use 3,700 billion gallons of water more than what is replaced in waterway systems. In addition, LEED-CI notes that large volumes of water cause greater maintenance and increase the life-cycle costs of equipment. Extensive water consumption also requires municipalities to consume more resources for water treatment operations. Water conservation strategies must be implemented to ensure adequate water for current and future generations. Residential and commercial buildings consume a great amount of water. Approximately half of the water from municipalities is consumed in residences. Commercial buildings, especially offices, hotels, and schools, also consume high quantities of water. Water conservation strategies aimed at these facilities can significantly help to sustain freshwater. The LEED-CI suggests that in commercial buildings, conservation strategies can reduce water consumption by at least 30 percent.

The two primary means to conserve water are to consume less water by using water-efficient equipment and to engage in water reclamation and reuse. To consume less water, the Energy Policy Act (EPAct) of 1992 developed minimum consumption standards for a variety of technologies, including toilets or water closets (WCs), showerheads, and faucets (see Table 6.4). For LEED-certified buildings it is expected to exceed the requirements established by EPAct. Table 6.4 also indicates water use recommendations for flush and flow fixture types. Low-flow, ultra-low-flush, and composting water closets are sustainable solutions. Waterless urinals are the preferred choice for this fixture. Sustainable solutions also include low-flow lavatories, kitchen sinks, and showerheads. However, water consumption practices with flow fixtures tend to be based more on behavior than technologies. For example, the water consumed for washing dishes is based on how much water is in the sink, rather than the flow from the fixture. Thus, in these situations, to conserve water people must be consciously aware regarding washing practices.

The requirements prescribed in Table 6.4 should be applied when specifying new WCs and urinals. In addition, inefficient technologies or leaking units should be replaced with new equipment. Research has found that a great deal of water is being wasted by faulty and inefficient technologies. In analyzing water conservation in California, the Pacific Institute stated, "indoor residential use could be reduced by approximately another 40 percent by replacing remaining inefficient toilets, washing machines, showerheads, and dishwashers, and by reducing the level of leaks, even without improvements in technology" (2003, p. 37). The Pacific Institute noted in California residences: WCs (33 percent) consumed the greatest amount of water, followed by showers and baths (22 percent), faucets (18 percent), washing machines (14 percent), leaks (12 percent), and dishwashers (1 percent). Water consumed for WCs is even more significant in commercial buildings. Pacific Institute reported that in California, hospital and hotel WCs consumed approximately three-quarters of the water used in restrooms. The study also indicated that compared with the industrial sector, commercial

Table 6.4
Energy Policy Act (EPAct) of 1992 Minimum Water Consumption Standards

Fixture	EPAct Flow Requirements
Faucets (GPF)	2.2
Replacement aerators (GPM)*	2.2
Showerheads (GPM)	2.5
Urinals (GPF)	1.0
Water closets (GPF)	1.6

*At flowing water pressure of 80 pounds per square inch (psi)

Flush Fixture Type	Gallons per Flush (GPF)
Conventional water closet	1.6
Low-flow water closet	1.1
Ultra-low-flow water closet	0.8
Composting toilet	0.0
Conventional urinal	1.0
Waterless urinal	0.0

Flow Fixture Type	Gallons per Minute (GPM)
Conventional lavatory	2.5
Low-flow lavatory	1.8
Kitchen sink	2.5
Low-flow kitchen sink	1.8
Shower	2.5
Low-flow shower	1.8
Janitor sink	2.5
Hand wash fountain	0.5

SOURCE: U.S. Government: Energy Policy Act of 1992.

facilities have the greatest potential for saving large quantities of water.

Using ultra-low-flow WCs and low-flow showerheads rather than conventional technologies can conserve significant amounts of water. Dual-flush toilets have two flushing systems that use different quantities of water. Depending on flushing needs, one button releases one gallon of water per flush and the other button controls 1.6 gallons of water. Depending on how a user consumes water, low-flow faucets can save water. Some of the technologies that can help to conserve water at lavatories are water-restricting aerators, automatic shutoff devices, and self-closing faucets operated by infrared sensors. Using efficient washing machines that have a horizontal rather than a vertical axis can conserve water. Front-loading washing machines use less water, detergent, and energy than top-loading machines. Leaks represent a substantial amount of water consumption. This consumption is not only unnecessary, but leaks can cause considerable damage to interiors and can contribute to unhealthy mold and mildew. Leak detection and repair must be performed on a regular basis.

Water reclamation and reuse are the other primary means to conserve water. The EPA (2004) indicates that to accommodate the world's population in the future, water reclamation and reuse have become a necessity. The EPA also notes that 25 states in the United States and several other countries are using water reclamation for nonpotable reuse. **Potable water** is for human consumption. Municipal wastewater treatment plants perform processes associated with water reclamation. Reclaimed water can come from domestic wastewater, industrial process waters, or agricultural irrigation systems. Reclaimed water is treated for nonpotable uses, which can include WC flushing, fire protection, and landscape irrigation. The EPA (2004) estimates that 1.7 billion gallons per day of wastewater are used each year. Florida reclaims the greatest amount of water, followed by California, Texas, and Arizona.

Wastewater can be **blackwater** and graywater. Blackwater is wastewater from WCs and urinals, and can include kitchen sinks and dishwashers. According to the Uniform Plumbing Code, graywater is "untreated household wastewater which has not come into contact with toilet waste. Graywater in-

cludes used water from bathtubs, showers, bathroom wash basins, and water from clothes-washers and laundry tubs. It shall not include wastewater from kitchen sinks or dishwashers." **Graywater heat recovery (GWHR)** systems are available that recapture heat from graywater and redistribute the energy to hot water systems. Some of the most likely applications of GWHR systems are commercial buildings that consume large quantities of warm water, such as laundries, restaurants, and apartment buildings. As with all building systems, state and local codes must be followed in determining compliance requirements.

To conserve energy, many buildings use **solar water heating systems**. High-temperature solar water heaters can provide hot water and hot water heat for residential, commercial, and industrial buildings. There are various passive and active systems, but the overall technology is the same. Most systems have glazed flat plate collectors mounted on a roof, which absorb the heat from the sun. The collectors have tubes filled with water or a heat-transfer fluid. The fluid in the tubes is heated by the sun and then can be transferred to the plumbing of the building's water heater. If the heat is the desirable temperature, the liquid is ready for use. If the temperature is too low, as can occur during cloudy days, the water heater heats water to the required temperature. The DOE estimates that solar water heating systems can provide approximately two-thirds of the hot water needed for a building.

Rainwater harvesting is becoming popular as a means to capture valuable rain and use the resource for a variety of applications. Rainwater harvesting is important for conserving water and can help to reduce problems associated with stormwater runoff. Generally, to harvest rainwater, a unit on the roof of a building collects the rain and directs the water to a **cistern**, or storage unit. Water stored in the cistern can then be used for nonpotable purposes, such as flushing WCs or landscape irrigation. Water can be conserved by installing controls on irrigation systems and by designing **xeriscaping** plans. This landscaping method uses plants that are native to a locality and drought-tolerant. In conventional settings, storm-water that strikes an impermeable surface collects pollutants as it flows to storm sewers. Thus, harvesting rainwater is an effective means to reduce surface runoff and the subsequent contaminants in waterways.

Summary

- To accommodate the needs of people and economic activities, building sites in urban settings will have to be conserved, restored, and well planned.
- Ecological factors must be considered during the construction phase and after the building exists.
- In urban settings a major concern is heat islands. This occurs from the significant amount of heat-absorbing materials, such as streets, roofs, and parking lots.
- The location of the building should help to sustain ecosystems by reducing the impact to the environment caused by cars traveling to and from the site.
- In focusing on reducing consumption of resources, site selection should focus on smaller lots and reducing the square footage of a building.
- Reducing the size of buildings requires more attention to efficient space utilization, or spatial strategies.
- Sustainable designs require a whole-building design approach. This entails considering and planning all of the elements of a building, such as the site, orientation, building envelope, mechanical systems, equipment, products, needs of its users, and economical issues.
- An important element of the whole-building design approach is proper commissioning.
- Given the depleting supplies of nonrenewable natural resources, increases in pollution levels, and the high cost of energy, buildings must be designed to optimize energy.
- To improve IAQ and the thermal comfort of people, sustainable design strategies have focused on underfloor air distribution and access floor systems.
- Specifying efficient lighting systems can optimize energy performance. Lighting is responsible for approximately 40 percent of the electricity that is used in commercial buildings.
- A lighting system consists of electricity, lamps, luminaires or fixtures, ballasts, controls, maintenance, and service. Each component of the system should be energy efficient, and to maximize efficiencies it is very important that all of the elements of the system are compatible.
- To reduce excessive energy consumption, LEED-CI requires that the lighting power density be *below* what is allowed by ANSI/ASHRAE/IESNA Standard 90.1-2004.
- Analyzing energy-efficient approaches to the building envelope is an excellent way to examine passive solar heating.
- Using effective insulation in the walls and roof is an excellent approach to reducing thermal exchanges. An R-value, or thermal resistance, is a means to rate insulation materials.
- An adequate number of windows and skylights are required to have sufficient ventilation, improve indoor air quality, provide views, and maximize natural daylight.
- The elements of a window that determine energy-efficiency are glass coatings, gas fills, warm edge spacers, and framing materials.
- Fenestration characteristics that affect energy performance are the U-factor, solar heat gain coefficient (SHGC), visible transmittance (VT or T_{vis}), and air leakage rating.
- Sustainable designs must conserve water. The LEED-CI indicates, "On an annual basis, the water deficit in the United States is currently estimated at about 3,700 billion gallons" (2005, p. 103). Thus, every year consumers use 3,700 billion gallons of water more than what is replaced in waterway systems.
- The two primary means to conserve water are to consume less water by using water-efficient equipment and to engage in water reclamation and reuse.

Key Terms

Air leakage rating

Blackwater

Building's footprint

Building management systems (BMS)

Chromaticity

Cistern

Color-rendering index (CRI)

Commissioning

Compact fluorescent lamp (CFL)

Dark Sky Association (DSA)

Daylight harvesting

Displacement ventilation system

Efficacy

Fluorescent lamp

Gas fills

Global-warming potentials (GWPs)

Graywater heat recovery (GWHR)

Halogen lamp

Heat islands

High-intensity discharge (HID) lamps

Incandescent lamp

Infilling

Insulated ceiling–air-tight (IC–AC)

Light-emitting diodes (LEDs)

Light output

Light pollution

Low-emittance (Low-E)

Lumens

Lumens per watt (lpW)

National Fenestration Rating Council (NFRC)

Organic light-emitting diodes (OLEDs)

Ozone-depleting potentials (ODPs)

Potable water

Rainwater harvesting

Solar heat gain coefficient (SHGC)

Solar water heating systems

Spatial strategies

U-factor

U-value

Visible transmittance (VT or T_{vis})

Warm edge spacers

Whole building design approach

Xeriscaping

Exercises

1. In urban settings, a major concern is heat islands. To counteract the effects of heat islands, some people are constructing green roofs. Identify a building that could qualify for a green roof. Design a plan for the garden that integrates the interior with the exterior. In a summary report, identify appropriate products for the green roof and manufacturers' specifications.

2. Minimizing the size of a building while maximizing the effectiveness of an interior is important for existing buildings and new construction. Reducing the size of buildings requires more attention to spatial strategies. Locate three different residential floor plans and determine spatial strategies. Summarize the results in a written report, and include drawings, illustrations, photographs, or sketches.

3. Specifying efficient lighting systems can optimize energy performance. Identify a commercial floor plan and specify an energy-efficient system. Manufacturers' specifications should include lamps, luminaires or fixtures, ballasts, controls, maintenance, and service. Summarize the results in a written report, and include illustrations, photographs, or sketches.

4. There are many important sustainable considerations related to windows and skylights. Research manufacturers of energy-efficient windows and skylights. Develop a resource file that includes product specifications for the following items: casement, awning, hopper, double-hung, single-hung, horizontal sliding, skylights, light pipes, and roof monitors.

CHAPTER 7

Sustainable Strategies for Indoor Environmental Quality

THE SEVENTH PLANET then was the Earth.

The Earth is not just another planet!

To give you a notion of the Earth's dimensions, I can tell you that before the invention of electricity, it was necessary to maintain, over the whole six continents, a veritable army of four-hundred-sixty-two thousand, five hundred and eleven lamplighters.

Seen from some distance, this made a splendid effect. The movements of this army were ordered like those of a ballet.

—ANTOINE DE SAINT-EXUPÉRY

Objectives

- Understand the importance of daylighting and identify approaches to integrating natural light with electrical sources.
- Describe methods to enhance daylighting and control sunlight.
- Identify important considerations for outdoor views and describe the impact on people.
- Understand how HVAC systems affect the quality of the indoor environment.
- Describe how the environment affects people and apply an understanding to the built environment.
- Identify how chemical contaminants affect indoor air quality.
- Describe how the contents of finishes and furnishings can affect indoor air quality.

CHAPTER 6 EXPLORED many attributes of the building envelope and its effect on the environment. The primary focus was identifying ways to conserve energy by selecting energy-efficient materials, equipment, and technologies. Conserving electricity, heat, and cooling helps to reduce emissions and decrease consumption of nonrenewable fossil fuels. This chapter begins an in-depth analysis of sustainable design within the context of the interior environment.

A distinction is made between indoor environmental quality (IEQ) and indoor air quality (IAQ). Indoor environmental quality is a comprehensive approach to many of the elements that affect users' perception of a space, including daylight, ventilation, temperature, humidity, noise, electrical light sources, and personal control of a setting. These characteristics affect users' satisfaction, productivity, and overall performance of tasks. Creating an enjoyable environment is not only good for human factors but also helps to reduce the likelihood of a renovation or the construction of a new structure. Consequently, existing materials do not become waste and additional resources are not being consumed for new construction. Discussion regarding IAQ will focus on materials and products that affect the health of people. Toxins emitted by numerous interior products, such as paint and furniture, can have serious physical effects. An interior designer must be knowledgeable about the products that cause problems and be cognizant of materials that are safe for people.

INDOOR ENVIRONMENTAL QUALITY: DAYLIGHTING

A very critical element of IEQ is having well-designed daylight that enters every room where people live or work. In addition, people should be able to enjoy a pleasant view of the outdoors. The quality of natural light is determined by understanding the difference between **daylight** and **sunlight**. Daylight is the desirable natural light that should be designed for interiors. Daylight is a soft, indirect, diffused light that avoids glare, harsh shadows, and heat gain. Sunlight is the direct light from the sun that can be overpowering to people due to its high level of brightness and its annoying glare. Sustainable interiors maximize daylight and minimize sunlight.

Another important element of quality daylighting is to *design* the light for its users and the specific characteristics of a room and building. Quality daylighting provides the proper illumination level for the tasks while conserving electricity by integrating natural light with electrical sources. Quality daylighting must have the appropriate solutions for controlling the negative effects associated with sunlight. To accomplish quality daylighting requires a great deal of planning, from the pre-design phase of a project to post-occupancy evaluations. Solutions that specify walls of glazing for daylighting fail to optimize the positive attributes of natural light and can contribute to unnecessary heat gain or loss.

Sustainable strategies must also conserve energy, protect the environment, and enhance economics. Electricity for commercial buildings represents approximately one-third of the energy costs. Daylighting that is properly designed results in some lights being turned off and dimming other lamps. Estimates reveal that electricity used for luminaires can be reduced by approximately 80 percent when a room has quality daylighting. In addition, decreases in the waste heat from lamps help to reduce the amount of energy used for operating air-conditioning systems. Reductions in the costs for electrical and HVAC systems provide a client with significant economic savings.

Designing Daylighting: An Integrated Approach

For new construction projects, the most effective approach to quality daylighting and daylight harvesting is to locate a site that can provide optimum solutions. Many factors associated with a site affect daylighting, including its latitude, topography, trees, and adjacent buildings. A site's latitude and the time of year affect the amount of daylight and the angle of the sun. For example, at 40 degrees north latitude, in January sun angles are low; in July the sun angle is high (see Figure 7.1). Latitudes farther from the equator have more variability associated with the angles of the sun and the amount of radiation. In addition, locations far from the equator experience the greatest variances between summer and winter months. To design daylighting, it is critical to know how the changing position of the sun varies during the day and throughout the year. This information helps to

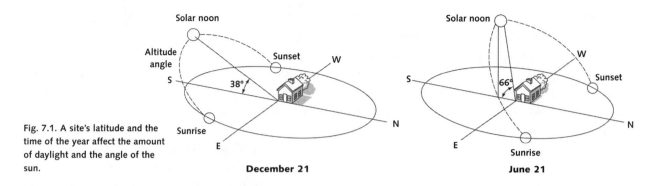

Fig. 7.1. A site's latitude and the time of the year affect the amount of daylight and the angle of the sun.

December 21

June 21

determine how to optimize the location of windows to enhance the diffusion or the control of daylight.

The landscape or surrounding buildings affect daylighting. A hill, mountain, or trees can prevent daylight from entering a building. In urban settings, where buildings are located close to one another, some spaces may not be exposed to direct sunlight. This can frequently occur in rooms located on the lower floors of a building. In addition to the availability of sunlight on a clear day, designing daylighting requires an analysis of other climatic conditions that affect the quality of light in a space. Every location in the world has unique sky conditions that affect daylighting. Some communities have a high number of sunny days and others have many cloudy conditions. Moreover, each location varies with respect to daylight availability. For example, in Alaska during the winter months there are very few hours of daylight, and the opposite occurs during the summer. To design daylighting, the sky conditions and sunlight availability must be considered to have the optimum illumination levels in every room throughout the year.

In analyzing the elements that affect daylighting, it is also important to consider other climatic conditions that impact sustainable designs. For example, many of the considerations that affect daylight impact natural ventilation. A site's topography, trees, and buildings can affect the wind's direction, speed, and frequency. These factors can impact the adequacy of natural ventilation flowing through a building during the warm summer months and the amount of cold wind striking a building in the winter. Thus, an integrated approach to buildings simultaneously considers all of the factors that affect the thermal comfort level of a building.

The building's form and the location, size, and orientation of windows affect daylighting. Figure 7.2 illustrates some forms of buildings that can maxi-

Fig. 7.2. A building's form affects the availability of daylighting. These shapes can allow for daylight in all of the rooms located in the perimeter of the structures.

mize the availability of daylight to rooms. As shown in the drawings, the goal is to have a form that allows for living spaces to have windows. To accomplish this, generally buildings should be narrow. Narrow buildings, rather than deep structures, allow for daylight to penetrate as many rooms as possible. Prior to the invention of electricity, architecture had to be designed to maximize the availability of daylight. Every room that people used had to have daylight for illumination. Consequently, architects focused on specifying the location of the structure to maximize daylight infiltration. The configuration of windows and characteristics of the interior were also designed to ensure the greatest amount of illumination possible. As illustrated in Figure 7.3, to emphasize the importance of daylight and its effect on an interior, many artists painted rooms while sunlight was streaming through large windows. Studying historical structures and the characteristics of their interiors is an excellent approach to understanding how to maximize daylighting in spaces. As will be discussed later in this chapter, classical architecture also provides outstanding examples of how to incorporate natural ventilation in a structure.

To optimize daylighting, a building's orientation, location, and size of windows must be carefully planned. In most locations the best orientation for daylighting is the south side of a building, followed by the north side. The south and north sides are ideal because these sides of a building are not exposed to the direct sunlight from sunrise or sunset. Windows located on the south side of a building are exposed to the benefits of solar gain in the winter. During the summer months, solar heat gain can be reduced by appropriate shading techniques, which are discussed later in this section. The quality of light penetrating northern windows has an even spectral quality throughout the year. Thus, many artists prefer to paint in rooms on the north side of a building. Windows on the east and west sides provide a good quantity of daylight, but the directional variability caused by the sun's movement makes it very difficult to simultaneously allow for light to enter the room and

Fig. 7.3. To emphasize the importance of daylight and its effect on people and an interior, many artists painted rooms with sunlight streaming through windows.

eliminate glare. If possible, when planning room configurations of a building, the goal should be to locate rooms frequently occupied on the south and north sides. The east and west sides could be used for storage, closets, equipment, or rooms that are used infrequently, such as bathrooms.

The location of windows within a room affects the quality of daylighting. Daylight can enter a space with **sidelighting** or **toplighting**. Sidelighting is from windows located in walls and toplighting occurs with units mounted in the ceiling, such as a skylight. Generally, locations that enable light to be reflected off of light-colored surfaces will provide the greatest quantity of daylight in a space. For example, windows located close to a white-colored ceiling provide high illumination levels, because light coming through the window strikes the ceiling's surface and then reflects into the space (see Figure 7.4a). **Clerestories** are an excellent choice for this purpose; however, the location can eliminate views to the outdoors. As shown in Figure 7.4b, a sloped ceiling close to a window also emits more light into a space. In contrast, windows low on a wall result in less reflected illumination because minimal light is reflected from a floor. Windows located close to an adjacent wall can also help to emit more daylight. The shape, depth, color, and texture of surfaces closest to a window affect the quantity and quality of daylight. To maximize the quantity of daylight, the window should be deeply recessed and the surfaces surrounding the opening should have splayed reveals (see Figure 7.5). The adjacent surfaces should be white or light-colored and matte finish. The reflectance of a ceiling should be at least 80 percent, and walls should have a reflectance greater than 50 percent. Floors, which reflect the least amount of light, should have a reflectance of approximately 20 percent.

Ideally, to maximize daylighting, windows should be located on two different walls. When the walls are across from each other, this **bilateral** arrangement can help to provide an even distribution of light in the room. To illuminate an entire room with daylight, the room should have a maximum depth. Generally, the depth of the room should be no longer than 2.5 times the height of a window. For example, when a window is four feet (120 cm) high, the depth of the room should be no greater than 10 feet (300 cm). In situations where the depth of the room

Fig. 7.4a. (left, top) Windows located close to a white-colored ceiling provide high-illumination levels because light coming through the window strikes the ceiling's surface and then reflects into the space.
Fig. 7.4b. (left, bottom) An angled ceiling close to a window can enhance illumination levels in a room. The ceiling should be a white-colored surface.
Fig. 7.5. (above) Illumination can be enhanced with recessed windows with splayed reveals. Adjacent surfaces should be white or light-colored and matte finish.

does not allow for daylight to strike the opposite side of the windows, toplighting should be considered for illumination. Careful consideration should be given to any obstruction that prevents the spread of daylight throughout a room, such as partitions. Whenever possible, to allow for daylight, glazing should be inserted into these obstructions. Adding glazing to walls that separate a room from a hallway is an excellent approach for providing daylight to the hallway. For example, transoms above doors can be an effective solution and operable units help to circulate natural breezes.

There are other daylighting considerations regarding the size and location of a window. Generally, a horizontally shaped window or arrangement is preferred to vertical because it is more natural for the eye to move side to side than up and down. Thus, eyes can perceive more illumination from a horizontally shaped window than vertical glazing. In addition, a wide view of the horizon is the most pleasing view to the outdoors. The continuous flow of light from **strip windows** can provide excellent daylight, but design strategies should focus on reducing glare and solar heat gain in the summer (see Figure 7.6a). Generally, **punched windows** are not as effective because the arrangement makes it more difficult to place furniture (see Figure 7.6b). In addition, the contrast between the bright window and the dark wall can create **disability glare**. Disability and dis-

comfort glare are conditions that affect the user's ability to function in a space. Disability glare can pose serious safety issues because the glare prevents someone from seeing objects or engaging in an activity. Discomfort glare is an annoyance, but an individual is able to see objects and activities. To help reduce glare, glazings should have a low VT. To help balance daylight transmittance and glare, an effective solution is to use high VT glazings in windows located close to the ceiling and low VT glazings in windows that are parallel to people. Another index that is useful for daylight glazing is the **luminous efficacy constant (Ke)**. The Ke is referred to as a coolness index because it reveals the glazing's relative performance in deflecting solar heat while allowing for the transmission of daylight. Higher Ke values are best for daylighting.

Toplighting can be a very effective approach to daylighting because the direction of light is the natural distribution of sunlight and the transmittance is continuous. Toplighting is able to provide continuous daylighting because many of the elements that can obstruct light in sidelighting applications do not exist. For example, generally, trees or buildings will not prevent light from transmitting through a skylight. Moreover, window treatments for privacy are not necessary with toplighting. As with sidelighting, there are many ways to increase the illuminance from toplighting. For example, skylights installed in deep wells with splayed edges can emit high quantities of daylight (see Figure 7.7). As with all apertures, care must be taken to avoid excessive heat gain or loss.

For buildings with multiple floors, light pipes can be installed from the roof through the floors of the structure. The quantity of illumination continuously decreases from the roof to the lower floors, but daylight is still available to occupants on the first floor. New technologies are being developed to improve the quantity of illumination emitted from light pipes. For example, to increase the quantity of light, some units have solar tracking lenses or mirrors located on the roof. Currently, a small town in Europe that has *no* direct sunlight during the winter months

due to the shadow from a mountain is exploring the use of a large tracking mirror. Sunlight will reflect off the mirror and beam toward the town. If the technology is successful, for the first time the community will experience sunlight during the long winter months.

To determine the amount of daylight in a space, LEED-CI allows applicants to use a computer simulation model, or to calculate the **daylight factor (DF)**. The LEED-CI requires a minimum level of illumination at 25 footcandles. The DF, expressed as a percentage, is the ratio of exterior illumination to interior illumination. The variables recommended by LEED-CI for determining the DF are the

Fig. 7.6a. (left, top) The continuous flow of light from strip windows can provide excellent daylight. Integration strategies should include reducing glare and solar heat gain in the summer.

Fig. 7.6b. (left, bottom) Punched windows can provide high-illumination levels. A disadvantage to this window arrangement is the interruption of views to the outdoors and restrictions imposed on the design of the interior.

Fig. 7.7. (above) Skylights installed in deep wells with splayed edges can emit high quantities of daylight. Toplighting can be a very effective approach to daylighting because the direction of light is the natural distribution of sunlight and the transmittance is continuous.

floor area, window area, window geometry, visible transmittance, and window height. The LEED-CI requires a minimum 2 percent DF at the back of the space. Windows above 7'-6" (230 cm) are daylight glazing and windows 2'-6" (76 cm) from the floor up to 7'-6" (230 cm) are vision glazing. Any windows located below 2'-6" (76 cm) from the floor must be excluded from the calculations. Please refer to LEED-CI for the DF calculations.

Controlling Sunlight

Successful daylighting can occur only when the negative effects of sunlight are minimized and when energy is conserved by effectively integrating natural light with electrical sources. Controlling sunlight can be achieved by using external and internal techniques. The choice of units is dependent on the architectural aesthetics, orientation, and characteristics of the interior design. Technologies for controlling sunlight are important for daylighting and passive solar applications. External shading devices are excellent for controlling solar heat. Externally mounted units are more effective for controlling solar radiation than interior shading devices, because heat is absorbed prior to entering the building.

There are several external techniques that can be used to control sunlight. Natural vegetation can be a solution outside windows; however, excessive shading from plants or trees reduces the amount of daylight entering a space. Deciduous trees can be an effective approach to controlling the heat gain from sunlight. When the leaves are gone during the winter, the radiant heat from the sun can penetrate windows; during the hot summer, the leaves of the trees provide shade from the sunlight. Plant materials with vines can accomplish the same function as deciduous trees. The deciduous vines can be trained to serve as an awning or grow along wires installed in the front of windows. During the summer the leaves provide protection from the sun; in the winter the bare vines allow sunlight to penetrate the glazing.

There are many external shading units that can shield sunlight from interior spaces. External units are available in fixed or movable configurations. The choice is dependent on a variety of factors, including the aesthetic design of the architecture, the orientation, and the surrounding characteristics of the site.

External solar control units include light shelves, overhangs, fins, sun louvers, roller shades, deep recesses, and double skin systems. Movable units are available in manual and motorized versions. Some have photosensors embedded in the units to automatically adjust to the variability of sky conditions. Light shelves are designed to shade a window and, when appropriate, the shelf can reflect light toward the ceiling of the interior (see Figure 7.8a). Light shelves are an effective approach to shielding the sun on the south side of a building but are less successful on the east or west side. Overhangs can be made from a variety of materials and positioned in several directions (see Figure 7.8b). Overhangs can be fabricated from a soft material, as in a canvas awning, or made from a hard material, such as wood or concrete. Generally, the material choice is determined by the architectural design. The position of the overhang is determined based on the orientation and characteristics of adjacent materials.

Fins and sun louvers are components designed to shield a window from sunlight (see 7.9 a and b). Fins are vertical units that can shield an interior from sunlight. Fins are most effective on the south-facing side of a building, although manufacturers produce specially designed vertical units for windows on the east and west sides. Horizontal and vertical sun louvers are available in a variety of materials, including wood, metal, and glass. Some sun louvers are perforated to allow light to enter a space while controlling for glare. Roller shades are manufactured in fabrics that vary in openness from being very translucent to providing blackout properties.

Many buildings, especially in warm climates, have deep recesses that help to control sunlight. Some of the elements provide a decorative facade to a building (see Figure 7.10). In designing buildings for locations in the desert, Louis Kahn created architecture that integrated shading units within the form of the structure (see Figure 7.11). Other architectural approaches to controlling sunlight include balconies, deep reveals, and arcades. To enhance daylighting and to incorporate passive solar elements, some contemporary buildings have double skin systems. The double wall of glazing has a space between the two vertical surfaces that helps to prevent solar heat gain and loss. In addition, often the units have operable windows, which helps to ventilate the building.

Fig. 7.8a. (top left) Light shelves can shade a window and enhance illumination levels by reflecting light toward the ceiling of the interior. Light shelves can be installed on the interior and the exterior of a building.

Fig. 7.8b. (middle left) An awning is an effective method to help control sunlight and provides an interesting structural element to the building's facade.

Fig. 7.9a–b. (top and middle right) (a) Fins and (b) sun louvers are components designed to shield a window from sunlight.

Fig. 7.10. (bottom left) Many buildings, especially in warm climates, have deep recesses that help to control sunlight. Some of the elements provide a decorative facade to a building.

Fig. 7.11. (bottom right) To control sunlight, Louis Kahn designed architecture that integrated shading units within the form of the structure.

When the open space is planned to facilitate air movement, the gap serves as the building's exhaust. Using the space in this manner can eliminate shafts from some buildings.

In the interior of a room, a variety of devices can control sunlight and help to prevent heat gain or loss. Internal units include light shelves, blinds, roller shades, shutters, fabrics, skylight-tension systems, and pleated or accordion shades. Internally mounted light shelves have the same characteristics as external units but are most effective when used to increase illumination levels. This is accomplished when daylight strikes the top of the shelf and reflects to the ceiling of the room. Light reflected from the ceiling provides more illumination to the areas of the room located away from windows. Light-colored treatments should be specified, and the directional orientation of blinds should be based on the direction of the sun's movement. For example, windows on the south side of a building should have window treatments with horizontal louvers. Windows on the east and west sides should have vertical louvers.

To provide flexibility in the quantity of illumination, window treatments can have a split configuration. For example, to provide high levels of illumination, the top section of a window treatment could be a translucent material, and the bottom portion could provide more shading. Shades, shutters, and horizontal and vertical blinds are available in a variety of materials and colors. Units are manually operated or the motorized window treatments function by a switch, remote control, and/or timer. Skylight-tension systems are mounted in the ceiling next to the skylight. Customized configurations are available that can be fabricated in a variety of sizes and shapes. Fabric openness is in a range from very translucent to total blackout.

Integrating Daylighting with Electrical Sources

Sustainable designs must use daylighting to conserve energy. Reducing electrical consumption helps to decrease greenhouse gases and conserve nonrenewable fossil fuels. To successfully integrate daylight and electrical sources requires pre-design planning. The goal is to design a seamless lighting system that works in unison with the variability of daylight. For example, the users in the space should not be able to notice light level changes when there is a transition from electrical to natural light. When daylight illumination levels decrease from clouds, the electrical sources should gradually replace the light loss. Within the perimeter area of a room, illumination levels should not fluctuate from being bright to dark. To accomplish effective daylighting, conceptualize how the design of the architecture will enhance daylight and then design the electrical system to support the integration of the two sources.

There are various approaches to integrating daylight and electrical sources. Photosensors are excellent controls for combining daylight and electrical sources. Photosensors can be mounted close to a window or in a window treatment. The sensors can be programmed so lights are on, off, or dimmed depending on the level of daylight illumination. Switching is a common technique for controlling lamps, but **stepped controls** and dimming are more satisfactory. Switching is an abrupt method to turn lights on and off. Stepped controls allow a smoother transition in illumination levels by controlling multiple lamps within a luminaire. The stepped process works by progressively turning lamps on or off. In this approach a lamp remains on; thus, the transition from one illumination level to the next is gradual. Dimming lamps is the most desirable approach to transitioning illumination levels because the changes are smooth. In addition, dimming can help to conserve energy.

Proper design of lighting circuits and switching systems are also important for successful integration methods. Manual or automatic systems should be circuited to allow separate control of various luminaires. In this arrangement luminaires close to a window can be turned off or dimmed when adequate daylight is present. Simultaneously, fixtures located far from the window can be left on. Some integrated systems use timers based on the activities that occur in the space. For example, luminaires connected to timers can be programmed to turn lights on or off depending on daylight hours. Timers can pose a problem with fluctuations in sky conditions. In addition, timers must always be carefully planned to allow people adequate time to safely exit a room.

Daylight integration with electrical sources must be calibrated to respond to prescribed illumination levels. The **International Engineering Society of**

North American (IESNA) has recommended illuminance levels in units of footcandles (fc) for a variety of activities. This organization can be contacted for specific requirements and the appropriate methods to use in calculating illuminance levels. After the illumination level has been determined for activities and zones within a room, the lighting system can be programmed to maintain a specific level regardless of sky conditions. Control systems can be programmed to change illumination levels during various times of day within a zone. For example, in most offices light levels remain uniform at all times of the day. This approach lacks the variability that helps to create interesting environments. To make a more stimulating setting, lighting could be programmed to change by having lower levels during transition times, such as early in the morning or prior to leaving the office. Light levels could be the brightest when people are working at their peak. The same conceptual variability could be programmed for daylight changes during the day and throughout the year. Summer light levels could be dimmer, and winter light levels could be brighter. Lighting systems are available that enable users to control fixtures within their workstation. Thus, regardless of the surrounding lighting, individuals can determine whether their lights will be on, off, or dimmed. This personal control of one's environment is a very important element of sustainable designs. Control of one's lighting is one of the elements in the built environment that is important for the health and well-being of people. (Other elements of an environment that individuals should be able to control are discussed in the next section of this chapter.)

INDOOR ENVIRONMENTAL QUALITY: PERSONAL COMFORT

The impact of the built environment on natural resources is vital to the importance of sustaining a healthy planet for current and future generations. However, sustainable development also includes an examination of the impact of activities on people and the economy. Thus, sustainable designs must focus on how to create interiors that are healthy and are able to accommodate the needs of their users. A focus on environmental quality emphasizes all of the factors that can affect how people perceive a space. Improvements in technology are making it possible to personalize a work environment. Thus, with the appropriate system and controls, individuals can regulate the temperature, ventilation, and lighting within their workstation. Many research studies have found that satisfaction with an interior environment results in enhanced productivity, lower absenteeism, and greater retention of employees. This results in increases in profits and the subsequent benefits associated with enhanced economics.

Views and Spatial Strategies

In addition to the importance of daylight for the health and well-being of individuals, people need a view of the outdoors. Outdoor views are so critical to people that every building assessment system provides credit for views. There are many factors that affect success with providing views to the outdoors. The building must be oriented to provide people with something pleasant to see. To enhance the visibility of the view, the proper window should be selected. Generally, horizontally shaped windows provide optimum views. However, to avoid an unpleasant view, a vertical application might be more appropriate.

The size of the window should also be determined by the elements that create an attractive view. In situations where quantities of daylight are compromised, it may be necessary to screen an undesirable view with an appropriate interior window treatment. Whenever possible, the interior layout of a building should be designed to ensure that the best views are seen from the most frequently used rooms. This should include views external to the building and pleasant views of enclosed spaces, such as courtyards or atriums.

Within each room the view must be maintained by carefully positioning partitions, furniture, and any other element that might obstruct the view. To ensure unobstructed viewing lines, the relationship between views and the interior must be analyzed from a variety of positions. For example, in spaces where people typically are standing, such as hallways or a kitchen, objects should not obstruct the view from an average standing position. In rooms where people are sitting for most of the time, such as a conference or living room, an unobstructed view to the

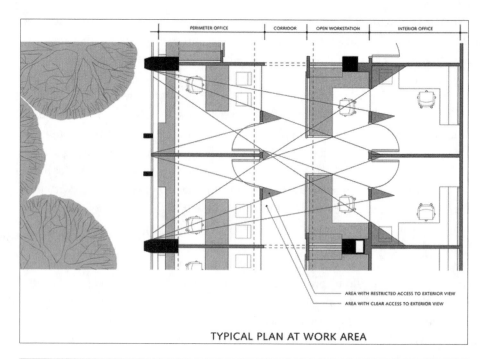

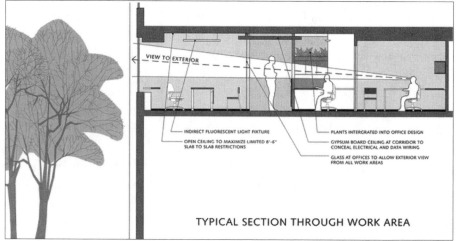

Fig. 7.12. (top) To determine views to the outdoors, LEED-CI requires sight lines drawn on the plan view.

Fig. 7.13. (bottom) To determine views to the outdoors, LEED-CI requires sight lines drawn in the section view.

outdoors should exist from the seated position. Thus, in determining clear lines of view, it is important to examine a room from both plan and elevation perspectives.

To determine these views, LEED-CI (2005) requires two calculations: (1) *direct line of sight to perimeter glazing*, and (2) *horizontal view at 42 inches* (106 cm). The direct line of sight to perimeter glazing is used to determine that at least 90 percent of the occupied space has a view to the outdoors. The LEED-CI defines occupied space as any area where people sit or stand. Nonoccupied spaces include rooms used for janitorial services. The view is based on LEED-CI's vision glazing requirements [2'-6" (76 cm) – 7'-6" (230 cm)] and any full-height interior partitions (see Figure

7.12). The horizontal view at 42 inches (106 cm) is the measurement used to ensure that views to the outdoors exist once furniture has been installed (see Figure 7.13).

To maximize views to the outdoors, buildings are frequently designed with large spans of glass. This approach can provide a wonderful view and high quantities of daylight; however, there are problems associated with this technique that must be addressed for a successful sustainable design. The large area of light penetrating a space can create either disability or discomfort glare. This can be a problem for tasks that are adjacent to a window. To help solve problems associated with glare, contrast differences must be reduced between the brightness emitted from glazing and the comparatively dark area surrounding the windows. For example, electrical lighting can be added to increase the level of illumination in dark areas. To reduce illumination levels from sunlight, a window treatment with some translucence can be installed. In addition, surfaces surrounding windows should not be a dark color. Dark surfaces will intensify extreme contrasts. Direct sunlight on tasks should always be avoided due to the high level of brightness. Frequently, a concern is computer monitor screens or any other material with high reflectivity properties.

To help reduce glare, some solutions have focused on applying a tint, film, or coatings on glazes. These materials can help to reduce the glare; however, any substance with added colorants distorts the colors of objects outdoors, and some cause the glass to absorb heat. The VT and SHGC of the glazing become important factors in determining the best solution for allowing visible light to pass through a window and control solar heat gain. For many climates, to enhance daylighting, windows should have a high VT and a moderate or low SHGC. Glare from windows can come from sunlight and any highly reflective material outdoors. For the comfort and safety of people, views should be analyzed for any surface that could reflect excessive brightness into a room. The analysis should be done at various times during the day to account for variances that occur from the movement of the sun. To help reduce glare, surfaces close to windows should have a matte finish. Glossy finishes increase glare and can create annoying reflectances.

A window with a view is wonderful to see during the day; however, depending on what is outdoors, in the evening the view can become a black hole. An evening view of city lights is attractive, but generally a large body of water or a forest is total darkness. In addition, glass with a dark background functions like a mirror. The surface reflects images, which can be a safety issue and annoying to occupants in the space. When planning the overall design of windows, careful consideration should be allotted to providing a pleasing view to the outdoors during the evening hours. Techniques to reduce reflectances should also be employed. Generally, solutions will focus on reducing the contrasts between the indoors and outdoors. For example, landscape lighting can create a pleasing view and can help to reduce indoor reflectances.

HVAC and Indoor Environmental Quality

Research has demonstrated the importance of quality environmental conditions. The HVAC system plays an important role in delivering comfortable temperatures, healthy air, and optimum humidity levels. A significant concern of sustainable designs is the IAQ. To protect the health, welfare, and safety of people, all building assessment systems have categories that focus on IAQ. In LEED-CI, IAQ is included in the IEQ category (2005). BREEAM has requirements for IAQ in the Health and Well-being category. In highly developed countries, the health consequences are not as serious as in developing countries. People in developing countries are reliant on biomass, such as wood and coal, for cooking and heating. These materials have extremely serious health effects, especially since the materials are burned on open fires with poor ventilation. Consequently, the World Health Organization (WHO) estimates that every year "indoor air pollution is responsible for the death of 1.6 million people—that's one death every 20 seconds" (2005, p. 1).

Understanding the sources of IAQ and approaches to ensuring healthy air is a critical element of sustainable interiors. In providing recommendations for healthy air in commercial buildings, LEED-CI indicates that indoor chemical contaminates are formaldehyde, particulates, total volatile organic compounds (TVOC), 4-phenycyclohexene (4-PCH), and carbon monoxide (CO) (2005). (The next section in this chapter provides details regarding these contaminates.) The LEED-CI also provides maximum concentration levels for each of these contaminates. Mechanical engineers (or a more recent term, *climate engineers*) are responsible for designing HVAC systems. However, as a member of the project's team, interior designers should be knowledgeable regarding how the systems operate and the impact of interior materials on IAQ.

To contribute to the comfort and well-being of users of a space, LEED-CI has a requirement for minimum IAQ performance. The HVAC systems manipulate air to provide ventilation and to regulate the thermal environment in a space. Ventilation can be provided by a mechanical unit, natural airflow, or mixed mode, which is a combination of the two methods. To provide minimum IAQ performance, the LEED-CI reference standard is ASHRAE 62.1-2004. This standard prescribes minimum guidelines for the rates that fresh air should enter a building. The rate is dependent on the density of people in an area and the type of activities. The number of people in a space is important because of the concentrations of carbon dioxide that people produce from breathing. In addition, people contribute to humidity levels and odors. Thus, minimum outdoor airflow rates must be regulated to account for the negative air qualities that can occur from large numbers of people. The type of activity also affects the airflow rates because spaces designated for considerable movement, such as a fitness center, require higher ventilation rates. The LEED-CI also provides credit for systems that increase ventilation rates at least 30 percent more than the minimum referenced standard.

An important consideration of IAQ performance is the quality of the outdoor air. The fresh air intakes should be installed in a location that avoids any surrounding sources of pollutants, such as automobile traffic, outdoor smoking areas, or waste disposal units (see Figure 7.14). The LEED-CI stresses the importance of avoiding a ventilation system that is overdesigned or underdesigned. An overdesigned system can waste energy by allowing too much heat or cooling to leave a building. An underdesigned system results in poor indoor air quality. However, to ensure quality indoor air, it may be necessary to contend with increases in energy costs. As discussed later in this chapter, quality indoor air is not only a healthy approach to sustainable interiors: Research indicates that the positive environment increases productivity and satisfaction with a building and reduces absenteeism.

To help protect the health of occupants, controlling tobacco smoke is a prerequisite of LEED-CI (2005). The acceptable approaches to dealing with tobacco smoke involve prohibiting smoking in the building and providing designated smoking areas that have very controlled requirements. Smoking areas outside of buildings must be "at least 25 feet [760 cm] away from entries, outdoor air intakes, and operable windows" (LEED-CI, 2005, p. 265). The LEED-CI has several requirements that are mandated for

Fig. 7.14. An important consideration of IAQ performance is the quality of the outdoor air. The fresh air intakes should be installed in a location that avoids any surrounding sources of pollutants, such as automobile traffic, outdoor smoking areas, or waste disposal units.

smoking rooms in a building. The requirements focus on ensuring that the HVAC systems are designed to have smoke directly exhausted to the outdoors and to avoid any infiltration to other areas of the building. All HVAC systems must be tested to ensure that smoke cannot enter any nonsmoking area of a building. For consistent quality indoor air, LEED-CI provides a credit for systems that have outdoor air delivery monitors (2005). Monitoring systems are designed to test the airflow and CO_2 levels within a building. An alarm signals when the monitoring system detects that the minimum ventilation requirements are not in compliance.

The aforementioned strategies impact the design of the HVAC system and the configuration of the building. To ensure quality indoor air from the onset, LEED-CI provides credit for projects that employ strategies that help to reduce contaminants in the building from construction activities and prior to occupancy. The purpose of the credit is to encourage contractors to reduce or eliminate contaminants starting at the construction phase. During the construction phase, large amounts of emissions from new products can be introduced to the environment, and building processes produce enormous amounts of dust. To help eliminate contaminants from buildings during construction, LEED-CI suggests several approaches, including (1) the development of an IAQ management plan, (2) protecting the HVAC system from dust and odors, (3) exhausting air directly to the outdoors during installation of VOC-emitting materials, (4) proper housekeeping procedures, and (5) a well-designed schedule of operations (2005).

The LEED-CI suggests an IAQ management plan that starts at preconstruction and continues throughout the life of the project (2005). Controlling airborne contaminants is essential for the well-being of the future occupants and the workers who are exposed to the environment during construction. The management plan should involve all of the stakeholders of the construction phases, including subcontractors, architects, engineers, and interior designers. Generally, the contractor is responsible for executing and coordinating the plan. The management plan serves to emphasize the importance of protecting the IAQ and helps to inform people of their roles and responsibilities for each phase of construction. For example, the management plan should indicate when and how the HVAC equipment is sealed. The plan should also specify the ideal time to schedule the installation of any materials that are highly absorbent, such as insulation, ceiling tiles, carpeting, and gypsum wallboard. Many materials can absorb contaminants that could remain after people occupy the building. Thus, proper installation sequencing can avoid contact with contaminants and subsequently enhance IAQ.

Prior to occupancy, LEED-CI recommends thorough housekeeping procedures and **flush-out** activities that help to eliminate air quality problems from the construction process (2005). The LEED-CI suggests that a construction project should have prescribed housekeeping activities during the construction phases and prior to occupancy. The purpose is to try to contain contaminants as soon as they are produced. Cleaning methods could include extensive vacuuming and wet applications to collect construction dust. Flush-out methods are fairly complex, and LEED-CI provides detailed procedures. Fundamentally, the process involves using the HVAC system to remove airborne contaminants. Fresh air is forced through the HVAC system to displace any off-gassed toxins. The process is done after construction and the installation of interior finishes and prior to occupancy. Thus, LEED-CI emphasizes the importance of allowing adequate time in the management plan for a thorough flush-out. In addition, IAQ testing must be scheduled before people move into the space. The LEED-CI also recommends the installation of new filtration media prior to occupancy. Knowledge of these important procedures can help interior design-

ers coordinate the appropriate time for deliveries of interior products and furniture to the site.

Humidity is the measure of the amount of moisture, or water vapor, that is in the air. For most people, comfortable humidity levels in a room are at least 30 percent and no more than 60 percent. The ANSI/ASHRAE Standard 55-2004 addresses the appropriate moisture loads for HVAC systems. Humidity is one of the considerations related to thermal comfort. Humidity is included in the criteria for thermal comfort in LEED-CI's *Indoor Environmental Quality* category. There are many factors that affect the humidity in a building, including the climatic conditions, the design of the structure's envelope, construction, and the HVAC system. The latitude of the site and proximity to water affect humidity levels. Generally, regions closest to the equator and locations next to water have high humidity levels. Damp, tropical climates have problems with humidity throughout the year. Due to the lack of water, deserts have low humidity levels of approximately 10 percent. Outdoor humidity levels vary throughout the day and during the year. Frequently, humidity levels are high in the morning due to the presence of dew and fog. Generally, humidity levels are high in warm climates and during the summer months in cold regions. The opposite occurs in cold regions during the winter months, when humidity levels are generally too low and moisture must be added to interior environments.

The building envelope design and how the construction was executed affect humidity levels. Excess water or moisture affects the health of people and causes some of the most significant damage to structural components and interior materials. The building's envelope must be designed and constructed to prevent moisture infiltration. Water can enter a building from leaks in the foundation, walls, roof, and windows. Internally, water can pose a problem from plumbing leaks, moisture-generating appliances, or the drip pans of HVAC systems. Inspections should be conducted on a regular basis to locate any condensation or wet spots in a building. The sources of the problem should be identified and rectified as soon as possible. The longer water remains in an area or on a surface, the more damage that will occur to the object and to the IAQ.

Too much moisture creates problems with mold

and mildew. Mold can create a variety of health effects and symptoms, including allergic reactions. In addition, eventually mold will destroy most materials, especially building materials, furnishings, fabrics, wood, carpet, drywall, and plaster. Routine inspections should be performed throughout a building to detect mold. The survey should include closets, attics, basements, the perimeters of rooms, and especially rooms with high moisture activities, such as bathrooms and kitchens. Mold can be deceptive because a material, such as a wallcovering, may not reveal mold on the side facing a room but the backside might have mold. Some of the problems to look for include condensation, wet stains, moisture blisters, rust, rotted wood, cracked masonry, and musty-smelling odors. The EPA recommends that if mold is detected in the HVAC system, the unit should not be used until the entire system has undergone remediation, including the air handler, air diffusers, ducts, and returns (2001). See the EPA guidelines for safe remediation procedures.

Sustainable designs must have the proper moisture load in a building. Frequently, the focus is on the ill effects of too much moisture—which is a major problem—but too little humidity is also a detrimental environmental condition. Too little moisture has health consequences, such as contributing to dry skin and irritating the nose, throat, and lungs. Dry environments are also detrimental to wood structures and furniture and contribute to static electricity. Low water vapor in an interior can cause wood to become brittle, and finishes can peel and crack (see Figure 7.15).

In ancient times, to create a cooler environment, the Egyptians, Greeks, and Romans hung a wet mat in front of windows and other large openings. The water helped to cool the wind as it flowed through the mats. The fundamental technology of circulating air and using a cooling medium is applied to current mechanical systems. The HVAC systems and local units are designed to monitor and control the thermal comfort in interiors. Air conditioners or dehumidifiers help to remove moisture from the air, and some units filter out dirt and pollen. To help protect the health, well-being, and safety of occupants and preserve the built environment, HVAC systems must be routinely inspected and maintained. To reduce the moisture level in the air, all leaks must be re-

Fig. 7.15. Dry environments are detrimental to wood. Low water vapor in an interior can cause wood to crack.

paired and ventilation rates must be adjusted. Mold occurs when moisture and warmth are present. Increasing ventilation rates will help to prevent moisture. To help remove excess moisture, odors, and pollutants, exhaust fans are installed at specific locations, such as bathrooms, laboratories, and kitchens. To help conserve electricity, exhaust fans could be connected to occupancy sensors, automatic humidistat controllers, or timers.

Humidity levels affect the perceived temperature of a space. Warm temperatures and high humidity are uncomfortable to most people because perspiration does not evaporate easily. Generally, the room temperature can be higher or lower than average when the humidity level is appropriate. For example, in the summer when the humidity level in a building is lower, people feel comfortable at warmer temperatures. During the winter the opposite effect can occur. People can tolerate a lower room temperature when the humidity level is comfortable. Using an appropriate humidity level to alter people's perception of the thermal climate can help to conserve energy.

Impact of Indoor Environmental Quality on People

In recent years a great deal of research has focused on the impact of the IEQ on people. Chapter 2 reviewed many of the physical effects on people caused by pollutants. In addition to these detrimental consequences, there are other effects associated with the IEQ. Most of the IEQ research examines the effects on people in offices, retail stores, and schools. The most frequent variables studied are the effects of daylight, air quality, thermal comfort, ventilation, noise, electrical lighting, and personal control of an environment. These variables can affect SBS symptoms, productivity, absenteeism, illness, performance, and overall satisfaction with an environment.

Benefits associated with daylight have been documented by research. The most frequently cited research is the extensive work conducted by the Heschong Mahone Group for the California Energy Commission. In 1999, the Heschong Mahone Group conducted a study on the effect of daylighting in schools. The research found that daylighting in the classroom positively affected the performance of students on standardized math and reading tests. In studying the results, people identified follow-up questions regarding the findings. Consequently, in 2003 the Heschong Mahone Group conducted a reanalysis of the study by focusing on the following tasks: a teacher survey, an analysis of teacher bias, a grade level analysis, and an analysis of absenteeism. Heschong found that the reanalysis confirmed the findings of the 1999 study. According to the Heschong Mahone Group, the reanalysis found that "elementary school students in classrooms with the most daylight showed a 21 percent improvement in learning rates compared to students in classrooms with the least daylight" (2003, p. i). Heschong found that teacher assignment bias did not affect the results and the daylighting effect did not vary by grade. In addition, the physical classroom characteristics did not have an effect on student absenteeism. Heschong concluded, "Daylight has a positive and highly significant association with improved student performance."

In another study examining the effects of daylighting, the Heschong Mahone Group analyzed the effects of daylight and retail stores for the California Energy Commission. From 1999 to 2001 the Heschong Mahone Group studied 73 store locations of a major retailer in California. Twenty-four of the stores had significant amounts of daylight illumination. This study was a follow-up to a study performed by Pacific Gas and Electric (PG&E) in 1999. To compare results, Heschong utilized a different retail sector than PG&E. Both studies reveal that retailers experienced higher sales in daylit stores than in similar non-daylit stores. Heschong reported that "increased annual hours of useful daylight per store were strongly associated with increased sales, but at a smaller magnitude than a previous [PG&E] study" (2003, p. i). Heschong noted that the retailer reported a reduction in operating costs due to daylighting; however, the profit from increased sales was worth more than the energy savings. Employees of the retailer indicated a slightly higher satisfaction with the daylighting conditions compared to the non-daylit stores.

In addition to daylighting, many research studies have examined the impact of the IEQ, including air quality, on people. In a study by Mendell and Heath, the results indicate that IEQ in schools affected student health, performance, and absenteeism (2005). The study found that IEQ improvements, which are beneficial to the health of students, are likely to enhance performance and attendance rates. Specifically, Mendell and Heath recommended that schools should prevent dampness, provide adequate ventilation, and reduce exposure to contaminants. Pollutants identified were nitrogen dioxide, formaldehyde, and any pollution associated with high densities. In another study for the California Energy Commission, the Heschong Mahone Group examined whether daylight and other aspects of the indoor environment affected student learning in elementary schools. The attributes of the classroom that were studied included ventilation, IAQ, thermal comfort, acoustics, electric lighting, quality of view to the outdoors, and type of classroom. Heschong found in the study that the "visual environment is very important for learning" (2003, p. ix). To enhance student outcomes, the classroom should have (1) "an ample and pleasant view"; (2) elimination of glare on writing surfaces and from direct sunlight; (3) window treatments used to control glare that are controllable by the teacher; (4) an effective acoustical environment by eliminating annoying sounds or excessive noise from outside the classroom; (5) proper ventilation and IAQ; and (6) satisfactory physical characteristics of classrooms, especially quality windows.

The Heschong Mahone Group found that windows and a pleasant view were also important to office employees (2003). In another study prepared for the California Energy Commission, Heschong examined the influences of daylight and view on office worker performance. A secondary focus was the effects of ventilation and thermal comfort. Better performance was consistently reported when office workers had access to views, appropriate daylight levels, and effective ventilation. Heschong found that the size of the window and the type of objects outdoors affected worker productivity. Office employees had the highest performance when they could look out large windows and when the view was vegetation. Office workers also reported better health conditions. In contrast, people without a view indicated greater fatigue. Desktop glare had a negative effect on productivity, and higher cubicle partitions were associated with slower performance.

Many research studies have examined the performance of office employees and IEQ. The academic publication *International Journal of Indoor Environment and Health* has published several articles regarding the effects of indoor air on office employees. These studies have focused on how productivity is affected by IAQ, ventilation properties, thermal comfort, humidity, noise, SBS symptoms, and absenteeism. Research has found that good indoor air quality is beneficial for the health, comfort, and productivity of people (Wargocki, Lagercrantz, Witterseh, Sundell, Wyon, and Fanger, 2002; Wyon, 2004). Poor IAQ contributes to decreases in productivity and overall dissatisfaction with an environment. Research suggests that, in general, to improve IAQ the most energy-efficient solutions focus on selecting low-polluting building materials and eliminating the sources of pollution. To conserve energy, these strategies should be employed prior to increasing the outdoor air supply rates.

Other studies examined the combined effects of ventilation rates, thermal comfort, and humidity on perceived air quality and SBS symptoms. Indoor air temperature and humidity affect the perception of air quality, productivity, and SBS symptoms. Many studies emphasized the importance of effective ventilation rates and recommended rates above the minimum levels prescribed in standards and guidelines (Fang, Wyon, Clausen, and Fanger, 2004; Heschong Mahone Group, 2003; Wargocki, Wyon, Sundell, Clausen, and Fanger, 2000). A large manufacturer found that the cost of additional ventilation might be offset by the savings from reduced sick leave (Milton, Markglencross, and Walters, 2000). In addition, effective ventilation has positive impacts on health and

productivity by reducing the prevalence of airborne infectious diseases (Seppanen and Fisk, 2004). Consequently, there are fewer sick days.

To maximize the benefits associated with healthy ventilation, pleasant views, and passive solar energy, some buildings are being designed to encourage interaction with the natural environment. Initially, the introduction of electricity and air-conditioning encouraged architects to design buildings that facilitated the conditioned air and eliminated unwanted noise from the outdoors. An excellent example of this is the Larkin building by Frank Lloyd Wright (see Figure 7.16). Since this time, the totally enclosed building has been replaced by interiors that are healthy and comfortable for people. Increasingly popular architectural features are sky gardens, sky lobbies, or wintergardens (see Figure 7.17). The purposes of the sky gardens are to provide an accessible area for people to interact with vegetation, improve natural ventilation by incorporating operable

Fig. 7.16. (top) In 1903 Frank Lloyd Wright designed the Larkin Building in Buffalo, NY, to maximize conditioned air and eliminate unwanted noise from the outdoors.

Fig. 7.17. (bottom) Sky gardens provide areas for people to interact with vegetation and can enhance ventilation and daylight. Rendering of the sky gardens in the SOM Master Plan.

windows, and increase exposure to daylight. Air and light flow through the facades and the gardens, which enhances the IEQ for its occupants. In some situations the natural ventilation moves through the building by a **chimney action**. In operating like the chimney of a fireplace, air flows into the building at openings near the lower level and then moves vertically to openings near the roof. When working on the interior design of these buildings, it is important to avoid obstructions that would constrict the natural flow of air.

Research indicates that people prefer to have personal control of their thermal comfort, ventilation, and lighting. Personalized controls can improve occupants' perceived air quality and decrease the intensity of SBS symptoms (Kaczmarczyk, Melikov, and Fanger, 2004). Sustainable designs should have environments that have the proper thermal comfort, ventilation, and humidity levels. Whenever possible, the preferred solution is to provide the users of the space with the ability to control their environment. New systems are available that include personal controls at every workstation in an office (see Figure 7.18). These individual environmental controls, or personalized ventilation systems, can be located at the floor or mounted on a work surface or within a workstation. Kaczmarczyk et al. recommend that more efficient air terminal devices should be designed (2004). Other researchers report that desk-edge-mounted ventilation systems could increase the effective ventilation rate by 50 percent (Faulkner, Fisk, Sullivan, and Lee, 2004).

Research has emphasized the importance of controlling noise in various settings, including offices, schools, homes, and neighborhoods (Heschong Mahone Group, 2003). Noise distractions in open office plans can increase fatigue and have many negative effects on the performance of office work (Witterseh, Wyon, and Clausen, 2004). The Environmental Health Officers in England and Wales reported that one of the most common disputes between neighbors is noise. The agency reported that 74 percent of the noise complaints they received in 2001–2002 were from domestic premises (EcoHomes, 2005). Sustainable interiors and communities must focus on controlling noise emitted from the built environment. Some solutions include installing sound-absorbing materials between interior walls, spec-

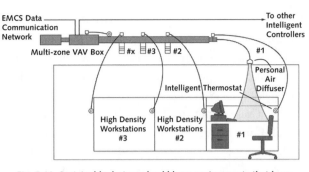

Fig. 7.18. Sustainable designs should have environments that have the proper thermal comfort, ventilation, and humidity levels. Systems are available that include personal controls at every workstation in an office.

ifying quiet HVAC and lighting systems, isolating loud equipment, and using sound-masking systems. Sound-masking systems can provide an unobtrusive background noise sometimes referred to as *white sound*.

INDOOR AIR QUALITY: MANAGEMENT OF MATERIAL EMISSIONS

The structural components of a building, products, and materials affect the IAQ of all residential and commercial interiors. Chapter 2 briefly identified the contaminants and their effects on people and the built environment. This section focuses on analyzing many of the products involved in specifying materials and products for interiors. The LEED-CI indicates that before occupancy the following chemical contaminants must be tested to ensure maximum concentration limits are not exceeded: formaldehyde, particulate matter (PM10), total volatile organic compounds (TVOC), 4-phenycyclohexene (4-PCH), and carbon monoxide (CO) (2005). The VOCs are a particular concern of interior designers because they are present in thousands of interior products. Ideally, products for sustainable interiors should not contain any contaminants. If this is not possible, the product should have low-emitting materials.

To reduce the quantity of indoor air contaminants, LEED-CI applies several referenced standards (2005). The products that can receive LEED-CI credit for complying with prescribed requirements are adhesives, sealants, paint, coatings, carpet systems, composite wood, laminate adhesives, and systems furniture and seating. For adhesives, sealants, and sealant primers, the referenced standard is South

Coast Air Quality Management District (SCAQMD) Rule 1168 (2003). **Green Seal Standard 36 (GS-36)** (2000) applies to aerosol adhesives. The referenced standards for topcoat paint and anticorrosive/anti-rust paint are GS-11 (1993) and GS-03 (1997), respectively. The **Carpet and Rug Institute's Green Label Plus** testing and product requirements are used for carpet and the carpet pad. To determine the indoor air concentrations of systems furniture and seating, LEED-CI applies the EPA's *Environmental Technology Verification (ETV) Large Chamber Test Protocol for Measuring Emissions of VOCs and Aldehydes* (1999).

Chemical Contaminants and IAQ

Chapter 2 introduced indoor air pollutants by providing descriptions of contaminants, their primary sources, and potential health effects (see Table 2.8). This section will focus on the relationship between specific products and the contaminants identified in LEED-CI's *Indoor Environmental Quality* category. Formaldehyde is a chemical used in numerous interior products. Formaldehyde in materials is released as a colorless gas into the air. A very dominant source of formaldehyde is pressed-wood products made with urea-formaldehyde (UF) resins. The UF resins are used as adhesives in particleboard, hardwood plywood, oriented strand board, and medium-density fiberboard. Many of these woods are used to construct subfloors, cabinets, shelves, hardwood plywood wall paneling, laminated flooring, and doors. Formaldehyde can also be present in glues, adhesives, carpets, paint, coating products, composite wood furnishings, and permanent-press clothing and draperies. To receive LEED-CI credit item EQ 3.2, "the total [formaldehyde] emissions from all building materials must not result in an indoor concentration greater than 50 ppb (parts per billion) with the building ventilation system operating in the minimum outside air mode" (2005, p. 303). To help reduce exposure to formaldehyde, the EPA recommends using PF pressed wood products, maintaining moderate temperature, reducing humidity, and increasing ventilation, especially when a new product is placed in a room (2005).

Particulate matter (PM10) is the term for a variety of substances in the air, such as dirt, dust, and soot. The number 10 represents the size of test sample par-

ticles. An aerodynamic diameter less than or equal to a nominal 10 micrometers qualifies for PM10. Concentrations at this level are associated with asthma, respiratory symptoms, and chronic bronchitis (EPA, 2005). The LEED-CI requires that "total emissions from all building materials must not result in an indoor concentration greater than 50 µg/m3 (micrograms per cubic meter) with the building ventilation system operating in the minimum outside air mode" (2005, p. 303). To help reduce PM, LEED-CI recommends that precautions should be performed during construction and prior to occupancy. In addition, maintenance and cleaning services should have detailed procedures regarding the removal of particulates in the air and on surfaces, especially carpet. To remove dirt, dust, dust mites, and other sources of allergens, carpet should be vacuumed thoroughly on a very regular basis. Some environments should be vacuumed daily. Entryway track-off systems are very useful in helping to attract dust, dirt, and moisture from shoes as people enter a building. Most track-off systems are metal grates or floor mats.

The colorless liquid 4-PCH is associated with the "new carpet" odor. The source is the styrene butadiene rubber (SBR) that can be used to bind carpet fibers to the backing material. The health effects associated with 4-PCH include headaches, nausea, and eye irritation. Some carpet does not have SBR. When SBR is present, the LEED-CI prescribes that the maximum concentration level of 4-PCH is 6.5 µg/m3 (2005).

The LEED-CI maximum concentration levels for carbon monoxide (CO) are 9 ppm (parts per million) and no greater than 2 ppm above outdoor levels (2005). Indoor CO occurs from the incomplete combustion of products including woodstoves; unvented kerosene and gas space heaters; leaking chimneys and furnaces; gas water heaters; tobacco smoke; and automobile exhaust from attached garages (EPA, 2005). Carbon monoxide can cause flulike symptoms and is fatal at very high concentrations. To reduce exposure to CO, some of the recommendations provided by the EPA are to properly adjust gas appliances, vent space heaters, use the proper fuels in kerosene space heaters, install exhaust fans vented to the outdoors over gas stoves, and open flues when using a fireplace (2005) (see Figure 7.19).

Building materials and interior products emit

Fig. 7.19. To reduce exposure to carbon monoxide, exhaust fans from equipment such as kerosene heaters should be vented to the outdoors.

hundreds of VOCs into the air, and collectively the contaminants comprise the TVOC. The chemicals are emitted as gases. Thus, to determine the true TVOC of a product, testing should be performed on its content and emissions. The products that emit VOCs include adhesives, glues, sealants, paint, coatings, pressed wood products, carpet, composite wood furnishings, pesticides, and dry-cleaned fabrics. To reduce exposure to VOCs, the EPA suggests to increase ventilation when using products with VOCs and to carefully follow label instructions (Figure 7.20). In addition, limited quantities should be purchased and unused contents should be thrown away according to the local toxic waste procedures. Due to the potentially serious side effects, the EPA recommends avoiding emissions from products containing methylene chloride, benzene, and perchloroethylene. Methylene chloride is found in paint strippers, adhesive removers, and aerosol spray paint. Benzene is in environmental tobacco smoke, stored fuels, and paint supplies. Perchloroethylene is present in newly dry-cleaned materials. For LEED-CI credit, "the total emissions from all building materials must not result in an indoor concentration greater than 500 µg/m3 (micrograms per cubic meter) with the building ventilation system operating in the minimum outside air mode" (2005, p. 303).

The Air Resources Board (ARB) of the State of California conducted a comparative analysis of three major programs that test products for the presence of VOCs. The programs examined were Green Seal, California Section 01350—Special Environmental

Requirements, and GREENGUARD Certification Program. Green Seal is an independent nonprofit organization that tests products based on the content of VOCs. Green Seal does not test for product emissions performance. Green Seal standards include GS-36, GS-11, and GS-03. California Section 01350 was created to test materials for the 1.5-million-square-foot *Capital Area East End Complex* in Sacramento, California. According to the ARB, Section 01350 is important for the development of IAQ guidelines, but due to its purpose, more testing needs to occur prior to being used for other projects. The GREENGUARD Certification Program tests for more than 2,000 individual VOCs in a product and reports the emission levels. As an indoor air quality program, GREENGUARD assists manufacturers in producing low-emitting products.

The report provides consumer awareness of how the programs test products and how to evaluate information. The ARB reports that IAQ performance must be determined by using an environmental chamber-testing unit. The ARB indicates that "there is a common misconception that products that do not contain VOCs do not release VOCs into the indoor environment" (2004, p. 2). Thus, products labeled as "formaldehyde free," "low VOC," "IAQ

Fig. 7.20. Designing a healthy IAQ requires a close examination of the content of building materials and interior products. Reading content labels of interior products is essential.

friendly," or "safe" might reflect the content, but not its emissions. Other considerations that should be researched when determining a product's VOC include the date of a test report, the selection of the representative product sample, the chain-of-custody procedures, and the type of chemicals tested in a program. To determine the IAQ performance of a product, the ARB recommends that test reports should not be older than one year. For accuracy, the product specified should have the same characteristics as the item that was tested. The ARB notes that this can be very difficult to accomplish because one furniture item may be available in hundreds of different combinations based on the wide availability of fabrics, stains, and finishes. The chain-of-custody process should ensure that the manufacturer complied with the certifying program's guidelines for packaging and shipping the product to the testing facility. The ARB recommends that for an IAQ program to be effective, testing should involve all VOCs emitted. Some programs only test for a relatively small number of VOCs.

Finishes and IAQ

To have healthy IAQ requires a close examination of the content of building materials and interior products. Content labels of interior products should be scrutinized in the same manner as food labels (see http://www.howproductsimpact.net). Now that scientific research has confirmed the presence of indoor contaminants and studies have identified the negative effects to the health of people, it is imperative that interior designers acquire complete information regarding a product prior to specification. Understanding how to read labels and knowing if the information provided by the manufacturer is complete is essential when specifying sustainable interiors. Ethically, and most likely legally in the future, interior designers are responsible for the products they recommend to clients. The increased awareness of sustainable products, and the considerable interest in attaining certifications for buildings, has prompted many manufacturers to produce products that are good for the environment. As the demand grows, more products will be designed and prices will continue to decrease.

There are many products in *CSI Division 9: Finishes*

that should be reviewed for their impact on the IAQ. This number and product category is based on the Construction Specifications Institute (CSI) Master-Format numbering system. In examining the effects of materials on the IAQ, the products reviewed are adhesives, sealants, paint, coatings, and flooring systems. SCAQMD Rule 1168 is LEED-CI's referenced standard for adhesives, sealants, and sealant primers. Rule 1168 has several sections: purpose, applicability, definitions, requirements, record-keeping requirements, methods of analysis, test methods, and exemptions. The purpose of Rule 1168 is to "reduce emissions of VOCs and to eliminate emissions of chloroform, ethylene dichloride, methylene chloride, perchloroethylene, and trichloroethylene from the application of adhesives, adhesive bonding primers, sealants, sealant primers, or any other primers" (SCAQMD, 2005, p. 1). This rule applies to the sale and application of the aforementioned materials.

Adhesives are defined as "any substance that is used to bond one surface to another surface by attachment. Adhesives include adhesive bonding primers, adhesive primers for plastics, and any other primer[s]" (SCAQMD, 2005, p. 1). Rule 1168 defines sealants as "any material with adhesive properties that is formulated primarily to fill, seal, or waterproof gaps or joints between two surfaces. Sealants include sealant primers and caulks" (SCAQMD, 2005, p. 8). A sealant primer is "any product applied to a substrate, prior to the application of a sealant, to enhance the bonding surface" (SCAQMD, 2005, p. 8). The requirements focus on the VOC limits for architectural applications (see Table 7.1). According to Green Seal (GS-36), an aerosol adhesive is "a mixture of rubber, resins, and liquid and gaseous solvents and propellants packaged in a container for hand-held application" (Green Seal, 2000, p. 1). Table 7.1 provides Green Seal's VOC limits for aerosol adhesives.

In working with a client, an interior designer would most likely be involved with products that require adhesives. The two primary products that may require adhesives are flooring and wallcoverings. Generally, floor manufacturers provide recommendations for the most suitable adhesives for their product. To reduce problems associated with IAQ whenever possible, flooring adhesive should be solvent-free, low- or zero-VOC, and water-based. Wallcovering adhesives should be low-VOC. A spe-

Table 7.1
Volatile Organic Compounds (VOCs)
Limits for Adhesives (GS-36)

Adhesive Type	VOC Weight (grams/liter minus water)
ABS welding	Not provided
Carpet pad installation	400
Ceramic tile installation	150
Contact bond	130
Contact bond-specialty substrates	250
Cove base installation	400
CPVC welding	150
Indoor floor covering installation	490
Multipurpose construction	150
Nonmembrane roof installation/repair	200
Other plastic cement welding	300
Outdoor floor covering installation	510
PVC welding	250
Rubber floor installation	510
Single-ply roof membrane	150
Installation/repair	250
Structural glazing	100
Perimeter bonded sheet vinyl flooring	660
Installation	170
Waterproof rescorcinol glue	150
Wood flooring adhesive	Not provided

ADHESIVES APPLICATION
ONTO SUBSTRATE

Flexible vinyl	250
Fiberglass	200
Metal-to-metal	30
Porous material	120
Plastic foams	120
Rubber	250
Other substrates	250

AEROSOL ADHESIVES

General-purpose mist spray	65% VOCs by weight
General-purpose web spray	55% VOCs by weight
Special-purpose aerosol adhesives (all types)	70% VOCs by weight

SOURCE: Green Seal (2000), *Commercial Adhesives (GS-36)*.

cial concern related to wallcoverings is materials that are highly absorbent, such as natural grass fibers. Since these materials require a greater amount of adhesives, the emissions can have higher levels of VOCs. In addition to VOCs emitted from adhesives, vinyl and polyvinyl chloride (PVC) wallcoverings have the potential to pose many environmental problems. Vinyl wallcoverings can emit high levels of VOCs, and burning the material emits highly dangerous chemicals. This can be a problem for outdoor air pollution and for firefighters combating building fires. In addition, the inherent properties of a vinyl wallcovering can encourage the growth of mold and mildew next to the wall surface. Any nonporous material must be monitored for the extremely detrimental growth of mold.

GS-11 and GS-03 are LEED-CI's standards for paint and anticorrosive paint, respectively. Table 7.2 provides the VOC limits for interior paint and anticorrosive paint in the following types: non-flat, flat, gloss, and semigloss. In addition to VOC limits, Green Seal has performance requirements for paint, which include scrubbability, hiding power, and washability. These requirements are important for sustainable interiors because they enhance the durability of paint and reduce the quantity of resources. Paint that can be scrubbed and washed does not have to be reapplied often. Paint with good opacity or hiding power requires fewer coats to cover a surface. GS-11 and GS-03 identify several chemical compounds that should not be used in paint, including methylene chloride, benzene, and formaldehyde. GS-03 stipulates that the paint can and its contents cannot be manufactured with lead.

Table 7.3 also includes the VOC limits for architectural coatings as prescribed by SCAQMD Rule 1113. The purpose of Rule 1113 is to "limit the VOC

Table 7.2
VOC Limits for Interior Paint (GS-11) and
Anticorrosive Paint (GS-03)

Paints (GS-11)	VOC Weight (grams/liter of product, minus water)
INTERIOR COATINGS—Coating Type	
Non-flat	150
Flat	50
EXTERIOR COATINGS—Coating Type	
Non-flat	200
Flat	100
ANTICORROSIVE PAINTS (GC-03)— **Coating Type**	
Gloss	250
Semigloss	250
Flat	250

SOURCES: Green Seal (2005), *Paints (GS-11)* and Green Seal (2005), *Anti-Corrosive Paints (GC-03)*.

Table 7.3
VOC Limits for Architectural Coatings as Prescribed by SCAQMD Rule 1113

Coating	Limit (grams of VOC per liter of coating, less water and less exempt compounds)
Bond breakers	350
Clear wood finishes	
Varnish	350
Sanding sealers	350
Lacquer	680
Clear brushing lacquer	680
Concrete-curing compounds	350
Dry-fog coatings	400
Fire-proofing exterior coatings	450
Fire-retardant coatings	
Clear	650
Pigmented	350
Flats	250
Floor coatings	420
Graphic arts (sign) coatings	500
Industrial maintenance (IM) coatings	
High-temperature IM coatings	420
Zinc-rich IM primers	420
Japans/faux finishing coatings	700
Magnesite cement coatings	600
Mastic coatings	300
Metallic pigmented coatings	500
Multicolor coatings	420
Non-flat coatings	250
Pigmented lacquer	680
Pretreatment wash primers	780
Primers, sealers, and undercoaters	350
Quick-dry enamels	400
Quick-dry primers, sealers, and undercoaters	350
Recycled coatings	
Rust-preventative coatings	420
Shellac	
Clear	730
Pigmented	550
Specialty Primers	350
Stains	350
Stains, interior	250
Waterproofing sealers	400
Waterproofing concrete/masonry	
Sealers	400
Wood preservatives	
Below-ground	350
Other	350

SOURCE: SCAQMD Rule 1113, *Architectural Coatings* (2004).

content of architectural coatings used in the District or to allow the averaging of such coatings, as specified, so their actual emissions do not exceed the allowable emissions if all the averaged coatings had complied with the specified limits" (SCAQMD, 2004, p. 1). The SCAQMD defines a coating as "a material which is applied to a surface to beautify, protect, or provide a barrier to such surface" (2004, p. 2). Coatings can include varnishes, lacquer, fire-retardant coatings, shellacs, and stains.

In specifying paint for a client, the contents should have low-VOCs or zero-VOCs. These paints are typically water-based, or interior latex. Some oil-based paint is available in low-VOC. To have products that are more environmentally responsible, some manufacturers have developed paint that is made from plants, minerals, and milk (see Figure 7.21). As with other products, the label should be reviewed to determine VOCs. Some materials can contain natural VOCs. Milk-based (food-grade) paint should only be used indoors and in dry conditions. Some food-grade paint has fungicides to help prevent mold. Colorants can increase VOC emissions, but some manufacturers have products with tints that are zero-VOC colorants. Generally, zero-VOC paint is available in flat, eggshell, satin, and semigloss finishes. There are a variety of chemicals that should not be present in paint, including formaldehyde, ammonia, mercury, lead acetate, crystalline silica, or ethylene glycol. Preferred products have contents that are safe for people who are chemically sensitive; have low-toxins, non-petroleum-based, or minimum biocides; and are odor-free. Recycled paint is available from a few manufacturers. The source of recycled paint can be derived from community toxic waste collections or from remanufactured paint.

Wood finishes and stains are coatings that are often specified by an interior designer. According to Green Seal, in 2004 wood finish products resulted in sales of approximately $2 billion (2005). Waterborne coatings that are low in VOCs and without aromatic solvents and heavy metals are starting to dominate the market. A wood finish is available in a liquid, paste, or gel form. There are basically two types of wood finishes (Green Seal, 2005). Some finishes form a coating on wood, such as varnish, shellac, lacquer, and stains. The other type of finish has an oil base

Fig. 7.21. To have products that are more environmentally responsible, some manufacturers have developed paint that has milk content.

that penetrates the wood. These finishes include tung oil, linseed oil, and oil-based stains. Other materials in finishes are pigments, resins, solvents, and thinners. Additives, such as substances that help to prevent fungus or mildew, can also be contained in finishes. To improve the health of people and the environment, Green Seal indicates that there is resurgence in creating varnishes in the manner that was done for centuries. The original content of varnishes was natural resins and oils. Subsequently, synthetic resins were created from petroleum-based products. Currently, these are the substances that are being eliminated from finishes. Manufacturers are returning to the centuries-old practice of using pure oils and other natural ingredients. For wood coatings and stains, Green Seal (2005) recommends that products should not contain the following chemicals and compounds: VOCs exceeding 350 g/L for coatings (250 g/L for stains); carcinogens (i.e., 1,4-dioxane, acetaldehyde); aromatic solvents (toluene, xylene); phthalates; heavy metals (i.e., lead, cobalt, zinc) and their compounds; reproductive toxins; and ozone-depleting chemicals (i.e., 1,1,1-trichloroethane).

To enhance IAQ, all materials used in flooring systems should have low-VOC emissions, including the substrate, finishes, and adhesives. This is to help protect the health of installers, occupants, and maintenance crews. Particleboard, which may be used for an underlayment, should not contain formaldehyde.

Water-based finishes and adhesives should have low VOCs. Adhesives used for tile setting may also have VOCs. Whenever possible, natural oils, such as tung or linseed oil, should be used for finishes. Cleaning products and procedures should be environmentally safe and healthy for the maintenance staff and the occupants. The VOC content of products used to strip and finish floors should be low, and the products should not contain carcinogens. Many floor maintenance products have high levels of VOCs, including glycol ethers. These are potentially hazardous when inhaled and when the substance comes in contact with skin. The following numbers identify glycol ethers: 111-76-2 (ethylene glycol butyl ether—EGBE); 109-86-4 (ethylene glycol methyl ether—EGME); and 110-80-5 (ethylene glycol ethyl ether—EGEE) (Green Seal, 2004).

When using rubber or recycled flooring, precautions must be taken for any potential off-gassing. Frequently, rubber flooring is recommended only for outdoor use or buildings with extensive ventilation systems, such as athletic facilities. Some binders used in floorings, such as cork, are made of UF. Linoleum can be an excellent choice for sustainable flooring because it is made from the natural materials of linseed, wood flour, and pine resins. However, the curing of linseed oil can produce off-gassing of VOCs. This can be a problem for people who are *highly* sensitive to chemicals.

There are many environmental and IAQ aspects related to carpet systems. Nylon, the fiber most often used for carpet, is made from petroleum, which is a nonrenewable resource. The methods associated with processing petrochemicals and constructing the carpet require significant amounts of energy and water. In addition, the processes can emit high levels of pollutants in the air and waterways. Carpet becomes another problem when large quantities are deposited in landfills. Green Seal estimates that in 1999 approximately 2.44 million tons of carpet were landfilled (2001). Green Seal also noted that this amount could completely cover New York City. Besides the serious environmental impacts associated with carpet, the materials used in the fibers, sealants, and adhesives are harmful to the IAQ. The indoor and outdoor detrimental environmental effects present a serious challenge to interior designers. This is especially critical when examining the amount of carpet that is specified every year. Green Seal estimates that in 1999 more than 1.9 billion square yards of carpet were produced in the United States (2001). The United States manufactures approximately 45 percent of the carpet purchased every year worldwide. Approximately three-quarters of the carpet is for residential dwellings, and the remainder is used in commercial buildings. As a primary specifier of carpet, interior designers must be knowledgeable regarding the most sustainable solutions.

In addition to considering the effects of carpet on the IAQ, care must be taken in specifying the carpet pad, adhesives, seam sealants, installation residues, and cleaning products and procedures. The LEED-CI (2005) requires that the carpet and carpet pad must meet or exceed the criteria established by the Carpet and Rug Institute's (CRI) Green Label Testing Program. Table 7.4 provides the maximum emission factors for carpet and carpet pads. The contaminants that are a problem for carpet and carpet pads are TVOCs, 4-PC, and formaldehyde. According to the LEED-CI, the carpet adhesive must meet the criteria for adhesives described earlier in this chapter. Carpet adhesives can emit high quantities of VOCs. This can be especially problematic for commercial buildings, because carpet installations often require adhesives. Whenever possible, tacking carpet rather than gluing is a healthier solution. Carpet should always be installed on a dry flooring underlayment. Moisture eventually ruins the carpet and fosters the growth of mold and mildew.

Removing old carpet and installing new carpet can pose IAQ problems. Dust, dirt, and other contaminants in old carpet can be released into the air when the carpet is removed. Thus, old carpet should be vacuumed and be carefully rolled as it is removed from the room. The highest levels of VOC gases are emitted with new carpet. Some estimates indicate that after the first 72 hours the VOC off-gassing subsides significantly. Thus, whenever possible, new carpet should be allowed to air out outside the building, and people should wait several days before occupying the rooms.

Cleaning products and procedures affect IAQ. Carpet can be especially problematic to IAQ because the fibers can trap soil, dust, particulates, dust mites, and soot. The CRI recommends high-performance

Table 7.4

Maximum Emission Factors for Carpet and Carpet Pads as Prescribed by SCAQMD Rule 1168

Architectural Applications	Current VOC Limit (grams of VOC per liter of coating, less water and less exempt compounds)
Indoor carpet adhesives	50
Carpet pad adhesives	50
Outdoor carpet adhesives	150
Wood flooring adhesives	100
Rubber floor adhesives	60
Subfloor adhesives	50
Ceramic tile adhesives	65
VCT and asphalt tile adhesives	50
Dry wall and panel adhesives	50

SOURCE: SCAQMD Rule 1168, *Adhesive and Sealant Applications* (2005).

vacuum cleaners and recognizes products that meet CRI criteria through its *Green Label Testing Program.* Vacuum cleaners must be effective in removing contaminants and should not disperse dust during the vacuuming process.

To improve the health of IAQ, the LEED-CI provides credit for specifying composite woods, agri-fiber products, and laminate adhesives that have low-emitting materials (2005). Specifically, these materials, including core products, must not have any added UF resins. The LEED-CI defines composite wood as a product that has "wood or plant particles or fibers bonded together by a synthetic resin or binder" (2005, p. 320). Examples of composite board include plywood, particleboard, strawboard, wheatboard, door cores, medium-density fiberboard (MDF), and oriented-strand board (OSB). For LEED-CI credit, the material must be inside the exterior moisture protection. For example, UF binders must not be present in plywood or particleboard, which can be used in finish carpentry, cabinets, and countertops. A substitute binder that does not off-gas any formaldehyde is methyl diisocyanate (MDI). Boards can be made by pressing the MDI binder with bamboo, or straw harvested from oats, rice, and wheat.

Furnishings and IAQ

Systems furniture and seating are also concerns related to indoor air contaminants. The LEED-CI defines systems furniture as "either a panel-based workstation comprised of modular interconnecting panels, hang-on components, and drawer/filing components or a freestanding grouping of furniture items and their components that have been designed to work in concert" (2005, p. 322). Seating is defined as task and guest chairs that are used with systems furniture. The LEED-CI identifies limits associated with the following chemical contaminants: TVOC, formaldehyde, total Aldehydes, and 4-PC (as an odorant) (2005). To receive credit from the LEED-CI, systems furniture and seating must have the GREENGUARD IAQ certification or the products must have been tested using an independent air quality testing laboratory (2005). The EPA has responsibility for the **Environmental Technology Verification (ETV) Program** for indoor air products. The EPA has a cooperative agreement with the Research Triangle Institute (RTI) in North Carolina to (1) perform the tests, (2) evaluate the data, (3) prepare the verification report, and (4) supply the verification statement. The testing is for emissions of aldehydes and VOCs from office furniture. The testing occurs by creating conditions that are similar to a commercial office environment.

Furniture systems and seating are tested within a controlled environment for several days. Emissions can be affected by compositions that are different from the materials tested in the chambers. Thus, when specifying a fabric or finish that is different from the testing protocol, the LEED-CI recommends that the variances should be discussed with the manufacturer. Potential environmental considerations are fabrics that have been treated with chemicals or manufactured with heavy metals or toxins. Paint and coatings can pose problems with IAQ, as described earlier in this section. Furniture systems and seating should also be made with low-emitting adhesives, sealants, and wood composites.

Cushioning foams can adversely affect the IAQ. To construct polyurethane foam, some products have HCFCs, which are being phased out in developed countries. Green Seal indicated that materials such as isoproprene, acetone, and pentane are being used as a substitute for HCFCs (2005). These compounds are "less harmful to the environment." For flame-retardant purposes, foam is often treated with polybrominated diphenyl ethers (PBDEs). Green Seal notes that new concerns are emerging regarding PBDEs and their effect on the health of people. In addition, PBDEs persist in the environment; thus, discarded furniture that is landfilled has become a serious problem.

Some materials used to metal-coat furniture are potentially dangerous to people due to their toxicity. Green Seal indicates that a common plating process involves hexavalent chromium (CrVI) and copper/nickel-plate is applied as an undercoat (2005). The electroplating process can release heavy metals. The EPA considers CrVI and nickel dust as human carcinogens. Thus, Green Seal has several recommendations for metal plating on furniture: use tin-cobalt alloy, nickel-alloy, or trivalent chromium (CrIII) rather than CrVI plating; avoid designs that require metal plating by using the powder coating process; design uncoated metal furniture; and use water-based, low-VOC metal paint (2005). The powder-coating process is a sustainable solution because the process does not include heavy metals and has zero-VOC emissions. Powder coatings use resins and dry pigment particles.

All adhesives, paint, coatings, resins, and finishes used on furniture should have low-VOC or zero-VOC emissions. Some manufacturers use hot-melt glue and double-sided tape as substitutes for adhesives with high-VOC. Green Seal delineates that finishes for furniture that produce low emissions of VOCs are: two-component, catalyzed coating that uses a polyurethane base; supercritical carbon dioxide/solvent-based finish; and a coating that uses ultraviolet light as a curing agent (2005).

Green Seal surveyed more than 25 U.S. manufacturers of office furniture to determine how their products affect the environment and IAQ. With respect to concerns regarding IAQ, Green Seal requested manufacturers to indicate the materials they used in the furniture and emissions information. Desirable characteristics related to IAQ were using powder coating (or electrodeposition without CrVI) and formaldehyde-free adhesives. Manufacturers reported using the following nontoxic products: polyurethane foam, water-based adhesives, and hot melt adhesives. The products also meet IAQ standards for GREENGUARD certification by using powder coating, powder resins, zero-VOC emissions, and electrodeposition without CrVI.

Summary

- Indoor environmental quality (IEQ) is a comprehensive approach to many of the elements that affect users' perception of a space, including daylight, ventilation, temperature, humidity, noise, electrical light sources, and personal control of a setting.
- Many factors associated with a site affect daylighting, including its latitude, topography, trees, and adjacent buildings.
- The building's form and the location, size, and orientation of windows affect daylighting.
- Successful daylighting can occur only when the negative effects of sunlight are minimized, and when energy is conserved by effectively integrating natural light with electrical sources.
- There are many external shading units that can shield sunlight from interior spaces. External solar control units include light shelves, overhangs, fins, sun louvers, roller shades, deep recesses, and double skin systems.
- In the interior of a room, a variety of devices can control sunlight and can help to prevent heat gain or loss. Internal units include light shelves, blinds, roller shades, shutters, fabrics, skylight-tension systems, and pleated or accordion shades.
- Sustainable designs must use daylighting to conserve energy. There are various approaches to integrating daylight and electrical sources.
- Sustainable designs must focus on how to create interiors that are healthy and accommodate the needs of their users.
- In addition to the importance of daylight for the health and well-being of individuals, people need a view of the outdoors.
- The HVAC system plays an important role in delivering comfortable temperatures, healthy air, and optimum humidity levels.
- Humidity is the measure of the amount of moisture or water vapor that is in the air. Too much moisture creates problems with mold and mildew.
- In recent years a great deal of research has focused on the impact of the IEQ on people. The most frequent variables studied are the effects of daylight, air quality, thermal comfort, ventilation, noise, electrical lighting, and personal control of an environment.
- Research indicates that people prefer to have personal control of their thermal comfort, ventilation, and lighting.
- Products that can receive LEED-CI credit for complying with prescribed requirements are adhesives, sealants, paint, coatings, carpet systems, composite wood, laminate adhesives, and systems furniture and seating.
- Building materials and interior products emit hundreds of VOCs in the air, and collectively the contaminants comprise the TVOC. Products that emit VOCs include adhesives, glues, sealants, paint, coatings, pressed wood products, carpet, composite wood furnishings, pesticides, and dry-cleaned fabrics.
- There are many environmental and IAQ aspects related to carpet systems. Nylon, the fiber most often used for carpet, is made from petroleum, which is a nonrenewable resource. The methods associated with processing petrochemicals and constructing the carpet require significant amounts of energy and water.

Key Terms

Bilateral

Carpet and Rug Institute's Green Label Plus

Chimney action

Clerestories

Daylight

Daylight factor (DF)

Disability glare

Discomfort glare

Environmental Technology Verification (ETV) Program

Flush-out

Green Seal Standard 36 (GS-36)

International Engineering Society of North America (IESNA)

Luminous efficacy constant (Ke)

Punched windows

Sidelighting

South Coast Air Quality Management District (SCAQMD)

Stepped controls

Strip windows

Sunlight

Toplighting

Exercises

1. Identify a commercial building in your local community. Analyze the site to determine the most effective approaches to quality daylighting and daylight harvesting. The analysis should include a summary of the building's latitude, topography, trees, and adjacent buildings. In a written report, identify suggestions for daylighting and approaches to controlling sunlight.

2. A focus on environmental quality emphasizes all of the factors that can affect how people perceive a space. Develop and conduct a survey of individuals working in a commercial building. The purpose of the survey is to determine individuals' perceptions regarding personalizing a work environment. Items on the survey should include the individuals' ability to control temperature, ventilation, and lighting within their workstation. Combine the results with other members in your class. In a written report, summarize the findings of the study and provide recommendations for future practice.

3. In ancient times, people had to use available materials to provide heating, cooling, lighting, and ventilation. Research various ancient approaches for the IEQ. Summarize the results in a written report, and include illustrations, photographs, or sketches. Provide recommendations for how the techniques could be applied to current buildings.

4. To have healthy IAQ requires a close examination of the content of building materials and interior products. Content labels of interior products should be scrutinized. Research sustainable products and provide a summary of the content labels for adhesives, sealants, paint, coatings, and flooring systems. Develop a resource file that includes manufacturers' specifications.

CHAPTER 8

Sustainable Strategies for Building Components, Finishes, and Furnishings

"It's a question of discipline," the little prince told me later on.

"When you've finished washing and dressing each morning you must tend your planet."

—ANTOINE DE SAINT-EXUPÉRY

Objectives

- Describe sustainable strategies for specifying wood and plastic building components.
- Identify sustainable characteristics of doors, windows, and equipment.
- Apply sustainable characteristics of doors, windows, and equipment to the built environment.
- Describe sustainable characteristics associated with interior finishes.
- Describe sustainable characteristics associated with furnishings.
- Apply sustainable characteristics of finishes and furnishings to the built environment.
- Understand the importance of cleaning and maintenance of the built environment.

CHAPTER 7 EXAMINED factors associated with IAQ that should be considered when designing sustainable interiors. Quality indoor air and connections with the outdoors are required for the health of occupants. Quality environmental conditions contribute to enhanced productivity, reduced absenteeism, and greater satisfaction with interiors. This chapter expands on criteria presented in previous chapters by reviewing additional attributes that are critical for sustainable interiors. A primary focus is examining resource reuse, recycled content, and rapidly renewable materials.

This chapter explores items that either are specified by an interior designer or are merely recommended to a client. Materials and products that are specified, and usually supplied by an interior designer, are finishes and furnishings. Finishes include acoustical ceilings, hard flooring, resilient flooring, carpet systems, wallcoverings, and paint. Interior furnishings comprise fabrics, window treatments, furniture, and seating. Items that may require recommendations from an interior designer are the sustainable characteristics of windows, doors, and residential appliances. Knowledge of these components of the built environment is important for understanding how sustainable strategies integrate with all elements of a building. To design sustainable interiors, a designer must understand the integration of the building's structure, finishes, furnishings, lighting, equipment, and the mechanical and electrical systems.

SUSTAINABLE STRATEGIES FOR BUILDING COMPONENTS

A critical element of specifying sustainable interiors is to consider the materials' life cycle analysis (LCA). The overarching operating principle should focus on reduction: reducing the size of buildings; reducing the consumption of new resources; reducing energy needs; reducing wasteful water practices; reducing outdoor and indoor pollutants; reducing negative impacts on the environment; and reducing waste. In assessing the characteristics of products, some of the considerations include how materials impact natural habitats, biodiversity, and the availability of the resource for future generations. The manufacturing process is examined to determine the

degree of energy consumption, the amount of waste, and the level of pollutants emitted to the air and water. Preference should be afforded to products with low **embodied energy**, or minimal amounts of energy to produce. Transportation modes and mileage are reviewed to reduce the impact on the environment. Whenever possible materials and products should be purchased from local and regional suppliers.

A product that consumes energy should be efficient and cost-effective and conserve resources. Products should minimize emissions, be durable, enhance the IEQ, and have a long-lasting, classical aesthetic. Interiors and the contents therein must be properly cleaned and maintained for a sustainable built environment. Materials and products that are designed according to the principles of biomimicry can be sustainable solutions. By mimicking nature's respect for limitations and operating as an interdependent system, interior finishes and furnishings can exhibit the principles of sustainable development. Many sustainable solutions should reflect a simple approach that reflects the design of interiors prior to the invention of electricity. After use, a sustainable product design closes the LCA loop. A **closed loop** design indicates that the materials can be reused or recycled or can safely decompose in a landfill.

CSI Division 6: Wood and Plastics

CSI Division 6 is the category for wood and plastics that are used in the built environment. From an interior perspective, the most relevant materials and products in Division 6 are finish carpentry and architectural woodwork. Interior millwork can include casings, aprons, cornice molding, chair rails, baseboards, fascia, and paneling. Sustainable considerations include reusing products, selecting products with recycled and/or recovered content, specifying rapidly renewable materials, and specifying products that have been extracted and manufactured either locally or from the immediate region of the project's site. To conserve resources, **salvaged wood** and **remilled lumber** are excellent choices (see Figure 8.1). Salvaged or *reclaimed wood* is a material derived from a previous use, such as wood from buildings that are being demolished. When salvaged wood has old paint, care must be taken to ensure that lead

Fig. 8.1. To conserve resources, designers can specify the use of salvaged wood and remilled lumber. The door in this room was made from salvaged wood.

remnants are not present. Some salvaged wood is remilled into new products, such as flooring and millwork.

New wood products, including millwork and wood veneer panels, should have Forest Stewardship Council (FSC) certification. Trees that are in danger of extinction or old-growth timber should be specified infrequently, and in small amounts. To acquire the list of endangered wood species, contact the **Convention on International Trade and Endangered Species (CITES)**. Whenever possible, **clear wood**, or wood without knots, should *not* be specified because to have enough wood of this high quality requires considerable waste during the fabrication process.

Due to high costs, and the desire to have surfaces in a consistent color and graining pattern, most cabinetry and furniture is made from wood composite panels. The panels can be particleboard, plywood, or medium-density fiberboard (MDF). As reviewed in Chapter 7, for a healthy IAQ the panels should not have UF binders. Wood composite panels are often

used for a substrate for decorative laminates, flooring underlayment, cabinet door fronts, and office furniture. Sustainable solutions for flooring underlayment include products made from recycled paper, straw fibers, or recycled textiles. Some manufacturers produce flooring underlayment with acoustical control, and other products have open supports and air slits to allow for airflow. Air movement helps to reduce moisture and the subsequent mold growth.

Particleboard can be made from wood fiber or **ag-fiber**. Wood fiber particleboard should be FSC-certified. Ag-fiber can be made from materials that are considered agricultural waste, such as straw and sorghum. Straw particleboard is made from the fibers of various agricultural products, such as wheat, oats, barley, buckwheat, and rye grass. These alternative agricultural materials are non-food and non-feed. Biocomposite products have agricultural content, such as soy-based flours and resins. Some manufacturers produce paneling, plywood, and veneers that are made from the rapidly renewable straw, or bamboo. These materials can be used for cabinetry, furniture, and interior paneling. Wood products should be solvent-free and zero-UF or minimally low-UF.

In specifying custom cabinets and countertops, there are important environmental characteristics to consider, including the type of particleboard, source of veneers, VOC emissions, recycled content, durability, and impact on natural resources if the products are landfilled. Custom cabinets are available in particleboards made from agricultural residues. Wheatboard is a common material for case materials, millwork, and doors. Hardwood veneers must have FSC certification. Products should have water-based adhesives, low-VOC finishes, and be formaldehyde- and solvent-free. Countertops are available in products made from recycled-glass aggregate/chips, post-industrial waste from carpet manufacturing, and pre-consumer and post-consumer waste paper. Recycled-glass chips can be embedded in concrete, masonry, or cement. Frequently these countertops have a terrazzo-like appearance. Butcher block countertops are available using FSC-certified woods.

CSI Division 8: Doors and Windows

There are many sustainable characteristics that must be considered when making recommendations for doors and windows. Two excellent resources for the energy performance of products are ENERGY STAR and the National Fenestration Rating Council (NFRC). The NFRC is an independent organization that rates and labels the energy performance of doors, windows, and skylights (see Figure 8.2); **NFRC 100** is the standard for rating the U-factor of windows, doors, and skylights. Rated items have an NFRC label or a label certificate (see www.nfrc.org for a listing of certified products).

The performance of door systems is determined by the U-factor and the SHGC. In cold climates doors should have a low U-factor to reduce the amount of heat that can be emitted from a building. The NFRC reports U-factor ratings between 0.20 and 1.20 (2005). For cold climates the U-factor should be 0.40 or less (NFRC, 2005). The SHGC becomes important for warm climates. A low SHGC rating will help to prevent solar heat gain from entering a building through the door. The SHGC ratings for warm climates should be 0.40 or less (NFRC, 2005). Since doors are installed as a separate component from the building, the NFRC label includes the type of door, type of glass, and amount of glass.

Wood is a common material for interior and exte-

rior doors and windows. As with other wood products mentioned in this chapter, wood doors should be FSC-certified or made from salvaged woods. Exterior doors should be durable, and proper maintenance must be performed to help prevent damage from water or insects. Generally, composite entry doors with foam insulation have better energy conservation properties than wood doors. Important considerations are formaldehyde-free materials, excellent weather stripping, and the R-value. Composite doors such as steel should be factory primed and exterior doors should have magnetic seals. Doors with glazing should avoid heat loss or gain.

The NFRC label for windows and skylights includes the ratings for the U-factor, SHGC, VT, air leakage (AL), and condensation resistance (CR). The NFRC reports U-factor ratings between 0.20 and 1.20 (2005). Windows and skylights are rated by their thermal transmission, or total U-factor. The lower the U-factor, the better the energy performance. A window's U-factor considers its conductivity, airflow around the window, and its ability to absorb infrared heat, or emissivity. Energy-efficient windows and skylights have low conductivity and low emissivity ratings. The NFRC 100 rates the total fenestration unit, including the frame and glass. Low SHGC ratings and high VT numbers are desirable for sustainable interiors. Windows with **spectrally selective glass** are either tinted or coated with a material that blocks solar heat from entering a space. To maximize daylighting and reduce infrared and UV rays, some skylights have prisms embedded in the glazing. Skylights are also available with photo-cell-controlled louvers, which continuously monitor the quantity of daylight. The louvers open when light levels are low and close during sunny days. AL measures the amount of outside air that penetrates into a space. The NFRC ratings are between 0.1 and 0.3. The lower the number, the better a window can prevent outdoor air from entering a space.

Condensation resistance measures a window's ability to resist condensation, and is rated between 1 and 100. The higher the number, the better the fenestration unit can prevent condensation. To reduce condensation, the glazing unit's frame and edges should be thermally efficient. In addition, windows should have dual glazing, insulated glass units, and edge spacers. The manufacturer does not always

Fig. 8.2. NFRC is an independent organization that rates and labels the energy performance of doors, windows, and skylights. Rated items have an NFRC label or a label certificate.

provide the CR rating. Some windows may have an acoustical performance rating, which demonstrates the amount of sound transmission through a window into the building. For replacement windows, doors, and skylights, the **International Energy Conservation Code (IECC)** has U-factor and SHGC requirements that are based on the heating degree-days for various climate zones.

The emphasis on daylighting, ventilation, passive solar heat gain, and views to the outdoors necessitates energy-efficient windows and skylights. The inherent properties of glass and the potential air infiltration associated with openings in a building's envelope require products that are made from sustainable materials and conserve energy. Windows are available in wood, vinyl, metal, and fiberglass. The window sash and molding are frequently made from solid wood. Whenever possible, the frame materials should be FSC-certified. As reviewed in Chapter 6, to conserve energy, windows should have low-e coatings, multiple panes, gas fills, and low-conductivity materials. Assemblies should be durable and easy to maintain, and preference should be given to units with recycled content. Recycled content is especially critical for vinyl windows, because of the negative environmental effects associated with PVC.

CSI Division 11: Equipment

Interior designers can be involved with specifying several items listed in *CSI Division 11: Equipment*, including recycling equipment and residential appliances. A very important area related to sustainable interiors is to design for recycling equipment. This involves planning for the ideal placement of recycling equipment and designing units that are aesthetically pleasing. To encourage people to recycle waste, an interior designer should consistently integrate facilities into the design of commercial and residential interiors. Recycling equipment placed in a convenient location encourages people to recycle. Generally, recycling equipment in commercial buildings consists of blue containers in hallways or in the corners of eating facilities. Most often residential dwellings do not have any area designated in the kitchen for recycling equipment. Any recycling containers or bins are generally in an inconvenient location, such as a basement or garage. In commercial and residential

interiors, recycling equipment should become an integral part of the design of the interior. Recycling equipment should be included with other items that are included in spatial strategies, such as the location of bedrooms, conversation areas, and workstations.

To determine ideal locations of recycling equipment it is important to analyze how people use the space. Specifically, observations should be made regarding where people use materials that can be recycled, such as paper and aluminum cans. Observational results should be used to plan the location of recycling equipment. Ideally, the equipment should be located in convenient proximity to where people are ready to dispose of the waste. For example, in an office environment, people working at their desk routinely have paper for recycling. Thus, recycling equipment should be designed as an attractive and integral part of the workstation. This could be accomplished by integrating a recycling bin into the base of a workstation. A kitchen is an important area for recycling equipment. Bins placed in slide-out units can be located in base cabinets (see Figures 8.3a and b). The design can include one or several bins to accommodate different types of waste, such as plastics, glass, and paper. Building several bins into the base cabinets is preferable because it encourages people to sort and to recycle several products. The base corner cabinet with a rotating shelf is an effective means to have several bins (see Figure 8.3c).

In addition to integrating recycling equipment into the design of interiors, the equipment should be an attractive component of the interior and reflect the conceptual design. Generally, recycling equipment is made from an unattractive material and has an "institutional" appearance. Most designs of recycling equipment give the impression that the only suitable location for the units is hidden in a closet, or in the waste area of a building. While it is important that the equipment is available, delegating recycling equipment to inconvenient locations fails to encourage spontaneous recycling. Placing recycling equipment in locations that encourages immediate disposal increases the likelihood that people will recycle products, rather than placing the items in garbage containers. The creative talents of interior designers should be used to design recycling equipment that meets the ergonomic needs of people and becomes an integral component of the interior's

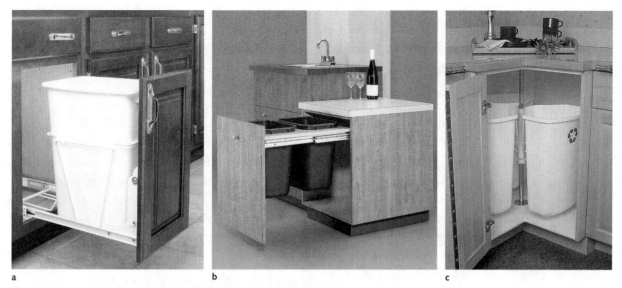

a

b

c

Fig. 8.3a. Bins placed in slide-out units can be located in base cabinets.
Fig. 8.3b. Units can have one or several bins to accommodate different types of waste, such as plastics, glass, and paper. Building several bins into the base cabinets is preferable because it encourages people to sort and recycle several products.
Fig. 8.3c. The base corner cabinet with a rotating shelf is an effective means to have several bins.

aesthetics. In addition, whenever possible, the contents of the equipment should be derived from recycled contents. For example, some recycling bins are made from recycled milk jugs.

Sustainable residential interiors should have appliances that are energy-efficient and conserve water. ENERGY STAR is an excellent resource for determining ratings on appliances, such as clothes washers, dishwashers, refrigerators, freezers, dehumidifiers, and room air conditioners. ENERGY STAR–rated clothes washers use 50 percent less energy than standard washers (ENERGY STAR, 2005). To measure the energy used by washers, ENERGY STAR uses the **Modified Energy Factor (MEF)**. MEF measures the energy used to operate the machine, to heat the water, and to dry the clothes (see Figure 8.4). Energy used for drying in washers is related to the spin cycle. Most ENERGY STAR washers extract high amounts of water during the spin cycle, which helps to conserve energy used for drying clothes. Reducing drying time also helps to lessen fiber deterioration of clothing. High MEF ratings indicate an efficient washer. The MEF is an excellent means to compare different clothes washers. ENERGY STAR does not rate clothes dryers because there are minimal differences in energy consumption between products. In addition to the energy-efficiency of a washer, ENERGY STAR tests machines for the amount of water used to clean clothes. According to ENERGY STAR,

most standard washers use 40 gallons of water per load. ENERGY STAR–rated washers use 18–25 gallons of water per load. Dishwashers are also rated for their energy-efficiency and water-consumption rates. ENERGY STAR–rated dishwashers use 25 percent less energy than minimum federal standards and much less water than conventional models (ENERGY STAR, 2005).

Refrigerators and freezers rated by ENERGY STAR use half the amount of energy compared with appliances manufactured prior to 1993. ENERGY STAR indicates that frequently the refrigerator is the appliance that consumes the most energy in a residence (2005). ENERGY STAR rates the refrigerator's compressor, insulation, precision of the temperature, and the defrost mechanism. In addition to ratings, ENERGY STAR recommends that refrigerators should not be located next to an appliance that generates heat, such as an oven. To conserve energy, the condenser coils should be cleaned regularly and adequate air should circulate around the coils. Door seals should be tight. Old refrigerators can be recycled.

ENERGY STAR dehumidifiers are rated according to energy efficiency and the units' ability to remove moisture. As an important element of IEQ, an efficient and effective dehumidifier is critical to sustainable interiors. ENERGY STAR units have efficient refrigeration coils, compressors, and fans.

Other factors that can affect a dehumidifier's performance are capacity, placement, and relative humidity. The proper dehumidifier capacity is essential for the comfort of people. This is based on the size of the space and the environmental conditions of the space (see ENERGY STAR for dehumidifier calculations: www.energystar.gov). The dehumidifier should be in a location that allows air to circulate around the unit. Windows and doors adjacent to the unit should be closed, and a dehumidifier should not be located in an area with high volumes of dust and dirt. If the unit has a hose that directs the water to a drain, care must be taken to ensure that water flows down the drain. Leaks create moisture, which promotes the growth of mold and mildew. **Relative humidity** is the amount of water vapor in the air compared with the amount of water that air can contain at a particular temperature. ENERGY STAR recommends a relative humidity range between 30 and 50 percent. To prevent condensation on windows during the winter, the range should be between 30 and 40 percent.

ENERGY STAR also rates room air conditioners. These products use at least 10 percent less energy than standard models. Some of the units have timers that can conserve energy by turning the air conditioner off when people are not using the space. ENERGY STAR emphasizes that many people purchase room air conditioners that are too large for the space. Frequently, people believe that a larger unit will result in a cooler room. ENERGY STAR indicates that the opposite condition occurs. An oversized unit wastes energy and fails to perform effectively because the unit cools the room too quickly. Consequently, cooling the room quickly does not allow the unit to satisfactorily remove the humidity. Thus, the room can be cool but also can feel damp. See ENERGY STAR for calculations regarding the proper size for room air conditioners.

SUSTAINABLE STRATEGIES FOR CSI DIVISION 9: FINISHES

Interior designers generally specify most of the products within the CSI divisions related to finishes and furnishings. Products categorized in the *finishes* division include acoustical ceilings, hard flooring, resilient flooring, carpet systems, wallcoverings, and paint. Chapter 7 of this text reviewed paint; this section reviews the other products associated with *CSI Division 9*. The products included in *CSI Division 12: Furnishings* are fabrics, window treatments, furniture,

Fig. 8.4. To measure the energy used by washers, ENERGY STAR uses the Modified Energy Factor (MEF). Clothes washers with a horizontal axis conserve water.

Fig. 8.5. A common width for carpet is 12 feet. To minimize the amount of carpet for a room, the dimensions should be based upon the standardized width of 12 feet.

and seating. Products associated with finishes and furnishings are reviewed by examining the LCA. The exploration includes the impact on ecosystems, IEQ, durability, maintenance, recycling, and disposal practices.

To conserve resources when specifying finishes for an existing structure, preferences should be to reuse as much of the installed materials as possible. Therefore, walls, ceilings, and floors should be thoroughly examined to assess their current condition. Whenever possible, finishes such as flooring or wallcoverings should be cleaned and/or restored rather than replaced. The cleaning process should utilize nontoxic substances and the least amount of energy. (Cleaning and maintenance is discussed in the final section of this chapter.)

When it is imperative to replace finishes, careful consideration should be given to accurate measurements and material calculations. Inaccurate measurements and miscalculations can waste resources, time, money, and labor and can create an adversarial relationship with a client. When too much of a product is ordered, usually the excess cannot be returned to the supplier. Thus, the excess often is landfilled. If insufficient amounts are ordered, waste can occur by a manufacturer's minimum requirements and/or piecing that may have to be done to complete the installation. The situation can become worse if the product is discontinued. When this occurs, materials that are already installed have to be removed and may become waste. Subsequently, a substitute product has to be selected and then approved by the client. A new order must be placed with the supplier, followed by another installation.

To conserve resources, another important consideration is designing the size of rooms to correspond with standardized sizes of products. For example, a very common width for carpet is 12 feet (see Figure 8.5). Therefore, to minimize the amount of carpet for a room, the dimensions should be based on the standardized width of 12 feet. Designing spaces based on industry standardizations can be applied to a variety of other products, such as windows, kitchen cabinets, or acoustical ceiling tiles. As an overall summary of specifying finishes for sustainable interiors, preference should be given to reducing consumption by reusing existing materials, followed by using recycled and recyclable materials. To specify the correct quantity of a product, the measurements must be accurate, the calculations without errors, and the room dimensions aligned with industry standardized sizes.

Acoustical Ceiling Products

Acoustical ceiling tiles and panels can affect sustainable interiors in a variety of ways. Most often acoustical ceilings are installed in commercial buildings; thus, the product has extensive applications. This results in the specification of large quantities, and eventually determining a safe means of disposal or finding a manufacturer that accepts the material for recycling. From a sustainable design perspective, the characteristics of acoustical units must be analyzed for their content, ability to control noise, flame-spread rating, and reflective properties. Acoustical ceiling tiles and panels are made from a variety of materials, including mineral fibers, volcanic perlite, clay, fiberglass, metal, compressed-straw, cornstarch, and gypsum fillers. To conserve resources, acoustical ceiling products are available with recycled content, including recycled newspapers, and post-consumer and post-industrial wastes. Some tiles and panels are available that have 80 percent or higher recycled content.

Acoustical ceiling products that are made from mineral fibers should have an element that controls moisture. The inherent properties of mineral fibers can prompt the growth of mold and mildew when exposed to moisture. Some products shed the mineral fibers, which can negatively impact the IAQ. In addition, materials containing UF should be avoided. Another consideration regarding the content of acoustical ceiling products is its ability to be recycled. Products are available that can be 100 percent recyclable. This is an important consideration, because acoustical ceiling products can pose problems for landfills.

Acoustical ceiling products are important for enhancing the IEQ by helping to control noise. Systems are rated for noise control by the **noise reduction coefficient (NRC)**, **sound transmission class (STC)**, and a relatively new standard, the **outside-indoor transmission class (OITC)** (NAIMA.org). An NRC number indicates how well a material absorbs sound. The range for NRC is .00 to 1.00, whereby ratings close to 1.00 provide the greatest absorption of sound. The STC provides information regarding an assembly's ability to prevent the transfer of noise from one area to another. A particular assembly can be a wood stud partition, plywood, or wallboard. The STC number is in decibels. As a point of reference, a quiet room is approximately 20 decibels, a phone ringing is 60, and street noise can be 90. Hearing loss can occur at 85 decibels. High numbers reflect an assembly's ability to block the transmission of sound. The OITC standard is a single number that reflects the system's sound transmission loss from factors external to the building, including ground and air transportation. Higher decibel numbers indicate greater reduction of noise. A variety of other materials for the built environment are rated for noise control, including windows and carpet. To improve the IEQ in interiors, considerations should include the STC and OITC ratings of windows. For example, the OITC number can be very important for buildings close to an airport.

Another consideration related to IEQ is quality lighting conditions. Acoustical ceiling units with high reflectance properties, such as ratings over 70 percent, can help to increase illumination levels from sunlight and electrical sources. For the safety of people and to reduce the destruction of buildings, refer to the product's flame spread and smoke provided by the **American Society for Testing and Materials International (ASTM)**; ASTM E84-05 is the standard test method for the surface burning behavior of materials as determined by the flame spread. Materials are tested in simulated conditions in a laboratory. Thus, to determine the burning characteristics of acoustical ceiling products, the entire ceiling system is installed in a room at the testing facilities.

Hard Flooring: Bamboo and Wood

As reviewed in Chapter 7, to have quality indoor air, the flooring materials should be low- or zero-VOC. This applies to various products associated with flooring, including adhesives, sealants, paints, and finishes. Other considerations related to sustainable interiors include the LCA, durability, acoustical properties, thermal mass for passive solar applications, flame resistance, and ease of maintenance. Flooring materials to be considered for sustainable interiors include bamboo, brick, stone, certified wood, reclaimed wood, and recycled-content tile. Hard flooring materials have the important sustainable characteristic of improving the health of IAQ. Hard materials do not harbor dust, dirt, or allergens in the same manner as soft flooring, such as carpet. It is difficult to remove undesirable particles in carpet from the edges of a room or around furniture. Thus, with proper and routine maintenance, it is easier to remove contaminants from hard flooring than from soft materials.

As an excellent substitute for wood, bamboo flooring is growing in popularity in the United States. This is due to the material's rapid renewable growing characteristic, its low embodied energy qualities, and the aesthetics of its graining and color. Bamboo is a perennial grass, not a tree (see Figure 8.6). Thus, the growth time for bamboo is considerably shorter than trees that are used for hardwood flooring, such as oak. The bamboo fiber can grow to a harvestable size of four-to-six-inch (10–15 cm) diameters in 4 to 15 years depending on the species. In comparison, an oak tree takes between 100 and 120 years to grow to maturity. Thus, using bamboo for flooring, rather than hardwoods, helps to conserve old timber and preserve the ecosystem associated with the forest. Contrary to some beliefs, bamboo harvested for products does not deprive panda bears of their food source. Pandas live in higher elevations than the location of bamboo plantations.

The primary source for bamboo is China, but bamboo can also be imported from Indonesia, Japan, Vietnam, and Costa Rica. For countries outside Asia, transportation costs negatively affect bamboo's low-embodied energy characteristics. However, the other environmentally favorable attributes of bamboo outweigh using nonrenewable resources for transportation. Bamboo is dimensionally stable, flame resistant, and the material exhibits the same hardness as red oak. The graining of bamboo flooring is available in horizontal or vertical grain versions. Vertical graining materials can be sanded more frequently than horizontally laminated flooring. For sustainability purposes this is an important characteristic. The ability to sand a material increases the life of a product because the refinishing process results in a new appearance. The more frequently a product can be sanded, the longer the life of the product.

Bamboo can be manufactured in strip or plank flooring. Frequently, the boards have a tongue and groove edge, which provides a smooth installation

and allows the boards to expand and contract with changes in the seasons. In addition to flooring, bamboo for interiors is also available for trim molding, stair parts, thresholds, baseboards, and vent registers. The color choices are the light natural hue and dark amber carbonized version. For areas with high traffic, some manufacturers produce flooring with an added scratch-finish. Some bamboo flooring incorporates UF in the glues that bind the planks together. The greatest quantities of UF are generally found in poor-quality bamboo flooring. This is a good example of why product specifications must always be reviewed when specifying sustainable materials. Since bamboo is a fairly well known sustainable material, many people do not examine the other contents of the flooring product. For example, bamboo flooring could be selected under the premise that someone is purchasing a sustainable product. The bamboo is a sustainable material, but the entire floor system may not be sustainable if VOCs or any other toxic materials are present.

Under the proper conditions, wood is an excellent choice for sustainable interiors. As discussed in Chapter 5, any wood product for furniture or finishes should be FSC-certified forest products. Wood is a renewable resource and has a low embodied energy. Wood consumes little energy for processing; however, logging, milling, and transportation impact the environment. Specifying local and regional materials helps to reduce the impact from transportation. For sustainable interiors, wood flooring must be derived from trees grown in managed forests, or alternative solutions are **reclaimed** and **remilled wood**. Wood

Fig. 8.6. Bamboo flooring is an excellent substitute for wood. Bamboo is rapidly renewable and creates a beautiful floor. The bamboo fiber can grow to a harvestable size of four-to-six-inch (10–15 cm) diameters in 4 to 15 years. In comparison, an oak tree takes between 100 and 120 years to grow.

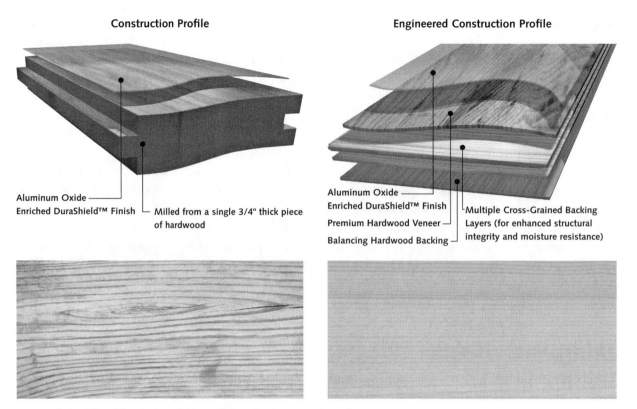

Construction Profile

Aluminum Oxide Enriched DuraShield™ Finish — └ Milled from a single 3/4" thick piece of hardwood

Engineered Construction Profile

Aluminum Oxide Enriched DuraShield™ Finish
Premium Hardwood Veneer —
Balancing Hardwood Backing ┘

└ Multiple Cross-Grained Backing Layers (for enhanced structural integrity and moisture resistance)

Fig. 8.7a–b. (top) Wood flooring is available in solid wood and engineered wood.
Fig. 8.8a–b. (bottom) Depending upon the characteristics of the wood, the material is classified by grade. The best grade is **clear**, without knots, streaks, spots, or other imperfections.

flooring made from virgin materials is available in **solid wood** and **engineered wood** (see Figure 8.7a and b). Solid wood is made from hardwood and softwood species. Pine is one of the fastest growing trees; however, because the wood is relatively soft, flooring can dent easier than an oak or maple floor. Quartersawn wood boards are more durable than plainsawn. Depending on the characteristics of the wood, the material is classified by a grade. The best grade is *clear*, or without knots or other imperfections, such as streaks or spots (see Figure 8.8a and b). To compile enough wood of the best quality requires more logging. Thus, to conserve natural resources, flooring should be selected in lower grades that have interesting *character*. A relatively new addition to flooring is **palm wood**. This flooring is a by-product of coconut palms and is a rapidly renewable material. The mature palm trees used for flooring no longer produce coconuts.

Engineered composite wood has a face veneer that is laminated to a substrate material. Solid wood flooring may be preferred to engineered wood flooring in sustainable interiors, because solid wood can be refinished many times and is easier to salvage. With proper maintenance, solid wood floors can last at least 100 years. Due to the extremely thin face veneer, engineered wood can only be refinished once or twice. This attribute also makes it almost impossible to salvage an engineered wood flooring from a building.

Preserving natural materials is critical to sustainable interiors. Thus, every strategy to maintain a wood floor should be considered when specifying the product. To preserve a wood floor, some important considerations include planning the most appropriate location in a building, ensuring a proper installation, creating suitable climatic conditions in the room, and using appropriate maintenance products and procedures. Wood is affected by moisture, sunlight, heavy traffic, and humidity, and some substances can stain wood. Thus, these factors should be considered when determining which rooms will have wood flooring. Close proximity to rooms with excessive moisture, such as bathrooms, can be very problematic.

Wood is a material that expands and contracts

based on climatic conditions. In high humidity, wood expands; the opposite occurs during dry periods, such as the winter. To allow for the inherent movement of the material, wood flooring should be installed with proper space allowances. In addition, wood flooring should not be installed until *after* any jobs that have high quantities of moisture associated with the installation process, such as installing ceramic tile. To protect newly installed wood flooring, the installation should not be done until the heating has been regulated in the building. Temperature and humidity conditions should be carefully monitored after occupancy. In addition, a wood floor should be cleaned regularly with a damp mop or sponge. Toxic cleaning materials should be avoided, and any substance that can stain or mar wood should be removed immediately.

Reclaimed wood and remilled wood are excellent choices for sustainable interiors. Reclaimed and remilled woods are recycled materials. Reclaimed wood is from a variety of sources, such as wood from structures planned for demolition or logs salvaged from the bottom of waterways. Reclaimed wood can also come from trees that must be removed for a variety of reasons, including being diseased, new roads, or new residential developments. Industrial wood blocks can create a very durable and aesthetically interesting flooring material. Reclaimed wood is salvaged from old buildings, railroad ties, pickle vats, bridge timbers, old water and wine tanks, barns, mills, warehouses, and industrial buildings. Remilled wood uses wood that is salvaged from structures to create a product such as flooring, siding, or other millwork. Reclaimed and remilled wood are outstanding materials to use in interiors because natural resources are preserved, materials are not landfilled, and the beauty of naturally antiqued wood cannot be duplicated. The splendor of antiqued wood can be created only after 100 or more years. In addition to the aesthetic effects of time and use on wood, many of the materials salvaged are extinct or no longer available from current suppliers, such as chestnut wood. Thus, using reclaimed wood is an excellent means to having products made from exotic or extinct species. Interior designers can acquire reclaimed wood from manufacturers, architectural salvage warehouses, antique dealers, and deconstruction sales.

Labels on wood and bamboo flooring should be carefully examined to ensure substrates are formaldehyde-free materials, and the adhesives are low- or zero-VOC and water-based. As reviewed in Chapter 7, natural oils and waxes that penetrate the wood, such as tung oil or beeswax, are effective solutions for a healthy IAQ. Moreover, penetrating natural finishes create a surface that can be easily refinished in the future. To reduce emissions from the finishing process, generally it is preferred to specify finished rather than unfinished flooring. This approach helps to reduce pollutants because factories must comply with regulated emission standards. Finished flooring can also be healthier for the installer and future occupants.

For sustainable interiors, the preferred installation method for bamboo and wood flooring is nailed or screwed to a surface, rather than adhesives. Fastening the flooring eliminates any VOCs that might be contained in adhesives. In the event of a future deconstruction, materials that are nailed rather than glued are easier to salvage. Replacement of strips or planks that are nailed or screwed is also an easier process than working with adhesives. Flooring can be fastened to plywood subfloor or **wood sleepers** (see Figure 8.9). Generally, wood sleepers are 2" × 4" (5 × 10 cm) wood members spaced 12 inches (30 cm) on center. Wood sleepers provide some resiliency to

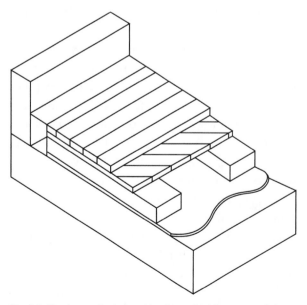

Fig. 8.9. Flooring can be fastened to plywood subfloor or wood sleepers. Generally, wood sleepers are 2" × 4" (5 × 10 cm) wood members spaced 12" (30 cm) on center. Wood sleepers provide some resiliency to the floor.

the floor, which provides more cushion than a plywood subfloor. This surface is more comfortable for people and helps to reduce stress on the joints of a body. A wood sleeper installation also provides air space under the flooring. Wood is easily damaged by water; thus, the air space allows air to flow through the flooring. Airflow helps to dissipate moisture, condensation, and humidity. Due to problems associated with water, wood flooring generally should not be installed below grade, such as in a basement. A vapor barrier should always be added for installations that are slab-on-grade.

Hard Flooring: Concrete and Tile

Concrete and tile are materials that can be used for flooring in high-traffic and water-intensive applications. Both materials are resistant to abrasion, dirt, water, and fire. Concrete and tile can be made to be resistant to frost, stains, and slippage. Since these materials are excellent for heat-storage mass, they are effective choices for absorbing, storing, and radiating solar energy. Thus, concrete and tile are very effective for rooms or areas that are designed to maximize passive solar energy, such as sunrooms. Under specific conditions, concrete can be an appropriate sustainable flooring material. For example, concrete can be the finished flooring when the material is used for slab-on-grade construction on the ground floor. Eliminating an additional flooring material that normally would be installed over the concrete helps to conserve resources and reduce waste. Concrete can be an attractive finish floor by adding materials to the substance during the mixing process. Additives that are aesthetically interesting are colorants and aggregates with various surfaces and colors. An attractive texture can be applied to the surface of concrete before the material sets. Some textures can help to provide slip resistance. Conventional concrete is made of portland cement, which is a high-embodied-energy product. To reduce portland cement's impact to the environment, a preferred alternative is fly ash concrete. Fly ash is a waste product of coal power plants and performs exceedingly well.

Tile flooring is available in baked clay, glass, and stone. Tile is made from virgin materials, but for sustainable interiors, products should be selected that are made from recycled-content materials. Ceramic tile is a preferred sustainable choice for a variety of reasons, including its durability, stain resistance, and ability to repel water and dirt. In addition, the product has color permanence and the contents are available in sufficient quantities. Ceramic tile is a product that has been used for centuries throughout the world. Ceramic tile can be installed on floors, walls, and ceilings. Thus, the material can be used for a variety of applications, including counters, backsplashes, shower enclosures, and baseboards. Basically, ceramic tile is made from an assortment of clays that are shaped and then fired at very high temperatures (see Figure 8.10).

Ceramic tiles are glazed and unglazed. Glazed tiles have a nonporous coating that prevents stains but is slippery when wet. The strength of a glaze is dependent on several factors, including the firing temperature, color, and level of gloss. The hardest glazes are fired at higher temperatures, have a light-color glaze, and have a matte or satin finish. These factors

Fig. 8.10. Ceramic tile is a product that has been used for centuries throughout the world. In the village of Dabakaha in Africa, Senufo potters use old-world techniques to make pottery. The handmade vessels are extremely durable.

are important when specifying sustainable products because tiles with greater strength resist wear and consequently last longer. Be alert to any lead-based glazes. Some glazed tile produced outside the United States may be lead based. Unglazed tiles have the advantages of being slip resistant and are extremely durable due to their inherent color properties and an increased thickness. Unglazed tiles include quarry, porcelain, and terra cotta.

The density and the hardness of ceramic tiles affect its durability, which is a critical characteristic of sustainable interiors. Tile density is measured by determining the amount of water the material absorbs. Tiles with the highest densities have fewer air pockets, which results in a more durable product. Density also affects whether the tile can be used only indoors. Tile classifications in increasing order of density are nonvitreous, semivitreous, vitreous, and impervious. Nonvitreous and semivitreous tiles absorb the greatest amount of water, and they can be used only indoors. Vitreous and impervious tiles are rated as frost resistant; thus, these products can be used indoors and outdoors. Tiles are measured for their hardness using the **Porcelain Enamel Institute (PEI)** rating system with a scale from zero to five. A material rated at zero should not be used for flooring, and the tile becomes more durable as the rating increases on the scale. Ratings of one and two indicate the tile is suitable for light traffic, such as residential interiors. Rating three is appropriate for residential and light commercial applications. Tiles with either a four or five rating are intended for commercial interiors, whereas the latter number is for heavy traffic areas.

To reduce waste and energy consumption, tiles are made from post-consumer and post-industrial recyclable content. These products are the preferred materials when very durable flooring is needed in sustainable interiors. Recycled-content tiles include ceramic, glass, pavers, and terrazzo. Tiles are available using 30 to 100 percent recycled solid waste. Post-consumer recycled materials include granite dust and clear and colored glass from windowpanes, bottles, windshields, and aviation. Post-industrial recycled materials include plate glass and grinding paste from the computer industry. Some companies employ sustainable practices by manufacturing products by zero-discharge and recycling waste cre-

ated during the production process within a short distance from the factory.

Sustainable considerations for tile include protecting the IAQ and reducing waste. Additional materials required to install tile are substrates, adhesives, grout, mortars, and sealants. All of these products should be zero- or low-VOC, and without petroleum or plastic substances. Tile adhesives should be water based, rather than solvent based. Larger tiles reduce the amount of grout needed for the flooring. To help ensure a durable product, which reduces waste in the future, tile must be installed properly. An essential installation requirement is ensuring that the floor is structurally sound, and the substrate must be a rigid material. The substrate must be level and clean prior to installation of the tiles. If a tile or concrete floor must be demolished, the materials can be salvaged and recycled. Maintenance of ceramic tile is very easy. Sweeping with a broom and washing with nontoxic substances and a mop can clean ceramic tile. Due to the abrasive reaction associated with grit and sand, these materials should be removed from the flooring as soon as possible.

Resilient Flooring

Resilient flooring has the advantage of providing comfort and cushion to the users of the space. This characteristic is especially important in areas where people stand for long periods of time, such as working in a kitchen. The best resilient floorings for the environment and IAQ are **earthen**, cork, and linoleum. For sustainability purposes, earthen flooring is becoming an alternative to other materials. The primary content of earthen flooring is the earth. To create a suitable material for indoor environments, additional substances are compacted with the earth, such as straw, oils, clay, and other natural fibers. Earthen flooring can be on a ground floor that is below or on grade. To eliminate dust, the surface should be sealed with natural oils, such as hemp or linseed. Earthen flooring is extremely durable and can be easily repaired. The embodied energy is extremely low and recyclability is not a factor. With a proper mixture and installation, earthen flooring can be resilient, durable, and aesthetically pleasing.

Cork and linoleum are available in sheets or tiles. The materials are resilient, biodegradable, antistatic, antimicrobial, and recyclable, and they are thermal or acoustical insulators. Cork is a natural material derived from the bark of the Mediterranean oak trees. Cork is cut from the outer layer of the trunks of oak trees after approximately nine years. Cork is a highly renewable resource because removing the layer does not require the tree to be felled, and after cork is removed, the tree replenishes the bark. Pressing together cork particles, binders, and resins, followed by baking the substance, creates composite cork flooring. Binders should be UF-free. In addition to finish flooring, cork can be an excellent resilient underlayment for hard materials, such as wood or ceramic tile. Cork is sensitive to heat; thus, the material should not be used for passive solar applications, or when a room has an underfloor heating system. Cork is not advisable in rooms with excessive moisture, such as bathrooms. However, cork has excellent hypoallergenic qualities, is mold resistant, fire resistant, and has a nonskid surface.

Natural materials are used to produce linoleum flooring (see Figure 8.11). The content of linoleum is linseed oil extracted from the flax plant, wood flour, natural pigments, and limestone dust. These materials are bonded to a natural jute-fiber backing. The contents of linoleum are locally available and require minimal energy for processing. Linoleum is manufactured in Europe, but the environmental and financial costs associated with transportation are minimal, compared to the benefits of linoleum. In addition to flooring, linoleum can be used for counters and writing surfaces. Linoleum has easy maintenance by sweeping with a broom or a damp mop. Cleaning substances should be light detergents, and solvents should be avoided that have ammonia or an alkaline-base. Linoleum is impervious to grease, solvents, and most stains. Since the material is antistatic, the amount of dust is reduced and the possibility of electrical shock is minimized. The antimicrobial characteristic helps to control dust mites. The pattern and colors are solid throughout the material; thus, rubbing with a soft brush or pad can easily perform repairs.

Cork and linoleum require a proper subfloor preparation and installation. These materials should not be installed over a moist surface. A damp-proof membrane might have to be used to prevent moisture from coming in contact with the material. To

Fig. 8.11. Natural materials are used to produce linoleum flooring. Linoleum flooring can be made in a variety of colors and patterns.

avoid indentations and irregularities on the surface of the flooring, the subfloor should be dry and clean. In addition joints and the screw heads used to attach the subfloor must be filled and sanded smooth. Linoleum should acclimate to the room's environment approximately seven to ten days prior to the installation. If adhesives are used, the materials should be zero- or low-VOC.

Vinyl is resilient flooring that became popular when the material was invented in the 1960s. To design sustainable interiors, vinyl flooring should *not* be specified. The content of vinyl is nonrenewable petroleum-based materials, and the manufacturing process generates toxic pollutants. The IAQ is negatively affected by vinyl's VOC emissions. Vinyl is not very durable, as demonstrated by lasting approximately 10 years. After its short life, vinyl is not biodegradable and cannot be recycled. Vinyl flooring can be substituted by the environmentally positive attributes associated with linoleum. The price of linoleum is comparable to higher quality vinyl flooring. Since the life of linoleum is approximately three times as long as vinyl flooring, there are also significant long-term economic benefits that can accrue with specifying linoleum. Rubber flooring, another resilient material, is also not recommended for most interior applications due to its detrimental off-gassing properties. The only appropriate installations for rubber flooring are buildings with considerable ventilation.

Carpet Systems

For many health and environmental reasons, carpet decisions should be based on careful research and analysis. For healthy IAQ, carpet systems should be certified by the *CRI Indoor Air Quality* standards, also known as the *CRI Green Label* program. Another program is California's *Indoor Air Emission Standard 1350*. As discussed previously in this text, the carpet manufacturing process consumes great quantities of energy and water. Furthermore, to produce synthetic fibers, the process emits poisonous air pollutants, VOCs, and toxic dyes into waterways. After carpet is installed in a space there can be emissions that affect the health of occupants. In addition, the carpet pile creates a texture that can easily collect and retain allergens, dust, and dust mites. Most of the carpet that is removed from buildings is not salvaged and is transported to landfills. This results in millions of pounds of nonbiodegradable carpet in landfills every year. Since interior designers specify a significant amount of the carpet that is purchased every year, the profession is in a formidable position to have a positive impact on the environment and IAQ.

The basic components of a carpet system are the carpet, carpet backing, carpet cushion or padding, and installation method. There are many important characteristics associated with carpet systems; however, for the purpose of this text, the discussion focuses on the attributes that affect sustainable designs. To specify carpet systems that reflect the principles of sustainable design, it is critical to examine the type of fiber, construction method, durability factors, cushion characteristics, installation method, maintenance procedures, and means of disposal. Most of these attributes can also be applied to area rugs.

For environmental and health reasons, area rugs, rather than wall-to-wall carpet, are recommended for sustainable interiors. Specifying area rugs rather than carpet is important for numerous sustainability reasons. Using area rugs and an environmentally appropriate hard flooring can help to conserve resources and reduce waste in landfills. Products that consume large quantities of resources, such as flooring, should always be prioritized for sustainability qualities. Durability is a critical characteristic of sustainable interiors because product longevity helps to reduce consumption. A considerable amount of a building's area is floors. Using carpet for floors consumes considerable resources, and the bulky nature of the product contributes enormous tons of waste. Thus, sustainable solutions emphasize using hard flooring, and when desired, area rugs can be added for comfort, warmth, and aesthetics. Area rugs can be easily changed after their life, and create far less waste than carpet and its cushion. Quality area rugs can last for decades with proper cleaning and maintenance. This is evident by the many auction houses, throughout the world, that routinely sell thousands of contemporary and antique rugs every year. Hard flooring and area rugs can also help the IAQ because of the allergens that can be harbored in carpet. Area rugs are easier to maintain because it is difficult to vacuum carpet that is next to walls and the areas around furniture.

The primary fibers for carpet are natural and synthetic. Natural fibers are wool, cotton, hemp, linen, jute, sisal, reed, coir, seagrass, mountain grass, and rubber (see Figure 8.12a and b). To conserve water, the preferred coloration technique is the **solution-dyed** method. This dyeing method adds color pigments to the melted polymer prior to extrusion into a fiber. In addition to conserving water, solution-dyed fibers are highly resistant to fading and are able to retain their original color characteristics for many years. These attributes can help to conserve resources and reduce landfilled materials when the carpet is not replaced early in its life. To promote using carpet for a long period of time, its color and pattern should be an enduring design, rather than trendy. The colors and pattern should be carefully selected to conceal dirt, stains, and wear. Using carpet for a long period of time is better for the environment and the economics of the client.

Wool has been used for centuries and sets the standards for synthetic fibers. The fiber is expensive; however, when a client can afford a wool carpet, the selection has excellent sustainability characteristics.

Wool is a renewable material, and compared with synthetic fibers, the manufacturing process consumes far less energy and water. Wool is extremely resilient, which enhances comfort, appearance, and durability. Carpet that consistently appears attractive for many years is an important sustainability characteristic because, most often, carpet is replaced due to a worn appearance rather than a disintegrated product. The wool fiber is also resistant to flame, static electricity, soil, and wear. To deter moths, some wool products have chemical additives. These toxic substances should be avoided. The natural plant and grass materials such as sisal and seagrass create a relatively rough surface but are extremely durable. The inherent variation of colors and textures of these materials results in timeless, interesting patterns, which can be used in commercial and residential interiors.

Nylon is the most common fiber used for carpet today. The synthetic fiber is strong, inexpensive, and resistant to wear, static electricity, and most stains. Due to the enormous quantities of nylon carpet that are sold and landfilled every year, manufacturers are

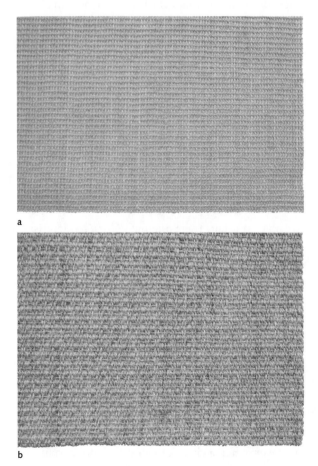

Fig. 8.12a–b. Examples of sisal rugs.

researching products that have less of an impact on the environment and the health of people. Ideally, companies are working to create a nylon carpet that is made from recycled content and can be recycled or is biodegradable. These criteria must be reflected in the **face fiber**, which is the surface or pile of the carpet, and its primary and secondary backings. Currently, nylon 6 and nylon 6,6 are recyclable fibers, but according to Green Seal there are environmental concerns regarding production processes (2001). The production of nylon 6 involves the potentially carcinogenic chemical benzene. Hydrogen cyanide gas, an exceptionally poisonous substance, is used to manufacture nylon 6,6. A fundamental difference in the performance of the two materials is related to durability. In comparing the two nylon products, nylon 6,6 has demonstrated better stain resistance.

Polyester is a synthetic fiber that is not as strong as nylon but has a comfortable *hand*, or aesthetic qualities to the touch. Polyester is resistant to mildew and abrasion, and it has good resiliency and colorfastness. Polyester carpet or polyethylene terephthalate (PET) can be produced from post-consumer recycled plastic drink bottles. Polypropylene, commonly referred to as olefin, is extremely durable. Thus, the synthetic fiber is used for indoor and outdoor carpet. Olefin demonstrates colorfastness, has a low melting point, and is inexpensive, easy to maintain, and highly resistant to staining. The manufacturing process requires less energy than other synthetic fibers, such as nylon. However, olefin lacks an attractive appearance and hand. The fiber has an unappealing sheen and lacks resistance to crushing. Thus, there are limited indoor applications.

Backing is all of the materials in a carpet except the pile. In tufted carpet the primary back is a fabric that is interwoven with the pile yarns during construction. A secondary back, or *scrim*, is a material that is applied to the backside of the carpet. The secondary back improves the durability of the carpet by providing dimensional stability. For sustainable interiors, the materials that are used for the primary and secondary backing should be examined for their content. Polypropylene is frequently used for the backing; however, some manufacturers produce the backing in natural fibers, such as hemp-cotton, jute, and natural latex rubber. Common backcoating chemical compounds are ethylene vinyl acetate,

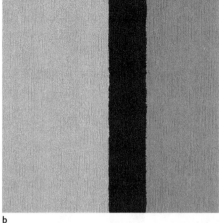

Fig. 8.13a–b. Fusion-bonding is the construction method used to create carpet tiles, also referred to as carpet modules. A common size for carpet tiles is 16" × 16" (457 × 457 mm). Carpet tiles can be an excellent sustainable choice due to their small size and ease of replacement.

a

b

polyvinyl chloride (PVC), and synthetic SBR latex. Synthetic backings can off-gas VOCs. According to Green Seal, in lieu of natural fibers, the backing should be 100 percent recovered materials with a preference for post-consumer content.

Currently, the three primary carpet construction methods are woven, tufted, and fusion-bonded. Weaving, the oldest technique, involves interlacing the pile and backing yarns. Due to the stability factor associated with weaving, generally the carpet does not require a secondary backing. The tufting construction process is used to make most of the carpet that is produced today. Tufting is similar to sewing, whereby a series of needles stitch through the backing material. To adhere the loops, an adhesive is applied to the underside of the primary backing. To provide stability, a secondary backing is then adhered to the backside of the carpet.

Fusion-bonding is the construction method used to create **carpet tiles**, also referred to as **carpet modules** (see Figure 8.13a and b). The surface pile is attached to the backing material by using an adhesive rather than weaving or stitching. A common size for carpet tiles is 16" × 16" (457 × 457 mm). A variety of adhesives are used to install carpet tiles, including peel-and-stick adhesives. From a sustainability perspective, when an application requires wall-to-wall carpet, tiles are an excellent choice. The replacement characteristic of carpet tiles extends the life of the flooring: New carpet tiles can replace soiled, stained, or worn tiles. In addition, removing and adding carpet tiles facilitates remodeling projects and provides easy access to any wiring that might be located under the floor. The small size of the units

also reduces the environmental impacts associated with transportation and landfilling.

To specify sustainable interiors requires a close examination of the performance characteristics of carpet. In addition to determining VOC off-gassing and recyclability issues, important considerations include durability, flammability, electrostatic propensity, thermal properties, and acoustical factors. Selecting a carpet that is durable is essential. Factors important for durability are how well the carpet wears, its resiliency, and retaining aesthetic qualities. These attributes are determined by examining the fiber, the pile yarn density, tuft bind, delamination strength of secondary backing, colorfastness, carpet tile dimensional stability, and flammability. The sources for this information are the ASTM, **American Association of Textile Chemists and Colorists (AATCC)**, and ISO. The ASTM tests the characteristics listed above except for colorfastness and carpet tile dimensional stability. The AATCC and ISO are the organizations that test colorfastness and carpet tile stability, respectively.

The *pile yarn density* is critical for durability. The calculation for this characteristic is the weight of the pile yarn within a prescribed area of the carpet. The highest quality carpets have a high pile yarn density. Carpet with high yarn densities lasts longer and springs back instantly after people repeatedly walk on the surface. The *tuft bind test* determines the amount of force that is necessary to pull the carpet from its primary backing. A carpet that withstands a high amount of force lasts longer, and the original appearance is preserved due to fewer snags. Another test of force is the *delamination strength of secondary backing*.

This test measures the amount of force required to remove the secondary backing from the carpet. Generally, this problem is most likely in spaces that have heavy traffic, such as an airport. Carpet specified for heavy-use areas should be able to withstand a great amount of force.

Colorfastness tests examine how well the color of the carpet withstands rubbing or exposure to light. Ideally, a carpet should have no, or minimum, color transference from rubbing. Color loss should be none, or minimum after exposure to light. The dimensional stability test for carpet tiles measures the product's ability to retain its shape in varying moisture conditions. This test is important because the small size of carpet tiles can easily be affected by excessive moisture. Dimensional stability is essential for the wear, appearance, and safety of carpet tiles. Carpet in the United States must pass the flammability test as directed by *16 CFR 1630*. The test is *ASTM D2859* or the **methenamine pill test**; ASTM D2859 tests carpet to determine its response to a burning methenamine pill. To determine a floor system's reaction to radiant heat, the **International Building Code (IBC)** also requires the *flooring radiant panel test* or *ASTM E 648*. To adhere to regulations, current local, state, and federal requirements should always be researched and applied to specifications.

Carpet cushion, or padding, is another component of the carpet system that should be good for the environment and the IAQ. Carpet cushion provides many benefits related to sustainable designs. Padding increases the life of a carpet, enhances resiliency, absorbs sound, and provides additional comfort to the users of a space. There are a variety of carpet cushion materials. Product availability includes recycled content, natural fibers, and synthetic materials. Carpet cushion is available in 100 percent post-consumer content. Natural materials include wool, jute, and natural rubber. Since the cushion is installed directly to the floor, care must be taken to ensure a dry surface. Moisture that is in contact with the cushion and/or carpet can eventually ruin the products and promote the growth of mold. Some carpet cushion has brominated flame-retardants, which has the potential to be detrimental to the environment and the health of people.

The method used to install carpet can affect the impact on the environment and the IAQ. The basic

methods of installation are direct glue-down or stretched-in installation (see Figure 8.14a and b). The carpet cushion is stapled or glued to the subfloor. For sustainable interiors, whenever possible, avoid adhesives and specify a method that does not emit VOCs. In addition, carpet that has been fastened to the underlayment is easier to remove for recycling purposes. The stretched-in installation method does not require any adhesives. Tack strips can be nailed or stapled to the perimeter of a room, and then the carpet is attached by stretching the material over the

a

b

Fig. 8.14a–b. The method used to install carpet can affect the impact on the environment and the IAQ. The basic methods of installation are (a) direct glue-down and (b) stretched-in installation. Whenever possible, avoid adhesives and specify a method that does not emit VOCs.

strips. The mechanics of stretching carpet prohibits the method in large rooms or over concrete. Thus, most commercial interiors use the direct glue-down method. For these applications, the material should be a low- or zero-emitting material. To help reduce any emissions from VOCs, carpet should be aired out prior to installation and occupants should wait several days prior to using the space.

Due to the significant environmental problems associated with synthetic fibers, carpet systems should be selected that are refurbished, or have recycled content in the face fiber and backing. Product specifications should be examined thoroughly to determine the percentage of recycled content. Some carpet is advertised as having recycled content, but the amount might be minimal, such as less than 10 percent. Recycled carpet can have recovered materials content and/or post-consumer and post-industrial content. The preferred sustainable strategy is recycled materials from post-consumer and/or post-industrial content. When reading specifications, be sure to examine carefully the content of recycled materials. For example, content descriptions that indicate a product has "75 percent total recycled content" may only have a small percentage of a previously consumed material. Thus, when an interior designer initially reads the specifications it might be assumed that the "75 percent recycled content" is *all* post-consumed materials. All products that have recycled content can be good for the environment; however, in trying to maximize sustainability practices, the preferred solution is to specify products with post-consumer and post-industrial recycled content. Some manufacturers certify the recycled content of a product via the **Scientific Certification Systems**.

To encourage refurbishment, reuse, and recycling, some manufacturers are involved with **carpet reclamation programs**. Recycling materials for reuse is sometimes referred to as a **repurposed** product. Basically, via the reclamation program a manufacturer accepts used carpet and then either refurbishes the product for reuse or recycles the materials. When a carpet is in good condition, the product undergoes refurbishment. This involves cleaning, retexturing, and restoring its fibers by redyeing and reshearing. In a recent study an analysis was conducted to compare recycled and newly manufactured carpets (Watson

and Warnock, 2003). The results indicate that a recycled polyester carpet is a good choice due to less color change, ability to retain its original density, and greater compression and recovery of face fibers. Some manufacturers clean carpet that is in good condition and then donate the product to a charity.

Carpet that is not suitable for refurbishment may be separated by the type of material, and then remanufactured into new nylon yarns or other products, such as automobile parts. Some manufacturers also have leasing or return programs for carpet. The premise of the program is to encourage the reuse and recycling of carpet. For example, a manufacturer can lease carpet tiles to a business. When a tile becomes worn or severely soiled, the product is returned to the manufacturer for refurbishment or recycling. In selecting a manufacturer, care must be taken to ensure that returned carpet is reused or recycled, rather than transported to the landfill.

Wallcoverings

For thousands of years some type of covering, other than paint, has been used on walls. Originally, most wallcoverings were used to prevent air infiltration and to help keep a room warmer. Rugs and tapestries are examples of wallcoverings that were used to warm the interior and served a decorative purpose. Fabrics were tacked to the walls of a room, but in early times, due to its high cost, only wealthy people could afford to use fabrics in this manner. Eventually, an inexpensive substitute for fabric became wallpaper. Thus, for practical as well as aesthetic reasons, people have always expressed concerns regarding an appropriate wallcovering. For sustainable interiors, desirable performance characteristics of wallcoverings are durability, insulating properties, and sound absorbency. The content of the material should be made from recycled matter, free of VOCs, recyclable, and biodegradable.

Important durability properties of wallcovering, are colorfastness, washability, scrubability, and its resistance to abrasion, stains, and tears; ASTM F793, *Standard Classification of Wallcoverings by Durability Characteristics*, provides the testing results of wallcoverings. There are three grades of wallcovering, which are based on its durability or serviceability. A Type I wallcovering is suitable only for *light duty*, such as hotel rooms and offices. Type II is intended for *medium duty* and Type III is rated for *heavy duty*. Examples of applications for a Type II wallcovering are dining rooms, classrooms, and public corridors. Type III can resist rough abrasion; thus, these wallcoverings are suggested for hospital or food-service areas. A primary difference between the three grades is the backing material. Type I wallcoverings have a loose material that lacks dimensional stability and, by contrast, Type III backing materials are very dense and firm.

Major types of wallcoverings are vinyl, wallpapers, and textiles. Vinyl wallcoverings are frequently specified for commercial interiors because they are durable and relatively inexpensive. However, most vinyl wallcoverings are PVC-based; thus, VOCs are emitted, especially during the initial weeks after installation. In addition, combustion of PVC, which can occur in a waste incinerator or a building fire, creates toxins that can be dangerous to people and the environment. Another problem with most vinyl wallcoverings is fungal growth, which can occur when moisture is present in gypsum wallboard. This can easily occur in warm and humid climates or from flooding. Mold and mildew may not appear on the surface of the wallcovering, but the backside might be covered with fungal growth. Thus, for sustainable interiors, alternatives to vinyl should be specified. Options include synthetic and natural products. All wallcoverings should be installed with zero- or low-VOC adhesives or tacked to surfaces. The contents of any primer, sealant, or sizing used to install wallcoverings should also be scrutinized for its effect on people and the environment.

In researching wallcoverings for sustainability, some of the attributes to search for in product specifications are recycled content, durability characteristics, fire-rating, ink properties, recyclability, and presence of PVC and chlorine. Products are available that are made with a variety of recycled content, such as paper, glass, and wood fiber. Some of the natural materials used to manufacture wallcoverings are flax, mulberry fibers, sisal, linen, cork, honeysuckle vines, and cellulose. From a color perspective, preferred contents are water-soluble ink and water-based vegetable dyes. Ideally, a wallcovering should be fully recyclable, breathable, and free of PVC and chlorine.

Cork and grass cloth wallcoverings are natural materials made from renewable resources, and have the additional benefits of absorbing sound and providing insulation. Cork wallcovering is made in tiles and sheets. As with cork flooring, products are made in a variety of patterns and colors. Grass cloth wallcoverings are made from several different woven native grasses and can be combined with other natural materials, such as bamboo. Natural textured wallcoverings are made from cane, raffia, jute, reed, bamboo, maize, and sisal. Backing materials can be paper or fabric. Wallcoverings that are relatively thick can help to reduce imperfections in a wall surface but require higher quantities of adhesives. Wallcovering adhesives are available that are made from natural materials and require only water when mixing the substances.

In specifying sustainable interiors, an interesting solution is to revert back to previous customs of using fabrics, tapestries, and rugs on the walls. Fabrics made from natural fibers, such as linen, flax, cotton, wool, and silk, are adhered to a backing, or the fabric itself can be directly applied to walls. Fabrics supported by a paper or vinyl backing are installed in the same manner as traditional wallcoverings. Applying fabrics directly to a wall can be done by gluing, tacking, or using an **upholstered wall system**, or what is referred to as a **stretched-fabric wall system** (see Figure 8.15). For dimensional stability, the weave of the fabric should be dense and firm. (Characteristics of textiles are examined in the next section of this chapter.) Some upholstery fabrics are ideal for stretched-fabric wall systems, because they are less likely to sag or ripple in the months after an installation. Glued installations can be difficult to remove when being replaced, and the content of the adhesive should be free of VOCs. Tacking the fabric to a wall eliminates VOCs and enables the material to be removed fairly easily with minimum damage to the surface of the wall. An upholstered wall system uses a track to stretch and hold the fabric. Upholstered walls can include padding behind the fabric for additional insulation, sound absorption, and an aesthetically soft appearance.

When nails are used to hang objects, or when the wall is used as a tackable surface, the fabric should be carefully selected to ensure easy repair and avoid snags. Frequently, a fabric with a heavy yarn is a good choice (see Figure 8.16). The relatively simplest

Fig. 8.15. (left) Applying fabrics directly to a wall can be done by using an upholstered wall system. For dimensional stability, the weave of the fabric should be dense and firm.
Fig. 8.16. (right) To ensure easy repair and avoid snags, a heavy yarn is a good choice for fabric for walls.

method of having a textile wallcovering is to hang a fabric, tapestry, or rug on a wall. This installation method avoids any adhesives, has the least damage to the surface of the wall, and the item can be easily removed for cleaning. For a healthy IAQ, dust and dirt must be removed from the surface of a textured wallcovering on a regular basis. In addition, depending on the characteristics of the material, substances such as grease or oil can be extremely difficult to remove from textured wallcoverings.

SUSTAINABLE STRATEGIES FOR CSI DIVISION 12: FURNISHINGS

An interior designer is extensively involved with the specification of furnishings. In following the categories established by CSI, this section reviews sustainable strategies for fabrics, window treatments, furniture, and seating. To conserve resources, buildings, finishes, and furnishings must be properly maintained. The final section of the chapter reviews overall recommended cleaning and maintenance procedures for the built environment.

To specify sustainable interiors, the furnishings must be healthy for people and the environment. This requires an examination of the product's LCA and the best solutions for the IAQ. A primary focus is to reuse and restore existing furnishings, rather than specifying new products. The nature of the field of interior design helps to facilitate this process, because there are thousands of resources that sell previously owned furniture and decorative accessories. Antique stores, auctions, estate sales, and online bidding operations are excellent examples. When furniture, wall finishes, or fabrics need to be refurbished, there are many local professionals who can perform the task, such as upholsterers and furniture restoration ex-

perts. The practice of reusing furnishings, rather than specifying new products, can be detrimental to an interior designer who is compensated by a commission that is based on sales. In these situations, alternative compensation methods should be developed. (Compensation methods that do *not* encourage increased consumption of resources are presented in Unit III of this text.)

Fabrics

Interior designers specify millions of yards of fabric every year. A textile, which is any material that contains fibers, is extensively used in commercial and residential interiors. Applications include upholstery, window treatments, wallcoverings, flooring, wall-mounted panels, systems furniture panels, and linens. There are many concerns related to fabrics, including the manufacturing process, VOC emissions, and the environmental impact of disposing of the material in landfills. In addition, textile manufacturing processes can involve heavy metals and toxins. The enormous quantity of fabrics that is produced and used every year makes it imperative to carefully research and specify products that are appropriate for sustainable interiors.

The development of fabrics occurred thousands of years ago, and some of the materials still exist, such as linen, which was used to wrap around mummies. This aspect contradicts a common assumption that fabrics lack durability. Thus, for sustainable interiors, it is imperative to understand the performance characteristics of textiles that affect durability and other aspects related to sustainability. Understanding textiles requires an examination of fibers, yarns, weaves, performance characteristics, dyeing methods, and fabric finishing. As with carpet, the basic fibers used to produce fabrics are natural, synthetics, and blends with various types. However, due to the lack of concern regarding hard wear, additional fibers can be used to produce fabric. Natural fibers used for fabric are derived from plants and animals, which are biodegradable. Fibers derived from plants are cotton, coir, flax, hemp, ramie, and sisal. Sustainability concerns related to these fibers include the use of pesticides and toxic chemicals. For example, extensive use of pesticides is typically required to control the insects that destroy the cotton plant. To help alleviate this problem, interior designers can specify organically grown cotton. Some cotton is grown to have a natural color other than the traditional off-white (see Figure 8.17).

Flax, which is the fiber that is used to create linen, is important for sustainable interiors. Linen is extremely strong and resistant to insects, mildew, pilling, stretching, and static electricity. These characteristics result in a durable fabric, and flax can be grown with minimal amounts of chemical fertilizers and pesticides. Linen wrinkles easily, which affects its appearance; however, the material has a luxurious sheen. Linen is relatively expensive compared to cotton. Other fibers from plant materials, such as jute and sisal, generally have a coarse hand. To enhance the texture, coarse fibers are often blended with softer fibers, such as cotton. Wool and other fibers from animals, such as silk (silkworm cocoon) and mohair, are susceptible to insects, sunlight deterioration, and shrinking. However, fibers from animals have many positive attributes, as described previously in this chapter, including resistance to soil, stains, and wrinkling. The silk fiber is very strong and takes excellent color, but it is quickly damaged by sunlight, moisture, abrasion, and soiling. Natural materials' propensity to be attractive to moths and susceptible to fungus growth prompt many manufacturers to apply toxic chemicals to the fibers. Therefore, product specifications must be thoroughly examined to avoid substances that negatively impact the health of people and the environment.

Since petroleum-based synthetic fibers are also used for fabric, research should be conducted to locate materials that have less of an impact on the environment. Generally, synthetic fibers are durable, dimensionally stable, inexpensive, and resistant to chemicals and sunlight. The positive attributes of

Fig. 8.17. Some cotton is grown to have a natural color other than the traditional off-white. Colors available are muted greens, beige, browns, whites, and peach.

synthetic fibers provide the rationale for specifying fabrics with a variety of contents, such as polyester, nylon, acrylic, and olefin. For sustainable interiors, whenever an application requires synthetic fibers, the fabric specified should have recycled content and be 100 percent recyclable. For example, some manufacturers use recycled PET for the polyester fiber in fabrics. Coated polypropylene fabrics can be recycled. In addition, the fabric should be manufactured without using solvents. The fabric should be without ultraviolet (UV) or flame inhibitors, including being free of antimony, which is a metallic oxide used for flameproofing. To facilitate processes, fabrics intended for recycling or composting should not have chemical backing. To demonstrate the positive environmental impact of their products, some manufacturers have their fabrics with synthetic fibers seek MBDC (McDonough Braungart Design Chemistry) C2C certification. This new certification program tests fabrics based on the following categories: materials, material reutilization/design for environment, energy, water, and social responsibility (MBDC, 2005). When fabrics qualify for the certification, the manufacturer should provide the designated level of compliance. The MBDC ecological design protocol has a 5-level system, wherein a level 5 is the best certification designation.

Fibers are twisted or spun into yarns. The basic yarn classifications are spun or filament. Spun yarns use staple fibers that are twisted together. Natural or staple fibers have short lengths, except for silk, which can be extremely long and continuous. Filament yarns are long and continuous strands of synthetic fibers or silk. Forcing a liquid polymer through the holes of a spinneret makes synthetic fibers (see Figure 8.18). This production method enables synthetic fibers to be made in any prescribed length. Twisting increases the strength of yarns. Plied yarns, which are formed by combining multiple yarns together, provide greater strength and thickness. The type of yarn affects the fabric's performance. From a sustainability perspective, important factors to examine are durability, ease of care, and appearance. For durability purposes, filament yarns are stronger than spun yarns, but filament yarns tend to run and unravel. Compared to simple yarns, plied yarns provide greater strength to a fabric. Ease of care is an important consideration for retaining appearance, thus increasing the life of a fabric. Two important considerations related to care are soil resistance and snagging. Filament yarns tend to resist soil but are easily snagged.

Yarns are woven into fabrics. Weaving is still the most common method for constructing fabrics for interiors. Weaving is done on looms, which interlace the warp (lengthwise yarns) and weft yarns (widthwise yarns). The closeness of the yarn, or the thread

Fig. 8.18. Filament yarns are long and continuous strands of synthetic fibers or silk. Forcing a liquid polymer through the holes of a spinneret makes synthetic fibers.

count, is determined by the number of warp and weft yarns that are present in one square inch (6 cm) of fabric. There are several basic weaves, including the plain, twill, satin, pile, and jacquard. Generally, a particular weave is used to create a type of fabric. For example, the jacquard weave is used to produce damask and tapestry fabrics. The type of weave can affect the fabric's durability and ease of care. In comparison to other weaves, the plain and twill weaves can have the highest thread count. A high thread count helps to provide strength, dimensional stability, and water repellency and can enhance fire-retardant properties. The satin weave can have a high thread count, but the long warp yarn that is floated over the filling yarns snags and can be easily abraded during use. Balanced fabrics that are woven with an even number of warp and weft yarns, such as a plain weave, are less prone to slippage in a stitched seam. This can be important for the durability of installations that require heavy fabrics, or long lengths of fabric, as with floor-to-ceiling window treatments. Seam slippage can also affect the durability of upholstered furniture. To retain the shape of a cushion, the fabric should not pull away from the stitched seams. Reduced seam slippage is especially important for furniture that is used by a high number of people on a daily basis.

Sustainability factors related to fabrics also involve coloring and printing methods. Textile colorants can be added in various stages of the construction process. **Greige goods** is the term for fabrics before dyes or finishes have been added. These fabrics have the potential to become very popular for sustainable interiors because they do not have many of the environmental consequences associated with dyes and finishes. To produce colors and patterns, fabrics can be dyed, printed, or a combination of both processes. The coloring and printing method can affect the environment and the fabric's durability. Colorfastness is an important characteristic to enhance durability. To improve colorfastness requires the appropriate match between a fiber and the dye method. Colorfastness is best achieved with fiber dyeing. As mentioned earlier in this chapter, to conserve water the preferred coloration technique is the solution-dyed method. For sustainable interiors, fabrics should be selected that are either dyed naturally, have nontoxic chemical dyes, or have no dye at all.

Fabric finishing is done to improve the performance of natural and synthetic fibers. Sustainability concerns related to finishes focus on environmental effects that occur during manufacturing processes, VOC emissions during use, and how the chemicals in a finish affect natural resources when the fabric is landfilled. Finishes are applied to a fabric with chemical treatments and mechanical processes. Both methods can negatively affect the environment; thus, in specifying fabrics, the products selected should have the least environmental impact. Solutions should focus on identifying fabrics with nontoxic chemicals. From a positive viewpoint, fabric finishes can increase the fabric's functional properties, appearance longevity, and durability. Fabric finishing can strengthen fibers and improve resistance to flames, stains, soil, moths, fungus growth, static electricity, water, and shrinkage. To be in compliance with building and fire codes, flame resistance is essential. Polymer or saline treatments are applied to fabrics for flame resistance. Fabric finishes can also be applied to reflect radiant heat and to provide insulation.

The performance characteristics of fabrics that are important for sustainable interiors include durability, maintenance, functional properties, and economic considerations. In selecting fabrics for sustainable commercial and residential interiors, durability is essential for reducing the consumption of natural and human-made resources. Thus, fabrics should be specified that are dimensionally stable and repairable and are resistant to abrasion, soil, stains, and tears. To encourage people to keep and restore existing fabrics, the ability to retain their appearance is extremely important. The appearance characteristics to consider are colorfastness, texture retention, and resistance to pilling, snagging, and running. Appearance retention is also affected by how well a fabric can hide soil, stains, and wear. For this purpose, the fabric's colors, patterns, and texture become critical considerations. Generally, light colors, small or no pattern, and smooth textures tend to reveal dirt and stains. In contrast, dark colors, large patterns, and rough textures can help to conceal the effects of use over time.

A common practice of the interior design profession is to use the same fabric on multiple surfaces and furnishings in a room (see Figure 8.19). Some rooms

Fig. 8.19. Some rooms have the same fabric for walls, the ceiling, upholstered pieces, window treatments, and accessories. From a sustainability perspective, these applications are very problematic due to the waste that can occur when people become tired of the fabric or when fabric is damaged on only one piece.

have the same fabric for walls, the ceiling, upholstered pieces, window treatments, and accessories. The aesthetics might be appealing; however, from a sustainability perspective, these applications are very problematic. The primary concern is the waste that occurs when people become tired of the fabric. In this situation the entire room must be refurbished, regardless of the condition of the materials. The waste is detrimental to the environment and can be extremely significant in commercial installations, such as hundreds of guest rooms in a hotel. To conserve resources and waste, interiors should be designed with a variety of textures, patterns, and colors in a room.

Fabrics have numerous functional expectations related to sustainability. From an environmental perspective, fabric can provide insulation, control noise, reduce the spread of fire, minimize static electricity, and control glare from sunlight. In addition, fabric on upholstered furniture can improve comfort and reduce the fatigue of users. Economic considerations related to fabrics include the purchase price, delivery, installation fees, and maintenance. Whenever possible, fabrics should be purchased close to the point of fabrication and subsequent deliveries. For example, the fabric mill for upholstered furniture should be in close proximity to the furniture manufacturer. Ideally, furniture should be selected from manufacturers that are local or regional to the site of installation. The cost of installation is important for the initial phase but can become even more critical when a fabricated piece must be removed for cleaning or repair. Maintenance requirements affect the durability of fabrics and the likelihood of keeping a product made with fabric for a long period of time.

Window Treatments

Fabrics are frequently used for window treatments in commercial and residential interiors. Thus, in selecting and/or designing a window treatment, the previously discussed fabric characteristics related to sustainability must be applied to these solutions. In addition to selecting appropriate fabrics, considerations for sustainable window treatments include a product's LCA, insulation, noise control, and privacy; reducing glare from sunlight or exterior lighting; and maximizing daylighting and views to the outdoors. To accommodate the increased emphasis on ventilation, daylighting, and views, buildings will have more surface area dedicated to glazing. Window treatments with solar protection are available for skylights. Thus, it is essential that the material components of window treatments reflect the principles of sustainability, including recycled content; biodegradability; antimicrobial characteristics; resistance to UV degradation; and use of water-based glues, stains, and finishes.

In operating as an interdependent element of the built environment's system, window treatments should help to improve the performance of mechanical systems, lighting, finishes, and furnishings. For example, window treatments can help to conserve energy, which contributes to the efficiency of HVAC systems. Integrating window treatments with lighting systems can maximize daylighting and reduce the need for electrical sources. Fibers, fabrics, carpet, and furniture will last longer when protected by an appropriate glazing and window treatment. People will have greater satisfaction with an environment when a window treatment reduces glare, brightness, and solar heat gain, while being able to see the view outdoors.

Generally, to conserve energy, the best approach is to specify high-performance windows. This is an effective approach for new construction or window replacements. However, when these two options are not available, window treatments that are designed to be energy efficient are an excellent solution. To reduce air infiltration, convection, and radiation, an effective approach is to install an insulated shade system that has a high R-value. To reduce heat loss and gain, the shade system should have a tight seal on all four sides of the treatment. Some products have magnetic strips, or tracks that seal the treatment to the wall. Drapery lining fabrics are also available with blackout and insulating properties. Lining is not only important for insulation; the additional layer of fabric also helps to preserve the window treatment. Since lining is exposed to the outdoors, most of the deterioration that can be caused by sunlight and condensation impacts the lining instead of the fabric. Over a period of time, the window treatment's fabric could be in excellent condition, but the lining might be faded, yellowed, water-stained, and in shreds. In this situation new lining fabric can replace the irreparable lining. This solution conserves resources and can significantly extend the life of a window treatment.

When privacy or darkness is required in a room, draperies and curtains can be good solutions. Other solutions are window treatments made from natural fibers, such as grasses, reeds, and bamboo (see Figure 8.20a). Some manufacturers use neither pesticides nor chemicals to grow the fibers and use solar energy to dry the materials. An alternate solution is accordion-folded shades that have a series of pockets (see Figure 8.20b). The pockets trap air, which can help to control heat loss or gain. These shades are available with reflective layers and have room-darkening options.

Technological advancements have improved the performance of screen shades (see Figure 8.21a–d). Screen shades are manufactured for interior and exterior installations. Screen shades can be an excellent solution for sustainable interiors, because they can be visually transparent while providing solar protection against brightness, glare, and heat gain. Visual transparency enables users of the space to enjoy the benefits of daylighting, and a view of the outdoors, without the ill effects of sunlight. Screen shades can enhance the visual comfort of a space and reduce eyestrain. Screens are available with blackout materials when all sunlight must be blocked. For example, a room needs to be dark during an AV presentation in a conference room. Generally, screen shades are preferable to blinds and shutters because the transparent fabric covers the entire area of glazing. Openings in blinds or shutters can produce glare and allow UV penetration and heat gain. The only way to eliminate these problems is to completely close the openings, which reduces daylighting and eliminates views to the outdoors.

Shading systems are available in manual and motorized systems. To save energy and costs whenever possible, manual systems should be specified. When a treatment is heavy or in a remote location, motorized systems should be installed. Shade systems are also available with sun-tracking software, which programs shades to open and close depending on the location of the sun. Shade systems can be integrated with building management software systems. This allows for centralized control of window treatments

a

b

Fig. 8.20a. Window treatments can be made from natural fibers, such as grasses, reeds, and bamboo. This hand-woven natural shade is in "Barbados Pecan."
Fig. 8.20b. Accordion-folded shades have a series of pockets, which trap air, helping to control heat loss or gain.

and facilitates the integration of electrical light sources and dimming controls. For recycling purposes, some manufacturers allow shades to be returned after use.

Specifications of screen shades have characteristics that are important for sustainable interiors and are similar to glazing. These attributes include a product's transmittance, reflectance, and absorptance qualities. As sunlight strikes the glazing of a building some of the light passes through, is reflected, and is absorbed by the glazing. To demonstrate how various materials affect this occurrence, shade and screen manufacturers provide **solar transmittance**, **visible transmittance**, **UV transmittance**, **solar reflectance**, **solar absorptance**, and **shading coefficient (SC)**. Manufacturers express these factors as percentages. Solar and visible transmittance is the amount of solar energy and visible light, respectively, that passes through a material such as a screen shade. Visible transmittance percentages reflect the amount of glare and natural light that passes through a material. Lower visible transmittance percentages indicate that the material is better for glare control. Higher percentages designate that the material will emit more natural light.

Ultraviolet transmittance refers to the amount of UV rays that penetrate a material. The UV transmittance is associated with a material's **openness factor**. The openness factor is the percentage of material area that is open. For example, when a sheer fabric has an openness factor of 5 percent, the UV blockage is 95 percent. A 10 percent openness factor results in blocking 90 percent of the UVs. Solar reflectance is the measure of the amount of sunlight reflected by the surface material. Solar absorptance refers to the amount of solar energy that a fabric absorbs.

Shading coefficient indicates the amount of heat gain generated by the sun that passes through the glazing and the window treatment. The lower the SC rating, the less heat gain. In specifying window treatments, an interior designer should research the various characteristics of materials and select the fabric that provides the optimum light and thermal condition for each space in a building. For example, on the north side of a building it might be desirable to have a screen with a high visible transmittance. Rooms facing west might require a window treatment with a low visible transmittance.

Fig. 8.21a–d. Screen shades can be an excellent solution for sustainable interiors because they can be visually transparent, while providing solar protection against brightness, glare, and heat gain.

Furniture and Seating

Furniture and seating have been designed and constructed for thousands of years. Some furniture in museums is from the earliest built environments. These examples serve to demonstrate the potential longevity of furniture and should serve as a basis for criteria used to specify furniture for sustainable interiors. Furniture can last for centuries when the appropriate materials are selected, suitable con-

struction techniques are employed, people take care during use, proper cleaning and maintenance is performed, and its appearance reflects a skillful application of the principles of design. The first priority should focus on specifying existing furniture. Millions of furniture pieces exist in buildings, and millions of *used* furniture pieces are for sale at stores, auctions, estate sales, and online. Refurbished and remanufactured office furniture is available from many companies. Refurbished furniture also has the

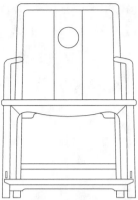
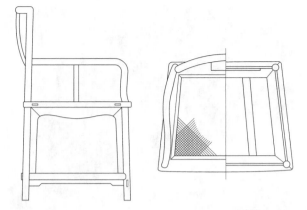

Fig. 8.22. The structural stability of furniture is based upon the type of material, design of components, and construction techniques.

economic advantage of lower costs compared to new pieces. Many used pieces do not need refurbishment, or a piece may require minor repairs, refinishing, or new upholstery. Professionals in most every community are available to refurbish furniture by refinishing surfaces and reupholstering seating. In selecting a refurbishing firm, identify a business that employs practices that minimize impacts on the environment. When it is absolutely not possible to specify used furniture, an interior designer must examine the item's LCA and select products that reflect the principles of sustainable design.

In selecting used or new furniture, sustainability considerations focus on its being durable for the prescribed function and the users of the space. Durability is critical to conserve natural resources and energy, and to reduce landfilled materials. Furniture must have structural stability, quality operating mechanisms, appearance retention properties, and timeless aesthetic qualities. In addition, furniture that is well designed for the purpose of the task and its users is most likely to be retained and not discarded to a landfill. Solutions should focus on the principles of universal design and be ergonomically functional. This requires a thorough examination of how people function in a space and interact with the furniture. Often this is a site-specific and user-specific requirement. For example, functional needs in a waiting room of a hospital are different from a waiting room in a train station. From users' perspectives, eight-month-pregnant women in a doctor's waiting room have furniture needs that differ from those of other adults.

Sustainability factors associated with many of the materials used to construct furniture, such as wood, have been reviewed in previous sections of this text.

Thus, furniture with wood content should be FSC-certified, and whenever appropriate, components should have post-consumer and post-industrial recycled content. Products should be free of formaldehyde, PVC, chrome, benzene, lead, mercury, solvents, and brominated flame-retardants. Coating-free or powder-coated metal finishes are preferred, and substances should have zero or low VOCs. Furniture should be able to be refurbished and, when necessary, easily disassembled for recycling. Materials should be biodegradable or recyclable. Relatively new products that are available from manufacturers are reclaimed-wood furniture and recycled-content furniture. Some of the materials used for recycled-content furniture include recycled paper, sunflower seed hulls, post-consumer plastics, wheat straw, and discarded used parts from automobiles, machinery, and bicycles. Systems furniture is available that is specifically designed to facilitate remodeling. The systems are built with access flooring, which can be used to house HVAC ducting, cables, and electrical wiring.

The structural stability of furniture is based on the type of material, design of the components, and construction techniques (see Figure 8.22). For durability and appearance retention, furniture that is used the most frequently, by high numbers of people, should be carefully selected for its structural stability. Steel is an extremely strong material for furniture and is available with recycled content. Furniture made with co-injected plastics should be avoided because the material is problematic to recycle. Furniture hardware, such as handles, pulls, hinges, casters, glides, and tilt mechanisms should be of a high quality and easy to replace or repair. Hardware should be sturdy and firmly attached to the furniture piece. To contribute to the life of furniture, quality hardware is worth the extra cost. This is especially important for movable hardware, such as hinges and door glides. Metals should be resistant to rust and corrosion. The design of each element of a furniture piece should be the appropriate height, width, and length to effectively fulfill its function. For example, a leg of a table should be the appropriate size that can support the weight of the tabletop. Table legs should also be able to support activities that require the tabletop and any items that are placed on the table. A table used for library books requires different structural properties than a table that is used just for eating.

Furniture that lasts for centuries has strong construction techniques and quality materials and finishes (see Figure 8.23). The construction of wood-frame furniture should be solid wood that is FSC-certified. Joinery methods are interlocking and mechanical (see Figure 8.24). Both of these methods use glue to increase strength and stability. Mortise-and-tenon joints are very strong. For residential furniture, durable pieces have dovetail joints for drawer sides and a dado joint at the ends of fixed shelves. Mechanical joints are used to reinforce the corners

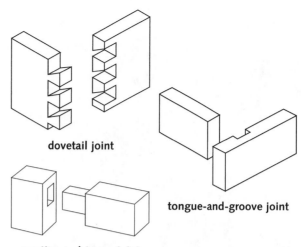

dovetail joint

tongue-and-groove joint

mortise-and-tenon joint

Fig. 8.24. Interlocking joinery methods. The methods use glue to increase strength and stability.

of furniture. A common example for seating is a screwed corner block. For durability, screws should be used rather than nails, staples, or metal fasteners. Durability concerns focus on how well a surface can resist scratches, dents, and stains. Edges, legs, and bases of furniture are especially prone to damage, because people and cleaning equipment can easily come in contact with these elements. Whenever possible, visible elements of a furniture piece should not come in contact with a floor and exposed parts should be protected with a hard material. To reduce soiling and wear on upholstered pieces, arms should not be covered with fabric and the back should be too low for a head to rest, or should be of a material that is easily cleaned. For dining rooms, the seats of chairs should be easy to clean, repair, and reupholster.

Upholstered furniture should be made with fabric that adheres to the sustainability characteristics described previously in this chapter. In addition, important considerations include the quality of the frame, the suspension system, its cushions, and elements associated with human factors (see Figure 8.25). It is very important to determine the quality of the frame and the suspension system, because these components affect the durability of the piece and the success of future refurbishing. Since these elements are hidden in upholstered pieces, an interior designer should locate the details in written specifications provided by a manufacturer. Over the years consumers and interior designers have learned which manufacturers produce furniture that lasts and

Fig. 8.23. Furniture that lasts for centuries has classic details, strong construction techniques, enduring materials, and quality finishes.

5/4" Hardwood Frames

Soft Cotton for Shape and Comfort

Coil Back Springs

Cotton and Foam Back

Highly Resilient
Polyurethane Cushions

Soft Fiber for
Shape and Comfort

Fabric Patterns
Matched

5/4" Solid Hardwood
Construction

Double Cone Coil Springs
Eight-Way Hand Tied

Double-Doweled Joints

Corner Blocks

Fig. 8.25. Important considerations of upholstered furniture include the quality of the frame, the suspension system, its cushions, and elements associated with human factors.

which products are shoddy. Hence, word-of-mouth and experience can provide reliable information regarding upholstered furniture.

The frame of upholstered seating should be kiln-dried hardwood that is FSC-certified. Glued mortise-and-tenon and double-doweled joints are extremely strong. Seat corners should be reinforced with glued and screwed corner-blocks. The suspension system should be resilient and be structured for long wear. To support the cushions, springs and webbing tapes are attached to the frame. The most durable system for the seat is the traditional eight-way tied coil springs. Springs should be spaced at a distance that avoids uncomfortable gaps and prevents rubbing against each other. Sinuous wire springs are usually applied to the back of seating. Webbing systems, which are frequently used for commercial furniture, use a material that is stretched across the seat and then tacked to the frame.

Cushions provide extra comfort to seating and can improve durability when the cushion is loose and reversible. Welt cording sewn in the seams of cushions and other areas of seating can improve the durability of the cover fabric. Welts can improve the longevity of furniture because welts are sewn in the areas that are rubbed when people move in a

chair. Rubbing is abrasive to all fabrics. Polyurethane foam is frequently used for cushions and should be made by using water as the blowing agent or other substances that minimize the impact on the environment. To determine the performance of foam cushions, an interior designer should examine their **density**, **indentation load deflection (ILD)**, and the **support ratio** or the **compression modulus**. These characteristics are important to review, because cushions significantly affect the wearability of seating. The density of foam is the mass per unit volume and is expressed as the pounds per cubic foot (kg/m^3). Density is extremely important to the life of a cushion. High densities provide the greatest support. The ILD measures the indentation qualities of a foam cushion. Higher ILD ratings provide the greatest firmness. The support ratio reflects the amount of support provided by the foam. Higher support factors indicate an ability to support more weight. To improve the life of a cushion, a fabric should be wrapped around the foam. Flammability is a serious concern with the cover fabric and cushion materials. Thus, content of materials should be scrutinized to determine the presence of additives that have high toxins.

To encourage reuse of furniture and seating, the design should support human factors. This is especially important for office seating. To accommodate the ergonomic needs of a variety of people, office seating should be selected that has the most adjustability. Seating should help to reduce fatigue and provide the appropriate support that the body requires for a specific task. Chairs with casters should be carefully selected to provide adequate safety and reduce wear on flooring. For safety purposes, chairs with casters should have a five-legged base. Hard casters with rounded-wheel edges are best for carpet. Chairs with soft casters should be used on hard and resilient flooring. Sophisticated office seating is mechanically very complex. To facilitate repairs and recycling, chairs with a minimum number of components are preferred.

Cleaning and Maintenance

Proper cleaning, care, and maintenance are essential for sustainable interiors. Finishes and furnishings must be properly cared for on a regular basis. Floors in particular need routine care. Mats at doorways help to reduce soil and pollutants entering a building. These should be cleaned daily. Carpet should be vacuumed as often as possible to eliminate particulates and to remove soil that is abrasive to the fibers. To conserve electricity, a damp mop or broom should be used to clean hard and resilient flooring. Clean rooms also improve the IAQ by eliminating particulates that affect the health of people, including substances associated with sick building syndrome. Proper cleaning products and procedures can dramatically increase the life of products. Manufacturers provide the appropriate cleaning recommendations for their products. This should be the first source to research when developing cleaning and maintenance protocols for a client. Other reliable sources are Green Seal, the **EPA Environmentally Preferable Purchasing Program**, the General Services Agency, and the Scientific Certification Systems.

For sustainable interiors, the products used for cleaning should be healthy for the environment, the person responsible for doing the cleaning, and the occupants of the space. Frequently, household cleaning substances can be products that are inexpensive, easily obtainable, and do not have chemicals or toxins. For example, products that can be used for cleaning purposes are baking soda, white vinegar, and rubbing alcohol. A common assumption is that to remove difficult stains, such as mold and mildew, requires toxic cleaning products. However, most often these problems can be alleviated with mild substances and more physical effort. Thus, *elbow grease* frequently can substitute for a toxic substance that requires spraying, waiting, and wiping. Whenever possible, cleaning recommendations should prioritize human exertion and specify products that are biodegradable and nontoxic. Labels and manufacturer's recommendations should be carefully scrutinized for harmful ingredients.

Sustainable environments require the preservation of current materials and products. A responsible practice is to provide a client with appropriate information regarding cleaning and maintenance procedures. Often this is a detail that does not receive adequate attention when the details of a project are planned and implemented. Frequently, when a client and interior designer are planning a project, the focus is on trying to stay within the project's budget. The initial cost of a project can be easily surpassed by unanticipated overruns. This situation fosters a focus on simply trying to complete the project with the least number of changes or deletions. Consequently, any *future* costs associated with a building are generally not considered during the planning and execution phases of a project. To help ensure proper maintenance procedures, a fund should be established for this purpose. The amount of money in the fund could be estimated by reviewing the maintenance requirements of the products specified in the project. These details are available from manufacturers. Annual maintenance costs should be calculated starting at the first year of occupancy through several decades in the future.

A maintenance fund would have been very useful to preserve buildings that are currently in serious disrepair. For example, most buildings on college campuses do not have maintenance endowments. When construction estimates were prepared, the projected costs for maintenance and repairs were rarely included. Consequently, maintenance over the years has been deferred in deference to other needs that are perceived to be more important. As a result, campuses throughout the United States have buildings in severe disrepair that are only 30 to 40 years old. Unfortunately, since the maintenance has been deferred for such a long period of time, the cost for the neglected repairs is extremely high. Due to years of neglect, the complexity and time required for renovation have multiplied extensively. These concerns become even more serious given the fact that most buildings constructed in the mid-twentieth century contained asbestos. Asbestos has been abated in buildings; however, there is still a significant amount of asbestos that must be removed for the health of people. The asbestos abatement process is very extensive and expensive, which extends the elimination of this serious problem. A maintenance fund could include contingency funds for any unanticipated costs, such as asbestos abatement.

Summary

- A critical element of specifying sustainable interiors is to consider the materials' life cycle analysis (LCA).

The overarching operating principle should focus on reduction: reducing the size of buildings; reducing the consumption of new resources; reducing energy needs; reducing wasteful water practices; reducing outdoor and indoor pollutants; reducing negative impacts on the environment; and reducing waste.

- CSI Division 6 is the category for wood and plastics that are used in the built environment. Sustainable considerations include (1) reusing products, (2) selecting products with recycled and/or recovered content, (3) specifying rapidly renewable materials, and (4) specifying products that have been extracted and manufactured either locally or from the immediate region of the project's site.

- There are many sustainable characteristics that must be considered when making recommendations for doors and windows. Two excellent resources for the energy performance of products are ENERGY STAR and the National Fenestration Rating Council (NFRC).

- A very important area related to sustainable interiors is to design for recycling equipment. To encourage people to recycle waste, an interior designer should consistently integrate facilities into the design of commercial and residential interiors.

- To conserve resources, an important consideration is designing the size of rooms to correspond with standardized sizes of products.

- Acoustical ceiling products are important for enhancing the IEQ by helping to control noise. Systems are rated for noise control by the noise reduction coefficient (NRC), sound transmission class (STC), and a relatively new standard, the outside-indoor transmission class (OITC).

- As an excellent substitute for wood, bamboo flooring is growing in popularity in the United States. This is due to the material's rapid renewable growing characteristic, its low embodied energy qualities, and the aesthetics of its graining and color.

- For sustainable interiors, wood flooring must be derived from trees grown in managed forests. An alternative solution is reclaimed and remilled wood.

- Concrete and tile are materials that can be used for flooring in high-traffic and water-intensive applications. Since these materials are excellent for heat-storage mass, they are effective choices for absorbing, storing, and radiating solar energy.

- Resilient flooring has the advantage of providing comfort and cushion to the users of the space. The best resilient floorings for the environment and IAQ are earthen, cork, and linoleum.

- For healthy IAQ, carpet systems should be certified by the CRI Indoor Air Quality standards, also known as the CRI Green Label program.

- For sustainable interiors, desirable performance characteristics of wallcoverings are durability, insulating properties, and sound absorbency. The content of the material should be made from recycled matter, free of VOCs, recyclable, and biodegradable.

- To specify sustainable interiors, the furnishings must be healthy for people and the environment. A primary focus is to reuse and restore existing furnishings rather than specifying new products.

- There are many concerns related to fabrics, including the manufacturing process, VOC emissions, and the environmental impact of disposing of the material in landfills.

- In addition to selecting appropriate fabrics, sustainable considerations for window treatments include a product's LCA, insulation, noise control, privacy, reducing glare from sunlight or exterior lighting, and maximizing daylighting and views to the outdoors.

- Furniture and seating has been designed and constructed for thousands of years. Furniture can last for centuries when (1) the appropriate materials are selected, (2) suitable construction techniques are employed, (3) people take care during use, (4) proper cleaning and maintenance is performed, and (5) its appearance reflects a skillful application of the principles of design.

- Proper cleaning, care, and maintenance are essential for sustainable interiors.

Key Terms

Ag-fiber

American Association of Textile Chemists and Colorists (AATCC)

American Society for Testing and Materials International (ASTM)

Carpet modules

Carpet reclamation programs

Carpet tiles

Clear wood

Closed loop

Compression modulus

Convention on International Trade and Endangered
    Species (CITES)

Density

Earthen

Embodied energy

Engineered wood

EPA Environmentally Preferable Purchasing Program

Face fiber

Greige goods

Indentation load deflection (ILD)

International Building Code (IBC)

International Energy Conservation Code (IECC)

Methenamine pill test

Modified Energy Factor (MEF)

NFRC 100

Noise reduction coefficient (NRC)

Openness factor

Outside-indoor transmission class (OITC)

Palm wood

Porcelain Enamel Institute (PEI)

Reclaimed wood

Relative humidity

Remilled lumber

Remilled wood

Repurposed

Salvaged wood

Scientific Certification Systems

Shading coefficient (SC)

Solar absorptance

Solar reflectance

Solar transmittance

Solid wood

Solution-dyed

Sound transmission class (STC)

Spectrally selective glass

Stretched-fabric wall system

Support ratio

Upholstered wall system

UV transmittance

Visible transmittance

Wood sleepers

Exercises

1. A critical element of specifying sustainable interiors is to focus on reduction. Develop suggestions for a client that would help to reduce the consumption of interior finishes and furnishings. Prepare a written summary of the suggestions and develop an oral presentation. Compare and contrast your recommendations with the other students in your course.

2. A very important area related to sustainable interiors is to design for recycling equipment. This involves planning for the ideal placement of recycling equipment and designing units that are aesthetically pleasing. Design recycling equipment that could be used in commercial and residential interiors. To encourage people to recycle waste, identify the best locations for the units. Summarize the results in a written report and include illustrations, photographs, or sketches.

3. To conserve resources, an important consideration is designing the size of rooms to correspond with standardized sizes of products. Identify products that are typically specified for a residential interior. Research standardized sizes and include the information in a product resource file.

4. Create a product resource file that includes sustainable characteristics. Products should include items from CSI Divisions 6, 8, 9, 10, and 11. Locate specification data for each product. Compile the resources in a file that is organized by CSI Division.

UNIT III Integrating Sustainability with the Design Process

CHAPTER 9

Sustainable Strategies for Commercial and Residential Interiors

He tells himself, "My flower's up there somewhere . . ."

But if the sheep eats the flower, then for him it's as if, suddenly, all the stars went out.

And that isn't important?

—ANTOINE DE SAINT-EXUPÉRY

Fig. 9.1. Illustration from *The Little Prince.*

Objectives

- Identify characteristics of historic buildings that inform sustainable practices and understand how to integrate the techniques with contemporary buildings.
- Describe sustainable benefits associated with reusing and preserving buildings.
- Understand how to apply these four basic approaches for the treatments of properties to sustainable interior environments: preservation, rehabilitation, restoration, and reconstruction.
- Identify approaches to integrating historic preservation with requirements in building assessment programs.
- Analyze the relationships between sustainability and commercial interiors.
- Analyze the relationships between sustainability and residential interiors.

THE PURPOSE OF UNIT III is to examine how to integrate sustainable strategies with the design process. Units I and II focused on providing an overview of sustainable development and its effects on people, the environment, and economics. Applying this information to practice is critical to the lives of people living presently and for future generations. An effective strategy for implementing the principles of sustainability is to demonstrate how the components should be addressed at each phase of the design process. This is a constructive approach because interior designers are already familiar with the phases of the design process, and an examination of each phase helps to ensure a comprehensive integration.

The first section of this chapter reviews how early architectural designs and building materials can be applied to the designs of sustainable interiors. In establishing a historical perspective, the importance of preserving buildings is examined. Most notable is explaining the major approaches to preservation as defined by the **U.S. National Park Service (NPS)**. Approaches to reusing buildings are **preservation**, **rehabilitation**, **restoration**, and **reconstruction**. All of these approaches are excellent means to conserve resources, materials, land, and energy and divert waste from the landfills. **Adaptive reuse** is also examined as a strategy for sustainability.

This chapter also reviews sustainable strategies that are specific to commercial and residential interiors. Many of the sustainable guidelines and practices are applicable to all interiors. However, as evidenced by assessment standards, which are specifically written for designated purposes, such as BREEAM's guidelines for retail stores, there are some sustainable recommendations that are unique to commercial and residential interiors. Generally, interior designers focus on a particular area of specialization. However, during the course of a career it is very likely for a client to ask a designer to work on a variety of projects. Thus, to consistently promote sustainability an interior designer should have an understanding of sustainable considerations for commercial *and* residential environments.

SUSTAINABLE STRATEGIES AND EXISTING BUILDINGS

A focus on existing buildings is absolutely essential for conserving resources, minimizing impacts to the environment, and reducing materials that are landfilled. Reusing buildings, finishes, and furnishings must be the preferred solutions when designing interior environments. In serving in an advisory role with a client, interior designers can have a significant impact on the number of buildings that are reused and the quantity of materials and products that are retained. Providing optimum solutions requires a good understanding of the principles of sustainable design and knowledge of how to preserve and refurbish interiors. A critical aspect of being successful is identifying local tradespeople who can execute quality restoration and refurbishment. As the interest in historic buildings continues to intensify, there will be even more professionals who are skilled in performing restoration. Buildings 50 years and older are considered historic properties.

Historic Buildings: Looking Backward to Look Forward

Imagine meeting with a client who outlines the following requirements for a proposed project: "I would like to have a building that will last at *least* 500 years, is built with only local materials, has no mechanical or electrical means for HVAC or lighting, requires very minimal maintenance, emits no VOCs, and has convenient accessibility." In today's world the client would be told this is an impossible request. Yet, these requirements exist in numerous buildings worldwide. Examples include the pyramids in Giza, Egypt (ca. 2550–2460 B.C.E.); the Pantheon in Rome (ca. 118–128 C.E.); Hagia Sophia in Constantinople (532–537); Horyuji Temple in Nara, Japan (670–714); The Great Mosque in Córdoba (833–988); Fogong Temple in Yingxian, China (1056); and Chartres Cathedral in France (1194–1230). Buildings, finishes, and furnishings can be built to last, and this is essential for sustainability. The techniques and materials employed in historic buildings provide excellent lessons in understanding how to preserve and specify enduring environments. An informative and interesting

Fig. 9.2. (left) Natural light enters the nave of this cathedral through the clerestory windows.
Fig. 9.3. (right) The glass ceiling in the GUM department store in Moscow provides an abundance of daylight.

resource is the writings of Vitruvius in *The Ten Books on Architecture*. For example, in describing how to construct buildings in the first century B.C.E., the Roman architect and engineer Vitruvius provided examples of how to create "permanent durability." Given the permanence of the buildings that were constructed using the techniques described by Vitruvius, contemporary society can gain insights that are applicable to the current practice of sustainability.

Most civilizations throughout the world have lived without electricity and mechanical HVAC systems. Thus, structures that were built prior to the twentieth century are excellent resources for understanding how to design sustainable interiors. Furthermore, characteristics of these buildings, and their accompanied city planning strategies, can provide inspiration for developing approaches to fulfilling credit requirements of building assessment standards. For example, every assessment program provides credit for daylighting. Buildings constructed prior to the twentieth century demonstrate excellent techniques for maximizing daylight because, without electricity, people were dependent on natural light. These structures should be examined by designers of sustainable interiors for methods to enhance natural ventilation, control sunlight, conserve heat, plan spatial arrangements, provide views to the outdoors, maximize space, and specify finishes. These

items and others, such as using local materials, are desirable characteristics when a building assessment program such as LEED certifies a building.

When buildings were reliant on daylighting, some of the techniques that were employed to maximize natural light included clerestories, transoms, deep openings with reflected surfaces, and room configurations that allowed light to penetrate the entire space. An extraordinarily large building such as a cathedral was designed with large windows surrounding the perimeter of the floor plan, and the nave had a higher ceiling with clerestory windows (see Figure 9.2). These windows provided natural light for the center section of the cathedral. Glass ceilings were used to provide extraordinary illumination and shield occupants from the weather. For example, as shown by the GUM (1888–1894) department store in Moscow, both of these attributes are especially important in cold climates that experience many hours of darkness in the winter (Figure 9.3). Beginning with the plans of Ur, Mesopotamia (Iraq, ca. 2100 B.C.E.), cultures worldwide have built center courtyards for the purposes of providing daylight, enhancing ventilation, controlling sunlight, and creating views to the outdoors (see Figure 9.4). The centralized arrangement enabled people to enjoy the outdoors while providing privacy and security.

Japanese dwellings are superb examples of integrating the interior with the beauty of a garden (see Figure 9.5). Openings in external walls are carefully planned to ensure the best vista of the most interesting natural elements in the garden. These examples are outstanding references for creating views to the outdoors. Incorporating large spans of glazing should not fulfill the requirements associated with views to the outdoors. Optimum solutions specifically plan openings that provide the most interesting views of the outdoors.

For thousands of years, buildings have been designed to control the sun. Exterior strategies include the use of arcades, verandas, deep overhangs, and recessed walls (see Figure 9.6a). Arcades and verandas controlled sunlight and provided a shelter from the

a

b

Fig. 9.4. (above, top) The use of center courtyards is evident in the plans of Ur, Mesopotamia (Iraq), ca. 2100 B.C.E.
Fig. 9.5. (above, bottom) Japanese dwellings integrate the interior with the beauty of a garden.
Fig. 9.6a. (left, top) Light wells are used to provide daylight in this residence in the Knossos in Crete (ca. 1700–1380 B.C.E.).
Fig. 9.6b. (left, bottom) The deep overhangs control sunlight in the Horyuji Temple in Nara, Japan (670–714).

elements. As shown in Figure 9.6a, some of the areas in the Knossos (ca. 1700–1380 B.C.E.) in Crete were constructed with light wells. The toplighting technique controlled sunlight while providing daylight. Deep overhangs (9.6b) shielded sunlight and helped to preserve the surfaces of the exterior walls by preventing rain from striking the building.

Using topography to maximize the benefits of nature is evident in the Villa Rotunda in Italy (1566–1580), by Andrea Palladio. Locating the residence on the top of a hill and designing numerous windows on all four sides of the building provided each room with the benefits of nature. Rooms of the residence have cross-ventilation, an abundance of daylight, and extraordinary views of the countryside. To enhance airflow, the interior of the villa has corridors that extend from one end of the building to the other (see Figure 9.7). Cross-ventilation also occurs by openings in the interior walls located across from windows. The Villa Rotunda is a remarkable example

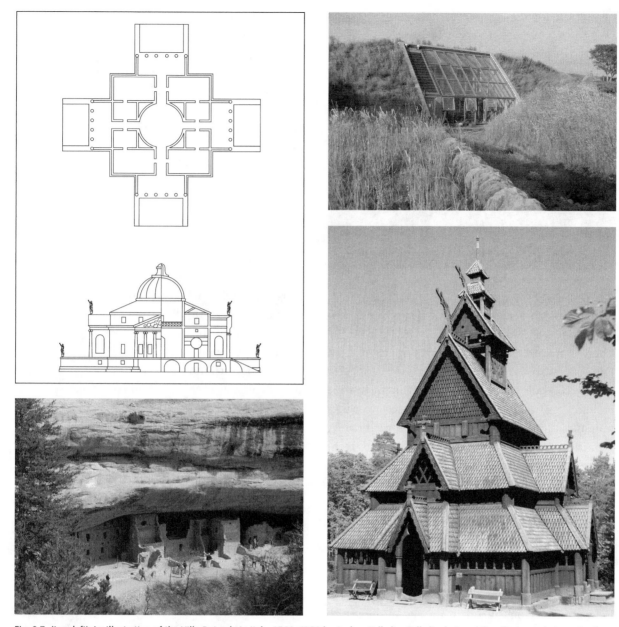

Fig. 9.7. (top, left) An illustration of the Villa Rotunda in Italy, 1566–1580 by Andrea Palladio. Palladio designed the villa to maximize natural ventilation and views of the countryside.

Fig. 9.8a. (top, right) To conserve energy, this residence has been partially submerged in the earth.

Fig. 9.8b. (bottom, left) Mesa Verde cliff houses. To maximize solar radiant heat and to avoid harsh winds from the north, the Anasazi Indians built their dwelling in the south side of the mountain.

Fig. 9.9. (bottom, right) The oldest stave church in Norway was designed with a very steep roof to prevent snow and ice from accumulating on the structure.

of designing the built environment to optimize the interaction with warm climatic conditions. Designing a building that successfully responds to weather conditions is especially important in cold climates and areas prone to flooding. To resolve temperature changes, many cultures have used the earth to help cool or warm a building. For example, buildings have been partially submerged in the ground or con-

structed into the side of a hill (see Figures 9.8a and b). As shown in Figure 9.8b, locating the dwelling on the south side of the mountain enabled people to enjoy the benefits of solar energy while sheltering them from the cold northerly winds. The oldest stave church in Norway was designed with a very steep roof to prevent snow and ice from accumulating on the structure (see Figure 9.9). To prevent flood

Fig. 9.10. Some older homes in New Orleans were constructed by elevating the first floor. These structures suffered minimal damage from Hurricane Katrina in 2005.

damage, older homes in New Orleans were constructed by elevating the first floor (see Figure 9.10). These structures suffered minimal damage from Hurricane Katrina in 2005.

For economic and practical reasons, many historic buildings were designed to conserve space by using a minimal number of rooms, reducing or eliminating transitional areas, and incorporating various techniques that suggested greater volumes of space. For example, as shown in Figure 9.11, the Romans provided interest in small spaces by strategically planning the axial arrangement. Walking through the residence produces a variety of sensations created by the altering of the heights of rooms, sizes of spaces, levels of illumination, and exposures to the outdoors. In addition, frequently a trompe l'oeil drawing was painted on the wall at the end of the axis to extend the illusion of space and provide visual interest. Roman and Greek buildings provide excellent examples of how to make small interiors interesting and a sensory experience. Thermal comfort was also addressed by altering the use of rooms according to the season of the year and locating activities such as cooking away from the primary living areas of people.

Due to restrictions in means of transport, previous civilizations were reliant on local materials and skills. This situation helped to conserve resources and contributed to the character of **vernacular architecture**. It is astonishing to find the finishes and materials that are still in remarkable condition after centuries of use. A close examination of original fin-

ishes and furnishings in buildings that are several centuries old provides evidence of durable materials, quality installations, and proper maintenance. Some of the materials are inherently durable, such as stone, but many products reflect an emphasis on quality materials, structural integrity, outstanding craftsmanship, and suitability for the climatic conditions and the intended use. For example, the glazed bricks on the Ishtar Gate in Babylon, Mesopotamia (Iraq, ca. 612–539 B.C.E.), are still in excellent condition (see Figure 9.12). Mosaics used in Islamic architecture have endured since at least 687, when the Dome of the Rock in Jerusalem was constructed.

To produce permanent colors for interior finishes, natural materials were used. For example, in *Book VII* Vitruvius explains where to find the products for yellow ochre, red earths, Paraetonium white, and green chalk. Vitruvius indicates, "Red earths are found in abundance in many places, but the best in only a few, for instance at Sinope in Pontus, in Egypt, in the Balearic islands of Spain" (Morgan, 1960, p. 214). As shown in Figure 9.13, wood, which is often viewed as being nonpermanent, has demonstrated extreme durability, as evidenced by the Great Hall of the Buddha in Japan (ca. 732–752) and the Fogong Temple in Yingxian, China (1056). Wooden ceilings in English Gothic cathedrals are still in beautiful condition.

To conserve resources, Vitruvius suggested material reuse: "When gold has been woven into a garment, and the garment becomes worn out with age

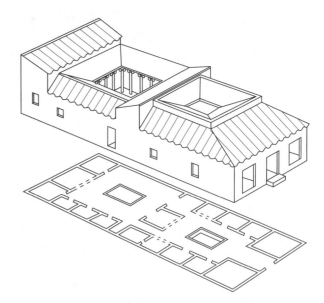

Fig. 9.11. The plan of the Roman domus allowed natural light to fill interior spaces.

Fig. 9.12. The glazed bricks on the Ishtar Gate in Babylon, Mesopotamia (Iraq), ca. 612–539 B.C.E., are excellent examples of durable materials.

so that it is no longer respectable to use, the pieces of cloth are put into earthen pots, and burned up over a fire" (Morgan, 1960, pp. 215–216). As explained by Vitruvius, the gold that remains in the ashes can be used for other purposes. To encourage building reuse, Vitruvius suggested that "the broken bits of marble or 'chips,' as they are called, which marble-workers throw down as they work, may be crushed and ground and used in stucco after being sifted" (Morgan, 1960, p. 213).

In addition to using local and natural materials, buildings that have endured were constructed to respect and respond to climatic elements. Vitruvius wrote several chapters that focused on addressing the impact of weather and the climate on buildings. For example, in *Book VII* Vitruvius described how to apply stucco in dry and damp conditions. In *Book I* Vitruvius outlined the directions of streets based on climatic conditions and the winds. Vitruvius also described construction methods that could be used to facilitate the replacement of worn components. In concluding *Book VI* Vitruvius noted, "As for replacing

tiles, roof timbers, and rafters, we need not be so particular about them as about the parts just mentioned, because they can easily be replaced, however defective they may become. Hence, I have shown by what methods the parts which are not considered solid can be rendered durable, and how they are constructed" (Morgan, 1960, pp. 191–192). This philosophical perspective and the prescribed techniques contributed to the longevity of Roman buildings. The intent was to repair and replace components that were expected to deteriorate. The practice at this time was not to demolish structures but to employ methods and materials that would make a structure permanent.

To create permanent buildings required techniques and materials that protected the structure from the elements. Buildings had architectural elements designed to protect the structure, and the materials selected were suitable to the climatic conditions. Structures were frequently designed with components that deflected moisture and encouraged runoff. For example, as illustrated in Figure 9.9, buildings in cold climates often have very steep roofs, which cause snow and ice to glide off surfaces. In addition, shingles were designed in a shape and material that deflected moisture. The deep overhangs on Chinese and Japanese buildings shielded the sun and protected the exterior siding of the structures. The *permanent* bricks used for the Ishtar Gate served a decorative purpose, and the finish protected the structural components of the building by providing resistance to the weather (see Figures 9.12 and 9.13). Vitruvius consistently described materials and building methods within the context of permanence.

Fig. 9.13. The Great Hall of the Buddha in Japan, ca. 732–752, is an excellent example of long-lasting wooden materials.

For example, in *Book VI* Vitruvius reviews appropriate foundations for residences: "Houses which are set level with the ground will no doubt last to a great age, if their foundations are laid in the manner in which we have explained in earlier books" (Morgan, 1960, p. 189). To warn against inappropriate methods, Vitruvius again provides suggestions within the context of permanence: "For if the load of the walls or columns rests on the middle of spans, they can have no permanent durability" (Morgan, 1960, p. 189). These sustainable practices are the approaches that should be applied to contemporary interiors.

Benefits of Reuse

Some of the benefits associated with preserving buildings are readily apparent, such as conserving resources and energy; however, there are also societal benefits connected to sustaining cultural heritages. This becomes evident when society bemoans the demolition of buildings that had either architectural significance or historical import. For example, much to the dismay and outcries of many people, the Chicago Stock Exchange building designed by Dankmar Adler and Louis Sullivan in 1893 was demolished in 1972. The entire interior of the trading room was dismantled and subsequently reassembled at the Art Institute in Chicago, but the loss to current and future generations is immeasurable. A demolition example that occurred centuries ago, but still evokes regret, is the Abbey church of Cluny III in Burgundy, France. The enormous monastery was started in 1088 and completed in 1130 (see Figure 9.14). Originally, to accommodate thousands of worshippers, the church had six towers, two transepts, and numerous chapels. Today, all that is left of the church is one transept and the baptistry. The massive destruction started during the French Revolution and concluded with much of the original structure being sold for demolition purposes.

The sense of disappointment that accompanies the loss of a magnificent structure, and a part of our cultural history, serves as a hard lesson for preventing future demolitions. Cultures worldwide have recognized the importance of preserving buildings, not only for economic incentives but to preserve the heritage that is embodied and reflected in the built environment. The built environment has no

Fig. 9.14. The Abbey church of Cluny III in Burgundy, France. Originally, the enormous monastery could accommodate thousands of worshippers. Today the church only has one transept and the baptistery. Destruction of the building started during the French Revolution.

inhibitors, such as language, to understanding cultural differences. The visual elements inherent in a building enable visitors from any country to gain an understanding of how a culture lives and what the people value, and a glimpse of their history. The uniqueness of a culture's architectural style is most evident in historic structures. When travel was limited, people living in a region developed vernacular architecture; they were not familiar with styles used in other parts of the world. People traveling today are able to benefit from the regionalism by experiencing different architectural styles throughout the world. There is a sense of deep appreciation for the diversity embedded in ancient Indian, Southeast Asian, Roman, Greek, Pre-Columbian Americas, Islamic, Renaissance, and Baroque architecture. Preservation is the only way to continue this architectural legacy. Encouraging building reuse and using local or regional materials are effective approaches to preserving this vernacular architecture.

BUILDING REUSE: PRESERVATION, REHABILITATION, RESTORATION, AND RECONSTRUCTION

Designing and building permanent structures with durable finishes and furnishings is essential for sustainability. The aforementioned buildings provide excellent examples of sustainable techniques and approaches that can be applied to the current built environment. These exemplary structures, and many others, demonstrate the importance of preserving buildings for future generations.

Approaches to Building Reuse

The preservation movement started in Europe in the 1800s but did not have a significant impact in the United States until the mid-twentieth century. To retain historic structures and preserve our cultural heritage, the historic preservation movement gained prominence in the United States in the 1960s. Congress established the **National Historic Preservation Act (NHPA)** in 1966, which has been amended through 2000. The Secretary of the Interior, NPS, is responsible for administering the program. In establishing the NHPA, Congress declared that "(1) the spirit and direction of the Nation are founded upon and reflected in its historic heritage; (2) the historical and cultural foundations of the Nation should be preserved as a living part of our community life and development to give a sense of orientation to the American people; (3) historic properties significant to the Nation's heritage are being lost or substantially altered, often inadvertently, with increasing frequency; [and] (4) the preservation of this irreplaceable heritage is in the public interest so that its vital legacy of cultural, educational, aesthetic, inspirational, economic, and energy benefits will be maintained and enriched for future generations of Americans" (16 U.S.C. 470, Section 1b). The fourth purpose of the NHPA is especially relevant to sustainability in acknowledging an association between preservation and its economic and energy benefits.

The Secretary of the Interior developed standards for the treatment of historic properties. After revisions, these standards were codified as 36 CFR Part 68 in 1995 (see Appendix B). The *Secretary of the Interior's Standards for the Treatment of Historic Properties* can be used by anyone working with historic properties. However, the standards become regulatory for development grant-in-aid projects and to qualify for the *Federal Historic Preservation Tax Incentives*. These tax incentives are available for buildings that (1) are National Historic Landmarks, (2) are listed in the National Register, and (c) contribute to National Register Historic Districts and certain local historic districts (www.cr.nps.gov). Financial incentives may help to motivate a client to engage in sustainability practices by reusing a building instead of ordering new construction. Data from the NPS illustrate that tax incentives have been effective for preserving and renovating historic properties. Since 1976, tax incentives have resulted in the rehabilitation of more than 32,000 historic properties; stimulating over $33 billion in private investment; rehabilitating more than 185,000 housing units; and developing more than 140,000 housing units, which includes more than 75,000 low- and moderate-income units (www.cr.nps.gov).

The Secretary of the Interior's Standards have four approaches for the treatment of properties: preservation, rehabilitation, restoration, and reconstruction. (Appendix B gives the standards for each treatment.) In defining each of the treatments, the NPS indicates, "*preservation* places a high premium on the retention of all historic fabric through conservation, maintenance, and repair. It reflects a building's continuum over time, through successive occupancies, and the respectful changes and alterations that are made" (www.cr.nps.gov). According to the NPS, an exemplary preservation project is Drayton Hall in South Carolina (see Figure 9.15). Constructed in 1767–1771, the building has been maintained in its original condition to serve as an example of an eighteenth-century plantation house and landscape.

The *rehabilitation* treatment "emphasizes the retention and repair of historic materials, but more latitude is provided for replacement because it is assumed the property is more deteriorated prior to work." The standards emphasize that preservation and rehabilitation "focus attention on the preservation of those materials, features, finishes, spaces, and spatial relationships that, together, give a property its historic character." Frequently an interior designer is involved with rehabilitation projects. A very common application of this treatment is adaptive reuse

Fig. 9.15. (top) An example of the *preservation* treatment. Drayton Hall in South Carolina, constructed in 1767–1771, has been maintained in its original condition to serve as an example of an eighteenth-century plantation house and landscape.

Fig. 9.16. (middle) An example of the *rehabilitation* treatment. Le Musée d'Orsay in Paris was originally a 1900 railroad station and hotel. The structure was saved from demolition and converted into an art museum in the 1970s.

Fig. 9.17. (bottom) An example of the *restoration* treatment. The sixteenth-century Palace of Schönbrunn near Vienna, Austria. In the eighteenth century the original entrance was replaced by two symmetrical stairways. In a subsequent restoration the stairways were retained for their historical significance.

projects, which involve rehabilitating a building for a new use. Some common examples are converting commercial buildings, such as abandoned warehouses and schools, into condominiums or retail stores. Many former railroad stations have been rehabilitated and converted to hotels, retail stores, and museums. An outstanding example is le Musée d'Orsay in the heart of Paris (see Figure 9.16). The original 1900 station and its hotel were scheduled for demolition, but the structure was saved and converted into an art museum in the 1970s. The museum is an excellent example of how to retain architecturally interesting elements, which contribute to historic character, while reinterpreting an existing building for new uses.

The NPS indicates that *restoration* "focuses on the retention of materials from the most significant time in a property's history, while permitting the removal of materials from other periods." Restoration involves returning a building to a particular period of time. When a building has been altered throughout the years, a decision must be made to determine which appearance has the most important significance. This may involve removing or retaining elements that were not present when the building was originally constructed. For example, since the original hunting lodge of the sixteenth century, the Palace of Schönbrunn near Vienna, Austria, has undergone a series of renovations and additions (see Figure 9.17). During the reign of Maria Theresa in the eighteenth century, the original entrance was replaced by two symmetrical stairways. Due to this historical significance, the stairs still exist today even though they were not the original entrance. Decisions regarding historical significance should be conducted with the assistance of historians.

Finally, *reconstruction* "establishes limited opportunities to re-create a non-surviving site, landscape, building, structure, or object in all new materials." Reconstruction occurs when a significant building has been destroyed by a variety of means, such as a fire, vandalism, or a demolition. A very unique example of reconstruction has been occurring in Colonial Williamsburg. The Peyton Randolph House had several outbuildings, which included a smokehouse, kitchen, and granary (see Figure 9.18a). Based on archaeology and architectural research, the buildings have been reconstructed on their original site by using eighteenth-century building methods, materials, and tools (see Figure 9.18b). Since Colonial Williamsburg is a living history museum, carpenters *interpreted* the reconstruction and documented the process. The historical significance of interpreting colonial Virginia's history is an excellent reason for engaging in reconstruction. However, since this approach is new construction, the treatment does not have the sustainable advantages associated with reuse. To enhance the sustainability of reconstruction projects, a recommendation is to specify original building materials that are available at local businesses. These items might be derived from salvaging that occurred during demolition, or from other buildings that were built in the same period and style.

Retaining and reusing existing buildings is a significant priority of sustainability. The four treatments defined by the NPS are useful for determining the appropriate strategy for building reuse. To identify the best treatment, the NPS indicates that considerations are the building's relative importance in history, physical condition, proposed use, and mandated code requirements. To evaluate a building's *importance in history*, it should be determined whether the building (1) is a "nationally significant resource —a rare survivor or the work of a master architect or craftsman" and (2) was the site of an important event (www.cr.nps.gov). The NPS suggests that "National Historic Landmarks, designated for their 'exceptional significance in American history,' or many buildings individually listed in the National Register often warrant preservation or restoration. Buildings that contribute to the significance of a historic district but are not individually listed in the National Register more frequently undergo rehabilitation for a compatible new use" (www.cr.nps.gov).

In examining the *physical condition* of a building, the NPS recommends that the following questions should be answered: (1) "What is the existing condition—or degree of material integrity—of the building prior to work?" (2) "Has the original form survived largely intact or has it been altered over time?" and (3) "Are the alterations an important part of the building's history?" (www.cr.nps.gov). In providing suggestions for the appropriate treatment

a

b

Fig. 9.18a. An example of the *reconstruction* treatment. In Colonial Williamsburg the Peyton Randolph House had several outbuildings, which included a smokehouse, kitchen, and granary. These buildings have been reconstructed on the site.

Fig. 9.18b. Buildings with the Peyton Randolph House were reconstructed on their original site using eighteenth-century building methods, materials, and tools. Since Colonial Williamsburg is a living history museum, carpenters *interpreted* the reconstruction and documented the process.

Fig. 9.19a. Many buildings have integrated historic preservation with building assessment programs. The "before" photograph of the headquarters of Conservation Consultants, Inc. (CCI) in Pittsburgh. The CCI received the LEED-EB, v1, rating at the gold level.
Fig. 9.19b. A "during construction" photograph of the headquarters of Conservation Consultants, Inc. (CCI) in Pittsburgh.
Fig. 9.19c. An "after" photograph of the headquarters of Conservation Consultants, Inc. (CCI) in Pittsburgh.

based on the physical condition of a building, the NPS recommends that preservation might be "appropriate if distinctive materials, features, and spaces are essentially intact and convey the building's historical significance." Rehabilitation is the likely treatment when a building requires extensive repair, replacements, alterations, or additions. *Proposed use*

considerations focus on whether the building will continue to be used as originally intended, or if the project will be adapted to a new use. When a building is a reuse project the goal should be to minimize any damage to the historic character and integrity.

Mandated code requirements are a very important consideration. Any treatment performed on a building must adhere to life safety and accessibility codes. To minimize damage to the historic character, building code requirements must be identified at the earliest stages of the project and then integrated with the final design. For historic buildings, the NPS indicates that some of the primary code considerations are (1) seismic upgrades, (2) abatement of lead paint and asbestos, and (3) accessibility requirements under the Americans with Disabilities Act (ADA) of 1990. In addition, the most recent fire safety codes must be followed. To minimize the elimination of original elements of the building or changes to its historic appearance, careful planning must include all of the members of the project's team, including structural, mechanical, and electrical engineers.

Sustainability and Historic Preservation

In addition to the considerations outlined by the NPS, an interior designer should review a treatment within the context of sustainability and economic considerations. Integrating historic preservation *with* building assessment programs has been achieved in many communities. For example, the headquarters of Conservation Consultants, Inc. (CCI), in Pittsburgh, Pennsylvania, is an adaptive reuse project; CCI received the LEED-EB, v1 rating at the gold level (see Figures 9.19a–c). Some of the features from the original building that were reused include interior brick walls, chimneys that were converted to ventilation stacks, floor systems in restrooms, hardwood floors, metal ceilings on the third floor, and the kitchen. The project also reconstructed, reused, and refurbished kitchen cabinets, office partitions, and furniture. The Bazzani Associates Headquarters renovated a historic 1918 building in Grand Rapids, Michigan (see Figure 9.20). The building attained the LEED-NC, v2 rating at the silver level. The building was renovated according to the Secretary of the Interior's Standards for Rehabilitation (www.usgbc.org).

One of the oldest historic buildings to achieve

LEED certification is the Cambridge City Hall Annex, in Cambridge, Massachusetts (see Figure 9.21). Built in 1871, the building was closed in 2000 when mold spores were detected at unhealthy levels. The city of Cambridge renovated the building and then received the gold level of LEED-NC, v2 certification. The city of Portland, Oregon, has also been involved with renovating a historic building with the intent of achieving LEED certification (see Figure 9.22). The Jean Vollum Natural Capital Center is a restoration and adaptive reuse project that received the gold level. Originally the 1895 brick and timber building was a warehouse. The renovation converted the warehouse into a multipurpose building, which houses a major retail store, the headquarters of EcoTrust, and several tenants who have an environmental mission.

To integrate sustainability with historic preservation requires special considerations. The factors to consider can be reviewed by examining the categories for LEED's rating system. For example, credits in LEED's *Sustainable Sites* category can be achieved by renovating historic properties. The building might qualify for urban or brownfield redevelopment. Since many historic properties are located in the center of cities, it is likely that credits can be achieved for access to public transportation. Credits in the *Water Efficiency* category might be possible with some of the water conservation methods that were frequently used with historic properties, such as cisterns. Many of the inherent characteristics of historic properties enhance energy performance, which is identified in LEED's *Energy and Atmosphere* category. The lack of mechanical cooling in buildings constructed prior to the twentieth century required forms of the building plan and features that maximized natural energy sources and fresh air. For example, in cold climates buildings were constructed with masonry walls with few windows. Buildings constructed in warm climates had porches, balconies, courtyards, deep roof overhangs, awnings, high ceilings, and various approaches to maximizing ventilation. Maximizing the flow of fresh air throughout a building was accomplished by operable windows, cross ventilation, roof monitors, skylights, centralized towers with vents, and operable transoms in windows and doors. Operable exterior and interior shutters were used in all climates to enhance the thermal comfort. Shutters could be closed to reduce the penetration of cold air

Fig. 9.20. (top) The Bazzani Associates Headquarters is located in a renovated historic 1918 building in Grand Rapids, MI. The building received the LEED-NC, v2, rating at the silver level.

Fig. 9.21. (middle) One of the oldest historic buildings to achieve LEED certification is the Cambridge City Hall Annex in Cambridge, MA. The city of Cambridge renovated the 1871 building and received the gold level of LEED-NC, v2, certification.

Fig. 9.22. (bottom) The Jean Vollum Natural Capital Center is a restoration and adaptive reuse project that received the LEED gold level. Originally, the 1895 building was a brick and timber warehouse.

and opened for solar energy gain during the day. In warm weather, by adjusting louvers in the optimum position, interior shutters had the flexibility of deflecting solar energy, while allowing fresh air to enter the room. These inherent attributes of historic properties contribute to achieving minimum levels of energy efficiency. Historic properties were also designed to maximize natural daylight by the form of the plan and using many of the same components that enhanced ventilation, such as windows and skylights. Thus, the ability to use natural light optimizes energy performance by reducing lighting power density, and provides people with the psychological benefits associated with daylight.

There are many attributes of historic properties that might qualify for credits in LEED's *Materials and Resources* category. Building reuse credits can be derived from maintaining the existing shell and interior nonstructural components. Generally, the construction processes associated with reusing a building result in reducing construction waste and diverting high percentages of waste from landfills. The focus on retaining historic materials, features, and finishes can contribute significantly to resource reuse. These are the elements that are *essential* to retain in historic properties. Reused resources can include many historic materials, such as flooring, wall paneling, cabinetry, doors, stair balustrades, mantelpieces, beams, or posts. Resource reuse can also include furniture and furnishings. Again, these are the desirable items to reuse in historic properties. The focus on authenticity in historic renovations provides the impetus for using local and regional materials. Thus, renovation projects have the potential to achieve *Material and Resources* credits for using regional materials.

To maintain the highest percentage of a building's shell and reused resources, a useful approach is to follow the recommended steps for rehabilitation as delineated by the NPS. The process involves documentation, evaluation, assessment, and planning. *Documentation* involves researching the history of the building and then recording the current condition of the exterior and interior. *Evaluation* should be performed within the context of the history of the building. The elements that should be evaluated are the floor plan, arrangement of spaces, features, finishes, lighting, mechanical systems, and plumbing. Items identified in the evaluation process are *assessed*

to determine their condition and subsequent actions. Resources should be reused whenever possible. Thus, any broken features or defective materials should be repaired. Interior components that must be replaced should be assessed to determine their potential to be recycled or salvaged for another use. The *planning* process includes methods for protecting the health of the workers who perform the renovation and safeguarding interior components.

Historic properties also have characteristics that are important in LEED's *Indoor Environmental Quality* category. Historic buildings were reliant on natural ventilation for fresh air and cooling. Thus, to increase ventilation for the improvement of IAQ, the plan's form and operable windows in historic buildings can supplement natural or mechanical ventilation systems. The size and abundant number of windows in older buildings also enhance daylighting and views to the outdoors. Generally, windows in historic buildings comply with LEED's requirements for the direct line of sight to perimeter vision glazing from standing and seated positions. Products and materials that have high VOC contents may not be present in historic buildings. For example, many buildings had wood flooring and area rugs rather than carpet systems. Composite wood and laminate adhesives were not developed until the mid-twentieth century. Buildings older than this time period would not have these materials unless they were added in a renovation. Older buildings with original furniture would not have systems furniture and seating, which can contain chemical contaminants. However, hazardous contents that were present in older buildings, such as lead in paint and asbestos, must be safely remediated. The next section reviews problems related to historic buildings that must be addressed to create healthy and sustainable environments.

Sustainable Considerations for Renovating Interiors

As delineated in the previous sections of this chapter, historic properties have many attributes that are important to sustainable interiors. However, these buildings can have problems that must be addressed for the benefit of the users, for the environment, and for economic considerations. To adhere to the standards provided by the Secretary of the Interior, the proceeding information is based on their requirements and recommendations (www.cr.nps.gov). The most critical issues focus on the finishes, approaches to conserving energy, and controlling moisture. When renovating an interior, surfaces are usually repaired and repainted. Historic properties often have many layers of paint on walls, ceilings, doors, trimwork, window moldings, door moldings, wainscoting, baseboards, mantelpieces, ornamental plaster, and floors. From a sustainability and a historical perspective, preferences are to retain the components whenever possible. Therefore, a careful analysis of its contents and the condition of the paint should be performed at the start of a project.

As mentioned previously in this text, a major concern is lead-based paint, especially in buildings with children. All exterior and interior paint made before 1950 had lead in its contents. To determine the presence and quantity of lead in paint requires an analysis performed by professionals. A public health official should be able to provide the names of qualified inspectors and testing laboratories. Removing lead-based paint and repainting requires adherence to local, state, and federal laws. Scraping or sanding paint creates lead-laden dust that is a health hazard. Using heat to remove lead-based paint creates toxic fumes. Both processes can result in lead-laden particles remaining in the room well after the painters are gone. Lead can infiltrate a body's system through the lungs by breathing and by penetrating skin pores. Thus, all surfaces must be cleaned thoroughly after paint removal, including using **high-efficiency particulate air (HEPA)** vacuum cleaners. For the health of users and painters, lead abatement must be performed according to **OSHA's 29 CFR Part 1926, Lead Exposure in Construction**, standards. The abatement process involves using HEPA respirators and HEPA filters.

The condition of the paint can reveal structural problems with the building that must be repaired for safety and preservation purposes. For example, cracks, flaking, or blistering could indicate moisture problems from a leaky roof or defective plumbing. These problems must be fixed before any repainting or other finishing work. The condition of the paint can also indicate points of excessive wear and the level of cleanliness in the rooms. Knowing where surfaces are damaged provides insights for determining appropriate finishes for future installations. Typical locations of damage are baseboards, lower sections of walls, surfaces around handles, and stair railings. Abused components must have durable finishes. Protecting surfaces results in retaining materials and keeping resources from landfills. Defective paint finishes can indicate that incompatible paints were applied when surfaces were repainted (www.cr.nps.gov). Paints with a strong film, such as acrylic latex, should not be applied over weaker paints. Stronger paints can pull a weaker paint from its surface. Acrylic latex is considered to have the strongest film, followed by alkyd/oils, and the weakest substance is water-based. Applying the wrong type of paint can result in a waste of materials, resources, and human effort when surfaces must be repainted. Paint failure can also occur when a surface was not properly prepared prior to painting. The problem could be soil, an inappropriate primer, or lack of a primer. Proper surface preparation must always be performed prior to applying new paint or a wallcovering.

Historic properties often have durable materials and components, such as plaster, built-in cabinets, wood flooring, and ceramic tile. In most every situation, the goal should be to extend the life of these materials as long as possible. Frequently, these elements are made from materials or skills that are no longer available or extremely expensive. For example, wood from old timber is an extremely valuable resource today. Plasterwork is highly specialized work. To execute quality installations requires knowing techniques that are only attainable from years of experience. In the United States, due to the lack of interest in plaster walls for the last several decades, many of these professionals are elderly. The resurgence in renovating interiors and the desire for durable, quality surfaces could encourage younger people to learn the trade before it is too late.

With proper care, materials have the potential to last for numerous decades. The materials should be inspected, repaired, and cleaned. Wood flooring should be sanded only when necessary, because the refinishing process removes a layer of the wood, which reduces the life of the flooring. For durability purposes, ceramic tile was often installed in areas prone to moisture, such as entries, kitchens, and bathrooms. A defective tile surface is often an

a

b

Fig. 9.23a. High-pressure water left marks on the surface of this granite stone.
Fig. 9.23b. Abrasive cleaning caused permanent damage to the bricks of this structure.

indication of a problem with mortar or grout. Removing and then replacing the grout can generally repair this problem. For resource reuse purposes, broken tiles should be repaired without removing the piece. Repair is often safer than replacement because the removal process can damage other tiles. When a group of tiles are defective and must be removed, the preferred solution is to design a new pattern that retains as much of the original tile as possible.

To enhance the longevity of finishes, furniture, and furnishings requires proper cleaning methods and solutions. Generally, historic properties have unique cleaning challenges because of the years of use, abuse, or neglect. Frequently the solution is an **abrasive cleaning** technique. The NPS has identified many of the problems associated with abrasive cleaning, which can permanently damage surfaces and materials (see Figures 9.23a and b). This type of destruction can result in materials being landfilled immediately or much sooner than the expected life of durable materials. The NPS defines abrasive cleaning as the "use of certain materials which impact or abrade the surface under pressure, or abrasive tools and equipment" (www.cr.nps.gov). Abrasive cleaning can destroy or erode the surface of interior and exterior materials. The NPS suggests that commercial and residential interiors should *never* be cleaned by abrasive methods. The NPS indicates that tools and equipment that can be abrasive to materials include wire brushes, rotary wheels, power sanding disks, belt sanders, and highly pressurized water. A common example of using an abrasive approach to cleaning is sandblasting a surface to remove undesirable substances, such as paint, soot, soil, or pollution. Grit blasting an exterior masonry wall can damage the surface and reduce its impermeable characteristics. Blasting can cause cracks between the bricks and mortar, which creates openings for moisture.

Abrasive cleaning can damage most materials used in buildings, including bricks, stone, terra cotta, plaster, stucco, and wood. Abrasive methods can also irreversibly damage architectural metalwork made from tin, zinc, lead, and copper. Removing paint from wood has unique problems. The presence of VOCs in chemical paint removers is a significant IAQ issue. Using a heat gun or heat plate can cause a fire or can char the wood. These surfaces cannot be repainted. When paint contains lead, a heat application causes the emission of toxic vapors. Propane torches or any type of flame should never be used to remove paint. It is easy to mar wood by scraping, sanding, or using a wire brush. The NPS recommends several gentle alternative means to remove soil or paint from surfaces: (1) low-pressure water wash; (2) avoid scrubbing, but when the technique is necessary, a natural bristle (never metal) should be used; and (3) steam cleaning (www.cr.nps.gov). In the future it may be possible to safely use pulsed laser beams and xenon flash lamps for cleaning surfaces.

Controlling moisture is a significant problem with historic properties and furnishings. Time and the elements take a toll on buildings that eventually affects the impermeability of the structure. Damage from moisture can be irreparable and can result in the unfortunate demolition of the building. Problems associated with water damage can be avoided by proper control of moisture. The first step is to search for moisture damage and identify the source of the problem. Determining the source of moisture damage can require considerable time because the problem could exist far from the water damage. In addition, the cause may be derived from a weather condition that only occurs during one season of the year. It is critical to be confident of the source of the moisture problem due to solutions that might damage the integrity of a building or treatments that may not control water. After the problem has been verified, the appropriate treatment must be implemented, and then the subsequent proper maintenance.

To resolve moisture problems requires identifying the source, followed by appropriate monitoring and maintenance. As suggested by the NPS, Box 9.1 lists visible signs and smells to search for when identifying moisture damage. The NPS indicates that the most likely sources for moisture damage in older buildings are leaking plumbing pipes; heating, cooling, and climate systems; and use or occupancy of the building. Common sources of moisture can be derived from moisture entering a building from above or below grade. Excessive water may be used in maintenance and construction materials. For example, grit blasting processes use considerable water, which can penetrate the exterior siding and the building's foundation.

Conserving energy in historic buildings is essential for sustainable buildings. As reviewed previously in this chapter, historic buildings have many inherent characteristics that help to conserve energy. To reinforce this fact, according to studies conducted by the Energy Research and Development Administration, buildings constructed before 1940 were found to be more energy efficient than buildings constructed after 1940 and before 1975 (www.cr.nps.gov). Buildings constructed after 1975 are found to be fairly efficient because the energy crisis in the 1970s necessitated the development of energy-efficient materials, technologies, and methods. Inherent characteristics of older buildings provide an excellent foundation for energy conservation, but these structures have other features that should be improved for energy efficiency. The NPS recommends two approaches for conserving energy in historic properties: passive measures and preservation retrofitting. Passive measures are the first priority, because they minimize the impact to the building, use the least amount of resources, and are easily performed. Passive strategies can involve programming the HVAC and lighting systems to accommodate when people utilize a building. Many buildings are occupied only during specific hours of a day and week. Controls can be programmed to provide the optimum thermal comfort when people are in the space and then readjust the system to conserve energy when rooms are unoccupied. Maximizing natural light and using fresh air for

---

Box 9.1

Visible Signs Associated with Moisture Damage in Buildings

The NPS has identified several signs of moisture damage (www.cr.nps.gov):

- Presence of standing water, mold, fungus, or mildew
- Wet stains, eroding surfaces, or efflorescence (salt deposits) on interior and exterior surfaces
- Flaking paint and plaster, peeling wallpaper, or moisture blisters on finished surfaces
- Dank, musty smells in areas of high humidity or poorly ventilated spaces
- Rust and corrosion stains on metal elements, such as anchorage systems and protruding roof nails in the attic
- Cupped, warped, cracked, or rotted wood
- Spalled, cracked masonry or eroded mortar joints
- Faulty roofs and gutters including missing roofing slates, tiles, or shingles and poor condition of flashing or gutters
- Condensation on windows and wall surfaces
- Ice dams in gutters and on roofs, or moisture in attics

SOURCE: National Park Service, *39 Preservation Briefs: Technical Preservation Services, Controlling Unwanted Moisture in Historic Buildings,* by Sharon C. Park, AIA.

---

ventilation are also means to passively conserve energy. Maintenance is critical for energy conservation. Mechanical equipment, radiators, and forced-air registers should be routinely serviced.

Preservation retrofitting should supplement passive measures. This is a critical element of sustainable interiors; however, solutions have been implemented that are not effective for historic buildings. As identified by the NPS, there are three major problems that have accompanied what was intended to be approaches to energy conservation: (1) inappropriate building alterations, including removal of historic windows, and adding insulated aluminum siding or dropped ceilings; (2) moisture-related deterioration problems due to buildings that are too tightly insulated; and (3) materials that are not compatible with existing materials or are improperly installed (www.cr.nps.gov). Material incompatibility is a serious concern when using cellulose insulations with ammonium or aluminum sulfate (www.cr.nps.gov). According to the NPS, the sulfates react with moisture in the air, which can then damage metals in the building, plumbing, wiring, stone, brick, and wood. A very important consideration for conserving energy in historic buildings is to be certain that the action will actually improve energy efficiency, enhance the thermal comfort of users, and maintain the integrity of the building as much as possible.

Prioritized retrofitting measures for historic buildings include controlling air infiltration; ensuring adequate attic insulation; installing storm windows; insulating crawl spaces, basements, ducts, and pipes; and using awnings and other shading devices. According to the NPS, other measures such as replacement windows and wall insulation frequently are not the most effective solutions, and the technical difficulties associated with the techniques can cause considerable damage to the original structure. Many of the problems associated with older windows are caused by air infiltration. The most effective means to resolve this problem are to add weather stripping and to caulk openings in joints and cracks. Providing or adding attic insulation is another effective means to conserve energy. Since warm air rises, a great amount of heat in a building can be lost through the roof. To preserve the insulating qualities of insulation, the space must have adequate ventilation. When it is not possible to add insulation in the attic, the NPS suggests exploring the possibility of constructing a new insulated ceiling in rooms located underneath the attic. However, ceilings with significant architectural or decorative details may not be good candidates for replacement. When ceiling replacement is appropriate, care must be taken to prevent any damage to other elements in the space.

Installing storm windows is an effective approach to improve the energy efficiency of windows. Storm windows can help to compensate for the heat loss associated with single-pane windows and help to reduce air infiltration. To conserve energy, installing storm windows is preferred to window replacement because the combined properties of storm windows and the original window can result in a better R factor than a new double-paned window unit. In addition, retaining original windows contributes to resource reuse and sustains the historical character derived from the original style, materials, and colors. Storm windows can be installed on the exterior or interior of a building. In either installation, care should be taken to avoid damaging surrounding structural elements. Storm windows may need to be painted to blend with the architectural details of the original window. Interior installations of storm windows can create condensation. To avoid problems with moisture, the windows should be routinely monitored. When water is present, an appropriate remedial treatment should be performed as soon as possible. To eliminate the moisture, a simple solution might be to slightly open the storm window for a short period of time.

Another approach to conserving energy in historic buildings is to insulate crawl spaces, basements, ducts, and pipes. Frequently, older homes do not have insulation in these spaces or around elements used for the distribution of a heated or cooled medium, such as hot water pipes. Adding insulation in these spaces can be performed relatively easily, and does not alter or damage historical components. Crawl spaces and basements have moisture-related problems; thus, it is critical to install the vapor barrier in the proper direction. In addition, as with insulating attics, it is imperative to have adequate ventilation. Energy is lost when heated or cooled air travels through HVAC ductwork. Energy is also lost when hot water moves through pipes. The greater the distance, the more energy is lost. Insulating ducts and pipes helps to conserve energy and is a solution that does not impact the architectural integrity of the building. Energy conservation approaches that do not affect the architectural character of a building are also important for resource reuse. Strategies that minimize contact with finished elements help to protect these resources and extend their life.

When working on a project that does not have a means to control the heat from sunlight, interior and exterior devices should be considered. As described in previous chapters in this text, awnings, operable shutters, and shading devices are excellent approaches for controlling sunlight and can help to conserve energy. Historically, in addition to deciduous trees, buildings have used these units to protect the interior from the heat in the summer and the glare from sunlight. During the winter, units can be removed to allow the penetration of solar radiant energy. Given the propensity for using awnings or other shading units on historic structures, it is fairly easy to research an appropriate style, material, and color.

The NPS indicates that installing a modern mechanical system is one of the most common updates performed on historic buildings. From a sustainability perspective, this can be a positive strategy when the new system conserves energy and reduces pollutants. However, there are problems that can occur when installing new HVAC systems that should be addressed when working with a client. Installing a modern system can damage materials and finishes, which can reduce building and resource reuse. When these materials cannot be recycled, the waste is diverted to landfills. New HVAC systems can introduce an additional weight to a structure, which was not included in the original structural calculations. This can result in structural damage and/or a loss of original materials. To accommodate air-conditioning systems, a common solution is to install a dropped ceiling in rooms. The new ceiling might hide or destroy a surface that has unique ornamentation. The insertion of grilles and registers can also cause these same problems. The placement of the ceiling often obstructs natural daylight and perhaps ventilation. Both of these features are critical to sustainable interiors.

A critical problem associated with new mechanical systems is altering the overall thermal and moisture properties of the building. Throughout the years, a building becomes accustomed to the collective conditions of its mechanical components, materials, building use, and climate. An important element of this adaptation is the natural expansion and contraction that occurs with changes in the weather. These natural fluctuations are necessary for the longevity of the structure. Introducing a new system can negatively affect the original interdependency of the building's components and environment. Consequently, a variety of problems can occur, such as excessive moisture in the summer, dryness in the winter, and alterations in the natural flow of circulating air. A new system can also create dust, new vibrations, and unforeseen noise. These problems can contribute to poor IAQ and can damage finishes and furnishings. Some new HVAC installations involve permanently sealing windows. For a healthy IEQ, this action should always be avoided. Thus, when a new HVAC system must be installed in a historic building, extensive planning should be conducted to minimize damage to the building, finishes, and the structure's ability to naturally expand and contract. Due to any anticipated mechanical upgrades in the future, the system should also be designed for ease in removal and replacement.

SUSTAINABLE STRATEGIES FOR COMMERCIAL AND RESIDENTIAL INTERIORS

Most of the sustainable content reviewed in this text is applied to both commercial and residential interiors. However, as evidenced by separate building assessment guidelines, such as BREEAM's EcoHomes and LEED-CI, there are some distinctions between these two areas that should be addressed when designing sustainable interiors. Some of the variations affect the design process, which is reviewed in the next three chapters in this book. This section examines some of the factors that should be considered when designing sustainable commercial and residential interiors. For the purpose of this analysis, commercial interiors discussed are offices, educational facilities, health care institutions, hotels, restaurants, and retail stores. The discussion focuses on these interiors because interior designers are extensively involved with these projects.

Interior designers have been designing commercial and residential interiors for many years. The background and experience derived from designing thousands of square feet must now be integrated with the principles of sustainability. To accomplish the integration requires a thorough understanding of sustainability and the elements that create successful commercial and residential interiors. The successful integration then results in cost-effective interiors that accommodate the needs of the users and reduce the impact on the environment.

To design sustainable interiors, all commercial and residential buildings are planned using the basic categories prescribed by building assessment programs: site selection, water efficiency, energy and atmosphere, materials and resources, and indoor environmental quality. Thus, all commercial and residential interiors must be constructed on a sustainable site, use water efficiently, optimize energy performance, conserve materials and resources, and have a healthy IEQ. Interiors must be designed to encourage the user's involvement with sustainable practices, such as providing recycling containers in convenient locations or planning accessible lighting controls. All commercial and residential interiors must be designed by focusing on *reducing consumption, reusing resources*, and *recycling*.

Space must always be strategized to reduce square footages while maintaining accessibility, safety, and security. Reducing the square footage needed for each activity results in less energy consumption. Consuming less energy reduces the environmental impacts associated with producing energy, including greenhouse gas emissions. Minimizing the square footage reduces the requirements for HVAC and lighting systems. Smaller spaces reduce the amount of materials needed for flooring, wall finishes, ceiling surfaces, lighting, and furniture. Consequently, fewer materials reduce maintenance and waste.

To identify unique sustainable considerations associated with commercial and residential interiors requires a solid understanding of the purpose of a space and how users function in the environment. This information is unique to every project. All interiors should be reviewed, evaluated, and designed based on the unique qualities of the users of the space, its site, and the characteristics of the built environment. Interior designers must gather information about the site and its users every time they begin a project. The process must be repeated even when a designer renovates a space that he or she previously had designed.

The proceeding sections in this chapter review commercial and residential interiors by providing examples of sustainable considerations that are unique to commercial and residential interiors. The focused content is not intended to be a summary of all the sustainability strategies that should be incorporated into commercial and residential interiors. The purpose is to identify some of the sustainable factors that are unique to a specific type of interior. These considerations should serve only as a guide for thinking about how to integrate the principles of sustainability with the unique needs of commercial and residential interiors.

Sustainable Strategies for Task-Oriented Commercial Interiors

Based on the missions of organizations, offices, educational facilities, and health care institutions could be considered task-oriented facilities. Customer-oriented facilities are discussed in the next section of this chapter. There are some sustainability factors that affect all commercial interiors because these facilities are impacted by large numbers of people. For example, the public and frequent use of facilities requires durable and serviceable materials, finishes, and furniture. Sustainable interiors should be designed to optimize the life cycle of all the components of the built environment. Public buildings have continuous opening and closing of exterior doors. Thus, commercial spaces need entryways that are designed to conserve energy. Since many people visit commercial interiors, the setting makes an excellent tool for teaching people about the principles of sustainability.

Offices represent a significant quantity of space that is consumed in buildings and generate a considerable amount of work for an interior designer. Due to the hundreds of thousands of square feet of office space in the United States alone, sustainable interiors can have a significant impact on the millions of people working in offices, the environment, and the financial viability of an organization. Thus, interior designers are in a formidable position to have a significant impact on people, the environment, and the economy by designing sustainable interiors and promoting sustainable practices.

The amount of square footage dedicated to offices indicates a clear need to strategize space. Spatial organization of commercial office space has changed throughout the decades. Most changes have occurred from new approaches to business practices and, most important, technological advancements. Changes in the work environment are continuous. For example, to have a global competitive edge, organizations today are in constant flux by continually reorganizing. At a moment's notice, a corporation may downsize or increase its number of employees. Businesses change their work and management styles, such as instituting collaborative teamwork, telecommuting opportunities, or emphasizing all forms of telecommunications. Whenever possible, offices should be designed to be adaptable to changing activities, employees, and technology. The sustainable approach is to design spaces that allow for change while retaining as many resources as possible. Spaces should be identified that are specifically designed to serve multiple purposes. Interior systems should be designed to allow for easy changes in technology and workstations. This is especially important to provide access to thermal comfort controls and views to the outdoors.

Regardless of what is transpiring with changes, a business is always focused on productivity. Research studies have focused on designing interiors that improve productivity. Specifically, studies have examined how daylight, electrical sources, and the IAQ affect productivity. (See the reference section in Appendix D for research sources.) These are essential elements of a sustainable interior. Thus, by incorporating sustainable strategies in an office environment, productivity should be enhanced.

Technology has dramatically changed the office environment by encouraging telecommuting, virtual offices, and videoconferencing. These activities can be excellent for reducing the impact of transportation on the environment. Interior designers must plan for the infrastructure, which is required for the technology and the anticipated changes in the future. This requires ceiling and/or floor systems that enable technological changes while not damaging finishes. The floor plan must have the flexibility to accommodate technological changes in the workplace without altering wall partitions, ceiling systems, and flooring.

Information technology is also extremely important for educational facilities. Classrooms utilize technology for presentations, demonstrations, and communication. As with the offices, educational facilities must be planned to accommodate technology and its conduit without damaging existing structural components, finishes, and furnishings. Another important sustainability factor specific to educational facilities is the consumption of energy during days, weeks, and months when buildings are not being used. Educational facilities consume a significant amount of square footage. This is apparent by examining all the buildings at each educational level: preschool, kindergarten, elementary, middle (junior high) school, high school, junior college, college,

and postsecondary. Energy conservation can occur by installing well-commissioned centralized controls of mechanical and electrical systems. Centralized controls can help to monitor the thermal comfort of spaces and regulate lighting systems. Temperatures and lighting systems can be programmed to respond to scheduled occupancies. Controlling lighting systems is especially critical for the successful integration of daylight in classrooms. As discussed in previous chapters, research has demonstrated improvements in academic performance when daylighting is effectively designed in the classroom.

When classes are not in session, communities may want to examine approaches to utilizing K–12 educational facilities for alternative purposes. In addition, many colleges and universities have large campuses with many buildings, which could be available for other purposes when classes are not in session. Educational facilities are also in the formidable position to use their sustainable interiors as learning tools. This is especially important at the kindergarten and elementary levels. Children can be introduced to the benefits of sustainability and learn practices that will last a lifetime. Sustainable development should also be integrated into curriculums throughout the educational system.

Health care involves many different types of facilities, including hospitals, outpatient clinics, nursing homes, physician offices, and psychiatric facilities. Significant sustainable issues for health care facilities are the consumption of large quantities of energy and water. According to the U.S. DOE, medical facilities spend $5.3 billion each year for energy (www.eere.energy.gov). The DOE also indicates that many facilities are not well insulated and have outdated HVAC equipment. These facilities need renovations that focus on minimizing heat gain or loss and upgrading equipment. Installing centralized energy management units and energy-efficient light systems would help to conserve energy. Efficient use of space can help to conserve energy and materials for finishes and furnishings. Installing low-flow fixtures can help to conserve water.

As with other commercial interiors, health care facilities are susceptible to technological changes and variable approaches to conducting business. Thus, health care facilities' interiors should also be flexible and adaptable. For example, in the near future more attention will be focused on designing spaces for acoustical and visual privacy. These changes are the result of new health insurance and accountability regulations. These requirements can affect space configurations and the location of medical records. Solutions should focus on being able to change spaces as the needs of an organization vary in time with minimum damage to structural components, finishes, and furnishings. Health care facilities have a significant need for daylighting and views. Several research studies have indicated that natural daylight can help the healing process and helps patients know the time of the day after being asleep or sedated.

Sustainable Strategies for Customer-Oriented Commercial Interiors

Hotels, restaurants, and retail stores rely on customer satisfaction for their income and profits. Therefore, for the owners of these facilities to engage in sustainable practices, they must be convinced that the investment will result in profits. Profits associated with sustainable design can be derived from long-term capital investments such as energy-efficient equipment, insulation, or durable furnishings. An indirect source of profits can occur from customers who are interested in environmentally conscious facilities and products. Thus, to encourage a client to invest in sustainable interiors requires an understanding of their customers and how sustainability supports their interests.

Hotels serve guests from various regions of the world. Many hotel guests travel on a regular basis and consequently are exposed to a variety of practices. Sustainability is a practice that varies by city, state, and country. Thus, someone who travels frequently is likely to encounter sustainable practices at a hotel. It is this exposure and experience that can often prompt hotel owners to engage in sustainable designs. For example, many hotels initiated the practice of asking guests to reuse their towels to conserve water and energy. Once exposed to this sustainable practice, many guests expect other hotels to follow this environmentally responsible custom. Hotels have also demonstrated sustainable practice by using energy-efficient lamps in guest rooms and nonpublic areas. In addition, signs have been posted in rooms requesting guests to turn off lights and the television when leaving the room. In larger hotels, **submetering systems** have been installed to identify areas of energy waste and defective equipment. Submetering is a technological means to measure and collect information regarding energy consumption from one or multiple areas within a facility. Hotel owners can use the energy summary data to understand problematic areas, identify performance hindrances, and develop strategies to improve energy consumption. Submetering can be an effective tool for any large facility, such as department stores.

People have become accustomed to some sustainability practices in guest rooms, but the focus on healthy environments has prompted guests to request even more sustainable amenities. For example, based on demands from guests, some hotels have focused on sustainable tourism and "eco" products in the guest rooms. Guests are also asking for rooms that have healthy IAQ and operable windows. Thus, there is a demand for guest rooms that provide natural ventilation, have low-emitting materials, and have zero environmental tobacco smoke. To provide healthier rooms, hotels should use HEPA vacuums and filters. Guestroom bathrooms must be void of mold and mildew. Mild cleaning products are very important to guests who have multiple chemical sensitivity syndromes.

In addition to the importance of a healthy guestroom, hotel owners are concerned about the high cost of energy and water. Most of the energy consumed by a hotel is for the electrical needs in guestrooms, water heating, and the HVAC in common areas. Thus, energy efficiency is critical to hotel owners and can be improved by ensuring that space utilization is cost-effective. Transitional spaces do not produce income for hotel owners, yet these spaces consume energy and require finishes, furnishings, and maintenance. Thus, the hotel plan should minimize spaces for circulation, registration, lobbies, and guestroom corridors.

Changes in lifestyles and technology impact the interiors of hotels. For sustainable interiors, the spaces, finishes, and furnishings must be designed to be flexible, adaptable, and very durable. Durability is especially critical when specifying the finishes and furnishings for the guest rooms. A compilation of all the products used in thousands of hotel guestrooms is astounding. The need to rapidly replace these materials due to wear is a tremendous waste of resources and a tremendous expense for the hotel owner. The products for guestrooms must be durable, and the materials should not be trendy or easily reveal wear. Ease of replacement of damaged components is also an important attribute. For example, carpet tiles in guest corridors and any high-traffic area can be a sustainable solution.

Specific sustainability concerns with restaurants focus on energy conservation and durable materials, furnishings, and finishes. Durable materials that do not show wear and can be easily replaced are also important for restaurants. Spillage from food and drinks places an enormous toll on materials. Additionally, the rapid turnover in foot traffic from customers can easily damage and wear flooring materials. Depending on the type of restaurant and the size of the space, other concerns focus on energy conservation. Some areas of concern are lighting applications, unused dining areas, and heat gain or loss at the entrance. To conserve energy, daylighting should be integrated with electrical sources for breakfast and lunch service. Energy-efficient light sources should be used for evening dining, and automated control systems can provide the changes in illumination that are needed from dining to cleaning. Large restaurants should be designed to provide the flexibility to close sections during slow serving times. To save energy, each area would have to be engineered to adjust to the variability in temperatures. Entrances should have a vestibule that helps to retain heating and cooling in a building.

The energy efficiency of lighting systems is a very important sustainable concern of retail stores. There are two potential causes for this problem. First and foremost, retailers are dependent on lighting to make their products appear appealing to the customer. People do not purchase products that have unattractive colors and textures. Unfortunately, lamps that have some of the best color-rendering properties consume the most energy. These lamps also generate heat, which can contribute significantly to increasing the loads on air conditioners. Many retailers have not retrofitted fixtures to accommodate energy-efficient lighting systems. The escalating potential of LEDs will significantly help to improve energy inefficiencies in retail stores. Sustainable retail interiors must be designed to optimize lighting while

reducing energy consumption. Another reason for high-energy consumption for lighting systems can be the contractual arrangements between retailers and the landlord. Many leases require the landlord to pay utilities. Thus, the retailer does not have a financial incentive to use energy-efficient lighting systems. To transfer costs to the user, the implementation of submetering and separate utility metering can help to alleviate this problem. Thus, with these units, the retailer can be charged the electrical costs and consequently may have an incentive to conserve energy.

The rapidly increasing popularity of online buying places a greater emphasis on well-designed retail stores. In trying to make the retail store an *experience* for their customers, retailers may focus on reducing the size of spaces to enable people to shop efficiently. Reducing the size of spaces is a sustainable strategy. To create unique retail environments, some retailers might be interested in operating the store in an adaptive-reuse building, which can also be positive for sustainability. To find a niche, a retailer might elect to promote "environmentally" or "ecologically" focused retailing. To reinforce the concept, the store could be designed according to the principles of sustainability by having low-emitting materials, recycled content, rapidly renewable materials, and certified wood products. In addition, the design could accentuate a connection with the environment by incorporating daylighting, and perhaps an adjacent courtyard with a patio and garden. The critical element for interior designers is to promote sustainability whenever an opportunity presents itself. Recreating the retail experience could be an ideal format for educating people about sustainability by allowing them to experience the benefits.

In promoting sustainable lifestyles, retailers as well as other public spaces should encourage recycling by providing bins for recyclable items in locations for customer use. A retail store receives packages and shipments on a daily basis. Procedures for separating, collecting, reusing, and recycling packaging materials should become standard practice. A waste management and recycling program should be included in the employees' training manual, including appropriate recycling/disposal practices for packaging materials. Another pollution-related concern for some retailers is refrigerant use for food storage. To reduce emissions to the atmosphere, refrigerant leak detection and recovery procedures should be delineated. For example, proper maintenance procedures are critical for reducing pollution problems associated with refrigerant leaks.

Sustainable Strategies for Maintenance

Proper operation and maintenance procedures are extremely important for sustainable residential and commercial interiors. Appropriate implementation of operational and maintenance practices helps to extend the life of equipment, finishes, and furnishings. Equipment that is properly monitored and maintained will last longer and is required for optimum energy efficiency, thermal comfort, proper ventilation, and healthy IAQ. Finishes and furnishings that receive proper care will also last longer and retain their new appearance, and they are more likely to be reused. A very extensive strategy for preventative practices is **reliability-centered maintenance (RCM)**, a comprehensive approach to all phases of maintenance, including reactive, time-based, condition-based, and proactive tasks (www. wbdg.org). *Reactive* maintenance resolves problems of small items or components with a known redundancy of needed repair. *Time-based* practices are preventative maintenance procedures. *Condition-based* procedures are used for random failures. *Proactive* maintenance focuses on performing tasks that help to eliminate future failures of an entire system. The RCM approach is an excellent investment by saving money in the long term. Savings can be derived from maximum energy conservation, avoiding replacement costs, and any problems that can be caused by the loss of equipment, such as temporary closings of a business.

To ensure proper operational and maintenance procedures, training must be provided to managers and personnel responsible for equipment, finishes, and furnishings. In addition, manuals should be developed that include specification data from manufacturers, an inventory of components, and proper products and methods for cleaning. When cleaning information is not available from a manufacturer, some excellent sources are the EPA's *Database of Environmental Information for Products and Services*, Green Seal, Scientific Certification Systems (SCS), CRI, and the

SCAQMD. An interior designer should develop a manual for the client that includes products specified and/or supplied by the designer.

Important procedures that should be included in training and the operational/maintenance manual are approaches to the building commissioning process. Building commissioning is a process that helps to ensure all building systems operate as prescribed by the original specifications. The building systems that should be commissioned include mechanical, plumbing, electrical, and life safety systems. The process helps to ensure the proper operation of equipment, which can maximize the IAQ, thermal comfort, energy efficiency, and costs associated with operations and maintenance. Building commission is done with new construction and retrocommissioning is performed to existing buildings. The commissioning process should begin at the pre-design phase and continue through the design phase, bidding phase, construction phase, and warranty period. Each phase is accompanied by roles and responsibilities of each team member and documentation procedures. Commissioning should be delineated in contract documents, training sessions, and operation/maintenance manuals.

Sustainable Strategies for Residential Interiors

Residential interiors include many different arrangements, such as single or multiunit dwellings, apartments, condominiums, and congregate senior housing. Residential interiors are often in historic buildings; thus, the strategies described previously in this chapter are excellent references. The popularity of the message from architect Sarah Susanka serves as an excellent protocol for promoting small, but quality interiors. The dramatic increases in the size of single-unit residences, with no relationship to the number of people in a household, are a significant concern for sustainability. Interior designers should encourage their clients to invest in residences with quality finishes and furnishings, rather than planning spaces with unnecessary square footage. The goal should be to reduce the building's footprint. Another sustainability benefit of quality interiors is investing in materials that have longevity.

An important element of designing manageable

residential interiors is planning for flexibility and adaptability. The household composition can change when people are living in a dwelling for many years. Sustainable interiors are designed to adapt to changes in the seasons and the composition of the residents. The importance of space flexibility can be traced back to the writings of Vitruvius. To contend with climatic changes in the seasons, Vitruvius indicated that special purposes in different rooms required the optimum conditions. This required shifting the use of a space based on the time of the year and its associated climatic conditions. For example, Vitruvius explains, "winter dining rooms and bathrooms should have a southwestern exposure, for the reason that they need the evening light, and also because the setting sun, facing them in all its splendour but with abated heat, lends a gentler warmth to that quarter in the evening. Bedrooms and libraries ought to have an eastern exposure, because their purposes require the morning light, and also because books in such libraries will not decay" (Morgan, 1960, pp. 180–181). In demonstrating how the function of rooms should change according to the seasons, Vitruvius continues, "Dining rooms for Spring and Autumn to the east; for when the windows face that quarter, the sun, as he goes on his career from over against them to the west, leaves such rooms at the proper temperature at the time when it is customary to use them. Summer dining rooms to the north, because that quarter is not, like the others, burning with heat during the solstice" (Morgan, 1960, p. 181).

The multiplicity of space use demonstrated by Vitruvius should be incorporated into today's residences. In cold climates, rooms on the south side should be maximized during the winter; the opposite arrangements could be done in the summer. Colder rooms could be closed off during the winter months. Adaptable spaces do not have a defined purpose. Japanese interiors are excellent examples of how to create interiors that enable a space to function for a variety of needs. Japanese screens, interspersed throughout the dwelling, are an excellent means for providing flexibility in the size of a room (see Figure 9.24). The conceptual design of Japanese interiors could be adapted to western residences. In adapting the layout of Japanese residences, other possibilities are minimizing transitional spaces, hallways, fur-

Fig. 9.24. Japanese screens are an excellent means for providing flexibility in the size of a room.

nishings, and ornamentation. The Japanese provide excellent examples of integrating the interior with the outdoor landscaping. A natural integration is essential for daylighting and maximizing views. A comprehensive sustainable approach is to practice safe gardening procedures by using nontoxic fertilizers and pesticides. Surface areas such as pavements, driveways, and patios should allow for water penetration rather than surface runoff.

Residences can be designed to encourage sustainable lifestyles. Incorporating accessible and well-designed recycling areas, as discussed previously in this text, can promote sustainability. To encourage a reduction in transport, residential offices should be emphasized, and access to bicycles should be convenient. Residential offices should be designed with objectives similar to those used in commercial offices. The workstation should be ergonomically appropriate for the users. All of the requirements for technology must be integrated with the design. Daylighting and views are also essential elements of the residential office.

Sustainable energy practices can also be part of the residential lifestyle. To conserve energy, the thermostat can be raised or lowered, and natural ventilation substituted for air-conditioning. The proliferation of electrical appliances is astounding. The majority of new appliances are not needed for cooking, cleaning, and grooming. Reducing or eliminating convenience appliances is an easy approach to conserving electricity. Energy-efficient lighting systems and turning lights off when not needed are also important for sustainable interiors. In addition, as a continuing practice in the field of interior design, clients should be encouraged to reuse and refurbish furniture. An examination of promoting sustainable practices continues in the next three chapters, which focus on the phases of the design process.

Summary

- A focus on existing buildings is absolutely essential for conserving resources, minimizing impacts to the environment, and reducing materials that are landfilled. Reusing buildings, finishes, and furnishings must be the preferred solutions when designing interior environments.
- Most civilizations throughout the world have lived without electricity and mechanical HVAC systems. Thus, structures that were built prior to the twentieth century are excellent resources for understanding how to design sustainable interiors.
- For thousands of years, buildings have been designed to control the sun. Exterior strategies include the use of arcades, verandas, deep overhangs, and recessed walls.
- For economic and practical reasons, many historic buildings were designed to conserve space by (1) using a minimum number of rooms, (2) reducing or eliminating transitional areas, and (3) incorporating various techniques that suggested greater volumes of space.
- To retain historic structures and preserve our cultural heritage, the historic preservation movement gained prominence in the United States in the 1960s. To support historic preservation, Congress established the National Historic Preservation Act (NHPA) in 1966.
- The Secretary of the Interior's Standards specify four approaches for the treatment of properties: preservation, rehabilitation, restoration, and reconstruction.
- In addition to the considerations outlined by the NPS, an interior designer should review a treatment within the context of sustainability and economic considerations.
- To integrate sustainability with historic preservation requires special considerations. The factors to consider can be reviewed by examining the categories for LEED's rating system.
- Historic buildings can have problems related to sustainability, which must be addressed for the benefit of the users, the environment, and economic considerations.
- Conserving energy in historic buildings is essential for sustainable buildings.
- All commercial and residential interiors must be designed by focusing on reducing consumption, reusing resources, and recycling.
- Offices represent a significant quantity of space that is consumed in buildings. Due to the hundreds of thousands of square feet of office space, sustainable interiors can have a significant impact on the millions of people working in offices, on the environment, and on the financial viability of an organization.
- A significant sustainable issue for health care facilities is the consumption of large quantities of energy and water.
- Hotels, restaurants, and retail stores rely on customer satisfaction for their income and profits. Profits associated with sustainable design can be derived from long-term capital investments, such as energy-efficient equipment, insulation, or durable furnishings.
- Appropriate implementation of operational and maintenance practices helps to extend the life of equipment, finishes, and furnishings. Equipment that is properly monitored and maintained will last longer and is required for optimum energy efficiency, thermal comfort, proper ventilation, and healthy IAQ.

Key Terms

Abrasive cleaning
Adaptive reuse
High-efficiency particulate air (HEPA)
National Historic Preservation Act (NHPA)
OSHA's 29 CFR Part 1926, Lead Exposure in Construction
Preservation
Reconstruction
Rehabilitation
Reliability-centered maintenance (RCM)
Restoration
Submetering systems

U.S. National Park Service (NPS)
Vernacular architecture

Exercises

1. Techniques and materials employed in historic buildings provide excellent lessons in understanding how to preserve and specify enduring environments. An informative document is the writings of Vitruvius in *The Ten Books on Architecture.* Read the book and develop a summary of the recommendations provided by Vitruvius that could be applied to practice today.

2. The Secretary of the Interior's Standards set out four approaches for the treatment of properties: preservation, rehabilitation, restoration, and reconstruction. Research an example of each treatment. In a written report, summarize how the building addresses a treatment and include illustrations, photographs, or sketches.

3. Review characteristics of a local office, health care institution, restaurant, and retail store. Identify sustainability factors that affect each commercial interior. Summarize the results in a written report, and include illustrations, photographs, or sketches.

4. Residential interiors include many different arrangements. An important element of designing manageable residential interiors is planning for flexibility and adaptability. Identify a residential floor plan and develop drawings that reflect how the structure can be flexible and adaptable.

CHAPTER 10

Sustainable Strategies for Management and the Initial Phases of the Design Process

"Anything essential is invisible to the eyes," the little prince repeated, in order to remember.

"It's the time you spent with your rose that makes your rose so important."

"People have forgotten this truth," the fox said. "But you mustn't forget it.

"You become responsible forever for what you've tamed.

"You're responsible for your rose . . ."

—ANTOINE DE SAINT-EXUPÉRY

Objectives

- Understand management strategies for sustainable interior environments and how to apply the methods to practice.
- Apply an understanding of the principles of sustainability to the goals and objectives of a sustainable environment.
- Describe strategies for enhancing the collaborative activities, which are essential to a sustainable project.
- Synthesize the methods for collecting data in the programming phase of a sustainable project.
- Understand how to analyze information gathered in the programming phase.
- Identify how a charrette can be used to analyze the results of programming.
- Comprehend how a charrette can develop the architectural program of a sustainable project.

THE MATERIAL COVERED in preceding chapters in this text provides the background for understanding sustainable development within the context of the built environment. An essential element of this content is relating sustainability to people, the environment, and economics. To effectively incorporate the content into practice requires a thorough study of the information, and then understanding how to integrate sustainability with the design process. To provide the background for the design process, this chapter begins by examining management concerns that are related to sustainable environments. There are specific management requirements associated with sustainable interiors. Thus, an understanding of these responsibilities assists in developing the plans for the project and helps to identify costs associated with the requirements.

This chapter and the remaining two chapters in this text focus on delineating approaches to assimilate the principles of sustainability with the phases of the design process: (1) pre-design: comprehensive planning, (2) pre-design: comprehensive programming, (3) schematic design, (4) design development, (5) contract documentation, (6) contract administration, and (7) evaluation. Sustainability must be integrated with the other considerations of the project. This chapter examines pre-design activities, which involves comprehensive planning and programming. An assessment of the design process continues in Chapter 11 by describing recommendations for schematic designs and design development. Chapter 12 concludes the phases of the design process by relating sustainability to contractual documents, contract administration, postoccupancy, and evaluation.

MANAGEMENT STRATEGIES FOR SUSTAINABLE INTERIOR ENVIRONMENTS

Sustainable design and development introduces additional considerations when designing interior environments and new approaches to business policies and practices. To design sustainable interiors requires an understanding of additional managerial responsibilities associated with sustainable buildings. These requirements impact procedures and costs to a client and subsequently affect the work of an interior designer. In addition to creating special managerial

responsibilities, designing sustainable interiors may alter the practice of an interior designer, such as allocating time and resources to collaborative activities.

Collaboration involves all of the professionals on a project and the potential to engage in shared arrangements with other interior designers within the community. To successfully design sustainable interiors requires a designer's commitment to the principles of sustainability. To demonstrate their shared philosophical beliefs, an interior design firm should have sustainable policies and practices. A client who is interested in investing in a sustainable built environment expects the design firm and the other professionals involved with the project to engage in sustainable practice. For some firms, this may require a transformation of current procedures, policies, and the characteristics of the firm's built environment. An excellent starting point is for the firm to achieve certification from a building assessment program, such as LEED. In addition, employees should be educated regarding the principles and practices of sustainability, and individuals should seek professional accreditation.

Sustainable Management

Management is responsible for ensuring that the sustainable attributes of the built environment are properly implemented, operate effectively, and are well maintained. BREEAM and Green Star—Australia have details regarding specific management responsibilities for organizations and businesses that are seeking certification. These requirements can serve as a foundation for developing management policies and procedures for sustainable environments. Some of the initial policies that must be developed focus on construction activities. BREEAM's assessment criterion requires compliance with managing a construction site by reducing waste, energy, water, and pollution. Construction waste should be minimized and then recycled whenever possible. Wood that is used for temporary building purposes should be from sustainably managed sources. After use the wood should be recycled or reused at other construction sites. Energy consumption should be monitored and then subsequently reduced. A primary use of energy on a construction site is transportation. Schedules should be coordinated to minimize transport to and from the site. This could involve construction workers, electricians, plumbers, inspectors, and material deliveries. Water consumption on the site should be minimized, and precautions must be enacted to avoid ground and surface water pollution. Air pollution from a construction site is primarily from dust. This can be harmful to the workers and potentially can impact the IAQ after occupancy. Thus, procedures must be developed to suppress dust and thoroughly clean the site on a very regular basis. Another important requirement identified by BREEAM is *considerate contractors*. Credit within the management category is given to construction sites that are "managed in an environmentally considerate and accountable manner" (BREEAM Retail 2005, p. 5).

Once occupancy occurs, there are many required management policies and procedures. Corporate or organizational policies must be developed that reflect the principles of sustainability. The policies should outline roles, responsibilities, required operation and maintenance (O&M) activities, purchasing specifications, suggested time frames, building operating manuals, and training programs. BREEAM stresses the importance of ensuring that policies are endorsed at the board and local levels. The policies and subsequent follow-up reports should be communicated to all of the employees. Environmental policies should be comprehensive by focusing on the major categories of a building assessment program: sustainable sites; water efficiency; energy and atmosphere; materials and resources; and indoor environmental quality. (See Chapter 5 and Appendix A for a listing of environmental categories and intent statements.) The policies for O&M must be comprehensive and well understood by the managers and the personnel assigned to undertake the required activities.

One of the most important requirements is commissioning. Personnel must be assigned to monitor commissioning. Extremely complex systems require a specialist commissioning agent. Pre-commissioning, commissioning, and quality monitoring must be performed. An independent commissioning provider can perform commissioning services, as can an individual a contractor hires, such as a *test engineer*. The commissioning agent can be hired at the planning stage and should continue to work through the design, bid, construction, and warranty phases of the project. Systems that can be commissioned can be HVAC, electrical systems, lighting controls, life safety, emergency power generators, security, and plumbing. A commissioning agent is expected to provide documentation that confirms a facility is performing according to the requirements of the original design. During the first year of occupation, BREEAM requires seasonal commissioning. An energy audit should be executed every three years, and documentation must provide any corrective actions. To encourage conservation practices, BREEAM recommends that energy consumption should be disseminated to all employees. Policies should require the retention of energy data. These historical records are used to calculate usage comparisons over years of operation. The data also serve as the basis for identifying improvement targets. As with all sustainability practice, strategies must be developed to continuously improve energy consumption and reduce environmental impacts.

Corporate policies should also include monitoring schedules for water consumption and procedures for correcting any problems. As with energy consumption, water usage data must be retained and used to improve conservation practices. Policies and management responsibilities should include encouraging employees to use public transportation and to ride bikes to and from work. After a business has installed the amenities associated with riding bikes, such as storage and showers, employees must be continuously reminded to use these facilities.

Communication is essential for encouraging sustainable practices and to rectify any problems. BREEAM provides credit for procedures that enable people to communicate malfunctions, such as defective ventilation systems or lamps. Communication should also include a process for informing employees when the corrective actions have been completed. Corporate policies should also include recycling procedures. This should include what should be recycled, the locations of recycling containers, hazardous material disposal procedures, and policies regarding removals from the site.

BREEAM encourages schools to disseminate to the community the environmental impacts of the building and the accompanying management strategies that minimize the effects. A sustainable school and its site can serve as a learning resource to the children, parents, and community. Schools can demonstrate conservation practices, healthy IAQ, recycling practices, sustainable materials, the importance of biodiversity, and waste reduction. BREEAM encourages schools to share their facilities with the community whenever possible. While using the facilities, people can learn from the sustainable practices and multipurpose spaces can help to reduce the construction of new buildings.

PRE-DESIGN: COMPREHENSIVE PLANNING

Successful projects require a thorough planning process. Expending the time and energy very early in the development of a project results in an optimum design, completed according to the schedule and the client's budget. Comprehensive planning in the pre-design phase is absolutely essential for sustainable buildings. To integrate sustainability with the other elements of the built environment, an exploration of how it can be accomplished is required at the very earliest stage of a project. For successful integration, sustainable components must be identified in the plans for the project. This requires thorough research, creative problem solving, and a strategy for involving all the stakeholders.

One of the initial steps in the planning process is to identify the members of the design team. Team members can include the client, architect, engineers, interior designer, users, maintenance specialists, commissioning provider, material suppliers, community representatives, and perhaps the contractor. When seeking LEED certification, at least one member should be an accredited professional. This person can serve as the team leader for the certification process. The requirements associated with acquiring certification, such as providing submittal documentation materials, necessitates at least one person who is responsible for coordinating the activities. Large projects require a certification team with an assigned leader.

The formulation of the design team is essential to successfully integrate all of the elements of a sustainable building. All team members should be knowledgeable of the principles of sustainability. Team members who are unfamiliar with sustainable development must express a sincere interest in the essence of the philosophy and then receive appropriate education. The design team is responsible for developing the project's goals, objectives, and priorities and meeting the criteria for a sustainable building. Responsibilities also include developing a cost analysis, estimated budget, projected schedule, and strategies for collaborative activities. The team must research applicable building codes, laws, and standards. The governance structure of the design team should encourage participation from all of the team members and delineate proper communication channels. Communication is critical at all phases of the design process, especially when modifications must be addressed during the construction.

The collaborative nature of a sustainable project necessitates identifying team members who are cooperative, have similar work ethics, and are receptive to exploring new concepts and ideas. Previous work with sustainable projects is important; however, the experience is most valuable when the person is also energized by the principles of sustainability. Members of the design team should demonstrate an affinity for pursuing the goals of sustainability. A personal commitment to sustainability enhances the resultant design. Past participants in sustainable projects have repeatedly indicated the importance of identifying team members who have a sincere interest in designing sustainable buildings. Successful sustainable buildings require a new way of conceptualizing the structure's design, operations, and maintenance. Sustainable buildings are more than installing energy-efficient systems. Truly sustainable buildings have the appropriate equipment and materials *and* foster a behavior in people that is sustainable for society, the environment, and the economy. These *living sustainable buildings* require new and creative problem solving, which requires sincere support for the principles of sustainability.

To design, construct, operate, and maintain this type of building requires a client and design team members who are committed to sustainability. The client especially must be willing to dedicate the time, energy, and resources required for sustainable buildings. A design team that is committed to sustainability is willing to work together to overcome obstacles that occur with nonconventional building processes. For example, laws and building codes may prohibit some of the new approaches to sustainable buildings, such as the use of graywater. Frequently, this requires perseverance and collaborative planning with local officials. Equally challenging is being able to use an innovative product design that is not available from manufacturers. The new technologies and methods associated with sustainable buildings require creative problem-solving skills. For example, the team members might also have to develop inventive financial arrangements to help fund the project, such as grants, government programs, or tax incentives.

Goals and Objectives for Sustainable Environments

A comprehensive approach to developing the goals and objectives of the project is critical to success. The goals and objectives should encompass the most salient elements required to select the ideal site and to design, construct, operate, maintain, and evaluate the project. The project's goals and objectives should serve as the criteria for determining the effectiveness of the building's performance, users' satisfaction, impact on the environment, and financial conditions. An important goal to establish is whether the client is seeking to have the building certified. For example, if attaining LEED certification is the goal, then equally important is determining the desired level of certification. For example, the LEED-CI platinum rating requires 42–57 points. The number of points for a certified rating is 21–26 points. The differences in the requirements for platinum and certified ratings need unique strategies. Thus, the desired rating is important to know at the pre-design phase. The rating goal enables the team to identify the parameters of the project and to begin the process of collecting and recording required documentation. In addition, establishing the certification goal during the pre-design phase enables the team to enlist an accredited professional at the earliest stage of the design process. Some clients that are interested in having a sustainable building do not desire certification. These projects are also extremely important, but they may require different goals than a potentially certified building. A client that might not be aware of LEED certification could elect to undertake the process with adequate information. Costs associated with certification should be explained to the client; these include resources for documentation, commissioning processes, registration fees, and certification reviews.

The goals and objectives of sustainable buildings focus on the fundamental categories of a certification process: (1) management, (2) sustainable sites, (3) water efficiency, (4) energy and atmosphere, (5) materials and resources, and (6) indoor environmental quality. The emphasis within each category can fluctuate with each project. For example, a building in an area with water shortages should focus attention on developing water-efficiency strategies. Buildings in cold climates emphasize heating-conservation measures. A school district might want to dedicate abundant resources to integrating daylight in all classrooms. In addition, every project has goals and objectives that are very specific to the interests of the client. For example, a client may want to create a work environment that is friendly and encourages collaboration. A hotel owner wants guestrooms that are clean and safe for guests. A client who is seeking National Register status, or has a building in a National Register Historic District, has additional standards. Environmental, personal, and business-oriented principles must all be incorporated within the project's goals and objectives. Realistically, a client will not be able to do all of the desirable features and plans. Thus, prioritization is a very important task for the design team. The team should collaboratively determine criteria and then use these as the basis for prioritizing goals, objectives, and activities.

An important goal for all projects should be to promote a payment or compensation structure that rewards sustainable practice and performance. This type of compensation structure is contrary to some traditional forms used today. Some traditional fee structures, such as compensation based on commissions, encourage increases in consumption of materials and resources. Since a primary goal of sustainability is to *reduce*, a client should focus on fee structures within their contracts that optimize sustainable practices.

Collaboration Strategies for Sustainable Environments

An essential element of sustainable designs is collaborative activities. A design team typically consists of people who have diverse interests, motivations, and opinions. Thus, at the pre-design stage, the design team should establish policies and procedures for facilitating communication and decision making. Effective governance systems establish a means to encourage participation, create consensus, and facilitate the assignments of the team. Guidelines should be developed that delineate the purposes of the design team, the roles and responsibilities of each member, a timeline for participation, means of communication, spending authorization policies, and strategies for decision making, including who is responsible for final decisions.

Sufficient time should be allotted to developing the governance guidelines, and team members should have the opportunity to participate in the process. Many teams have not been successful because a governance structure was not established. For example, a lack of governance guidelines can lead to confusion regarding who is responsible for completing a task. As a result, a task may never be completed or could become cost prohibitive at a later date. In addition, without proper communication channels someone might not be informed about a design change that can significantly impact his or her work on the project. Consequently, projects can be delayed and costs can escalate. Furthermore, a dysfunctional team can cause people to decline participation. In circumstances when an individual is required to attend, his or her feelings of resentment can taint the entire collaborative process. The communication plan should identify all individuals involved with the project and the most appropriate time and means to communicate with them. A very important element of the plan is the communication process when changes occur in a project. When alterations from the original design must be done, it is imperative to inform all individuals and firms whose work might be impacted by the changes.

In recent years, the management profession has been developing effective strategies for executing the work of collaborative teamwork. There are many structured collaborative processes that a design team can use when it must solve problems and make decisions. Examples include structured processes for brainstorming and determining interrelated factors, pathways to achieve goals, chain of events analysis, and prioritization matrices. Detailed descriptions of how to use the processes can be found in many management books and articles. Some of the most noted authors are W. Edwards Deming; GOAL/QPC; and T. J. Peters and R. H. Waterman. These processes became very popular in the 1980s when the *total quality management (TQM)* movement stressed the importance of teamwork in corporations and higher education. The design team can review various approaches and then collectively determine the process that will be the most effective for their operational needs. An important reason for using structured collaborative processes is having an effective and productive means to work in teams. These processes are structured to allow everyone to participate, and gather a significant amount of information in a relatively short period of time. Some of the processes also have a structure that enables a team to prioritize issues by consensus. Given the limited time that most professionals have to devote to teamwork, it is critical to use every means possible to ensure smooth and productive sessions.

PRE-DESIGN: COMPREHENSIVE PROGRAMMING

Structured collaborative processes can be used for some programming activities. Based on the goals and objectives of the project, a comprehensive programming plan should be developed by the design team. Figure 10.1 illustrates elements of programming and how the outcomes of the activities inform the design of the project. Integrating a building with the environment and the community is one of the unique features of sustainability. Programming processes provide the means to accomplish successful integration. Comprehensive programming is important for sustainable buildings because the essence of sustainable development is the multidisciplinary involvement of the stakeholders. Thus, to be inclusive it is essential to acquire feedback and to have participation from people who will be impacted by the built environment. The plan for programming should focus on identifying the information that needs to be collected, how the data will be acquired, and a respective timeline. The information gathered is critical to determining the budget, feasibility of the project, required resources, and schematic designs.

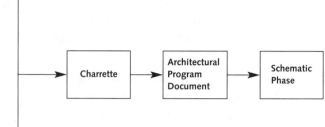

Fig. 10.1. Flow chart diagram of components of the programming design phase.

Programming Phases and Sustainable Environments

The programming process has two basic phases: gathering relevant information and then analyzing the data collected. Design team members can be involved with gathering the information, or an outside consultant might be hired to conduct some of the data collection. All of the members of the design team should be involved with determining what information is needed, and members should have the opportunity to review all of the data. Individuals responsible for collecting the information usually perform the analysis. (A review of the analysis process follows the description of gathering data.) Information required to develop the initial design concept includes the following:

- Program requirements from the client/owner
- Feedback from users of the space and community representatives
- An analysis of the area and site of the building
- Assessment of the features of the built environment
- An analysis of space use
- An inventory of finishes, furnishings, and equipment
- Initial budget and life-cycle costs
- Current codes, regulations, standards, and certification requirements
- Contemporary sustainability practices and products
- Projected schedule

The project can be a renovation of a client's building or a new site. When a client is seeking a new location, the design team should be involved with the selection process. There are many sustainable considerations associated with the site of a building and its respective area. Thus, the design team should explore several different sites to select the building that can incorporate as many of the principles of sustainability as possible. A building that already has certification can be an excellent choice. In urban areas a brownfield redevelopment has benefits for the environment and community. Priority should be given to selecting an existing building rather than new construction.

The team should visit various sites and perform an analysis of existing sustainable elements and the potential for developing additional features. Certification criteria can be used to evaluate sustainable features (see Chapter 5 and Appendix A). The LEED-CI has many items in the *Sustainable Sites* category that can be used to evaluate a building and its site. In addition, LEED-CI identifies features in its other categories that affect site selection. For example, within the *Materials and Resources* category, LEED-CI includes environment credits for the storage and collection of recyclables. Thus, when reviewing various sites, the design team should search for recyclables provisions. When these do not exist, the team should record the information and analyze the site for potential locations for the storage and collection of recyclables. Table 10.1 provides a list of LEED-CI credit categories that should be explored when reviewing the site (2005). To select the ideal site, the data collected from various sites should be used for the schematic design phase.

A variety of techniques can be used to collect information in the pre-design phase. To acquire information from people, some methods are interviews, **focus groups**, surveys, observations, and charrettes.

Interviews must be done with the client and should be conducted with users of the space and members of the community. In nonpublic commercial interiors, such as an office, people from the various corporate divisions should be interviewed. In public commercial buildings, as with retail stores, employees should be interviewed and, if possible, representative samples of the firm's customers. Interviews can be conducted face-to-face, or several people can be interviewed at one time. There should be a single list of questions that are asked to each individual. However, variations in questions will occur when interviewing people in different divisions. Table 10.2 provides examples of questions that can serve as a guide for developing an instrument for designing sustainable interiors. These items can also be used as a guide in developing topics for focus groups. Conducting focus groups can be an effective method to acquire perspectives from employees, customers, or community representatives. Basically, focus groups are a structured means to discuss topics for a few hours. A facilitator structures the discussion and is responsible for ensuring the involvement of participants. At the conclusion of a focus group, the facilitator develops a summary of the perspectives of each individual and the group itself.

Surveys are another method to gather information from users of the space and members of the community. The types of items included in a survey are similar to questions in an interview. Before distributing a survey to individuals, the instrument should be tested on people not involved with the study. By pretesting and performing appropriate revisions, the survey is more likely to be successful. Pretesting helps to identify problems people may have with understanding a question or providing a response. In addition, individuals pretesting the survey may be able to suggest additions and deletions that would help improve the instrument. To attain as much information from interviewees as possible, it is recommended to include open-ended questions on the survey. Open-ended questions provide people with the opportunity to provide more information by being able to freely write personal reactions to issues and concerns.

Observations of a space can accomplish many objectives. One of the most enlightening aspects of field observations is to gain an understanding of how people function in a space. People can respond to items on a survey or questions during an interview. However, it is very difficult for people to describe *how* they function in a space. Observations enable an interior designer to study and record movements, activities, and problems. By observing people functioning in a space, a designer can determine which aspects of the built environment are effective and can identify any problematic features. Table 10.3 is an example of an observational form that can be used to record activities and details related to sustainability. An interior designer should complete the form while conducting observations. An important element of observations is dedicating adequate time to the activity. Activities performed in a space can vary by the time of day, week, and season. Moreover, the number of people in the space affects activities. Thus, to attain a true assessment of a space requires observations at various times of the day and week, with different quantities of people. Since daylighting and views are important elements of sustainable interiors, observations should be performed at the various times of the sun's path. Recordings should include problems from the glare of sunlight and areas without daylight. Views should be analyzed to determine desirable attributes and any problems from surrounding structures or surfaces, such as glare from adjacent windows.

Other sustainable issues that can be observed are energy consumption patterns, such as thermostat settings, lighting habits, and effectiveness of controls.

Table 10.1
LEED-CI (2005) Site Selection Credit Categories

SS1 Site Selection
Select LEED Certified Building
Brownfield Redevelopment
Stormwater Management: Rate and Quantity
Stormwater Management: Treatment
Heat Island Reduction: Non-Roof
Heat Island Reduction: Roof
Light Pollution Reduction
Water Efficient Irrigation: Reduced Potable Water
　Consumption
Water Efficient Irrigation: No Potable Use or No Irrigation
Innovative Wastewater Technologies
Water Use Reduction: 20% Reduction
Onsite Renewable Energy
Other Quantifiable Environmental Performance

Table 10.2

Examples of Items for Interview Guides or Focus Groups

Name: Location:

Health Concerns Related to Indoor Environmental Quality (allergies, asthma, headaches, eye irritation, sinus congestion, chemical sensitivities, etc.):

PART I: Overall Knowledge of Sustainable Development and Design

Describe your understanding of sustainable interiors.

Describe your understanding of global environmental concerns.

Describe your perceptions of engaging in sustainable practice.

PART II: Neighborhood Characteristics

Identify amenities of a neighborhood that are important to you.

What is your preferred means to get to the building (drive, walk, public transportation, bike)?

Describe your use of public transportation.

What are your impressions of the neighborhood surrounding the building?

PART III: Use of Water, Energy, Materials, and Resources

Describe approaches to conserving water.

What are your perceptions regarding water-conservation practices in this building?

Describe approaches to conserving electricity.

What are your perceptions regarding energy-conservation practices in this building?

What are your perceptions regarding energy used for lighting in this building?

Describe approaches to reducing consumption of materials and resources.

What are your perceptions regarding material conservation practices in this building?

Do you recycle?

   If yes, please explain further.

      What do you recycle?

      Where do you recycle?

      Are the recycling containers in a convenient location? If no, why?

Describe your understanding of recycled content.

Describe your understanding of rapidly renewable materials.

PART IV: Perceptions of Indoor Environmental Quality

Describe your understanding of indoor air pollution.

What are your perceptions of the quality of the air in this building?

Identify any problems associated with tobacco smoke in or around this building.

Identify any outdoor pollutants that affect the interior of this building.

Do you perceive any allergic reactions from materials or spaces in this building?

Is the temperature comfortable? If no, what is the problem with the temperature?

Do you have control over the temperature in your space?

Is the humidity comfortable? If no, what is the problem with the humidity?

Do you have adequate ventilation?

Do you have adequate fresh air?

Is your lighting effective for the tasks you must perform? If not, explain your concerns about your lighting.

Do you have control of your lighting?

Identify any problems with noise in the building.

PART V: Anticipated Changes in the Future

1. Anticipated changes in occupants.
2. Anticipated changes in space needs.
3. Anticipated changes in activities/tasks.

Supplemental Items for Commercial Projects

Business-Related Data

   Purpose of the business/organization.

   Mission/goals/objectives of the business/organization.

   Image of the business/organization.

   Building owned or leased.

   Elements contributing to profits and ROI (return on investment).

   Energy and environmental conservation policies and practices.

   Current societal events affecting the business/organization.

   Current involvement with the community.

   Demographic profile of employees (gender, ages, ethnic and cultural backgrounds).

   Absentee records:

      Operation and maintenance manual?

      Operation and maintenance educational sessions?

      Occupant operational manuals?

      Occupant operational educational session?

   Cleaning procedures and products.

SOURCE: Adapted from Winchip, S. (2005), *Designing a Quality Lighting Environment.* New York: Fairchild Publications.

Table 10.3
Commercial Observation Form to Record Activities and Details Related to Sustainability

Project:	Location:
Observation Date: Observation Start Time:	Observation Finish Time:

Describe people in the space (number of people, employee, customer, approximate ages, special needs).	Describe any behavior that suggests undesirable thermal comfort.
Describe activities in the space.	Describe recycling practices of the occupants.
Describe how people interact with the neighborhood.	Describe any behavior that suggests allergic reactions to the materials and/or substances in the building.
Identify areas within the building that are not being used by the occupants.	Describe any behavior that suggests problems from outdoor pollutants.
Identify areas within the building that appear to be preferred by the occupants.	Describe any behavior that suggests problems with glare (sunlight or electrical).
Describe any practices that contribute to water being wasted.	Describe any behavior that suggests people are unable to see views to the outdoors.
Describe any practices that contribute to energy being wasted.	Describe any behavior that suggests problems with noise.
Describe any behavior that suggests the lighting system is not effective.	Describe any behavior that suggests undesirable airflow.
	Describe any other behavior related to sustainability.

SOURCE: Adapted from Winchip, S. (2005), *Designing a Quality Lighting Environment*. New York: Fairchild Publications.

Problems associated with the IEQ should be recorded. This can include musty smells, ventilation effectiveness, tobacco smoke, outdoor pollutants, and any scents from materials emitting VOCs. It should be noted whether people are sneezing, coughing, or have watery eyes. This can be an indication of problems with the IAQ. This is especially disconcerting when there are many people in one area that have these health problems. Particular attention should be given to observing recycling habits. Are people using the receptacles? What is being recycled? Safety problems should be recorded, such as areas where people frequently fall or slip.

Observations can also provide important details regarding the features of the built environment. Photographs of the site are very helpful in the schematic and design development phases. Sketches with sustainability features can be done of the plan, elevations, and ceiling. Coding via symbols can identify problems associated with sustainable interiors (see Figure 10.2). For example, an *energy* symbol could be used next to leaky windows. A *water* symbol could be drawn next to faulty plumbing or an *IAQ* symbol could be drawn where mold exists. An assessment and inventory must be conducted of finishes, furnishings, and equipment. As illustrated in Table 10.4,

information that should be recorded includes the condition of materials, products likely to have VOC content, and refurbishment suggestions.

Project Analysis and Charrettes

After collecting all of the information from the various methods, an analysis of the data must be conducted. The analysis process involves thoroughly reviewing the information collected and then determining what appear to be the most important considerations for the design. The basic process for conducting the analysis involves identifying similar and contrasting responses. The design team uses the consistent responses to inform the development of the initial design of the project. In analyzing the data, it may be necessary to resolve conflicting information. For example, when completing a survey, several people may report a problem with the ventilation. In contrast, data from observations may indicate that the building's ventilation is acceptable. In these circumstances it is important to conduct follow-up activities to determine the reasons for the discrepancies. In performing follow-up interviews and/or observations it may be discovered that the ventilation problem exists in only one area of a building.

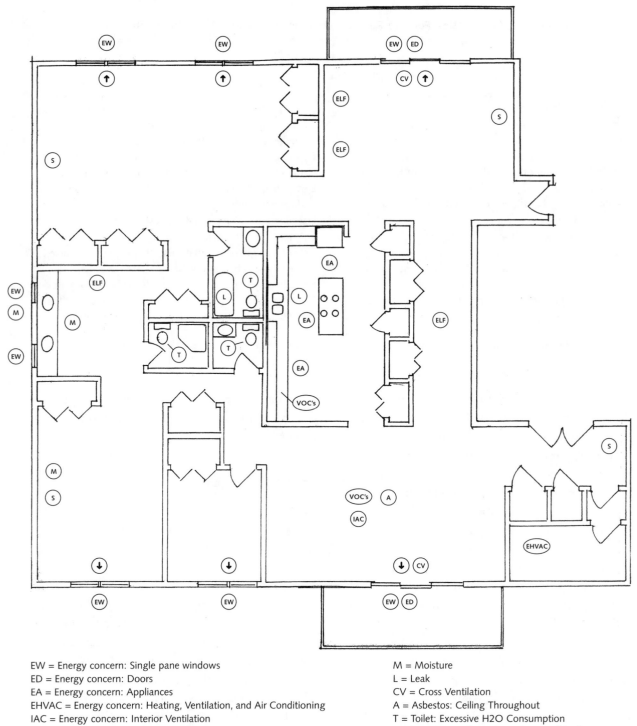

EW = Energy concern: Single pane windows
ED = Energy concern: Doors
EA = Energy concern: Appliances
EHVAC = Energy concern: Heating, Ventilation, and Air Conditioning
IAC = Energy concern: Interior Ventilation
ELF = Energy concern: Light Fixtures
➜ = Energy concern: Exterior View

M = Moisture
L = Leak
CV = Cross Ventilation
A = Asbestos: Ceiling Throughout
T = Toilet: Excessive H2O Consumption
VOC's = Carpet fibers throughout and kitchen counter
S = Sustainable Feature: Plaster Walls

Fig. 10.2. Plan view of coding that can be used to identify problems associated with sustainable interiors.

Table 10.4
Site and Built Environment Assessment

Client:	Location:				
		Existing		Not Existing	
Categories	Description of Existing Condition	Recommendations for Improvements	N/A	Implementation Feasibility	Implementation Concerns
MANAGEMENT					
Educational sessions for operations and maintenance					
Operations and maintenance manuals					
Occupant guides					
Preventative maintenance plan					
Building commissioning plan					
NEIGHBORHOOD					
Walking distance to public transportation					
Walking distance to amenities (grocery, dry cleaners, post office, etc.)					
Walking distance to restaurants					
Walking distance to public outdoor areas (parks, waterfront, bike paths, etc.)					
Feasibility of biking to and from building					
Neighborhood density (high, medium, low)					
Accessibility of public parking					
Potential glare problems from surrounding buildings					
Potential light trespass from surrounding light sources					
Potential hazardous air emissions					
SITE SELECTION					
Existing greenfields (prime farmland, park, forestry, etc.)					
Flood zone					
Existing natural habitats					
Other natural resources to be protected					
Existing vegetation					
Shading trees					
Irrigation system					
Rainwater harvesting					
Brownfield site					
Features affecting stormwater management (location of gutters, overhangs, etc.)					
Surfaces affecting stormwater management (parking lots, driveways, etc.)					
Features affecting stormwater management during construction					
Surfaces affecting heat island (parking lots, driveways, etc.)					
Roof contributing to heat island					
Exterior lighting contributing to light pollution					
BUILDING SELECTION					
Certified building					
Orientation					
Reasonable footprint					

(continued)

Table 10.4 (continued)

Categories	Existing			Not Existing	
	Description of Existing Condition	Recommendations for Improvements	N/A	Implementation Feasibility	Implementation Concerns
Ability to design flexible spaces					
Feasibility of sharing facilities					
Historical building					
Important exterior features to retain					
Important interior features to retain					
Area for bike storage					
Accessible bike storage area					
Area for shower facilities for bikers					
Feasibility of green roof					
WATER USAGE ASSESSMENT					
Low-water-capacity toilets					
Low-water-capacity dishwashers					
Low-volume faucets					
Low-volume shower					
Dry urinals					
Leaky faucets					
Other water leaks					
Condensation on pipes					
Front- or top-loading clothes washer					
Submetering					
Water-recovery methods					
ENERGY AND ATMOSPHERE					
Energy efficiency of windows					
Energy efficiency of doors					
Adequacy of caulking					
Seal of cracks and joints					
ENERGY STAR–rated appliances					
Energy efficiency of window treatments					
Thermostat settings					
Location of thermostats					
Renewable energy use (solar, wind, water, geothermal, etc.)					
Equipment with CFCs					
Submetering					
Energy-efficient lamps					
Energy-efficient wattages					
Energy-efficient luminaires					
Motion sensors					
Photosensor controls					
Time controls					
Energy management system					
Dimmers					
Multiple switching plans					
Daylighting integrated with electrical lighting sources					
Adequacy of commissioning					
MATERIALS AND RESOURCES					
Recycling containers					
Recycling containers with separate waste units					

Table 10.4 (continued)

Categories	Existing			Not Existing	
	Description of Existing Condition	Recommendations for Improvements	N/A	Implementation Feasibility	Implementation Concerns
Centralized recycling facilities					
Waste amount (light, medium, heavy)					
Architectural elements to retain					
Wall finishes					
Ceiling treatment					
Flooring					
Casework and trim					
Built-in cabinetry					
Interior doors					
Exterior doors					
Furniture					
Window treatments					
Items to be salvaged					
Demolition items for recycling					
Demolition items for return to manufacturer					
Demolition items for charity					
Areas for reducing square footage usage					
INDOOR ENVIRONMENTAL QUALITY					
Walk-off grilles at entries					
Sources of contaminants					
Outdoor pollutant sources					
Location of smoking areas/rooms					
CO_2 sensors					
Asbestos					
Radon					
New carpet scent					
Cleaning equipment					
Cleaning products					
Natural ventilation					
Mechanical ventilation					
Exhaust ventilation					
Location of outside air intakes					
Signs of mold or mildew					
Signs of dust					
Rooms or areas with chemicals (copy rooms, chemical storage, etc.)					
Programmable controls for HVAC system					
Programmable controls for lighting system					
Surface colors next to windows, skylights					
Surface finishes next to windows, skylights					
Recess depths of windows, skylights					
Occupant control of temperature					
Occupant control of ventilation					
Luminaires and lamps					
Lighting controls					
Occupant control of lighting					
Occupant(s) exposure to daylighting					
Occupant(s) view to the outdoors					
Glare from sunlight					
Controls for sunlight					

(continued)

Table 10.4 (continued)

Categories	Existing			Not Existing	
	Description of Existing Condition	Recommendations for Improvements	N/A	Implementation Feasibility	Implementation Concerns
Skylights					
Roof windows					
Sidelighting					
Glare from sunlight on tasks					
Glare from electrical light sources on tasks					
Noise levels					
Waste storage during construction					

Thus, maintenance must work on correcting the problem in that particular zone, rather than assuming that perhaps the entire system needs to be repaired or replaced. Acquiring information from a variety of sources helps tremendously in verifying conditions and requirements. Therefore, the comprehensive programming process is critical to successful sustainable interiors. After completing an analysis of the information, a summary report with supporting documentation should be given to the design team for review.

The emerging and ever-changing field of sustainable development requires a design team to locate current codes, regulations, standards, and certification requirements for every project. Policies and requirements change on an annual basis. For example, there have been several versions of building assessment programs. If a client would like to achieve LEED certification, as of 2006, the design team would need to use the *LEED Green Building Rating System Version 2.0*. Significant problems could occur when a project is planned using the wrong version. Compliance issues for a client may also involve international standards. Thus, researching regulations may require locating standards from organizations outside of the United States.

Nearly every day new sustainable products and materials are introduced. This is tremendous for designing sustainable interiors, but these continuous improvements require interior designers to constantly keep abreast of new finishes and furnishings. Countless national and international resources are available online. Sustainable products and new practices are posted online. There are several free "green" newsletters available online. Computers provide an easy and accessible source of information. However, the vast amount of information can be overwhelming and discouraging. An item looked up on Google that results in hundreds of sites can appear far too difficult to review and excessively time consuming. Key to sorting through all of the sites is to rely on credible organizations. Generally, government-sponsored agencies and research-oriented organizations provide reliable information. Thus, in reviewing a website it is critical to read the information that describes the organization and its background. In addition to using the Internet, information may be available from books, journal articles, and professional organizations. (See a list of resources in Appendix C.) Case studies of certified buildings can be an excellent source for understanding elements that are important for the design, financing, construction, and evaluation. Researching multiple sources helps to identify consistent solutions, which is an indication of reliability.

The information derived from the data collection and analysis processes is an excellent source of data for conducting a charrette. A team can determine the desired outcome of a charrette; however, for the purpose of the design process, a suggestion is to develop a document that serves as the basis for the architectural program. As described in Chapter 4, the charrette is a method to gather information from a variety of stakeholders. Thus, individuals involved with the charrette should include the design team and any other individuals who have a stake in the project, including legal and financial representatives. Firms designing sustainable buildings have been utilizing charrettes, because the process helps to facilitate the complicated task of integrating suggestions from several people who represent multiple disciplines. As described throughout the text, sustainable designs require the involvement of all the stakeholders. A charrette provides the structure for collaborative activities. An extremely important element of a charrette is dedicating several consecutive days for the process. According to the National Charrette Institute (NCI), to conduct a charrette requires four to seven days. This concentrated and committed time provides the framework needed to involve all the stakeholders, analyze the data, and develop guidelines for the architectural program.

The location of the charrette should be on or near the site of the project. This location enables the participants to experience the space. A location near the site allows people to visit when necessary. Locating the charrette at the site also improves the attendance of community representatives, and participants acquire a sense of the community. The structure of the charrette is a series of meetings that involves the participation of the stakeholders. Concepts of the project are presented and reviewed, which ultimately results in a document that summarizes the scope of the project. For sustainable design projects, the concepts should be analyzed within the context of people, the environment, and economics. For example, if a team is examining the attributes of a specific building, the analysis should explore the impact of the building on its users, people in the immediate community, the natural habitat, and the client's financial resources. With the assistance of the financial representative, the team should be able to develop an estimated budget for the project.

The charrette is also an opportune time to examine to what extent the project meets the criteria for certification. Characteristics of each option can be cross-referenced with each category in a building assessment program. As a result of this analysis, the client should have an initial profile of the credits the building can receive and the applicable rating level. The client will also have an idea what must be done to achieve specific credits and the associated estimated costs. In following LEED-CI requirements, this stage of the design process is an excellent time to develop the commissioning plan. The LEED-CI program outlines the specific required components of the commissioning plan, such as the identification of the commissioning team and a list of the systems that are involved with the process.

The NCI recommends that from the onset of the process, participants should agree to a schedule of progressive outcomes. A regimented schedule of outcomes helps to ensure progress and recommendations for the project at the conclusion of the charrette. The document produced by the team is then used for the schematic phase of the design process. The collaborative nature of the charrette process helps to develop a shared vision of the project. This helps tremendously in gaining acceptance from the community for sustainability and assists with educating many individuals regarding the benefits of sustainable developments. Before proceeding to the schematic design phase, the client should review the results of the programming phase. Based on the client's reaction, more data might have to be collected by the team. The client should approve the outcomes of each phase of the design process. The next chapter continues the review of the phases of the design process by examining schematic design and design development.

Summary

- To design sustainable interiors requires an understanding of additional managerial responsibilities associated with sustainable buildings.
- Management is responsible for ensuring that the sustainable attributes of the built environment are properly implemented, operate effectively, and are well maintained.
- One of the most important requirements is commissioning. Personnel must be assigned to monitor commissioning.
- Team members can include the client, architect, engineers, interior designer, users, maintenance specialists, commissioning provider, material suppliers, community representatives, and perhaps the contractor. When seeking LEED certification, at least one member should be an accredited professional.
- The collaborative nature of a sustainable project necessitates identifying team members who are cooperative, have similar work ethics, and are receptive to exploring new concepts and ideas.
- The client must be willing to dedicate the time, energy, and resources required for sustainable buildings.

- The goals and objectives should encompass the most salient elements required to select the ideal site and to design, construct, operate, maintain, and evaluate the project.
- At the pre-design stage, the design team should establish policies and procedures for facilitating communication and decision making.
- Based on the goals and objectives of the project, a comprehensive programming plan should be developed by the design team. Integrating a building with the environment and the community is one of the unique features of sustainability.
- The programming process has two basic phases: gathering relevant information and then analyzing the data collected.
- A variety of techniques can be used to collect information in the pre-design phase. Information can be acquired through interviews, focus groups, surveys, observations, and charrettes.
- The analysis process involves thoroughly reviewing the information collected and then determining what appear to be the most important considerations for the design.
- The information derived from the data collection and analysis processes is an excellent source of data for conducting a charrette.
- The NCI recommends that from the onset of the process, participants should agree to a schedule of progressive outcomes.

Key Term

Focus groups

Exercises

1. To design sustainable interiors requires an understanding of additional managerial responsibilities associated with sustainable buildings. Analyze a client's commercial building and determine managerial responsibilities associated with sustainability. The requirements should include procedures, anticipated costs to a client, and commissioning specifications.

2. Comprehensive planning in the pre-design phase is absolutely essential for sustainable buildings. Develop a list of activities that should be completed during the comprehensive planning stage. The description of activities should include individuals, anticipated timeline, and resources. Summarize the comprehensive plan in a written report. Compare and contrast your plan with those of other students in the class.

3. The design team should develop a comprehensive programming plan. Identify elements of programming that are important for sustainable interiors. Recommendations should include integrating a building with the environment and the community. Summarize the comprehensive programming plan in a written report. Compare and contrast your plan with those of other students in the class.

4. Develop a plan for a project's charrette. The plan should include the structure for collaborative activities, including the location, stakeholders, agendas, and anticipated outcomes. Discuss the structure of a charrette with other students in the classroom. Develop a written report that includes a reflective statement of the group discussion.

CHAPTER 11

Sustainable Strategies for Design Process: Design Phases

What moves me so deeply about this sleeping little prince is his loyalty to a flower—

the image of a rose shining within him like the flame within a lamp, even when he's asleep. . . . And I realized he was even more fragile than I had thought.

Lamps must be protected: A gust of wind can blow them out . . .

—ANTOINE DE SAINT-EXUPÉRY

Objectives

- Understand how to develop sketches that illustrate sustainable features of the built environment.
- Identify and describe elements of the lighting system related to sustainability that should be analyzed during brainstorming sessions.
- Identify and describe how to analyze sustainable materials and resources during brainstorming sessions.
- Identify and describe how to analyze important considerations for the indoor environmental quality during brainstorming sessions.
- Understand how to develop sustainability features on the drawings and specifications created in the design development phase of the design process.
- Describe the important sustainability features that should be included in a project manual for a sustainable environment.
- Understand important sustainability elements that should be included in an oral presentation to a client.

CHAPTER 10 INITIATED the design process by reviewing recommendations for pre-design activities. Comprehensive planning and programming were described within the context of sustainable design. The chapter concluded by examining procedures and outcomes of a charrette. A recommendation is for the outcome to be a document that serves as the basis for the architectural program. The purpose of this chapter is to demonstrate how the results of the charrette can be used to develop initial and final design solutions. Some firms are using building information modeling (BIM) software to assist with the design, construction, delivery, operations, and management of a building. Autodesk Revit, ArchiCAD, and Bentley Systems are examples of platforms that can support BIM software. (See the manufacturers' websites for further information.)

Initial design solutions are explored in the schematic design phase. The design team explores a variety of solutions for the project. Upon approval from the client, the team then proceeds to the design development phase. At this stage, final details of the project are determined and incorporated into the working drawings and specifications. Upon approval from the client, these documents can be distributed for bids. As with the preceding phases of the design process outlined in Chapter 10, this chapter examines the schematic and design development phases within the context of sustainability. The intent is to review the sustainable concepts that are important to consider while engaged in these phases. In working on a project, these elements are integrated with all of the other important components of the built environment. To ensure a comprehensive approach to sustainability, an effective approach is to explicitly dedicate time and attention to the project's sustainable solutions.

SCHEMATIC DESIGNS AND SUSTAINABILITY

The schematic design phase is the most creative stage of a project. Individuals responsible for developing the design, such as the architect, interior designers, and accredited professionals, conduct multiple brainstorming sessions. Primary topics discussed are spatial strategies and attributes of products. At each session the team members explore various ideas by discussing and sketching possibilities until the team has consensus on the best design. All members of the team should be encouraged to participate, and everyone's ideas should be respected and considered as a possible solution. For sustainable projects, an effective approach to organizing the process is to structure the brainstorming sessions according to the credit categories of building assessment programs. Thus, to demonstrate how the schematic design phase can be conducted for sustainable projects, the following explanations use the credit categories of LEED-CI (2005). For projects that are seeking LEED certification, this phase of the design process is a good time to register the project.

The purpose of the brainstorming sessions is to explore all possible solutions for the project. The results of the programming phase serve as the basis for developing ideas. The team should use an existing floor plan or develop a preliminary plan for new construction projects. Preliminary site plans, elevations, sections, and ceiling plans should also be used for the sessions. Tracing paper is a useful material that can be used as an overlay. Every sheet should be saved, and new designs should start with a clean overlay. This practice saves time and enables the team to easily return to previous thoughts. Notes that describe the rationale for a solution and any remarks related to the design should accompany the sketches. Notes and subsequent discussions should include how various solutions impact people, the environment, and economics. Another useful aspect of sketches is the ability to relate a solution to other elements of the design. For example, when designing options for the smoking room, potential solutions must be reviewed within the context of other aspects of the design. Thus, a significant problem can occur if what appears to be a good location in the building for the smoking room results in polluting an adjacent outdoor courtyard.

In working on the schematic designs, the team develops and discusses numerous options, including any potential growth requirements. A matrix can be a useful tool for assembling ideas and evaluating the appropriateness of the solution. Table 11.1 illustrates an example of a matrix that could be used to evaluate proposed solutions. An important element of the

Table 11.1

Matrix of Lighting Criteria and Proposed Solutions

	Lighting Option Manufacturer A	Lighting Option Manufacturer B	Lighting Option Manufacturer C	Lighting Option Manufacturer D
Sustainability Criteria Durable				
Sustainability Criteria Rapidly renewable material				
Sustainability Criteria Biodegradable				
Sustainability Criteria Regional source				
Total +				
Total −				

NOTES:

1. Identify lighting criteria and several illumination options. You may list as many as possible.
2. Every member in a team should evaluate how well each illumination solution accommodates the lighting criteria. Provide a rating using the following scale:

+++	Strong relationship
++	Moderate relationship
+	Weak relationship
−	Weak nonrelationship
− −	Moderate nonrelationship
− − −	Strong nonrelationship

3. Total the number of +'s and −'s for all team members.
4. The best illumination options will have the greatest number of +'s.

SOURCE: Adapted from Winchip, S. (2005), *Designing a Quality Lighting Environment.* New York: Fairchild Publications.

matrix is developing well-conceived criteria. Various solutions are evaluated against each criterion. Thus, to attain a valid assessment of each proposed concept requires appropriate criteria. The criteria should reflect best sustainable practices, and the team should agree with the criteria that are included in the matrix. As shown in Table 11.1, the criteria can be listed in the rows and proposed design solutions in the columns. Each member of the team can review the matrix and assess how well each solution addresses each criterion. A summation of all the results is then tabulated. The solutions that address the most criteria can serve as a basis for developing the initial designs.

The holistic aspects of sustainability are evident in the importance of designing the built environment in response to the area surrounding the building and its site. The surrounding environment affects the solutions that are needed to design a sustainable building. Therefore, whenever possible, selection of the site and the design concepts for the built environment should be explored simultaneously. To have a building that has exemplary sustainability properties requires selecting a site that can maximize the sustainability of the structure, and vice versa. The site and the building are an interdependent system that must be planned together. The schematic phase is the ideal stage for creating the integration between a community, the site, and the built environment.

Schematic activities related to sustainability focus on spatial strategies and attributes of products within the context of the credit categories. This can be accomplished by drawing sketches that illustrate solutions and/or brainstorming the ideal finishes, furnishings, and equipment. To commence the schematic phase, a good starting point is to review the various sites and their surrounding areas, which were studied in the programming stage. A site plan, local map, public transit maps, and photos/videos of the neighborhood are needed to develop schematic designs. The site plan provides the building's footprint, orientation, attributes of landscape features, and a view of the relationship between the building and its surrounding area. The local map helps to identify the location of public transportation stations and the location of other amenities that can be important to employees and customers. Since a sustainable building encourages walking, the team should calculate the distances between the potential sites and needed services, such as train stations, post offices, grocery stores, and dry cleaners. A map and accompanying photographs can help to gauge development density and location of parking lots. The local map can also indicate the location of any bike paths and/or community bike facilities.

The public transit map assists the team in identifying a site's relationship to bus and/or train stops. Photographs/videos help the schematic process in a variety of ways: (1) to gain an insight of the neighborhood's culture; (2) to distinguish the location of any natural habitats; (3) to identify any surrounding reflective materials of adjacent buildings, which could create glare in a proposed building; and (4) to locate sources of potential problems with stormwater and surfaces that contribute to urban heat. Photographs taken during the evening can illustrate sources of light pollution and light trespass. Photographs can also help the design team to study the facade of the potential building. The team can identify architectural features and materials that should be retained and the style of windows.

Sketches for Sustainable Environments

The site plan is an excellent tool for determining the best way for a building to interact with its surroundings. Sketches can be drawn to explore how the interior can be designed to accommodate the elements that surround the building. The design team could sketch various interior solutions that address the needs of the users at each entrance of the building. For example, entrances of the building that are the closest to train stations could have services and accommodations for commuters. Entries adjacent to bike paths should have facilities for bike storage and showers. Sketches of the site could also be used to integrate interior space with a roof garden. Ideally, people should have access to the outdoor space. The

team could develop sketches to explore various ways people could access the roof garden. In addition, schematics could review how space adjacent to a roof garden could have a view of the vegetation.

Site sketches could also identify characteristics of the surrounding area that impact the design of the interior. Items that are important to record are the sources of light trespass, reflective surfaces, desirable views, and walkable amenities close to the building. These sketches should be referred to when developing interior layouts. For example, areas impacted by light trespass could be planned for people who only work in the space during the day. To encourage people to walk to services in the neighborhood, the interior plan could include an attractive entrance that links the building to the sidewalk. This should also be done with any pleasant outdoor space, such as a lakefront or a park.

The site and/or building selection stage is the ideal time to strategize space. Planning the space for an existing building or new construction must always focus on reducing square footage needs. The first strategy is to reduce the size of the building's footprint by strategizing spatial arrangements. Reducing the square footage needed for each activity, room, area, and structure results in less energy consumption. Consuming less energy reduces the multiple environmental impacts associated with producing energy, including greenhouse gas emissions. Reducing the building's footprint has a ripple effect on all the other needs for a building, such as structural components, HVAC & Refrigeration requirements, flooring, wall finishes, ceiling surfaces, lighting, and furniture. Reducing spatial requirements should be implemented on existing buildings and new construction. The task is easier to accomplish with new construction; however, spatial strategies can be performed with existing buildings by creatively considering new uses for unused space. When a client is the sole occupant of a building, unused space could be leased to other businesses or organizations. As a considerate gesture to the community, unused space could be available to local nonprofit organizations at no cost. When these options are not possibilities, a client may want to consider blocking off unused areas by closing doors and recalibrating the HVAC system to accommodate nonuse.

To ensure the most efficient use of space, an

important task in the schematic design phase is to *constantly* calculate the square footage. Square footages should be calculated with every scheme and within each area of a building. For example, if a design team creates five different plans of a building, each of the five sketches should be accompanied by square footage estimates for each activity, area, circulation space, storage, and overall dimensions. Special notes should be recorded for multipurpose spaces. It is important to acknowledge that using space for multiple purposes can reduce the square footage required for the building. When a client is relocating to another existing building, efficient spatial strategies can reduce the rent, the cost of utilities, and the impact on the environment.

Brainstorming sessions for strategizing water efficiencies should focus on products and spatial strategies for minimizing plumbing lines. The team should review several products that conserve water, such as low-flow fixtures and occupant sensors. By studying manufacturers' specifications, the team could determine the best water-efficient fixtures and controls for the project. Products ultimately specified should reduce water consumption and wastewater. The team could also explore graywater possibilities and how the interior layout could accommodate the technology. To reduce plumbing lines, the interior plan should consolidate spaces that are used in the graywater system. Reducing the length of plumbing lines is especially important for hot water. Locating hot-water heaters close to where the supply is needed conserves energy. Sketches are excellent tools for examining how an interior designer can reduce the length of plumbing lines by planning efficient spatial strategies.

There are many ways the work of an interior designer can contribute to the energy and atmosphere performance of a building. The first strategy is to reduce the size of the building's footprint. As explained earlier in this chapter, reducing the square footage results in less energy consumption and lessens the impacts on the environment. The size of a space is a significant factor in the specifications of HVAC systems. Efficient spaces use less energy to operate the HVAC systems and lighting. Thus, an interior designer has a critical responsibility in conserving energy by designing efficient spaces that accommodate multiple purposes whenever possible.

Sustainability Sketches: Lighting Systems

In addition to designing efficient interiors, the work of an interior designer can optimize energy performance by designing quality lighting systems. Within the LEED-CI *Energy and Atmosphere (EA)* category, several credits are associated with lighting. The *EA 1.1* and *1.2* credits focus directly on optimizing energy performance via lighting power and controls. Indirectly, lighting affects the outcome of other EA categories, such as meeting "minimum energy performance" and commissioning requirements. Thus, at the schematic phase of the design process, the design team should examine various approaches to develop quality lighting throughout the building. The team should also brainstorm the ideal products for the lighting system.

For existing buildings, luminaires in each space should be evaluated to determine their efficiency and functional success. In brainstorming the lighting plan, the design team should closely examine luminaires that are inefficient and do not fulfill the intended purpose. Before eliminating and replacing luminaires, the team should explore approaches that can enhance the performance of the lighting system. For example, an existing luminaire might be able to be retrofitted to accommodate more efficient lamps. A simple solution might be to simply clean the luminaire and its lamps. A luminaire that does not appear to fulfill the functional needs of its users might be installed in the wrong location or perhaps might need a different diffuser. From a sustainability perspective, alternative solutions should always be explored prior to removing the fixture and delivering it to the landfill. Luminaires that are no longer needed could remain in place, but inoperable, or the fixtures could be donated to a local organization. Donating items that are in good condition to a charitable organization is a preferable solution to being landfilled.

The team should draw sketches to explore new strategies for a revised or new lighting plan. To conserve energy and resources, the plan should fulfill the needs of the users of the space by using an appropriate number of fixtures. The number of fixtures can be reduced when light is aimed in the optimum direction and has the appropriate illumination level. A lighting plan that is designed in a grid pattern with the same luminaire and lamps throughout the space can waste energy and resources. *Quality* lighting must replace *quantity* illumination. Each activity area of a room should be evaluated to determine the optimum lighting solution. Lighting solutions must be activity based. For example, circulation areas do not require the same level of illumination as someone working at a desk.

Designing specific lighting solutions for each activity and space becomes very important when integrating daylighting with electrical sources. During the day, perimeter areas next to windows require less illumination from electrical sources. However, variations can occur next to windows when an adjacent building is close enough to shield sunlight. Trees located close to the windows can also reduce the amount of daylight entering the space. Using appropriate photosensors can accommodate the variations that occur from outdoor elements. Skylights are also a source of daylighting that can help to reduce the energy required for electrical sources. To examine the relationship between various light sources, the design team can develop sketches that diagram the various lighting zones. A visual representation of how light is distributed in the interior can help a designer to identify areas that have duplicative sources, such as when daylight and electrical lights combine to create light levels that waste energy. Sketches can also be useful in determining the relationship between the location of luminaires, furniture, wall partitions, and activities.

The team can brainstorm a variety of ways to provide the most effective and efficient lighting. The goal should be to minimize the interior lighting power while maintaining a lighting plan that meets the needs of the users. Chapter 6 reviewed various equations specified by the LEED-CI for determining interior lighting power allowances. In developing various lighting solutions, the design team should refer to these equations and perform calculations for each plan. Computer simulation models can help perform space-by-space lighting power calculations. Solutions should explore identifying luminaires that are more efficient by distributing illumination on a task, specifying energy-efficient lamps, and carefully determining appropriate lighting controls.

Controls are critically important for energy-efficient solutions. The technologies of controls have improved dramatically in the last several years. An important advancement is enabling the users of the space to control their own lighting. This can conserve energy, and individual controls enable the users to create the optimum lighting for their needs. For the work of an interior designer, these improvements translate to dedicating more time and thought to selecting optimum controls, which are installed in the most appropriate locations, including convenient locations for individual controls.

The design team should carefully review the various controls and how they operate, and then brainstorm optimum locations. In addition to plan views, sketches should be done that illustrate the location of control mechanisms in the vertical plane. For example, occupancy sensors must be located in a position that enables the technology to identify a person or movement. Thus, an elevation or a perspective drawing can help to identify any obstructions in the space that would prevent the sensor from recognizing occupancy. The design team should explore the possibility of using programmable controls that automatically conserve energy based on predetermined schedules. A vertical analysis of the interior also helps to understand how daylighting is affecting the lighting plan and the environment that is adjacent to the windows.

The design team should dedicate considerable time and thought to a review of the various components of a lighting system and then develop recommendations that are energy-efficient, fulfill functional needs, and are cost-effective. Industry research is constantly focused on improvements in lighting systems. Thus, each element of a system should be reviewed to determine optimum solutions. Specifications from several manufacturers should be compared and contrasted. Photometric data from luminaire manufacturers are especially relevant for exploring how light will be distributed and determining specific quantities of light within the illuminated areas. Lamps should be selected that maximize the efficiency of the luminaire and minimize the overall energy consumption of the built environment.

Sustainability Sketches: Materials and Resources

In the schematic design phase, the design team has many areas to explore in LEED-CI's *Materials and Re-*

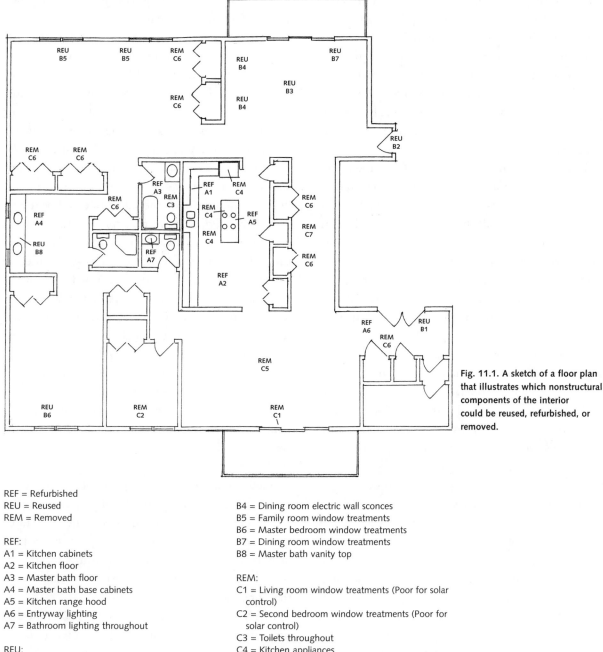

Fig. 11.1. A sketch of a floor plan that illustrates which nonstructural components of the interior could be reused, refurbished, or removed.

REF = Refurbished
REU = Reused
REM = Removed

REF:
A1 = Kitchen cabinets
A2 = Kitchen floor
A3 = Master bath floor
A4 = Master bath base cabinets
A5 = Kitchen range hood
A6 = Entryway lighting
A7 = Bathroom lighting throughout

REU:
B1 = Front door
B2 = Second entrance
B3 = Dining room ceiling fixture
B4 = Dining room electric wall sconces
B5 = Family room window treatments
B6 = Master bedroom window treatments
B7 = Dining room window treatments
B8 = Master bath vanity top

REM:
C1 = Living room window treatments (Poor for solar control)
C2 = Second bedroom window treatments (Poor for solar control)
C3 = Toilets throughout
C4 = Kitchen appliances
C5 = Carpet throughout
C6 = Interior door
C7 = Hallway light fixture

sources category. In exploring various solutions, the design team should focus on reducing, reusing, and recycling materials and resources. Finishes and furnishings should be carefully examined to determine the optimum sustainable solution. Items to consider include flooring, rugs, wall finishes, ceilings, lighting fixtures, interior doors, moldings, built-in case goods, furniture, and decorative pieces. The team could draw sketches of a floor plan that illustrate which nonstructural components of the interior could be reused, refurbished, or removed (see Figure 11.1).

These sustainable strategies should be applied to existing buildings and new construction. For relocations and new construction projects, the design team should analyze the client's current furnishings and then provide the most sustainable recommendations. For example, the design team should examine each furniture piece and determine if the item can be reused. If the piece needs to be updated and/or repaired, the team should provide refurbishment recommendations. When on-site reuse is not possible, the design team should brainstorm which items could come from off-site reuse sources. Many nonstructural building components and furnishings can be acquired from architectural salvage operations, auctions, and antique stores.

In reviewing finishes and furnishings, the design team should identify any items that should be removed for safety reasons or to improve the IAQ. For example, any materials that have been severely damaged by mold most likely will have to be removed. Objects or surfaces that have been painted with lead-based substances must be remediated. Proper disposal procedures must be used for any materials that have toxic substances. When an item, such as a furniture piece, is in good condition but the client does not want to keep the piece, a sustainable approach is to donate the item to a charity. If the client has many items, a possibility is to have an auction of the pieces with the proceeds being donated to a local charity. The schematic design phase is an ideal time to develop reuse solutions that benefit people, the environment, and the client's budget.

When it is necessary to specify new products, one of the most important tasks is to review the LCA of products and the manufacturers' sustainability practices. The design team should focus on recommending products that minimize the impact to the environment during the extraction stage, manufacturing process, transport, use, and post-use. In addition, the manufacturer of the product should be ethically responsible by engaging in practices that reduce the impact to the environment. These are critical considerations when the design team is brainstorming products for the project. Brainstorming sessions should focus on durability features of a product and content composition. Preference should be given to products that have pre-consumer recycled materials and are recyclable. Post-consumer recycled materials are also desirable. The team should show a preference for products that are made with rapidly renewable materials. Products made with wood should have certified wood content. When sustainable characteristics are not possible, the design team

should brainstorm alternatives that cause minimal impact to the environment.

To help visualize solutions, and to ensure that sustainable considerations are afforded to all elements of the interior, an effective strategy is to draw floor plans that are keyed to sustainable features. As illustrated in Figure 11.2, sketches could include a floor plan that is drawn specifically to identify sustainable elements. A combination of symbols, notes, and descriptions in schedules could illustrate sustainable features. All of the sustainable features could be drawn on one plan, or the sketches could be drawn on several overlays. Items that could be marked on a drawing include products and materials that possess these characteristics: (1) on-site or off-site reuse, (2) salvaged on-site or off-site, (3) recycled content, (4) manufactured regionally, (5) rapidly renewable content, and (6) certified wood. These drawings should supplement the conventional set of architectural plans, elevations, and sections. Developing drawings that are specific to sustainability is an excellent approach to demonstrate the importance of the practice. Drawings that include sustainable features also help to demonstrate how the principles of sustainability should be integrated with all the elements of the built environment.

Sketches in the schematic design phase should include strategies for recycling. To emphasize and focus attention on recycling practices, sketches should be drawn that focus only on this purpose. Floor plan overlays could be used to brainstorm the location of collection and storage. When exposed locations for the containers are preferred, the design team may want to explore a design that is attractive and has unity with the other elements of the interior. Based on the purpose of the building and the client's preference, the design team should review variable characteristics of recycling containers, such as the size of units and sorting capabilities. The LEED-CI (2005) has recycling guidelines based on the building's square footage and business type. For example, offices are considered to create light waste and retail establishments generate heavy waste. The design team also has to strategize the ideal location for the storage of recyclables. Interiors should be designed with a specific area for this specific purpose. The location should be convenient for the maintenance staff and

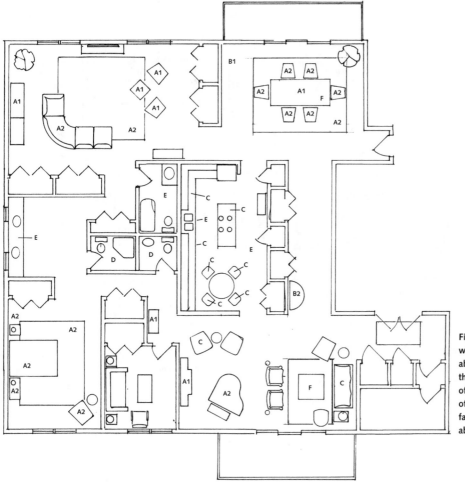

Fig. 11.2. Sketch of a floor plan with the identification of sustainable elements. Items marked on the drawings include on-site or off-site reuse, salvaged on-site or off-site, recycled content, manufactured regionally, rapidly renewable content, and certified wood.

A1 = On-site reuse
A2 = Off-site reuse
B1 = Salvaged on-site
B2 = Salvaged off-site

C = Fabrics/countertops (Recycled content)
D = Manufactured regionally (Floor)
E = Rapidly renewable (Cabinets and floors)
F = Certified wood

easily accessible for central collection purposes. Generally, for central collection and pickup the storage area should be located close to elevators or a loading dock.

Diverting construction waste from landfills is also a sustainable practice. The design team can contribute to this effort by brainstorming locations for construction waste in existing buildings. Thus, sketches could be drawn that illustrate potential sites within the building that could be used to store construction waste (see Figure 11.3). As the construction proceeds, additional plans could illustrate new waste sites. Thus, the design team could develop a strategy that enables the contractor to have space for construction waste through all phases of construction. These plans should also include construction management issues related to IAQ. To enhance IAQ, construction should progress in a manner that prevents contaminants from being absorbed in finish materials, such as gypsum board. The construction waste plans could be integrated with an appropriate schedule for installations. In addition, the sketches should indicate the items and areas that should be protected with plastic, such as HVAC returns.

Sustainability Sketches: Indoor Environmental Quality

There are many considerations within the *Indoor Environmental Quality* category for the work of an interior designer. In the schematic design phase, the design team should brainstorm strategies for enhancing

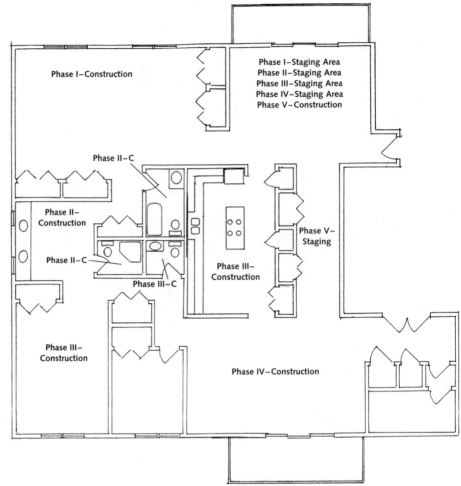

Phase I–Construction

Phase I–Staging Area
Phase II–Staging Area
Phase III–Staging Area
Phase IV–Staging Area
Phase V–Construction

Phase II–C

Phase II–Construction

Phase II–C

Phase III–C

Phase V–Staging

Phase III–Construction

Phase III–Construction

Phase IV–Construction

Fig. 11.3. A sketch of a floor plan illustrates potential sites within the building that could be used to store construction waste.

ventilation, specifying low-emitting materials, reducing indoor chemical sources, and providing for personal controls, daylighting, and views. The team should develop several sketches that demonstrate the airflow through a building. Chapter 6 provides examples of drawings with airflow patterns. To study airflow patterns throughout a building, the team should draw plan views and sections. Any interior elements that restrict airflow should be identified, and the team should brainstorm effective solutions. The design team should also study the plan views and elevations to ensure that occupants can see the alarm system for ventilation systems.

Natural ventilation is critical to a healthy environment. The design team should explore various operable windows and determine locations that enhance cross-ventilation. In analyzing the cross-ventilation paths, partitions may need openings and/or transoms. Airflow sketches of natural ventilation should also include window openings that are exposed to

pollution and/or excessive noise. Knowing this information, the design team might be able to strategize the space plan by locating rooms used by people away from these openings. Window treatments should not restrict airflow. To maximize the flow of natural ventilation, the team might want to explore using louvered window treatments.

To ensure that outdoor pollutants are not entering the HVAC system, the team could also examine the location of air intakes. The site plan and exterior photographs could help in identifying the source of any problems, such as outdoor smoking areas. The design team might have to plan space for an indoor smoking area. A smoking room must be carefully planned to avoid the infiltration of tobacco smoke to other rooms in the building. The team can strategize a location that is removed from areas that are typically used by many people. The smoking room should not be located close to rooms with children. The design team can be involved with recommending a door to the room that is tightly sealed. The LEED-CI (2005) recommends using weather stripping to minimize air leakage.

The design team must brainstorm various approaches to specify low-emitting materials. As identified in many discussions throughout the text, materials that can emit contaminants are adhesives, sealants, paint, coatings, carpet systems, composite wood, laminate adhesives, furniture, and seating. In exploring various options for the finishes, the design team can identify alternative materials for the interior. For example, to eliminate IAQ problems associated with carpet systems, the design team may explore other flooring materials, such as wood or linoleum. In reviewing various products for finishes, the design team must carefully study manufacturers' literature. The products recommended by the team must be accompanied by explicit specification requirements. (Chapter 12 has information for writing sustainability bids and product specifications.)

To reduce indoor chemical sources, the design team should determine the most effective means to collect contaminants that can enter a building on the shoes of people. There are many ways to collect particles at the entryway. Thus, the team can design a system that blends with the design of the entry. The team should also strategize the location of equipment that can emit chemicals, such as copy machines. Frequently, a copy machine is placed in a hallway without consideration of its emissions. To improve the IAQ, any equipment that emits toxins should be in a room with excellent ventilation. Furthermore, any room that requires the use of indoor chemicals should be located away from where people work. Spatial strategies developed by the design team can help to reduce the users' exposure to contaminants and chemicals.

The IEQ also involves designing interiors that enable individuals to control their lighting, ventilation, and thermal comfort needs. To contribute to creating this environment, the design team should examine the plan and determine sources of potential problems. Once problems are identified, the team can strategize solutions that are related to the work of an interior designer. Individual controls for lighting were previously discussed in this section. These controls should be integrated with electrical sources and daylighting. Lighting controls should enable users to have an illumination level that is appropriate for their needs regardless of the lighting levels that are surrounding them. Controls for general lighting should be separate from individual task lighting.

Thermal comfort is affected by the temperature, ventilation, and humidity. Thus, the design team should analyze the building to identify any sources that can affect these factors. For example, excessively warm temperatures occur from solar radiant energy. Therefore, in areas close to windows, strategies should be designed to reduce the thermal impact from the sun. The design team could explore window treatments that help to control heat while emitting daylight and natural ventilation. The team might focus on external shading devices that blend with the design of the interior. In identifying sources of excessive heat, the design team should identify activities or equipment that generate heat. For example, activities in exercise facilities generate heat. Vending machines and other refrigeration systems emit heat.

Cold can also affect the thermal comfort of people. The team should examine potential cold areas, such as entryways and spaces close to windows, and determine any problems. From an interior design perspective, brainstorming sessions could focus on solutions that involve spatial strategies. For example, people working in a cold zone could be relocated or wall partitions could be added to shield people from the cold. The latter solution is most likely to be used at an entryway. Areas close to windows require solutions that do not prohibit the flow of natural ventilation and exposure to views. For these conditions, the design team should review the cause of the problem. A common cause for cold temperatures next to windows is air infiltration. In this situation the design team should examine caulking solutions. The team could also examine the specifications of window treatments to find solutions that can help to reduce the cold. Overlay sketches should be drawn that identify thermal problematic areas, followed by drawings of potential solutions.

Daylighting and views are very important to IEQ. Previous sections in this text have suggested various approaches to integrating daylight and views with the built environment. These are possibilities the design team can brainstorm in the schematic design phase, from which to create various sketches. The site plan and photographs of the area surrounding the building are excellent sources for determining how structures and vegetation affect the quality of natural light that enters the building. To integrate daylighting with the interior, some of the responsibilities of an interior designer are to develop strategies that enhance daylighting while controlling the undesirable effects of direct sunlight. Approaches to maximizing daylight focus on using surfaces around apertures to intensify illumination levels. This applies to sidelighting and toplighting installations. To accomplish this, the indirect source of daylight requires white or light-colored surfaces, matte finishes, deep recesses, and rounded surfaces at the edges of openings. Windows close to ceilings and light shelves also enhance daylighting by providing a surface for light to reflect off and disperse into the room.

To control the harmful effects of sunlight, the design team can explore various strategies, such as external shading devices and window treatments. The team should review each space to identify areas experiencing glare, excessive solar radiation, and fading and/or deterioration of materials. Controls with photosensors, which are connected to window treatments, are an effective means to control sunlight and allow daylight into the room. The team should acquire footcandle (lux) readings of daylight in several areas within each space, at various times during the day. This provides the team with information regarding the adequacy of daylight for all occupants in a space. The LEED-CI (2005) requires at least 25 footcandles, or a minimum daylight factor of 2 percent in regularly occupied areas. Areas with excessive levels of daylight require controls. Areas within a room that have inadequate levels of daylight need to be supplemented with electrical sources and/or new sources of daylight. Additional daylight sources can include openings in walls, the insertion of interior glazing in wall partitions, or toplighting from skylights, windows, roof monitors, and light pipes.

To ensure views throughout a room from various positions, the design team should sketch the drawings provided by LEED-CI (2005) (see Figures 7.14 and 7.15 in Chapter 7). The team could use an overlay on the floor plan to determine the direct lines of sight throughout each room. The team should also draw elevations or sections to analyze the horizontal views

from a seated position. The team should identify any obstructions to the views and develop solutions. Approaches to providing views include interior glazing, openings in walls, and lower interior partitions. The LEED-CI program considers the vertical vision glazing area to be a maximum of 60 inches starting at 2 to 6 inches above the finished floor.

At the completion of brainstorming sessions, the design team develops approaches to presenting various solutions to the client. For sustainable interiors, this can be structured in a variety of ways. Sustainability presentations should be organized by examining solutions within the context of how the design benefits and impacts people, the environment, and economics. The presentation should also include analyses of the LCA. When a client is seeking certification, the design team could organize the presentation by illustrating various approaches to the program's categories. For example, for LEED-CI certification, alternative solutions could focus on multiple ways to address the five major categories. In this situation, a design scenario might concentrate on achieving all the credits within the *Sustainable Sites* area and fewer points for *IEQ*. An alternate solution might enable the client to gain marginal credits in the *Energy and Atmosphere* category and all the points in *Materials and Resources*. Other alternatives could demonstrate how the project may qualify for different levels of ratings. For example, the team could develop the optimum solutions for achieving the silver and platinum ratings.

Presentations to clients who are not seeking certification could still be organized by describing scenarios that demonstrate which sustainable characteristics are emphasized and areas that have less of an impact on the project. The focus should be based on the preferences of the client and the results of programming. For example, programmatic results might reveal the importance of having quality IAQ and less concern regarding water efficiency. Thus, the design team could develop the presentation to focus on these solutions, as well as other scenarios that demonstrate the inherent balancing that occurs within the parameters of the project. Developing various solutions provides the client with the opportunity to select the optimum design within their budget, timeline, and prioritized sustainability issues. The presentation to the client should be an interactive discussion that includes a thorough review of the analysis of the problem and the various solutions. Based on the discussion, the design team may have modifications to make to the design. The schematic design phase should conclude with the client signing an agreement to the preliminary design.

DESIGN DEVELOPMENT AND SUSTAINABILITY

Upon the client's approval, the design team can proceed to the design development stage. At this stage the details of the project are developed and specifications are delineated. The schematic design phase created the solutions. The design development stage is used to carefully examine all of the aspects of the project and determine how ideas impact one another. Conflicting solutions are resolved in the design development phase, which enables the team to draw detailed drawings and the project's budget.

Drawings and Specifications for Sustainable Environments

The design development phase is the stage to create detailed drawings and specifications. Executed by hand, or by using a computer, typical drawings include the floor plan, reflected ceiling plan, elevations, sections, perspectives, and axonometric drawings. This section does not review the details of how to create these drawings. The purpose of this section is to review formal drawings and details that should be used to indicate features associated with sustainable interiors. This section also reviews important sustainable details that should be included with specifications. It is critical to develop drawings and specifications that specifically focus on sustainability. Sustainable design is a relatively new concept that has not been a primary consideration when designing a project. Therefore, due to the natural tendency to focus on conventional practices, to avoid having sustainable features be forgotten or overlooked, the design team should develop drawings and details that focus on sustainability.

Based on the outcome of the schematic design meeting with the client, the design team may have to develop revisions. After the client has approved solutions, the team can begin to develop the formal drawings. The team should refer to the original goals and objectives to ensure that the final solutions meet the criteria. The design team works through the details of sustainable features by interacting with the suppliers, manufacturers' representatives, contractors, local building inspectors, community representatives, Department of Energy (DOE), EPA, ANSI/ASHRAE, and any other organization that can provide assistance. The various sketches described in the schematic design phase of this chapter are developed into formal drawings. The team can develop a style and format that is appropriate to the design firm and addresses the needs of the client. Developing drawings that focus on sustainability is a new approach for the design profession. Therefore, the design team can be very creative in developing effective means to visually communicate important sustainable features. As described in the schematic design section, sustainable features can be illustrated on floor plans, elevations, and sections. Perspective and axonometric drawings can also be used to illustrate the three-dimensional aspects of the interior.

Table 11.2 provides of list of potential sustainability sketches. The design team should consider which sketches would be appropriate to develop into formal drawings. As a supplement to conventional formal drawings, the team should identify the illustrations that reinforce the most salient issues for the project. For example, when a client is very interested in promoting the use of public transportation and connecting with the community, a drawing should be developed from the sketch that includes the site plan and its surrounding area. Drawings could also be developed that illustrate how various sustainability elements are integrated together. An example of this is a plan view that illustrates the integration of ventilation, thermal comfort, lighting, furniture, and window treatments. To reinforce the importance of sustainability, several formal drawings should be developed. These drawings can be used in the presentation to the client and can be referenced during the construction phase of the project. In addition, many of these drawings could be developed to accommodate documentation requirements of certification programs.

As the team is developing the formal drawings, the specifications of the project should be written. Specifications must be consistent with the details

Table 11.2

Examples of Sustainable Sketches

Sustainable Site Sketches

Access and views of the roof garden

Building footprint that illustrates light pollution, light trespass, parking garages, local services, public transportation stops, undesirable and desirable views, amenities in walking distance, bike paths, parks, water

Water Efficiency

Plumbing lines and the relationship to spatial strategies—graywater possibilities

Energy and Atmosphere

Evaluation of lighting—luminaires to eliminate, replace, or add

Controls—occupancy sensors

Materials and Resources

Building reuse for nonstructural components—what to keep, refurbish, eliminate (includes ceilings, floors, walls, wall partitions, doors, built-in case goods, furniture)

Collection and storage areas for recycling

Construction waste areas for disposal phased through the construction process [includes IEQ schedule for absorbing materials (carpet, gypsum wall board, ceiling tiles) and HVAC protection returns)]

Reused/salvaged on-site and off-site; recycled contents; regional materials; rapidly renewable materials; certified wood

Indoor Environmental Quality

Ventilation airflow patterns plan view and elevations; location of operable windows; noise and pollution around open windows

Smoking-room analysis

Location of low-emitting materials

Temperature problems, thermal comfort—humidity, ventilation, temperature

Daylighting—exterior influences—shading from trees or buildings

Plan showing access to daylight (LEED-CI)

Elevation showing access to views (LEED-CI)

---

provided in the drawings. In developing the specifications, the team should verify the contents of materials to ensure that the products and materials possess the requirements of sustainable interiors. For example, the team should research the specifications of finishes and furnishings to ensure that the materials conserve natural resources, avoid emissions, reduce the impact to the environment, and contribute to a healthy IEQ. For certification projects, the team should review material and resource criteria to en-

sure compliance. Products claiming to have recycled content should be reviewed to determine the source of the materials. In particular, the content should be analyzed to verify the percentages of virgin and pre- and post-consumer materials. Materials should be examined to determine the local/regional availability and their biodegradability characteristics. The team should contact organizations and agencies that are involved with certifying green products, such as Green Seal, Global Ecolabeling Network (GEN), FSC, ENERGY STAR, CRI, and GREENGUARD. These organizations can verify products that advertise certification and can provide recommendations when a substitution is necessary. Specifications should identify which products have certification from third-party testing agencies.

To develop specifications and the project's budget, the team should verify the life cycle assessment (LCA) of products. The LCA is critical for determining and comparing the environmental impact of products, services, or processes. Chapter 4 provided detailed information regarding LCA procedures developed by the ISO. The team can refer to the ISO for the life cycle assessment framework. Acquiring the information from manufacturers can be challenging. Manufacturers' data may reflect industry averages or information may be incomplete. It is easier to acquire LCA data from European manufacturers than from corporations in the United States. An organization that has a database in North America is the Athena Sustainable Materials Institute, a not-for-profit organization established to promote sustainability of the built environment (www.environmental-expert. com). Athena has a database of comparable LCA for building materials and products. Currently, products in the database are structural and envelope systems of commercial and residential buildings. The organization is working on LCA for other materials. The goal for the design team is to acquire information regarding the extraction and refining of raw materials; manufacturing process; operational costs of the product/material/equipment, including energy consumption, maintenance, and repair; proper use of the item; and proper disposal or recycling capabilities. When data are not available, the design team should try to review a product by conducting an LCA with specifications provided by the manufacturer and industry standards. These team-developed

LCAs can provide some data that can help inform the specification process. In particular, these data can help to compare products from different manufacturers. As sustainability becomes more mainstream in the United States, it will become easier to acquire LCA data.

All of these requirements should be included in the specifications and/or in a project manual that is provided to the client. In addition, information attained from the product's LCA can also provide data for the long-term costs of the project. When first or upfront costs are high, the long-term budget projections become very important. Thus, products that are durable and last a long time are very positive for the long-term costs of the project. The LCA can provide the anticipated costs of operation and maintenance, and an approximate date for replacement. This information can be used to calculate the **life-cycle costs** of the product. Generally, a product that is well made has a higher upfront cost, but due to its quality, the item will last longer. Specifications should include the first costs, operating costs, and life-cycle costs of products and equipment. This information is also included in the estimated budget for the project. While working with manufacturers, the team should also attain cutsheets, current prices, product availability, estimated delivery dates, and possible installation requirements.

Project Manual for Sustainable Environments

For projects seeking certification, the team should create a list of the required submittal documents. Certification submittal documents should be coordinated with project specifications and the formal drawings. To achieve certification, building assessment programs require submittal documentation. The LEED-CI program has specific documentation that must be submitted for every credit in each category. For example, the submittal documents for the resource reuse credit are to complete the LEED-CI letter template and create a table that includes a list of salvaged materials, modifications made to materials, and replacement value (www.usgbc.org). Collecting data for submittal documentation must be done at the start of the project. Thus, the design development phase is an excellent time to plan the documentation process. The team should determine what data must be collected, who is responsible, and a timeline. A critical requirement is the building commissioning. The building systems that should be commissioned are HVAC systems, life safety systems, and lighting controls. A commissioning provider can assist in developing the design documents, specifications, and commissioning plan. Computer simulations may be used to collect energy-related information. The Department of Energy has energy analysis software programs, such as DOE-2 and ENERGY-10, which can be used to improve the design of a building, operations, and HVAC systems (www.eere.energy.gov).

The design development phase is also the stage to develop an initial schedule for the project. From a sustainability perspective, there are many important considerations. The team should develop a sequencing plan that minimizes inconveniences to people, reduces the impact to the environment, and avoids any additional costs. These factors should be examined at every stage of the construction process. Thus, considerable time should be dedicated to "walking through" each stage and discussing the schedule with all of the people involved with the project. For example, to avoid compaction of the soil, heavy equipment should be at the site only when it is needed. To avoid additional transportation costs, materials and supplies should be delivered at the appropriate time. Unnecessary transportation costs also apply to subcontractors, inspectors, or any other tradesperson who travels to the site at designated stages of the construction. In addition, a schedule must include the proper sequencing of activities for other purposes. For example, a sequenced plan is important for the commissioning process and the IAQ. Many of the commissioning activities must occur prior to and after occupancy. The schedule must allocate time for the commissioning process to ensure that HVAC systems and lighting are installed and operating according to design. As discussed previously in this text, to have a healthy IAQ there are many precautions that should be implemented during construction. This involves a schedule that delineates the proper sequencing of installations and construction. For example, materials prone to collect or absorb substances, such as gypsum board, must be installed after any construction activity that involves contaminants. A schedule for carpet systems must be carefully orchestrated to avoid contaminants during construction and to prevent exposure to any VOC emissions after installation. Adequate time must be provided for flush-out procedures and IAQ test procedures. These procedures must be properly sequenced with move-in.

A well-designed schedule is useful for the occupants of the building. A schedule that is followed enables people to plan for moves and activities at the appropriate time. Careful planning provides the occupants with the opportunity to arrange activities based on the move-in and any construction details that must be done after occupancy. This is especially important when people remain in the building during construction. A well-developed schedule also helps to avoid unnecessary costs. Delays always increase the cost for the client, contractor, and any other parties involved with the project. A restaurant that is unable to open due to construction delays can be extremely expensive for a client. When the client must rent space during construction, any delays increase the cost of the lease and utilities. A tentative schedule should be discussed with people who are significantly involved with the project. The finalized schedule should be given to all parties involved with the project, including community representatives.

An important task in the design development stage is to develop a document that describes policies and procedures for change orders. For a variety of reasons, a completed project does not have all of the elements proposed in the original design. Products can be discontinued, a client has a change of mind during construction, cost overruns result in some aspect being eliminated, or a particular architectural detail does not work for the site. Alterations from the original design can have a significant impact on the sustainability of the built environment. For example, the elimination of efficient water fixtures results in wasting water. Eliminating the facilities for bike riders may result in people not biking to work. Specifying the wrong fabric for a shade may increase the temperature of the room. This slight alteration could affect all energy-related systems in the building. Ultimately, the combined change orders could prevent a building from being certified. The LEED-NC program does not certify or rate a building at the design stage. The combined design and construction submittals determine project certification

and the rating level (leedonline.usgbc.org). Thus, the team should develop policies and procedures for all change orders. The policies must include a communication plan that involves all of the people who are impacted by any changes from the design. How the changes are processed should be delineated and the individuals responsible for approvals should be identified.

The design development stage also involves creating a comprehensive budget for the project. From the sustainability perspective, the design team should determine the life-cycle costs of the project. The budget for the project should include first costs, operating costs, employee productivity costs, maintenance/repair costs, replacement costs, and disposal costs. These costs should be projected over several years to determine the true cost of the project. To emphasize the importance of durability and thinking in the long term, the life-cycle costs should be calculated for as many years as possible. Costs associated with structural components could be calculated in years, decades, and centuries. The life of finishes and furnishings should be determined by manufacturers' specifications, and it can be very informative to discuss product durability with clients who have experience with the item. For items that can be refurbished, such as furniture, cost projections for products should be calculated for years and decades. A comprehensive analysis of the costs helps to justify the investment in sustainable building systems, finishes, and furnishings. In addition, projecting costs over the life of the project/products focuses attention on future expenses the client should expect to expend. For example, knowing anticipated costs for maintenance and repair enables the client to establish a fund for this purpose at the initial phases of the project. Employee productivity costs can demonstrate the net gain from investing in environments that have daylighting, healthy IAQ, the ideal thermal comfort, proper ventilation, and quality lighting.

In addition to identifying comprehensive costs for the project, the team should develop a profile of the direct and indirect benefits associated with a sustainable environment. This involves an analysis of the project's impact on society, the community, employees/customers, the environment, and economics. Investing in sustainable environments can demonstrate that a business or corporation is a good steward and a responsible member of the global community. Environmental stewardship can lead to a global competitive advantage and new business opportunities. An important element of sustainable design is its origin's focus on development. The concept of sustainable *development* encourages what is referred to as the three *P*'s: people/planet/profit. As described in the Brundtland Report, "technology and social organization can be both managed and improved to make way for a new era of economic growth" (WCED, 1987, p. 24). Successful corporations that have embraced sustainable development and demonstrated *smart growth* can be used to demonstrate that sustainability can be profitable in the long term.

Sustainability Perspectives: Oral Presentation

The organization of the presentation and its content should focus on sustainability and its importance to current and future generations. To help reframe people's approach to designing the built environment, the presentation should be different from conventional approaches. The content should be structured around the principles of sustainability, and the choice of presentation media should reflect sustainable practices. In developing the content, the design team should consider that some people attending the presentation might not be familiar with the principles of sustainability. The term is basically unfamiliar to most people, or sustainability is assumed to be a synonym for "green" or "environmental" design. Therefore, the presentation should begin by explaining the principles of sustainability and focus on the importance of reducing, reusing, and recycling. The description should *not* be a bulleted list of characteristics. A list tends to give people the impression that it represents the totality of a concept. Consequently, checking off items on the list means that the task has been accomplished. In addition, providing people with a list of sustainability characteristics gives them the impression that they have all the information they need for sustainable interiors; thus, they do not have to study further. Sustainability is a concept that requires continuous learning and improvement. Therefore, lists of sustainability characteristics can be detrimental to fully comprehending the concept and can hinder someone from understanding how to integrate the philosophy into practice.

Meaningful and long-lasting sustainable development requires changes in lifestyles and transformational ways of thinking about the built environment. This is the message that should be communicated in the presentation. Thus, depending on the audience, the presentation should begin by explaining sustainability within the context of global concerns involving society, environmental conditions, and economic realities. The global context serves as the foundation for describing international sustainable development initiatives. The presentation can proceed by explaining sustainability and the built environment. Prior to reviewing an analysis of the project, the design team should discuss sustainability with the audience to respond to questions and clarify information.

To organize the presentation of the design, a tempting approach is to separate the conventional elements of a building and the sustainability factors. In contrast, the presentation should be organized to demonstrate the integration of sustainability with the built environment. From this perspective, the client gains a better understanding of the importance of viewing sustainability as an interdependent element of the environment. To emphasize the importance of sustainable development, each section of the presentation should demonstrate the integration of sustainability with the built environment. For example, when reviewing the floor plan with the client, the presenter should describe each area in a building by discussing conventional elements of the built environment with the sustainability features. Thus, in describing the layout of furniture, the presenter should include how the furniture is positioned to maximize daylight and views. At the same time the presenter could include information regarding the furniture's low-VOC emissions.

Problems related to sustainability should also be presented in a manner that integrates solutions with conventional building components. For example, the presenter could show photographs of mold and mildew on ceilings and walls. An explanation of the problem could include health and structural problems associated with fungi. The presenter could then demonstrate how the building's new HVAC and ventilation system helps to arrest the hazardous situation. As an effective visual tool, matrices could be developed to demonstrate the integration of sustainability with the conventional components of the built environment.

In using a traditional format for a presentation, sustainability should be integrated within the introduction, analysis of the problem, descriptions of goals and objectives, explanations of solutions, and conclusion. An important aspect of the presentation is to repeatedly address the design intent of developing a sustainable interior. When a client is seeking certification, the presentation should include a summary of how the project addresses the criteria and the projected rating. The presenter should be sensitive to sustainability terminology that may not be familiar to the audience. The presenter may need to explain a term during the presentation or during a question/answer session. The design team wants the stakeholders to understand the principles of sustainability. Knowledge of the principles establishes the foundation for sustainable practice. The project's budget should be thoroughly explained to the client within the context of life-cycle costing. Generally, it is more effective to discuss the budget after the presentation. Figures and costs can divert attention from the design. Furthermore, an extensive discussion of the budget provides the design team with the opportunity to explain the value of a long-term investment in the project.

The presentation media and materials should reflect sustainable practice. Handouts should be minimized and when necessary, any materials should be printed with soy ink on recyclable paper. Whenever possible, a CD-ROM should be distributed to the audience rather than paper. Materials that can be included with the presentation are the concept statement integrated with sustainability features, drawings, product specifications, finish samples, budget estimates, bidding/purchase order recommendations, maintenance/commissioning manual, and projected timelines. Whenever possible, material samples, such as upholstery fabric, should be borrowed from suppliers and returned to the company after the presentation. The design could be presented using computer software such as PowerPoint. Computer-generated images are an excellent tool for demonstrating virtual interiors and an animated walkthrough.

Following the presentation and the budget discussion, the design team may have to conduct revisions to the program. Prior to proceeding to the contract document phase, the client must approve the design by signing a contract. The next phase of the design process is to create the contract documents. Registered professionals, architects, and engineers develop the contract documents for the design team. Documents can include working drawings, specifications, sections, cutsheets, and purchase orders. The next chapter explains the contract document, contract administration, and postoccupancy evaluation phases within the context of sustainable design.

Summary

- The schematic design phase is the most creative stage of a project. Individuals responsible for developing the design, such as the architect, interior designers, and accredited professionals, conduct multiple brainstorming sessions. Primary topics discussed are spatial strategies and attributes of products.
- The site plan is an excellent tool for determining the best way for a building to interact with its surroundings.
- Brainstorming sessions for strategizing water efficiencies should focus on products and spatial strategies for minimizing plumbing lines.
- In addition to designing efficient interiors, the work of an interior designer can optimize energy performance by designing quality lighting systems.
- The design team should dedicate considerable time and thought to reviewing the various components of a lighting system and then develop recommendations that are energy efficient, fulfill functional needs, and are cost-effective.
- In exploring various solutions, the design team should focus on reducing, reusing, and recycling materials and resources.
- When it is necessary to specify new products, one of the most important tasks is to review the LCA of products and the manufacturers' sustainability practices.
- In the schematic design phase, the design team should brainstorm strategies for enhancing ventilation, specifying low-emitting materials, reducing

indoor chemical sources, and providing for personal controls, daylighting, and views.

- Sustainability presentations should be organized by examining solutions within the context of how the design benefits and impacts people, the environment, and economics. The presentation should also include analyses of the LCA.

- The design development phase is the stage to create detailed drawings and specifications.

- As the team is developing the formal drawings, the specifications of the project should be written.

- For projects seeking certification, the team should create a list of the required submittal documents.

- The design development stage involves creating a comprehensive budget for the project. From the sustainability perspective, the design team should determine the life-cycle costs of the project.

- In addition to identifying comprehensive costs for the project, the team should develop a profile of the direct and indirect benefits associated with a sustainable environment.

- The organization of the presentation and its content should focus on sustainability and its importance to current and future generations.

Key Term

Life-cycle costs

Exercises

1. The site plan is an excellent tool for determining the best way for a building to interact with its surround-ings. Identify a commercial building and develop sketches of how the interior could be designed to accommodate the elements that surround the building. Write a summary of the recommendations, and submit all sketches with photographs of the building.

2. In the schematic design phase, the design team has many areas to explore in LEED-CI's Materials and Resources category. A team of designers should create sketches of a floor plan that illustrate which nonstructural components of the interior could be reused, refurbished, or removed. In addition, the team should create sketches that demonstrate strategies for enhancing ventilation, specifying low-emitting materials, reducing indoor chemical sources, and providing for personal controls, daylighting, and views. Write a summary of the recommendations, and submit all sketches with photographs of the building.

3. The design team should consider which sketches created in Exercises 1 and 2 would be appropriate to develop into formal drawings. As a supplement to conventional formal drawings, the team should identify the illustrations that reinforce the most salient issues for the project. Develop a set of drawings for the structure.

4. To achieve certification, building assessment programs require submittal documentation. LEED-CI has specific documentation that must be submitted for every credit in each category. Identify the documentation required for LEED-CI certification and write a summary of the requirements. Include in the summary suggested timelines for documenting the data and who is responsible for the respective activities.

CHAPTER 12

Sustainable Strategies for Design Process: Final Phases

The important thing is what can't be seen . . .
It's the same as for the flower.
If you love a flower that lives on a star, then it's good,
at night, to look up at the sky.
All the stars are blossoming.
—ANTOINE DE SAINT-EXUPÉRY

Objectives

- Describe how to verify sustainable elements of a project when developing working drawings, specifications, and schedules.
- Understand important details of specifications that must be included for sustainable environments.
- Identify important aspects of bidding a sustainability project.
- Describe elements that should be considered when developing the schedule and budget of a sustainability project.
- Identify and describe strategies for site administration for a sustainable environment.
- Determine effective approaches for developing manuals and education sessions for a sustainable environment.
- Describe important elements of postoccupancy evaluation for a sustainable environment.

CHAPTERS 9 AND 10 started the review of identifying which elements of sustainability must be considered at each phase of the design process. The client's approval of the architectural program initiates the development of contract documents. This phase of the design process is followed by contract administration and postoccupancy evaluation. Each phase has sustainability considerations that the design team must address. These three phases have many sustainability aspects that affect the work of an interior designer.

To understand the interior designer's responsibilities, this chapter has a section for each of the three phases. The first section examines the contributions the designer provides for creating the project's contract documents, including the development of working drawings and specifications. The next section reviews how the interior designer is involved with contract administration for a sustainable interior. The postoccupancy and evaluation phase concludes the chapter. This phase is generally considered the last phase of the design process. However, in conceptualizing the built environment from the sustainable development perspective, data derived from the evaluation phase should be used to inform future practice. An effective model to follow is the continuous process depicted in PDCA cycles. The PDCA cycle reviewed in Chapter 4 can serve as a model for continuously improving sustainable interiors.

SUSTAINABILITY AND CONTRACT DOCUMENTS

Contract documents for a project include working drawings, specifications, and schedules. The contract document phase is a critical stage for the success of sustainable interiors. The documents must be drawn and written to ensure that the designed project is actually constructed. General contractors, subcontractors, and vendors understand conventional building techniques. Given the fact that sustainability is an emerging concept in the United States, many contractors are not aware of specific requirements and/or have not had experience with constructing a sustainable building. Therefore, the design team must develop comprehensive and detailed contract documents.

To continuously focus on the design intent of the built environment, the team should revisit the project's goals and objectives. Feedback acquired from stakeholders during the design development phase should be reviewed to determine any revisions to the goals and objectives. Establishing consensus on the project's goals is essential for developing contract documents. The project's goals and objectives set the tone for the construction of the project. Thus, goals and objectives should be the first introduction to the project in the contract documents. The emphasis on sustainability reflected in the goals demonstrates to the contractor that this is a priority of the project. The goals and objectives should serve as a guide throughout the construction of the project. For example, during the course of construction a project is always subjected to alterations and substitutions. When these changes occur, the goals and objectives should serve as the basis for making decisions.

Emphasizing sustainability in the contract documents should encourage the involvement of contractors and vendors who are interested in or committed to the philosophy. Hiring a contractor who has experience with constructing sustainable buildings, or a sincere interest in learning how to build sustainable environments, is *essential* to the success of the project. Many of the elements of a sustainable environment are dependent on the work of the contractor. A contractor who lacks interest in sustainability may not fulfill requirements, or when decisions must be made that are not prescribed in the specifications, the contractor may not consider the optimum solution for a sustainable environment. Furthermore, apathy can affect interactions with the design team. This can seriously alter the collaborative spirit, which is an essential element of sustainable development and design.

Working Drawings

The drawings developed in the design development phase are used to create the contract documents. To help ensure the accuracy of the working drawings and the specifications, several people on the design team should review all of the documents. The team must also verify that the working drawings are accurately cross-referenced with the written specifications. Working drawings include plans, elevations, sections, and details. The basic categories are the construction and FF&E (furniture, furnishings, and equipment) contract documents. An interior designer can be involved with developing drawings associated with the basic floor plan, furniture layout, interior elevations, and a reflected ceiling plan. Sustainable interiors use the same drawings as conventional construction projects; however, to clarify specific details associated with sustainability requirements, the design team may want to include **resource drawings**. Resource drawings are not included with the construction contract but are used to help clarify project requirements. For example, Chapter 11 provided examples of sketches and drawings that illustrate sustainable features. These drawings are an effective means to communicate requirements, such as the preferred locations for storing construction waste or identifying the nonstructural components intended for building reuse.

Resource drawings can help to visualize sustainability features. In addition, the novelty of the illustrations can help to direct attention to the importance of the practice. For example, the design team might want to develop resource drawings that demonstrate integrated building systems. Integrating building systems is essential to sustainable environments. Thus, to emphasize this importance, resource drawings that specifically illustrate the integration can be very informative to the project's contractor, electricians, and plumbers. To demonstrate the importance of integrating building systems with furnishings, an interior designer could develop plans and elevations that demonstrate integration. For example, a sustainable interior should provide the users with the ability to control their lighting, temperature, and ventilation. For this to be effective requires the proper integration of the furniture layout and the mechanical and electrical systems. This integration could be illustrated in a resource drawing.

To implement the integrated sustainable design requires examining multiple aspects of the project. Therefore, in developing the construction documents, an interior designer should be involved with verifying many architectural and engineering working drawings. For example, an interior designer should review the final details of the site plan to verify the position of existing and new trees, because vegetation can affect daylighting and any passive solar energy applications. The working-drawing floor plan should be examined to verify the location of doors, windows, and partitions. The accuracy of this plan has significant implications for many features of a sustainable interior, such as daylighting, views, and natural ventilation. The floor plan should be checked to ensure that any special areas are included, such as the bike storage, changing rooms, and an indoor smoking room when the space is applicable. The roof plan is important to review when the building has a roof garden. In addition, the roof plan can be used to verify the location of any skylights, roof windows, or roof monitors.

The finish schedule that is keyed to rooms on the floor plan should be thoroughly studied to ensure that the proper materials are specified for the ceilings, walls, base, trim, wainscot, and floor. These materials and the furnishings should be accurately cross-referenced to details provided in the specifications. The furniture schedule must be checked for accuracy. The window and door schedules and their detail drawings should also be thoroughly reviewed for accuracy. An interior designer should review the exterior elevations and cross-sections to verify that windows and doors are in the correct locations. In addition, the drawings should be verified for the dimensional accuracy of windows, doors, overhangs, and any outdoor-shading device. Accurate overhangs and shading units are required for the design of daylighting and control of sunlight.

There are many elements that should be verified by reviewing the interior elevations. For example, elevations illustrate elements that can affect the quality and quantity of daylight. Thus, an interior designer should analyze the location of windows, openings, and finish materials. Interior elevations and/or sections should be carefully reviewed for the location of skylights, roof windows, roof monitors, and light shelves. The area surrounding an aperture should be analyzed to check the accuracy of the depth and angle of recessed surfaces. The length of suspended fixtures should be examined to make sure that the unit does not interfere with views, door swings, path of airflow, or any structure in the space. Interior elevations and floor plans should be used to verify the site lines for views. The interior elevation should include furniture to confirm views from the seated position.

To help ensure the accurate integration of the

interior with mechanical and electrical systems, an interior designer should study the mechanical, plumbing, and electrical working drawings. The mechanical and electrical floor plans must be checked to ensure that the drawings indicate the components that are needed for thermal comfort and lighting. Elements on the HVAC floor plan that should be verified are the duct/grille locations and sizes; locations of exhaust fans; the direction of airflow through registers; and the locations of CO2 sensors. Electrical and lighting working drawings must be examined to check for the location of luminaires (fixtures), outlets, and controls. The luminaire schedule must coincide with the specification documents. Lighting data must be analyzed to ensure an accurate list of fixtures, lamps, lens, color, ballast, controls, mounting application, manufacturers, and product numbers. The plumbing floor plan is reviewed to ensure proper placement. The plumbing schedule is checked to verify the correct flush and flow fixtures.

Specifications

Specification contract documents provide written instructions for procedures, details, and performance requirements. A great deal of the critical information related to sustainability requirements can be detailed in the specifications. As a contract document, the specifications must be written in a very clear and concise manner. This helps to ensure that the building will be constructed as designed, which is especially important to achieve the optimum performance that is expected of sustainable buildings. In addition, specifications that can be understood by the contractor should help to avoid overpricing bids, which can occur when a contractor is uncertain how to execute a requirement. Whenever uncertainty exists regarding how much time and resources will be required for an activity, contractors tend to overbid the project to ensure that their expenses will be covered. This is more likely to occur with sustainable projects because many contractors are unfamiliar with the requirements. The relative novelty of sustainability may also contribute to a contractor's lack of awareness of various standards. Generally this is not a problem with conventional construction methods. Thus, these specifications may simply reference a commonly used standard, and the contrac-

tor understands how to apply the requirements to the building. To avoid any confusion with unfamiliar standards, the design team may include the details of the requirements in the specifications, rather than citing just the name of the standard. Providing the details can also help to ensure that the most important information is not overlooked.

The two basic types of specifications are closed and open. **Closed specifications** are used when an exact product is required. Closed specifications delineate a specific manufacturer, the product name or number, and any other descriptors required to order the item. **Open specifications** do not specify a particular product, but indicate the requirements for a material or item. The three open specifications are descriptive, performance, and reference standards. Descriptive specifications include information related to the characteristics of a product, such as the type of material, construction method, and finish. Performance specifications are written by concisely describing the desired end results. Reference standard specifications identify a particular standard for the product's material, performance, or installation method. For example, ANSI/ASHRAE standards are often cited in these specifications.

Open specifications must be *carefully* written for sustainable interiors. The newness of the concept and terminology requires specifications that have concise descriptions and corresponding instructions. For example, ambiguity exists in understanding the differences between recycled content, post-consumer content, and pre-consumer content. The open specifications for these products require very concise descriptions and definitions. Unfortunately, accurate descriptions may not be provided because many spec writers do not have experience in writing specifications for sustainable built environments.

Open specifications for these products may result in products or materials that do not comply with standardized testing and product requirements. To achieve sustainable interiors, closed specifications may need to be used to ensure that the product or material complies with the prescribed requirements. For example, to help ensure a healthy indoor environment, the closed specification would provide the exact manufacturer, product, and item number for the low-emitting materials, including adhesives, sealants, paints, coatings, carpet systems, composite wood, laminate adhesives, furniture, and seating. Closed specifications may be especially critical with commonly purchased products, such as carpet systems. A contractor is accustomed to reading conventional carpet specifications. Thus, when a specific product is not identified, as in an open specification, the sustainability description and instructions might not be understood or could be overlooked. The end result may be a carpet system that results in unhealthy VOC emissions from the carpet, pad, and adhesive. For products with recycled content, specification details should include the desired percentages of virgin, pre-consumer, and post-consumer contents.

An interior designer might provide exact product, material, and equipment information to a spec writer. In North American commercial projects, the Construction Specifications Institute's (CSI) Master-Format™ is the most common standard used to organize information by construction practices. In providing information to a spec writer, an interior designer should be familiar with the document's division numbers and titles. *MasterFormat 2004 Edition* has a six-digit format. The first two numbers represent a *division*. The next two numbers are used for the *Level Two Classification*, and the last two digits are the *Level Three Classification*. Some items have a fourth level that is indicated by adding a point after level three, followed by two numbers. For example, the number for *Plaster Restoration* is *09 01 20.91*. The *09* indicates that plaster restoration is in *Division 09*. The next two numbers, *01*, represent the *Maintenance of Finishes* classification. The numbers for the third level, *20*, indicate the classification of *Maintenance of Plaster and Gypsum Board*. The two numbers to the right of the point, *91*, denote the fourth level: Plaster Restoration. The MasterFormat standardization may appear complicated, but in reality the system provides the consistency that is needed to organize the contents of project manuals used in the professions.

MasterFormat 2004 has many more numbers and titles than the 1995 edition. The additional categories are very useful to people who are writing specifications for sustainable buildings, because CSI included divisions that are applicable to sustainability. According to CSI, the growing interest in green building and sustainability contributed to the need to have more categories. Contractors and vendors will eventually become accustomed to these divisions, which should result in an enhanced understanding of sustainability. Some of the divisions that could be used with sustainability projects are *Division 40—Process Integration*; *Division 41—Material Processing and Handling Equipment*; *Division 44—Pollution Control Equipment*; and *Division 48—Electrical Power Generation*. Some of the divisions associated with the work of interior designers are *Division 09—Finishes* and *Division 12—Furnishings*. The CSI did not change the numbering system for these two divisions; however, the division associated with lighting was changed. Division 16, which included electrical and lighting topics, was transferred to *Division 26—Electrical*.

CSI's **SectionFormat**™ is used to organize sections in a project manual. The three divisions of the format are *Part 1—General*, *Part 2—Products*, and *Part 3—Execution*. The content of the general section includes descriptions and instructions for overall procedures and administrative requirements associated with the project, such as the scope of the work, submittals, product delivery, storage and handling, job conditions, and alternatives. The *Products* division describes the requirements for products and fabrication. *Part 3—Execution* provides the details for on-site activities, such as inspections, installations, adjustments, cleaning, and schedules. Sustainable projects will have many unique requirements with each of these divisions. Thus, the design team should carefully review each section to ensure procedures, administrative terms, products, activities, and schedules adhere to sustainability requirements.

To help ensure a sustainable project is constructed as designed requires a very careful analysis of the language used in the specifications and the coordination with the working drawings. Specification language, especially for sustainable interiors, should not be ambiguous or incomplete. The design team should be cautious with any words that can provide a choice or are ambiguous, such as "either," "and/or," and "etc." The novelty of sustainability requires consistency with the terms used for products, procedures, and policies. The design team should develop definitions for terms related to sustainability and consistently use them on all contract documents, including the working drawings. The definitions should be included in the project manual.

Careful attention should also be afforded to the coordination between working drawings, schedules, and specifications. Again, the newness of sustainable projects requires an emphasis on consistency and accuracy. The contract documents must be coordinated to ensure that each part fulfills a unique purpose without duplications. For example, information provided in the working drawings, such as the size of rooms, does not have to be duplicated in the specifications. While avoiding duplication, the design team must ensure that the contract documents do not have any omissions. A checklist of project requirements can help to ensure the contract documents are complete and employ the same terminology and symbols.

In the United States, writing specifications for sustainable buildings is a relatively new undertaking for construction projects. To supplement specifications, the design team may want to provide additional information regarding sustainability in the project manual. To provide guidance in writing supplemental material, a good source is the state of California's *Section 01350—Special Environmental Requirements*. Section 01350 is an important specification for reducing the project's impact on the environment by focusing on energy conservation and efficiency, indoor environmental and air quality, and resource-efficient materials and systems. The document includes environmental requirements for general specifications, including design requirements; submittals; quality assurance; delivery, storage, and handling; and project conditions and sequencing. The section on products includes details for chemicals of concern and substitutions. The execution section delineates instructions for field quality control, cleaning, and protection. Environmental requirements for specific products are found in *Section 01565: site waste management program*; *Section 01600: product requirements*; *Section 01810: building commissioning*; and *Section 01820: system demonstration*.

California's *Section 01350—Special Environmental Requirements* provides helpful details for sustainability projects. Thus, in writing specifications and supplemental documents for the project manual, the design team should review Section 01350 and California's other sections related to the environment and sustainability. Some noteworthy examples of the content include a focus on teamwork by encouraging suggestions from the construction team, extensive procedures for testing indoor air emissions, protocols

for paint testing, and a comprehensive list of "chemicals of concern." The list of 78 chemicals includes chronic reference exposure levels and the system or organ that may be affected by the substance. For example, ammonia is listed as a "chemical of concern" and the targeted area is the respiratory system.

The requirements for substitutions delineated in Section 01350 provide useful details for how the process should occur for environmental issues. Since product or procedural substitutions can significantly impact the outcome of a sustainability project, substitution specifications must be very prescriptive. For example, in addition to the protocols established in California's *Section 01630—Product Substitution Procedures*, environmental issues must comply with the following:

1. Indicate each proposed substitution complies with requirements for VOCs.
2. Owner, in consultation with Architect, reserves right to reject proposed substitutions where data for VOCs are not provided or where emissions of individual VOCs are higher than for specified materials.
3. Comply with specified recycled content and other environmental requirements (California, 2002, p. 19).

Specifications for a sustainability project must provide detailed instructions for packaging, project conditions, sequencing, field quality control, and cleaning. There are many aspects related to these requirements that affect the work of an interior designer. An interior designer is actively involved with ordering products and equipment for the project. Thus, these items should have specifications that require recyclable or reusable packaging. Suppliers should be encouraged to minimize packing materials and avoid nonbiodegradable plastics. At the site the contractor must have a process for separating, reusing, and recycling packaging materials and other construction waste. Any unused materials or products that can be returned to the manufacturer should be designated in the specifications. Scraps from biodegradable materials such as linoleum can be composted. Any materials delivered with mold or mildew are not acceptable and should be disposed of in an environmentally responsible manner.

An interior designer should make certain that

specifications include requirements for handling any materials that have VOC emissions. This includes delineating conditioning requirements before and after installation. Sequencing instructions must be provided to avoid contamination of porous materials and to allow adequate time before the building flushout procedures. An interior designer must review the cleaning specifications to ensure proper procedures for finishes and furnishings. Toxic and volatile substances should be avoided, and carpet should be vacuumed with a HEPA vacuum cleaner.

For projects seeking certification, the project manual should include information regarding the organization's requirements, including the anticipated rating. The document should include a list of the submittal documents required for certification. In addition, the project manual may delineate suggested approaches, implementation, and strategies for acquiring each credit. Commissioning requirements should be very explicit and delineate the prescribed activities required for construction, prior to occupancy, after occupancy, and the extended commitment. Specifications should include any equipment required to perform testing. The instructions should also indicate the contractor's responsibilities related to commissioning. The LEED online certification process has three steps: (1) *registration*, (2) *design submittal*, and (3) *construction submittal and project award*. Registration should be done in the early stages of the design process. Design submittal occurs with the development of the construction documents. The LEED has a list of the credits that are eligible for the design stage submittal. The USGBC reviews the documents and determines whether credit is anticipated or denied. After most of the construction is completed, the USGBC reviews the construction credits and determines credit achievements or denials. To determine the certification award and a rating level, the USGBC reviews the results of the design submittal and construction submittal.

CONTRACT ADMINISTRATION

The completion of the contract documents initiates the contract administration phase. It should be noted that the design team has dedicated a tremendous amount of work and time to reach this phase of the project. This important aspect of sustainability is also apparent by the distribution of content in Unit III of this text. A significant amount of information was introduced prior to the discussion of the construction phase. For a sustainable built environment to be successful requires considerable upfront planning, designing, and collaboration. The construction phase is gratifying because all of the upfront work is finally developed into reality; however, to ensure that the building is constructed as designed, the design team must be continuously involved through the postoccupancy phase.

Most projects undergo a bidding process. However, to execute a sustainability project, some clients request a two-step process. The purpose of two stages is to prescreen applicants prior to the bidding process. The first phase is the request for qualifications (RFQ). Elements of the RFQ can include qualifications and experience with sustainability projects. The RFQ phase can be important for sustainability projects because many contractors are unfamiliar with the requirements. In addition, since many projects are awarded to the lowest bidder, a list of prequalified applicants results in bids from contractors who have the desired qualifications.

The design team reviews the qualifications of all submittals from the RFQ and may elect to interview potential firms. From this pool of applicants, the design team and client determine which firms are requested to bid the project. The novelty of sustainability projects may require the design team to have a pre-bid session with the potential contractors. At this meeting the team could review the goals and objectives of the project and conduct a question/answer session. The preselected contractors review the contract documents and then bid the job. Upon receiving the bids, the design team should carefully examine the proposal to determine the acceptability of substitutions and identify any omissions or additions. Intentional or unintentional substitutions can frequently occur with sustainability projects because of unfamiliar products, materials, and procedures.

An interior designer should specifically examine elements related to materials, resources, lighting, and the IEQ. For each substitution, the design team should determine if the change is acceptable. From the sustainability perspective, the decision should focus on how the substitution may affect criteria specifically related to the principles of sustainability.

For example, if the contractor proposed an alternative luminaire, the team should determine how the new product might affect energy efficiency, quantity of illumination, daylighting systems, individual controls, installation procedures, maintenance requirements, and the thermal and visual comfort. Substitutes should also be reviewed by examining how the alternative affects the LCA and life-cycle costs. After reviewing the proposal, the design team may present the client with recommendations regarding the substitutions and other elements of the bid. Subsequently, the client negotiates a contract with the contractor that is the most qualified, and selects a bid that conforms to the requirements of the project at a fair price.

Project Schedules and Budget

After the contract has been signed, the design team should review the project's schedule and budget with the contractor. As mentioned previously in this text, construction schedules for sustainability projects are very complex because of additional procedural requirements and the proper sequencing that must occur with a variety of activities, such as commissioning and flush-outs. The schedule must include all the variables and determine the proper time to order products and materials and hire tradespeople. The design team's experience with conventional construction schedules and budgets is very helpful in developing these items for a sustainability project. Using conventional construction experiences as an overall structure and a thorough knowledge of sustainability, the design team is able to integrate these essential elements together. As a result, the team can develop a reasonable and comprehensive schedule and budget. For large projects, management software is used to develop the schedule, but the team has to make certain that all of the elements and contingencies are provided to the program.

The development of a schedule and budget should coincide with finalizing the communication plan. The communication plan must identify who is involved, what is conveyed, the medium, and the location. The team is involved with many of the individuals, businesses, and organizations involved with the project, including the client and the community. An interior designer is actively involved with communicating with the client, design team, manufacturers, and tradespeople. Communicating to all of the stakeholders is a unique and necessary requirement for sustainability projects. Thus, the communication plan must identify all of the stakeholders and determine what information each party needs and when. For sustainability projects, the goals and objectives of the project should be communicated on a regular basis. All of the details and complications of a construction project can easily distract from the original design intent. Making a conscious effort to revisit the goals can help to ensure a successful sustainability project. This can occur at job meetings and through memos.

The chosen communication medium should be determined by what needs to be discussed with whom. Critical updates and decisions that impact the integrity of the design should be discussed with the design team and other relevant individuals in a face-to-face meeting or a teleconference arrangement. Routine sustainability updates should be communicated to all of the stakeholders, and could be done through e-mail or memos. Another form of communication that is essential to sustainability projects is maintaining records. Records must include documents that detail the construction process and the development of as-built drawings and specifications. When a project is seeking certification, there are many requirements associated with documenting and recording construction details. Documentation can include certificates and letter templates that must be signed by the authorized agent. For example, to fulfill fundamental commissioning requirements, LEED-CI submittals must include the "LEED-CI letter template, signed by the commissioning authority and tenant."

The design team is routinely involved with visiting the construction site. However, the majority of the time, individual members of the design team visit the site rather than the entire team. The involvement of the entire team throughout the design process becomes a valuable asset during site visits. The comprehensive knowledge of the project can be applied when each person is at the site. Collectively, the design team monitors all of the features related to sustainability. For example, when an interior designer visits the job site, in addition to carrying out his or her required activities, the designer can also review other aspects related to sustainability, such as the construction waste management, ventilation practices, and the protection of flora and fauna. An important activity to monitor is the overall construction practices. The construction activities for a sustainable building should reflect the principles of sustainability. Therefore, the design team should monitor the site to examine many aspects associated with sustainability, such as ensuring minimal impact to the environment, controlled storm runoff, managed construction IAQ, no smoking on site, management of waste, separation and recycling of materials, management of noise, containment of dust, minimal use of toxic substances, and adherence to local toxic disposal practices. Many of these conditions are especially important to monitor when people are occupying other sections of the building during construction. Lights used during construction should also be monitored to avoid excessive energy consumption and control annoying glare to occupants of surrounding buildings. Sustainability projects are also concerned about the overall health conditions of the workers. Thus, the design team should monitor job site conditions to ensure precautions are executed that minimize workers' exposure to contaminants and toxic substances. This includes monitoring to ensure that areas are isolated from off-gassing volatile finishes. In addition, the team should monitor the impact of the construction on the occupants of the surrounding buildings and attempt to resolve as many problems as possible.

Strategies for Site Administration of Sustainable Environments

During the construction phase, there are several specific tasks that are associated with the work of an interior designer. For example, the interior designer prepares purchase orders for finishes, furniture, and furnishings. Subsequently, the designer monitors their respective delivery dates and installations. A project can take several years to complete; it is likely that the original products and/or materials may become discontinued. Thus, to ensure the designed sustainability features remain intact, an important task is to constantly monitor any substitutions that may occur during the progression of the construction process. When the project involves renovation,

the interior designer is involved with making certain that the specified nonstructural components are protected and retained. The designer can be involved with ensuring that the reuse building materials, such as flooring or ceiling tiles, are salvaged on or off the building site. The designer typically monitors the retention of any existing furniture or furnishings that are salvaged. This activity might require the designer's involvement with overseeing any refurbishments that might be needed, followed by identifying a safe storage facility. For certification purposes, documentation submittals often require photographs of the before and after conditions. In addition, certification may require records that document sources of reused items.

Other responsibilities for the interior designer that are associated with sustainable interiors include verifying products and installation procedures. Generally, an interior designer is involved with monitoring and approving products used for finishes, furniture, lighting, and furnishings. These items are either specified or ordered by an interior designer. As deliveries are made for the project, the designer must verify that the products and materials are in the proper condition and correct quantity. As mentioned previously in this chapter, any items with mold or mildew may not be used. An indication of this problem is water stains on packaging materials. Items must also be examined to verify that the correct product was delivered. Important issues related to sustainability that must be verified include manufacturers' recycled content percentages, confirmation of regional content, rapidly renewable contents, FSC certificates, chain of custody certificates, and confirmation of VOC levels in products. Flush and flow fixtures should be verified by examining the manufacturer's product data that accompany the fixtures. For certification purposes, documents that should be retained are manufacturers' literature, specifications, and certificates or statements verifying the contents.

An interior designer is also involved with activities required for daylighting, electrical lighting, and views. During the construction phase, these elements of the interior must be ordered, delivered, inspected, installed, and commissioned. An interior designer should monitor these activities to ensure that the interior has the designed IEQ. For effective daylighting, the designer should ensure that surfaces are painted with the correct color and finish. The window treatment should operate in concert with the controls and electrical sources. The lighting system must be checked to make sure the correct luminaire is installed in the proper location. All controls must be checked for proper location and functional capabilities. Lamps for all fixtures must be verified, and a reference guide should be developed that provides the exact lamp specifications for each fixture. A reference guide is very useful for the maintenance staff when lamps must be replaced. The directional aim of exterior fixtures should be examined to ensure proper safety and minimize light pollution and/or light trespass. The designer must verify that furniture is coordinated with the location of each person's controls for lighting, temperature, and ventilation. The designer must verify that the placement of furniture does not interfere with views to the outdoors. Required commissioning procedures require the involvement of the designer to verify that the lighting is properly installed and functioning as designed. Commissioning will also include tests to determine if the lighting system is capable of operating as designed and can be efficiently maintained. Documentation of the commissioning tests must be recorded and included in the O&M manual for the building operators and maintenance personnel. Any modifications to the systems must be recorded on the as-built drawings and specifications.

After construction and the installation of finishes, furniture, and furnishings, the design team must do a thorough walk-through of the building and develop a *punch list* of missing or defective items. These items should be submitted in writing to the client, contractor, architect, and engineers. Prior to move-in, the team should monitor the building flush-out and cleaning procedures. The responsible party performing the flush-out test must record all levels of contaminants revealed by the testing procedures. The design team should ensure that the least toxic substances are used for cleaning, and that HEPA vacuums are used to clean carpet. Cleaning procedures should also minimize the use of water for conservation purposes, humidity control, and reducing the potential of fungal growth. Lamps in fixtures should be cleaned, or they may need to be replaced if they were used for years during construction. The team should verify that all recycling storage containers have been installed in the proper location. In addition, the team should check to be certain that all waste is properly removed from the site and recycled materials are delivered to local recycling centers. Excess materials should either be returned to manufacturers or donated to local charities.

POSTOCCUPANCY AND EVALUATION

The design team monitors the progress of move-in activities to ensure that the process is smooth and performed in a safe manner. The team should make certain that procedures are in place to prevent any problems with the IEQ and damage to the built environment. The design team should provide the client and the occupants with a variety of documents related to operating and maintaining a sustainable environment, including O&M manuals, occupant guidelines, product warranties, as-built contract documents, and, if applicable, certification requirements.

Manuals and Educational Sessions for Sustainable Environments

The O&M manuals are developed by the contractor, engineers, and commissioning provider. Manuals for sustainable projects should be developed in a format that illustrates the integration of the building systems, structure, environment, occupants, and maintenance staff. A comprehensive O&M manual is essential for maintaining the built environment for the long-term use of the occupants, community, and future generations. To have buildings with endurance requires adherence to the recommendations of manufacturers and equipment suppliers. An important element of the manual is the commissioning procedures during the warranty phase, which can be one to two years. The mechanical, plumbing, and electrical systems must be commissioned after occupancy to ensure that the systems are functioning properly for the optimum energy efficiency and for the thermal comfort of the occupants.

The O&M manual should have preventative maintenance requirements. Preventative maintenance conserves resources by extending the life of materials, finishes, and equipment. The O&M manual should be accompanied by educational sessions with maintenance staff and equipment handlers. A videotape of educational sessions can be an effective approach to reinforcing operating procedures for equipment. Individuals who need refresher sessions and new staff can use the videotapes. Advantages to videotapes include a consistent demonstration of the procedures and the easy access to all staff.

The design team should also provide recommendations for educational sessions and guidelines for the occupants of the building. Videotapes may also be made of educational sessions that are developed for occupants. Successful sustainable interiors require more than incorporating energy-efficient systems and low-emitting materials. Successful sustainable environments require the occupants to practice the principles of sustainability. Individuals working and living in sustainable interiors must understand sustainability in order to engage in best practices that optimize the design intent. Ideally, the principles of sustainability transform the behavior of people and become integrated with their lifestyle. To help develop a culture of sustainability requires education. People must understand sustainable development and its relationship to society, the environment, and economics. Collaboration should be emphasized and the design team should explain how the collaborative efforts of the users are essential to the success of a sustainable environment. People should learn the goals of the project, the strategies designed to accomplish the goals, and their benefits. This content should be the foundation for reviewing how to use equipment and the proper care for finishes, furniture, and furnishings.

Encouraging and promoting a sustainable lifestyle and environment should be woven through the occupant guidelines and educational sessions. A suggested outline of the contents includes (1) an explanation of sustainable development and international initiatives; (2) benefits of sustainability for the users, community, society, the environment, and economics; (3) goals of the project and how they were developed; (4) sustainable strategies designed to accomplish the goals; (5) operation and maintenance instructions for equipment, lighting systems, and individual controls; (6) procedures for recycling; and (7) providing suggestions for continuous improvement. Throughout the guidelines and educa-

tional sessions, the integration between the goals of the project, the design, and the occupants should be emphasized. For example, the guidelines and the educational sessions could explain that a goal of a sustainable environment is to have a healthy IEQ. Occupants could be told that to accomplish this goal, the built environment has many special features, such as individual control of lighting, temperature, and ventilation. After understanding the relationship between a healthy IEQ and the individual controls, the users should have a greater interest in learning how to operate the system and should be prudent when using the equipment. The users will also have a better understanding of functional problems that should be reported to the maintenance staff. In the educational sessions, knowledge of the thermal comfort systems could be supplemented with the designed energy efficiency of the building. An understanding of energy conservation should be demonstrated when operating the thermal comfort systems.

Postoccupancy Evaluation

A very essential activity for sustainable environments is postoccupancy evaluation (POE), a process for determining user satisfaction with the environment and the success of the built environment. The design team should develop a POE program that identifies (1) who should be asked to participate, (2) information to be collected, (3) the most effective means for collecting the information, (4) when the data should be collected, (5) procedures for rectifying any problems, and (6) a means of dissemination. Conventional building projects generally involve the client and the users of the space in the POE. For sustainability projects, these individuals should be asked to participate in the POE, but other people who should also be included are the contractor, engineers, architects, suppliers, community representatives, and any other stakeholders. The design team should also conduct a self-assessment of the project and the phases of the design process.

Data should be collected at various intervals. An assessment should be conducted soon after occupancy, six months later, and then on an annual basis. A review of a project normally is not conducted over several years; however, there are good reasons to maintain contact with the occupants of a sustainable environment. Regular involvement with the occupants demonstrates a commitment to sustainability, the importance of the long-term perspective, and the practice of continuous improvement. The information collected from all the stakeholders should be used to inform future practice and educate the community and other professionals interested in becoming involved with designing sustainable environments. The design team should disseminate the results of the sustainability project by presenting the results at community meetings and professional conferences. The project could be featured in newsletters, journals, and the local newspaper. In addition, to advance sustainability practices the design team may establish a local network of people who are involved with sustainability projects. Collaborative discussions could focus on improving sustainable environments, learning new technologies, and identifying strategies to get more people involved with sustainable development. The network could be a means for people to learn from one another how to best practice the principles of sustainability for the current and future generations.

Summary

- The contract document phase is a critical stage for the success of sustainable interiors. The documents must be drawn and written to ensure that the designed project is actually constructed.
- Emphasizing sustainability in the contract documents should encourage the involvement of contractors and vendors who are interested in or committed to the philosophy.
- Specification contract documents provide written instructions for procedures, details, and performance requirements. A great deal of the critical information related to sustainability requirements can be detailed in the specifications.
- The two basic types of specifications are closed and open.
- In North American commercial projects, the Construction Specifications Institute's (CSI) MasterFormat™ is the most common standard used to organize information by construction practices.
- To supplement specifications, the design team may want to provide additional information regarding sustainability in the project manual.
- Specifications for a sustainable project must provide detailed instructions for packaging, project conditions, sequencing, field quality control, and cleaning.
- For projects seeking certification, the project manual should include information regarding the organization's requirements, including the anticipated rating.
- The design team is routinely involved with visiting the construction site. The comprehensive knowledge of the project can be applied when each person is at the site.
- To ensure the designed sustainability features remain intact, an important task is to constantly monitor any substitutions that may occur during the progression of the construction process.
- Responsibilities for the interior designer that are associated with sustainable interiors include verifying products and installation procedures.
- The team should make certain that procedures are in place to prevent any problems with the IEQ and damage to the built environment.
- The design team should provide the client and the occupants with a variety of documents related to operating and maintaining a sustainable environment.
- The design team should provide recommendations for educational sessions and guidelines for the occupants of the building.
- An essential activity for sustainable environments is the postoccupancy evaluation (POE). The POE is a process for determining user satisfaction with the environment and the success of the built environment.

Key Terms

Closed specifications
Open specifications
Resource drawings
SectionFormat™

Exercises

1. Contract documents for a project include working drawings, specifications, and schedules. Identify the most important sustainability details that should be provided in contract documents. Include specifics for working drawings, specifications, and schedules.

2. The design team is routinely involved with visiting the construction site. Your design team is to identify the features related to sustainability that should be noted when visiting the construction site. Your team should develop a written summary of the sustainability features and project a timeline for when activities should be observed.

3. Manuals for sustainable projects should be developed in a format that illustrates the integration of the building systems, structure, environment, occupants, and the maintenance staff. Your design team should create a manual and respective educational sessions for a client building a sustainable interior. Submit a mock manual and presentation details for sustainability education sessions.

4. Your team should identify end-users of a commercial space. For the purpose of conducting a POE related to sustainability, develop a list of questions for interviews and surveys. Questions should be specific to the end-users of the space and sustainability. In a written report, include the following information: (1) a list of the questions related to sustainability; (2) an outline of the plan for interviewing and surveying end-users; and (3) a description of how the results will be used for future sustainability projects.

BREEAM CREDIT CATEGORIES FOR RETAIL AND SCHOOLS

Table A.1

BREEAM Credit Categories and Aims for Retail

Credit Categories	Aim of Categories
MANAGEMENT SECTION	
Commissioning—monitoring	To recognize and encourage an appropriate level of building services commissioning and ensure that commissioning is carried out in a coordinated and comprehensive manner.
Commissioning—responsibilities	To recognize and encourage constructors (main contractors, subcontractors, specialist contractors) to carry out commissioning as required by BSRIA/CIBSE guidelines.
Seasonal commissioning	To recognize and encourage seasonal commissioning of building services to ensure optimum performance under actual occupancy conditions, particularly during extremes of weather.
Considerate constructors	To recognize and encourage construction sites managed in an environmentally considerate and accountable manner.
Construction site impacts	To recognize and encourage construction sites managed in an environmentally sound manner in terms of resource use, energy consumption, waste management and pollution.
Environmental management system	To recognize and encourage companies to monitor and manage their own environmental impacts by ensuring adequate management systems are in place.
Environmental responsibility	To recognize and encourage the appointment of named individuals who can take ownership and responsibility for monitoring and implementing strategies to avoid environmental impacts.
Tenant engagement	To raise awareness on environmental issues in general, and in particular the ways in which the building management team is responding to them practically.
Customer information and interface	To recognize facilities that provide information on environmentally related issues concerning the development's operation and its customer's environmental impacts. And also provide a platform for customer feedback on concerns regarding the development's daily operation and associated environmental impacts.
Public information dissemination	To encourage the dissemination of information concerning the building-related environmental impacts and management minimization strategies to reduce those impacts.
Building users' guide	To recognize and encourage the provision of guidance to enable a building user to understand and operate the building efficiently, in line with current good practice.
Building user education	To facilitate the structured and systematic provision of training that enables building users to understand and operate the building efficiently and in a manner that reduces and minimizes operational environmental impacts.
Company environmental policy	To recognize and encourage a formal company environmental policy that addresses and aims to reduce organizational environmental impacts.
Company purchasing policy	To recognize and encourage a formal company environmental purchasing policy that addresses and aims to minimize the environmental impacts from supply and purchasing of materials/goods.

(continued)

Table A.1 (continued)

Credit Categories	Aim of Categories
HEALTH AND WELL-BEING SECTION	
Fail-safe humidification	To avoid risk of illness related to microbial contamination of humidification systems.
Contamination of domestic water systems	To minimize the risk of microbial contamination within domestic water systems.
Office space	To recognize steps taken to provide a good working environment in the office areas within the retail development.
High-frequency lighting	To reduce risk of health problems related to frequency of fluorescent lighting.
External lighting levels	To ensure external lighting is provided at a level of illumination suitable for its task, and to ensure safety and security.
Internal lighting levels	To ensure that internal lighting is designed to provide a level of illumination suitable for the task.
Secure car parks	To recognize retail developments that provide safe and secure car parks that reduce public fears and restrict opportunities for crime to be completed.
Internal air pollution	To reduce the risk to health associated with poor indoor air quality.
Maintenance schedules	To reduce the risk to health associated with poor indoor air quality from poorly maintained air-conditioning and/or mechanical ventilation systems and have planned preventative maintenance procedures in place.
Smoking policy	To minimize the risk to health from passive smoking.
Ventilation rates	To ensure adequate provision of fresh air.
Indoor air quality	To ensure adequate indoor air quality conditions.
ENERGY SECTION	
Building fabric heat loss	To recognize and encourage buildings that have minimized the emission of CO_2, produced in meeting the building's space hearing requirements, through considered fabric design, building form, and system specification.
Internal/external lighting efficiency	To recognize and encourage light fittings that consume less energy, for the same task, than more traditional fittings.
Display lighting	To recognize and encourage display light fittings that consume less energy, for the same task, than more traditional fittings.
Internal lighting strategy	To recognize developments that employ a lighting strategy that minimizes the need for general internal lighting.
External lighting strategy	To recognize buildings that control the level of external lighting and lighting for signs in balance with daylight levels.
Energy submetering	To recognize the provision of energy metering for the purposes of monitoring and targeting of energy consumption for the whole development.
Tenancy submetering	To recognize and encourage the provision of energy submetering to facilitate energy monitoring by tenant or end user.
Specification of space heating plant	To encourage the specification of an energy-efficient heating system.
Specification of water heating plant	To recognize and encourage energy-efficient hot water plant and distribution.
Specification of mechanical ventilation plant	To recognize and encourage the specification of energy-efficient cooling strategies.
Specification of air-conditioning plant	To recognize and encourage the specification of energy-efficient cooling strategies.
Maintenance schedules	To reward procedures that ensure building services are maintained and calibrated for optimum performance.
Building management systems	To identify and minimize potential energy-inefficient operations and procedures through adequate monitoring and control of the major energy consumers.
Lighting maintenance survey	To ensure energy-efficient operation, maintenance, and replacement of light fittings and strategy.
Renewable and low carbon energy use	To encourage the use of a source of energy that emits zero or low carbon emissions to meet part of the building energy demand.

Table A.1 (continued)

Credit Categories	Aim of Categories
Avoiding air infiltration	To avoid air infiltration and subsequent heat loss from the development.
Passive solar design	To ensure the design maximizes the benefits, and takes into consideration the effects, of solar radiation and light.
Services whole life performance	To encourage the selection of viable options for the main building services on the basis of their CO_2 emissions over the course of the building's life cycle.
Cold food storage—cabinets	To encourage energy-efficient specification and operation of cold food cabinets and thus reduce electricity demand and subsequent CO_2.
Cold food storage—cold store	To encourage energy-efficient specification and operation of cold food stores and thus reduce electricity demand and subsequent CO_2.
Cold drink coolers	To recognize and encourage the specification of cold drink dispensers that minimize energy use.
Kitchen and bakery layout	To encourage a kitchen and bakery layout and specification that is complementary to energy efficiency.
Laundry equipment	To encourage the specification of energy-efficient equipment for laundry use.
Dry cleaning equipment	To recognize the energy-efficient operation of dry cleaning equipment.
Lifts	To encourage the specification of energy-efficient transportation systems.
Escalators and traveling walkways	To encourage the specification of energy-efficient transportation systems.
Energy management	To encourage energy efficiency through best practice management of energy consumption.

TRANSPORT SECTION

Proximity to public transportation	To recognize developments that are in close proximity to good public transport links, thereby increasing the likelihood of staff and customers using public transport.
Quality partnership public transport	To improve the efficiency of public transportation and increase the opportunity for non-car travel through closer ties between retailers and local operators.
Quality partnership freight transport	To improve the efficiency of freight transport and reduce its impact on the local environment.
Travel survey	To assess the travel patterns of building users so that the information may be used to develop or update travel plans.
Travel plan	To recognize the development of a travel plan that will encourage building users to maximize the use of environmentally friendly forms of transport.
Travel information space	To encourage the provision of up-to-date travel and transport information for customer use and, thereby, encourage greater use of car alternatives for travel.
Bicycle racks	To provide adequate facilities for customers and staff who choose to cycle to the development and encourage more customers to do the same.
Cyclists' changing facilities	To encourage building occupants to cycle by ensuring adequate cyclists' facilities are or will be present on the site.
Cycle lanes on site	To provide infrastructure that helps to encourage staff and customers to cycle and, thus, reduce congestion and pollution caused by other means of travel.
Pedestrian routes	To recognize and encourage the provision of safe and secure pedestrian routes.
Remote purchase of goods	To reduce unnecessary journeys and, thus, potential congestion and pollution.

WATER SECTION

Water-efficient sanitaryware	To minimize the consumption of freshwater in sanitary applications to a level that saves water while still performing the desired function.
Water-efficient urinals	To minimize the consumption of freshwater for urinal flushing.
Sanitary supply shutoff	To reduce risk of minor leaks in toilet accommodation.

(continued)

Table A.1 (continued)

Credit Categories	Aim of Categories
Maintenance of sanitary fittings	To recognize the provision of a good level of maintenance for all water fittings, thereby ensuring ongoing efficient performance.
Water meter	To ensure systems are capable of being monitored and managed, leading to subsequent reductions in water consumption.
Major leak detection	To reduce the risk of major water leaks.
Reclaimed water: rainwater	To reduce high-quality water consumption for WC flushing, irrigation, laundries, or vehicle washes.
Reclaimed water: graywater	To reduce high-quality water consumption for WC flushing and irrigation.
Irrigation methods	To reduce the consumption of freshwater used for plant and landscape irrigation.
Water recirculation: vehicle wash	To minimize the volume of freshwater used by vehicle-washing facilities.
Water consumption monitoring	To ensure that monitoring and targeting of water consumption is carried out.

MATERIALS AND WASTE SECTION

Reuse of building facade	To recognize and encourage the reuse of any existing facades from buildings that had previously occupied the site.
Reuse of building structure	To recognize and encourage the reuse of existing structures that previously occupied the site.
Recycled aggregates	To recognize and encourage the use of recycled aggregates in construction, thereby reducing the demand for virgin material.
Embodied impacts: building	To recognize and encourage the use of materials that have less impact on the environment, taking account of the full life cycle of materials used in the major specifications.
Embodied impacts: external surfaces	To recognize and encourage the use of materials in construction that have less impact on the environment, taking account of the full life cycle of materials used to provide external hard surfaces.
Embodied impacts: site boundary	To recognize and encourage the use of materials in construction that have less impact on the environment, taking account of the full life cycle of materials used for the site boundary.
Low-impact paints and varnishes	To recognize and encourage the use of paints and varnishes that have a lower embodied environmental impact.
Sustainable sourced timber	To recognize and encourage the specification of responsible sources of timber for primary building elements.
Vehicle impact protection	To ensure that exposed parts of the development are protected from damage by vehicles, forklift trucks, and trolleys.
Waste minimization	To recognize and encourage measures adopted to minimize waste produced on site as a result of building operation.
Recycling facilities household waste	To encourage the provision of facilities on site for the collection of customers' recyclable waste, therefore preventing such waste going directly to landfill.
Recycling facilities for customers	To recognize and encourage retailers who have dedicated "recyclable waste" bins throughout the development for customer use.
Recycling facilities for retailers	To encourage the provision of adequate facilities to cater for the collection and storage of recyclable waste materials generated from the retailers' daily operations.
Waste disposal facilities	To recognize the provision of facilities that enable the efficient and hygienic operation of waste sorting and storage facilities.
Composting	To encourage the provision of facilities for composting of organic waste, thereby reducing waste from the development going directly to landfill.
Asbestos	To recognize and encourage the use of alternatives to asbestos (i.e., materials that do not present the same health risks to occupants.

Table A.1 (continued)

Credit Categories	Aim of Categories
LAND USE AND ECOLOGY SECTION	
Reuse of land	To encourage the reuse of land that has been previously occupied by building developments and discourages the use of previously underdeveloped land for building.
Contaminated land	To encourage positive action to use contaminated land that otherwise would not have been developed.
Land of low ecological value	To encourage, wherever possible, development on land that already has a limited value to wildlife and discourage the development of ecologically valuable sites.
Change of ecological value	To encourage, wherever possible, development on land that already has a low ecological value and thereby discourage the development of more ecologically valuable sites.
Ecological enhancement	To encourage the protection, enhancement, and/or introduction of ecological features on site.
Protection of ecological features	To protect existing ecological features from substantial damage during the clearing of the site and completion of construction works.
Long-term impact on biodiversity	To minimize the long-term impact of the development on the site's and surrounding area's biodiversity.
POLLUTION SECTION	
Building services refrigerant use	To reduce the potential for long-term damage to the earth's stratospheric ozone layer through the accidental release of ozone-depleting substances to the atmosphere.
Cold food storage refrigerant use	To reduce the potential for long-term damage to the earth's stratospheric ozone layer through the accidental release of ozone-depleting substances to the atmosphere.
Refrigerant leak detection	To reduce the emissions of refrigerants to the atmosphere arising from leakages in cooling plants.
Refrigerant recovery	To reduce and prevent unnecessary loss of refrigerants in the event of a leak.
Refrigerant leak detection procedures	To ensure that effective procedures are in place to cover the management and maintenance of refrigeration plants to minimize refrigerant leaks.
NO_x emission from heating source	To encourage the use of space heating that minimizes NO_x emissions, and so reduces pollution in the local vicinity and/or from fossil-fueled power stations.
Minimizing pollution to watercourse	To reduce the potential for pollution to natural watercourses from surface water runoff from buildings and hard surfaces.
Minimizing site water runoff	To delay water runoff from hard surfaces to public sewers and watercourses, thus reducing the risk of localized flooding, pollution, and other environmental damage.
Minimizing artificial light pollution	To ensure that nighttime lighting is concentrated in the appropriate areas and that upward lighting is minimized, reducing unnecessary energy consumption, light pollution, and nuisance to neighboring properties.
Insulant use for services and structure	To reduce the potential for long-term damage to the earth's stratospheric ozone layer and the potential for increased global warming from substances used in the manufacture or composition of insulating materials.
Insulant use for cold food storage	To reduce the potential for long-term damage to the earth's stratospheric ozone layer and the potential for increased global warming from substances used in the manufacture or composition of insulating materials.
Noise attenuation	To reduce the likelihood of complaints of noise from the occupants of nearby noise-sensitive buildings, such as homes, hospitals, and schools.

SOURCE: Building Research Establishment, Ltd. (November 2005), *BREEAM Retail 2005: Scope of the Method*. United Kingdom: Building Research Establishment, Ltd.

Table A.2

BREEAM Credit Categories and Aims for Schools

Credit Categories	Aim of Categories
MANAGEMENT SECTION	
Site investigation	To recognize and encourage detailed site investigation to enable the building to be designed to take account of the conditions and make any remedial action required.
Whole life costing	To recognize and encourage the development of a *whole life cost (WLC)* model for the project to improve design, specification, and through-life maintenance and operation.
Ease of maintenance	To recognize and encourage specification of a building and its mechanical and electrical plant that can be easily maintained during its life span.
Commissioning	To recognize and encourage an appropriate level of building services commissioning and ensure that commissioning is carried out in a coordinated and comprehensive manner.
Building users' guide	To enable the building users to understand and operate the building safely and efficiently, in the manner envisaged by the design team.
Shared facilities	To recognize and encourage flexibility in the design to enable the building to be used as a shared facility with the local community.
Security	To recognize and encourage the implementation of the effective measures in reducing the opportunity for crime.
Considerate constructors	To recognize and encourage construction sites that are managed in a clean, considerate, and respectful way in regard to the local environment.
Construction site impacts	To recognize and encourage construction sites that monitor and reduce environmental impacts.
Publication of building information	To recognize and encourage the publication of information related to the features of the design that reduced the overall environmental impact of the building.
The development as a learning resource	To recognize and encourage the utilization of the building structure and school site as a learning resource to demonstrate environmental issues, such as energy or water conservation, biodiversity, and waste reduction.
HEALTH AND WELL-BEING SECTION	
Daylighting	To improve level of daylighting for building users.
Glare	To reduce problems associated with glare in internal occupied areas.
View out	To allow occupants to refocus their eyes from close work and so reduce the risk of eyestrain.
High-frequency ballasts	To reduce risk of health problems related to the frequency of fluorescent lighting.
Lighting design	To ensure lighting has been designed in line with best practice for suitability and visual comfort.
Lighting controls	To optimize the level of lighting control available to building occupants.
Thermal zoning	To recognize the provision of controls that allow independent adjustment of heating and cooling systems to reflect differing loads.
Thermal comfort	The aim of this credit is to encourage the use of design tools to ensure that thermal comfort is achieved, and to encourage it to be optimized without resorting to mechanical cooling.
Rain noise	To attenuate noise from rain falling on the roof and roof lights in teaching and study spaces.
Acoustic performance	To encourage adoption of good acoustic performance standards and testing to confirm that standards have been met on site.
Microbial contamination	To reduce risk of microbial contamination of hot and cold water systems.
Ventilation rates	To provide sufficient, controlled, and controllable ventilation for indoor air quality and health and hygiene.

Table A.2 (continued)

Credit Categories	Aim of Categories
Drinking water	To provide an appropriate and available supply of drinking water to pupils and staff throughout the day.
Indoor air pollution	To reduce risk of indoor air pollution resulting from external sources.
Occupant-controlled natural ventilation	To enable adequate ventilation to ensure BB87 requirements are met, and to show that the natural ventilation strategy allows for occupants to control the ventilation to provide draft-free fresh air.
Volatile organic compounds	To recognize and encourage the specification of finishes and fittings with low solvent content.
ENERGY SECTION	
Submetering	To recognize and encourage the provision of energy submetering to facilitate energy monitoring of services.
Net carbon dioxide emissions	To recognize and encourage buildings that contain features that help to minimize the CO_2 emissions associated with their operational energy consumption.
Free cooling	To reduce the dependency of the school on mechanical refrigeration to provide thermal comfort conditions, and so reduce energy and CO_2 emissions and also the pollution aspects of refrigerant use.
Light fittings	To recognize and encourage buildings where high-efficacy light fittings are specified.
TRANSPORT SECTION	
Transport plan	To recognize and encourage the development of a school transport plan.
Cyclists' facilities	To encourage building occupants to cycle and so avoid unnecessary car use by ensuring adequate cyclist facilities are present on site.
Pedestrian/cyclist safety	To recognize and encourage provision of safe pedestrian/cycling routes.
Provision of public transport	To recognize and encourage the selection of sites well served by public transport.
WATER SECTION	
Water consumption	To encourage the specification of low-water-consuming sanitary fittings.
Mains leak detection	To reduce the risk of unnecessary water consumption via undetected major leaks within the school or its grounds.
Water meter	To provide appropriate systems to allow the building occupier to monitor, benchmark, and manage efficiently the school's water consumption, avoiding unnecessary or wasteful use of water supplies.
Sanitary supply shutoff	To reduce water being wasted as a result of minor leaks in toilet blocks from sanitary fittings.
Rainwater or graywater use	To encourage the collection and use of wastewater or rainwater to meet toilet flushing needs and reduce the demand for potable freshwater.
MATERIALS AND WASTE SECTION	
Environmental impact of floor covering	To recognize and encourage the use of construction materials that have less impact on the environment, taking account of the full life cycle of materials used as floor coverings.
Environmental impact of upper floor slab	To recognize and encourage the use of construction materials that have less impact on the environment, taking account of the full life cycle of materials used as upper floor slabs.
Environmental impact of external walls	To recognize and encourage the use of construction materials that have less impact on the environment, taking account of the full cycle of materials used in external walls.

(continued)

Table A.2 (continued)

Credit Categories	Aim of Categories
Environmental impact of internal walls	To recognize and encourage the use of construction materials that have less impact on the environment, taking account of the full cycle of materials used for internal walls and partitions.
Environmental impact of roof	To recognize and encourage the use of construction materials that have less impact on the environment, taking account of the full cycle of materials used in roof construction.
Environmental impact of windows	To recognize and encourage the use of construction materials that have less impact on the environment, taking account of the full cycle of materials used in windows.
Environmental impact of hard landscaping and fencing	To recognize and encourage the use of construction materials that have less impact on the environment, taking account of the full cycle of materials used as hard landscaping and/or fencing.
Reuse and recycling	To recognize and encourage the development of both corporate policies and operational procedures for recycling consumables, and the provision of storage space for recyclable waste.
Reuse of structure	To recognize and encourage the reuse of existing structures that previously occupied the site.
Reuse of facade	To recognize and encourage the reuse of any existing facades from buildings that had previously occupied the site.
Recycled aggregates	To recognize and encourage the use of recycled aggregates in construction, thereby reducing the demand for virgin material.
Sustainable timber	To recognize and encourage the specification of timber from responsible sources and harvested forests/plantations for primary building elements.
Designing for longevity	To recognize and encourage the protection of exposed parts of the building and landscaping.
Asbestos	To recognize and encourage the use of alternatives to asbestos (i.e., materials that do not present the same health risks to occupants).
LAND USE AND ECOLOGY SECTION Reuse of land	To encourage the reuse of land that has been previously built on or used for industrial purposes within the last 50 years.
Use of contaminated land	To encourage positive action to use contaminated land that otherwise would not have been developed.
Consultation with students and staff	To encourage the design team to include pupils and staff in the design of the school grounds.
Land of low ecological value	To encourage, whenever possible, development on land that already has a limited value to wildlife and discourage the development on land that already has a limited value to wildlife and discourage the development of ecologically valuable sites. This is affected by previous uses and the presence of ecological features such as trees, hedges, watercourses, wetlands, meadows, etc.
Local wildlife partnerships	To encourage the design team to form a partnership with a local group that has wildlife expertise, in order to benefit from their knowledge and ongoing support.
Ecological enhancement	To encourage the enhancement of ecological value during development.
Change in ecological value	To minimize the ecological impact of a school development project and maximize the enhancement of a site for both new and existing buildings.
Protection of ecological features	To protect ecological features from substantial damage during the clearing of the site and completion of construction works.
Long-term impact on biodiversity	To minimize the long-term impact of the completed development on biodiversity.

Table A.2 (continued)

Credit Categories	Aim of Categories
POLLUTION SECTION	
Water pollution	To reduce the potential arising as a result of water runoff from the site, buildings, and hard surfaces to natural watercourses.
Water runoff	To prevent and attenuate water runoff from the hard surfaces of the site to public sewers and watercourses, and thus reduce the risk and impact of flooding.
Refrigerant ODP/GWP	To reduce the potential release of refrigerants with global warming potentials exceeding 5, ozone-depleting substances, and substances hazardous to health; from refrigeration systems; or cold rooms, where present.
Insulant ODP/GWP	To reduce the potential for long-term damage to the earth's stratospheric ozone layer from ozone-depleting substances used in the manufacture or composition of thermal insulants.
NO_x emissions of heating source	To encourage the use of NO_x emitting boilers and reduce pollution to the local vicinity.
Nighttime light pollution	To reduce the impact of external light fittings on levels of nighttime pollution.
On-site renewable energy	To reduce atmospheric pollution by encouraging locally generated renewable energy to supply a significant proportion of the building's energy demand.

SOURCE: Building Research Establishment, Ltd. (November 2005), *BREEAM Schools Assessment 2005.* United Kingdom: Building Research Establishment, Ltd.

STANDARDS FOR PRESERVATION, REHABILITATION, RESTORATION, AND RECONSTRUCTION

Standards for Preservation

The Secretary of the Interior's Standards for the Treatment of Historic Properties, 1995

- A property will be used as it was historically, or be given a new use that maximizes the retention of distinctive materials, features, spaces, and spatial relationships. Where a treatment and use have not been identified, a property will be protected and, if necessary, stabilized until additional work may be undertaken.
- The historic character of a property will be retained and preserved. The replacement of intact or repairable historic materials or alteration of features, spaces, and spatial relationships that characterize a property will be avoided.
- Each property will be recognized as a physical record of its time, place, and use. Work needed to stabilize, consolidate, and conserve existing historic materials and features will be physically and visually compatible, identifiable upon close inspection, and properly documented for future research.
- Changes to a property that have acquired historic significance in their own right will be retained and preserved.
- Distinctive materials, features, finishes, and construction techniques or examples of craftsmanship that characterize a property will be preserved.
- The existing condition of historic features will be evaluated to determine the appropriate level of intervention needed. Where the severity of deterioration requires repair or limited replacement of a distinctive feature, the new material will match the old in composition, design, color, and texture.
- Chemical or physical treatments, if appropriate, will be undertaken using the gentlest means possible. Treatments that cause damage to historic materials will not be used.
- Archaeological resources will be protected and preserved in place. If such resources must be disturbed, mitigation measures will be undertaken.

SOURCE: www.cr.nps.gov.

Standards for Rehabilitation

The Secretary of the Interior's Standards for the Treatment of Historic Properties, 1995

- A property will be used as it was historically or be given a new use that requires minimal change to its distinctive materials, features, spaces, and spatial relationships.
- The historic character of a property will be retained and preserved. The removal of distinctive materials or alteration of features, spaces, and spatial relationships that characterize a property will be avoided.
- Each property will be recognized as a physical record of its time, place, and use. Changes that create a false sense of historical development, such as adding conjectural features or elements from other historic properties, will not be undertaken.
- Changes to a property that have acquired historic significance in their own right will be retained and preserved.
- Distinctive materials, features, finishes, and construction techniques or examples of craftsmanship that characterize a property will be preserved.
- Deteriorated historic features will be repaired rather than replaced. Where the severity of deterioration requires replacement of a distinctive feature, the new feature will match the old in design, color, texture, and, where possible, materials. Replacement of missing features will be substantiated by documentary and physical evidence.
- Chemical or physical treatments, if appropriate, will be undertaken using the gentlest means possible. Treatments that cause damage to historic materials will not be used.
- Archaeological resources will be protected and preserved in place. If such resources must be disturbed, mitigation measures will be undertaken.
- New additions, exterior alterations, or related new construction will not destroy historic materials, features, and spatial relationships that characterize the property. The new work shall be differentiated from the old and will be compatible with the historic materials, features, size, scale and proportion, and massing to protect the integrity of the property and its environment.
- New additions and adjacent or related new construction will be undertaken in a such a manner that, if

removed in the future, the essential form and integrity of the historic property and its environment would be unimpaired.

SOURCE: www.cr.nps.gov.

Standards for Restoration

The Secretary of the Interior's Standards for the Treatment of Historic Properties, 1995

- A property will be used as it was historically or be given a new use that reflects the property's restoration period.
- Materials and features from the restoration period will be retained and preserved. The removal of materials or alteration of features, spaces, and spatial relationships that characterize the period will not be undertaken.
- Each property will be recognized as a physical record of its time, place, and use. Work needed to stabilize, consolidate, and conserve materials and features from the restoration period will be physically and visually compatible, identifiable upon close inspection, and properly documented for future research.
- Materials, features, spaces, and finishes that characterize other historical periods will be documented prior to their alteration or removal.
- Distinctive materials, features, finishes, and construction techniques or examples of craftsmanship that characterize the restoration period will be preserved.
- Deteriorated features from the restoration period will be repaired rather than replaced. Where the severity of deterioration requires replacement of a distinctive feature, the new feature will match the old in design, color, texture, and, where possible, materials.
- Replacement of missing features from the restoration period will be substantiated by documentary and physical evidence. A false sense of history will not be created by adding conjectural features, features from other properties, or by combining features that never existed together historically.
- Chemical or physical treatments, if appropriate, will be undertaken using the gentlest means possible. Treatments that cause damage to historic materials will not be used.

- Archaeological resources affected by a project will be protected and preserved in place. If such resources must be disturbed, mitigation measures will be undertaken.
- Designs that were never executed historically will not be constructed.

SOURCE: www.cr.nps.gov.

Standards for Reconstruction

The Secretary of the Interior's Standards for the Treatment of Historic Properties, 1995

- Reconstruction will be used to depict vanished or nonsurviving portions of a property when documentary and physical evidence is available to permit accurate reconstruction with minimal conjecture, and such reconstruction is essential to the public understanding of the property.
- Reconstruction of a landscape, building, structure, or object in its historic location will be preceded by a thorough archaeological investigation to identify and evaluate those features and artifacts which are essential to an accurate reconstruction. If such resources must be disturbed, mitigation measures will be undertaken.
- Reconstruction will include measures to preserve any remaining historic materials, features, and spatial relationships.
- Reconstruction will be based on the accurate duplication of historic features and elements substantiated by documentary or physical evidence rather than on conjectural designs or the availability of different features from other historic properties. A reconstructed property will re-create the appearance of the nonsurviving historic property in materials, design, color, and texture.
- A reconstruction will be clearly identified as a contemporary re-creation.
- Designs that were never executed historically will not be constructed.

SOURCE: www.cr.nps.gov.

PROFESSIONAL ORGANIZATIONS, GOVERNMENT AGENCIES, AND TRADE ASSOCIATIONS

Advanced Buildings, www.advancedbuildings.org

Advanced Desiccant Cooling and Dehumidification Program, www.nrel.gov/desiccantcool

Advanced Transportation Technology Institute, www.atti-info.org/

Advanced Waste Management Systems, Inc., www.awm.net/iso14000.htm

Air Quality Management District (AQMD), www.aqmd.gov

Alliance for Sustainable Jobs and the Environment, www.asje.org/

Alliance of Foam Packaging Recyclers, www.epspackaging.org/

Alliance to Save Energy, www.ase.org/

American Concrete Pavement Association, www.pavement.com/

American Council for an Energy-Efficient Economy (ACEEE), www.aceee.org/

American Environmental Health Foundation, www.aehf.com/

American Farmland Trust, www.farmland.org

American Gas Cooling Center, www.agcc.org

American Institute of Architects, www.aia.org

American Lung Association, www.lungusa.org

American Nature Study Society (ANSS), www.members.aol.com/anssonline/

American Rainwater Catchment Systems Association, www.arcsa-usa.org/

American Rivers, www.amrivers.org

American Society of Heating, Refrigerating, and Air-Conditioning Engineers (ASHRAE), www.ashrae.org

American Solar Energy Society, www.ases.org/

American Water Works Association, www.awwa.org/

Amsterdam Environmental and Building Department, www.dmb.amsterdam.nl/

Analysis of the Performance of Students in Daylit Schools, www.innovativedesign.net/studentsperformance.htm

Architects/Designers/Planners for Social Responsibility (ADPSR), www.adpsr.org

Art of Daylighting, www.edcmag.com/CDA/ArticleInformation/features/BNP_Features_Item/0,4120,18800,00.html

Associated Air Balance Council (AABC), www.aabchq.com

Association for Commuter Transportation, tmi.cob.fsu.edu/act/

Association for the Environmental Health of Soils (AEHS), www.aehs.com

Association of Environmentally Conscious Builders, www.aecb.net/

ASTM International, www.astm.org

Australian Building Greenhouse Rating Scheme, www.abgr.com.au/

Benefits of Using Alternative Transportation Costs Calculator, www.metrocommuterservices.org/cost.htm

BEQUEST, www.surveying.salford.ac.uk/bqextra/main.htm

Best Workplaces for Commuters, www.bestworkplacesforcommuters.gov/index.htm

Bicycle and Pedestrian Program, U.S. Department of Transportation, www.fhwa.dot.gov/environment/bikeped/

Bicyclinginfo.org, www.bicyclinginfo.org

Bike to Work, www.biketowork.com

Bioenergy Information Network, www.esd.ornl.gov/

Biological Diversity, www.biodiv.org

Biomimicry, www.biomimicry.org

Bread for the World, www.bread.org

BREEAM, http://products.bre.co.uk/breeam/

British Urban Regeneration Association (BURA), www.bura.org.uk/

Building Commissioning Association, www.bcxa.org

Building Energy Codes Program, U.S. Department of Energy, www.energycodes.gov

Building Environment and Thermal Envelope Council, www.nibs.org/

Building for Environmental and Economic Sustainability, www.bfrl.nist/gov/oae/software/bees.html

BuildingGreen, www.buildinggreen.com

Building Materials Reuse Association (formerly the Used Building Materials Association), www.ubma.org

Building Research Establishment, www.bre.co.uk/

Business for Social Responsibility (BSR), www.bsr.org

California Integrated Waste Management Board, www.ciwmb.ca.gov

California Integrated Waste Management Board, www.ciwmb.ca.gov/CalMAX

California Integrated Waste Management Board, www.ciwmb.ca.gov/WasteChar/

Canadian Environmental Protection Act (CEPA), www.ec.gc.ca

Canadian Institute of Chartered Accountants, www.cica.ca/

Carbon Trust, www.thecarbontrust.co.uk

Carpet and Rug Institute, www.carpet-rug.com

Center for Ecoliteracy, www.ecoliteracy.org

Center for Holistic Management,
www.holisticmanagement.org

Center for Marine Conservation, www.cmc-ocean.org

Center for Maximum Potential Building Systems,
www.cmpbs.org/

Center for Our Common Future, http://habitat.org/
projects/cocf.html

Center for Plant Conservation, www.mobot.org/CPC/

Center for Renewable Energy and Sustainable Technology
(Crest) Sustainable Energy and Development Online
(Solstice), http://solstice.crest.org/

Center for Resourceful Building Technology (CRBT),
www.crbtdb.ncat.org/

Center for Resourceful Building Technology (CRBT),
www.crbt.org/

Center for Resourceful Building Technology (CRBT),
www.montana.com/crbt/

Center for Science in the Public Interest, www.cspinet.org

Center for Social and Environmental Accounting Research,
www.dundee.ac.uk/

Center for the Built Environment,
www.cbe.berkeley.edu

Center for Watershed Protection, www.cwp.org

Center of Excellence for Sustainable Development,
www.sustainable.doe.gov

Centre for Alternative Technology, www.cat.org.uk/

Centre for Environmental Informatics (CEI),
http://cei.sunderland.ac.uk/envrep/iso14000.htm

Chartered Institute of Building Services Engineers,
London, www.CIBSE.co.uk

Chesapeake Bay Foundation, www.cbf.org

Choosing a Toilet, www.taunton.com/finehomebuilding/
pages/h00042.asp

Citistates, www.citistates.com/

Citizen's Clearinghouse for Hazardous Waste,
www.essential.org/cchw/

City Bikes, www.citybikes.com

Clean Energy, Union of Concerned Scientists,
www.ucsusa.org/clean_energy

Clean Sites, http://clu-in.org/programs/clnsites/
cleaninc.htm

Clean Water Act, www.epa.gov/watertrain/cwa

Clean Water Action Project, www.cleanwateraction.org

Clean Water America, www.cleanwateramerica.org

Climate Solutions, www.climatesolutions.org/

Coalition for Environmentally Responsible Economies
(Ceres), www.ceres.org

Cohousing Network, www.cohousing.org

Commission for Architecture and the Built Environment,
www.cabe.org.uk/

Common Cause, www.commoncause.org

Community Transportation Association of America,
www.ctaa.org

Commuting Guide for Employers,
www.self-propelled-city.com/employ-comm_html

Composting Toilet Reviews, www.buildinggreen.com

Congress for the New Urbanism, www.cnu.org

Congress Watch, www.citizen.org/congress

Conservation International, www.conservation.org

Construction Materials Recycling Association,
www.cdrecycling.org

Consumer Product Safety Commission,
www.cpsc.gov

Contractors' Guide to Preventing Waste and Recycling,
Resource Venture, www.resourceventure.org

Cool Roof Rating Council, www.coolroofs.org

Co-op America's National Green Pages,
www.coopamerica.org

Coral Reef Alliance, www.coral.org

CoreNet Global Corporate Real Estate Network,
www.corenetglobal.org

Council on Economic Priorities (CEP),
www.2.realaudio.com/cep/home.html

Crest, www.sol.crest.org

Critical Mass Energy Program, www.citizen.org/cmep

Deep Ecology Platform, www.deepecology.org

Defenders of Wildlife, www.defenders.org

Design for Homes, www.designforhomes.org/

Development Center for Appropriate Technology (DCAT),
www.dcat.net

Directory of Green Building Professionals,
www.directory.greenbuilder.com

Directory of Green Building Professionals,
www.cfd.rmit.edu.au/programs/sustainable_buildings/
directory_of_green_building_professionals

DOE2, www.doe2.com

Ducks Unlimited, www.ducks.org/

Earth 911, www.earth911.org/master.asp

Earth Architecture: An Overview WebPage, www.ran.org/

Earth Charter Initiative, www.earthcharter.org

Earth Island Institute, www.earthisland.org

Earth Pledge Foundation, www.earthpledge.org/

Earthwatch Institute, www.earthwatch.org

Ecologia, www.ecologia.org

Ecological Design Association, www.seda2.org

Ecological Design Institute, www.ecodesign.org

Eco-Portal, www.eco-portal.com/

ECOS Corporation, www.ecoscorporation.com/

Ecotrust, www.ecotrust.org

Employer's Guide to Encouraging Bicycle Commuting,
Bicycle Coalition of Maine, www.bikemaine.org/
btwemployer.htm

Energie-Cités (association of European local authorities
promoting local sustainable energy policy),
www.energie-cites.org/

Energy and Environmental Research Center (EERC),
www.eerc.und.nodak.edu

Energy Crossroads, http://eetd.lbl.gov/EnergyCrossroads/
EnergyCrossroads.html

Energy Design Resources,
www.energydesignresources.com

Energy Efficiency and Renewable Energy Network DOE
(EREN), http://es.epa.gov/cooperative/websites/
eren.html

Energy Efficient Building Association (EEBA),
www.eeba.org

Energy Guide, www.energyguide.com

Energy Ideas Clearinghouse, www.energy.wsu.edu/

Energy Information Administration (EIA),
www.eia.doe.gov/

Energy Outreach Center (EOC), www.eoc.org/

Energy Rated Homes of America, www.erha.com/

ENERGY STAR Reflective Roofing Products,
www.energystar.gov/index./cfm?c=roof_prods.pr_
roof_products

ENERGY STAR, www.energystar.gov

English Partnerships, www.englishpartnerships.co.uk/

ENVEST Building Research Establishment,
www.bre.co.uk/services/ENVEST.html

Envirolink, www.envirolink.org/

Environmental Access Research Network (EARN),

Environmental Building News (EBN),
www.buildinggreen.com/ecommerce/ebn.cfm?

Environmental Careers Organization (ECO), www.eco.org

Environmental Defense Fund, www.edf.org

Environmental Defense, www.environmentaldefense.org

Environmental Design + Construction, www.edcmag.com

Environmental Law Institute, www.eli.org

Environmental Organization Web Directory,
www.webdirectory.com/

Environmental Profiles, www.bre.co.uk/services/
Environmental_Profiles.html

Envirosense, www.envirosense.org/

EPA Sustainable Redevelopment of Brownfields Program,
www.epa.gov/brownfields

European Commission:

Energy: www.europa.eu.int/comm/energy/

Environment: www.europa.eu.int/comm/environment/

Transport and Energy: www.europa.eu.int/comm/dgs/
energy_transport/

Transport: www.europa.eu.int/comm/transport

FacilitiesNet, www.facilitiesnet.com

Fish and Wildlife Reference Service

Forest Certification Resource Center,
www.certifiedwood.org

Forest Stewardship Council, www.fscus.org

Forum for the Future, www.forumforthefuture.org.uk/

Freedom from Hunger, www.freedomfromhunger.org

Friends of the Earth, www.foe.org

FTC Guides for the Use of Environmental Marketing
Claims, www.ftc.gov

General Green Building Links, www.ci.san-jose.ca/esd/
GB-LINKS.HTM

George Washington University Environmental Information
Resources, www.gwu.edu/

Global Action Plan, http://empowermentinstitute.net/

Global Ecovillage Network, http://gen.ecovillage.org

Global Environment and Technology Foundation,
www.getf.org/

Global Environment Management Initiative (GEMI),
www.gemi.org

Global Environment Options, www.geonetwork.org

Global Network of Environment and Technology (GNET),
www.gnet.org

Global Reporting Initiative, www.globalreporting.org

Global Water Partnership, www.sida.se/gwp

Government Institutes, www.govinst.com

Green Architect, http://archrecord.construction.com/
features/green/

Green Building Advisor, www.greenbuildingadvisor.com/

Green Building Challenge, http://greenbuilding.ca.iisbe/
gbc2k2/gbc2k2-start.htm

Green Building Council of Australia, www.gbcaus.org/

Green Corps, www.greencorps.com.au/

Green Seal Standard, www.greenseal.org

GreenClips, www.greendesign.net/greenclips

GreenClips Archives, http://solstice.crest.org/sustainable/
greenclips/info.html

Green-e Program, www.green-e.org

Green-e Renewable Electricity Certification Program,
www.green-e.org

Greenguard, www.greenguard.org

Greenpeace, USA, www.greenpeace.org

Greenroofs.com, www.greenroofs.com

Greenware Environmental Systems, www.greenware.ca

Groundwork, www.groundwork.org.uk/

Growth and Water Resources, www.epa.gov/watertrain/
smartgrowth

Guidance Specifying Management Measures for Sources of
Non-Point Pollution in Coastal Waters, January 1993,
www.epa.gov/owow/nps/MMGI

Guide to Resource-Efficient Building Elements,
www.crbt.org

Habitat for Humanity International, www.habitat.org

Heat Island Effect, U.S. Environmental Protection Agency,
www.epa.gov/heatisland

Heat Island Group—Cool Roofs, Lawrence Berkeley
National Laboratory, http://eetd.lbl.gov/HeatIsland/
Cool-Roofs/

Heat Island Group, Lawrence Berkeley National
Laboratory, http://eetd.lbl.gov/HeatIsland/

Heifer Project International, www.heifer.org

Holistic Management, www.holisticmanagement.org

Home Energy Rating Systems (HERS) Council,
www.herscouncil.org

"Home Energy Rating Systems (HERS) Required
Verification and Diagnostic Testing," California Low
Rise Residential Alternative Calculation Method
Approval Manual, www.energy.ca.gov

Home Energy Ratings, www.energystar.gov/default.shtml

Home Power Magazine, www.homepower.com

How to Conserve Water and Use It Effectively, U.S. Environmental Protection Agency, www.epa.gov/OW/you/chap3.html

HUD (U.S. Department of Housing and Urban Development), www.hud.gov/

IAQ Standards Program, State of Washington, www.aerias.org

ICLEI Global, www.iclei.org

Illuminating Engineering Society of North America, www.iesna.org

Indoor Air Quality Information Clearinghouse, www.epa.gov/iaq/iaqxline.html

Indoor Air Quality Page, http://ttsw.com/AirJT.html

Inform: Strategies for a Better Environment, www.informinc.org

Institute for Earth Education, www.eartheducation.org

Institute for Local Self-Reliance (ILSR), www.ilsr.org

Institute of Scrap Recycling Industries (ISRI), www.isri.org

Interface Sustainability, www.interfacesustainability.com

Intergovernmental Panel on Climate Change, www.ipcc.ch/

International Alliance for Sustainable Agriculture, www.mtn.org/iasa

International Chamber of Commerce, www.iccwbo.org

International Council for Local Environmental Initiatives, www.iclei.org/

International Dark-Sky Association, www.darksky.org

International Energy Agency Solar Heating and Cooling Programme, www.iea-shc.org

International Food Policy Research Institute, www.ifpri.org/

International Initiative for Sustainable Built Environment, www.iiSBE.org/

International Institute for Bau-Biologie and Ecology (IBE), www.bau-biologieusa.com

International Institute for Sustainable Development, www.iisd.org/

International Network for Environmental Management (INEM), www.globalreporting.org

International Organization for Standardization, www.iso.org

International Performance Measurement and Verification Protocol, vol. 1 (2001), www.ipmvp.org

International Rivers Network, www.irn.org

International Union for the Scientific Study of Population, www.iussp.org

International Water Management Institute, www.iwmi.cgiar.org

Investor Responsibility Research Center (IRRC), irc@aol.com

Iris Communications (Resources for Environmental Design Index), www.oikos.com/redi/index.html

Irrigation Association, www.irrigation.org

ISO 14000 Infocenter, www.iso14000.com/

Izaak Walton League of America, www.iwla.org

Janitorial Products Pollution Prevention Project, www.westp2net.org/janitorial/jp4.htm

Lady Bird Johnson Wildflower Center, www.wildflower.org

Lakenet, www.worldlakes.org

Land Institute, www.midkan.com/theland/

Land Trust Alliance (LTA), www.lta.org

Lawrence Berkeley National Laboratory, www.lbl.gov/

League of Conservation Voters, www.lcv.org

League of Women Voters of the United States, www.lwv.org

Lighting Research Center, www.lrc.rpi.edu

Living Lakes Partnership, www.livinglakes.org

Local Government Commission (LGC), www.lgc.org/

Local Power, www.local.org

Management Institute for Environment and Business, www.wri.org/wri/meb/

Marine Stewardship Council, www.msc.org

Measurement and Verification Documents, http://ateam.lbl.gov/mv

Millennium Development Goals, www.developmentgoals.org/

Millennium Ecosystem Assessment, www.millenniumassessment.org

Million Solar Roofs Initiative, www.eren.doe.gov/

MIT Technology, Business, and Environment Program, www.envirolink.org/resource.html?itemid=710201144631&catid=1

National Agricultural Library, www.grande.nal.usda.gov/wqic

National Arbor Day Foundation, www.arborday.org

National Association of Conservation Districts (NACD), www.nacdnet.org

National Association of Home Builders Research Center, www.nahbrc.com

National Association of Regulatory Utility Commissioners, www.naruc.org

National Audubon Society, www.audubon.org

National Australian Building Environmental Rating System, www.ea.gov.au/

National Center for Environmental Decisionmaking Research (NCEDR), www.ncedr.org/guides

National Center for Photovoltaics (NCPV), www.nrel.gov/ncpv/

National Climatic Data Center, www.ncdc.noaa.gov/oa/ncdc.html

National Coalition Against the Misuse of Pesticides, www.ncamp.org

National Council for Science and the Environment, www.ncseonline.org/

National Database on Environmental Management Systems, http://ndems.cas.unc.edu/

National Drought Mitigation Center, www.drought.unl.edu

National Environmental Balancing Bureau (NEBB), www.nebb.org

National Ground Water Association (NGWA), www.ngwa.org

National Institute for Occupational Safety and Health (NIOSH), www.cdc.gov/niosh/npg.html

National Institute of Building Sciences, www.nibs.org

National Lead Information Center (NLIC), www.epa.gov/lead/pubs/nlic.htm

National Materials Exchange Network (NMEN), www.earthcycle.com/nmen

National Park Foundation, www.nationalparks.org

National Parks Conservation Association, www.npca.org

National Pesticides Telecommunications Network (NPTN), ace.orst.edu/info/nptn/index.html

National Renewable Energy Laboratory Energy-10™ Program, www.nrel.gov/buildings/energy10.html

National Renewable Energy Laboratory, www.nrel.gov

National Safety Council's Air Quality Program, www.nsc.org/EHC/airqual.htm

National Solid Wastes Management Association (NSWMA), www.envasns.org/nswma

National Strategies for Sustainable Development, www.nssd.net

National Technical Information Service, www.ntis.gov

National Trust for Historic Preservation, www.nthp.org

National Water Resources Association, www.nwra.org/index.cfm

National Wildlife Federation, www.nwf.org

Nationwide Rivers Inventory, www.ncrc.nps.gov/rtca/nri

Natural Home Magazine, www.naturalhomemagazine.com

Natural Logic, www.natlogic.com/

Natural Resources Conservation Service Backyard Water Conservation, www.nrcs.usda.gov/feature/backyard/watercon.html

Natural Resources Defense Council, www.nrdc.org

Natural Step Canada, www.naturalstep.ca

Natural Step (TNS), www.naturalstep.org

Nature Conservancy, http://nature.org/

Nature Conservancy, www.tnc.org

New Buildings Institute, www.newbuildings.org

New Buildings Institute's Productivity and Building Science Program, www.newbuildings.org

New England Light Pollution Advisory Group, http://cfa-www.harvard.edu

New Ideas in Pollution Regulation (NIPR), www.worldbank.org

NIST Multizone Modeling Software, www.bfrl.nist.gov/IAQanalysis/Software.htm

North American Lake Management Society, www.nalms.org

Northeast Recycling Council (NERC), www.nerc.org/

Northeast Sustainable Energy Association (NESEA), www.nesea.org

Northwest Earth Institute, www.nwei.org

NSF International Strategic Registrations, www.nsf-isr.org

Nuclear Information and Resource Service (NIRS), www.nirs.org

Office of Transportation and Air Quality, U.S. Environmental Protection Agency, www.epa.gov/otaq/

Oikos Green Building Source, www.oikos.com/

One World Network, www.oneworld.net/

Online TDM Encyclopedia, www.vtpi.org/tdm

Oregon Natural Step, www.ortns.org

Oxfam America, www.oxfamamerica.org

Passive Solar Industries Council (PSIC), www.psic.org

PECI Model Building Commissioning Plan and Guide Specifications, Portland Energy Conservation Inc., www.peci.org

Penn State Center for Green Roof Research, http://hortweb.cas.psu.edu/research/greenroofcenter/

Performance Review Institute, www.pri.sae.org

Permaculture, www.permaculture.biz

Pew Center on Global Climate Change, www.pewclimate.org/

Photovoltaic Systems Assistance Center (PVSAC), mfnl.xjtu.edu.cn/gov-doe-sandia/pv/pvsac.htm

Physicians for Social Responsibility, www.psr.org

Planned Parenthood Federation of America, www.plannedparenthood.org

Planning and Development Network, www.planetizen.com/

Plants for Clean Air Council (PCAC), www.plants4cleanair.org

Pollution Prevention and Energy Efficiency Yellow Pages, www.p2.org/yellow_pages96/p2e2.html

Population Action International, www.populationaction.org

Population Connection, www.populationconnection.org

Population Institute, www.populationinstitute.org

Population Reference Bureau, www.prb.org

Post-Construction Storm Water Management in New Development and Redevelopment, U.S. Environmental Protection Agency, http://cfpub.epa.gov/npdes/stormwater/menuofbmps/post7.cfm

President's Council on Sustainable Development, www.whitehouse.gov/pcsd/

Protected Harvest, www.protectedharvest.org

Public Citizen, www.publiccitizen.org

Rachel Carson Council, http://members.aol.com/rccouncil/ourpage/rec_page.htm

Radiance Software, radsite.lbl.gov

Rails-to-Trails Conservancy, www.railstotrails.org

Rainforest Action Network (RAN), www.ran.org

Rainforest Alliance, www.rainforest-alliance.org

Recycling and Waste Management During Construction, www.metrokc.gov

Recycling at Work, U.S. Conference of Mayors, www.usmayors.org\

Reef Relief, www.reefrelief.org

Renewables for Sustainable Village Power, www.rsvp.nrel.gov

Renew America, http://sol.crest.org/environment/ renew america/

Residential Energy Services Network (RESNET), www.natresnet.org

Resource Renewal Institute Green Plans, http://greenplans.rri.org

Resource Renewal Institute, www.rri.org/

Resources for Global Sustainability, www.environmentalgrants.com

Resources for the Future, www.rff.org

Reuse Development Organization (ReDO), www.redo.org

Rocky Mountain Institute, www.rmi.org

Saline Lakes of the World, lakes.chebucto.org/saline1.html

Salvaged Building Materials Exchange, Green Building Resource Guide, www.greenguide.com/exchange/ search.html

Save the Dunes Council, savedunes.org

Scenic America, www.scenic.org

Schumacher Society, www.schumachersociety.org/

Scientific Certification Systems Forest Conservation Program, www.scscertified.com/forestry/

Scientific Certification Systems, www.scscertified.com/

Scorecard: The Pollution Information Site, www.scorecard.org

Second Nature, www.secondnature.org

Sewage World, www.sewage.net

Shack/Slum Dwellers International, www.sdinet.org/

Sheet Metal and Air Conditioning Contractors' National Association (SMACNA), www.smacna.org

Sierra Club, www.sierraclub.org

Sky and Telescope, http://skyandtelescope.com/resources/ darksky/default.asp

Smart Architecture in The Netherlands, www.smartarch.nl/

Smart Communities Network, www.sustainable.doe.gov/ efficiency/weinfo.shtml

Smart Commute, www.smartcommute.org/

Smart Growth Network, www.smartgrowth.org

Soil and Water Conservation Society, www.swcs.org

Solar City, www.solarcity.org/

Solar Energy International, www.solarenergy.org

Solari, www.solari.com

Sourcebook for Green and Sustainable Building, www.greenbuilder.com/sourcebook/ ConstructionWaste.html

South Coast Air Quality Management District, www.aqmd.gov

Southface Energy Institute, www.southface.org/

Southwest Network for Environmental and Economic Justice, www.sneej.org/

Sprawl Watch Clearinghouse, www.sprawlwatch.org/

Standard Practice for the Testing of Volatile Organic Emissions from Various Sources Using Small-Scale Environmental Chambers (State of California Standard 1350), Section 9, www.dhs.ca.gov

State of Arizona Telecommuting Program, www.teleworkarizona.com

Steel Recycling Institute, www.recycle-steel.org

Stockholm Partnerships for Sustainable Cities, www.partnerships.stockholm.se/

Stormwater Authority, www.stormwaterauthority.org/ stormwater_stockpile/default.aspx

Stormwater Manager's Resource Center, www.stormwatercenter.net

Student Conservation Association (SCA), www.sca-inc.org

Sustainability, www.sustainability.ca/

SustainAbility, www.sustainability.com

Sustainable Architecture, Building, and Culture, www.sustainableabc.com

Sustainable Building Sourcebook, www.greenbuilder.com/

Sustainable Building Technical Manual, Public Technology, www.pti.org

Sustainable Buildings Industry Council, www.sbicouncil.org/

Sustainable Business.com, www.sustainablebusiness.com/

Sustainable Cities, European Sustainable Cities Project and Campaign

Sustainable Communities Network, www.sustainable.org/

Sustainable Development, www.sustainable-development.gov.uk/

Sustainable Development Commission, www.sd-commission.gov.uk

Sustainable Living Sourcebook, www.greenbuilder.com

Sustainable Production, www.sustainableproduction.org

Sustainable Sources, www.greenbuilder.com

Teletrips, www.secure-teletrips.com

Telework Collaborative, www.teleworkcollaborative.com

Terry Love's Consumer Toilet Reports, www.terrylove.com/crtoilet.htm

Towards Sustainability, www.towards-sustainability.co.uk/

TreePeople, www.treepeople.org/

Tropical Forest Foundation (TFF), www.tropicalforestfoundation.org/

Trust for Public Land (TPL), www.tpl.org/

UNEP maESTro, www.maestro.unep.or.jp

UN Global Compact, www.unglobalcompact.org

Union of Concerned Scientists (UCS), www.ucsusa.org/

United Nations Commission on Sustainable Development, www.un.org/esa/sustdev/csd.htm

United Nations Environment Programme (UNEP), www.unep.org

United Nations Framework Convention on Climate Change, http://unfcc.int

United Nations-Habitat Best Practices Database, www.bestpractices.org/

United Nations Population Fund (UNFPA), www.unfpa.org

Urban Agricultural Network, www.cityfarmer.org/ TUAN.html

Urban Ecology (UE), www.urbanecology.org/

Urban Land Institute, ULI Washington, www.washington.uli.org

URBED (Urban and Economic Development Group), www.urbed.co.uk/

U.S. Bureau of Reclamation, www.usbr.gov

U.S. Department of Commerce (DOC), www.commerce.gov

U.S. Department of Energy, www.energy.gov

U.S. DOE Energy Efficiency and Renewable Energy Clearinghouse, www.eere.energy.gov/

U.S. Environmental Protection Agency (EPA), www.epa.gov

U.S. EPA Comprehensive Procurement Guidelines Program, www.epa.gov/cpg/products.htm

U.S. EPA Environmental Technology Verification (ETV) Large Chamber Test Protocol for Measuring Emissions of VOCs and Aldehydes (September 1999), Research Triangle Institute and U.S. EPA, www.epa.gov/etv/pdfs/ vp/07_vp_furniture.pdf

U.S. EPA Office of Ground Water and Drinking Water, www.epa.gov/OGWDW

U.S. EPA Office of Science and Technology, www.epa.gov/ost

U.S. EPA Office of Solid Waste and Emergency Response, www.epa.gov/swerrims/index.htm

U.S. EPA Office of Water, earth1.epa.gov/OWOW

U.S. EPA River Corridors and Wetlands Restoration, www.epa.gov/owow/wetlands/restore

U.S. Geological Survey National Water Quality Assessment Data Warehouse, www.infotrek.er.usgs.gov/traverse/ f?p=NAWQA:HOME:4927518673983675534

U.S. Geological Survey—The Water Cycle, www.ga.water.usgs.gov/edu/watercycle.html

U.S. Geological Survey Water Use in the United States, www.water.usgs.gov/watuse/index.html

U.S. Green Building Council (USGBC), www.usgbc.org

U.S. House of Representatives, Law Library/Bill Status, law.house.gov/

U.S. Office of Science and Technology Policy (White House), www.whitehouse.gov/WH/EOP/OSTP

U.S. Public Interest Research Group, www.pirg.org

U.S. RCRA Superfund and EPCRA Hotline, www.epa.gov/epaoswer/hotline/index.htm

U.S. Water News Online, www.uswaternews.com/ homepage.html

Used Building Materials Exchange, www.build.recycle.net

Waste Spec: Model Specifications for Construction Waste Reduction, Reuse and Recycling, Triangle J: Council of Governments, www.tjcog.dst.nc.us/cdwaste.htm

Watercenter.org, www.watercenter.org

Water Closet Performance Testing, www.ebmud.com/ conserving_&_recycling/toilet_test_report/ NAHBRC%20Toilet%20Report.pdf

Water Efficiency Manual for Commercial, Industrial and Institutional Facilities, www.p2pays.org/ref/01/00692.pdf

Water Efficient Gardening and Landscaping, University of Missouri Extension, http://muextension.missouri.edu/ xplor/agguides/hort/g06912.htm

Water Environment Federation, www.wef.org

Water Librarians' Home Page, www.interleaves.org/ ~rteeter/waterlib.html

Water Reuse (CIWEM), www.ciwem.org/resources/water

Water Wiser: The Water Efficiency Clearinghouse, www.awwa.org/waterwiser/

Wetlands, Oceans, and Watersheds U.S. EPA, www.epa.gov/ owow

Whole Building Design Guide, www.wbdg.org/design/ greenroofs.php

Whole Earth, www.wholeearth.com/

Wilderness Society, www.tws.org

Wildlife Society, www.wildlife.org

World Conservation Union, www.iucn.org/

World Resources Institute, www.wri.org

World Society for the Protection of Animals (WSPA), www.wspa.org.uk/home.html

World Watch Institute, www.worldwatch.org

World Water Council, www.worldwatercouncil.org

World Wildlife Fund, www.worldwildlife.org

Zero Population Growth (ZPG), www.zpg.org

APPENDIX D REFERENCES

Abley, I., and J. Heartfield. 2001. *Sustaining Architecture in the Anti-machine Age*. New York: John Wiley & Sons.

ABN AMRO. 2004. *Sustainable report 2004*. New York: ABN AMRO Holding N.V.

Aerias. 2005. *Aerias air quality sciences: IAQ resource center*. www.aerias.org (accessed September 2005).

Agogino, A. M. 2005. *Intelligent commercial lighting: Demand-responsive conditioning and increased user satisfaction*. Berkeley: University of California Energy Institute.

Air Resources Board (ARB). 2004. Air quality, emissions, and modeling. www.arb.ca.gov (accessed November 2005).

Akbar, K. F., S. Pakistan, W. H. G. Hale, and A. D. Headley. 2003. Assessment of scenic beauty of the roadside vegetation in northern England. *Landscape and Urban Planning* 63 (3): 139–144.

Al-Kodmany, K. 2001. Bridging the gap between technical and local knowledge: Tools for promoting community-based planning and design. *Journal of Architectural and Planning Research* 18 (2): 110–130.

Altschuler, A., C. P. Somkin, and N. E. Adler. 2004. Local services and amenities, neighborhood social capital, and health. *Social Science and Medicine* 59 (6): 1219–1229.

American Society of Interior Designers (ASID). 2005. Toward ethical design. www.asid.org (accessed September 2005).

Anderson, R. C. 1998. *Mid-course Correction: Toward a Sustainable Enterprise: The Interface Model*. Atlanta: Peregrinzilla Press.

ANSI (American National Standards Institute). 2002. *Standard S12.60. Acoustical performance criteria, design requirements, and guidelines for schools*. Washington, DC: ANSI.

———. 2004. *Building commissioning*. Washington, DC: ANSI.

ANSI/ASHRAE. 2004. *Standard 55-2004. Thermal environmental conditions for human occupancy*. Washington, DC: ANSI.

Arriaza, M., J. F. Cañas-Ortega, J. A. Cañas-Madueño, and P. Ruiz-Aviles. 2004. Assessing the visual quality of rural landscapes. *Landscape and Urban Planning* 69 (1): 115–125.

ArTech. 2003. *The kids' ISO 14000 programme*. Tokyo: ArTech.

———. 2005. The kids' ISO 14000 programme. www.iso.org (accessed September 2005).

ASHRAE (American Society of Heating, Refrigerating, and Air-Conditioning Engineers). 2004. *Standard 62.1. Ventilation for acceptable indoor air quality*. Washington, DC: ASHRAE.

Auld, J. W. 2001. Consumers, cars, and communities: The challenge of sustainability. *International Journal of Consumer Studies* 25 (3): 228–237.

Aultman-Hall, L., M. Roorda, and B. W. Baetz. 1997. Using GIS for evaluation of neighborhood pedestrian accessibility. *Journal of Urban Planning and Development* 123 (1): 10–17.

Australian Environmental Labelling Association (AELA). 2003. *Environmental product declaration: Environmentally innovative product: Flooring—overseas recognition framework*. Weston Creek: Australia: AELA.

Ayala, H. 1996. Resort ecotourism: A master plan for experience management. *Cornell Hotel and Restaurant Administration Quarterly* 37 (5): 54–61.

Bansal, P., and W. E. Kilbourne. 2001. The ecologically sustainable retailer. *Journal of Retailing and Consumer Services* 8 (3): 139–146.

Bartlett, J. G., D. M. Mageean, and R. J. O'Connor. 2000. Residential expansion as a continental threat to U.S. coastal ecosystems. *Population and Environment* 21 (5): 429–468.

Bastin, L., and C. D. Thomas. 1999. The distribution of plant species in urban vegetation fragments. *Landscape Ecology* 14 (5): 493–507.

Battle, G., and C. McCarthy. 2001. *Sustainable Ecosystems and the Built Environment*. Hoboken, NJ: Wiley-Academy.

Beisi, J. 1995. Adaptable housing or adaptable people? Experience in Switzerland gives a new answer to the questions of housing adaptability. *Architecture and Comportement/Architecture and Behaviour* 11 (2): 139–162.

Benjamin, L. W. 1983. *Art of Designed Environments in The Netherlands*. Amsterdam: Stichting Kunst en Bedrijf.

Bennett, E. M. 2003. Emancipatory responses to oppression: The template of land-use planning and the old order Amish of Ontario. *American Journal of Community Psychology* 31 (1,2): 157–171.

Bennett, R. J., and R. J. Chorley. 1978. *Environmental Systems: Philosophy, Analysis, and Control*. Princeton, NJ: Princeton University Press.

Benyus, J. M. 1997. *Biomimicry: Innovation Inspired by Nature*. New York: HarperCollins.

Berke, P. R., J. MacDonald, N. White, M. Holmes, D. Line, K. Oury, and R. Ryznar. 2003. Greening development to protect watersheds: Does new urbanism make a difference? *Journal of the American Planning Association* 69 (4): 397–413.

Birkeland, J. 2002. *Design for Sustainability: A Sourcebook of Integrated, Ecological Solutions*. Sterling, VA: Earthscan Publications.

Birkin, F. 2003. Ecological accounting: New tools for a sustainable culture. *International Journal of Sustainable Development and World Ecology* 10 (1): 49–61.

Block, M. R. 1999. *Identifying Environmental Aspects and Impacts*. Milwaukee, WI: ASQ Quality Press.

Block, M. R., and I. R. Marsh. 2002. *Integrating ISO 14001 into a Quality Management System*. Milwaukee, WI: ASQ Quality Press.

Block, P. 1996. *Stewardship: Choosing Service over Self-interest*. San Francisco: Berrett-Kowhler Publishers.

Bohdanowicz, P. 2005. European hoteliers' environmental attitudes: Greening the Business. *Cornell Hotel and Restaurant Administration Quarterly* 46 (2): 188–204.

Bontje, M. 2004. From suburbia to post-suburbia in The Netherlands: Potentials and threats for sustainable regional development. *Journal of Housing and the Built Environment* 19 (1): 25–47.

Bosselmann, P., E. Macdonald, and T. Kronemeyer. 1999. Livable streets revisited. *Journal of the American Planning Association* 65 (2): 168–180.

Boubekri, M., M. Z. Yin, and R. Guy. 1997. A neural network solution to an architectural design problem: Design of a light shelf. *Architectural Science Review* 40 (1): 17–21.

Bowman, N., J. Goodwin, P. Jones, and N. Weaver. 1998. Sustaining recycling: Identification and application of limiting factors in kerbside [curbside] recycling areas. *International Journal of Sustainable Development and World Ecology* 5 (4): 263–276.

Boyce, P. R. 2004. Lighting research for interiors: The beginning of the end or the end of the beginning. *Lighting Research and Technology* 36 (4): 283–294.

Brandon, P. S., and P. Lombardi. 2005. *Evaluating Sustainable Development in the Built Environment*. Oxford, UK: Blackwell Science.

Brassard, M. 1989. *The memory jogger plus +*. Methuen, MA: GOAL/QPC.

BREEAM (Building Research Establishment Environmental Assessment Method). 2005. How does BREEAM work? www.breeam.org (accessed November 2005).

———. 2005. BREEAM for offices. www.breeam.org (accessed November 2005).

———. 2005. BREEAM retail. www.breeam.org (accessed November 2005).

———. 2005. BREEAM schools. www.breeam.org (accessed November 2005).

———. 2005. EcoHomes. www.breeam.org (accessed November 2005).

Breuste, J. H. 2004. Decision making, planning, and design for the conservation of indigenous vegetation within urban development. *Landscape and Urban Planning* 68 (4): 439–452.

Brody, S. M. 2003. Implementing the principles of ecosystem management through local land use planning. *Population and Environment* 24 (6): 511–539.

Brown, L. R. 2001. *Eco-economy: Building an Economy for the Earth*. New York: W.W. Norton.

Buckminster Fuller Institute. 2005. Comprehensive anticipatory design science. www.bfi.org (accessed September 2005).

Building Design and Construction (BDC). 2003. Green building industry awareness study. www.edcmag.com (accessed September 2005).

Burmil, S. 2004. An integrated approach to landscape and planning. *Journal of Architecture and Planning Research* 21 (2): 140–151.

Busch, D. E., and J. C. Trexler, eds. 2003. *Monitoring Ecosystems: Interdisciplinary Approaches for Evaluating Ecoregional Initiatives*. Washington, DC: Island Press.

Bush, M. B. 2003. *Ecology of a Changing Planet*. Upper Saddle River, NJ: Prentice Hall.

Cairns, J. 2003. Materialphilia, biophilia, and sustainable use of the planet. *International Journal of Sustainable Development and World Ecology* 10 (1): 43–48.

California. 2002. California section 01630—product substitution procedures. www.chps.net (accessed December 2005).

Carrus, G., M. Bonaiuto, and M. Bonnes. 2005. Environmental concern, regional identity, and support for protected areas in Italy. *Environment and Behavior* 37 (2): 237–257.

Carson, R. 1962. *Silent Spring*. New York: Fawcett Crest.

Carter, D. J. 2002. The measured and predicted performance of passive solar light pipe systems. *Lighting Research and Technology* 34 (1): 39–52.

Casado, M. A. 1999. Balancing urban growth and landscape preservation: The case of Flagstaff, Arizona. *Cornell Hotel and Restaurant Administration Quarterly* 40 (4): 64–69.

Casault, A. 2001. House hunting, or I've never "lived" in my house. *Traditional Dwellings and Settlements Review* 12 (2): 45–55.

CASBEE—Japan Sustainable Building Consortium (JSBC). 2005. Assessment tool. www.ibec.or.jp (accessed September 2005).

Cerviño, J., and J. M. Cubillo. 2005. Hotel and tourism development in Cuba: Opportunities, management challenges, and future trends. *Cornell Hotel and Restaurant Administration Quarterly* 46 (2): 223–246.

Chang, Y., H. L. Chen, and S. Francis. 1999. Market applications for recycled post-consumer fibers. *Family and Consumer Sciences Research Journal* 27 (3): 320–340.

Cherrill, A., and C. McClean. 1997. The impact of landscape and adjacent land cover upon linear boundary features. *Landscape Ecology* 12 (4): 255–260.

Cheung, K. P. 1997. An alternative solar chart and its use in a case study. *Architectural Science Review* 40 (1): 23–32.

Chicago Department of the Environment (DOE). 2005. Department of Environment. www.cityofchicago.org (accessed September 2005).

Chiesura, A. 2004. The role of urban parks for the sustainable city. *Landscape and Urban Planning* 68 (1): 129–138.

Chikkodi, S. V., R. D. Mehta, and S. Khan. 1995. Effects of biofinishing on cotton/wool blended fabrics. *Textile Research Journal* 65 (10): 564–569.

Chirarattananon, S., P. Chaiwiwatworakul, and S. Patanasethanon. 2003. Challenges of daylighting with the luminosity and variability of the tropical sky. *Lighting Research and Technology* 35 (1): 3–10.

Choi, A. S., K. D. Song, and Y. S. Kim. 2005. The characteristics of photosensors and electronic dimming ballasts in daylight responsive dimming systems. *Building and Environment* 40 (1): 39–50.

Chow, W. K., and S. K. Fong. 1997. Typical meteorological year for building energy simulation in Hong Kong. *Architectural Science Review* 40 (1): 11–15.

Colborn, T., D. Dumanoski, and J. P. Myers. 1997. *Our Stolen Future: Are We Threatening Our Fertility, Intelligence, and Survival? A Scientific Detective Story*. New York: Penguin Group.

Committee on the Environment (COTE). 2005. AIA/COTE. www.aia.org/cote (accessed September 2005).

Conine, A., W. Xiang, J. Young, and D. Whitley. 2004. Planning for multi-purpose greenways in Concord, North Carolina. *Landscape and Urban Planning* 68 (2,3): 271–287.

Construction Specifications Institute (CSI). *CSI MasterFormat™*. Alexandria, VA: The Construction Specifications Institute.

Council on Environmental Quality (CEQ). 1997. *Considering cumulative effects under the national environmental policy act*. Washington, DC: National Environmental Policy Act (NEPA).

Covington, G. A., and B. Hannah. 1997. *Access by Design*. New York: Van Nostrand Reinhold.

Crosbie, L., and K. Knight. 1995. *Strategy for Sustainable Business: Environmental Opportunity and Strategic Choice*. New York: McGraw-Hill.

Crosbie, M. J. 1994. *Green Architecture: A Guide to Sustainable Design*. Washington, DC: American Institute of Architects Press.

Crump, J. R. 2003. Finding a place in the country: Exurban and suburban development in Sonoma County, California. *Environment and Behavior* 35 (2): 187–202.

Daher, R. F. 1999. Gentrification and the politics of power, capital, and culture in an emerging Jordanian heritage industry. *Traditional Dwellings Settlements Review* 10 (2): 33–45.

Davis, M. 1998. Stepping outside the box: Water in Southern California. UCLA Environment Symposium, March 3, 1998.

Dean, A. M. 2003. *Green by Design: Creating a Home for Sustainable Living*. Salt Lake City, UT: Gibbs Smith.

Dean, A. O. 2002. *Rural Studio: Samuel Mockbee and an Architecture of Decency*. New York: Princeton Architectural Press.

Deming, W. E. 1986. *Out of the Crisis: Quality, Productivity, and Competitive Position*. Cambridge: Cambridge University Press.

Deng, S. M., and J. Burnett. 2002. Water use in hotels in Hong Kong. *International Journal of Hospitality Management* 21 (1): 57–66.

Department for Environment, Food, and Rural Affairs (DEFRA). 2005. Agri-environment scheme. www.defra.gov.uk (accessed September 2005).

Dubois, M. C. 2003. Shading devices and daylight quality: An evaluation based on simple performance indicators. *Lighting Research and Technology* 35 (1): 61–76.

Duncan, B. W., S. Boyle, D. R. Breininger, and P. A. Schmalzer. 1999. Coupling past management practice and historic landscape change on John F. Kennedy Space Center, Florida. *Landscape Ecology* 14 (3): 291–309.

Duncanson, W. 2002. Transformation in the traditional Himalayan landscape: The rise of the Trekking hotel in Nepal. *Traditional Dwellings and Settlement Review* 13 (2): 7–21.

Dwyer, J. F., and G. M. Childs. 2004. Movement of people across the landscape: A blurring of distinctions between areas, interests, and issues affecting natural resources management. *Landscape and Urban Planning* 69 (2,3): 153–164.

Earth Pledge Foundation. 2000. *Sustainable Architecture White Papers*. New York: Earth Pledge Foundation.

EcoHomes. 2005. EcoHomes 2005—the environmental rating for homes. www.ecohomes.org (accessed December 2005).

Edmonds, I. 2005. Daylighting high-density residential buildings with light directing panels. *Lighting Research Technology* 37 (1): 73–87.

Edwards, A. R. 2005. *The Sustainability Revolution: Portrait of a Paradigm Shift*. Gabriola Island, Canada: New Society Publishers.

Edwards, B., ed. 2001. Green architecture. *Architectural Design* 71 (4).

Edwards, B., ed. 2003. *Green Buildings Pay*. New York: Spon Press.

Ellis, C. D., S. W. Lee, and B. S. Kweon. 2006. Retail land use, neighborhood satisfaction, and the urban forest: An investigation into the moderating and mediating effects of trees and shrubs. *Landscape and Urban Planning* 74 (1): 70–78.

Emmel, J., K. Parrott, and J. Beamish. 2003. Technology and dishwashers: Are users still wasting water? *Canadian Home Economics Journal* 52 (2): 14–18.

Energy Information Administration (EIA). 2005. International Energy Outlook (IEO). www.eia.doe.gov (accessed September 2005).

ENERGY STAR. 2003. 2003 Annual report. www.energystar.gov (accessed November 2005).

———. 2005. Clothes washers. www.energystar.gov (accessed November 2005).

———. 2005. Dishwashers. www.energystar.gov (accessed November 2005).

———. 2005. Refrigerators and freezers. www.energystar.gov (accessed November 2005).

———. 2005. Residential windows, doors, and skylights. www.energystar.gov (accessed November 2005).

———. 2005. What is ENERGY STAR? www.energystar.gov (accessed November 2005).

Engler, M. 1995. Waste landscapes: Permissible metaphors in landscape architecture. *Landscape Journal* 14 (1): 10–25.

Engvall, K., C. Norrby, and D. Norbäck. 2003. Ocular, nasal, dermal, and respiratory symptoms in relation to heating, ventilation, energy conservation, and reconstruction of older multi-family houses. *Indoor Air* 13 (3): 206–211.

Engvall, K., P. Wickman, and D. Norbäck. 2005. Sick building syndrome and perceived indoor environment in relation to energy saving by reduced ventilation flow during heating season: A one year intervention study in dwellings. *Indoor Air* 15 (2): 120–126.

Environment Canada (EC). 1997. Environment Canada's sustainable development strategy 1997. www.ec.gc.ca (accessed September 2005).

Enz, C. A., and J. A. Siguaw. 1999. Best hotel environmental practices. *Cornell Hotel and Restaurant Administration Quarterly* 40 (5): 72–77.

European Union (EU). 2005. European Union: Delegation of the European Commission. www.eurunion.org (accessed September 2005).

Ewing, R., R. Pendall, and D. Chen. 2002. *Measuring sprawl and its impact.* Smart Growth America, www.smartgrowth america.org.

Fang, L., D. Wyon, G. Clausen, and P. O. Fanger. 2004. The effects of indoor air quality on performance and productivity. *Indoor Air: International Journal of Indoor Environment and Health* 14 (7): 92–101.

Faulkner, D., W. Fisk, D. Sullivan, and J. H. Lee. 2004. Ventilation efficiencies and thermal comfort results of a desk-edge-mounted task ventilation system. *Indoor Air: International Journal of Indoor Environment and Health* 14 (8): 92–97.

Finster, M., P. Eagan, and D. Hussey. 2002. Linking industrial ecology with business strategy. *Journal of Industrial Ecology* 5 (3): 107–125.

Fjørtoft, I. 2004. Landscape as playscape: The effects of natural environments on children's play and motor development. *Children, Youth, and Environments* 14 (2): 21–44.

Forest Stewardship Council (FSC) U.S. 2003. *Looking to the future.* Washington, DC: Forest Stewardship Council.
———. 2005. Forest Stewardship Council (FSC) U.S. www.fscus.org (accessed September 2005).

Foundation for Interior Design Education and Research (FIDER). 2005. FIDER website. www.fider.org (accessed September 2005).

Francis, M. 2002. Village homes: A case study in community design. *Landscape Journal* 21 (1): 23–41.

Frank, L. D., and P. O. Engelke. 2001. The built environment and human activity patterns: Exploring the impacts of urban form on public health. *Journal of Planning Literature* 16 (2): 202–216.

Friedman, A. 1997. Design for flexibility and affordability: Learning from the post-war home. *Journal of Architectural and Planning Research* 14 (2): 150–170.

Fujii, S., C. Hiun, N. Kagi, H. Miyamura, and Y. S. Kim. 2005. Effects on air pollutant removal by plant absorption and adsorption. *Building and Environment* 40 (1): 105–112.

Fullan, M. 1991. *The New Meaning of Educational Change.* London: Cassell.

Gage, S. A., G. R. Hunt, and P. F. Linden. 2001. Top down ventilation and cooling. *Journal of Architectural and Planning Research* 18 (4): 286–301.

Gensler Architects. 2005. Gensler: Architect of ideas. www.gensler.com (accessed September 2005).

Gheewala, S. H., and P. H. Nielsen. 2003. Central and individual air conditioning systems: A comparison of environmental impacts and resource consumption in a life cycle perspective. *International Journal of Sustainable Development and World Ecology* 10 (2): 149–155.

Gilpin, A. 2000. *Environmental Economics: A Critical Overview.* New York: John Wiley & Sons.

Gipe, P. 1995. *Wind Energy Comes of Age.* New York: John Wiley & Sons.

Global Ecolabeling Network (GEN). 2004. Global Ecolabeling Network (GEN) information paper: Introduction to ecolabeling. www.gen.gr.jp (accessed November 2005).
———. 2005. What is the GEN? www.gen.gr.jp (accessed November 2005).

Gobster, P. H., and L. M. Westphal. 2004. The human dimensions of urban greenways: Planning for recreation and related experiences. *Landscape and Urban Planning* 68 (2,3): 147–165.

Gordon, P. J. 2001. *Lean and Green: Profit for Your Workplace and the Environment.* San Francisco: Berrett-Koehler Publishers.

Gouldson, A., and P. Roberts. 2000. *Integrating Environment and Economy: Strategies for Local and Regional Government.* New York: Routledge.

Grant, J. 2003. Exploring the influence of new urbanism in community planning practice. *Journal of Architectural and Planning Research* 20 (3): 234–253.

Grasso, M. M., B. D. Hunn, and A. M. Rewerts. 1997. Effect of textile properties in evaluating a directional shading fabric. *Textile Research Journal* 67 (4): 233–247.

Gratia, E., and A. De Herde. 2003. Design of low energy office buildings. *Energy and Buildings* 35 (5): 473–491.

Green Building Council Australia (GBCAUS). 2005. Green Star environmental rating tools. www.gbcaus.org (accessed September 2005).

Greenberg, M. R., J. Renne, and E. J. Bloustein. 2005. Where does walkability matter the most? An environmental justice interpretation of New Jersey data. *Journal of Urban Health* 82 (1): 90–100.

GREENGUARD Environmental Institute (GEI). 2005. GREENGUARD Environmental Institute. www.greenguard.org (accessed November 2005).

Green Party. September, 2005. Greens condemn EPA rule waiver after Katrina. *Common Dreams News Center.* www.commondreams.org (accessed November 2005).

Green Seal. 1993. Paints (GS-11). www.greenseal.org (accessed December 2005).

———. 1997. Anti-corrosive paints (GC-03). www.greenseal.org (accessed December 2005).

———. 2000. Commercial adhesives (GS-36). www.greenseal.org (accessed December 2005).

———. 2001. Greening your purchase of carpet. Washington, DC: United States Environmental Protection Agency.

———. June 2004. Floor-care products: Finishes and strippers. Washington, DC: United States Environmental Protection Agency.

———. February 2005. Wood finishes and stains. Washington, DC: United States Environmental Protection Agency.

———. July 2005. Office furniture. Washington, DC: United States Environmental Protection Agency.

Guerin, D. A., B. L. Yust, and J. G. Coopet. 2000. Occupant predictors of household energy behavior and consumption change as found in energy studies since 1975. *Family and Consumer Sciences Research Journal* 29 (1): 48–80.

Gunnarsen, L., and A. M. B. Santos. 2002. Reduced heat stress in offices in the tropics using solar powered drying of the supply air. *Indoor Air* 12 (4): 252–262.

Gunter, P. 1971. *The Big Thicket: A Challenge for Conservation.* New York: Jenkins Publishing Company.

Gupta, R., and G. N. Tiwari. 2005. Modeling of energy distribution inside greenhouse using concept of solar fraction with and without reflecting surface on north wall. *Building and Environment* 40 (1): 63–71.

Guzowski, M. 2000. *Daylighting for Sustainable Design.* New York: McGraw-Hill.

Hackley, B. 2003. Lead poisoning in pregnancy: A case study with implications for midwives. *Journal of Midwifery and Women's Health* 48 (1): 30–38.

Hagerhall, C. M. 2000. Clustering predictors of landscape preference in the traditional Swedish cultural landscape: Prospect-refuge, mystery, age, and management. *Journal of Environmental Psychology* 20 (1): 83–90.

Haghighat, F., and H. Li. 2004. Building airflow movement—validation of three airflow models. *Journal of Architectural and Planning Research* 21 (4): 331–349.

Hanna, K. S. 2005. Planning for sustainability: Experiences in two contrasting communities. *Journal of the American Planning Association* 71 (1): 27–40.

Harrison, E., P. Wheeler, and C. Whitehead, eds. 2004. *The Distributed Workplace.* New York: Spon Press.

Health Canada. 2005. Environmental contaminants. www.hc-sc.gc.ca (accessed September 2005).

Heiskanen, E., and M. Jalas. 2003. Can services lead to radical eco-efficiency improvements? A review of the debate and evidence. *Corporate Social Responsibility and Environmental Management* 10 (4): 186–198.

Hemmati, M. 2002. *Multi-stakeholder Processes for Governance and Sustainability: Beyond Deadlock and Conflict.* Sterling, VA: Earthscan Publications.

Herlocker, C. E., J. D. Foubert, and S. T. Allison. 1997. Intended and unintended overconsumption of physical, spatial, and temporal resources. *Journal of Personality and Social Psychology* 73 (5): 992–1004.

Herman Miller. 2005. A better world together. www.hermanmiller.com (accessed September 2005).

———. 2005. Celle chairs. www.hermanmiller.com (accessed September 2005).

Heschong Mahone Group (HMG). 1997. *The lighting efficiency technology report, vol. I: California lighting baseline.* For the California Energy Commission (May).

———. 1999. *Skylighting and retail sales, and daylighting in schools.* For Pacific Gas & Electric (August). www.pge.com.pec/daylight.

———. 2003. *Daylighting in schools: Reanalysis report.* For the California Energy Commission (October).

Higgitt, N. C., and J. A. Memken. 2001. Understanding neighborhoods. *Housing and Society* 28 (1,2): 29–46.

Hilty, L. M., E. K. Seifert, and R. Treibert. 2005. *Information Systems for Sustainable Development.* Hershey, PA: Idea Group Publishing.

Hirst, J. 1996. Values in design: "Existenzminimum," "maximum quality," and "optimal balance." *Design Issues* 12 (1): 38–47.

Hodgson, A. T., A. F. Rudd, D. Beal, and S. Chandra. 2000. Volatile organic compound concentrations and emission rates in new manufactured and site-built houses. *Indoor Air* 10 (3): 178–192.

Howard, J. 2004. Toward participatory ecological design of technological systems. *Design Issues* 20 (3): 40–53.

Howes, H. 2004. An environment for prosperity and quality living accommodating growth in the Thames valley. *Corporate Social Responsibility and Environmental Management* 11 (1): 35–47.

Huhtala, A. 2004. What price recreation in Finland? A contingent valuation study of non-market benefits of public outdoor recreation areas. *Journal of Leisure Research* 36 (1): 23–44.

Hyde, R. 2000. *Climate Responsive Design: A Study of Buildings in Moderate and Hot Humid Climates.* New York: Spon.

Hyllegard, K. H., J. P. Ogle, and B. Dunbar. 2003. Sustainability and historic preservation in retail design: Integrating design into a model of the REI Denver decision-making process. *Journal of Interior Design* 29 (1,2): 32–49.

Inam, A. 2002. Meaningful urban design: Teleological/catalytic/relevant. *Journal of Urban Design* 7 (1): 35–58.

InformeDesign. 2005. InformeDesign: Where research informs design. www.informedesign.org (accessed September 2005).

Interface. 2005. Our vision. www.interface.com (accessed September 2005).

Interior Design Educators Council (IDEC). 2005. IDEC Interior Design Educators Council. www.idec.org (accessed September 2005).

International Design Center for the Environment (IDCE). 2005. Our mission. www.idce.org (accessed September 2005).

International Energy Agency (IEA). 2005. The IEA: An overview. www.iea.org (accessed September 2005).

International Finance Corporation (IFC). 2005. International Finance Corporation: World Bank Group. www.ifc.org (accessed September 2005).

International Initiative for a Sustainable Built Environment (iiSBE). 2005. iiSBE overview. www.iisbe.org (accessed September 2005).

International Interior Design Association (IIDA). 2005. Key facts. www.iida.org (accessed September 2005).

International Organization for Standardization (ISO). 2004. ISO 14000. www.iso.org (accessed September 2005).
———. 2005. ISO family of international standards. www.iso.org (accessed September 2005).

International Union of Architects (UIA). 2005. The International Institute of Architects. www.uia-architectes.org (accessed September 2005).

Jaakkola, J. J. K., H. Parise, V. Kislitsin, N. I. Lebedeva, and J. D. Spengler. 2004. Asthma, wheezing, and allergies in Russian schoolchildren in relation to new surface materials in the home. *American Journal of Public Health* 94 (4): 560–561.

Jannadi, M. O., and S. Ghazi. 1998. Earth-sheltered housing: The way of the future? *Journal of Urban Planning and Development* 124 (3): 101–114.

Joerger, A., M. A. Noden, and S. D. DeGloria. 1999. Applying geographic information systems: Siting of coastal hotels in Costa Rica. *Cornell Hotel and Restaurant Administration Quarterly* 40 (4): 48–59.

Johnson, L. C. 2003. From hybrid housing to cybrid neighborhoods: Case Studies of five decentralized tele-workspaces. *Journal of Architectural and Planning Research* 20 (2): 136–152.

Johnson, M. K., and K. R. Parrott. 1995. A logistic regression analysis of factors affecting recycling behavior in apartment communities. *Housing and Society* 22 (3): 41–52.

Kaczmarczyk, J., A. Melikov, and P. O. Fanger. 2004. Human response to personalized ventilation and mixing ventilation. *Indoor Air: International Journal of Indoor Environment and Health* 14 (8): 17–29.

Kambezidis, H. D., T. I. Oikonomou, and D. Zevgolis. 2002. Daylight climatology in the Athens urban environment: Guidance for building designers. *Lighting Research and Technology* 34 (4): 297–312.

Kaplan, R., M. E. Austin, and S. Kaplan. 2004. Open space communities: Resident perceptions, nature benefits, and problems with terminology. *Journal of the American Planning Association* 70 (3): 300–312.

Kasim, A. 2004. BESR in the hotel sector: A look at tourists' propensity towards environmentally and socially friendly hotel attributes in Pulau Pinang, Malaysia. *International Journal of Hospitality and Tourism Administration* 5 (2): 61–83.

Kaya, Y., and K. Yokobori, eds. 1997. *Environment, Energy, and Economy*. New York: United Nations University Press.

Khattak, A. J., and Y. Yim. 2004. Traveler response to innovative personalized demand-responsive transit in the San Francisco Bay area. *Journal of Urban Planning and Development* 130 (1): 42–55.

Kibert, C. J. 2005. *Sustainable Construction: Green Building Design and Delivery*. New York: John Wiley & Sons.

Kiuchi, T., and B. Shireman. 2002. *What We Learned in the Rainforest: Business Lessons from Nature: Innovation, Growth, Profit, and Sustainability at Twenty of the World's Top Companies*. San Francisco: Berrett-Koehler Publishers.

Kim, J. 2004. Physical and psychological factors in sense of community: New urbanist Kentlands and nearby orchard village. *Environment and Behavior* 35 (3): 313–340.

Kim, K. B. 2005. Toward sustainable neighborhood design: A sustainability evaluation framework and a case study of the Greenwich Millennium Village project. *Journal of Architectural and Planning Research* 22 (3): 181–203.

Kim, S., S. Oah, and A. M. Dickenson. 2005. The impact of public feedback on three recycling-related behaviors in South Korea. *Environment and Behavior* 37 (2): 258–274.

Kline, K., and D. Wichelns. 1998. Measuring heterogeneous preferences for preserving farmland and open space. *Ecological Economics* 26 (2): 211–224.

Knight, K. 2003. Risk management: An integral component of corporate governance and good management. *ISO Bulletin October 2003*.

Koch, K., and T. Domina. 1999. Consumer textile recycling as a means of solid waste reduction. *Family and Consumer Sciences Research Journal* 28 (1): 3–17.

Kotler, P., and N. Lee. 2005. *Corporate Social Responsibility*. New York: John Wiley & Sons.

Kyle, G. T., A. J. Mowen, and M. Tarrant. 2004. Linking place preferences with place meaning: An examination of the relationship between place motivation and place attachment. *Journal of Environmental Psychology* 24 (4): 439–454.

Lafferty, W. M., and J. Meadowcraft, eds. 2000. *Implementing Sustainable Development: Strategies and Initiatives in High Consumption Societies*. New York: Oxford University Press.

LaGro, J. A. 1998. Landscape context of rural residential development in southeastern Wisconsin (USA). *Landscape Ecology* 13 (2): 65–77.

Lange, E., and W. A. Schmid. 2000. Ecological planning with virtual landscapes: Three examples from Switzerland. *Landscape Journal* 19 (1,2): 156–165.

Lawhon, L. L. 2003. Planners' perceptions of their role in socially responsive neighborhood design. *Journal of Architectural and Planning Research* 20 (2): 153–163.

Lawrence Berkeley Laboratory (Berkeley Lab). 2005. Earth sciences division. www.lbl.gov (accessed September 2005).

Lee, Y. L., R. De Young, and R. W. Marans. 1995. Factors influencing individual recycling behavior in office settings: A study of office workers in Taiwan. *Environment and Behavior* 27 (3): 380–403.

Leech, J. A., M. Raizenne, and J. Gusdorf. 2004. Health in

occupants of energy efficient new homes. *Indoor Air* 14 (3): 169–173.

LEED Steering Committee. 2004. *The treatment by LEED of the environmental impact of HVAC refrigerants.* Washington, DC: United States Green Building Council (USGBC).

Leibrock, C., and J. E. Terry. 1999. *Beautiful Universal Design: A Visual Guide.* New York: John Wiley & Sons.

Leo A Daly. 2005. Sustainability is our nature. www.leoadaly.com (accessed September 2005).

Leopold, A. 1949. *A Sand County Almanac.* New York: Oxford University Press.

Levi, D. J. 2005. Does history matter? Perceptions and attitudes toward fake historic architecture and historic preservation. *Journal of Architecture and Planning Research* 22 (2): 148–159.

Lewitus, A. J., L. B. Schmidt, L. J. Mason, J. W. Kempton, S. B. Wilde, J. L. Wolny, B. J. Williams, K. C. Hayes, S. N. Hymel, C. J. Keppler, and A. H. Ringwood. 2003. Harmful Aegal blooms in South Carolina residential and golf course ponds. *Population and Environment* 24 (5): 387–413.

Li, D. H. W., and J. C. Lam. 2004. Predicting daylight illuminance by computer simulation techniques. *Lighting Research and Technology* 36 (2): 113–129.

Li, F., R. Wang, J. Paulussen, and X. Liu. 2005. Comprehensive concept planning of urban greening based on ecological principles: A case study in Beijing, China. *Landscape and Urban Planning* 72 (4): 325–336.

Lindsey, G. 2003. Sustainable and urban greenways: Indicators in Indianapolis. *Journal of the American Planning Association* 69 (2): 165–180.

Lippiatt, B. C. 2002. *BEES 2.0: Building for environmental and economic sustainability, peer review report.* Gaithersburg, MD: U.S. Dept. of Commerce, Technology Administration, National Institute of Standards and Technology, Building and Fire Research Laboratory.

Littlefair, P. J., and A. Abdul Motin. 2001. Lighting controls in areas with innovative daylighting systems: A study of sensor type. *Lighting Research and Technology* 33 (1): 59–73.

Liu, A. J., and N. Guy. 2001. Analysis of landscape patterns in coastal wetlands of Galveston Bay, Texas (USA). *Landscape Ecology* 16 (7): 581–595.

Lyle, J. T. 1994. *Regenerative Design for Sustainable Development.* New York: John Wiley & Sons.

Lynn, N. A., and R. D. Brown. 2003. Effects of recreational use impacts on hiking experiences in natural areas. *Landscape and Urban Planning* 64 (1,2): 77–78.

Macy, S., and J. A. Thompson. 2003. Residential design implications of consumers' recycling behaviors. *Journal of Interior Design* 29 (1,2): 17–31.

Marsh, G. P. 1864. *Man and Nature.* New York: C. Scribner.
———. 1864. *The Earth as Modified by Human Action: Man and Nature.* New York: C. Scribner.

Martin, M. D. 2001. Returning to Radburn. *Landscape Journal* 20 (2): 156–175.

Mayer, F. S., and C. M. Frantz. 2004. The connectedness to nature scale: A measure of individuals' feeling in com-

munity with nature. *Journal of Environmental Psychology* 24 (4): 503–515.

McDonough Braungart Design Chemistry (MBDC). 2005. MBDC cradle to cradle certification. www.c2ccertified.com (accessed September 2005).

McDonough, W., and M. Braungart. 2002. *Cradle to Cradle: Remaking the Way We Make Things.* New York: North Point Press.

McGregor, S. M., and N. B. Trulsson. 2001. *Living Homes: Sustainable Architecture and Design.* San Francisco: Chronicle Books.

McNeill, J. R. 2001. *Something New under the Sun: An Environmental History of the Twentieth-century World.* New York: W.W. Norton & Company.

McWilliams, C. 1946. Quoted in M. Davis. 1998. Stepping outside the box: Water in Southern California. Paper presented at the UCLA Environment Symposium, March 3, 1998.

Meade, B., and A. D. Monaco. 2001. Introducing environmental management in the hotel industry: A case study of Jamaica. *International Journal of Hospitality and Tourism Administration* 1 (3,4): 129–142.

Mendell, M., and G. Heath. 2005. Do indoor pollutants and thermal conditions in schools influence student performance? *Indoor Air* 15 (1): 27–52.

Mendler, S. F., W. Odell, and M. A. Lazarus. 2006. *The HOK Guidebook to Sustainable Design.* Hoboken, NJ: John Wiley & Sons.

Merriam-Webster Dictionary. 2005. Merriam-Webster online. www.m-w.com (accessed August 2005).

Milton, D. K., P. Markglencross, and M. D. Walters. 2000. Risk of sick leave associated with outdoor air supply rate, humidification, and occupant complaints. *Indoor Air* 10 (4): 212.

Mirovitskaya, N., and W. Ascher, eds. 2001. *Guide to Sustainable Development and Environmental Policy.* Durham, NC: Duke University Press.

Moore, C., and A. Miller. 1995. *Green Gold: Japan, Germany, the United States, and the Race for Environmental Technology.* Boston: Beacon Press.

Moore, S. M., and N. B. Trulsson. 2001. *Living Homes: Sustainable Architecture and Design.* San Francisco: Chronicle Books.

Moore, T., D. J. Carter, and A. I. Slater. 2003. Long-term patterns of use of occupant controlled office lighting. *Lighting Research and Technology* 35 (1): 43–59.

Morgan, M. H., trans. (1960). *Vitruvius: The Ten Books on Architecture.* New York: Dover Publications.

Moussatche, H., and J. Languel. 2002. Life cycle costing of interior materials for Florida's schools. *Journal of Interior Design* 28 (2): 37–49.

Nathanson, J. A. 2003. *Basic Environmental Technology: Water Supply, Waste Management, and Pollution Control.* Upper Saddle River, NJ: Prentice Hall.

National Association of Realtors. 2005. Size of the average new home: U.S. Bureau of the Census. www.nahb.org (accessed October 2005).

National Audubon Society. 1994. *Audubon House: Building the Environmentally Responsible, Energy-efficient Office*. New York: John Wiley & Sons.

National Charrette Institute (NCI). 2005. National charrette institute: The art and science of creating healthy communities. www.charretteinstitute.org (accessed September 2005).

National Fenestration Rating Council (NFRC). 2005. The NFRC label. www.nfrc.org (accessed September 2005).

National Historic Preservation Act (NHPA). 2000. The national preservation act of 1966, as amended. www.achp.gov (accessed November 2005).

Ndubisi, F. 2002. Managing change in the landscape: A synthesis of approaches for ecological planning. *Landscape Journal* 21 (1): 138–155.

Nelson, A. C., and T. W. Sanchez. 1997. Exurban and suburban households; A departure from traditional location theory? *Journal of Housing Research* 8 (2): 249–276.

Neo, H. 2001. Sustaining the unsustainable? Golf in urban Singapore. *International Journal of Sustainable Development and World Ecology* 8 (3): 191–202.

Nepal, S. K. 1997. Sustainable tourism, protected areas, and livelihood needs of local communities in developing countries. *International Journal of Sustainable Development and World Ecology* 4 (2): 123–135.

———. 2002. Linking parks and people: Nepal's experience in resolving conflicts in parks and protected areas. *International Journal of Sustainable Development and World Ecology* 9 (1): 75–90.

Northridge, M. E., E. D. Sclar, and P. Biswas. 2003. Sorting out the connections between the built environment and health: A conceptual framework for navigating pathways and planning healthy cities. *Journal of Urban Health* 80 (4): 556–568.

Null, R. L., and K. F. Cherry. 1998. *Universal Design: Creative Solutions for ADA Compliance*. Belmont, CA: Professional Publications.

Nussbaumer, L. L. 2004. Multiple chemical sensitivity (MCS): The controversy and relation to interior design. *Journal of Interior Design* 30 (2): 51–65.

Occupational Safety and Health Administration (OSHA). 2005. OSHA technical manual. www.osha.gov (accessed September 2005).

Odell, E. A., D. M. Theobald, and R. L. Knight. 2003. Incorporating ecology into land use planning: The songbirds' case for clustered development. *Journal of the American Planning Association* 69 (1): 72–82.

Ó hAnluain, D. 2005. A P2P network for bikes. http://wired.com (accessed October 2005).

Olson, R., and D. Rejeski, eds. 2005. *Environmentalism and the Technologies of Tomorrow: Shaping the Next Industrial Revolution*. Washington, DC: Island Press.

Organisation for Economic Co-operation and Development (OECD). 2003. *Environmentally sustainable buildings: Challenges and policies*. Paris: Organisation for Economic Co-operation and Development.

Orr, D. W. 2002. *The Nature of Design: Ecology, Culture, and Human Intention*. New York: Oxford University Press.

———. 2004. *Earth in Mind: On Education, Environment, and the Human Prospect*. Washington, DC: Island Press.

———. 2004. *Nature of design: Ecology, culture, and human intention*. New York: Oxford University Press.

Pacific Institute. 2003. *California can slake its thirst via efficiency, conversation*. Oakland, CA: Pacific Institute.

Painter, K. A., and D. P. Farrington. 2001. The financial benefits of improved street lighting, based on crime reduction. *Lighting Research and Technology* 33 (1): 3–12.

Pan, D., S. de Blois, and A. Bouchard. 1999. Temporal (1958–1993) and spatial patterns of land use changes in Haut-Saint-Laurent (Quebec, Canada) and their relation to landscape physical attributes. *Landscape Ecology* 14 (1): 35–52.

Papanek, V. J. 1983. *Design for Human Scale*. New York: Van Nostrand Reinhold Co.

———. 1985. *Design for the Real World: Human Ecology and Social Change*. London: Thames and Hudson.

———. 1995. *Green Imperative: Natural Design for the Real World*. New York: Thames and Hudson.

Parikh, D. V., T. A. Calamari, P.S. Sawhney, E. J. Blanchard, F. J. Screen, J. C. Myatt, D. H. Muller, and D. D. Stryjewski. 2002. Thermoformable automotive composites containing kenaf and other cellulosic fibers. *Textile Research Journal* 72 (8): 668–672.

Pearson, D. 2005. *In Search of Natural Architecture*. New York: Abbeville Press.

Peters, T., and R. Waterman. 1982. *In Search of Excellence*. New York: Harper & Row.

Phillips, C. 2003. *Sustainable Places: A Place of Sustainable Eevelopment*. Hoboken, NJ: Wiley-Academy.

Pirages, D., and K. Cousins, eds. 2005. *From Resource Scarcity to Ecological Security*. Cambridge, MA: MIT Press.

Pitts, A. C. 2004. *Planning and Design Strategies for Sustainability and Profit: Pragmatic Sustainable Design on Building and Urban Scales*. Boston: Elsevier/Architectural Press.

Population Reference Bureau. 2005. 2005 world population data sheet of the Population Reference Bureau. www.prb.org (accessed September 2005).

Presidential Documents. 1999. Greening the government through efficient energy management. *Federal Register* 64 (109): 1–12.

Pressman, N. 2004. *Shaping cities for winter: Climatic comfort and sustainable design*. Prince George, B.C., Canada: Winter Cities Association.

Preston, M., and A. Bailey. 2003. The potential for high-performance design adoption in retail property portfolios. *Corporate Social Responsibility and Environmental Management* 10 (3): 165–174.

Purvis, M., and A. Grainger. 2004. *Exploring Sustainable Development: Geographical Perspectives*. Sterling, VA: Earthscan.

Ragan, G. E., C. J. Makela, and R. A. Young. 1996. Use of accelerated testing methods with survey data: How water quality affects appliance life. *Family and Consumer Sciences Research Journal* 24 (3): 254–271.

Raven, P. H., and L. R. Berg. 2004. *Environment.* 2nd ed. New York: John Wiley & Sons.

———. 2005. *Environment.* 3rd ed. New York: John Wiley & Sons.

Revilla, G., T. H. Dodd, and L. C. Hoover. 2001. Environmental tactics used by hotel companies in Mexico. *International Journal of Hospitality and Tourism Administration* 1 (3,4): 111–127.

Revkin, A. C. September 2005. Arctic ice cap shrank sharply this summer, experts say. *Chicago Tribune.* p. 10.

Ribe, R. G., E. T. Armstrong, and P. H. Gobster. 2003. Scenic vistas and the changing policy landscape: Visualizing and testing the role of visual resources in ecosystem management. *Landscape Journal* 21 (1,2): 42–66.

Robinson, L., J. P. Newell, and J. M. Marzluff. 2005. Twenty-five years of sprawl in the Seattle region: Growth management responses and implications for conservation. *Landscape and Urban Planning* 71 (1): 51–52.

Rocky Mountain Institute. 1998. *Green Development: Integrating Ecology and Real Estate.* New York: John Wiley & Sons.

———. 2005. *Rocky Mountain Institute.* www.rmi.org (accessed September 2005).

Rogan, R., E. Cowan, M. O'Connor, and P. Horwitz. 2005. Nowhere to hide: Awareness and perceptions of environmental change, and their influence on relationships with place. *Journal of Environmental Psychology* 25 (2): 147–158.

Romero, F. S. 2003. Open space preservation policies: An institutional case study. *Journal of Architectural and Planning Research* 20 (2): 164–176.

Rutman, E., C. Inard, and A. Bailly. 2005. A global approach of indoor environment in an air-conditioned office room. *Building and Environment* 40 (1): 29–37.

Ryan, J. C., T. Durning, S. J. Breslow, C. Halvorson, and A. Tohan. 1997. *Stuff: The Secret Lives of Everyday Things.* Seattle, WA: Northwest Environment Watch.

Ryan, R. L. 2005. Exploring the effects of environmental experience on attachment to urban natural areas. *Environment and Behavior* 37 (1): 3–42.

Ryan, R. L., J. G. Fabos, and M. S. Lindhult. 2002. Continuing a planning tradition: The New England greenway vision plan. *Landscape Journal* 21 (1): 164–171.

Safarzadeh, H., and M. N. Bahadori. 2005. Passive cooling effects of courtyards. *Building and Environment* 40 (1): 89–104.

Saint-Exupéry, A. D. 1943. *The Little Prince.* Trans. Richard Howard. Orlando, FL: Harcourt.

Sakr, W., H. N. Knudsen, L. Gunnarsen, and F. Haghighat. 2003. Impact of varying area of polluting surface materials on perceived air quality. *Indoor Air* 13 (2): 86–91.

Sauer, J., and B. Rüttinger. 2004. Environmental conservation in the domestic domain: The influence of technical design features and person-based factors. *Ergonomics* 47 (10): 1053–1072.

Schmandt, M. J. 1999. The importance of history and context in the postmodern urban landscape. *Landscape Journal* 18 (2): 157–165.

Schmandt, J., and C. H. Ward. 2000. *Sustainable Development: The Challenge of Transition.* New York: Cambridge University Press.

Schmuck, P., and W. P. Schultz, eds. 2002. *Psychology of Sustainable Development.* Boston: Kluwer Academic Publishers.

Schulze, G. G., and H. W. Ursprung, eds. 2001. *International Environmental Economics: A Survey of the Issues.* New York: Oxford University Press.

Sekhar, S. C., K. W. Tham, and K. W. Cheong. 2003. Indoor air quality and energy performance of air-conditioned office buildings in Singapore. *Indoor Air* 13 (4): 315–331.

Seo, D. 2001. *Conscious Style Home: Eco-friendly Living for the Twenty-first Century.* New York: St. Martin's Press.

Seppanen, O., and W. J. Fisk. 2004. *A Model to Estimate the Cost Effectiveness of Indoor Environment Improvements in Office Work.* Berkeley: Lawrence Berkeley National Laboratory.

Sherwin, C., T. Bhamra, and S. Evans. 1998. The "eco-kitchen" project—using eco-design to innovate. *The Journal of Sustainable Product Design* 1 (7): 51–57.

Shopsin, W. C. 1989. *Restoring Old Buildings for Contemporary Uses: An American Sourcebook for Architects and Preservationists.* New York: Whitney Library of Design.

Smith, G. R., and J. R. Taylor. 2000. Achieving sustainability: Exploring links between sustainability indicators and public involvement for rural communities. *Landscape Journal* 19 (1,2): 179–190.

Smith, M. B., and J. S. Sharp. 2005. Growth, development, and farming in an Ohio exurban region. *Environment and Behavior* 37 (4): 565–579.

Smith, M. T. 2003. The impact of energy efficient house construction on homeownership costs: A comparative study in Gainesville, Florida. *Family and Consumer Sciences Research Journal* 32 (1): 76–98.

Smith, P. F. 1979. *Architecture and the Human Dimension.* Westfield, NJ: Eastview Editions.

Smith, P. F. 2002. *Sustainability at the Cutting Edge: Emerging Technologies for Low Energy Buildings.* New York: Elsevier.

Smith, P. F. 2004. *Eco-refurbishment: A Guide to Saving and Producing Energy in the Home.* New York: Elsevier.

Smith, P. F. 2005. *Architecture in a Climate of Change.* New York: Elsevier.

Solomon, B. S. 1988. *Green Architecture and the Agrarian Garden.* New York: Rizzoli.

Sonery, L. 2004. Hearing as a way of dwelling: The active sense-making of environmental risk and nuisance. *Environment and Planning: Society and Space* 22 (5): 737–753.

South Coast Air Quality Management District (SCAQMD). 2003. Rule 1168: Adhesive and sealant applications. www.aqmd.gov (accessed October 2005).

———. 2005. Rule 1168: Adhesive and sealant applications. www.aqmd.gov (accessed October 2005).

———. 2004. Rule 1113: Architectural coatings. www.aqmd.gov (accessed October 2005).

Speir, C., and K. Stephenson. 2002. Does sprawl cost us all? Isolating the effects of housing patterns on public water and sewer costs. *Journal of the American Planning Association* 68 (1): 56–70.

Spiegel, R., and D. Meadows. 1999. *Green Building Materials: A Guide to Product Selection and Specification.* New York: John Wiley & Sons.

Starke, L., ed. 2004. State of the world, 2004: A Worldwatch Institute report on progress toward a sustainable society. New York: W.W. Norton & Co.

Stead, W. E., and J. G. Stead. 2004. *Sustainable Strategic Management.* New York: M. E. Sharpe.

Steinfeld, E., and G. S. Danford, eds. 1999. *Enabling Environments: Measuring the Impact of Environment on Disability and Rehabilitation.* New York: Kluwer Academic/Plenum Publishers.

Stiling, P. 2002. *Ecology: Theories and Applications.* 4th ed. Upper Saddle River, NJ: Prentice Hall.

Stitt, F. A. 1999. *Ecological Design Handbook: Sustainable Strategies for Architecture, Landscape Architecture, Interior Design, and Planning.* New York: McGraw-Hill.

Stone, B. 2004. Paving over paradise: How land use regulations promote residential imperviousness. *Landscape and Urban Planning* 69 (1): 101–113.

Suen, I. S. 2005. Residential development pattern and intraneighborhood infrastructure provision. *Journal of Urban Planning and Development* 131 (1): 1–9.

Susanka, S. 1998. *The Not So Big House.* Newtown, CT: Taunton Press.

Susanka, S. 2000. *Creating the Not So Big House.* Newtown, CT: Taunton Press.

Susanka, S., and M. Vassallo. 2005. *Inside the Not So Big House: Discovering the Details that Bring a Home to Life.* Newtown, CT: Taunton Press.

Syme, G. J., Q. Shao, M. Po, and E. Campbell. 2004. Predicting and understanding home garden water use. *Landscape and Urban Planning* 68 (1): 121–128.

Tajima, K. 2003. New estimates of the demand for urban green space: Implications for valuing the environmental benefits of Boston's big dig project. *Journal of Urban Affairs* 25 (5): 641–655.

Talen, E. 2001. Traditional urbanism meets residential affluence: An analysis of the variability of suburban preference. *Journal of the American Planning Association* 67 (2): 199–216.

Talloires. 2005. Programs: Talloires declaration. www.ulsf.org (accessed September 2005).

Tasci, A. D. A., and B. J. Knutson. 2004. An argument for providing authenticity and familiarity in tourism destinations. *Journal of Hospitality and Leisure Marketing* 11 (1): 85–109.

Tetri, E. 2002. Daylight linked dimming: Effect of fluorescent lamp performance. *Lighting Research and Technology* 34 (1): 3–10.

Thayer, R. L. 1994. *Gray World, Green Heart: Technology, Nature, and Sustainable Landscape.* New York: John Wiley & Sons.

Thomas, R., ed. 1999. *Environmental Design: An Introduction for Architects and Engineers.* New York: Spon.

Thompson, J. W., and K. Sorvig. 2000. *Sustainable Landscape Construction: A Guide to Green Building Outdoors.* Washington, DC: Island Press.

Topalis, F. V., M. B. Kostic, and Z. R. Radakovic. 2002. Advantages and disadvantages of the use of compact fluorescent lamps with electronic control gear. *Lighting Research and Technology* 34 (4): 279–288.

Ubbelohde, M. S. 2003. The dance of a summer day: Le Corbusier's sarabhai house in Ahmedabad, India. *Traditional Dwellings and Settlements Review* 14 (2): 65–80.

United Nations. 1987. *Development and international economic co-operation: Environment.* New York: United Nations.

———. 1992. *UN conference on environment and development.* New York: United Nations.

———. 1997. *The world conferences: Developing priorities for the twenty-first century.* New York: United Nations.

———. 1999. *United Nations Environment Programme (UNEP).* New York: United Nations.

———. 2002. *Report of the world summit on sustainable development.* New York: United Nations.

———. 2005. *Commission on sustainable development: Report on the thirteenth session.* New York: United Nations Economic and Social Council.

United States Census Bureau. 2005. International Data Base (IDB): Data access—display mode. www.census.gov (accessed September 2005).

United States Department of Energy (DOE). 1996. Clean Water Act. www.eh.doe.gov (accessed September 2005).

———. 2000. *How to buy energy-efficient compact fluorescent light bulbs.* Washington, DC: Department of Energy.

———. 2003. Resource Conservation and Recovery Act (RCRA). www.doe.gov (accessed September 2005).

———. 2005. DOE-2. www.eere.energy.gov (accessed September 2005).

United States Environmental Protection Agency (EPA). 1999. *Lead in your home: A parent's reference guide.* Washington, DC: United States Environmental Protection Agency.

———. 2000. *Environmental planning for communities.* Washington, DC: United States Environmental Protection Agency.

———. 2001. *An organizational guide to pollution prevention.* Washington, DC: United States Environmental Protection Agency.

———. 2001. *Mold remediation in schools and commercial buildings.* Washington, DC: United States Environmental Protection Agency.

———. 2002. *Brownfields handbook: How to manage federal environmental liability risks.* Washington, DC: United States Environmental Protection Agency.

———. December 2004. *Buildings and the environment: A statistical summary.* Washington, DC: United States Environmental Protection Agency.

———. 2004. *2004 Guidelines for water reuse.* Washington, DC: United States Environmental Protection Agency.

———. 2005. Chromium compounds. www.epa.gov (accessed September 2005).

———. 2005. Clean water act. www.epa.gov (accessed September 2005).

———. 2005. Environmental justice. www.epa.gov (accessed September 2005).

———. 2005. Resource Conservation and Recovery Act (RCRA). www.epa.gov (accessed August 2005).

———. 2005. Green buildings. www.epa.gov (accessed October 2005).

———. 2005. Hazardous waste: Subtitle C of RCRA. www.epa.gov (accessed September 2005).

———. 2005. Indoor air quality. www.epa.gov (accessed September 2005).

———. 2005. Medium density fiberboard manufacturing. www.epa.gov (accessed September 2005).

———. 2005. Municipal solid waste. www.epa.gov (accessed September 2005).

———. 2005. Sources of indoor air pollution. www.epa.gov (accessed November 2005).

———. 2005. Sources of indoor air pollution—carbon monoxide (CO). www.epa.gov (accessed November 2005).

———. 2005. Summary of the EPA municipal solid waste program. www.epa.gov (accessed September 2005).

———. 2005. Water recycling and reuse: The environmental benefits. www.epa.gov (accessed November 2005).

United States Federal Government. 1994. Executive Order 12902. www.archives.gov (accessed September 2005).

———. 1998. Executive Order 13101. www.archives.gov (accessed September 2005).

———. 1999. Executive Order 13134. www.archives.gov (accessed September 2005).

———. 1999. Executive Order 13123. www.archives.gov (accessed September 2005).

———. 1999. The Federal Register. www.archives.gov (accessed September 2005).

———. 2000. Executive Order 13148. www.archives.gov (accessed September 2005).

———. 2002. Clean Water Act (CWA). www.epa.gov (accessed September 2005).

United States Federal Government: National Energy Policy (NEP). 2001. Reliable, affordable, and environmentally sound energy for America's future. www.whitehouse.gov (accessed September 2005).

United States Green Building Council (USGBC). 2003. The GREEN Roundtable. www.usgbs.gov (accessed September 2005).

———. 2004. LEED Green building rating system. www.usgbs.gov (accessed November 2005).

———. 2005. *LEED-CI for commercial interiors: Reference guide version 2.0.* Washington, DC: United States Green Building Council (USGBC).

University of Michigan. 2005. Environmental stewardship at the University of Michigan. www.umich.edu (accessed September 2005).

Vale, B., and R. Vale. 1991. *Green Architecture: Design for a Sustainable Future.* London: Thames and Hudson.

Van der Ryn, S., and S. Cowan. 1996. *Ecological Design.* Covelo, CA: Island Press.

Vogt, C. A., and R. W. Marans. 2004. Natural resources and open space in the residential decision process: A study of recent movers to fringe counties in southeast Michigan. *Landscape and Urban Planning* 69 (3): 255–269.

Wackernagel, M., and W. E. Rees. 1996. *Our Ecological Footprint: Reducing Human Impact on the Earth.* Stony Creek, CT: New Society Publishers.

Wann, D., with Center for Resource Management. 1996. *Deep Design: Pathways to a Livable Future.* Washington, DC: Island Press.

Wargocki, P., L. Lagercrantz, T. Witterseh, J. Sundell, D. P. Wyon, and P. O. Fanger. 2002. Subjective perceptions, symptom intensity, and performance: A comparison of two independent studies, both changing similarly the pollution lad in an office. *Indoor Air: International Journal of Indoor Environment and Health* 12 (2): 74–80.

Wargocki, P., D. P. Wyon, J. Sundell, G. Clausen, and P. O. Fanger. 2000. The performance and subjective responses of call-center operators with new and used supply air filters at two outdoor air supply rates. *Indoor Air: International Journal of Indoor Environment and Health* 14 (8): 7–16.

Watson, S. A., and M. M. Warnock. 2003. Comparative analysis between recycled and newly manufactured carpets. *Family and Consumer Sciences Research Journal* 31 (4): 425–441.

Weaver, D. B. 2001. Ecotourism as mass tourism: Contradiction or reality? *Cornell Hotel and Restaurant Administration Quarterly* 42 (2): 104–112.

Werner, C. M., M. U. Rhodes, and K. K. Partain. 1998. Designing effective instructional signs with schema theory: Case studies of polystyrene recycling. *Environment and Behavior* 30 (5): 709–735.

White House, United States Federal Government. 2005. Energy security for the twenty-first century. www.whitehouse.gov (accessed September 2005).

Williamson, T., A. Radford, and H. Bennetts. 2003. *Understanding Sustainable Architecture.* New York: Spon Press.

Wilson, A., N. Malin, and M. Piepkorn, eds. 2005. *Greenspec Directory: Product Listings and Guideline Specifications.* 5th ed. Brattleboro, VT: Building Green.

Wines, J. 2000. *Green Architecture.* New York: Taschen.

Witterseh, T., D. P. Wyon, and G. Clausen. 2004. The effects of moderate heat stress and open-plan office noise distraction on SBS symptoms and on the performance of office work. *Indoor Air: International Journal of Indoor Environment and Health* 14 (8): 30–40.

Wong, N. H., and A. D. Istiadji. 2004. Effect of external shading devices on daylighting penetration in residential buildings. *Lighting Research and Technology* 36 (4): 317–333.

Wood, B. 1999. Intelligent building care. *Facilities* 17 (5,6): 189–194.

World Bank. 2001. *Making sustainable communities: An environment strategy for the world bank.* Washington, DC: The World Bank.

World Business Council for Sustainable Development (WBCSD). 2004. WBCSD sustainable project update. www.wbcsd.org (accessed September 2005).

World Commission on Environment and Development (WCED). 1987. *Our Common Future: The World Commission on Environment and Development.* New York: Oxford University Press.

World Green Building Council (WorldGBC). 2005. About the WorldGBC. www.worldgbc.org (accessed September 2005).

World Health Organization (WHO). 2005. Indoor air pollution and health. www.who.int (accessed November 2005).

Xia, Y. Z., J. L. Niu, R. Y. Zhao, and J. Burnett. 2000. Effects of turbulent air on human thermal sensations in a warm isothermal environment. *Indoor Air* 10 (4): 289–296.

Xu, P. 2002. Lightness and chroma of computer simulated surfaces lit by lamps of different spectra. *Lighting Research and Technology* 34 (4): 289–295.

Xu, P. 1997. Feng-shui as clue: Identifying prehistoric landscape setting patterns in the American southwest. *Landscape Journal* 16 (2): 174–190.

Yang, Z. 2002. Microanalysis of shopping center location in terms of retail supply quality and environmental impact. *Journal of Urban Planning and Development* 128 (3): 130–149.

Yeang, K. 1995. *Designing with Nature: The Ecological Basis for Architectural Design.* New York: McGraw-Hill.

Yu, F. W., and K. T. Chan. 2005. Electricity end-use characteristics of air-cooled chillers in hotels in Hong Kong. *Building and Environment* 40 (1): 143–151.

Yuen, B., and W. Y. Hien. 2005. Resident perceptions and expectations of rooftop gardens in Singapore. *Landscape and Urban Planning* 73 (4): 263–276.

Yust, B. L., D. A. Guerin, and J. G. Coopet. 2002. Residential energy consumption: 1987 to 1997. *Family and Consumer Sciences Research Journal* 30 (3): 323–349.

Zacharias, J. 2001. Pedestrian behavior and perception in urban walking environments. *Journal of Planning Literature* 16 (1): 3–18.

Zacharias, J., and A. Stamps. 2004. Perceived building density as a function of layout. *Perceptual and Motor Skills* 98 (3): 777–784.

Zimmerman, R. 2005. Mass transit infrastructure and urban health. *Journal of Urban Health* 82 (1): 21–32.

Abiotic Nonliving elements of the planet, such as sunlight, the atmosphere, soil, minerals, and water.

Abrasive cleaning The use of certain materials, abrasive tools, or equipment that impact or abrade a surface.

Acid deposition A type of air pollution, in wet or dry forms, that is primarily derived from sulfur and nitrogen oxides. Burning fossil fuels and other industrial processes produces the primary sources. Also referred to as acid rain.

Adaptive reuse Rehabilitating a building for a new use.

Ag-fiber A substance that is made from materials that are considered agricultural waste, such as straw and sorghum.

Asbestos A natural mineral that is a serious health concern in the built environment.

Biobased product An item that utilizes biological products or renewable domestic agricultural or forestry materials (Executive Order 13134, 1999).

Biodegradable A substance that can decompose by organic means.

Biodiversity The variety of living organisms in nature, including ecosystems and various species.

Bioenergy Biomass is used for the production of energy, including electricity, fuels (liquid, solid, and gaseous), and heat (Executive Order 13134, 1999).

Biomass Any organic matter that is available on a renewable or recurring basis, including dedicated energy crops and trees, agricultural food, feed crop residues, aquatic plants, wood, wood residues, and animal wastes. Biomass excludes old-growth timber or timber of a forest from the late successional stage of forest development (Executive Order 13134, 1999).

Biomimicry A method that examines how nature functions and then identifies ways the natural processes can be adapted to human needs.

Biosphere All of the earth's ecosystems, including the interactions between organisms, land, air, and water.

Biotic Living organisms of the planet.

Blackwater Wastewater from WCs, urinals, kitchen sinks, and dishwashers.

Brownfield Abandoned sites or buildings in urban areas that have the potential to contain chemical contaminants.

Building-related illness (BRI) An indoor air quality environmental problem that requires a physician's diagnosis and is considered more serious than sick building syndrome. Some of the illnesses associated with BRI are asthma, carbon monoxide poisoning, Legionnaire's disease (type of pneumonia), hay fever, and other infectious or allergic diseases.

Building's footprint The land area consumed for the plan of the building.

Charrette A term used to describe an interdisciplinary, collaborative activity that results in a design or a comprehensive plan.

Chimney action The flow of natural ventilation through a building that simulates the operation of a fireplace's chimney. Air flows in the building at openings near the lower level and then moves vertically to openings near the roof.

Chlorofluorocarbons (CFCs) Synthetic molecules containing chlorine and fluorine that can destroy the ozone. CFCs are used in a variety of products, including aerosol sprays, solvents, and refrigerants.

Chromaticity Indicates the degree of warmness or coolness of a light source and is measured by Kelvins (K). Also referred to as color temperature (Winchip, 2005).

Cistern A unit designed to store rainwater. Water stored in the cistern can then be used for nonpotable uses, such as flushing WCs or landscape irrigation.

Closed loop A sustainable process that indicates a product can be reused, recycled, or safely decomposed in a landfill.

Closed specifications Contract documents that delineate a specific manufacturer, the product name or number, and any other descriptors required to order the item.

Color rendering index (CRI) Measures how well a light source makes objects appear. The index ranges from 0 to 100. The higher the CRI number, the better the color rendering ability of the lamp (Winchip, 2005).

Commissioning Procedures to determine whether systems in a building are properly designed, installed, functionally tested, and capable of being operated and maintained (USGBC, 2005).

Communities Various populations coexisting within a prescribed area. The setting could be a forest, lake, coral reef, or tundra.

Compact fluorescent lamp (CFL) A lamp that is made with one or two small linear fluorescent lamps with a screw base. The ballast is a separate control gear or is built into the unit as an integral system (Winchip, 2005).

Composting A solid management waste method that utilizes nature to process organic materials and convert the waste into the humus substance.

Compression modulus A rating that reflects the performance of foam cushions by designating the amount of support provided by the foam. Higher support factors indicate an ability to support more weight. Also referred to as the support ratio.

Conservation The practice of preserving resources for current and future generations.

Contaminant Any substance that can negatively affect natural resources, including land, water, and air.

Cost-benefit analysis (CBA) A method to evaluate an investment with respect to the benefits.

Cost-effectiveness analysis (CEA) A method to evaluate the cost and the effectiveness of a program, service, or objective.

Cradle-to-grave A term used to describe the life cycle of a product beginning with the extraction of the raw materials and progressing until the item is disposed of as waste.

Daylight (skylight) The desirable natural light in a space (Winchip, 2005).

Daylight factor (DF) The ratio between the amount of daylight in specific areas in a room and the light outdoors (Winchip, 2005).

Daylight harvesting Term that describes capturing daylight for the purpose of illuminating interiors (Winchip, 2005).

Demography A subdiscipline of sociology that studies population trends.

Disability glare A distracting high illuminance level that prevents visibility (Winchip, 2005).

Discomfort glare A distracting high illuminance level that hampers visibility (Winchip, 2005).

Ecological footprints The average amount of land and ocean required for each person to live. The ecological footprint reflects the amount of natural resources required for shelter, food, transportation, energy, and waste.

Ecology The science that studies the interrelationships between and among organisms and their interaction with an environment.

Ecosystems An organizational level that includes an interacting community and its abiotic elements. Ecosystems are specific to a geographic area and place in time.

Efficacy A rating that is based upon the lumens per watt consumed. This reflects the energy efficiency of the lamp (Winchip, 2005).

Embodied energy The total energy that was consumed to produce and deliver a product or structure.

Engineered wood Wood with a face veneer that is laminated to a substrate material.

Environment All of the factors or conditions that surround an organism. This can include air, temperature, light, sound, plants, animals, and people. In addition, cultural, psychological, and social conditions affect the environment.

Environmental justice The fair treatment and meaningful involvement of all people regardless of race, color, national origin, or income with respect to the development, implementation, and enforcement of environmental laws, regulations, and policies (EPA, 2005).

Environmental science A specialization of ecology that focuses on the interaction of people and ecosystems.

Environmental stewardship The sustainable management and care of the planet's natural resources. Effective stewardship results in a healthy planet for future generations.

Face fiber The surface or pile of the carpet.

Fluorescent lamp An electric-discharge light source that generally uses electrodes, phosphors, low-pressure mercury, and other gases for illumination (Winchip, 2005).

Flush-out A procedure that helps to eliminate air quality problems from the construction process by using the HVAC system to remove airborne contaminants. The procedures are done after the installation of interior finishes and prior to occupancy.

Focus group A structured means to discuss topics for a few hours. A facilitator structures the discussion and is responsible for ensuring the involvement of participants.

Formaldehyde A colorless gas that is frequently used in materials for construction and products specified by interior designers, such as furniture and textiles. Primary sources of formaldehyde resins are urea-formaldehyde (UF) and phenol-formaldehyde (PF).

Fossil fuels Energy substances formed millions of years ago from the decay of organisms, such as skeletons or leaves that existed in a past geological age. Primary fossil fuels are crude oil, natural gas, and coal.

Geothermal The natural heat contained in the earth.

Glassphalt A material used for roads that contains recycled glass.

Graywater A conservation method to direct water from sink or tub drains to secondary usages, such as flushing toilets or watering the landscape.

Graywater heat recovery (GWHR) A system designed to recapture heat from graywater and redistribute the energy to hot water systems.

Greenfield A site that has not been developed.

Greenhouse effect The natural warming of the earth that is caused by gases that absorb and retain solar radiation.

Greenhouse gases Numerous gases, including carbon dioxide, chlorofluorocarbons, methane, nitrous oxide, tropospheric ozone, and water vapor, that are primarily created by the actions of people.

Greenwash Unfounded ecological claims regarding attributes of a product.

Greige goods Fabrics before dyes or finishes have been added.

Halogen lamp An incandescent lamp that uses a tungsten filament and halogen gas (Winchip, 2005).

Heat island Any large, paved area that causes an increase in the ambient temperature.

High-intensity discharge (HID) lamps Electric-discharge lamps have a light-producing arc that is stabilized by the temperature of the bulb. Lamps include mercury, metal halide, and high-pressure sodium (Winchip, 2005).

Hydrocarbons Organic compounds that contain only hydrogen and carbon.

Incandescent lamp A light source that uses an electrical current to heat the conductive material until incandescence is produced (Winchip, 2005).

Indentation load deflection (ILD) A rating that reflects the performance of foam cushions by designating the indentation qualities of the product. Higher ILD ratings provide the greatest firmness.

Indoor environmental quality (IEQ) Considerations associated with the built environment that must be employed for the health and well-being of people. Considerations include the availability of daylight, views to the outdoors, humidity levels, adequacy of ventilation, user control of human comfort, noise levels, and indoor air pollution.

Industrial smog A smoke pollution that contains sulfur oxides and particulates. Primarily derived from burning coal.

Integrated waste management (IWM) Sustainable waste policies and procedures that focus on source reduction, recycling, waste combustion, and landfilling.

Life cycle assessment (LCA) A tool used to help determine the comprehensive environmental impact of products, services, or processes. Most examples of life cycles depict five stages: (1) extraction of raw materials; (2) refining the raw materials; (3) manufacturing the product; (4) consumer use of the product; and (5) disposal and/or recycling.

Life-cycle costs An economic strategy used to project a budget for a project. Costs should include first costs, operating costs, employee productivity costs, maintenance/repair costs, replacement costs, and disposal costs. These costs are projected over several years to determine the true cost of a project.

Life cycle impact assessment (LCIA) The phase of the life cycle assessment that analyzes data to determine the environmental exchanges, or the impacts associated with the life cycle of an entity. The analysis requires a thorough examination of the production, transportation, energy consumption, and disposal processes.

Life cycle inventory (LCI) A phase of the life cycle assessment that has the purpose of gathering data regarding each stage of a product or service.

Light-emitting diodes (LEDs) As a semiconductor device, LEDs have a chemical chip embedded in a plastic capsule. The light is focused or scattered by using lenses or diffusers (Winchip, 2005).

Light pollution The excessive glow of light in the evening sky (Winchip, 2005).

Low-emittance (Low-E) coating A microscopically thin layer on windows or skylights that helps to suppress radiation.

Lumen (lm) A unit measurement of the quantity of light emitted from a light source (Winchip, 2005).

Lumens per watt (lpW) A rating that describes the amount of electricity that is consumed for a given amount of illumination (Winchip, 2005).

Methenamine pill test A carpet flammability test as directed by *16 CFR 1630*. Also referred to as the *ASTM D2859* test.

Modified Energy Factor (MEF) A rating that indicates the energy used to operate a washer, heat the water, and dry clothes. High MEF ratings indicate an efficient washer.

Municipal solid waste (MSW) Debris from residential and commercial buildings, including paper, yard trimmings, metals, plastic, food scraps, glass, and other substances.

Nitrogen oxides (NO$_x$) A greenhouse gas that is caused by burning fossil fuels and biomass.

Noise pollution An environmental problem that can affect the mental and physical well-being of people, including inducing stress-related illnesses. Noise can be any disturbing sound that is loud or annoying, interferes with tasks, or damages hearing.

Noise reduction coefficient (NRC) A rating that indicates how well a material absorbs sound. The range for NRC is .00 to 1.00, whereby ratings close to 1.00 provide the greatest absorption of sound.

Nonpoint source pollutant A pollutant that is deposited in water from an indirect source, such as runoffs from toxins from a nearby landfill, pesticides used on farmland, or poisons from the residue of rainwater.

Nonrenewable resources Elements of the earth that have a limited supply and cannot be replenished, such as fossil fuels and various minerals.

Nuclear energy Energy created by splitting atomic nuclei (fission) or combining atomic nuclei (fusion). In nuclear power plants, the fission process produces electricity.

Off-gas Unhealthy chemicals contained in interior products that can be expelled into the built environment.

Open specifications Contract documents that do not specify a particular product, but indicate the requirements for a material or item. The three open specifications are descriptive, performance, and reference standards.

Organic light-emitting diodes (OLEDs) A thin light-emitting diode that contains an organic emissive layer.

Organisms Living things, such as animals, insects, birds, plants, or microbes. Ecologists study how an organism functions and their requirements for shelter, sustenance, reproduction, and creating populations.

Outside-indoor transmission class (OITC) A rating that reflects the sound transmission loss from factors external to the building, including ground and air transportation. Higher decibel numbers indicate greater reduction of noise.

Ozone A gas that exists in the earth's troposphere and

stratosphere. Ozone in the troposphere is not good, and ozone in the stratosphere is essential. Troposphere ozone is one of the primary categories of air pollution.

Particulate matter Solid particles and liquid droplets floating in the air.

Payback principle An economic strategy for comparing short- and long-term costs of a product or service.

Photochemical smog A smoke pollution created by the interaction between sunlight and various chemicals in the air. The primary source of photochemical smog is car emissions. Photochemical smog is more prevalent in the summer and is visible by a brownish-orange-colored haze.

Photovoltaic Units that are able to convert the energy from the sun into electricity.

Planned obsolescence Refers to products that are intentionally designed for short-term use.

Plug loads All equipment plugged into electrical outlets.

Point source pollutant A water pollutant derived from one main source, such as a factory chimney or sewage pipe.

Polluter-pays principle An economic strategy for assessing costs to the individual or business responsible for the pollution.

Polychlorinated biphenyls (PCBs) A toxic material that was used in ballasts produced prior to 1978 (Winchip, 2005).

Population One species that is capable of interbreeding.

Post-consumer recycled content Products that contain materials derived from items that have fulfilled a useful purpose.

Post-industrial content Products that contain material that has not been used as part of a consumer product and would have been disposed of as waste. Also referred to as pre-consumer content.

Potable water Water that is for human consumption.

Pre-consumer content Products that contain material that has not been used as part of a consumer product and would have been disposed of as waste. Also referred to as post-industrial content.

Preservation A treatment for a building that retains the historic fabric through conservation, maintenance, and repair (www.cr.nps.gov).

Radon A radioactive gas that is derived from the natural breakdown of uranium in soil, rock, and water. Radon that is emitted to an enclosed space becomes dangerous to the inhabitants. The primary source of radon into a building is from the breakdown of uranium in the soil.

Rainwater harvesting The practice of collecting and storing rain for secondary usage.

Reclaimed wood Wood from various sources, such as timber from structures planned for demolition, logs salvaged from the bottom of waterways, or from trees that must be removed for a variety of reasons.

Reconstruction A treatment that re-creates a nonsurviving site, landscape, building, structure, or object in all new materials (www.cr.nps.gov).

Recycling A conservation method by converting a used material into a new product.

Rehabilitation A treatment for a building that emphasizes the retention and repair of historic materials (www.cr.nps.gov).

Remediation The process of cleaning up a contaminated site.

Remilled wood Wood salvaged from structures and recycled to create products, such as flooring, siding, or other millwork. Also referred to as salvaged wood.

Renewable resources Biological elements that have the potential to be replenished, such as water, trees, or soil.

Repurposed Recycled materials for reuse.

Resource drawing Document that can help to clarify specific details associated with unique requirements. For sustainable designs, resource drawings could illustrate the preferred locations for storing construction waste, or identifying the nonstructural components intended for building reuse.

Restoration A treatment for a building that focuses on the retention of materials from the most significant time in a property's history while permitting the removal of materials from other periods (www.cr.nps.gov). Restoration involves returning a building to a particular period of time.

Risk management A business strategy that helps to avoid risk or minimize any adverse impacts from a disaster.

Salvaged wood Wood salvaged from structures and recycled to create products such as flooring, siding, or other millwork. Also referred to as remilled wood.

Shading coefficient (SC) A rating that indicates the amount of heat gain generated by the sun that passes through the glazing and window treatment. The lower the SC rating, the less heat gain.

Sick building syndrome (SBS) An indoor air quality (IAQ) environmental problem that occurs when people who are working or living in the same building experience similar health problems, such as headaches, dizziness, nausea, depression, or eye irritations. When people who experience SBS leave the building, they no longer have the shared symptoms. SBS cannot be traced to any specific cause.

Sidelighting Daylight that enters from windows located in walls of a building.

Solar absorptance A rating that designates the amount of solar energy that a fabric absorbs.

Solar heat gain coefficient (SHGC) A rating that indicates how well a window or skylight blocks the heat from sunlight. The SHGC scale is 0 to 1, whereby the lower the rating, the less heat that will enter a room.

Solar reflectance A rating that designates the amount of sunlight reflected by a surface material.

Solar transmittance A rating that designates the amount of solar energy that passes through a material, such as a screen shade.

Sound transmission class (STC) A rating that provides information regarding an assembly's ability to prevent the transfer of noise from one area to another. The STC number is in decibels. High numbers reflect an assembly's ability to block the transmission of sound.

Spatial strategies Sustainable space planning methods that emphasize reducing the size of buildings by focusing on efficient space utilization.

Stakeholder An individual that can be affected by policies, procedures, and activities.

Stepped control A lighting control method that allows for a smoother transition in illumination levels by controlling multiple lamps within a luminaire. The stepped process works by progressively turning lamps on or off.

Stratosphere A layer in the atmosphere that contains ozone. Ozone in the stratosphere is a protective layer that helps to filter harmful rays of the sun.

Submetering system A technological means to measure and collect information regarding energy consumption from one or multiple areas within a facility.

Sustainable design Designs that reflect a respectful interaction between people and the earth by conserving resources for current and future generations. Criteria focus on developing designs that sustain societies, the environment, and the economy.

Sustainable development A concept credited to the 1987 report of the World Commission on Environment and Development (WCED) entitled "Our Common Future" (Brundtland Report). A concept that focuses on common concerns that threaten our future; the role of the international economy; equality; managing the shared oceans, space, and Antarctica; security; and institutional and legal proposals. Major themes are connections between poverty, inequality, and environmental degradation (WCED, 1987).

System A group of elements that simultaneously operate independently and interdependently.

Thermal pollution A pollution caused by industrial processes that emit heated water into the waterways. An unnatural water temperature alters the ecosystem's balance in a variety of ways, including accelerating the rate of decomposition and decreasing the supply of oxygen.

Toplighting Daylight that enters from windows or skylights mounted in the ceiling of a room.

Troposphere The layer of the atmosphere that is closest to the earth. This proximity to the earth results in a primary exposure to air pollutants.

U-factor (U-value) A measurement of the rate of heat loss or gain through a material. U-factor ratings range from .25 to 1.25, whereby the lower the rating, the better the insulating value.

User-pays principle An economic strategy that proposes consumers should pay the social costs associated with resources.

UV transmittance A rating that refers to the amount of ultraviolet rays that penetrate a material.

Vernacular architecture Features of a building that reflect the uniqueness of a culture and region.

Visible transmittance (VT or T_{vis}) A rating that indicates how much light penetrates the glazing. The rating scale is 0 to 1, whereby the higher the VT, the greater the amount of light that will enter a room.

Volatile organic compounds (VOCs) A category of organic compounds that contribute to air pollution. VOCs are carbon-based emissions and produce vapors quickly indoors.

Xeriscaping A landscape method that involves specifying native plant materials and employing water conservation practices.

CREDITS

Chapter 1

Figure 1.1: Illustration from *The Little Prince*, by Antoine de Saint-Exupéry. Reprinted with permission of Harcourt, Inc.

Figure 1.3: Source: UN Department of Economic and Social Affairs (2005). *Partnerships for Sustainable Development—Update*. New York: Commission on Sustainable Development.

Figure 1.5: Copyright © Greg Bledsoe.

Figure 1.9: John James Audubon, *Blue Yellow Back Warbler*. Collection of Mr. and Mrs. Paul Mellon. Copyright © 2006 Board of Trustees, National Gallery of Art, Washington.

Figure 1.10: Copyright © Picture History.

Figure 1.11: Courtesy of the Estate of R. Buckminster Fuller.

Figure 1.13: Courtesy © Alejandro Lapuerto Mediavilla/Shutterstock.

Chapter 2

Figure 2.1: Source: World Marketed Energy Consumption, Energy Information Administration, U.S. Department of Energy.

Figure 2.2: Source: History: Energy Information Administration (EIA), *International Energy Annual 2004* (May–July 2005), website www.eia.doe.gov/iea/. Projections: EIA, System for the Analysis of Global Energy Markets (2006).

Figures 2.3–2.5: Source: Energy Information Administration, U.S. Department of Energy.

Figure 2.6a–c: International Data Base, U.S. Census Bureau.

Figure 2.8a and b: Courtesy of Interagency Monitoring of Protected Visual Environments.

Figure 2.9: Copyright © Michael Ledray/Shutterstock.

Figure 2.10: Copyright © Michael M. Reddy, U.S. Geological Survey, U.S. Department of the Interior.

Figure 2.11: Source: U.S Environmental Protection Agency.

Figure 2.12: Courtesy of USG.

Figure 2.14: Copyright © U.S. Environmental Protection Agency.

Figure 2.15: Copyright © David Hyde/Shutterstock.

Figure 2.16a: Copyright © Erik H. Pronske, M.D./Shutterstock.

Figure 2.16b: Copyright © Justin Kim/Shutterstock.

Figure 2.17: Copyright © U.S. Environmental Protection Agency.

Chapter 3

Figure 3.1: Sources: Sandia National Laboratories and U.S. Department of Energy, Energy Information Administration.

Figure 3.2: Copyright © Simon Pederson/Shutterstock.

Figure 3.3: Copyright © U.S. Federal Trade Commission.

Figure 3.4: Source: United Nations Environmental Programme, *Global Environment Outlook 2000*.

Figure 3.5: Source: U.S. Central Intelligence Agency.

Figure 3.6: Copyright © Lyn Watson/Shutterstock.

Figure 3.7: Copyright © 2004 Conservation Design Forum, Elmhurst, IL.

Figure 3.8: Copyright © Murray Legge/LZT Architects, Inc.

Figure 3.9: Copyright © David Joseph.

Figure 3.10: Copyright © Tim Hursley, courtesy of Herman Miller, Inc.

Figure 3.11: Courtesy of Roy Kaltschmidt, Lawrency Berkeley National Laboratory.

Figure 3.12: Courtesy of Sherry Seybold, Lawrency Berkeley National Laboratory.

Figure 3.13: Courtesy of Rocky Mountain Institute, www.rmi.org.

Figure 3.14: Copyright © 2002, 2005 by the Regents of the University of Minnesota.

Chapter 4

Figures 4.3 and 4.4: This graphic is reproduced with the permission of ISO (International Organization for Standardization), www.iso.org.

Figure 4.5: Courtesy of Herman Miller, Inc.

Figure 4.7a: Copyright © Mian Kursheed/Reuters.

Figure 4.7b: Copyright © Jason Reed/Reuters.

Figures 4.8a and b and 4.11: Source: www.howproductsimpact.net.

Figure 4.14: Photo by Chris Barrett, courtesy of Herman Miller, Inc.

Figure 4.15: Photo by Beeldbank VenW.nl, Rijkswaterstaat, Adviesdienst Geo-Informatie en ICT, courtesy www.deltaworks.org.

Chapter 5

Figure 5.1: Illustration from *The Little Prince*, by Antoine de Saint-Exupéry.

Reprinted with permission of Harcourt, Inc.

Figure 5.2: Copyright © Waite Air Photos, www.globalairphotos.com.

Figure 5.3: Source: U.S. Central Intelligence Agency.

Figure 5.4: Copyright © DesignInc, Melbourne.

Figures 5.5, 5.6a and b, 5.7, and 5.8: Source: Institute for Building Environment and Energy Conservation (IBEC), www.ibec.or.jp/CASBEE/english.

Figure 5.9a: Courtesy of Moseley Architects.

Figure 5.9b: Copyright © 2003 Christian Richters/NBBJ.

Figure 5.10: Copyright © U.S. Green Building Council.

Figure 5.11: Copyright © Jose Fuste Raga/Corbis.

Figures 5.12 and 5.13: Source: Global Ecolabelling Network, www.gen.gr.jp.

Figure 5.14: Courtesy of Forbo Flooring.

Figure 5.16: Source: U.S. Environmental Protection Agency

Figure 5.17a–d: Courtesy of the Carpet and Rug Institute.

Figure 5.18: Copyright © 1996 Forest Stewardship Council A.C.

Figure 5.19: Source: National Institute of Standards and Technology, U.S. Department of Commerce.

Chapter 6

Figure 6.1: Copyright © 2004 Conservation Design Forum, Elmhurst, IL.

Figure 6.2: Copyright © AGE Fotostock.

Figure 6.3: Copyright © Shutterstock.

Figure 6.4a–c: Photos by Nathan Kirkman. Courtesy of Muller & Muller, Ltd.

Figure 6.5: Courtesy of JCDecaux.

Figure 6.6: Copyright © Yann Arthus-Bertrand/Altitude.

Figure 6.7: Copyright © Raf Makda/VIEW & Bill Dunster Architects.

Figure 6.12a: Copyright © Ioannis Ioannou/Shutterstock.

Figure 6.12b: Copyright © Raymond Kasprzak/Shutterstock.

Figure 6.14: Courtesy of Alliant Energy®.

Figure 6.16: Copyright © NASA/Goddard Space Flight Center, Scientific Visualization Studio.

Figure 6.17: Courtesy of Susan Winchip.

Figure 6.18: Source: U.S. Department of Environmental Protection

Chapter 7

Figure 7.3: Reprinted with permission of Kunsthistorisches Museum, Wien.

Figure 7.4a: Copyright © Potter Lawson Inc.

Figure 7.4b: Photo by Mark E. LaMoreaux. Courtesy of Lathrop Douglass Architects.

Figure 7.5: Courtesy of LEARN, London Metropolitan University.

Figure 7.6a and b: Courtesy of Pella Windows and Doors.

Figure 7.7: Copyright © Michael Mathers.

Figure 7.8a: Photo by Jon Zachary. Courtesy of Ramsay GMK Architects, Raleigh, NC.

Figure 7.8b: Copyright © 2006 Hunter Douglas.

Figure 7.9a: Copyright © Nigel Young/ Foster and Partners.

Figure 7.9b: Copyright © 2006 Hunter Douglas.

Figure 7.10: Copyright © Lakis Foundation/Shutterstock.

Figure 7.11: Photo by Dorrie Meeker; reprinted with permission.

Figures 7.12 and 7.13: Copyright © Envision Design, PLLC.

Figure 7.14: Copyright © Dundas Jafine.

Figure 7.15: Copyright © David Andrew Gilder/Shutterstock.

Figure 7.17: Copyright © 2002 Lower Manhattan Development Corporation.

Figure 7.18: Source: Public Works, Government Services, Canada.

Figure 7.19: Copyright © Dan C. Kopp, Valley Home Inspection, www.boise inspector.com.

Figure 7.20: Photo by Michael Lafferty. Courtesy of The Old Fashioned Milk Paint Co., Inc.

Chapter 8

Figure 8.1: Copyright © Leger Wanaselja Architecture.

Figure 8.2: Reprinted with permission from The National Fenestration Rating Council, Inc.

Figure 8.3a–c: Courtesy of Rockler Woodworking and Hardware, www.rockler .com.

Figure 8.4: Courtesy of Whirlpool.

Figure 8.5: Reprinted with permission of CTS Gyson, jcooper@ctsgroup.com.au.

Figure 8.7a and b: Copyright © 2000, Shaw Industries Group, Inc. Reprinted with permission.

Figure 8.8a: Copyright © WizData, Inc./ Shutterstock.

Figure 8.8b: Copyright © Javarman/Shutterstock.

Figure 8.10: Copyright © Sue Warga.

Figure 8.11: Courtesy of Forbo Flooring.

Figure 8.13a: Copyright © 2004 Bruce Quist. Courtesy of Interface.

Figures 8.13b and 8.14a: Courtesy of Carpet and Rug Institute.

Figure 8.14b: Copyright © Renata Hundley.

Figure 8.16: Copyright © EnviroTextiles. Photo by Joe Jenkin.

Figure 8.17: Copyright © Andy Piatt/Shutterstock.

Figure 8.18: Courtesy of Fluent Inc.

Figure 8.19: Courtesy of Channel House Hotel, Minehead, Somerset, UK, www.channelhouse.co.uk.

Figure 8.20a: Courtesy of Decorator Shades and Blinds.

Figure 8.20b: Copyright © Hunter Douglas.

Figure 8.21a–d: Copyright © 2006 MechoShade Systems, Inc. All Rights Reserved

Figure 8.25: Copyright © King Hickory Furniture Company.

Chapter 9

Figure 9.1: Illustration from *The Little Prince*, by Antoine de Saint-Exupéry. Reprinted with permission of Harcourt, Inc.

Figure 9.2: Copyright © Keith Levit/Shutterstock.

Figure 9.3: Copyright © Titus Paulsel/ www.Photocorral.com.

Figure 9.4: Copyright © the Trustees of The British Museum.

Figure 9.5: Copyright © Steve Yager/Shutterstock.

Figure 9.6a: Copyright © Grisel Gonzalez, http://grisel.net. All rights reserved.

Figure 9.6b: Copyright © Raul Razvan/Shutterstock.

Figure 9.8a: Copyright © Phil Reddy.

Figure 9.8b: Copyright © Wendy Kaveny Photography/Shutterstock.

Figure 9.9: Copyright © Tyler Olson/Shutterstock.

Figure 9.10: Copyright © Lee W. Nelson, www.inetours.com.

Figure 9.12: Copyright © Bildarchiv Preussischer Kulturbesitz/Art Resource, NY.

Figure 9.13: Copyright © W.H. Chow/Shutterstock.

Figure 9.14: Copyright © Hartill Art Associates, Inc.

Figure 9.15: Courtesy of Drayton Hall, Charleston, South Carolina.

Figure 9.16: Copyright © Albo/Shutterstock.

Figure 9.17: Copyright © Schönbrunn, Kultur und Betriens-GmbH.

Figure 9.18a and b: Copyright © The Colonial Williamsburg Foundation 2006.

Figure 9.19a–c: Copyright © Conservation Consultants, Inc.

Figure 9.20: Copyright © Bazzani Holdings LLC.

Figure 9.21: Copyright © Dan Gair, www.blinddogphoto.com.

Figure 9.22: Reprinted with permission of Ecotrust, www.ecotrust.org.

Figure 9.23a: Reprinted with permission of the Technical Preservation Services, National Park Services.

Figure 9.23b: Copyright © Barbara Krankenhaus.

Figure 9.24: Copyright © Mark Nedzbala/ Shutterstock.

INDEX